To Neill O'Quinn —
Congratulations on your third place finish in Random Lengths' Super Bowl XXVIII Contest!

Jan 30, 1994

Dave Evans

Random Lengths® Terms of the Trade

THIRD EDITION
Revised & Expanded

A Reference For The Forest Products Industry

Terms of the Trade

THIRD EDITION
Revised & Expanded

Copyright 1993, 1984, 1978
All Rights Reserved

Publisher: Jon P. Anderson
Editor: David S. Evans
Electronic Publishing & Design: Nancy West
Illustrator: Ken Brauner

Random Lengths Publications

Post Office Box 867
Eugene, Oregon 97440-0867
Phone: (503) 686-9925 • FAX: (503) 686-9629

Third Edition, 1993
Second Edition, 1984
First Edition, 1978

Library of Congress Catalog Card Number 77-95459
ISBN 0-9614042-8-0
Manufactured in the United States of America

FOREWORD

The forest industry has its own unique vocabulary. In fact, the industry is so greatly segmented by region, products, and activities that it has several vocabularies. One result of this diversity is that the experienced practitioner in one field often neither knows, nor has ready access to, the specialized terms that are common to those who support or supplement his activities.

Terms Of The Trade is designed to meet the needs of both the industry veteran and the beginner by gathering into one easily accessible source a great amount of information for a wide audience. This book defines words and phrases used in forestry, logging, primary and secondary manufacturing, marketing, futures trading, construction, and other related fields.

Use the book as you would a dictionary. You'll find it a valuable reference. Or browse through it for its wealth of current and historical information and its accurate illustrations.

Work on the third edition of **Terms Of The Trade** began almost immediately after the second in 1984. We have drawn heavily from many specialized references in order to provide the broadest range of terms and definitions. In addition, we have been able to draw on the knowledge and experience of a large number of persons directly involved in the diverse activities of the forest products industry. Their contributions and advice are gratefully acknowledged.

A special thanks to those Random Lengths staff members whose efforts helped make this book possible: Jon Anderson, Shawn Church, Burrle Elmore, Joe Heitz, and Jessie Taylor.

CONTENTS

Section I
Terms of the Trade

Section II
Abbreviations

Section III
Useful Information

Section I

TERMS of the TRADE

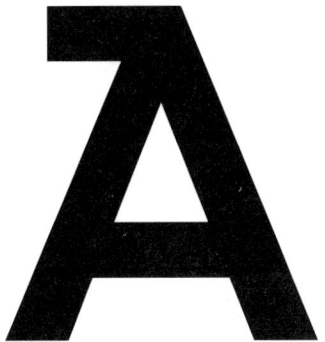

A1 – First class condition. Used in waterborne transportation to specify the type of hull (A) and the nature of stores and equipment (1). Lloyd's Register rates vessels A1, A2, etc. In American registry, vessels are rated in descending order by fractions: A1, A1-1/4, A1-1/2, etc.

AA Exterior – Sanded plywood with A-grade face and back plies and C-grade inner plies, bonded with exterior glue. The panel may be used in exterior or unprotected locations.

AA Grade – Plywood constructed of clear, or knot-free, faces and backs, both sanded; the highest regular grade of plywood.

AA Interior – Sanded plywood with A-grade face and back and D-grade inner plies; either interior or exterior glue may be used, but the panel is recommended for interior or protected applications.

Abacus – The top portion of a capital to a column.

Abatement – 1. A diminution from original size. The loss of volume in timber or lumber due to milling, shaping or seasoning, leading to a decrease in strength. 2. A suspension of proceedings. 3. A discount allowed in the payment of a bill. The extent is usually specified before payment is due, and the amount is deducted from the bill.

A B C D – Grades of softwood veneer which are combined in the manufacture of plywood to develop specific products. The highest grade is A, the lowest D. The most heavily produced combination is CD, used in construction sheathing.

AB Exterior – A plywood grade similar to AA Exterior, except that it has a B-grade veneer as the back ply. Used where appearance of one side is less important.

Abies – The botanical designation for the species Fir. In North America, this includes: Abies lasiocarpa, Alpine Fir; A. amabalis, Western Silver Fir; A. concolor, California White Fir; A. Fraseri, Fraser Fir; A. balsamea, Balsam Fir; A. grandis, Grand Fir, White Fir; A. magnifica, California Red Fir; A. procera, Noble Fir.

AB Interior – A sanded plywood grade similar to AA Interior except that a B-grade veneer is used as the back ply.

Abney Level – A type of clinometer, an instrument used to measure angles of elevation or inclination.

Abnormal Wood – Wood that has been

Terms Of The Trade   1

Above Ground Use

deformed during growth, such as compression wood found on the under side of a bent tree. Also can include callus growth, scars from fire, or other defects.

Above Ground Use – A designation for treated wood products intended for use in applications where the wood does not come in contact with the ground.

Abrasive Planing – A method of applying a smooth, finished surface to a product utilizing belts or drums coated with sandpaper. First developed for use in surfacing plywood and particleboard and later adapted for use on sawn wood, although most lumber still is surfaced by a planer equipped with knives. Abrasive planing results in less residue than knife planing and permits sawing very close to finished sizes, resulting in a greater lumber recovery factor.

Absolute Advantage – The ability to manufacture or sell a product, without incurring losses, below the cost of a competitor.

Absolute Humidity – The ratio of a mass of water vapor to the volume of the air in which it is contained. See Relative Humidity, Dew Point.

Absolute Liability – A condition in which a person or entity is responsible for all liability and not released from exemptions normally found in a bill of lading.

Absorbed Moisture – Water held in the cell walls of wood. See Bound Water.

Absorption – The process by which water or other liquid is drawn into a porous solid body, such as wood.

Absorption Rate – The volume of water absorbed by an item when it is partially immersed for one minute.

Abstract – A legal summary of the history of a plot of land from the date of the original deed.

Abutment Piece – The lowest structural member receiving and distributing the weight of an upright. The floor plate to which a stud is fastened.

Abutting Joint – The joint formed by the meeting of two structural pieces end to end, or at an angle to each other.

Abutting Tenons – Tenons entering a structural member from opposite sides, and

Acanthus

abutting in the center of a mortise.

Acanthus – An architectural ornament resembling the leaves of an acanthus plant. Often a distinguishing characteristic of the capital of a Corinthian column.

A-Cat – Traders' oral shorthand for AC grade sanded plywood.

Accelerated Aging – A method of determining the approximate ability of a material to withstand exposure. ASTM Standard D1037 provides for combinations of immersion, exposure to steam and water, heat and dry air, and freezing to accelerate aging.

Accelerated Air Drying – The use of equipment and procedures to accelerate air drying. Included are yard-fan drying, shed-fan drying, and forced-air drying.

Acceleration Clause – The section of a loan agreement that states the full amount of the loan is immediately due should the contract be broken.

Acceptance – The act of agreeing to the offer of another, creating a contract to which all parties are bound.

Accessorial Service – A service in addition to transportation rendered by a carrier, including storage, switching, etc.

Acclimatization – The process of stacking lumber at the jobsite to allow it to acclimate to the surrounding air prior to installation.

Accolade – The decorative use of moulding, in which two ogee curves meet above a door or window.

Actual Size

Accord & Satisfaction – The full settlement of a disputed claim through the performance of a specified act.

Account Analysis – The process of determining the profitability of an account by analyzing activity, balances, cost of handling, etc.

Accounts Payable – The amounts owed to creditors for goods or services.

Accounts Receivable – The amount owed by customers to a business for its goods or services.

Accouplement – 1. The placement of two columns close together to form a colonnade in pairs. 2. A brace or tie between two structural members.

Accretion – The increase made by natural growth, as in a forest, or by gradual additions due to natural causes, such as additions to land by flood deposits.

Accumulating Shear – Shear that increases with the passage of time.

Accumulation Items – 1. Those products that develop as a consequence of the manufacture of a specific item; the "fall down" or residual of manufacturing. 2. Products that tend to accumulate in surplus as other items are sold. The less-popular lengths, grades, or sizes, or combinations of these.

AC Exterior – A sanded plywood panel with A-grade face, C-grade back, and C-grade inner plies, bonded with exterior glue. Usually abbreviated ACX.

Acid Free Paper – Paper manufactured from alkaline pulp, so that it will resist deterioration due to age.

Acid Rain – Rain or other precipitation polluted by smokestack emissions such as sulphur dioxide, nitrogen dioxide, and other by-products of burning coal and petroleum products. Said to have a harmful impact on trees and freshwater lakes.

Acid Wood – Wood used to produce certain distilled products, such as wood alcohol.

Acknowledgment – A written verification of the acceptance of an order, sent by a seller, such as a manufacturer, to a buyer and listing the details of the transaction. These include a description of the goods, the price, shipping instructions, and other information.

Acoustical Materials – Fibrous material, including lumber or plywood with a face pattern, used in the control of sound.

Acoustic Construction – A method of building in which the reduction of sound transmission is a priority.

Acre – A unit of land measurement equal to 43,560 square feet.

Acre Foot – A unit of water measurement, equalling the volume of water one foot deep on an acre of land, or 43,560 cubic feet. Used to measure volumes of lakes, reservoirs, etc.

Across-the-Board – A uniform change, such as an increase in the prices of all widths of #2&Btr dimension.

Action – A legal proceeding in which a person demands or enforces a right.

Active Drying Period – In air drying, the period or season of the year when conditions are most favorable for drying wood.

Active Earth Pressure – Horizontal pressure on a wall from earth pushing against it.

Actual Freight – The term that differentiates the actual cost of shipping from the estimated cost determined prior to shipment. Any deviation from the estimated cost is for the shipper's account unless other arrangements are made.

Actual Measure – The actual net measurement of a product such as a piece of lumber as opposed to a nominal measurement. See Nominal Size.

Actual Merchantable – The volume of usable logs cut from a tree after eliminating defects, tops, etc.

Actual Placement – The location of a railroad car for loading or unloading at a point previously designated by the consignor or consignee.

Actual Size – The finished size, as opposed to the nominal size, of a piece of lumber. The minimum sizes to which lumber may be finished or dressed are specified in the American Lumber Standard for softwood lumber used in the U.S. and are listed in regional grading rules. Actual sizes may vary by type of product, moisture content at the time of dressing and, in some cases, by species. Panel products often are described by actual sizes.

Terms Of The Trade

Actual Weight

Actual Weight – The weight of a specific shipment of forest products as distinguished from an estimated weight established for that item. Actual weights vary according to species, products, the locale in which the timber was grown, by its density, and by moisture content. See Actual Freight.

Additive – As used in the particleboard industry, any special material incorporated in a panel in the course of manufacture to impart special properties. Examples are preservatives, water repellents, and fire retardants.

Add To Set – The overhang on the point of a sawtooth. This increases the thickness of the kerf, and makes the sawing easier.

Adhesive – Any substance used to bond the surfaces of two materials. Adhesives are made from inorganic and organic sources, with the former used principally on materials that will be exposed to weather.

AD Interior – A sanded plywood panel with A-grade face, D-grade back, and D-grade inner plies. Either interior or exterior glue may be used, but the panel is recommended for interior or protected applications.

Adirondack Spruce – Another name for White Spruce, Picea glauca.

Adirondack Standard – One of various log rules in which the volume in a log or group of logs was expressed in terms of the number of "standard" logs of equivalent cubic volume. An Adirondack Standard was defined as a log 13 feet long and 19 inches in diameter at the small end. It was usually regarded as equaling 200 board feet. Also called the Adirondack Market, Dimick Standard, Glens Falls Standard, and Nineteen-Inch Standard.

Adjustable-Rate Mortgage (ARM) – A mortgage in which the interest rate is changed periodically according to changes in another financial instrument, such as U.S. Treasury bills. The period between changes and the index to which changes are pegged are established at the time the mortgage is taken out.

Adjustment Factor – A change in a design value due to variations in use conditions such as extraordinary loads, load duration, wet conditions, etc.

Admiralty Shackle – A heavy shackle used in a skyline logging system to connect the skyline to an anchor line (stub) at the tail tree.

A-Dog – Traders' oral shorthand for AD sanded plywood.

Adsorbed Moisture – A liquid or dissolved substance condensed on the surface of an object.

Adsorption – The adhesion of vapor (gas or liquid) to a surface in a condensed layer during the drying process.

Adult Wood – Wood produced after the cambial cells have reached their maximum dimensions. Also called Mature Wood, Outer Wood, Stem-formed Wood.

Advanced Decay – A stage of decay in which wood becomes rotten and often crumbles to the touch.

Advise on Shipment – A notice that shipment of goods has been made. It usually includes details of loading and routing, and often is accompanied by an invoice.

Adz – A cutting tool shaped like a hoe, used to trim and shape logs by hand.

"A" End of the Car – The end of a rail car opposite the hand brake.

Aerial Cruise – A type of survey in which the volume of standing timber in a given area is estimated by flying over the stand and inspecting visually or by taking aerial photographs for later study.

Aerial Logging – A method of logging that employs helicopters, balloons, or skylines to lift and transport logs above the ground to a landing or loading site. Often used in ecologically fragile areas, or where road-building costs would be prohibitive.

A-Frame Car

Aerial Roading – Hauling logs by using a tramway or skyline.

Afforestation – Planting trees on land that has not recently been forested.

A-Frame – 1. An arch or framework, usually built of timbers, that supports a block used in hauling or loading logs. 2. A building with a steeply sloping roof extending to, or near, the foundation.

A-Frame Car – A railroad flat car with an A-shaped frame, running the length of the car, to which loads can be secured.

African Mahogany – A reddish brown, moderately soft wood used in cabinets and furniture. Most African Mahogany comes from Nigeria.

After Arrival of Car (AAC) – A credit term used in defining terms of payment of invoices.

After Cut – An old term for the final cut made in felling a tree. See Face Cut.

After Date of Invoice (ADI) – A credit term used to define conditions of sale. Certain discounts are often granted for payment within a specified period ADI.

After Deducting Freight (ADF) – A credit term used in defining terms of payment of invoices. Sometimes expanded to ADF&D, After Deducting Freight and Duty, or ADFD&E, After Deducting Freight, Duty and Entry Fees.

Age-Class Gap – A situation in which managed timberlands lack trees of diverse ages.

Agency – 1. In forest products, an organization of manufacturers established to oversee quality control operations. A grading or rule-writing agency. 2. The relationship between a principal and one authorized to act in his behalf.

Agency Plywood – A product bearing the mark of an authorized grading organization. See Mill Grade.

Agency Stamp – The grademark of an authorized grading agency.

Agent – One who works on another's behalf. Specifically, a Shipper's Agent.

Agents Pool – A system used by railroads to return empty cars back to their origin for storage and loading.

Aggregate-Coated Panel – A wood fiber-based panel coated with perlite or other material to produce a decorative or acoustical face.

Aging Machine – A device used to distress the surface of a panel in order to give it the look of being aged or weathered. Also called a Distressing Machine.

Aging of Accounts – The time span between the date of a receivable and when it is actually paid.

A Grade – 1. In plywood, a smooth, paintable face with limited repairs. Suitable for natural finish in some applications. 2. A clear grade of lumber; in Redwood, A Grade allows some sound sapwood or medium stain, and small checks that will not develop into splits.

Agreed Charges – The rail freight rates under which virtually all long-haul shipments of forest products once moved within Canada. These rates were established annually by contract between shippers and carriers. They committed the railroad to provide the agreed-upon rates from June l through May 31. They also committed producers to ship by rail a stated percentage of the forest products they move to the destinations covered in the contract.

Agropelter – A mythical beast said to inhabit the woods of the Upper Midwest. It lived in hollow trees and killed unwary loggers who strayed too close by causing limbs to fall on them.

A-Horizon – The upper layer of soil.

Air Bag – A large inflatable bag used as dunnage on rail cars.

Air Dried – Seasoned by exposure to the atmosphere, in the open or under cover, without artificial heat.

Air-Dried Paper – Paper that has been dried by moving through a hot-air chamber during the manufacturing process. The resulting product has a hard, slightly rough surface.

Air-Dry Ton (ADT) – A measure of wood pulp in which, of the 2000 lbs. in a ton, 1800 is pulp and 200 lbs is moisture. In terms of wood fiber content, one air-dry ton is equal to 0.9 ovendry tons.

Air Flotation

Air Flotation — A means by which different size particles can be segregated into groups of similar size and weight by passing them through a stream of moving air.

Air Jet Debarker — A log debarker using a concentrated jet of compressed air to remove bark, as contrasted with mechanical debarkers utilizing metal fingers to scrape the bark away.

Air Reversal — A change in direction of the air flowing through a load of drying lumber.

Air Saw — A powered saw driven by compressed air.

Air Seasoned — Seasoned by exposure to the atmosphere. See Air Dried.

Air Shed — An unheated building used in air drying lumber. Usually open on two or more sides to permit natural air movement.

Air Tongs — The loading tongs on a shovel-loader boom, activated by compressed air.

Alaska Fir — A common name for Western Hemlock, Tsuga heterophylla, exported from Alaska. Also called Alaska Pine.

Alaska Pine — Another name for Western Hemlock, Tsuga heterophylla.

Alaska Yellow Cedar — Chamaecyparis nootkatensis. This species is found along the Pacific Coast from Northern Oregon to Alaska. It is similar to Port Orford Cedar. Also called Yellow Cedar and Yellow Cypress.

Albany Board — A standard unit of measurement used when Albany, N.Y., was a major lumber marketing center. An Albany Board was a piece one inch thick, 10 inches wide, and 13 feet long.

Alberta Rule — Another name for the International 5/16th-inch Log Rule.

Alburnum — The sapwood, or outer part, of a tree trunk.

Aldehyde — A class of organic compounds used in adhesives.

Alder — Alnus rubra. Red Alder, a deciduous tree of the Pacific Northwest, having pinkish-brown wood that is used in interior finishing, furniture, and cabinetry. It is very receptive to stains. Other alders include A. glutinosa, British Alder; A. maritima, Formosan Alder.

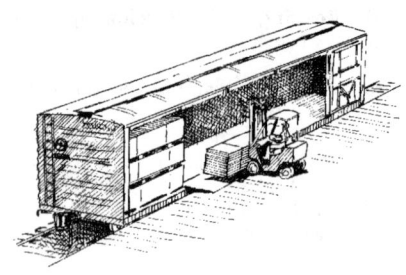

All-Door Car

Aligned Face — The face of an oriented strand board panel, as opposed to the random pattern of the face of a waferboard panel.

Alkyd — An oil-based coating used in paints, stains, and varnishes.

All-Age Management — A forest management system that includes trees of all ages and sizes.

All Current Closing Rate Method — A type of currency conversion in which all foreign currencies are translated at current exchange rates.

All Door Car — A boxcar on which the doors can be opened for the full length of the car for easier loading and unloading.

Alley — A passage between the piles of lumber air drying in a yard, parallel to the piles.

All Heart — Lumber of heartwood throughout, free of sapwood.

Alligator — 1. The cracking or separation of the surface layer of materials only, as in the breaking of a layer of paint; also called crocodiling. 2. A device used to lift the front end of a log to facilitate skidding it across wet grounds. Often fashioned from the fork of a tree. 3. A small boat used to handle logs in a pond.

Alligator Juniper — Juniperus deppeana. Native to the higher elevations of the U.S. Southwest, this species takes its common name from the checkered appearance of its bark, which resembles an alligator's hide. It is of little commercial value. Also called Checkered-Barked Juniper, Mountain Cedar, and Oak-Barked Cedar.

All-In Charges — In transportation, a single charge for all services.

Anchor Blocks

Allowable Cut – That volume of national forest timber designated by the Forest Service that may be offered for sale during any one year; the timber may or may not actually be cut that year. The allowable volume is based on an estimate of the amount that can be cut from a given area in perpetuity.

Allowable Cut Effect (ACE) – A timber management term describing the different results that may be obtained by using varying data or assumptions in calculating allowable harvests of timber. For example, different allowable cut levels may be obtained for a given area by making different assumptions about growth rate, intensity of management, insect damage, mortality, and fire hazard. For a specific application of allowable cut effect, see Earned Harvest.

Allowable Design Value – The tabulated design value of lumber, modified by various adjustment factors such as temperature, load duration, size, and others.

Allowable Load – The ultimate load, modified by a safety factor.

Allowable Sale Quantity (ASQ) – The amount of timber that can be sold from a public forest over a decade. Annual sales volumes may vary, but the total over the 10-year period should not be more than the allowable sale quantity.

Allowable Stress – The maximum load at which structural lumber or plywood can be used safely in construction. Allowable stress is determined by species, size, grade, moisture content, specific gravity, duration of stress, and temperature. Standard allowable stresses have been determined for most species, sizes, grades, etc., in laboratory and field tests.

All Weather Wood Foundation (AWWF) – A foundation system in which treated lumber and plywood are used in place of concrete. The name was changed in 1984 to Permanent Wood Foundation (PWF).

Along-Side Delivery – Delivery within reach of loading or unloading tackle on either a vessel or dock. See At Ship's Tackle.

Along the Grain – In the same direction as the grain; the stronger and stiffer direction in wood. In plywood, the same direction as the grain of the face ply.

Alpine Fir – Abies lasiocarpa; also called Subalpine Fir. A species included in the White Wood grouping.

Amabilis Fir – Abies amabilis. More commonly called Silver Fir, this species is included in the Hem-Fir grouping.

Ambrosia Beetle – Pinhole borers of the Scolytidae and Platypodidae families.

American Lumber Standard (ALS) – A voluntary product standard developed by the National Bureau of Standards in cooperation with wood producers, distributors, and users. The American Lumber Standard is designated PS 20-70 (Product Standard 20 issued in 1970). It establishes the dimensions for various types of lumber products, the technical requirements, and the methods of testing, grading, and marking.

American Lumber Standards Committee (ALSC) – A standing committee composed of representatives of producers, distributors, specifiers, and consumers of softwood lumber. The primary functions of the committee are to review and consider proposed changes or revisions to the American Softwood Lumber Standard, PS 20-70, which establishes requirements for sizes and types of various lumber products, and methods of grading, testing and marking the products. ALSC inspectors conduct field checks on certified grading agencies, and the committee's independent Board of Review has the power to discipline those committing infractions. The ALSC is operated under the aegis of the Commerce Department, U.S. Bureau of Standards.

American National Standards Institute (ANSI) – A private organization of manufacturers, specifiers, and consumers that establishes commercial standards for a variety of products.

American Terms – An exchange rate expressed as the number of currency units per U.S. dollar.

Amortized Mortgage – A mortgage on which both principal and interest are paid in regular, equal installments.

Amplitude of Cycle – In the kiln drying of lumber, the temperature difference between the low and high points of a complete drying cycle.

Anchor Blocks – Wooden blocks that are built into masonry walls, so that partitions or fixtures may be attached to them.

Terms Of The Trade

Anchor Bolt

Anchor Bolt – A bolt set in a concrete foundation or wall to tie down the frame of a structure.

Anchor Cable – A short line used to secure machinery, specifically to tie down the ends of a donkey sled to prevent tipping.

Ancient Forest – An old-growth forest; virgin timber.

Ancon – A right-angled projection at the top of a vertical piece such as a door or window casing.

...And Better – This designation, usually abbreviated "&Btr", indicates that lumber so graded contains an unspecified percentage of pieces that are of a higher grade than the lowest acceptable grade. Thus, Std&Btr will contain some pieces of the Standard grade, and some that are of higher grades, such as Construction. The proportionate distribution of grades is not guaranteed unless a maximum percentage of the lower grade is specified in the purchase order.

...And Longer – A designation, usually abbreviated "&Lgr", that indicates a given quantity of lumber contains lengths in excess of a certain size, such as in "16-foot&Lgr." This specification is generally understood to include all the lengths normally found in a random assortment; however, there is no guarantee of the number of pieces of each length unless these are specified at the time of sale.

...And Wider – A designation, usually abbreviated "&Wdr", that indicates a given quantity of lumber contains widths in excess of a certain size, such as in "2x6&Wdr." This is usually understood to mean all the widths normally found in a load, up to 12-inch; however, there is no guarantee as to the number of pieces of each width in the load unless these are specified at the time of sale.

Angiosperm – One of the two major classes of trees, including most deciduous types and commercial hardwoods. The other major class is the gymnosperms, which include the softwoods. Angiosperms produce seeds or fruits that are covered by a shell or other protection; gymnosperms have naked seeds.

Angle Bar – A vertical bar at the angle of a window.

Angle Bead – A bead attached to the projecting angle in a wall, to protect injury to the corner. Can be of wood or metal.

Angle Board – A board used as a guide in carpentry to plane lumber to a specific angle.

Angledozer – A tractor with a bulldozer blade that is centrally mounted so that it can be angled to either side. Used in road construction for sidecasting.

Angle Joints – Any of various joints connecting timbers not in the same straight line or plane.

Angle of Attack – See Cutting Angle.

Angle of Repose – The maximum degree of slope at which a hillside will remain stable.

Angle Post – A corner post in a half-timbered structure.

Angle Rafter – A hip rafter.

Angle Tie – A roof timber that ties together the wall plates.

Animal and Plant Health Inspection Service (APHIS) – A federal agency that regulates the import, export, and intra-U.S.A. movement of animals, plants, and pests.

Animal Logging – A logging method that uses animals, such as horses, mules, or oxen, to drag the logs from the cutting area to the landing. This logging method is no longer widely used, except on small tracts, or in thinning or prelogging, or on tracts that are environmentally fragile.

Anisotropic – Not having the same properties in all directions.

Annual Allowable Cut – The average volume that may be harvested annually in perpetuity from a given forest unit. See Allowable Cut.

Annual Average Increment – The average annual growth of a tree or trees in a stand, expressed in board feet, cubic feet, or annual growth rings per inch, over a certain period of time.

Annual Current Increment – The growth of a tree or trees, expressed in board feet, cubic feet, or diameter inches, for the most current year.

Annual Cut – The volume of timber harvested from a given area in any one year.

Annual Growth Ring – See Annual Ring.

Appearance Grade

Annual Leader – The annual vertical growth of a coniferous tree.

Annual Mortality – The volume of timber lost from the forest due to natural causes during a given year.

Annual Ring – The layer of growth added to the circumference of a tree in one year, including both springwood and summerwood.

Annular Nail – A type of pallet nail with circular rings on the shank.

Annular Nail

Annulet – A small, semicircular moulding circumscribing a column.

Anti-Checking Iron – A device, made of iron and of various shapes, which is driven into the ends of ties, poles or large timbers to prevent or reduce end checking.

Anti-Dumping Duty – A tariff designed to prevent the "dumping" of imported goods by selling them at prices below the regular prices charged in the country of origin.

Anti-Fungus Treated – Wood that has been treated by a dip or spray to retard the growth of fungi, and to help the wood retain its bright appearance.

Anti-Sag Bar – A tie-rod used to connect the ridge of a truss and the horizontal tie beam.

Anti-Sapstain Treated – A chemical treatment applied to lumber to prevent discoloration of the sapwood during storage or shipment.

Anti-Stain Treated – Lumber or other wood product treated with any of various chemicals to retard staining caused by exposure to weather or fungi.

Apache Pine – Pinus engelmannii. A minor, non-commercial species found in the Southwest.

APA Performance-Rated Panels – Structural panel products manufactured under an American Plywood Association standard covering wood by-products and species not provided for in Product Standard 1-83 for plywood. These meet criteria based on end use such as uniform and concentrated static and impact load capacity, fastener-holding ability, racking resistance, dimensional stability, and bond durability. The standard covers conventional plywood, composite panels (veneer faces bonded to reconstituted wood cores), and fully reconstituted wood panels including waferboard, oriented strand board, and structural particleboard. APA Performance-Rated Panels are recognized by model building codes through the National Research Board and Federal Housing Administration.

APA 303 Siding – Proprietary plywood products for exterior siding or fencing. The surface may be given a variety of treatments such as grooving, brushing, or embossing. 303/6 designates a panel with a maximum of six patches or repairs; 303/18 may have up to 18 patches.

APA Trademark – The registered trademark of the American Plywood Association. It is used as a grade mark to signify that a panel has been manufactured under the association's quality supervision and testing program.

Apgar Rule – A log rule. See Finch and Apgar Rule.

Apical Meristem – The tip of a growing stem; the point at which wood tissue divides and grows.

Apophyge – A small, curved part of a column joining the shaft to its base, especially in the Corinthian and Ionic orders.

Appearance Grade – A general term for lumber or plywood suitable for exposed use such as in siding, soffits, paneling, or trim.

Applied Moulding

Appearance grade items are mostly clear wood, although a limited number of sound, tight knots may be allowed.

Applied Moulding – A method of arranging moulding to give the appearance of paneling.

Appraisal – An estimate of the market value of property. In real estate, an appraisal is made to ensure that a home's value will cover the amount of the loan in case of default.

Appraised Price – A price set by the U.S. Forest Service, or other public agency, on a particular timber sale, based on an estimate of the actual market value of the timber. It is also the minimum acceptable price for the timber.

Approved Grader – A person, usually a manufacturer's employee, who has been trained and approved for grading lumber but is limited to the use of grade stamps only. See Certified Grader.

Apron – 1. A piece of finish moulding below the sill of a window, covering the rough edge of plaster or sheetrock. 2. A short ramp with a slight pitch. 3. A support placed in a staircase.

Arbitrage – Buying on one market and seeking to sell at a profit in another; i.e., an attempt to profit from a discrepancy in prices. In futures trading this often refers to the simultaneous purchase of a futures contract in one market or time period and the sale of a contract in another market. See Spread.

Arbitration – The settlement of a dispute by a person or persons chosen to hear both sides and reach a decision. In forest products trading, arbitration awards normally are binding and enforceable in court.

Arbor – 1. An axle or spindle that supports cutting tools that spin or rotate. 2. A latticework creating a shady place, usually supporting climbing vines; the place itself.

Arboreal – Pertaining to trees; treelike; living in or among trees.

Arborvitae – Trees of the genus Thuja of North America and Asia; a soft but strong and durable wood.

Arch – 1. A piece of logging equipment consisting of a U-shaped steel frame with wheels on each leg of the inverted U. Used to support one end of a log to facilitate skidding it to a landing with a crawler tractor. 2. A structural member, usually curved, that spans an opening and serves as a support for weight above the opening.

Archangel Fir – Pinus sylvestris. A Baltic red wood, named after the port of shipment.

Arch Band – The visible portion of a rib in a vault.

Arch Hook – A hook designed to allow several chokers to be attached to one line.

Architect Clear Decking – A decking grade developed by the Western Red Cedar Lumber Association. The highest decking grade designated by the WRCLA.

Arch and Tractor

Architect Knotty Decking – A decking grade developed by the Western Red Cedar Lumber Association.

Architectural Door – A type of door specification calling for above-standard materials and appearance.

Architectural Grade – See Appearance Grade.

Architectural Panels – Veneered panels (usually hardwood) that are matched with each other so that, when installed, they create a particular visual effect in a room.

Architectural Products – Custom-milled decorative millwork items.

Architectural Veneers – Hardwood veneers that are matched to create architectural panels with particular patterns.

Architrave – The moulding around a door or other rectangular opening.

Archivolt – A decorative band around an arch.

Archline – A line or wire rope run over an arch, to which chokers are attached.

Arch Ring – The load-bearing portion of an arch.

Arc Shake – Another name for cup shake, a type of lengthwise grain separation between or through the growth rings in wood.

Are – A metric unit of surface area; 100 square meters equals one are, 100 ares are equal to one hectare.

Area Salvage – A timber sale in which the U.S. Forest Service, or other public agency, sells dead timber within a given area. Such sales generally cover more than one operating season and require the operator to return annually to remove newly dead timber.

Aril – The fleshy, berry-like structure encasing the seeds of female yew trees.

Arizona Cypress – Cupressus arizonica. Wood from this species, native to the southwestern U.S. and Mexico, is sometimes used for fence posts and mine timbers.

Arizona Longleaf Pine – Another name for Apache Pine, Pinus engelmannii.

Ark – Another name for a wanigan, the floating cookhouse used in the days of river drives.

Arkansas House – A type of house, first built in Arkansas, that incorporated a variety of energy-saving ideas such as extra insulation, thicker walls, double-pane windows, etc. The prototype for construction that has become increasingly common in the North Central and Plains states.

Arkansas Rule – A log rule. See Doyle Rule.

Arm – A cross-arm.

Armillaria Root Disease – A destructive fungus, especially harmful to hardwoods.

Arm's Length Transaction – A sale involving two parties who are independent of each other. In such a transaction no special consideration, such as preferred pricing arrangements, special services, etc., is made because of one party's relation to the other. Sales within a company, or other transactions between parties having some legal, financial, or other common connection, are, by definition, not arm's length transactions.

Aromatic Red Cedar – Juniperus virginiana. An aromatic wood of Eastern North America. It is used in construction of cedar chests or as paneling in storage closets as a deterrent to insects.

Arris – A sharp ridge or edge formed by the meeting of two surfaces at an exterior angle.

Arrival Card – A self-addressed card sent by a shipper to a freight agent and designed to be returned to the shipper by the agent when the car reaches its destination. The card normally has blanks for the agent to fill in regarding arrival time, the total freight owed, and other information.

Arrow – A fancy-butt shingle pattern in which the exposed portion of the shingle roughly resembles the head of an arrow.

Arsneau – A derrick used to load logs.

Articulated Car – A railcar designed to flex around curves, capable of carrying overlength loads.

Asbestos – A fibrous mineral once used in various applications as fireproofing. The fibers were later found to be carcinogenic, and are now rarely used.

Asbestos Board

Asbestos Board – A fire-resistant panel made of a combination of cement and asbestos fibers.

Ash – Fraxinus americana, F. pennsylvanica, F. excelsior (in Europe). A flowering, red-fruited tree whose wood is used to produce hoops and bentwood items.

Ashe Juniper – Juniperus ashei. This species, found in a range from Southern Missouri to Northern Mexico, is used for posts, railroad ties, and fuelwood, as well as an ornamental.

Ashlar – 1. A short wall from the attic floor to the rafters. Also called a Knee Wall. 2. Building stones cut nearly true to permit use of very thin mortar joints. 3. A wall faced with such stones.

Asking Price – The price asked by a seller, usually a producer or wholesaler, for his stock. Also, the "list" price.

Asparagus – Small logs strapped into a bundle for ease of handling from the woods to a pulp mill.

Aspect – The view from a building in a specific direction, or the side or surface that faces a certain direction. In forest engineering, the direction a slope faces.

Aspen – Any of several species of poplar, including Populas tremuloides, and P. gradidentata. The leaves of this tree tremble in the slightest breeze, giving rise to one popular name, Quaking Aspen. The wood is used for pulp, in the manufacture of oriented strand board, and in roofing shakes.

Asplund Process – A method for reducing wood to fibers in the manufacture of pulp and fiberboard. Defibrating.

Assay Zone – The portion of a treated wood item in which the minimum quantity of preservative is specified and is to be determined by extraction or by chemical assay.

Assembly Time – 1. The time required to complete construction of a building or a component such as a roof truss or pre-hung door. 2. In plywood manufacturing, that period of time between the spreading of adhesive on surfaces to be joined and the application of pressure to the joint. See Open Assembly Time.

Assigned Railcar – A railcar assigned to a particular shipper for a specified time. It cannot be used by another shipper without specific permission.

Assignment – A written transfer of title or interest in a property.

Associated Species – A species found to be numerically more abundant in a particular forest successional stage as compared to other stages.

Association Weights – A schedule of the estimated weights of various forest product items published by an association of manufacturers for use by its members in calculating shipping costs. Although once a common practice, the publication of such schedules was discontinued by associations because of anti-trust implications. See Estimated Weights.

Astel – Planks used overhead in constructing a tunnel.

Astragal – A moulding pattern. There are two basic types, a T-astragal and a flat astragal. The T type is attached to one of a pair of doors to keep one door from swinging through the opening. The flat type is used for decorative purposes.

Athey Wheels – Endless treads, similar to those on dozers, used on logging trailers in soft ground.

Atlantic White Cedar – Chamaecyparis thyoides. This species is found in a narrow coastal belt from Maine to Florida and westward to Mississippi. It is not a major species. The wood is used most often for shingles, posts, and interior finishes.

Atlas Cedar – Another name for Atlantic Cedar. Chiefly British.

At Ship's Tackle (AST) – A term used in water transportation to indicate the point at which the price (mill cost, freight, insurance, etc.) is calculated. Generally, a.s.t. means the cargo is delivered and deposited on the receiving dock at the end of the ship's tackle, or unloading equipment.

Attached Columns – Columns which project from a wall.

Attached Housing – Private residences that are attached on one or both sides to other, similar, residences. For example, duplexes, fourplexes, row houses.

Attachment – The legal act placing a debt-

or's property in the custody of the law, pending the outcome of a creditor's suit.

At the Market – In futures trading, an order to buy or sell at the best price obtainable at the time the order is received.

Attic Base – The bottom part of a Doric or Ionic column.

Attrition Mill – A device for reducing wood to fibers or small chunks by friction; a hog.

Auction Sale – A method of selling timber, usually publicly owned, in which various potential buyers bid in an oral auction, with the highest bidder winning the right to buy the timber. Sealed bid "auctions" are also held. In this system, each bidder submits a single offer equal to, or higher than, the minimum bid price, with the sale awarded to the highest qualified bidder.

Auditing – A review of freight bills to determine whether errors in charges have occurred. Often done by an outside auditor for a percentage of the claims recovered.

Auger – A long drill bit used to make holes in trees or timbers.

Australian Brown Pine – Podocarpus elatus. Native to Australia, this softwood is not a true pine. Also called She Pine.

Australian Clears – A select grade that allows streaks or pockets of pitch. Graded high D Select, with the exception of the pitch allowance.

Australia Pine – Pinus radiata. Monterey Pine grown in plantations.

Austrian Pine – Pinus nigra. Also called Black Pine.

Authorized Grader – One who has been authorized to act as an agent for an approved grading agency. See Approved Grader, Certified Grader.

Autobucking – A system using an electronic scanner to measure long log geometry in order to maximize value of the log. The scanner determines such variables as diameter at various intervals along the log, as well as crook, sweep, and other factors. This information is then fed to a computer, which will calculate the optimum lengths to which to buck the log.

Autoclave – An airtight container used in pressure treating wood to prevent insect damage or rot.

Automatic Grade Mark Reader – A scanning machine that reads the marks placed on lumber by the grader, and automatically applies the appropriate grade stamp.

Average Agreement – An agreement between a shipper and a carrier under which demurrage debits are used to offset credits.

Average Annual Mortality – Mortality that occurs when a tree becomes unusable for timber because of damage, disease, insects, etc. The average annual mortality usually represents a stand of trees and is expressed as a percentage of the number in the stand that become unusable during the year. It may also be broken down by diameter class.

Average Customer Specifications – A descriptive term that indicates that a particular offering from a producer or wholesaler contains a typical assortment of the normally desired lengths, widths, grades, etc.

Average Demurrage Agreement – See Average Agreement.

Average Yarding Distance – The average yarding distance for a particular setting, obtained by dividing the total yarding distance for all turns by the number of turns.

Awarded Sale – A federal timber sale that has been let to a successful bidder through a formal contract.

Ax – An instrument used for chopping or splitting with a bladed head attached to a handle. A double-bitted ax is one with blades on opposite sides of the handle; usually one is knife-sharp for cutting across the grain while the other is blunt and used for splitting. A single-bitted ax has a broad end, or poll, opposite the blade which often doubles as a sledge.

Ax Handle Punch – A punch used to drive broken ax handles out of the ax head.

Axial Force – Compression or tension along the length of a member, measured in pounds.

Axial Stress – The axial force action at a point along the length of a member, divided by the cross-sectional area of a member, expressed in pounds per square inch.

Terms Of The Trade

Axil

Axil – The angle between the stem and a branch. –

Ax Man – A faller.

Azeotrope – A liquid, or mixture of liquids, having constant maximum and minimum boiling points and capable of being distilled without decomposition.

Azeotropic Drying – A method of drying wood in which a heated liquid mixture is used to draw out water. The azeotrope is recovered by distillation, while the water evaporates.

Babe – The name of Paul Bunyan's mythical blue ox.

Baby Square – A piece of lumber approximately four inches square produced for the Japanese market, usually of Western Hemlock. Net sizes are 3-9/16x3-9/16 inches (90x90mm) and 4-1/8x4-1/8 inches (105x105mm); lengths are mostly 3 and 4 meters.

Bacillus Thuringiensis (Bt) – A soil bacterium used as an organic insecticide to control insects such as the spruce budworm or the gypsy moth.

Back – The side of a piece of lumber or plywood opposite the face. The back is the side with the lower overall quality or appearance.

Back Arch – A concealed arch that carries the inner part of a wall, while the exterior facing is carried by a lintel.

Back Around – A turnaround; a wide area at the end of a logging road in which a log truck can be turned around.

Back Band – A rabbetted moulding used to surround the outside edge of a casing.

Back Bevel – A sloping cut on the back of a board or timber, as in beveled siding.

Back Block – Another name for a tail block, a pulley that is attached to an anchor stump, and through which a cable is passed and used to return the mainline and chokers to the cutting area from the landing.

Back Cant – A technique in which a cant hook is used to hold a log back instead of rolling it forward.

Back Cut – The second and final cut made when felling a tree. The first cut, called the undercut or face cut, is made on the side of the tree in the direction it is intended to fall. The back cut is then made on the opposite side of the tree.

Backer – A non-decorative laminate used on the back of a composite panel to protect the substrate from changes in humidity and to balance the panel construction.

Back Fill – To replace material such as earth removed during a construction project, especially around a foundation. Also, the material itself.

Back Fillet – The return of a fillet moulding.

Backfire – A blaze set by fire fighters in the path of a forest fire in an effort to check the wildfire by cutting off the fuel supply in its

Terms Of The Trade 15

Back Guy

path. A backfire is started where a fire trail has been cleared and is made to burn between that trail and the wildfire.

Back Guy — A support line on a spar tree, rigged so that it is opposite the mainline.

Back Haul — 1. The movement of goods by truck or rail on the return trip after a loaded outward-bound run. For example, a trucker delivering machinery from Chicago to Seattle may pick up a load of lumber as a back haul for the return trip. 2. A line, usually called a haulback, used to return chokers to the chokersetters after a turn of logs has been hauled to the landing.

Backing Board — See Dog Board.

Backing Grade — A grade of hardwood plywood.

Backline — Another term for haulback, the line used to return the mainline and chokers from the landing to the cutting area.

Back Lining — Thin boards used in construction of double-hung windows to enclose a box for the balance weights, and to keep the box free of mortar.

Back Months — The more distant months in which futures trading is being conducted. Also known as Deferred Months.

Backout — See Nail Pop.

Back Out — To groove or remove a portion of the wood on the unexposed face of a wood member to better fit over irregular surfaces.

Back Priming — The application of a coat of primer paint to the back side of a plywood panel, or piece of lumber siding, for the purpose of preventing warping or deterioration, especially due to dampness.

Back Saw — A type of thin saw used in carpentry work. The back (non- cutting) edge of the saw is stiffened with a steel or brass strip.

Back Spar — A tree or pole used to support one end of a skyline logging system. The back spar supports the end of the system away from the landing. Also called a Tail Tree, or Tail Pole.

Back Stamp — A grade mark on the back of a board to preserve the appearance of its face.

Back Strap — In logging, a line running from the rear of a donkey to an anchor, usually a stump, to keep the donkey in place while it is pulling.

Back Timber — A term used in the Lake States to describe timber that was located a distance from a river and had to be hauled by sleigh to a point for movement downriver.

Back-to-Back — A system of purchasing in which a wholesaler has a buyer for a particular order before the order is placed with the producer. This type of trading eliminates the speculative risk to the wholesaler; many restrict themselves to back-to-back purchases during periods of market weakness.

Backup Roller — A roller that holds a peeler block against the veneer lathe knife. See Powered Backup Roller.

Bacteria Mold Resistance — A requirement that plywood bonded with intermediate glue be made with an adhesive possessing a high degree of resistance to attack by bacteria and mold organisms.

Bad Car — See Bad Order Car.

Bad Fill — A customer order for a futures market transaction that is filled at an unfavorable price due to a sudden move in the market and the lack of orders on the opposite side.

Bad Order Car — A rail shipment that has been delayed by the carrier. The rail car may be taken out of service temporarily for repairs with the shipment still in it.

Bag Boom — A type of log boom, or raft, in which a number of logs are encircled by a chain of boomsticks, without regard for the arrangement of the logs. The simplest type of log boom.

Bag House — A sander-dust collector in a plywood plant.

Baguette — A bead or astragal used in finish carpentry.

Bait Log — See Trap Tree.

Baker Raft — An ocean-going log raft, consisting of a permanent frame enclosing a system of cross logs, each with a number of logs chained to it.

Balanced Construction — See Balanced Panel.

Banded

Balanced Matching – A method of laying up face veneers in which more than two pieces of uniform size are used in a single face.

Balanced Panel – A plywood panel having face and back veneers of uniform thickness. A balanced panel is less likely to warp.

Balance of Payments – A measure of financial transactions between the United States and foreign countries. A favorable balance occurs when incoming payments from foreign countries exceed U.S. payments to foreign creditors; an unfavorable balance occurs when outflow exceeds income.

Balance of Trade – The difference between the total values of exports and imports of goods and services.

Baldcypress – Taxodium distichum. This species, one of two deciduous softwoods, grows throughout the South. It is most often found in swamps or other watery sites. The heartwood of this species is highly resistant to decay and is used in a wide variety of applications where durability is a factor. The sapwood is less decay-resistant and is seldom used.

Balk – See Baulk.

Ball Hooter – In the early logging days, a worker who rolled logs down a hill.

Ball Milling – The hogging or grinding of particles.

Balloon Framing – A framing system in which joists are fixed to vertical studs running the full height of the building, from the ground sill or plate through intermediate floors to the head plate supporting the roof rafters. The opposite of platform framing.

Balloon Loan – A loan on which interest (and sometimes small amounts of principal) is paid periodically until, at the end of a stated period, the large balance becomes due in a lump sum. A method of interim financing while longer-term arrangements are made.

Balloon Logging – A system of logging in which a large, helium-filled balloon is used to lift the logs off the ground; the balloon, in effect, takes the place of the spar tree in a high lead operation.

Balsa – Ochroma lagopus. This wood, one of the lightest known, is native to Central and South America. Although relatively strong for its weight, it has no use in construction. However, it is widely used for such purposes as model building and packing material.

Balsam – A common name for some poplars or cottonwoods.

Balsam Fir – Abies balsamea. This species is native to the Upper Midwest, the Northeast, and Eastern Canada. Its wood is used mostly for pulp.

Balsam Pine – Another name for Eastern White Pine, Pinus strobus.

Baltic Pine – A name applied, chiefly in England, to any of a variety of red wood species originating in countries around the Baltic Sea.

Baltic Spruce – Another name for European Spruce, Picea abies.

Baluster – Columns of spokes used in a stair rail as support and/or for decorative effect.

Balustrade – A series of balusters joined by a rail to form an enclosure for balconies, stairs, etc.

Bandage Treatment – A preservative treatment using a slow-release chemical.

Banded – Lumber or plywood secured

Double Cutting Band Mill

Terms Of The Trade 17

Banding

Modern, Computerized Band Mill

with steel strapping for ease of handling.

Banding — Wood strips or veneers attached to the exposed edges of plywood or particleboard in the construction of furniture or shelves.

Band Joist — A horizontal lumber member that is butted against the ends of floor or ceiling joists to tie the joists together and add support. Also called a Ribbon Joist.

Band Mill — A sawmill using a toothed, endless steel blade for its saw.

Band Saw — A saw consisting of a continuous piece of flexible steel, with teeth on one or both sides, used to cut logs into cants and also to rip lumber.

Band Sticks — Sticks of wood between which shingles are packed in bundles.

Bangor Board — A unit of measurement of lumber used in Maine when Bangor was a major lumber marketing center. A Bangor Board was a piece one inch thick, 12 inches wide, and 12 feet long.

Bank Beavers — In the days of river drives, those workers who brought up the rear.

Banked Logs — Logs that were piled on the edge of a river in anticipation of rising water that would float them.

Banker — A worker who piled logs on a riverbank in preparation for a river drive.

Banking Ground — An area beside a river or other body of water on which logs were decked prior to floating them to the mill.

Bank Scale — The footage volume of logs piled in a banking ground.

Banksian Pine — Another name for Jack Pine, Pinus banksiana.

Bannister — A balustrade, especially one on the side of a staircase.

Baptist Cone — A steel cone placed over the front of a log in a ground yarding operation to facilitate skidding the log along the ground. Seldom used in the West, the Baptist Cone was most often seen in the Great Lakes region, where it was invented by William Baptist.

Bar — A narrow, rabbeted, horizontal, vertical, or diagonal sash door member, extending the total length or width of the glass opening.

Barber Chair — A tree that splits up the middle while being felled, whipping the butt of the tree toward the faller and endangering him, and leaving a stump with a vertical "chair back." Also called a Tombstone.

Barber Pole — A tree that has fallen against another, bending the latter tree over. A hazard to loggers.

Barcode — A label bearing a symbol consisting of a series of bars and spaces affixed to individual pieces of lumber or other merchandise. Used with a scanning device at the point of sale, barcodes improve inventory control and the speed and accuracy of clerks at checkout lines.

Bardon — A type of choker hook, used in logging.

Bare — Undersize; the opposite of full.

Bareboat Charter — A leasing arrangement in which a shipper charters a vessel only and is responsible for providing his own crew, and for supplying and servicing the vessel during the length of the contract.

Barefaced Tenon — A tenon with a "shoulder" on only one side, used in the construction of certain kinds of doors.

Bare-Root Seedling — A seedling grown together with others in a single mass of dirt instead of in its own separate container.

Barge — A flat-bottomed boat used to move freight. Barges are usually not powered, and are towed by other craft.

Barge Board – A board used to cover the ends of the purlins and ridge on the gable of a building. Barge boards are sometimes painted or carved as a type of ornamentation.

Bark – The outermost covering of a tree.

Bark Beetle – Any of various beetles that kill conifers by girdling the cambium layer with galleries in which eggs are laid. The tree dies because nutrients cannot be drawn from the soil, through the cambium layer, to the growing part of the tree.

Bark Blister – A type of disease attacking trees, particularly certain types of pines.

Barkboard – A type of panel constructed of bark particles.

Bark Dray – A sled used to haul bark from the woods in the early logging days.

Bark Eater – Slang for a logger or sawmill worker.

Barked – 1. Sniped. Refers to a log that has had one end rounded to facilitate pulling or skidding it along the ground. 2. A reference to a log that has had its bark removed.

Barker – 1. One who peels bark from trees. 2. A tool used for removing bark, or a machine designed for that purpose. Bark is removed from logs before sawing to segregate it from solid wood residues, which are converted to chips or particles for use in various products.

Bark Flour – An extender for adhesives, made from finely ground bark.

Bark Hack – A mark made on the bark of a log, designed to identify ownership; such marks were common before log brands were used. The hack was usually made with an ax.

Barking Ax – A small broad-ax used to ring the bark of a log before peeling with a barking iron.

Barking Drum – A drum in which small logs are rotated against knives to remove their bark preparatory to pulp manufacture.

Barking Iron – A tool used to remove bark from a log; a spud.

Barking Saw – A saw used to detect metal or other foreign matter that may damage a head saw. Removal of bark before sawing, and the use of electronic metal detectors, have reduced the use of barking saws.

Bark Mark – See Bark Hack.

Bark Marker – A person who marked logs with an identifying mark in the bark in the days before logs were branded on the ends.

Bark Percentage – The weight or volume of bark on a tree in relation to the complete tree.

Bark Pocket – A patch of bark partially or wholly enclosed in the wood.

Bark Side – The side of a piece of lumber which, if it were still part of the log, would be closest to the bark. The side on which the grain is least likely to raise or separate from the body of the piece.

Bark-to-Wood Bond – The degree of bonding between the bark and outer wood of a tree; this varies among species and in other circumstances.

Bark/Wood Separation – The segregation of bark from wood through the use of screens.

Barky – A log with the bark still on it.

Barky Strips – An early term for material used for crating.

Barnhart Loader – A steam-powered log loader mounted on a rail car.

Barometer – An index of market activity, based on statistics concerning production, sales, inventories, and shipments. Barometers are prepared using reports submitted by a sample of producers to their trade associations.

Barrel Saw – A type of saw in the shape of a drum having a toothed band attached to the free end. A hole-cutting saw.

Barrel Vault – A semi-circular arch. The simplest form of vaulting.

Bar Room – An early term for a building in a logging camp in which the loggers slept.

Barter – A form of trade in which two or more parties exchange goods of comparable value. Used in international trade in place of currency transactions.

Basal Area – The cross-sectional area of a tree, in square feet, measured at breast

Base

height. One method of measuring the volume of timber in a given stand.

Base – A type of moulding, used where floor and walls meet to protect the walls from kicks, bumps, and scuffs, and to cover the unfinished edge of plaster or gypsum board. Can be made of wood, vinyl, or other material. Also called a baseboard.

Baseboard Pull-Away – A condition that occurs when floor or ceiling joists with excessive moisture content are installed. As the lumber dries and shrinks, the floor or ceiling is pulled away from the baseboard moulding.

Base Line – The starting reference line used when doing surveying or timber cruising.

Base Period – The period of time, usually a year, which is assigned a value of 100 in a statistical series, with subsequent data expressed as a percentage of the base for comparison.

Base Shoe – A small moulding placed at the foot of a base moulding to trim the area where the base and floor meet.

Base Stock – In the manufacture of coated paper, the stock to which the coating is added.

Basic Building Code – The standard regulations governing building construction and occupancy.

Basing Point – A procedure for figuring delivered prices. The buyer figures his cost from the area used as a base, even though the product may not have been shipped from there.

Basis – 1. The difference between the cash price and the futures price of a specific commodity. 2. A method of measuring the output of panel mills, in which production volumes of different thicknesses are converted to a standard basis for calculation purposes. For example, plywood is generally measured on a 3/8-inch basis. Thus, a 4x8' panel with a 3/8-inch thickness would contain 32 square feet, while a 3/4-inch panel would contain 64 square feet.

Basis Grade – The grade of a commodity used as the standard of a futures contract. In lumber futures, the basis grade is Std&Btr. Also called Par Grade.

Basis Point – One one-hundredth of one percentage point, used to measure small differences in prices or yields.

Basis Trade – A futures trade that involves taking offsetting positions in futures and cash based on the price spread between the two.

Basis Weight – In papermaking, the weight of one ream of paper cut to basic size for its grade.

Bassett Pine – Another name for Loblolly Pine, Pinus taeda.

Basswood – Tilia glabra, T. americana, T. canadensis. A fine-textured, soft wood used in cabinet work and paneling. The Linden tree from which most excelsior is made.

Bast – See Bast Fiber.

Bastard Growth – A colloquialism describing fast-growing second-growth timber.

Bastard Sawn – Lumber that has been sawn so that the annual rings make angles of 30 to 60 degrees to the surface of the piece.

Bast Fiber – Tough and fibrous inner bark, sometimes used to manufacture nets and cordage. Ligneous fibers obtained from phloem tissue.

Batch Kiln – See Compartment Kiln.

Bateau – A flat-bottomed boat used on river drives.

Batt – A strip of insulating material, such as fiberglass, designed to be placed between framing members, such as studs or joists.

Batten – A narrow strip of wood used to cover the joints of boards or plywood used as siding; this siding pattern is referred to as board and batten.

Batter Board – A temporary framework used in locating corners when laying out the foundation for a building.

Batter Post – An inclined timber forming a side support to a tunnel roof.

Battery Stock – Wood with a fine, straight grain (usually a cedar) used as partitions between the cells of a battery. The wood is neutral to the acid used in a wet-cell battery.

Baulk – A sawn or hewn timber with dimensions of 4 inches by 4-1/2 inches or greater.

Bavins – Wastewood of various kinds, including firewood, chips, brushwood, etc.

Bay – In construction, a space between two main trusses or beams.

Bayonet Top – A tree whose top has been broken off and which has grown a new leader. The position of the new leader is often reminiscent of the way a bayonet is attached to a rifle.

BB Exterior – A sanded plywood panel with B-grade veneers on the face and back and C-grade inner plies bonded with exterior glue.

BB Interior – A sanded plywood panel with B-grade veneers on the face and back and D-grade inner plies; bonded with either exterior on interior glue but recommended for use in interior or protected areas.

BB Plyform – American Plywood Association trade name for a concrete form panel with B-grade face and back veneers and C-grade inner plies, bonded with exterior glue. Manufactured specifically for concrete form work. Plyform is marketed as Class I or Class II, depending upon timber species used in construction of the panels.

BC Exterior – A plywood panel with a sanded B-grade face; C-grade veneers are used in the back and inner plies. Bonded with exterior glue.

B.C. Fir – Another name for Douglas Fir.

B.C. Rule – See British Columbia Rule.

BD Interior – A plywood panel with a sanded B-grade face and D-grade back and inner plies. It is bonded with interior or exterior glue and recommended for interior or protected areas.

Beachcomb – To search along a beach or coastline for logs than may have escaped from a log boom or raft.

Bead – 1. A narrow, half-round moulding, either attached to or milled on a larger piece. 2. A square or rectangular trim of less than one inch in width and thickness. 3. A choker ferrule; the knob on the end of a choker.

Beaded – A piece of lumber decorated with a raised half-circle bead along its length.

Beads – Slang for the chain used to bind loads of logs; used chiefly in the early logging days in the Lake States.

Beak – A drip mould.

Beam – A structural member, usually larger than five inches in width and thickness, used horizontally to support a load.

Beam and Column – A type of construction consisting of a series of rafter beams supported by columns.

Beam Hanger – A strap, wire, or stirrup used to support a beam. See Joist Hanger.

Beam Pocket – An opening in a vertical member in which a beam is to rest.

Beam Stability Factor – One of various adjustment factors affecting the "Extreme Fiber Stress in Bending" design value for lumber. The tabulated design value is multiplied by all applicable adjustment factors to determine the allowable design value.

Bear – One who is pessimistic about the market's prospects. One who anticipates a slow pace and lower prices is said to be "bearish."

Bear Cat – A type of drag saw, with detachable wheels for ease of movement.

Bear Claw – A type of choker hook, used in early-day logging.

Bearing Area Factor – One of various adjustment factors affecting the "Compression Perpendicular to Grain" design value for lumber. The tabulated design value is multiplied by all applicable adjustment factors to determine the allowable design value.

Bearing Capacity – The maximum amount of pressure that a material such as soil can withstand without failure or settlement to a degree that is detrimental to the integrity or function of a structure.

Bearing Tree – A tree used to mark a corner when surveying.

Bearing Wall – A wall that supports a load, such as the weight of the floor above.

Bear Market – A falling market; one that is weak or shows potential for falling prices.

Bear Rassler – See Edgerpicker.

Bear Scratch Figure

Bear Scratch Figure – A type of figure resulting from indented or fluted growth rings; lumber cut from logs having these characteristics shows a jagged grain pattern that resembles wood that might have been scratched by a bear.

Bear Trap – 1. A log pile that could roll and injure a logger. 2. A dam gate used to hold back water when driving logs down a river.

Beat – Ornamental grain in wood, cut tangentially to the annual rings.

Beat Camps – In the days of river drives, camps located along the river to accommodate the men driving the logs.

Beating – The process of separating entwined fibrils, or outer layers of fiber walls, to increase the bonding with other fibrils in paper making. Also called fibrilation.

Beats – Sections of a river on a log drive; separate crews would handle the logs through their beats.

Beaver – A derisive term for an unskilled logger, especially one who cleared roads with an ax and a grub hoe.

Beavertail Bar – A type of chain saw bar, wider at the tip than at the motor end.

Bed – To level or smooth a path in which a tree is to be felled, to prevent the tree from breaking as it hits the ground.

Bed Moulding – A moulding placed at an angle between a vertical surface and an overhanging horizontal surface, such as between a sidewall and the eave of a building.

Bed Piece – A skid placed under a lumber pile.

Beech – Any of a number of hardwoods of the genus Fagus, having characteristics of straight, close grain and good workability. Often used in furniture, turnings, tools, and similar products.

Beehive Burner – See Wigwam Burner.

Belfast Truss – See Bowstring Truss.

Belgian Truss – Another name for a Fink Truss.

Bell – The part of a choker that receives the nubbin from the other end. The choker is passed around a log, and the nubbin is inserted in the bell.

Bell Arch – A semicircular arch supported by quarter-round corbels.

Bell Butt – A log with a swell on the butt end, resembling a bell.

Belly – Slack in a cable.

Belly Guy – A wire or line attached to a spar tree or pole at or near its midpoint, to stabilize the pole.

Belt Rail – Another name for a lock rail, the middle rail of a door that usually contains the lock.

Belt Sander – A type of machine used to impart a smooth finish to wood or other material, consisting of an endless belt of cloth or rubber coated with an abrasive.

Bending Moment – A design value important in determining the requirement for beams and other structural members. At any cross section of a beam, the bending moment is the algebraic sum of the moments of external forces acting on one side of the section.

Bending Press – A device utilizing steam to produce curvature in wood.

Bending Strength – The ability of wood to support a transverse load by bending without collapse. Bending strength is the relation between the load and the deflection at midspan.

"B" End of the Car – The end of a rail car where the hand brake is located.

Benson Hook – An early-day choker hook.

Benson Raft – A log raft designed by Simon Benson, an early-day lumberman in the Pacific Northwest. The raft was constructed by placing logs in a cradle and binding them tightly into a huge "cigar" shape using chains. Benson rafts contained up to six million board feet of timber and were towed from the Columbia River to Benson's sawmill in San Diego. Benson rafts successfully withstood the stresses of a long ocean voyage, where earlier rafts broke up more frequently than they arrived at their destinations.

Bent – In heavy timber construction, two or more posts braced together to form a support.

Bent Girt – A horizontal member used as

Big Sticks

a brace between two columns or posts.

Bent Wood – Wood bent to curved shapes by bending while plasticized by moist heat or other agency, and set by cooling and drying.

Bermuda Cedar – Another name for Eastern Red Cedar, Juniperus virginiana.

Berthing Fee – A charge levied on a vessel by a port for the use of a berth.

Best Conventional Technology (BCT) – Widely accepted, widely used technology, not necessarily the best or latest available.

Best Management Practices (BMPs) – State or local regulatory or non-regulatory guidelines for protecting waterways as required by federal statutes, including the Clean Water Act and the Water Pollution Control Act.

Best Opening Face System (BOF) – A computer program developed at the U.S. Forest Products Laboratory. The program determines the optimum sawing pattern to use on a log in order to maximize the lumber yield of the log. Using the system, the dimensions of the log, along with mill variables such as saw kerf, sawing method, etc., are fed into the computer. The computer compares all possible sawing patterns and determines which one is most efficient.

Best Order – An order to an agent to buy or sell foreign currency at the best price available, without stipulating a specific rate.

Bethel's Process – A treating process in which wood to be treated is placed in a cylinder, air is removed from the cylinder, and creosote is forced into the wood under pressure.

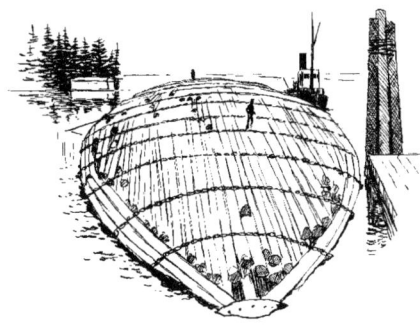

Benson Raft

Bettoni System – A method for rotary cutting of veneer.

Bevel Sawn – A term describing bevel siding that has been cut from board lumber. Boards are made into bevel siding by resawing them diagonally to gain the beveled dimensions.

Bevel Siding – A board that has been resawn diagonally to be used to clad the exterior of a building.

Bicycle – A carriage in a skyline logging system, running on an overhead cable between the spar tree and the tail tree.

Bid – An offer to buy at a specific price.

Bid-Ask Spread – The difference between the bid (buying) and ask (selling) prices of currency contracts.

Bid Rate – The rate at which a foreign exchange dealer will buy a currency.

Bid Ratio – In a public timber sale, the ratio or difference between the appraised value of the timber and the winning bid.

Big Bin – A proprietary name for a 300-gallon collapsible wooden bin constructed from 1-1/8-inch APA structural panels. The bin has a built-in pallet and a replaceable plastic liner that allows it to be used to ship a variety of wet or dry products. A smaller, 55-gallon version is called a Slim Bin.

Big Blue Butt – Loggers' slang for a large, good-quality log.

Big Bull – Same as Bull of the Woods.

Big Cone Douglas Fir – Pseudotsuga macrocarpa. A variation of Douglas Fir, found mainly in California.

Big Pine – Another name for Sugar Pine or Ponderosa Pine.

Big Square – See Falling on the Square.

Big Stick Loader – A mechanized system used to load pulpwood on a truck. The system consists of a vertical center post, a horizontal boom, a cable to which tongs are attached, and a winch powered by the truck engine.

Big Sticks – A term used in the Lake States to refer to "the woods."

Terms Of The Trade   23

Big Wheels

Big Wheels – Large wooden-spoked wheels, sometimes 10 feet or more in diameter, used to move logs in pre-mechanized days. The wheels had a high axle from which the log was slung; one end of the log was held off the ground in this way, making it easier for a team of oxen or horses to pull the rig.

Bilateralism – In international trade, the requirement that shipments between two countries be done on vessels flying the flag of one of the countries involved.

Bilge Saw – A type of cylinder saw, often used in cutting stock for cooperage.

Billet – A short length of wood; a bolt.

Bill of Exchange – A negotiable instrument drawn by one person, ordering a second person to pay a specified sum of money to a third party on demand. Also, a draft.

Bill of Lading – A document issued by a carrier, acknowledging receipt of the goods being shipped and serving as a contract for the shipment.

Bill of Sale – A document which the seller gives the buyer to convey title to, or interest in, personal property.

Biltmore Stick – A measuring device carried by timber cruisers and used to determine tree diameters and heights. It usually includes a tree volume table. Named for the Biltmore Forestry School. Also called a Cruiser's Stick.

Binder – 1. Chain or cable used to secure logs to a truck. 2. A beam carrying common joists in a double floor.

Binding Chain – See Binder.

Bin Sorter – A mechanical system in which lumber is sorted by length, width, or thickness by dropping or ejecting pieces into individual bins or compartments. Also called a Drop Sorter, Pocket Sorter.

Biocide – Any substance capable of destroying living organisms.

Biodegradable – Capable of decomposing naturally in the environment.

Biodiversity – The mix of living organisms that make's up the Earth's biological systems.

Biological Diversity – See Biodiversity.

Biological Opinion – A document stating the opinion of the Fish and Wildlife Service or the National Marine Fisheries Service as to whether a federal action is likely to jeopardize the continued existence of listed species or to result in the destruction or adverse modification of critical habitat.

Biological Oxygen Demand – The demand placed on a body of water to provide oxygen to aid in the decomposition of organic matter.

Biomass – The total volume of organic matter in a given area.

Bioregion – An area of land distinguished by its environmental characteristics, rather than by national or political boundaries.

Biosphere – That part of the Earth's crust, including the land, water, and atmosphere, capable of sustaining life.

Birch – Any of a variety of hardwoods of the genus Betula. The wood, usually strong and fine-grained, is used for plywood, furniture, and turnings.

Birch Hook – A small hook used for handling small timbers.

Bird Cage – A screen placed over the top of a smokestack or chimney to prevent sparks from escaping. A Spark Arrester.

Bird Damage – Damage to a tree or piece of wood caused by birds. See Bird Peck.

Bird Peck – A mark or wound in a tree or piece of wood caused by birds pecking on the growing tree in search of insects. Also, wood containing such marks.

Bird's Beak Moulding – A type of drip mold, often part of a Doric column.

Birdseye – A contortion of the grain in a piece of lumber in the shape of a small circle or ellipse, sometimes resembling the eye of a bird. Lumber with this feature is sometimes desired for its decorative effect.

Bird's Eye Pine – Another name for Ponderosa Pine, Pinus ponderosa.

Bird's Mouth – In carpentry, a cut in the end of a piece of lumber that allows it to fit the corner of a supporting timber.

Birl – To cause a log to roll in water by treading on it, usually while wearing caulked or spiked boots to provide a grip. Birling, or log rolling, is often a competitive event at timber carnivals and other such gatherings. In birling, two persons try to dislodge each other from the log by alternating rapid rotation with sudden stops in an effort to cause the opponent to lose his balance.

Biscuit – Logger's slang for the chunk of wood removed from the undercut when felling a tree.

Bishop Pine – Pinus muricata. This species is found in scattered locations along the California coast and in Baja California. It is of little commercial value.

Bitch Chain – A short, heavy chain used in logging, especially for loading logs.

Bitch Link – An extra-heavy link on the end of a chain.

Blackbird – A riverman skilled in riding logs in a river drive.

Black Check – Resinous bark pockets; black streak.

Black Cypress – Another name for Baldcypress, Taxodium distichum.

Black Gang – Loggers working to salvage timber after a forest fire. The name is derived from the loggers' appearance after working with wood covered by charcoal.

Black Gum – Another name for Tupelo, Nyssa sylvatica.

Blackjack Pine – See Suppressed Pine.

Black Knot – A resinous knot that has oxidized to a black color.

Black Label – A grade designation for Number 3 grade cedar shingles, as designated by the Cedar Shake and Shingle Bureau, a grading agency and trade association. See Blue Label, Red Label.

Black Liquor – A by-product of paper production, sometimes used as a fuel to power the plant.

Black Logs – Logs from timber that has been burned in a forest fire.

Black Oak – Quercus velutina. This species, common to the eastern half of the United States, takes its name from the color of the bark of the mature tree. The wood is hard and heavy. It is used for flooring, furniture, and other products.

Black Pine – An informal name for several pine species, including Jackpine and Loblolly Pine.

Black Spruce – Picea mariana. This species is found primarily in the Upper Midwest, the Northeast, and Eastern Canada. Its wood is used most often for pulp.

Black Walnut – Juglans nigra. Common to the Eastern U.S. and Canada, this species is a favorite for fine furniture and cabinetry as well as for its nuts.

Blade Protrusion – A defect resulting from one segment of a cutting tool penetrating the surface more than other segments.

Blank – A piece of lumber, sometimes rough, from which finished products such as such as pencils, handles, or various milled items are made.

Blanked Lumber – Lumber dressed to a size in excess of standard dressed size but scant of nominal size. It may involve any dressing from S1S to S4S. It is usually intended for later remanufacture.

Blanker – The machine used to produce wood blanks for further processing into a finished product.

Blanket Rate – A discontinued rail freight rate that at one time applied to shipments from the Western U.S. and Canada to the "Official Territory" in the Northeastern U.S.

Blanking – Cutting wood to a rough size for later remanufacture.

Blasting Wedge – In the early logging days, a wedge that was loaded with explosives and detonated to break a log too large for skidding.

Blaze – A mark made on a standing tree to designate a trail, a survey line, or similar path. Usually made by chipping bark off the tree with an ax, but sometimes made by hanging bits of survey tape or by spraying paint on the tree. Also, to make such a mark.

Bleeding – A defect in finishing in which pitch diffuses through paint or varnish, causing stain or discoloration.

Blemish – Anything marring the appearance of lumber or plywood.

Terms Of The Trade

Blender

Blender — A machine that blends wood particles and resin in the construction of panels such as particleboard.

Blind — An assembly of wood stiles, rails, and wood slats or louvers used in conjunction with doors and windows.

Blind Arch — An arch concealed behind a wall facing.

Blind Conk — Hidden decay in a tree. Conks are usually a visible sign of decay; they sometimes fall off the tree, however, and the defect may go undetected by a timber cruiser or log scaler.

Blind Floor — A subfloor.

Blind Mortise — A mortise for a stud tenon.

Blind Punk — A dark streak in wood, often resembling a knot.

Blindstop — A rectangular moulding in a window frame.

Blister — 1. A type of tree disease, characterized by the seeping of pitch onto the bark surface. 2. In wood finishing, a defect that occurs when volatiles leaving a film are trapped and expand inside the film.

Blister Figure — A blister-like appearance sometimes found on flat-sawn or rotary cut surfaces, caused by unevenness in the annual rings. The figure appears as high or low areas of rounded contour.

Blister Rust — A fungal disease that attacks various species, with pines especially vulnerable.

Block — 1. A log to be used in veneer production that has been cut to a designated length, usually 4 or 8 feet. Sometimes referred to as a bolt. 2. A section cut from a cedar log for shingle or shake manufacture. 3. A large pulley used in logging. 4. A section of a log raft. 5. A geographic area of trees or vegetation that is distinct from surrounding conditions.

Blockboard — A type of panel made by bonding thin pieces cut from wood blocks to an adhesive backing; used primarily for decorative purposes.

Block Conditioner — A vat or room in which veneer blocks are conditioned for peeling, usually by steaming or soaking in warm water.

Block Cut — 1. The cut made with a power saw to take out the undercut chunk. 2. A clear cut.

Block Cutting — A method of logging in which alternate stands of timber are clearcut or left standing. This type of cutting can produce a checkerboard pattern when viewed from above.

Block Design — One method of laying up veneers to form a particular pattern.

Block Flooring — A type of flooring in which squares of wood, each with tongues and grooves, are fitted tightly together. Sometimes these blocks are patterned with a particular design of inlaid wood; this is known as parquet flooring.

Blocking — 1. Apparatus placed within a container or box car to prevent the load from shifting. An example is the bulkheads constructed to stabilize a load that is shorter than the inside length of the car. 2. Improper and incomplete drying of the finish of a panel, where the surface is dry but the subsurface has not cured. 3. Short pieces of lumber fastened between joists to stabilize them. See Bridging.

Block Pallet — A pallet having blocks between the pallet decks or beneath the top deck.

Block Roundup — Veneer produced from a log before the lathe knife cuts cleanly across the entire block. Taper in logs, and defects near the outer portion of them, yield veneer that is odd-shaped or unusable in plywood production. The odd-shaped veneer is either fishtail or random width.

Block Sale — A large volume, typically involving several carloads of lumber or plywood. A block sale usually implies that the price has been reduced by the seller.

Block Saw — A large crosscut saw used to cut logs into veneer blocks of specified lengths.

Block Shear Specimen — A 2x2x2-1/2-inch wood block used in determining shear strength, or shear parallel to the grain, of various species of wood.

Block Tally — A method of tallying lumber without counting each piece. The lumber is stacked in even-size blocks, the blocks are

Boarding

measured, and the board footage is then calculated from these measurements.

Blodgett Foot – A unit of measurement used in log scaling. One log rule, the New Hampshire Rule, used the Blodgett Foot as the standard unit. It is based on a standard one foot long and 16 inches in diameter; this volume is taken to equal one cubic foot.

Blood Adhesive – An organic adhesive, not suitable where it will be exposed to severe weather or moisture conditions.

Bloom – Crystals formed on the surface of treated wood by exudation and evaporation of the solvent in the preservative solution.

Blow – A separation of a portion of veneers in a plywood panel, caused by a steam pocket that develops during the pressing process. When separation occurs on outer gluelines it can cause splits in the surface veneers.

Blow Down – A tree that has been felled by wind.

Blow Out – 1. A hole in a Red Cedar shake; a non-permissible defect in the shake. 2. A term describing a forest fire that crowns (burns into the highly flammable tops of trees) and becomes uncontrollable.

Blow Up – A forest fire that flares up explosively, burning in the tops of trees and jumping fire lines. See Blow Out.

Blue Butt – See Big Blue Butt.

Blue Goods – A reference to lumber or timber afflicted by blue stain, a discoloration of the wood caused by a fungus.

Blue Haze – An emission from veneer dryers; an air pollutant. Blue, or smoky, haze is also created by a growing forest on warm days and is responsible for the piney odor and "blue" color of some mountains.

Blue Label – A grade designation for Number 1 cedar shingles, as designated by the Cedar Shake and Shingle Bureau, a grading agency and trade association. See Red Label, Black Label.

Blue Nose – Slang for a logger from Nova Scotia.

Blue Pine – Pinus wallichiana. Native to India, this pine is used chiefly in that country for joinery, flooring, and other construction purposes. It is straight-grained and even-textured, but is quite soft for a pine.

Blue Spruce – Picea pugens. This spruce is usually found in conjunction with Engelmann Spruce, a species it closely resembles. The wood from this species is usually marketed under an Engelmann Spruce stamp. Also called Colorado Blue Spruce and used as an ornamental tree.

Blue Stain – A discoloration of wood caused by a fungus; usually occurring in the sapwood. It is particularly troublesome in Ponderosa Pine logs during the warmer months.

Board – A piece of lumber less than two inches in nominal thickness and one inch or more in width.

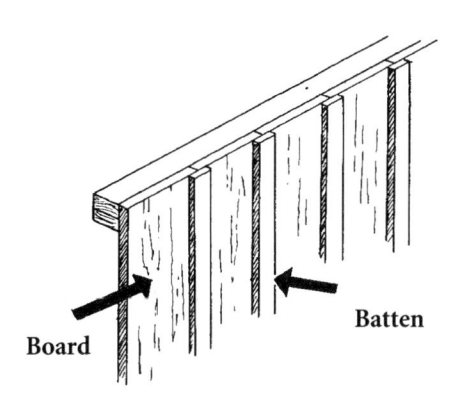

Board and Batten

Board & Batten – A type of siding in which narrow strips of wood are used to cover the joints of the boards or plywood used.

Board Foot – The basic unit of measurement for lumber. One board foot is equal to a 1-inch board 12 inches in width and 1 foot in length. Thus, a 10-foot long, 12-inch wide, and 1-inch thick piece would contain 10 board feet. When calculating board feet, nominal sizes are assumed.

Board Hole – A hole cut in a tree to accept a springboard.

Boarding – Any of various thin, usually wide, boards used collectively to board up or cover a wide surface.

Terms Of The Trade

Boarding Car

Boarding Car – A railcar used as a bunkhouse or cookhouse for loggers.

Board Measure – A term used to indicate that a board foot is the unit of measurement of lumber. For lumber with a nominal thickness of less than one inch, the number of board feet equals the product of the nominal width in feet and the length in feet.

Board of Review – An agency of the American Lumber Standards Committee that reviews the actions of grading agencies and others under the American Lumber Standard. The board can impose sanctions for violation of ALS provisions.

Board Rule Tally – A method of tallying certain grades and types of lumber; mainly S2S Shop and Moulding&Btr. The tallyman uses a flexible stick, or rule, to measure the width of each piece. Those that measure one-half inch or more above the last full inch are tallied as being the next full inch in width, while those less than one-half inch above the last full inch are dropped back. For example, a piece 11-1/2 inches in actual size is tallied as being 12 inches in widths, as is a piece 11-5/8 inches in width. However, a piece 11-3/8 inches in actual size is tallied as being 11 inches in width.

Board Up a Tree – To make a series of springboard holes, each higher than the last, to get to a point above the swell of the butt in a tree to be felled.

Boat Patch – An insert of sound wood used to replace defects in veneer or plywood. A boat patch is oval-shaped, with sides tapering in each direction to a point or to a small rounded end.

Bobber – A log that is partially sunk and bobbing up and down in the water.

Bobbin – 1. An insulated support for a traveling cable. 2. A reel on which thread is wound, as in stitching veneer.

Bob Cat – A crawler tractor logging without an arch.

Bob Tail – 1. A type of log truck with six wheels and no trailer. 2. A method of ground-skidding logs by hooking directly to the tractor without a lifting device to hold log ends off the ground.

Body Wood – That part of a tree consisting of clear, straight-grained wood, taken from the tree body below the limb area where most knots are found.

Bog – A lumber raft.

Bog Spruce – Another name for Black Spruce, Picea mariana.

Bogus – A corrugating medium made from reprocessed fibers from kraft or semichemical cuttings.

Boiler House – The steam plant in a sawmill.

Boiling in Oil – A special process for drying wood. Rough green wood products are submerged in an open hot bath of water-repelling liquid such as petroleum oil, creosote, or molten wax, which has a boiling point considerably above that of water.

Boiling Test – A means of testing the adhesion between parts of a piece of plywood or other laminated product by submitting the test piece to boiling water or other medium.

Boilproof Resin – A type of adhesive binder used in the production of oriented strand board and waferboard. When fully cured, it is not softened by heat or moisture.

Boker – A type of jack used to move logs in the early logging days. Named for its German inventor.

Bolander's Pine – Pinus bolanderi. A variation of Lodgepole Pine, P. contorta.

Bole – The trunk of a tree, especially that part immediately above ground.

Bolection Moulding – A type of rebated moulding in a door, with the face of the moulding standing above the face of the framing.

Bolman Truss – A type of truss used in the construction of timber deck bridges.

Bolster – A piece of wood, generally a nominal four inches in cross section, placed between stickered packages of lumber or other wood products to provide space for the entry and exit of the forks of a lift truck.

Bolt – 1. Raw material used in the manufacture of shingles and shakes. A wedge shape split from a short-length log and taken to a mill for manufacturing. 2. A short log to be sawn for lumber or peeled for veneer. 3. A wood section from which barrel staves are made.

Border Point

Bolter – A machine with one or more ripsaws. Used to cut small squares for furniture stock.

Bolt Hook – A steel hook used to handle pulpwood.

Bond – 1. To hold together or join two materials. 2. The adhesion between materials. 3. A type of paper, often used for stationery.

Bond Failure – The rupture of a glue or other adhesive bond.

Bond Strength – The measure of the force required to break an adhesive bond.

Bond Timbers – Timbers placed in a brick or masonry wall to serve as a base to which lath or battens are attached.

Bone Dry Lumber – Lumber that is dried to zero moisture content in a laboratory. Used in the calibration of moisture meters.

Bone Dry Ton – A quantity of wood pulp that weighs 2,000 lbs. at zero percent moisture content. Also called an Ovendry Ton.

Bone Dry Unit – A measure of wood chip volume equal to 2,400 pounds of bone-dry chips from which all the moisture has been removed.

Bookmatched – Consecutive flitches of veneer from the same log, laid up side by side so that the pattern formed is almost symmetrical from the common center line. Used in decorative paneling and cabinetry.

Book Offset – A type of paper, used for general commercial printing.

Boom – A group of logs floating in a river or other body of water. Also, the ring of logs or timbers fastened together to enclose the logs. A log raft.

Boomage – A booming ground. An area where log rafts are formed.

Boom Auger – A large tool used to bore holes in boomsticks, so that chains can be passed through them to form booms.

Boom Boat – A small, powerful boat used to herd logs around in a pond, to put together log booms, and to assist in towing. Also called a Bulldozer Boat.

Boom Buoy – A weight used to anchor log booms.

Boom Chain – A heavy chain used to tie logs together for towing.

Boom Company – A company engaged in the assembly and towing of log booms.

Boom Crew – The men who form and tow log booms.

Boom Dog – A steel wedge that is driven into a boom log and to which boom chains are attached.

Boomer – A small animal, also called a Mountain Beaver, that lives in the mountains of Western Oregon and Washington. The boomer forages on young coniferous trees and is thus considered a harmful pest by foresters.

Booming Ground – An area at the mouth of a river where log booms were held and/or sorted for ownership. Also called a Boom Works, Sorting Grounds, or Sorting Works.

Boom Jumper – A small boat used to round up logs in forming a boom.

Boomman – A person who arranges logs into a raft or boom. Part of a booming crew.

Boom Rat – A worker on a boom.

Boom Stay – A boom buoy.

Boomsticks – A series of logs chained together to form the outer boundaries of a log boom.

Boom Walker – A worker responsible for keeping log booms in good repair.

Boom Works – See Booming Ground.

Borate – A chemical retardant/suppressant used to fight forest fires. Aircraft, often reconditioned military bombers, "bomb" the fire with the chemical. Phosphate is more commonly used now.

Bordered Pits – Thin parts of radial cell walls in wood tissue through which moisture can move.

Border Point – A location along the U.S.-Canada border to which shipments of Canadian wood products are consigned. There they are broken down, reloaded on a truck or (less often) a railcar, and shipped to an ultimate destination. Also called reloads or lumber transfer yards.

Terms Of The Trade

Borer Hole

Borer Hole – A void made by a wood-boring insect, such as a grub or worm.

Boston Hip – A method of finishing the hip or ridge line of a shingled roof so that nails are not exposed to the weather.

Bottle Butted – A description of a tree with a large swell in the butt or lower trunk. Also called Swell Butted.

Bottle Hook – A wire wrapped around the neck of a saw-oil bottle, so that it could be hung on a stump or log. Oil, kerosene, and turpentine were used on saw blades to reduce friction caused by a buildup of sap and pitch.

Bottom – 1. In lumber trading, the point at which prices stop falling. Traders speak of the market "being at the bottom," or "bottoming out." 2. A low-level, marshy area. A swamp.

Bottom Chord – The horizontal member at the bottom of a truss.

Bottom Deck – A panel or assembly of deck boards comprising the bottom surface of a pallet.

Bottom Dropped Out – An expression describing a market in which prices dropped sharply, and continued to fall.

Bottomed Out – An expression signifying that a market decline has halted and prices have started to rise.

Bottom Loader – The member of a loading crew who attaches the tongs to the log.

Bottom Plate – The framing member that rests on a floor and to which studs are fastened. It provides a nailer to which surface materials can be fastened between studs.

Bottom Rail – Pieces of lumber, cut from shop, that are used to form the bottom horizontal member of a door.

Bottom Sill – The bottom log on a splash dam.

Bottom Skin – The bottom layer in a plywood stressed-skin panel, a composite system made up of plywood and framing lumber, glued together to act as a structural unit.

Bottom White Pine – Another name for Spruce Pine.

Boucherie Process – An unpressurized preservative treatment for wood, using waterborne chemicals.

Boulton Process – A wood preservative treatment utilizing intense heat in a vacuum.

Boundary Layer – A region of retarded air flow near the surfaces of an object being dried.

Bound Water – In wood technology, moisture that is intimately associated with the finer wood elements of the cell wall by adsorption and held with sufficient force to reduce the vapor pressure. Also Adsorbed Water, Hygroscopic Water.

Bow – Deviation flatwise from a straight line from end to end of a piece of lumber, measured at the point of greatest distance from the straight line.

Bow

Bow Boat – A small boat used to help steer a log raft.

Bow Saw – A type of chain saw in which the chain returns through a large metal frame bowed to curve around a tree trunk. The bow adds stability to the saw. Such saws were used primarily in felling eastern hardwoods; they were seldom used in the West due to the larger tree trunk sizes.

Bowstring Truss – A roof truss designed for long spans, but light loads.

Bowtell – A plain, round moulding.

Box Beam – A plywood, or plywood and lumber, beam engineered to combine light weight with great rigidity.

Boxboard – 1. Bundles of boards ready to be assembled into crates or boxes. Box Shook. 2. A classification of wagon stock made of hardwood.

Boxed Heart – A piece of lumber in which the heart, or pith, is enclosed within the four sides of the piece.

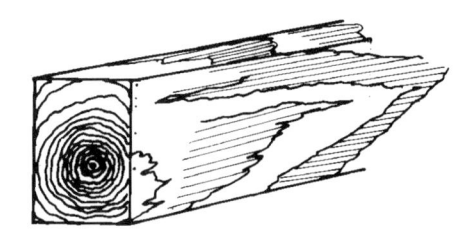

Boxed Heart

Boxed Heart No Defect (BHND) – A classification for lumber in which a piece with boxed heart is not considered defective.

Boxed Pith – Pith that is enclosed within the four sides of a piece of lumber.

Boxed Tenon – A right tenon on a corner post.

Box Grade – #3 common or better wood used in the manufacture of boxes.

Boxing Glove – An early-day choker hook.

Box Kiln – See Compartment Kiln.

Box Nail – A flat-headed nail used in rough framing. It is lighter and has a smaller shank diameter than a common nail.

Box Piling – A method of stacking random length lumber for drying. Full-length boards are placed on the outer edges of each layer, and shorter boards are alternated lengthwise to produce square-edged piles.

Box Scarf – A type of scarf joint used in the manufacture of wood gutters in which the overlapping joint is secured with screws and then usually painted.

Box Shook – Thin pieces of lumber used to make wooden boxes, usually cut to size and bundled together.

Brace Framing – A framing system in which all vertical structural elements of the bearing walls and partitions except the corner posts extend for one story only.

Bracing – See Bridging, Blocking.

Bracking – In the European timber trade, the act of grading or classifying wood products. It also implies a product whose quality is below the regular requirement.

Brackish Water Immersion – A level of treatment of wood products intended for use in, or in contact with, brackish water. As established by the American Wood Preservers Association, that level is 2.50 pounds of retained preservative per cubic foot of wood. This is the same level as required for salt water immersion.

Bracted Fir – Another name for Noble Fir.

Brag Load – In the early logging days, a very large load of logs, often created especially for a photograph.

Brail – A part of a log raft.

Brake Hickey – See Hickey.

Branch Knot – See Knot Occurrence.

Branchwood – Wood from branches.

Brand – An identifying mark on the end of a log, indicating the owner of the log. The brand is made on the log by hitting the end with a hammerlike device that bears the design of the brand. Also, paint sprayed on logs to indicate to the mill deck scaler which area the logs were from.

Branding Ax – A tool used to mark the ends of logs with a distinctive mark to designate ownership of the log. Also called a branding hammer.

Brashness – A condition of wood characterized by coarse, conspicuous annual rings. Such wood has a low resistance to shock and has a tendency to fail abruptly across the grain without splintering.

Brashy – A reference to wood afflicted with brashness.

Brazilian Cedar – Another name for Spanish Cedar, Cedrela mexicana.

Brazilian Pine – Another name for Parana Pine, Araucaria angustifolia.

Break – In carpentry, a change in the direction of a plane surface.

Breakage – That portion of a tree lost due to the break-up of the tree as it is felled. Trees may be badly broken if they are felled across other logs, stumps, etc.

Break Bulk – 1. To divide a large shipment into components to distribute to scattered destinations. 2. Ocean shipping of packaged goods that are not containerized.

Break Bulk Point

Break Bulk Point – A distribution point at which all or part of a load is unloaded and distributed.

Break Bulk Ship – A vessel designed to carry break-bulk, or non-containerized, cargo.

Break Cut – A cut made in a log to remove a portion that has suffered damage.

Break Down – To reduce a log to lumber or plywood.

Break Even Point – The point at which the selling price just equals the cost, leaving neither a profit nor a loss.

Breaking Radius – The limiting radius of curvature to which lumber or panels can be bent without breaking.

Breaking Strength – The greatest load that a material can withstand before failing. Also called Ultimate Strength.

Break Joints – A method of laying plywood sheathing so that the panels are offset and the ends do not line up in a single row. The same technique used when laying bricks.

Break Out – To release a log from a hang-up.

Breaks – Broken lengths or chunks of logs, usually not long enough to make into lumber, but suitable for pulpwood.

Breakup – The thawing of frozen ground; a term used in Canada and parts of the U.S. to denote that period when logging is hampered by road closures due to thawing ground. See Road Ban.

Breast – 1. The wide or heart side of a piece of lumber. 2. The toothed side of a crosscut saw. 3. A stair riser. 4. That portion of a wall from under a window sill to the floor level.

Breasted Shingles – Shingles cut from a block, using a splitting froe.

Breast Height – A standard height from average ground level. A point at which diameter, girth, and basal area of a standing tree are measured. Generally, 4.5 feet, or 1.37 meters, above ground level.

Breast Log – See Brow Log.

Brereton Scale – A log scale used extensively in the export and import trade. It is basically a cubic volume rule with multiplication by 12 for conversion to board feet.

Brewer Spruce – Picea breweriana. This species, also called Weeping Spruce, is characterized by long, string-like "branchlets" that hang down from its limbs. It is found at high altitudes in Southern Oregon.

Briar – A name for a crosscut saw.

Brickmould – A moulding that bridges the edge of brickwork and adjacent construction.

Bridging – Short pieces of lumber fitted between joists to act as bracing and to prevent the joists from shifting or tilting. Also called Blocking.

Bridle – 1. A system used to restrain logs when skidding them downhill. 2. A method of using two chokers to encircle a large log too big for a single choker.

Bright – 1. Unstained. 2. Untreated.

Bright Deal – In the British timber trade, a term describing lumber that has been sawn from logs that have not been floated in water and become discolored.

Bright, Dry, and Flat – A specification requiring lumber to have no discoloration, no warpage, and the required amount of drying.

Bright Sapwood No Defect – A term that indicates that sapwood is permitted in each

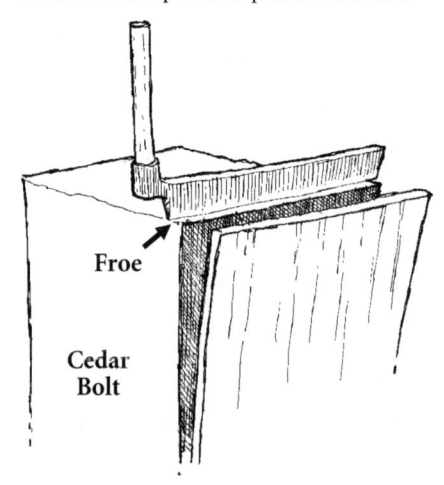

Breasted Shingles

Broomed Logs

piece of lumber, in any amount.

Bright Stock – Unstained or untreated wood.

Briquette – A compacted mass of fine material, usually compressed without a binder. There are various kinds of briquettes, including those made from charcoal, sawdust, bark, or shavings. All are used as fuel.

Briquettor – A machine that molds briquettes.

Bristlecone Fir – Abies bracteata. This rare species is found in the Santa Lucia Mountains of Northern California. Not a commercial species.

Bristlecone Pine – See Great Basin Bristlecone Pine, Rocky Mountain Bristlecone Pine.

Bristol – A type of paper used for index cards, file folders, etc.

British Columbia Fir – Another name for Douglas Fir.

British Columbia Firmwood Cubic Scale – The official log scale of British Columbia. This rule superseded the British Columbia Rule in 1972.

British Columbia Railway (BCOL) – This railroad is an important line involved in the movement of lumber in British Columbia. The line is owned and operated by the Province of British Columbia.

British Columbia Rule – A log scale that was used for many years in British Columbia. It was first used about 1895. In 1902, it became the official log rule for the province. It was replaced in 1972 by the British Columbia Firmwood Cubic Scale.

British Columbia Soft Pine – Another name for Ponderosa Pine. Chiefly British.

British Standards Institute (BSI) – An organization in the U.K. responsible for setting standards for a variety of commodities and industries in that country. Similar in purpose to the American National Standards Institute in the U.S.

British Thermal Unit (BTU) – The amount of heat required to raise the temperature of one pound of water one degree Fahrenheit.

Brittleheart – A defect in some tropical and subtropical hardwoods that develops when they are overmature. The defect is characterized by cracks in the heartwood of the tree, which can result in failure during sawing or later when the wood is in use.

Broadax – An ax with a large head, used for hewing timbers and cross ties.

Broadcast Burn – A deliberately set and controlled fire designed to reduce the danger of wildfire by consuming dangerous amounts of fuel such as slash, brush, etc.

Broadcast Seeding – A method of reforestation in which an area to be planted is sown with seed, often from an airplane or helicopter.

Broadleaf – A deciduous tree. A hardwood.

Broke – A British term for part of a forest marked for harvest.

Broken Flake – The breaking or loosening of the medullary ray, or flake, in quartered material; most frequently seen in oak.

Broken Grain – See Torn Grain.

Broken Stripe – Ribbon figure in which the stripe effect is not continuous.

Broken Unit – A number of pieces of lumber or plywood less than the number in a standard unit or package.

Broker – A person who buys or sells on behalf of another for a fee or commission.

Brokerage Fee – A fee charged by a broker for his services.

Broker Loan Rate – The fee banks charge securities dealers on loans backed by inventory. Securities dealers relend the proceeds to their clients buying stock on margin, or credit. This rate follows the federal funds rate.

Broker's Sale Measure – A method of determining the footage in logs, especially those used for furniture wood, such as mahogany. Also called Hoppus Measure. Used in the British timber trade.

Broomage – Extra length on a log, usually measured in inches, to allow for compensation for damage incurred during a river drive.

Broomed Logs – Logs whose ends become

Terms Of The Trade   33

Brow Log

damaged during a river drive.

Brow Log – A large log laid beside the track or road at a log dump or landing to prevent logs from swinging or kicking back when unloaded from railroad cars or logging trucks.

Browning Loader – A self-propelled, steam-powered log loader, mounted on a rail car.

Brown Rot – A type of decay found in wood and resulting from fungi. The fungi remove cellulose, leaving a dry, crumbly residue.

Brown Stain – A brown-colored discoloration of the sapwood of some pines, caused by a fungus that acts similarly to blue-stain fungus.

Brush – Loggers' slang for the woods.

Brush Ape – Slang for logger.

Brush Cat – Slang for logger.

Brushed Plywood – A type of plywood siding or paneling that has undergone a manufacturing process that abrades the soft portions of the wood to leave a raised grain pattern.

Brush Machine – A machine used to produce brushed plywood.

Brush Monkey – A slang term that can mean either a logger, timber cruiser, or other type of woods worker.

Brush Out – To clear brush away from a roadway or other area in the woods.

Brush Rabbit – Slang for choker setter.

Brush Scythe – A scythe used in "brushing out" an area in the woods.

Brush Treatment – A method of applying preservatives to lumber, using a brush.

Bubble – A short-lived market increase. Specifically, a market condition in which speculative buying has caused prices to surge without being supported by comparable end-use demand, resulting in a subsequent drop.

Bubble Cuffer – A log birler.

Bucheron – A name for a French-Canadian lumberjack.

Buck Cypress – Another name of Baldcypress, Taxodium distichum.

Bucker – A person who saws felled trees into logs.

Bucker's Break – A break or crack in a log caused by poor bucking technique.

Buck for Grade – To buck, or cut, a tree into various lengths in order to maximize the grade or quality of the logs. The opposite of cutting the tree into predetermined lengths, often equal, without regard to log grade.

Bucking Bar – A type of power saw designed to be used by one man; one lacking a handle on the bar end.

Bucking Prop – A limb or chunk of wood used to support a log so it will not bind the saw while being bucked.

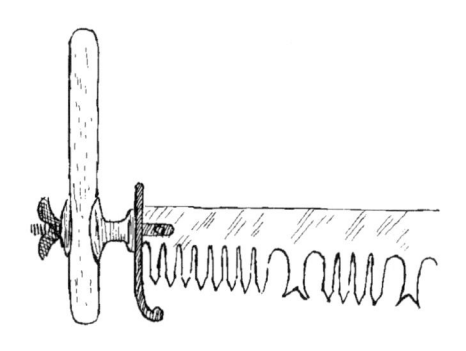

Bucking Saw

Bucking Saw – A crosscut saw used to cut, or "buck," felled timber into log lengths. A bucking saw was shorter and more rigid that a falling saw; it was straighter across the back and had a longer handle. A bucking saw usually was operated by a man at each end alternately pulling the blade through the log. However, on steep ground it was unsafe for a man to work on the downhill side of the log being sawn. Therefore, all bucking was done from the uphill side by a single bucker. Various mechanical devices were developed to take the place of one bucker, but success was limited until the advent of the gasoline-powered saw.

Buckle – See Veneer Buckle.

Buckling Strength – A measure of wood's ability to withstand a load applied with compression parallel to grain.

Buck Saw – A hand-powered saw used to cut firewood.

Buckskin – A snag. A standing dead tree or log whose bark has fallen partially or completely away and whose exposed wood has a bleached or "buckskin" appearance.

Buckwheat – A tree that was felled in such a manner that it lodged against another tree.

Buffer – A type of sanding machine used to smooth the finish between finishing coats.

Buffer Strip – An area of timber left uncut next to a stream, to minimize erosion and water pollution, or next to a road, for scenic considerations.

Buggy – A carriage on a skyline logging system.

Buggy Bell – A slang term for choker hook.

Bug Kill – An area of timber killed by an infestation of insects.

Bug Picker – An early-day tractor with three wheels, used in the Western Pine country.

Bug Tree – A tree infested with insects such as bark beetles.

Building Area – The greatest horizontal area of a building above grade, within the outside surface of exterior walls, or within the outside surface of exterior walls and the centerline of firewalls.

Building Board – Any of various kinds of wallboard, usually used as subwalls and ceilings and made of a variety of materials such as gypsum, wood particles, straw, etc.

Building Code – A set of regulations governing construction in a particular political subdivision, such as a city or county. The building code spells out certain requirements pertaining to such criteria as lumber strength values, grades, and spans.

Building Envelope – The sheathing of a building, to which exterior finishes are attached.

Building Height – The number of stories in a building, as measured from the floor of the first story to the roof.

Building Paper – A waterproof or water-resistant material used to form a vapor barrier under shingled roofs, or between sheathing and siding.

Building Permit – A certificate required by most cities, counties, or other political agencies before construction of a dwelling or other building may be undertaken. The number of building permits issued each month is an important measure of activity in housing construction.

Built Rib – A laminated member of a frame or structure. Chiefly British.

Built Up – The addition of one or more pieces to the width or thickness of a member.

Builtup Roof – A type of roof construction employing membranes laid over roof sheathing, with each layer covered in place by hot tar.

Builtup Timber – A timber produced by joining pieces of lumber together with mechanical fastenings.

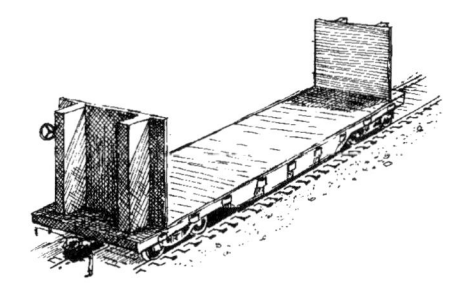

Bulkhead Flat Car

Bulk – A measure of the thickness of paper, expressed in pages per inch.

Bulk Cargo – Cargo that is not packaged or containerized when placed aboard a ship. Examples include grains, crude oil, and wood chips.

Bulk Carrier – A ship whose cargo space is suitable for the storage of loose or irregularly shaped commodities. Some common cargoes shipped on bulk carriers are grain, pulp, lumber, and plywood.

Bulk Density Factor – A method of comparing solid wood equivalent volume with the actual volume of processed wood such as chips, pulp, and particleboard. The solid wood equivalent volume is considered to

Terms Of The Trade

Bulker

have a bulk density factor of 1.

Bulker – A bulk carrier.

Bulkhead – An upright wall in a rail car or ship that separates one part from another.

Bulkhead Flat – A railroad flat car with a retaining wall at either end to provide additional load stability.

Bulk Space – The cargo capacity of a bulk carrier.

Bulk Transfer – The sale or transfer of goods in large volume outside the normal course of business. See Block Sale.

Bulk Weight – The weight shown by a carrier on a way bill or freight bill, for the purpose of assessing freight charges.

Bull – 1. One who is optimistic about the market's prospects. One who anticipates a quicker pace and higher prices is said to be "bullish." The opposite of "Bear." 2. A logging boss. See Bull of the Woods. 3. A tree whose limbs are close to the ground. 4. In loggers' slang, anything large, strong, or powerful.

Bull Block – In high-lead logging, the main line lead block.

Bull Buck – The lead man in a falling and bucking crew.

Bull Chain – A heavy chain used as a brake when skidding logs down a steep hill.

Bull Choker – A heavy-duty choker used on particularly big logs.

Bull Cook – A flunky in a logging camp; one who helped the cook and performed various other menial tasks.

Bull Donkey – A particularly large donkey.

Bulldozer – A crawler tractor with a heavy blade attached to the front. A bulldozer, or simply "dozer", is used both for roadbuilding and for logging.

Bulldozer Boat – A small but powerful boat used to herd logs around in a pond, to put together log booms, and to assist in towing. Also, a boom boat.

Bull Edger – The first and, usually, largest edger behind the headrig, to which low-grade cants are directed for ripping to widths

suitable for further manufacture on a resaw or trimmer.

Bull Engine – A logging locomotive.

Bull Gang – Any of various logging crews, especially one that did much of its work by hand rather than by machine.

Bull Hook – 1. A hook used to attach chokers to a line. 2. Any of various large hooks used in a logging system.

Bull Line – The main line in a high-lead logging system.

Bull Logging – A logging method in which bulls or oxen were used to drag the logs to the landing for loading. The common logging method in the early days of the industry.

Bull Market – A rising market, one that shows strength or upward potential.

Bullnose – The process of rounding an edge of a board used as shelving, stadium seating, stepping, etc.

Bull of the Woods – Logging superintendent or manager.

Bull Pine – See Suppressed Pine.

Bull Puncher – An ox driver; one who handled a team of oxen in bull logging.

Bulls – Oxen.

Bullseye – A timber or piece of dimension cut so as to center the pith. Boxed heart.

Bull Skinner – A Bull Puncher.

Bull Whacker – An ox or bull team driver. Also called a Bull Puncher.

Bully – A woods boss. See Bull of the Woods.

Bummer – A type of low-wheeled cart for moving logs, used in the early logging days.

Bumper – A diversion point; the point where a transit car is held until it is sold and shipped to its ultimate destination.

Bunch – 1. A turn of logs; one or more logs yarded at one time to the landing. 2. To gather logs together in a turn.

Buncher-Feller – See Feller-Buncher.

Butt Chain

Bunching Chain – A chain used to skid or drag a turn of logs.

Bunching System – A method of assembling small logs for subsequent handling.

Bunching Team – A horse team used in the Western Pine country to haul logs to a central point, where they were then moved by Big Wheels.

Bundling – A method of moving pulpwood in which a chain or cable is wrapped around a number of logs so that they may be dragged to a loading point.

Bundle – 1. A package of lumber, usually sorted by grade and/or size and most often consisting of narrow boards or strips. 2. A unit of shingles or shakes.

Bundled Lineal – A measurement of the combined length of all the bundles contained in a given shipment of bundled lumber. Bundled lineal is obtained by dividing the lineal footage of the entire shipment by the number of pieces per bundle. For example, if 90,000 lineal feet of lumber was packaged into six- piece bundles, the combined length of these bundles would be 15,000 feet "bundled lineal." The number of bundles in the shipment can then be calculated by dividing the bundled lineal measurement by the length of each bundle.

Bung – A stopper for the opening of a barrel or cask.

Bungalow – 1. A type of one-story house. 2. A type of siding, used to sheath the exterior of a building.

Bunk – A cross support on a logging truck or railcar that supports the logs.

Bunk Block – A wedge used to hold logs on a bunk. Also called a Cheese Block or a Chock.

Bunker Fuel – Fuel for ocean-going vessels.

Bunk Log – A log on the lower-most course when loading a truck or railcar; any log next to the bunk.

Bunya Pine – Araucaria bidwillii. This Australian wood is often grouped with species of similar characteristics under the name Queensland Pine.

Bureau – An agency with specific responsibility or authority, such as a scaling bureau or grading bureau.

Bureau of Land Management (BLM) – An agency of the U.S. Department of the Interior. The BLM has administrative control of large areas of public domain land in the West, including Alaska. It also administers the two million acres of forestland in the revested Oregon and California land grant in Western Oregon.

Bureau Scale – A log scale value established by any of various scaling bureaus and accepted by both buyer and seller as an independent and unbiased measure.

Burl – A distortion of grain, usually caused by abnormal growth due to injury to the tree.

Burn – An area of forest that has been burned by a forest fire. Usually referred to by as specific name, such as the "Tillamook Burn."

Burner – A receptacle in which mill wastes are burned. See Wigwam Burner.

Burnett's Process – The application of zinc chloride to timber or lumber by infusion, for the purpose of wood preservation.

Burning Brand Test – A process for testing the flammability of roofing materials by exposing the roof to a simulated airborne burning brand.

Burning Index (BI) – A number related to the degree of effort needed to contain a fire in a particular fuel type in a forest. A doubling of the index indicates that twice the effort will be needed to contain a fire in that fuel type.

Burr – Another name for a burl.

Bush – Canadian slang for "the woods."

Busheling – A system by which falling and bucking crews are paid by the volume of timber cut, rather than by the hour or other set rate.

Bush Ranger – A timber cruiser.

Butt – The lower end of a tree, or a log from that part of the tree closest to the stump.

Butt Chain – A short chain once used in logging in place of a choker. Also, a chain used between the butt rigging and the chokers in cat logging.

Butt Cut

Butt Cut – 1. The first log above the stump. 2. A slight vertical cut at the ends of bottom chord on a truss to ensure uniform span and provide clearance for sheathing. Also called a Heel Cut or Nub Cut.

Butt Diameter – A cross-sectional measurement of a log, taken at the butt end of the log.

Butt End – The end of a log nearest the butt, or stump end, of the tree.

Butterfly Hook – A type of choker hook once used on log skidders.

Butternut – Juglans cinerea. A member of the walnut family, this tree is also sometimes called White Walnut. Its wood is used for furniture, but is generally considered to be of lesser quality than Black Walnut.

Butt Flare – The swell of a log where a tree was cut close to the ground. Common in cedars.

Butt Hook – A heavy hook used to attach the chokers to the butt rigging.

Butt Joint – An end joint made by simply joining the square ends of two pieces of lumber or plywood. Butt joints are very weak.

Butt Lash – The tendency of a tree, when being felled, to jump out in an unexpected direction, with potentially fatal results to the faller.

Butt Line – Another name for a tag line, a short line connecting skidding tongs to the butt rigging.

Butt Log – The first log from the stump end of the tree.

Butt Plate – The end plate of a structural member.

Butt Rigging – A system connecting the haulback and mainlines to the butt hooks, from which chokers are fastened.

Butt Rot – Decay in the lower part of a tree.

Butt Saw – Another name for a crosscut saw.

Butt Veneer – Veneer marked with heavy curly figure, due to the way in which the tree roots are joined to the trunk.

Buyer – A generic term for anyone purchasing forest products. Specifically, one assigned to purchase products at the secondary or retail levels.

Buyer's Market – A situation in which supply exceeds demand, causing prices to fall and giving buyers an upper hand in negotiations.

Buyer's Option – An agreement by which a potential currency buyer can choose to take delivery of a currency contract at any time within the dates specified in the option.

Buyer's Right to Route – The right of a buyer of a commodity to specify the rail route of his shipment, when the seller does not pay freight charges. The seller is responsible for the buyer's instructions, while the buyer is responsible for freight charges stemming from a particular routing.

Buy-In – In futures trading, a purchase to cover a previous sale; short covering.

Buying Agent – One who buys forest products for a wholesaler or retailer, usually for a flat fee based on the volume purchased.

Buying Group – A cooperative.

Buying Hedge – The purchase of a futures contract to protect against possible increases in the cost of commodities that will be needed in the future.

Buying Service – A company that buys wood products for retailers or industrial users for a set fee or commission, but does not take title to the goods.

Buy List – A notice of a willingness to buy, usually at a stated price, certain lumber and plywood items, issued by wholesalers or other prospective buyers.

Buy On Close – In futures trading, to buy at the end of a trading session at a price within the closing range.

Buy On Opening – In futures trading, to buy at the opening of a trading session at a price within the opening range.

Buzzard Hook – A type of self-locking choker hook, used on skidders.

Buzz Saw – A circular saw.

Byatt – A timber placed horizontally in a trench to support decking or a walkway.

C

Cabinet Nailer – A bracing piece on the back of a cabinet, by which it is fastened to the wall.

Cabin Log – A small-diameter log used to construct a log cabin. There are machines that process logs for this purpose. Various patterns can be produced, including logs having flattened sides and a number of notch or groove patterns.

Cable Logging – A system of logging using wire rope in which the winches are in fixed positions.

Cable Moulding – A cylindrical molding with the appearance of woven, ropelike strands, as found in Norman architecture.

Cable Road – Originally an incline logging railroad; a tramway for carrying logs. See Incline Road.

Calabrian Pine – Pinus nigra maritima. One of various pines grouped under Corsican Pine.

Calathus – The bell or core of the Corinthian capital.

Calender – A series of steel rollers that gives a smooth finish to the surface of paper.

Calf's Tongue Moulding – Moulding with a series of pointed members in relief against a flat or curved surface.

California Juniper – Juniperus californica. A species with heavy, irregular-shaped branches, very similar to the Western Juniper.

California Mill – A lumber producer in Northern California, a region included in the Inland West.

California Red Fir – Abies magnifica. A member of the Hem-Fir group, this species is found mainly in California. A close variety, Shasta Red Fir, is found in the higher Cascades of Southern Oregon. Both are very close in appearance to Noble Fir.

California White Pine – A name used at various times for Sugar Pine or western white pines.

Caliper Rule – A type of log rule in which the diameter is measured at the center of the log.

Calks or Caulks – Boots with hobnail-like spikes designed to provide sure footing while walking on logs in the woods or on floating logs in a pond. Also, the spikes themselves. Usually pronounced "corks".

Terms Of The Trade

Calked Boots

Call – In futures trading, a buying and selling period designated by the exchange in order to establish a price or price range for a particular time.

Callus – Thicker tissue formed by friction or over a wound; an unnatural growth that has been incorporated with wood growth in a tree.

Calyx – The tightly bunched group of leaves forming the outer part of a bud or flower.

Camber – The curve or bend found in lumber when it is under no stress. A rising at the middle of a horizontal member to counteract sagging.

Camber Arch – An arch with a concave curve approaching the flat.

Camber Beam – The tie beam of a roof truss, specifically a kingpost truss.

Cambio Debarker – A device that removes bark from a log by abrasion. The bark's bond with the wood is broken at the cambium layer as the log revolves while it passes through the machine; cylindrical abrading heads with conical projections and knives combine to remove the bark.

Cambium – A cell layer in the outer part of the tree that produces new wood for the growth of the tree. The cambium encloses the other living parts of the tree. Cambial cells divide to produce wood cells on the inside of the cambium layer and phloem, or bark cells, on the outer side of the cambium.

Camel Back – A conveyor system in which lumber drops from an upper level of a sawmill to a lower level.

Campbellton Spruce – Canadian Spruce.

Camp Run – The total log output of a logging operation, unsorted by grade.

Canada Balsam – Turpentine from Abies balsamea. A clear, viscous liquid used chiefly for mounting objects on microscope slides and in the manufacture of lacquers.

Canada Hemlock – Another name for Eastern Hemlock.

Canada Measure – A measure of wood volume, about one-half that of a Petrograd Standard. It is equivalent to 1,000 board feet.

Canadian Black Spruce – Picea mariana, a close relative of Eastern Canadian Spruce.

Canadian Fir – Abies balsamea, Balsam Fir.

Canadian Lumber Standard (CLS) – The product standard governing sizes and grades of lumber manufactured in Canada. Lumber graded under CLS rules is accepted by U.S. building authorities.

Canadian Peaker – The top, or peaker, log in a load.

Canadian Plywood Standard – One of the product standards that govern the manufacture and grading of softwood plywood in Canada. There are two: CSA 0121- 1973, Douglas Fir Plywood (DFP); and CSA 0151- 1974, Canadian Softwood Plywood (CSP). Douglas Fir veneers are used on the faces and backs of Douglas Fir Plywood, with inner plies from any of several specific softwood species. CSP consists of faces, backs and inner plies from a number of coniferous species.

Canadian Red Pine – Pinus resinosa, also known as Norway Pine. A straight-grained, resinous, easily treatable species. It takes its name from the red color of the bark.

Canadian Softwood Plywood (CSP) – Veneered panels manufactured by Canadian producers who use S-P-F as their primary raw material.

Car

Canadian Spruce – Picea alba, P. glauca, P. canadensis.

Canadian White Pine – Another name for Eastern White Pine.

Canalis – A space, usually concave, between the fillets of an Ionic column.

Canary – 1. A long rod or pole with a hook at one end, used to pull a chain or cable under a load of logs. 2. A sarcastic name for a mule or donkey.

Canceling Date – The date by which a chartered vessel must be ready for loading.

Candy Side – A well-run logging show; one that is well-equipped, smoothly operated and efficient. Also, a site with big logs or flat ground that is easy to work.

Candy Wagon – A bus or truck used to transport loggers to the logging site. See Crummy.

Canker – Diseased tissue in a tree as a result of fungus.

Canned Specs – Tallies or loading specifications that are routinely manufactured or sought. Canned specs may be peculiar to an individual manufacturer or buyer, or they may be widely used.

Canoe Cedar – Another name for Western Red Cedar.

Canopy – An overstory or "roof" formed by intertwining tree branches.

Cant – A large slab cut from a log at the headsaw, usually having one or more rounded edges, and destined for further processing by other saws.

Canterbury – 1. A pattern used in parquet flooring. 2. A piano bench with a built-in container for sheet music.

Cant Hook – A wooden lever with an iron hook at the lower end, used in turning logs or cants. Also, a Cant Dog.

Cantilever – A rigid structural member projecting horizontally from a vertical support. A building component in which the upper part is in tension and the lower in compression to develop rigidity.

Cantilever Bridge – A bridge made of two projecting beams whose ends meet but do not support each other.

Cant Profiler – A primary breakdown machine that uses chipping heads to shape small logs into squared shapes.

Cant Sawing – Reducing logs to cants, or flat-sided squares or rectangles, for further manufacture at a different machine or site.

Canuck – A Canadian; a logger from Canada, especially a French Canadian. Offensive.

Cap – A covering for the top of a post for ornamentation, or to protect from weathering.

Capital – The ornamental top of a column or pilaster.

Capital Gain – The increase in value of an asset over a period of time. Long-term capital gains are taxed at lower rates than is ordinary income, an important consideration for timberland owners who often must hold their property for a long period before realizing a return on their investment.

Capping Rail – A rail that sits astride fence boards between posts.

Cap Plate – A piece at the top of a column or end of a beam, covering the exposed end.

Cap Sheet – The weather-exposed top sheet of composition roofing in a built-up roof.

Captive Pallet – A pallet used within a single facility or ownership. One that is not exchanged.

Captive Shipper – A shipper having access to only one railroad from origin to destination.

Car – A railroad car, either a boxcar or a

Cant

Terms Of The Trade

Carbide Tip Saw

flatcar. Also, a carload of lumber or plywood.

Carbide Tip Saw – A saw equipped with specially hardened teeth to resist wear.

Car Blocking – Material used for bracing, or securing, a load on a rail car; usually small timbers are used.

Carbolineum – A dark, heavy, liquid wood preservative combining anthracene oil and zinc chloride.

Carbotage – The requirement that coastal maritime shipments within one country be restricted to vessels of domestic registry.

Carbunk – The trolley used to carry lumber into dry kilns.

Car Camp – A railroad logging camp, when such existed.

Carcassing Grades – A European term referring to the framing grades of lumber used in general construction, as opposed to the higher, joinery grades.

Car Day – Each 24-hour period that a specific rail car is on a particular railroad line.

Cardboard – A panel product made from pulp and widely used in packaging.

Car Decking – Lumber designed for use as flooring for rail cars.

Card Process – A pressure-treating process, named after the originator, using creosote oil and zinc chloride.

Car Framing – Lumber used as the framework for rail cars.

Cargo – The load or freight of a ship; lumber carried by waterborne vessel.

Cargo Market – A consuming area that relies heavily on wood products shipped by water.

Cargo Ton – A unit of volume, equal to 40 cubic feet, used in waterborne shipping. Also called a Freight Ton or Measurement Ton.

Caribbean Pine – Pinus caribaea. Also called Cuban Pine.

Cariboo – A lumber producing region in Central British Columbia, bordered by the route from Quesnel to Cash Creek on the east and the North Thompson River on the west.

Car Lining – Lumber or plywood used to line the interior walls of rail cars.

Carload – A railroad car filled to normal capacity. The volume in a carload will vary widely, depending on the size of the car and how it is loaded. A carload of dimension lumber may range from 50,000 board feet to 80,000 or more. A carload of plywood may vary from 75,000 square feet to more than 90,000.

Car Loader – One who loads a railroad car with lumber, with or without the benefit of mechanical loaders.

Car Loading Diagram – See Loading Diagram.

Carloadings – The number of railroad cars loaded over a specific period, usually reported by product category.

Car Material – Any of various materials used in the construction of rail cars.

Car Number – The number assigned to a rail car by the railroad, used to identify the load on invoices, shipping orders, etc.

Carolina Hemlock – Tsuga caroliniana. A relative of Eastern Hemlock, this relatively rare species is found mainly in the Carolinas, Virginia, Tennessee and Northern Georgia. The wood is soft, relatively weak, and is not considered commercially valuable.

Carolina Pine – A common name for any of the softwood species making up the Southern Yellow Pine group.

Carolithic Column – A column with a shaft shaped like a leaf or leaves.

Carpenter Ants – Black or brown ants that excavate wood for shelter. Like termites, carpenter ants are social insects. They are often visible outside the wood they are destroying.

Carpenter Bees – Any of several species of large, non-aggressive bees resembling bumblebees which build nests in wood.

Carpet Strip – 1. A thin wood slat with protruding tack points that grip and hold carpeting. 2. A strip of carpeting placed underneath a door.

Carriage – 1. The framework to which a

Cash and Carry Wholesaler

Carriage

log is fastened during manufacture at the head saw. 2. A two-wheeled device suspended from a skyline that carries logs; the log carrier on a tramway system. The name is applied to various parts such as carriage dog. 3. The middle support underneath a wide stairway.

Carriage Dog – A device that holds a log steady while it is being passed by a saw on a carriage.

Carrier – A railroad, truck line, ship line, or other type of agency that transports goods.

Carrier Bunk – A specially designed wood beam on which parcels of lumber or other wood products are placed, enabling a straddle truck or carrier to pick up the unit for transport.

Carrier's Lien – The right of a carrier to hold property as security for freight charges.

Carroty – Short-grained wood.

Carrying Capacity – The maximum number of organisms that can be supported in a given area.

Carrying Charges – The cost of holding property for sale or delivery at a later date. Carrying charges include costs such as storage, interest, and insurance.

Car Seal – A device fastened to a lock on a rail car door that must be broken to open the door; a broken seal indicates that the car's contents may have been tampered with.

Car Service Rule – A rule imposed by the Interstate Commerce Commission governing car distribution, demurrage, per diem charges, and movement practices of the railroads.

Car Shortage – A condition that exists when the demand for rail cars exceeds the supply. This occurs periodically in the forest products industry and has a variety of causes, including heavy demand for wood products, labor problems, and the diversion of rail cars for the transport of other commodities, such as grain. Since the late 1970s, various incentives to load cars to their maximum capacity has resulted in more efficient car use, and fewer shortages.

Car Siding – A 1x4 piece of lumber, rarely produced today, that was used on the exterior of railroad boxcars. Car siding was manufactured in a standard flooring pattern with two edge Vs, most often in 8-foot lengths.

Car Stake – A short pole or post placed in sockets on the bed of a flatcar to hold a load in place.

Carstrip – See Car Lining.

Cartage – The moving of material by motor carrier to or from rail or cargo docks as one step in a shipment. Also called Drayage.

Cart Sorter – A sorting system that uses carts to receive the lumber for each sort.

Cascades Fir – Another name for Pacific Silver Fir, Abies amabilis.

Caseboard – See Boxboard.

Cased Opening – An interior opening in a structure without a door but finished with jambs and casings.

Casehardened – A condition of lumber in which varying degrees of stress occur at different depths below the surface, causing it to cup when resawn or worked.

Casein Glue – A protein precipitated from milk, casein forms the basis for an interior-type glue used in plywood manufacture.

Casement – A window sash that opens on hinges, usually attached to an upright side of its frame.

Casement Door – A hinged door or pair of doors featuring large glass surfaces.

Casework – The surrounding framework of a window or door; the casing.

Cash – See Cash Market.

Cash and Carry Wholesaler – One who performs all of the usual wholesale functions

Cash and Carry Yard

except financing and delivery.

Cash and Carry Yard – A retail operation that provides no credit to its customers, as contrasted with a full service yard that often will run a "tab" for contractors and regular customers. C&C operations often combine building materials with the sale of appliances and other products in "home centers."

Cash Discount – An incentive offered by a seller to obtain fast payment. In lumber and plywood transactions, a discount of 2% from the amount stated on the invoice is often allowed if payment is within a specified time after the date of the invoice, or after the arrival of the material.

Cash Flow – The amount of money generated from the operation of a business. Cash flow is determined from the net income of the business, less depreciation and non-cash expenses. Cash flow information helps a company plan and control its cash needs.

Cash Market – A term used in futures trading to describe the market for the physical commodity, as opposed to the market for futures.

Cash Price – In futures trading, the current price of the physical commodity; also called the spot price.

Cash Terms – 1. Terms of payment that allow a discount for payments within a specified time after the invoice date or after the arrival of the material. 2. Terms that require payment prior to shipment or on delivery before taking possession.

Casing – Trim applied around the tops and sides of windows and doors.

Casket Shook – Thin pieces of lumber used to make burial caskets, usually cut to size and bundled together.

Casting – An article cast in a mold, or the act of placing material in a mold.

Cast-off Hook – A device used to release logs from a tram.

Cat – A bulldozer or crawler tractor. Although originally derived from the "Caterpillar" brand of tractor, the term often refers to any brand of such tractor.

Catalyst – In wood finishing, a chemical that, when added to conversion coatings, initiates chemical bonding.

Cat Bummer – A log carrier mounted on endless treads and pulled by a tractor.

Catch Basin – A small reservoir to hold excess water, or a reservoir of water that can be pumped into a truck to be used in settling dust on a road or fighting fire.

Catch Boom – A boom, or string of logs, across a body of water to hold floating logs.

Catch Brand – A mark or brand used to identify stray logs caught in a river or lake by a log patrol, prior to returning the logs to their original owner.

Catch Mark – See Catch Brand.

Catch Shackle – In cable logging, a shackle with a bar welded across its throat, attaching the eye of the haulback to the skyline.

Cat Eye – A pin knot in lumber.

Cat Face – A scar on a tree or log, caused by fire or injury to the growing tree.

Cat Hook – A hook used in yarding logs, having a "barb" at the end to prevent chokers from falling off.

Catkin – A flowering spike on willow or birch trees.

Cat Ladder – A board to which cleats have been attached, laid across a roof to provide access for workmen. Also known as a duck board.

Cat Logging – A logging operation in which a "Cat," or crawler tractor, is used to yard the logs.

Cat Road – A crude roadway cut by a bulldozer.

Cats and Dogs – Odds and ends; various odd sizes, lengths, or grades of lumber and plywood. They are usually the less popular items in an inventory that are harder to sell.

Cat's Ass – A kink or snarl in a hauling line, or in a choker when it slips off a log and cinches up tight.

Cat Skinner – An operator of a bulldozer or crawler tractor.

Cat Spruce – Canadian Spruce.

Caul – In particleboard production, the flat metal plate on which wood particles are

Cellulose

formed into mats, conveyed, and processed.

Caulis – A piece of an architectural ornament patterned after a plant stem, normally used on the middle portion of a Corinthian column.

Caulk – A waterproof sealant used to fill joints or seams.

Caulless Process – A method of making hardboard and medium density fiberboard. The caul, or plate on which the mat of particles is formed, is removed from the press before the pressing operation is completed. Most high density board is manufactured in a process in which the caul remains in the press as the bottom plate.

Cauls – Clamps or presses used to hold veneers under pressure until the glue has set; the plates of a press.

Cavetto – A simple concave moulding; a cove.

Cavity Nesters – Wildlife that require holes in trees for nesting and reproduction.

CC Plugged Exterior – A touch-sanded plywood panel with a C-plugged grade face, and C-grade back and inner plies bonded with exterior glue. A plugged panel is one that has had a defect repaired with a wood patch or synthetic filler.

CD Exterior (CDX) – A grade of plywood; the standard grade of plywood sheathing. The "CD" represents the grades of veneer used for the face and back, respectively. The "X" signifies that an exterior-type glue has been used. However, despite the exterior glue, CDX plywood is classified as an interior type of plywood and is required to withstand only incidental exposure to the weather during construction.

CD Plugged Interior – A touch-sanded plywood panel with a C-plugged-grade face, D-grade back and inner plies, bonded with either interior or exterior glue but recommended for use only in protected locations.

Cedar – 1. A softwood with reddish heartwood and white sapwood. 2. A coniferous tree of the genus Cedrus, or Juniperus, or Thuja.

Cedar Ax – A light, single-bitted ax.

Cedar Itch – An allergic reaction to cedar pollen, often affecting loggers in late spring and early summer.

Cedar of Lebanon – Cedrus libani, a rare, fast-growing species now protected as a national treasure in Lebanon.

Cedar Pine – Another name for Spruce Pine.

Cedar Savage – A logger working in cedar.

Cedar Saw – A long, thin, cross-cut saw with no raker teeth.

Cedar Spud – A flat, long-handled tool with a blade like a chisel, used for removing bark from cedar poles and posts.

Cedro – Another name for Spanish Cedar, Cedrela mexicana.

Ceiling – A piece of patterned, tongue and grooved lumber, used to cover the ceiling of a room in older houses.

Ceiling Floor – Joists, beams or other supports for a ceiling.

Ceiling Joist – Lightweight joists installed below floor joists, designed to carry a lath and plaster ceiling or boards.

Ceiling Price – The highest legally allowable price under terms of the government's price regulations of 1971-73. These varied widely among producers, depending on individual circumstances.

Ceiling Strap – A strip of wood attached to floor joists or rafters, used for suspending ceiling joists.

Celery Top Pine – A softwood from Tasmania, used mainly for cabinet work, joinery, and carriage building.

Cell – The basic structural unit of plant and animal life.

Cellar Fungus – One of the fungi causing dry rot.

Cellular Structure – The construction of various species of woods. Hardwoods have a fairly complicated structure involving fibers, rays, and conducting cells. Softwoods are simple tracheids with thin walls and large cavities in springwood, and thicker walls in summerwood.

Cellulose – A polymeric carbohydrate making up the chief portion of wood and

Terms Of The Trade 45

Cellulose Sheet

other vegetable matter.

Cellulose Sheet – A sheet of flooring material made from sawdust, cork dust, or other materials, on a backing of woven jute.

Cembran Pine – A European species also known as Swiss Pine or Siberian Yellow Pine.

Cement-Bonded Board – A board constructed of either cellulose or mineral particles which are bound together by cement. Also called cement board.

Cement-Fiber Shake – A type of fire-resistant roof shake made from a combination of cement, fly ash, sawdust, and shavings.

Center Chain – On a railroad car loaded with logs, the middle chain binding the load and keeping it from moving.

Center Gap – See Core Gap.

Center Matched – Lumber that has been worked to contain a tongue in the center of one edge of each piece and groove in the center of the opposite edge, to provide a close tongue-and-groove joint by fitting the two pieces together.

Center Matched

Centers – Inner plies in a piece of plywood whose grain direction runs parallel to that of the outer plies.

Center-to-Center Spacing – The spacing between structural members determined by measuring from the center of one to the center of the next, e.g. "16-inches o.c."

Central Zone – An unofficial division of the Southern Yellow Pine producing region, consisting of the states of Alabama and Mississippi.

Certificate of Inspection – A document issued by a grading agency that assures the buyer that the shipment of lumber has been examined by a qualified inspector and that the lumber in the shipment is of the grade indicated. Often used for selects and timbers where a grade mark would not show, or where one would affect the use of the piece.

Certificate of Occupancy – A document issued by a government entity certifying that a structure meets legal requirements, allowing it to be occupied.

Certification Agency – Any of various accredited independent testing organizations that monitor required testing and evaluation programs to ensure conformance with applicable performance standards.

Certification Mark – An agency grade-mark.

Certified Grader – A person who has been certified to inspect and supervise the work of approved graders. He is authorized to issue certificates attesting to the grade of a shipment of lumber. See Approved Grader.

Certified Inspector – A person certified by the American Plywood Association to conduct quality assurance inspections at mills producing structural panels.

Certified Scaler – A log scaler employed by one of several independent log scaling bureaus. The scalers of these bureaus are trained and certified by the individual bureau.

Certified Stocks – Commodities designated and certified for delivery by a futures exchange under its trading and testing regulations at delivery points and/or warehouses specified and approved by the exchange.

Certified Tree Farm – Privately owned land dedicated to growing trees and certified by the American Forest Institute as conforming to AFI standards.

Certigrade – A registered trade name used by the Cedar Shake and Shingle Bureau in labeling Red Cedar shingles.

Certigroove – A registered trade name of the Cedar Shake and Shingle Bureau, designating shakes that have been processed for use as siding. These shakes are retrimmed to be square, often pre-stained, and fluted or grooved on the surface.

Certisplit – A trade name used by the Cedar Shake and Shingle Bureau in labeling Red Cedar shakes.

Chain – 1. A measuring device used in surveying, consisting of a chain of 100 lengths or

Charge

of a narrow ribbon of steel. A chain is 66 feet in length and is usually graduated in feet, tenths of feet, and hundredths of feet. 2. A unit of measurement equalling 66 feet. 3. A conveyor in a mill, as in "green chain." 4. A chain of stores; a retail chain.

Chain Boom – A group of floating logs corralled around the perimeter by other logs that have been chained together.

Chain Grab – A hook and chain used to anchor a cable network.

Chaining – 1. An attempt to improve forage in a dry, open forest area by dragging a heavy chain or cable, fastened between two tractors, through the woods to tear out brush and small trees. 2. Skidding logs with horses and chains. 3. The use of a chain or steel tape to make measurements in the field.

Chain Saw – A power-driven crosscut saw, usually powered by a gasoline engine, used to fell trees and buck logs. The teeth of the saw are attached to an endless, articulated chain.

Chain Swifter – A light chain used in assembling a log raft.

Chain Tightener – A lever-like device used to tighten the chains binding a load of logs on a truck or rail car.

Chain Yard – One of a series of retail lumber yards owned, and usually operated, by a single parent company.

Chair – A stump resulting when a tree falls before the cut is completed, leaving an upright section of wood on the stump. Also, Barber Chair.

Chair Rail – A type of moulding usually applied to a wall about one-third the distance from the floor and parallel to it. Originally used to prevent chairs from marring walls, it is used today primarily as a decorative element.

Chalking – The powdery coating that forms on a painted surface due to weatherizing.

Chamfer – A bevel or slope created by slicing off the square edge or end of a piece of wood or other material.

Chamfer Block – A chock or wooden beam used on flatcars to prevent a load from shifting.

Chamfer Strip – A triangular moulding often used in concrete forming work.

Chance – A reference to the ease or difficulty with which a particular logging show can be logged. Thus, a "good chance" would be one that is easy to log.

Channel – 1. A groove or furrow of rectangular shape, cut in the face of a board or panel. 2. Any structural member having the three sides of a rectangle. 3. The L- or T-shaped pieces that support the tiles of a suspended ceiling. 4. A route by which products are distributed.

Channel Dues – Charges levied against a vessel for using a channel.

Channel of Distribution – The path taken by goods in moving from producer to consumer.

Channel Siding – A type of siding used to sheath the exterior of a building.

Chap – A fissure or split in tree bark, caused by extreme heat or cold, and exposing the cambium layer.

Chapin Rule – A log rule, developed about 1883 and said to have been the most erratic of all log measurement rules. The Chapin Rule was reportedly developed by selecting values from other existing rules to suit the author.

Chapter VII – The broadest form of bankruptcy, consisting of total liquidation of all assets and all debt.

Chapter XI – Reorganization under the protection of a bankruptcy court with the aim of avoiding liquidation and creating a financially viable entity. Most Chapter XI filings involve businesses rather than individuals and typically involve restructuring to eliminate money-losing operations and a reduction in the amount of debt owed to creditors.

Characteristics – Distinguishing features which, by their extent and number, determine the quality of a piece of lumber or veneer.

Charcoal – The residue left after partial combustion of wood; an important commercial by-product of wood.

Charge – The total amount of wood products to be dried in a dry kiln, or to be treated

Terms Of The Trade

Charger

in a retort.

Charger — A system built into veneer green ends that automatically centers blocks on the lathe. The system is a modernization tool, which helps mills maximize recovery.

Charred Wood — Wood that has been scorched or partly burned by fire. As solid wood burns, it forms a charred layer that helps insulate inner portions from the heat.

Charring — A method of hardening or protecting wood by burning its outer parts; the charred portion becomes somewhat resistant to insects or decay.

Charter — To contract for the use of a vessel for a period ranging from a single trip to a specific destination to a period of up to several years. Also, the vessel itself.

Chartering Agent — The person or firm that handles the chartering of a vessel.

Charter Party Form — The contract covering the transport of wood (or other goods) from one point to another.

Charter Rate — Payment by a shipper to a ship owner to charter his vessel.

Chart Trader — A futures trader who bases his buying and selling decisions primarily on conditions that develop within the futures market rather than on developments in the market for the physical commodity. The name is derived from the trader's use of charts as an aid in following developments in the market. See Technical Trader.

Chase — A groove or decoration incised in a material, usually metal.

Chaser — The person in a logging operation who unhooks the choker from the log at the landing. He also cuts off any remaining limbs, brands logs, and acts as a general handyman.

Chatter — A defect in particleboard caused by sanding.

Cheat Stick — Slang for the measuring device used by log scalers to determine the volume of a log. See Scaler's Stick.

Check — A lengthwise separation of wood, normally occurring across or through the rings of annual growth and usually the result of seasoning. Classified for the purpose of grading as surface check, small, medium, or large; end check; and through check. Surface check occurs on the surface of a piece, end check occurs on an end, and through check extends from one surface through the piece to the opposite surface.

Check Dam — A small dam constructed in a stream or drainage ditch to minimize erosion.

Checked Joint — A joint designed to accommodate the rounding of inside corners.

Checkerboard Ownership — A pattern of land ownership in which every other section is in federal ownership. The result of federal land grants to early western railroads. See Oregon and California Lands.

Checkered-Bark Juniper — See Alligator Juniper.

Check Rail — A rail, usually beveled, that fills the space between the top and bottom sash of a double-hung window.

Check Stop — A piece of molding designed to hold the bottom sash of a double-hung window in place.

Cheeks — Any pair of vertical facing members, such as those found on a doorway.

Cheese Block — A chock that prevents a log from rolling. See Chock.

Chemically Modified Wood — Wood that has been altered by chemical processes to change its physical, biological or chemical properties.

Chemical Pulping — A pulp-making process in which wood chips are broken down chemically and the lignin removed. Finer, higher-quality paper is produced by chemical pulping; however, this method is more expensive than mechanical pulping and the yield, in terms of volume of pulp obtained from the same volume of raw material, is much less.

Chemical Seasoning — The application of certain chemicals to unseasoned wood for the purpose of reducing such defects as surface check during the drying process.

Chemical Stain — Stains that occur in lumber or logs through the oxidation of minerals or chemicals within the cells.

Chemical Wood — Trees used as a source of various chemicals such as acetic acid,

Chip Marks

methanol, and wood alcohol. Usually, timber that is not of sufficient size and/or quality to make lumber or plywood.

Chemi-Thermomechanical Pulping Process (CTMP) – A process of converting wood chips into fibers between metal disks, using heat, pressure, and chemicals.

Cheneau – The ornamental upper portion of a gutter or cornice.

Cherry – Prunus virginiana in North America. A hard, decorative wood used in the manufacture of furniture.

Cherry Picker – 1. A light log loader utilizing tongs or a grapple operated from a boom to pick up individual logs. 2. A hoist that raises a person, providing access to rigging. 3. In Britain, one who tows log rafts.

Cherry Picker

Cherry Stained – See Cherry Toned.

Cherry Toned – A patented process of anti-stain treatment used on Hemlock to enhance the appearance of the lumber.

Chestnut – Castanea dentata, a reddish-brown wood used in furniture. Also, the edible nut.

Chevron – 1, The place where rafters meet at the ridge of a roof. 2. A type of moulding with a zig-zag pattern.

Chicago Board of Trade (CBT) – A commodities exchange in Chicago where futures contracts are traded. See Exchange (Futures).

Chicago Mercantile Exchange (CME) – A commodities exchange in Chicago where the Western S-P-F futures contract is traded. See Exchange (Futures).

Chicago Stepping – 6/4x10 #2&Btr Ponderosa Pine used in the construction of steps and furniture. A major market for this product is in and around the Chicago area.

Chicken Tracks – Scars found on tropical hardwood veneers caused by the stems or hair roots of clinging vines. The scars often contain residue of the vine where it intergrew with the tree.

Chihuahua Pine – Pinus leiophylla var. chihuahuana.

Chil – Pinus wallichiana. A long-leafed pine from Northern India used for inexpensive furniture and joinery. Also called Blue Pine.

Chilean Pine – Araucaria araucana. A South American species also known in the U.S. and the United Kingdom as the monkey-puzzle tree.

Chimney – A vertical opening in a lumber pile to assist air circulation.

Chin Chopper – A tree that splits while it is being felled.

Chinese Fir – Cunninghamia sinensis. An important plantation tree in China and Taiwan.

Chip – A small piece of wood used to make pulp. The chips are either made from wood waste in a sawmill or plywood plant or from pulpwood cut specifically for this purpose. Chips are of generally uniform size, and are larger and coarser than sawdust.

Chip Angle – Same as cutting angle.

Chipboard – A type of panel board made with relatively large, discrete chips as the basic raw material, as opposed to the smaller fibers usually used in ordinary particleboard. Also, a term used loosely to describe all types of particleboard or fiberboard.

Chip Breaker – A pressure bar used in conjunction with some planing or moulding machines to prevent the knives from tearing the grain.

Chip Load – The quantity of wood removed by an individual saw tooth as it cuts on each pass.

Chip Marks – Shallow depressions or indentations on or in the surface of dressed lumber, caused by shavings or chips getting embedded in the surface during dressing.

Terms Of The Trade

"Chip-n-Saw"

Chipping Headrig

"Chip-n-Saw" – A brand of chipping headrig. Although this is one of several brands, the name has come into common usage as applicable to all such types of machines. See Chipping Headrig.

Chip Out – A defect in particleboard in which fines or flakes are removed or torn from the top or bottom face edges of a panel.

Chipped Grain – An area of the surface of a piece of lumber that is chipped or broken out in very short particles below the line of the cut. Not classed as torn grain and, as usually found, not considered a defect unless more than 25% of the surface is involved.

Chipper-Canter – A machine that makes cants from whole logs using chipping heads only and no saws.

Chipper Knives – The knives that reduce wood to chips for use in pulping or for the manufacture of compressed-wood panels. The design of the knife contributes to the shape of the chip.

Chippewa Pine – Select pine growing in the Chippewa River Valley of Wisconsin.

Chipping Edger – An edger utilizing chipping knives instead of a saw blade.

Chipping Headrig – A piece of machinery that mills small logs simultaneously into lumber and chips. The machine chips away the outer part of the log and saws the inner part, usually into 2x4s.

Chipping Slabber – A chipping headrig that chips away two sides of a small log, leaving a slab.

Chip Segregation – The separation, by screen or air pressure, of chips of different sizes and weights.

Chisel Hook – A type of cant hook having a hook with a chisel edge.

Chisel-Tooth Saw – A saw with a wedge-shaped cutting edge at the end of each tooth that is at right angles to the surface of the saw.

Chlorinated Organics – By-products produced during the bleaching process in paper manufacturing.

Chlorophyll – The substance that gives leaves and needles of trees their green color. Chlorophyll is part of the photosynthesis process by which plants produce their food.

Chock – A block used to prevent movement of a wheel or log; often wedge shaped.

Choice – A select grade of Idaho White Pine, equivalent to the C Select grade in other species.

Choker – 1. A wire rope or cable that is fastened around a log before pulling it into the landing. 2. A British term for a small log.

Choker Gun – A tool used in pulling the end of a choker under a log.

Choker Hole – A hole dug under a log to enable the end of a choker to be passed through.

Choker Hook – The device that hooks the choker cable to the main line for yarding logs. Generally, today a socket rather than a

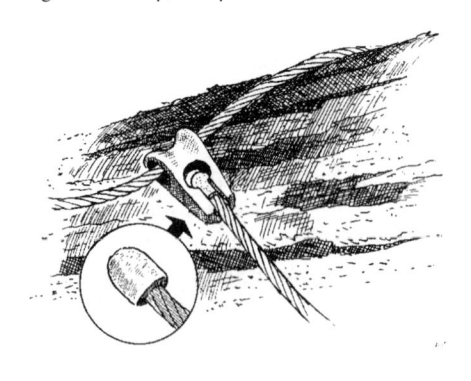

Choker

Circular Saw

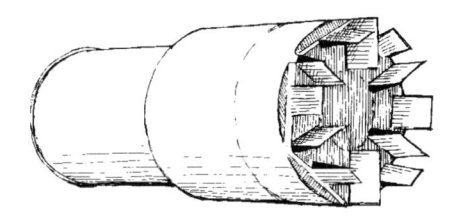

Lathe Chuck

hook is used because it makes a more secure fastener, yet can be released quickly.

Chokerman – See Choker Setter.

Choker Setter – The person in a logging operation who places the choker around a log, prior to the log being hauled to a landing.

Chopper – Another term for faller, used chiefly in the Northern California woods. Fallers in that region are also sometimes called cutters.

Chopping Board – See Springboard.

Chopping Iron – A logger's term for an ax.

Chopping Platform – A scaffolding sometimes built for fallers when trees were cut above the swell of the butt.

Chop Saw – A mechanical saw with the blade mounted on a movable arm for quick cuts, especially in making miter cuts.

Chord – The top or bottom member of a truss, to which the web members are attached.

Chore Boy – A bull cook; one who performs various menial tasks in a logging camp.

Christiana Standard – An obsolete lumber measure, equal to 120 pieces of lumber 1-1/4 inches thick, 9 inches wide and 11 feet long.

Chromated Copper Arsenate (CCA) – A water-soluble salt used in wood preserving.

Chuck Boat – A cook's raft that followed a log drive down river.

Chucking & Boring Machine – A machine that centers and clamps a wood piece so that a hole can be drilled longitudinally.

Chuck Marks – Indentations on both ends of a peeler core, caused by lathe chucks. These marks may limit the length of studs that can be manufactured from peeler cores.

Chucks – A pair of metal spindles with prong "fingers" that grasp a peeler log in a veneer lathe, holding the log firmly at both ends so that it can be turned against the knives to produce veneer.

Chunk Out – To clear stumps and debris from an area such as a road right-of-way or landing area.

Chunkrete – Concrete with woodwaste as the aggregate.

Churn Butt – A log cut just above the ground to include the swell of the butt.

Churn Moulding – A moulding with a zig-zag pattern, often seen in Norman architecture.

Chute – A dry trough used to move logs from the logging area to a landing, to a body of water for rafting or storage, or to a mill. The trough may be made of logs or lumber, or simply gouged in the earth.

Chute Tender – One who patrolled the troughs once used to transport logs. A chute was a three-sided affair that relied on gravity, water, or grease to speed the passage of the logs. A chute once in use near Klamath Falls, Ore., dropped more than 2,600 feet in elevation. See Flume Chaser.

Cigar Box Cedar – Cedrela odorata or C. mexicana, also known as Honduras Cedar. A light red, durable, easy-to-work species from Central America, often used in joinery, cabinet work, or cigar boxes.

Cigar Raft – A log raft assembled roughly in the shape of a cigar, smaller on each end than in the middle. See Benson Raft.

Circle Hook – A large, circular-shaped hook on the end of a skidding chain that is easily detached from its load.

Circle Saw – A round saw with teeth around the circumference. Also known as a rotary saw.

Circular Patch – A round patch used to fill voids caused by defects in the veneers of plywood panels. Also known as a Cookie Patch.

Circular Saw – A round saw having cut-

Terms Of The Trade

Cladding

ting teeth on its perimeter. Originally common as a head saw in sawmills, it has been largely replaced by thinner band saws. Circular saws remain widely used as trim and cut-off saws.

Cladding – Another name for siding. Chiefly British.

Claim – 1. To assert one's right to a property. 2. A complaint filed by the receiver of goods alleging that quality or quantity is less than promised in a transaction.

Clapboard – A narrow board, usually thicker at one edge than the other, used as siding.

Clarke Beam – A beam comprised of two or more joists bolted together, with short diagonal reinforcing pieces attached solidly along each side.

Clark's International Rule – See International 1/8-inch Rule.

Class I – A basic grade of concrete form limited to Group I species on face and back and other limitations on inner plies.

Class II – A basic grade of concrete form permitting the use of species of Groups I, II, or III on the face or back, and providing limitations on the inner plies.

Clean and Bright – A reference to freshly manufactured lumber.

Clean Bill of Lading – One that has not been modified by special limitations.

Clean Cutting – The removal of all merchantable timber from a stand.

Cleaner Teeth – The raker teeth of a saw that clean the kerf on each passage.

Clear – 1. Free or practically free of all blemishes, characteristics, or defects. 2. A select grade of lumber. 3. A member in good standing of the International Workers of the World (IWW).

Clear All Heart – See Clear Heart.

Clearance Angle – The angle between the back of a knife and the path of its cutting edge.

Clear Cut – A logging method in which all of the trees in a given area are harvested, regardless of size. It is used principally in even-aged stands and is considered essential to the reforestation of species that are not shade tolerant.

Clear Face – The side of a piece of wood that is without blemish.

Clear Grade – A general term referring to the highest grades of lumber, which are clear of defects, or nearly so.

Clear Heart – The highest grade of Redwood and Western Red Cedar. Finish, paneling and ceiling of this grade are often used for interior and exterior trim and cabinet work, where finest appearance is important.

Clearing & Grubbing – Cutting and digging vegetation, stumps, etc., to provide a clear space for road construction or a landing.

Clearinghouse – An agency of a commodity exchange through which all futures contracts are reconciled or settled. A clearinghouse may be a separate corporation or a division of the exchange.

Clear Length – That portion of a tree between the ground and the point where the lowest limbs join the trunk.

Clear Paneling – Interior wall paneling, free of defect.

Clear Space – The space between joists or other supports, an alternative to spacing from center to center.

Clear Span – The distance between supports of a beam.

Clear Wall – A grade of Eastern White Cedar shingles. Shingles of this grade are used mostly for interior applications.

Clear Wood – Wood that has no defects. In some instances, grading rules permit very small knots or pitch streaks. Small clear wood samples are used in laboratory tests to determine some strength properties of wood.

Cleat – A small piece of wood or other material used to prevent sliding. Narrow pieces are fastened to an inclined board to provide footing.

Cleated Plywood – Packaging plywood that has been fastened to solid wood cleats to add to the stiffness or strength of a container.

Cleavability – A measure of how well a specific type of wood can be split.

Closed Forest

Cleavage Test – A test designed to measure the strength of scarf-jointed and finger-jointed panels, following vacuum-pressure and boil tests, or vacuum soak tests. In conducting the cleavage test, a wedge or chisel is used to pry apart the joint without directly contacting the glue area.

Clevis – A U-shaped shackle used in logging; usually closed by a pin or bar.

CLF – An abbreviation for "hundred lineal feet."

Climax – A steam locomotive, first used in 1888 on logging railroads. It was driven by a central drive shaft geared to all axles.

Climax Forest – A forest in which the species are no longer subject to change. For example, a coniferous forest has reached climax when the predominant species is reproducing itself without significant competition from other types. Usually, the dominant species is highly shade tolerant and has taken over as trees of other species have died and fallen.

Climb Cutting – A method of machining with a cutting tool in which the tool is rotating in the same direction as the material being cut is traveling.

Climber – The person who removes tops and branches from a tree to enable its use as a spar pole for cable logging. Usually, he also does the rigging.

Climbing Irons – Metal spurs that are strapped to a logger's boots and legs to aid him in climbing a tree.

Climbing Irons

Climb Sawing – A method of sawing in which a circular saw blade rotates in the same direction that the material being sawn is fed into the saw. Also called Climb Cutting or Power Cutting.

Clinometer – A hand instrument used by foresters and timber cruisers to measure vertical angles. Such angles, when correlated with specific distances, indicate the height of a standing tree.

Clip – A device used as a substitute for lumber blocking in roof construction. The clip is used to join two panels, edge to edge, and provides support. Also called a Panel Clip.

Clipper – A machine used to cut veneer into individual pieces after it leaves the lathe in a continuous belt.

Clipper Board – A device used in conjunction with a clipper saw to produce parallel edges on shingles.

Clipper Saw – A machine used to make shingle edges parallel.

Clips-a-Minute – The number of times in a minute that a block carriage passes a shingle saw.

Clones – A group of genetically identical individuals.

Close – 1. The end of the daily trading session in futures markets. 2. The price at the time of closing. 3. To complete a transaction. In real estate, to sign the various documents completing the sale.

Close Couple – 1. To fasten objects closely together while allowing some freedom of movement between them. 2. A roof system consisting of pairs of rafters tied together at the feet to prevent them from spreading.

Closed Cornice – A box cornice enclosed by shingles above, a fascia board in front, and the wall of a structure behind it.

Closed Defect – See Hidden Defect.

Closed Face – A veneer surface not touching the veneer knife during peeling or slicing.

Closed Forest – A term used in international forestry to describe forests of high density; one where the crowns of trees often touch.

Closed Side

Closed Side – See Closed Face.

Closed Soffit – The underside of a roof overhang that has been closed, or finished, by applying plywood or boards to the underside of the rafters.

Close Grain – Wood grain characterized by an average of approximately six, but not more than approximately 30, annual rings per inch on either end of a piece of lumber.

Closely Associated Species – A species found to be significantly more abundant in a particular forest successional stage as compared to other successional stages.

Closing – The point at which a transaction is completed. In real estate, the time at which buyer and seller sign and deliver papers to one another. See Close.

Closing Costs – The total estimated costs customarily chargeable to a home buyer for items that are incidental to the transaction. These include the initial service charge of the mortgage, cost of title search, recording fees, charges for preparing deeds and mortgage documents, and similar items.

Closing Exchange Rate – In currency trading, the exchange rate prevailing on a financial reporting date.

Clothes Pin Bolt – A block of wood, usually Aspen, from which clothes pins are made.

Cluster Development – A design for a housing development in which homes are grouped closely together and common areas are left as open space to be shared by all of the residents.

Cluster Pine – Pinus pinaster. Also called Maritime Pine.

Clyde Skidder – A self-propelled steam skidder used in early railroad logging.

Coal Oil – Kerosene. Used to light lanterns and torches, and to lubricate hand-powered saw blades to prevent binding. Also called saw oil.

Coarse Grain – Wood with wide and conspicuous annual rings; wood with less than four rings per inch.

Coastal Cypress – Another name for Baldcypress, Taxodium distichum.

Coast Douglas Fir – Pseudotsuga menziesii var menziesii. See Douglas Fir.

Coaster – A ship used to transport goods between ports on the same coast, or on inter-island routes.

Coast Hem-Fir – See Hem-Fir (Coast).

Coast Index – A plywood pricing system that was the basis for a successful class-action suit against several major manufacturers. In

Coaster

the system, Southern Yellow Pine plywood prices were adjusted to provide a comparison with West Coast mill prices. The approximate delivered costs to the buyer could be calculated by adding freight on the Coast rate to the buyer's location. In the suit, the plaintiffs contended this system required them to pay a "phantom freight" charge.

Coast Region – In the U.S., the region of Washington and Oregon that is west of the Cascades, extending south into the Redwood region of California. In British Columbia, a region west of the Cascades, from Hope to Terrace.

Coastwise – Shipment between ports on the same coast.

Coated Paper – Printing paper with one of various coatings applied to enhance the display or retention of ink.

Cob Pile – In air drying lumber, a pile that is self-stickered with each course at right angles to adjacent courses, and having the same number of pieces.

Cockle Finish – A type of paper finish consisting of a slightly puckered surface on bond paper. This is achieved by passing the paper through an air drier during manufacture.

Code – See Building Code, Model Code.

Coded Lumber – A system of marking packaged lumber or plywood to ensure complete interchangeability of like packages.

Codominant Crown Class – The trees that make up the general canopy layer of a forest. Such trees receive light from above and only partial light from the side. They have some competition for space from neighboring trees. See Crown Classes.

Coefficient of Friction – A property of wood dependent on the moisture content and surface roughness. There is little variance among species, except in those containing high levels of oil or waxy extractives.

Coefficient of Thermal Expansion – The rate at which a material expands or contracts in response to temperature changes.

Coffered Ceiling – A ceiling comprised of sunken or recessed panels.

Cogeneration – Simultaneous production of electricity and steam.

Cold Bending – A method of forming lumber to a desired shape without first softening the wood with steam. Sometimes used to produce curved glulam timbers or furniture parts from veneer. The cold-bent items must be glued or mechanically held.

Cold Deck – A pile of logs stored for future use, commonly built through the summer and early fall to provide logs for late winter and early spring mill operations. See Hot Deck.

Cold Peel – Veneer manufactured without softening the log with steam or water prior to peeling.

Cold Press – A press that bonds veneers into a plywood panel without using heat in the process. Only certain types of glues are used in a cold press.

Cold Setting Adhesive – An adhesive effective for use in temperatures below 68 degrees Fahrenheit.

Cold Soak Treatment – A method of preserving dry wood by soaking it for hours or days in preservative oils. This method is not as effective as others using pressure. Pine can be successfully treated using this method, but other species do not fare as well.

Collapse – Irregular shrinkage in wood above the fiber saturation point, caused by the collapse of wood cells as free water is drawn out of the cell cavities without replacement with air or more water.

Collar – The small, semi-circular moulding pattern on a column.

Collar Beam – A horizontal tie beam on a roof truss, connecting two opposite rafters well above a wall plate.

Collarless Saw – A circular saw that attaches directly to a shaft, or arbor, and does not require a collar to secure it.

Collar Tie – See Collar Beam.

Collateral – Property or money pledged as security for a loan.

Collateral Security – A pledge given in addition to the principal security.

Collusion – An attempt by two or more competitors to manipulate prices or supplies to their advantage over customers or other competitors.

Colonial

Colonial — A grade of Idaho White Pine equivalent to the #1 Common (board) grade in other species. The highest common grade in Idaho White Pine.

Colonnade — A series of columns at regularly spaced intervals, usually supporting beams.

Colorado Blue Spruce — See Blue Spruce.

Colorado Bristlecone Pine — Pinus aristata var. aristata. Examples of this variation, found in Colorado and the Southwest, are among the oldest living trees.

Colorado Juniper — Juniperus scopulorum, also known as Rocky Mountain Juniper. Common to the higher elevations of the U.S. West, it is known for its tight grain.

Coloration — The distinctive color of wood. The appearance that helps distinguish one species from another.

Columbia Fir — Another name for Douglas Fir.

Columbia Pine — Another name for Douglas Fir.

Columbia River Rule — A variation of the Spaulding Log Rule that was used in parts of Oregon and Washington; now seldom used.

Columbia River Snipe — A snipe, or bevel, cut on the front end of a log to facilitate skidding.

Columbia River Spruce — Another name for Sitka Spruce.

Column — A vertical structural member, usually subject to longitudinal compression.

Column Stability Factor — One of various adjustment factors used in calculating compression parallel to grain in solid-sawn lumber.

Comb — The ridge of a roof.

Combed Joint — An angle formed by a series of tenons engaging in corresponding slots.

Comber — A beachcomber; one who searches along a coast or river's edge for stray logs from broken booms.

Comb Grain — The grain of quarter-sawn wood.

Combination Beam — A structural member consisting of two or more pieces of lumber bolted together, sometimes with a steel plate in the middle. Also called a Flitched Beam.

Combination Door — A door in which both screen and glazed sections are combined in the same frame. Also, a door in which separate screen and glazed sections are interchangeable.

Combination in Restraint of Trade — Any understanding between two or more parties designed to limit or eliminate competition.

Combination Rate — A through rate covering transportation through two or more carriers.

Combination Rule — A type of log rule that uses values from two or more rules, depending on the size of the logs being measured. For example, the Doyle-Scribner Rule uses values from the Doyle Rule for small logs, and from the Scribner rule for large logs.

Combined Stress — The combination of bending and axial stresses acting on wood; often seen in the bottom chord of a truss.

Combing — The top course of a shingle roof that projects above the ridge from the side of the prevailing winds.

Comeback Line — A haulback line that returns rigging to the woods in yarding logs.

Come-Back Road — See Go-Back Road.

Commercial — 1. A futures market term describing a trader who maintains both a physical and a futures position in a given commodity, usually for the purpose of hedging. 2. A grade of decking, ranking below the other grade of decking, "Selected." Lumber graded Commercial is recommended for the same purposes served by the higher grade when appearance is not of primary importance.

Commercial Credit — Credit used in the conduct of business.

Commercial Forest — That portion of the total forest which is capable of, and available for, growing trees for harvest. Parks and wilderness areas are not included.

Commercial Standards — See Product Standard.

Component

Commercial Thinning – The partial harvesting of a stand of trees with the intent of gaining some economic return from those that are cut and of accelerating the growth of the trees left standing.

Commercial Veneer – Ungraded, or lower grade, veneers used as core stock in plywood or in the concealed parts of furniture.

Commission Buyer – One who buys lumber, plywood, or other products for another party, for a set fee based on the type and volume of material purchased.

Commission House – A firm that buys or sells futures contracts on behalf of its customers and charges a percentage of the value of the transaction. A brokerage.

Commission Salesman – One who sells forest products for a producer and receives a certain fee for his efforts, with the fee based on the volume sold and the price received. Some commission salesmen work for the company for which they sell; others represent a number of companies and are self employed.

Commitment – A pledge, or obligation, to perform; e.g. to pay on receipt of invoice.

Commodity Exchange – See Exchange (Futures).

Commodity Item – A general term referring to those items of lumber, plywood, or other forest products that are sold in sizeable volume, usually in full carload quantities.

Commodity Quote – A rail rate quoted for a single commodity only.

Commodity Specific Tariff – A rail rate tariff that applies to one commodity only.

Common – 1. A term applied to the board sizes. 2. Lumber that is suitable for general construction and utility purposes. 3. Equal or shared characteristics, such as a common joist: the joists in a single floor. 4. An area shared by two or more entities, such as a wall between them, or the hallway of an office building.

Common Carrier – A person or firm in the business of transporting goods or persons, usually at a fixed, published rate, on a set schedule.

Common Garden Study – In forestry, an investigation in which seeds from different sources are grown in a uniform environment to examine genetic variation in traits.

Common Juniper – Juniperus communis. This species is found across a wide area of North America, usually as a bush. The trees have limited value commercially except as ornamentals.

Common Larch – Another name for European Larch, Larix decidua.

Common Market – The informal name for the European Economic Community, an economic association of Western European countries.

Common Spruce – European Spruce, Picea abies.

Community – All of a population in a given area.

Compacted – As applied to pulp and wood residues, a load that is pressed together as by settling in transit due to the weight of material above it.

Comparative Rate Schedule – A table showing the difference in shipping costs resulting from the use of various routes or modes of transportation.

Comparative Value Pricing – A method used in Canada to calculate stumpage prices.

Compartment Kiln – A type of dry kiln in which the entire charge of lumber is dried as a single unit. Also called a Charge Kiln, Box Kiln, Batch Kiln.

Compass Roof – A roof constructed of pairs of rafters having inclined ties which also serve as struts.

Compass Saw – A small handsaw with a thin blade designed for cutting a small circle.

Compensating Balance – Money that a lender requires a borrower to keep on deposit.

Comply – An American Plywood Association proprietary name for member-produced composite panels, consisting of veneer faces and backs with cores of reconstituted wood.

Com-Ply Stud – A composite stud manufactured by bonding strips of veneer to the edges of a particleboard core.

Component – 1. An element in something

Composer

larger; studs are a component of a wall, walls the components of a building. 2. Building sections assembled prior to erection, such as plywood boxed beams or stressed skin panels.

Composer – A machine that joins the edges of random width veneer to form full sheets. Composers employed today may use stitching, glue, or tape, though tape is nearly obsolete. The process increases veneer recovery and results in increased production efficiencies and a higher quality product. Also called a Veneer Composer or Veneer Welder.

Composite Arch – A pointed or lancet arch.

Composite Panel – A panel consisting of a veneer face and back and a core of particleboard.

Composite Price – Either of two widely watched indicators of market strength in lumber and panel markets. The Random Lengths Framing Lumber Composite Price is designed as a broad measure of price movement in the lumber market. It is a weighted average of key framing lumber prices, chosen from major producing areas and species. The Random Lengths Structural Panel Composite Price tracks price movement in structural panel markets. It is a weighted average of key structural panel items.

Composite Truss – A roof truss assembled from wood and steel. The wood is used in top and bottom chords connected (or held apart) by tensile members of steel.

Composition Board – A generic term for hardboard, insulation board, and particleboard.

Compound Arch – The arch that results from a series of concentric arches being placed successively within and behind each other.

Compound Beam – A beam built up from smaller pieces, as in lamination.

Compound Curvature – A structure, or assembly, having curved surfaces, no element of which is a straight line.

Compreg – Wood that has been impregnated with synthetic resin and compressed to increase its strength and density, and to reduce swelling and shrinking.

Compression – A force that tends to shorten a member. The opposite of tension.

Compression Damage – Deformation due to crushing.

Compression Failure – Minute ridges formed by crumpling or buckling of cell walls, resulting from excessive compression along the grain.

Compression Parallel to Grain – A measurement of the internal stress induced in a piece of wood when a load is applied to the end of the piece. This stress rating is indicated by the symbol: Fcll.

Compression Perpendicular to Grain – A measure of stress, expressed in pounds per square inch. This is an expression of the stress placed on a joist, beam or similar piece of lumber when it bears, or supports, a load. The load tends to compress the fibers and it is thus necessary that the bearing area is sufficient to prevent side grain crushing. This stress rating is indicated by the symbol: Fcl.

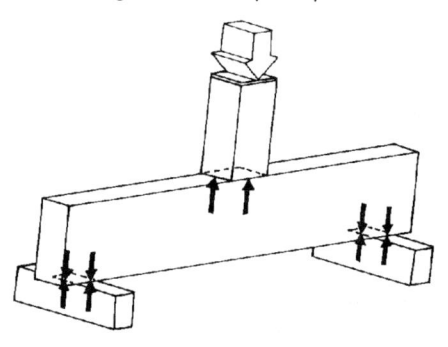

Compression Perpendicular to Grain

Compression Set – The tendency for wood to deform during compression, giving it a smaller-than-normal size after drying.

Compression Wood – Abnormal wood that forms on the lower side of leaning or crooked coniferous trees. It is characterized by its wide growth rings, color, hardness, brittleness, and generally lifeless appearance.

Compressive Strength – The resistance of a member to axial loading, expressed in pounds per square inch, and used in design calculations.

Concave Slope – A slope having a slightly hollowed-out appearance.

Concentrated Load – The weight or pressure applied to a structure over a very small area.

Concentrated Static Test – One of various tests designed to determine the glue bond quality of plywood.

Concentration Point – A location where less-than-carload shipments are brought to be combined into carload units.

Concentration Yard – A compound or area where materials are assembled for delivery to a construction jobsite.

Concrete Form – Plywood panels, usually 5/8-inch and 3/4-inch in nominal thickness, with B grade sanded faces on both sides. Used as forms or molds in pouring concrete. Plyform is a name registered by the American Plywood Association for concrete form.

Condenser Kiln – See Dehumidifier Kiln.

Conditioning – 1. The adjustment of the moisture content of wood to that existing in use, either through controlled drying in a kiln or by exposure to site conditions. 2. Steaming, in lumber to relieve the stresses present at the end of a controlled drying period, in plywood to prepare a peeler for the lathe.

Conditioning Vat – A vat, or room, in which hot water or steam are used to prepare a plywood peeler for the lathe. Veneer peels more readily and with less breakage from a conditioned block.

Condo – A condominium.

Condominium – A multi-family building in which the dwelling units are individually owned. Each owner receives a recordable deed enabling him to mortgage, or sell, his unit independent of other owners in the building.

Cone – The cone-shaped fruit or seed-bearer of conifers.

Cone Cutting – A method of removing a circular, beveled layer of veneer, similar to sharpening a pencil.

Cone Figure – The circular piece of veneer resulting from cone cutting.

Coneflower – Any of several herbs of the genus Rudbeckia or Echinacea, sometimes used as an anti-inflammatory agent.

Conference Carriers – A group of shipping lines whose members provide regularly scheduled ocean freight service at mutually agreed-upon rates.

Conference Rate – The rate charged for ocean freight space by a group of conference carriers.

Confirmation – A written verification of an order issued by a purchaser, listing the details of a transaction. See Purchase Order.

Conifer – Any of an order of mostly evergreen trees and shrubs, including those with true cones, such as pines, and with arillate fruit, such as yews.

Conk – A fungus growth that extends as a raised body from the trunk of a tree and indicates the presence of wood-destroying disease.

Conky – A term describing a tree that is rotten due to fungus growth.

Connecting Carrier – The railroad or trucking company that meets another at a certain place and continues the transportation of goods.

Connecting Girt – In timber joinery, a beam supporting two principal posts.

Connector Plate – A toothed metal plate used to join two or more members of a truss.

Conservationist – One who works to protect and preserve natural resources. Conservationists do not rule out use of a basic resource, such as land, to obtain its benefits, but do require that such use be designed to preserve or replace the resource. See Preservationist.

Consideration – The price or promise on which an agreement is based.

Consignee – The party to whom a shipment is consigned; the party entitled to receive a shipment.

Consignment – 1. The process of turning over stock to an intermediary to be sold, with the seller taking a percentage of the sales price as a fee for his services. Some small lumber producers consign their stock to another so that they do not have to employ a full-time salesperson. Some large producers consign a portion of their production to assure steady shipments. 2. In shipping, to consign (direct) a shipment to a specific point.

Consignor – The shipper or the party who gives forwarding instructions to a carrier.

Terms Of The Trade 59

Consolidation Point

Consolidation Point – A location where many small shipments are assembled for forwarding as full truck or rail car loads.

Constantine Measure – A method of measurement for cedar and mahogany logs.

Constancy – The frequency of occurrence of a species in a plant community type, expressed as a percentage of the total stand sampled.

Construction – A grade of lumber, characterized by good appearance, strength, serviceability, and the absence of serious defects.

Construction Common – A grade of Redwood that ranks below Construction Heart. Construction Common allows sapwood and is thus less resistant to decay than all-heartwood.

Construction Heart – A grade of Redwood consisting of all heartwood. Because of its high resistance to decay and insects, this grade is often used in applications where the wood will be exposed to the elements.

Construction Loan – Temporary funds advanced to finance construction.

Construction System – An assembly of construction members, whether site-built, preframed, or panelized. A floor system consists of joists, subfloor, and underlayment. The Permanent Wood Foundation is a construction system for foundations of light frame buildings.

Constructive Placement – A type of rail car storage for which a fee is charged.

Consumer Awareness Program – A program established by the Environmental Protection Agency to ensure that users of treated wood products are aware of the proper use, handling methods, and potential hazards of these products.

Consumer Information Sheet – A point-of-sale handout, established by the Environmental Protection Agency, that outlines use and handling precautions for treated wood products.

Consuming Area – An identifiable but inexact geographic region, such as the Northeast, Southwest, etc., viewed as a market for a particular product or species, or group of products and species.

Consuta Plywood – Stitched and glued plywood up to 5/8-inch thick used in shipbuilding and aircraft construction.

Contact Glue – An adhesive that adheres instantly to itself upon contact. A type of cement that bonds on contact between pieces being glued. Used primarily in installing wall paneling.

Container – A box in which goods are packed for shipment, permitting transfer from one shipping mode to another without repackaging. Ocean-going containers are up to 40 feet in length.

Container Ship

Contractor-Built House

Containerboard – A type of paperboard used in the manufacture of boxes. Usually constructed of two flat sheets, separated by a corrugated sheet.

Containerization – 1. The assembly of individual parts of a shipment into a container for ease in handling. 2. The growing of tree seedlings in degradable containers. The seedlings are planted while still in the containers, which then break down, allowing the roots to spread. Containerization of seedlings virtually eliminates damage to the roots during planting and permits use of fertilizer or other chemicals in the growing medium in the container.

Container on a Flat Car (COFC) – A shipping container placed on a flat car, from which it can be lifted to another car or truck to continue to destination. Often referred to as a "Piggyback" shipment.

Container Ship – A ship designed to carry containerized cargo.

Contiguous Habitat – Habitat, suitable to support the life needs of a species, that is distributed continuously, or nearly so, across a landscape.

Contiguous Service – Marine transportation to ports of a single nationality, located on the same land mass.

Continuous Beam – A beam supported at more than two points over two or more spans.

Continuous Header – The use of 2x6s turned on edge in place of a top plate of 2x4s. The header acts as a lintel over wall openings, eliminating fitting of separate headers.

Continuous Lumber Tester (CLT) – A brand of stress rating machine. The CLT tests individual pieces in a production line by measuring the force required to obtain a specified deflection. The CLT automatically codes each piece to indicate modulus of elasticity, a factor in assigning strength values to lumber. Actual grades are assigned to the lumber after visual examination.

Continuously Rising Temperature – A dry kiln schedule employing increasing dry-bulb temperature at a certain number of degrees per unit of time.

Continuous Press Line – In particleboard manufacturing, a belt that feeds a continuous mat of furnish into the press. Panels are cut to length after pressing.

Contour – An imaginary line connecting points of land with the same elevation.

Contour Felling – Timber felled parallel to the contour of the ground.

Contract – 1. An agreement between two or more parties to do or not do a certain thing. Specifically, an agreement between a buyer and seller in which both parties agree to certain terms of a transaction such as price, product specifications, delivery time, etc. 2. In futures trading, a commitment to deliver or receive a specified volume of a particular commodity at a future date. 3. In futures trading, a specific volume of a commodity. For example, one contract of wheat equals 5,000 bushels. One contract of lumber equals 160,000 board feet of Western S-P-F Std&Btr 2x4.

Contract Business – Long-term buying arrangements between shippers and buyers, usually involving regular shipments of certain items at agreed-upon intervals.

Contract Carrier – A carrier under contract to perform specific services for specified rates.

Contract Freight Rate – A reduced rail freight rate granted, in a confidential signed agreement, to a specific shipper, usually in exchange for a commitment by the shipper to route a stated volume of products over the carrier's lines.

Contract Grade – The grades of a commodity that are deliverable against a futures contract.

Contracting Out – The practice of hiring an outside company or individuals to complete a specific job or jobs. Often an issue in labor negotiations.

Contract Item – The specific item or items deliverable in a commodity futures contract.

Contract Month – The month in which futures contracts may be satisfied by making or accepting delivery.

Contractor – An individual or firm that agrees to perform specific services for a set price.

Contractor-Built House – A house built for owner occupancy on the owner's land, with construction under the supervision of a

Terms Of The Trade

Contractor Clear Decking

single general contractor.

Contractor Clear Decking – A decking grade developed by the Western Red Cedar Lumber Association.

Contractor Knotty Decking – A decking grade developed by the Western Red Cedar Lumber Association.

Contract Price – Selling levels that are established by producers, often at one-month intervals. Used to distinguish these prices from open market levels, which are established on a day-to-day basis.

Contract Rate – See Contract Freight Rate.

Contraflexure – The portion of a curve on a piece of lumber that is opposite to the direction of the stress being applied.

Contremaitre – A logging camp foreman in Quebec.

Controlled Burning – The use of fire to destroy logging debris, reduce buildups of dead and fallen timber that poses wildfire hazards, control tree disease, clear land, or perform other functions, such as clearing a buffer strip in the path of a wildfire.

Controlled Random Pattern – A method of installing decking or flooring in which random length pieces are arranged so that the end of one piece is not adjacent to the end of the piece next to it.

Controlling Kiln Sample – One of the wettest samples used to determine the progress of drying in a kiln.

Conventional Cutting – A method of sawing in which a circular saw rotates counter to the direction that the material being sawn is fed to it. Also called Countersawing.

Conventional Design – A design procedure using factors determined by widely accepted methods.

Conventional Loan – A mortgage loan made by a financial institution directly to a borrower without government insurance or guarantees.

Convergence – The tendency of expiring futures contracts to gravitate toward the price at which the physical commodity is trading.

Conversion – In wood finishing, the process of chemically bonding the resins in a film.

Conversion Period – The time required to completely remove old growth forests and convert them to young stands.

Convertible Currency – Any currency that can be converted to another without special permission of an exchange control authority.

Converting Plant – A manufacturing facility that produces corrugated paperboard and manufactures boxes from that board.

Convex Slope – A slope that pushes out or bulges slightly.

Conveyance – A written agreement by which property is transferred from one person to another.

Conveyor – A continuous belt or similar device used for moving materials.

Convoy Treated – Lumber treated with a proprietary product to resist staining during shipment.

Cookee – The cook's assistant in old logging camps.

Cookie Patch – See Circular Patch.

Cooler – A machine used in the manufacture of OSB and waferboard, usually positioned after the hot press. The cooler lets air circulate on both sides of a panel before it is routed to the trimmer.

Cooling Shed – A place where lumber is stored after kiln drying to allow it to cool before further processing.

Coon Tree – A hollow tree, or one with a good-sized hole in it. Such trees now are sometimes left standing to provide wildlife habitat. A Wildlife Tree.

Co-op – See Cooperative.

Cooperage – The process of making containers such as barrels, tubs, and kegs, using wooden staves and headings and metal hoops. There are two types of cooperage: 1. Tight cooperage is designed to produce containers that will hold liquids; 2. Slack cooperage produces containers designed for other products.

Cooperative – A group of retailers who operate independently but who organize for the

Core Wood

purpose of establishing a jointly owned purchasing office.

Cooperative Housing – A housing complex owned by a non-profit corporation, whose shareholders are residents of the complex. The co-op is governed by an elected board of members.

Coping – 1. A covering to protect a beam or post from weather. 2. A process in which two moulding strips are fitted together at an angle by cutting one to fit the design of the other.

Coping Saw – A narrow, thin-bladed saw used to fit two mouldings together at an angle.

Coppice (Copse) – A cutover area. In Europe, a plantation where trees are cut young to encourage the growth of shoots which are marketable.

Coppice System – A silvicultural system in which trees are regenerated from stump sprouts.

Co-Products – Bark, shavings, and other by-products of lumber and plywood manufacturing.

Corbel – A bracket, or projecting support, on the face of a wall.

Cord – A unit of measurement equal to a stack of wood 4x4x8 feet, or 128 cubic feet. Pulpwood is often measured in cords.

Corduroy Road – A road or pathway that has logs or poles placed crosswise to the road direction, to act as a firm surface upon which to haul or skid logs from the cutting area to the landing.

Cordwood – Small wood or branches cut for firewood or to make charcoal.

Core – 1. Inner plies in a piece of plywood whose grain direction runs perpendicular to that of the outer plies (See Crossband). 2. The inner portion, usually particleboard, of material covered by veneer or other products; generally used in the manufacture of furniture or cabinets.

Core Feeder – A worker who feeds core veneer into a glue-spreading machine.

Core Flake – A wood flake used in construction of the inner portion of particleboard or waferboard. Usually larger or heavier than the particles used in the construction of faces and backs.

Core Gap – An open joint extending through or partly through a plywood panel, occurring when core veneers are not tightly butted. When center veneers are involved, the condition is referred to as "Center Gap."

Core Lathe – A lathe designed to peel additional veneer from a peeler core after it has become too small to handle on the main lathe.

Core Layer – The person who assembles the core veneers of a sheet of plywood.

Core Layer

Core Line – The production area in a plywood plant where cores are assembled and glue is applied.

Core Marks – Traces of wood grain transferred through the face of a panel from rough core veneer. Also called Core Transfer.

Core Saw – A band saw used to cut stacks of core veneer to specific sizes.

Corestock – A type of particleboard or other fiberboard used as the inner core for counter tops, furniture, or such applications.

Core Stud – A stud manufactured from a peeler core, that part of the log remaining after it has been peeled on a lathe to yield veneer. Core studs are generally viewed as inferior to studs produced from logs.

Core Transfer – See Core Marks.

Core Void – See Core Gap.

Core Wood – Same as Juvenile Wood.

Terms Of The Trade

Coring

Coring – The slippage of the inner pieces of a lumber package, due to inadequate compression when strapping, or to slipperiness.

Corinthian – A type of architecture distinguished by intricately carved capitals.

Cork – The layer of dead cells on the outside of a stem or root that protects the inner, living cells against damage.

Corkbark Fir – Abies lasiocarpa var. arizonica. This fir, a variant of Subalpine Fir, is distinguished by soft, corky, light-colored bark. It is found in the southwestern U.S.

Corkboard – Compressed and baked granulated cork used in flooring and sound conditioning.

Cork Pine – A regional name for fine old-growth Idaho White Pine. 2. An Eastern White Pine tree yielding a superior grade of lumber.

Corks – See Calks.

Corkwood – Balsa wood, known for its light weight.

Corn Cribbing – A lumber grade used to specify boards used in the construction of corn cribs, or storage bins, and other farm buildings. Corn cribbing is 1x6, machined to pattern. It can be made from any species and be of any grade agreeable to buyer and seller. Usually it is the Superior grade of Finish. Corn cribbing was common through the 1930s, but is rarely made now.

Corner – The intersection of two adjacent faces in a piece of lumber.

Corner Bead – A reinforcing strip of formed galvanized steel placed on the corners of interior walls before plastering.

Corner Block – Blocks used in furniture construction to reinforce joints subjected to high stress.

Corner Board – A piece of trim for an external corner of a house or similar frame structure, against which the ends of the siding are finished.

Corner Knot – See Knot Occurrence.

Corner Post – Two or more studs nailed together to form a corner in a frame structure.

Corner Protector – A moulding installed on the outside corners of interior partitions to protect them and to finish the joint.

Corner Up – In felling a tree, to cut up to the corners of the undercut before cutting the main part of the holding wood in the center of the tree.

Cornice – Exterior trim used at the juncture of an outside wall and the roof. Also, interior trim used where wall and ceiling meet.

Cornice Trim – A building's outside finish where a sloping roof meets a vertical wall.

Corporate Lands – Forest land owned by corporate organizations other than those in the forest industry, such as utility companies, railroads, banks, etc.

Corridor – 1. A narrow tract of land, or strip of timber, serving as a connector to other land. 2. A common passageway in a building.

Corrugated Box – The common carton constructed of a face and back of flat sheets of heavy paper laminated to a corrugated inner ply to increase strength and stiffness.

Corrugating Medium – The fluted portion of corrugated (cardboard) box material which is sandwiched between two sheets of linerboard.

Corsican Pine – Any of various pines, such as Pinus calabrica, P. laricio, or P. nigra. Also called Austrian Pine.

Cortex – The part of a tree's bark between the endodermis and the epidermis.

Cost Accounting – A process in which all elements of cost involved in an activity are evaluated.

Cost & Freight (C&F) – A basis for quotation that includes the price of the goods (cost) and the expense of shipment (freight) to a specific destination.

Cost, Insurance, & Freight (CIF) – A term used in waterborne shipments to indicate that the price quoted includes all charges from the point of origin to the port of destination, including the original cost of the goods.

Cost, Insurance, Freight, & Exchange (CIF&E) – A similar term as above, plus an additional charge due to a difference in the monetary exchange rate between countries of origin and destination.

Cost Plus Pricing – Setting the selling price of an item by adding overhead costs and a profit to a base cost figure.

Cottage Roof – A type of roof consisting of common rafters, purlins, ridge, and wall plates, but lacking principal rafters or trusses.

Cottonwood – Populus deltoides, P. balsamifera, P. monilifera, and others. A poplar whose seeds are attached to fluffy white down, or "cotton," to aid in distribution. Used in box manufacture, for excelsior and veneer core. Locally in the West, sometimes referred to as Mormon Pine.

Coulter Pine – Pinus coulteri. This species, found in the coastal mountains of central and southern California, is closely related to Jeffery Pine. It is of limited commercial value except as fuelwood.

Coulisse – A piece of lumber grooved to accommodate a sluice or similar item.

Couch Roll – A device in paper manufacturing that pulls water from the paper sheet, enabling it to separate more easily from the wire web on which it was formed.

Count – The number of pieces or units of specific items in a shipment.

Counter – A counteroffer to buy at a lower price, made after a seller has quoted a price for a particular item. Usually made verbally and considered by both parties to be binding if accepted by the seller.

Counter Batten – A wooden piece fixed to the back of a wide board, or several boards, to deter warping.

Counterbracing – Diagonal braces which transmit stress in an opposite direction from the main bracing, such as those in a truss providing relief from transverse stress.

Counterclaim – A claim made by a defendant to offset a previous claim or accusation made by a plaintiff.

Counter Floor – In a floor with two layers, the bottom layer of floor boards.

Counteroffer – See Counter.

Counteroffset – See Counter.

Countersawing – See Conventional Cutting.

Counterstock – Lumber, usually select grade and in widths of 22 inches or more, used for counter tops and drain boards.

Countertop Grade – A grade of particleboard slightly lower in density than Industrial grade.

Countertrade – A parallel transaction in international trade in which a party in one country agrees to sell goods to a party in a second country, while also agreeing to buy other goods from the second party. Payment may be made in currency, goods, services, or a combination of all three. See Transit Trade.

Countervailing Duty – A duty levied on imports to offset a subsidy in the exporting country.

Counter Veneer – The bottom layer in a double veneer layup, used to prevent cracking in the face veneer.

Country Cut – A British term denoting full original sawn measure.

Couple – 1. To join two objects. 2. A pair of rafters.

Couple Roof – A short-span pitched roof, with common rafters and no tie beam.

Coupling Dog – A short chain or cable with dogs at each end, used to link logs end-to-end for skidding.

Course – A row of roof shingles, or a layer of boards in a stack of lumber.

Cove – A type of moulding with a concave profile used at corners, particularly as a ceiling cornice.

Cove Ceiling – A ceiling that curves in from the side walls.

Cover – 1. A purchase to offset a previous transaction in which an item was sold prior to having been bought. Used in reference to both futures and cash market trading. See Short Covering. 2. Vegetation used by wildlife for protection.

Cover Board – Pieces of plywood placed on the top of a plywood unit to protect the inside pieces from the elements while being shipped or stored. The cover boards are usually of a lower grade than the stock they are

Terms Of The Trade 65

Cow Cypress

protecting.

Cow Cypress – Another name for Baldcypress.

Cow's Mouth – The notch cut into the trunk of a tree to fell it. See Face Cut.

C-Plugged – A C-grade plywood face or back that has been patched where there was a defective portion. Such a patch may be sound wood, but is likely to be a synthetic filler of fiber and resin to provide a smooth, sound surface.

Cranage – A port charge assessed for the use of cranes to load or unload cargo.

Crating – An end-use application for structural panels, often in connection with the transport of new machinery.

Crawl – A defect in hardboard.

Crawler Tractor – A machine that moves by means of an endless tread rather than wheels.

Crawl Space – Space under the floor joists of a house that allows access to plumbing and wiring under the house.

Crazing – The cracks resulting from the expansion and contraction of wood in response to temperature changes; also called cold checking.

Crazy Wheel – A braking system used in the eastern woods to ease the descent of sleighs loaded with logs on icy hills.

Credit Line – The amount a seller will allow a customer to owe on goods purchased.

Creep – In wood drying, the inelastic strains that produce tension and compression sets in the wood.

Creosote – A wood preservative consisting mainly of aromatic hydrocarbons obtained by distillation of coal tar. Used to preserve wood products such as utility poles, fence posts, and the like that come into contact with the ground.

Crew Cab – A pickup truck or utility vehicle outfitted with an extended passenger compartment to accommodate more passengers. Often used for transporting logging crews and their equipment.

Crib – 1 Two or more layers of timbers or lumber laid across one another to support a heavy load. 2. An open framework of timbers filled with stone or concrete to construct a dam or a foundation, as for a bridge. 3. A stickered load of lumber prepared for seasoning in a dry kiln.

Cribwork – Any of various structures built up with criss-crossed logs or timbers, such as abutments, trestles, or retaining walls.

Cricket – A type of metal flashing often used above chimneys when applying a shingle or shake roof.

Crimping – See Ribbing.

Cripple – A short stud used above or below headers in window and door openings.

Cripple Patch – A rectangular patch with round corners used in voids caused by defects in the veneers of plywood panels. Similar in shape to the Davis (or router) patch, but usually two inches wide and up to six inches long and designed to cover larger defects.

Cripples and Header

Cripple Wall – A short stud wall between the floor and foundation of a house.

Critical Habitat – An area deemed essential to the survival of a threatened or endangered species.

Critical Habitat Unit (CHU) – A block of land designated by the U.S. Fish & Wildlife Service as essential habitat for survival of a species. In 1992, the service designated 190 CHUs, totaling 6.8 million acres, for the northern spotted owl.

Crocodile – See Alligator.

Crook – Deviation edgewise from a straight line from end to end of a piece of lumber, measured at the point of the greatest distance from the straight line.

Crook Reducer – A patented machine used by some Southern Yellow Pine manufacturers to reduce the crook in rough lumber by use of a cutterhead to develop a straight edge before the lumber passes through a planer.

Cross Aligned – The pattern in which inner layers of an OSB panel are arranged perpendicular to the length-wise alignment of the outer layers.

Cross Alley – In stickered units of air-dried lumber, the passageways that connect main alleys at right angles to the piled lumber.

Cross Arm – The horizontal cross member on a utility pole, designed to support electrical or telephone wires.

Crossband – A construction technique for plywood with five or more plies, in which veneer is laid at right angles to the core and front and back faces. This increases stability in uses such as underlayment. Also X-Band.

Crossband Gap – A void created when the veneer in a crossband does not butt firmly together.

Crossband Lap – A defect occurring when the edges of core veneer overlay one another.

Crossbar – In plywood, a type of figure or irregularity of grain resembling a dip in the grain and running at approximately right angles to the length of the veneer piece.

Cross Break – Separation of wood across the grain.

Crosscut – To cut with a saw across the grain. Also, a saw used for this purpose.

Crossfire – A type of distortion of the wood fibers of a tree which, when cut in a radial direction, produces figures and highlights resembling a corrugated surface. Also called a cross figure.

Cross Grain – An area in a piece of lumber in which the grain of the wood is distorted so that it runs across the piece from edge to edge instead of along the length of the piece. An example would be the deviation of the grain around a knot. Cross grain represents a weakness in the piece.

Cross Lamination – The basic method of plywood manufacture. Veneers are laid at right angles to each other, or cross-laminated, to increase the strength and stability of the panel.

Cross Out – A narrow strip of wood placed at right angles between layers of lumber to facilitate air circulation during drying. See Sticker.

Cross-Panel Stiffness – In plywood, stiffness in the direction perpendicular to the grain of the face ply; normally, stiffness in the 4-foot direction of a 4x8-foot panel.

Crossply – An inner ply in plywood laid at a right angle to the direction of grain on the face and back veneers. See Plugged Crossply.

Cross Rate – The rate of exchange between two foreign currencies.

Cross the Lead – To fall timber across previously felled timber.

Cross Tie – A cross member, usually of wood, used to support railroad rails in a roadbed.

Cross Tongue – A type of brace or stiffener made by cutting a piece of plywood or a strip of wood with diagonal grain and attaching the piece, usually by gluing, between two members to stiffen an angle joint.

Cross Trade – A trade route between two countries served by a vessel flying the flag of a third country.

Crotch Veneer – Veneer cut from the crotch, or fork, of a tree. Such veneer yields unusual grain patterns, including curly and flowery figures.

Crowder – A machine that digs by pushing its bucket or shovel away from itself.

Crow Foot – 1. A type of figured grain, resembling tracks made by a bird's foot. 2. Checks or cracks extending from the center of a log. 3. A mark or brand used to identify logs.

Crown – 1. The upper part of a tree. 2. A term denoting government ownership or

Terms Of The Trade 67

Crown Classes

control in Canada, as in "Crown Timber." 3. A slight camber on a horizontal member; such members are placed so the crown is on top.

Crown Classes – Trees compete for space in the forest canopy, with faster growing trees taking a larger share of the space. This occurs in mixed tree stands, where trees are of all ages. Crown classification categorizes faster and slower growing trees according to their position in the forest canopy. Four classes are used: Dominant, Codominant, Intermediate, and Overtopped.

Crown Cut – To saw tangentially to annual rings. Flat sawn.

Crowned Board – A condition in particleboard manufacturing in which the center of the width of a sanded panel is thicker than the two long edges of the panel.

Crown Fire – A forest fire that is burning in the crowns, or tops, of trees. A crown fire may start from a lightning strike, or be ignited by the intense heat of a ground fire. A fire that has crowned is more subject to the effect of wind than is a fire on the ground, and may result in a "blow out," an uncontrollable, fast-spreading blaze.

Crown-Formed Wood – Same as Juvenile Wood.

Crown Moulding – A moulding used where two surfaces meet at an angle; usually applied wherever a larger angle is to be covered.

Crown Piece – A short bearing timber on a wall, designed to carry the foot of a strut.

Crown Post – The short vertical post used near the middle of a hammerbeam roof.

Crown Timber – In Canada, timber owned by the government. From colonial days when such timber was literally the property of the crown.

Cruise – To estimate the volume and quality of a timber stand by visual examination of test plots or strips in the stand. A cruiser usually examines from 10% to 20% of the total stand.

Cruiser – One who estimates the volume and quality of a timber stand, by visual examination of the stand.

Cruiser's Mark – An identifying mark used by a timber cruiser to label witness trees.

Cruiser's Stick – A measuring device used by a timber cruiser, consisting of a long stick marked with graduations for measuring tree height, diameter, and estimated volume.

Crummy – A truck or bus used to transport a logging crew to and from the work area.

C-Type Ship – Any of various-sized break-bulk ships. The vessels are designated C-1, C-2, etc. depending on their gross tonnage.

Cuban One-Fifth Rule – A log rule used primarily in the imported hardwood trade.

Cuban Pine – Pinus caribaea. This species, also called Caribbean Pine and Honduras Pitch Pine, is similar to Long Leaf Pine.

Cuber – A person who splits shake blocks. This term is used primarily in British Columbia. Also called a cuberman.

Cubic Content – The volume of cubic feet in a room or structure, used as a basis for cost estimates in materials and construction.

Cubic Foot Log Scale – The standard tree and log measurement used by many forest products companies in the Pacific Northwest.

Cubic Meter Log Scale – The metric standard measure of log volume for most of the world.

Cubic Recovery – A measure of the actual cubic volume of lumber recovered from the original net cubic log scale volume. It is expressed as a percentage of the net log volume.

Cubic Scaling – The measurement of timber volume in cubic meters, rather than in board feet. The most common method of measurement, except in the United States.

Cubit – An 18-inch unit of linear measurement; now rarely used.

Cull – 1. A tree or log that is less than one-third useable for lumber or plywood because of excessive decay or other defects. Cull logs are often converted to chips for sale to pulp producers. 2. Lumber of the lowest quality, with little or no commercial value, usually below Economy or #5 grade. Lumber is sometimes purchased "mill run, culls out."

Culmination of Mean Annual Increment (MAI) – The point at which the average an-

Custom Milling

nual growth of a forest is at a maximum.

Culvertail – Another name for dovetail; chiefly British.

Cunit – A measurement of volume equal to 100 cubic feet.

Cup – Deviation flatwise from a straight line across the width of a piece of lumber, measured at the point of greatest distance from the line.

Cup Shake – A separation between the annual rings of a log, caused by a lack of nutrients, insect damage, wind, shock, or faulty seasoning. Also, Arc Shake.

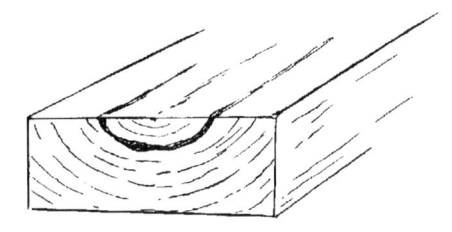

Cup Shake

Curb Roof – A roof comprised of four attached surfaces, with the bottom edge of each sloping outward. Also called a Mansard Roof.

Cure – The setting of an adhesive by chemical reaction, usually accomplished by the application of heat or a catalyst.

Cured – Dried; seasoned.

Cure Rate – The rate or time in which an adhesive or coating will develop maximum strength or hardness.

Cure Time – The length of time required for an adhesive or coating to develop maximum strength or hardness.

Curl – A spiral or curved marking in wood grain.

Curl Veneer – Veneer cut from the junction of a branch and the main trunk of a tree and favored for its attractive grain pattern.

Curly Grain – An ornamental grain pattern in wood.

Currency Adjustment Factor – A surcharge assessed shippers of ocean freight to make up for fluctuations in the U.S. currency against other world currencies.

Current Assets – Assets that can be turned into cash within 90 days.

Current Capital – A fixed asset, not readily converted into cash.

Current Liabilities – Debts that must be paid within 90 days.

Current Ratio – The ratio of current assets to current liabilities.

Current Weight – The weight of a kiln sample at any given time during the drying process.

Curved Beams – Glue-laminated beams available in a variety of configurations.

Curved Plywood – Stressed-skin or sandwich panels that are curved to varying degrees by being fastened over a framework, usually lumber.

Curved Sawing – A carriage system or resaw that feeds the log or cant through the saw in a curve parallel to the edges of the log or cant.

Customary Measure – A reference to a method of measuring logs or timbers in which allowances are made for wane and other defects.

Customary Square – In the British timber trade, a square of timber that may include a waney edge, as opposed to a Dead Square, which allows no waney edges.

Custom Clear Decking – A decking grade developed by the Western Red Cedar Lumber Association.

Customer Specifications – See Specifications.

Customer Specified Loading – A loading consisting of the exact lengths, widths, and grades specified by the customer.

Custom Knotty Decking – A decking grade developed by the Western Red Cedar Lumber Association.

Custom Milling – The surfacing or remanufacturing of lumber on a contract basis and to order. The lumber usually belongs to the person ordering the milling, with the mill receiving a fee for its services.

Terms Of The Trade   69

Customs Broker

Customs Broker – A person or firm licensed to act on behalf of importers and exporters in clearing shipments in international trade by preparing the necessary documents.

Customs District – Any one of a number of federal stations through which imports and exports are processed. Although a district is often identified by a state designation, exports passing through it may actually originate from a wider area than a single state.

Cut – 1. A reference to harvest volume in a forest, as in "annual allowable cut." 2. In a sawmill, a reference to output, as in "a daily cut of one million feet," or species, as in a "hemlock cut". 3. A railroad term referring to any number of cars moving as a unit.

Cut Alive – To saw logs on a headrig without turning them, as in a Scragg mill.

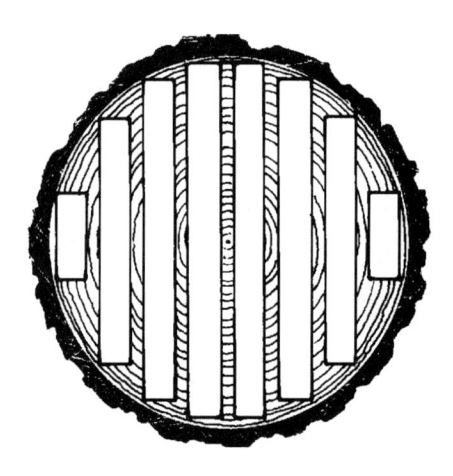

Cut Alive

Cut and Run – An accusation made against the forest industry generally and certain forest products companies specifically, especially in earlier days. A company was said to "cut and run" if it harvested all the profitable timber in an area without regard to reforestation efforts or to modern forestry practices. Current state and federal regulations discourage the practice by establishing minimum reforestation and providing tax incentives.

Cut-Full Lumber – Lumber intentionally manufactured in larger-than-normal thickness and width, usually to allow for shrinkage. This term is sometimes confused with "Full Cut," which means cut to measure fully to specified sizes.

Cuticle – The impervious outer coating of the epidermis providing protection and preventing water loss.

Cutline – The boundary separating an area to be logged from the remaining timber.

Cutoffs – Short pieces, trimbacks.

Cutoff Saw – A large saw, usually circular, used to trim logs to specific lengths before they enter a manufacturing plant. See Trimsaw.

Cutout – 1. An opening cut into a wall or structural member to accommodate something, as an electrical outlet. 2. A term designating that all of the timber in a specific area or ownership has been cut.

Cut Over – Land that has previously been logged.

Cut Stock – Small pieces of surfaced, partially worked or rough lumber in specified sizes suitable for further manufacture into specific products.

Cut Stuff – In the United Kingdom, timbers or deals resawn into smaller sections.

Cutter – A timber faller. See Chopper.

Cutter Head – Part of a moulding machine. Fitted with moulding knives, cutter heads are installed in a moulder, where they rotate at high speed to shape the moulding profile.

Cutting – A common name for sawn products cut to meet the specifications of an order; not mass produced. Usually applied to products of the Douglas Fir region, such as roof purlins, bridge stringers, and industrial items.

Cutting Alive – See Cut Alive.

Cutting Angle – The angle between the face of a cutting edge and a plane perpendicular to its cutting direction. Also called Angle of Attack or Rake Angle.

Cutting Bar – A flat steel bar on a power saw, around which the chain runs.

Cutting Circle – 1. The circle described by the outer rim or extremity of the teeth in a circular saw. 2. A general description of a timber-harvest area that is tributary to a group of manufacturing plants.

Cutting Crew –   The loggers who fell timber in a logging operation.

Cutting Line –   The boundary in a logging show between those trees to be harvested and those to be left standing.

Cutting Plan –   The schedule for harvesting timber in a given area.

Cutting Rights –   A contractual right to cut certain described timber over a long period on a specific property. Cutting rights do not involve ownership or control of the land and usually cover periods of 10 years or more. Sometimes called a "Timber Deed."

Cutting Teeth –   The teeth on a crosscut saw that actually do the cutting, as opposed to raker teeth which draw out the sawdust.

Cutting Unit –   An area of timber designated for harvest.

Cut-to-Size –   Lumber, plywood, or particleboard sawn to a specific size, usually designated by the buyer. Most often seen in items destined for remanufacture.

CWT –   Hundredweight; the standard designation for 100 pounds, used in determining freight costs in some cases when rates are quoted on a "per CWT" basis. In the U.K., a hundredweight is 112 pounds.

Cycle Time –   The time required for a process to be completed and to resume a new cycle.

Cyclone –   Part of a pneumatic conveyor system that transports various mill wastes including sander dust, planer shavings, chips, etc. to a central collection point. The cyclone, a conical shaped device, separates suspended particles from the air stream of the system. The air stream, with its load of particles, enters the cyclone, where the material is directed, by centrifugal force, against the walls of the cyclone. The particles lose velocity and fall into a collection bin, while the stream of air is vented through an exhaust in the top of the cyclone.

Cyclone Burner –   A waste burner, usually conical, that utilizes a stream of air to aid combustion.

Cyma –   A commonly used molding, similar in form to an italic letter f.

Cymbia –   A fillet.

Cypress –   See Baldcypress.

Cypress Pine –   Callitris glauca, or Queensland Cypress. Buff-colored and fragrant, this species is commonly used for construction, flooring, joinery, boats, and piles.

Terms Of The Trade

D

D4S – Dressed four sides.

Dado – 1. A groove cut into one piece to accommodate another piece. A dado is three-sided and cut into a board, usually across the grain, as opposed to a rabbet, which has two sides and is at the edge of a board. 2. Part of a column, between the base and the cap or cornice. 3. The lower part of an interior wall.

Dado Head – A type of saw blade, used to make a dado.

Dado Head

Damage Free Car – A type of rail car having internal bulkheads and other provisions designed to reduce the need for bracing and dunnage on the part of the shipper.

Damp Air – In air drying, air in and around the piles whose relative humidity is so high that little or no drying takes place. Also called Moist Air.

Dandy Roll – In papermaking, a wire-mesh drum used to press surface patterns and watermarks into the paper while it is still on the fourdrineir.

Danzig Fir – Pinus sylvestris, a major European species. Also called Baltic Redwood.

Dap – A notch cut in a timber to receive another timber or to allow passage of some object.

Dapple – A variegated figure, or fleck, in wood.

Dark Grain – Grain that is darker than the rest of the wood in a piece; this should not be confused with pitch streak.

Dating Nail – A nail showing a date or symbol on its head. Used to indicate the year of treatment or the date of installation.

Davis Patch – A rectangular patch with round corners. Used in voids caused by defects in the veneers of plywood panels. One of two patch designs allowed in A-grade faces. Also known as a router patch.

Terms Of The Trade 73

Davis Raft

Davis Raft – A type of seagoing log raft, in which a large number of logs are bound together with interwoven wire rope so that the finished raft forms a large bundle, sometimes containing a million board feet or more of logs.

Dawn Redwood – Metasequoia glyptostroboides. This rare tree, native to China, is cultivated as an ornamental. It is not a commercial species.

Day Faller – A timber faller who works for a daily wage, rather than on a piece-rate basis calculated on the volume of timber felled.

Daylight Width – The width of a window opening though which light can actually pass.

Day Order – In futures trading, an order that is placed for execution during only one trading session. If the order cannot be executed that day, it is automatically canceled.

Day-Time Drying – Discontinuous operation of a dry kiln, due to interruptions of steam, fuel, or power supply. Also called Part-Time Drying.

Day Trader – A futures speculator, usually a floor trader, who establishes and liquidates each of his positions within one trading session.

Deadening Felt – A building paper applied to a roof deck before shingles are laid.

Deadhead – 1. In road transportation, a truck traveling outbound or inbound without a load. 2. A saturated log that floats very low in the water and poses a hazard to small boats.

Dead Knot – A loose knot; one not firmly joined to the surrounding wood. A decayed knot.

Dead Load – The weight borne by a structure resulting from the presence of immobile objects such as furniture; a design factor in calculating the requirements for construction of a load-bearing surface such as a floor or roof.

Deadman – A buried or sunken weight, often a log, used to anchor a cable.

Dead Pack – A unit of lumber banded without stickers.

Dead Piled – Plywood fresh from the press, piled on a solid flat base, without stickers, and weighted down while it returns to normal levels of heat and moisture content. Also called Solid Pile.

Dead Rolls – Rollers that are not power driven, as opposed to live rolls.

Dead Square – Absolutely square, without wane. As opposed to customary square, which may contain some waney pieces.

Deadwood – Wood from dead, standing trees.

Deal – An inexact term referring to a board or plank of various sizes, usually 9 or more inches in width and 3 to 5 inches in thickness.

Dealer – A retailer; one who sells directly to builders, contractors, and other end users.

Debarker – A machine used to remove bark from logs prior to processing them into lumber, panels, or pulp.

Debarker

Debenture – An unsecured note or bond issued by a corporation to raise funds.

Debenture Timber – In the British timber trade, imported mining timbers, usually in the round.

Decay – Disintegration of wood substance due to action of wood-destroying fungi. Also known as dote, or rot. Among the types of decay recognized for grading purposes are: 1. Advanced (or typical) decay; an older stage of decay in which disintegration is readily recognized because the wood has become punky, soft, spongy, stringy, shaky, pitted, or crumbly. Decided discoloration or bleaching of the rotted wood is often apparent. 2. Incipient decay; an early stage of decay in which disintegration has not proceeded far enough to soften or otherwise change the hardness of the wood perceptibly. Usually accompanied by slight discoloration or bleaching of the wood. 3. Pocket rot; typical decay which appears as an area of soft rot, usually surrounded by apparently sound wood. 4. Water soak or stain; water-soaked area in heartwood, usually interpreted as the incipient stage of certain types of rot.

Decayed Knot – See Knot Quality.

Decay Resistance – A reference to a wood species' ability to resist attack by wood-destroying fungi under conditions favorable to their growth.

Deciduous – Trees that lose their leaves; usually broadleaved and usually classified as hardwoods.

Deck – 1. See Log Deck, Cold Deck, Hot Deck. 2. The surface of a floor or roof before finishing materials are applied. 3. The boards or panels making up the top and bottom surfaces of a pallet. 4. An outdoor deck.

Decking – Lumber used primarily in roofing and flooring applications. The most common sizes of decking are 5/4x6, 2x6, 2x8, 3x6, and 4x6. Decking is often sawn with tongues and grooves and in various patterns (double tongue and groove or single tongue and groove). Patterns are sometimes sawn on the face to be exposed. These patterns are often grooves of various shapes, depths, and sizes.

Deck Load – Freight carried on the open deck of a vessel.

Deck-on-Hip – A flat roof capping a hip roof.

Decorative Grades – Grades for lumber or panels that are based on the appearance qualities of the product, rather than the structural qualities.

Decorative Panel – An appearance grade panel with a rough sawn, brushed, grooved, or striated face. Used for paneling, accent walls, and other interior applications.

Deep Cutting – Resawing timber parallel to its face.

Deep Ecology – A branch of environmentalism in which one relates to the environment in a predominately spiritual or religious manner. Deep Ecologists subscribe to a belief that all things have an equal right to live or be.

Deeping – See Deep Cutting.

Defect – Any naturally occurring imperfection, or condition of wood, including decay, shake, checking, pitch seams, etc., that would make lumber or other finished wood products off grade.

Defective Car – A rail car in such a condition that is likely to damage the contents of the car.

Defect Scanner – A video camera system designed to identify defects in lumber, in order to determine grade and/or control sawing or trimming.

Defense Supply Agency – An agency of the Department of Defense that acts as procurement agency for the armed forces.

Defensive Pricing – A pricing strategy used by a producer when, for various reasons such as a long order file or short inventory, he wishes to discourage business. This is accomplished by raising list or asking prices to an artificially high level above current trading prices.

Deferreds – The more distant months in which futures trading is being conducted at a given time. Also known as Back Months.

Defibrator – A machine used to break down wood into fibers for use in various types of fiberboard.

Deficit Weight – The difference between the actual weight of a shipment and the minimum weight. If a particular freight rate required a minimum weight of 100,000 pounds for a shipment, but the actual weight was 80,000 pounds, the deficit weight would be 20,000 pounds.

Deflection – The movement of a horizontal member under load.

Deformation – Misshapenness or crookedness in construction, resulting from stress over a period of time.

Degrades – Pieces of lumber that on reinspection prove to be of lower quality than the grade originally assigned to them.

Dehorn – 1. To remove limbs from a log. 2. To remove a brand from a log, either due to a change of ownership, or to steal it with less chance of being caught with an identifiable log.

Dehumidification Drying

Dehumidification Drying – An alternative kiln drying process in which moisture removed from lumber is condensed, and the circulating air is reheated rather than vented from the kiln.

De-Inking – The process of removing ink and other substances from paper to be recycled.

Delamination – The separation of the layers of veneer in a plywood panel at the glueline, usually caused by moisture, mismanufacture, or defective glue.

Delignification – The process of removing lignin from wood by chemical treatment.

Delivered Price – The price of an item with the freight to destination included.

Delivery Month – A specified month within which delivery may be made under terms of a futures contract.

Delivery Notice – A written notice provided to the buyer of a futures contract by the seller, indicating his intention to deliver the physical commodity.

Delivery Ticket – A document verifying the receipt of a shipment by the consignee, usually used when the shipment is by truck. By signing the delivery ticket, the consignee acknowledges receipt of the goods.

Demising Wall – A Party Wall.

Demurrage – A charge assessed by a carrier for holding a rail freight car, truck, or ship. In the forest products trade, demurrage commonly refers to the charges assessed to a wholesaler who is unable to sell a transit car and must hold it temporarily at a diversion point.

Dendrochronology – The science of tree-ring dating. An examination of the annual rings of a tree can provide a wealth of information in such areas as the climate during a tree's lifetime, natural forces such as fires or insect damage, and when they occurred. Lumber can be dated by comparing its rings with trees from the same area. This has value in dating archeological finds.

Dendrology – The study and identification of trees.

Dendrometer – An instrument used to determine the height of a tree.

Dense – A reference to the specific gravity of wood. Lumber classified as "Dense" has six or more annual rings per inch, plus one-third or more summerwood, measured at either end. Pieces averaging less than six rings per inch also qualify if the rings average one-half or more summerwood.

Dense Industrial – A stress rated grade of Southern Pine with high design values for various industrial uses.

Dense Packing – To break up a unit of lumber or plywood and stack the pieces individually to use the maximum space available in a freight car or shipping container.

Densification – See Densified Wood.

Densified Wood – 1. Multiple layers of wood bonded with glue and then compressed to such an extent that the normal density is increased by 100% or more. Such wood is used in special applications where high strength is required, such as in airplane propellers. 2. Wood residue that has been compressed to form briquettes, fuel logs, or pellets. These are bound together under pressure, without a binder, and are used for fuel.

Densitometer – An instrument for measuring the density of an object.

Density – In particleboard manufacture, the weight of a panel as measured in pounds per cubic foot.

Density Gradient – The curve of the change in density that occurs through the thickness of a reconstituted panel. Surface layers are usually higher in density (containing smaller particles, more tightly compressed) than are core layers.

Dentil – A series of small, square blocks uniformly spaced and projecting like teeth. Often used in a cornice or as a mantel ornament.

Dentist – Loggers' slang for a saw filer, because he worked on saw teeth.

Department of Natural Resources (DNR) – An agency of the State of Washington responsible for administering state forest lands. Revenues from the sale of timber from state lands goes to the state's schools.

Departure – The act of departing from a non-declining flow policy in timber harvesting by cutting more than can be sustained by

Diamond Match

new growth.

Depressed Arch – An arch having less pitch than an equilateral arch.

Depression – A defect in particleboard that appears as a concave area on the surface.

Deregulation – The removal or easing of rules and regulations, especially by a government agency. The deregulation of the rail and trucking industries had major implications for forest products shippers, since relaxation of regulations dealing with rate setting greatly increased the number and variety of rates and their applications.

Desiccated – Thoroughly dry, without moisture.

Desiccator Test – A quality control procedure performed by particleboard plants to monitor formaldehyde emissions from the panel product.

Designated Conservation Area (DCA) – See Owl Conservation Area.

Design Strength – The weight-bearing capacity of a construction member, based on its design specifications.

Design Value – A measurement of strength in lumber, involving the basic properties of wood. These are: fiber stress in bending (Fb), tension parallel to grain (Ft), horizontal shear (Fv), compression perpendicular to grain (FcI), and modulus of elasticity (E).

Desorption – The loss of adsorbed moisture from a surface to the surrounding air.

Detached Housing – Single-family residences, each built on its own plot of ground.

Detail Man – A construction worker who does the final finish work in preparing a home or building for occupancy.

Detrusion – The shearing of wood fibers along the grain.

Dew Point – The air temperature at which dew will form. See Absolute Humidity, Relative Humidity.

Dex – An abbreviation for Decking.

DFPA – Originally, the Douglas Fir Plywood Association. The name was changed to the American Plywood Association when the softwood plywood industry started in the South. For product identification purposes, the DFPA initials were retained as "Division for Product Approval" until 1977, when the division was renamed the Quality Services Division.

Diagonal – An oblique line or marking.

Diagonal Grain – A deviation of the grain from a line parallel to the edges, which results from sawing a piece of lumber at an angle other than parallel with the bark.

Diagram Rule – One type of log rule, used to determine the net yield of a log. This rule uses diagrams representing the sawing pattern on the small end of the log. The diagrams take into account allowances for saw kerf, taper, thickness, and minimum width, as well as other factors.

Diameter at Breast Height (DBH) – A commonly used point of measurement in estimating the wood volume in a standing tree. See Breast Height.

Diameter Class – Tree diameters are measured in a sample survey of a stand of trees. These diameters are then grouped in size categories, usually by 2- inch increments, with a minimum base diameter as the starting point.

Diameter Inside Bark (DIB) – A measurement of wood volume in a standing tree or log in which the actual or estimated thickness of the bark is discounted.

Diameter Limit – A limit on the minimum size of the trees to be cut in a logging operation.

Diameter Outside Bark (DOB) – A measurement of tree size in which the bark is included.

Diameter Tape – A measuring device calibrated to give the diameter of a tree from the girth measurement.

Diamonding – A form of warp in which the cross section of a square-sawn piece of wood changes to a diamond shape during drying. This occurs where the growth rings pass through diagonal corners and is caused by the difference between tangential and radial shrinkage.

Diamond Match – A method of laying up veneers in which four pieces are used to make a veneer face, with the grain of each

Terms Of The Trade 77

Diamond Warp

piece running perpendicular to a line running diagonally across the whole panel; the resulting pattern resembles a diamond shape.

Diamond Warp — See Diamonding.

Diaphragm — An engineered component of roof, wall, or floor systems, combining panels and lumber. A diaphragm distributes stresses applied at one point throughout the component.

Dibble — A spade-like tool used to prepare planting holes for seedlings. Dibbles are most commonly used in the South, but their use has spread to other areas for the planting of containerized seedlings.

Dibble

Dieboard — Plywood, usually hardwood, used in making steel rule dies, which in turn are used to make boxes.

Differential — The difference between objects or things that are comparable.

Differentiation — The attributes or benefits of one product that sets it apart from similar competing products. Often used as a marketing tool.

Diffuse-Porus — A condition in which pores are spread throughout a growth ring to where there is little difference between the number and size of pores in springwood versus summerwood.

Diffusion — The spontaneous movement of heat, liquids, or gasses throughout an object.

Diffusion Treatment — A non-pressure process for treating wood in which green or wet wood is put into contact with a waterborne preservative. The preservative will diffuse out of the water of the treating solution and into the wood. One type of diffusion process for treating standing poles involves injecting the solution into the poles at ground level or applying the solution in a paste at ground level.

Digester — A type of retort in which wood chips and chemicals are combined and heated under pressure to produce pulp.

Digger Pine — Pinus sabiniana. A medium-sized tree growing in high valleys and foothills of the Coast Range and Sierra Nevada in California. So named because its seeds were a source of food for the "Digger" Indians.

Dimension — 1. Lumber that is from two inches up to, but not including, five inches thick, and that is two or more inches in width. Dimension also is classified as framing, joists, planks, rafters, etc. 2. In hardwood, pieces cut to full-inch dimensions.

Dimensional Stability — The ability of a material to maintain its original dimensions under variations of temperature, moisture, and physical stress.

Dimension Shingle — Shingles cut to a particular width, usually five or six inches, and used for special architectural effects, or to provide a uniform appearance.

Dimension Stock — Hardwood plywood that has been manufactured to precise requirements at the mill and sold to a user to meet a specific purpose or use. It is stock of specified thickness, width, and length, "pre-sized" for a particular buyer.

Dimethyl Sulfoxide (DMSO) — A byproduct of pulp manufacture, $(CH_3)_2SO$. A penetrating solvent, used as a carrier of medicine, and as a cleaner.

Dimick Standard — See Adirondack Standard.

Dimples — Small depressions in growth rings.

Dinkey — A small locomotive engine or crawler tractor, used in logging.

Dioecious — Plants having male and female reproductive parts in separate and distinct individuals.

Distressing Machine

Dioxin – An extremely toxic agent, sometimes found in certain herbicides, the most notorious being "Agent Orange," a defoliant used in Vietnam. Trace levels have been found in some herbicides used in spraying programs in connection with reforestation. This has been the source of considerable controversy between industry and environmental groups.

Dip Grained – Wood grain having a wave in fiber orientation, usually occurring in wood on either side of a knot.

Dip Tank – A vessel holding wood preservative, into which wood is briefly dipped to provide a superficial treatment. Such dipping provides only very limited protection for wood used in ground contact, but is often sufficient in applications where the wood will be painted or not exposed to the ground or severe moisture.

Dip Treatment – A wood preservative process involving absorption of preservative through submersion.

Directional Felling – A system of felling trees in a predetermined pattern, due to terrain considerations or to reduce breakage. Such a system often necessitates that trees be jacked or pulled to overcome natural lean.

Direct Mill Shipper – A producer who sells directly to retailers, bypassing the wholesale segment of the market.

Direct Quotation – A rate of exchange in which a certain number of units of foreign currency are determined to equal one unit of the home currency.

Direct Sale – A sale of a forest product from the primary producer directly to the retailer.

Direct Stress – Stress in lumber caused by compression or tension.

Dirty Stock – Waste paper being recycled for pulp.

Discoloration – A change in the color of a piece of lumber that affects only its appearance.

Disconnected Trucks – Railroad trucks used in early-day logging operations. The trucks could be adjusted to accommodate any length of log.

Discontinuous Rings – Growth rings formed on one side or part of a tree only, forming an incomplete or partial circle.

Discount – A deduction from a stated or list price, usually allowed for prompt payment.

Discount Rate – 1. The money value of time, a method of expressing the value of the future relative to the present. Discount rate calculations can be helpful in determining the cost of the time required to grow timber. 2. The rate charged by the Federal Reserve Bank and other central national banks on money loaned to member banks.

Discrete – A term describing the size of raw material particles used in the manufacture of particleboard or similar product. Discrete particles are those such as chips or hogged fuel that are distinct, individual pieces, as opposed to fine sawdust or similarly sized particles.

Dishing – A form of warp in which one face of a piece of lumber is concave due to a combination of bow and cup.

Dishonor – To refuse to pay a debt when due; to refuse to honor a negotiable instrument.

Disintermediation – The outflow of funds from one type of financial institution to other investments because a higher return is available.

Dispatch – A refund paid to a charterer of a vessel when full lay-time is not used. Opposite of demurrage.

Dissolving Woodpulp – Chemical pulp of special quality, with a very high alpha-cellulose content (usually 90% or more), readily adaptable for uses other than papermaking. These pulps are always bleached. They are used principally as the source of cellulose in the manufacture of such products as man-made fibers, plastics, lacquers, and explosives.

Distressed Offering – A load of lumber or other product that has reached a diversion point without being sold and is subject to daily demurrage charges. The owner of such a load will often attempt to sell it at a low price in order to avoid the demurrage charges.

Distressing Machine – A device used to apply a "distressed" surface to a piece of paneling, to give it the look of being aged or weathered. Also called an Aging Machine.

Distribution Center

Distribution Center – A facility where wood products are received, stored, and distributed to retailers, usually in truckload quantities. Essentially the same as a distribution yard, except that "centers" usually have the capacity for indoor storage.

Distribution Chain – 1. The system through which wood products move from the manufacturer to the end-user. Made up of companies that buy and sell the products on their way through the system. 2. A company that owns more than one distribution yard; purchasing and sales are often centralized.

Distribution Yard – A lumber yard operated by a wholesaler in which lumber is received from producers and distributed in smaller amounts to retail customers over a relatively large area.

Distributor – An umbrella term for companies who stock and distribute products to local markets. Used loosely, a synonym for stocking wholesaler, but this term can also apply to manufacturer-owned distribution networks.

Diversion Charge – An additional freight charge assessed by rail carriers for the privilege of changing the routing or destination of a shipment while en route. Often applied to transit cars when they are routed to their final destination after being sold.

Diversion Notice – A document instructing a district freight agent to divert a rail car from one destination to another, or from a hold point to a particular destination.

Diversion Point – A place at which a railroad car can be switched from one destination to another or held until a delivery point is designated by the consignee. Used by transit wholesalers to route their rolling cars to the final destination after they are sold. Also, Hold Point, Bumper, Hold Track.

Diversity – The variety, distribution, and abundance of difference plant and animal species and communities within a given area.

Division – A separate operation that is part of one corporation and which takes the parent corporation's credit rating.

Dockage – A payment to dock or harbor authorities for the use of a dock for loading or unloading. Also called Dock Dues.

Dock Dues – See Dockage.

Docker – A trimmer. A saw that cuts logs to length, or the ends off lumber in a sawmill. Also, the operator of such a machine.

Doctor Bar – A device used to regulate the amount of liquid glue on the rollers of a plywood glue spreader. Also called a Doctor Roll.

Doctor Roll – See Doctor Bar.

Dode – Decay in wood. See Dote.

Dog – 1. A device designed to bite into and hold something securely, such as a log on a mill carriage. 2. A spike designed to hold a chain or cable on a boom log when making up a log raft; a Rafting Dog.

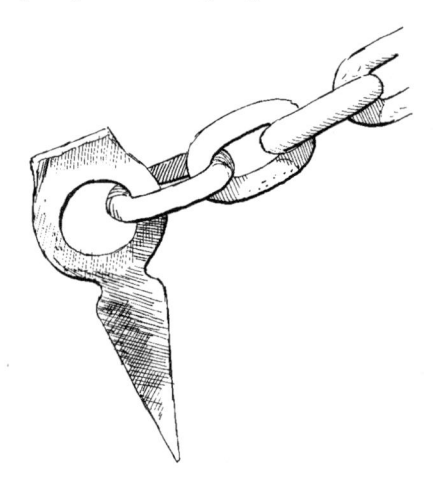

Rafting Dog

Dog Board – When sawing lumber on a headrig, the last board in a log to which the carriage dogs are attached.

Dog Boat – The hollowed log once used as a sled in the western woods to carry dogs and other tools between a logging area and a landing. Also, Pig.

Dogbone Patch – A plywood repair patch, larger on both rounded ends than in the middle and similar in shape to a dogbone. It is used to fill voids caused by defects in the veneers of plywood panels, usually those using the heavier veneers.

Doggy – Slow to move; hard to sell; sluggish.

Dog Hair – A thick stand of small, suppressed trees.

Door Stock

Dog Hairs – Fibers protruding from a sheet of paper, generally longer than fuzz.

Dog Hole – In the days of the lumber schooner, the term for various small bays on the California coast near Mendocino, where ships could find sufficient shelter to take on cargo.

Dog Hook – A short chain with hooks, used to link logs together when skidding with horses or oxen.

Dog Knocker – A light hammer or maul used to knock dogs out of logs.

Dog Maul – A tool used to drive dogs into logs.

Dogs and Cats – See Cats and Dogs.

Dog's Breakfast – 1. An unpopular assortment of items, usually the least-desired lengths, widths, or grades in lumber. 2. A customer specification covering a wide assortment of items.

Dogtooth – 1. An ornamental tooth-like design in mouldings or trim. 2. An orientation of brick in which each is laid so that a corner projects upward, creating a tooth-like appearance.

Do-It-Yourselfer (DIY) – A person, usually a homeowner, who does his own home construction and repair projects. Part of the "shoulder trade."

Dolbeer – The original donkey logging engine, built in the 1880s by a man named Dolbeer.

Dolly Varden – A type of siding, used to sheath the exterior of a building.

Domestic Cargo – Waterborne shipments of lumber from the U.S. West Coast to the East Coast. Broadened to include shipments from Western Canada.

Domestic International Sales Corporation (DISC) – A U.S. government program that allowed exporting firms to defer taxes on a portion of the income generated by overseas sales. See Foreign Sales Corporation.

Dominant Crown Class – This group includes trees that are higher than the general forest canopy and receive light from above and from the sides. Such trees usually have fully formed crowns and little competition from neighboring trees. See Crown Classes.

Dominant Species – The principal species in a stand of timber, not necessarily the climax species. See Climax Forest.

Doming – The process of rounding off the top of a post or piling; sometimes done by a producer for an extra service charge.

Donkey – A portable engine, powered by gas, diesel or, in the past, by steam. Used to drag logs from the cutting area to a landing. The engine is usually mounted on a sled and can be moved from place to place.

Donkey Puncher – The operator of a donkey engine.

Donkey Setting – An area in the woods cleared to make room for a donkey and the landing.

Donkey Tender – The fireman or boiler-tender on a donkey in the days of steam donkeys.

Donkey Wood – Firewood used to fuel a steam donkey.

Dook – A wooden plug.

Door Buck – A doorframe fashioned from rough material, to which the finished doorframe is attached.

Door Cheeks – Members of a door frame that run vertically.

Door Core Grade – A grade of particleboard. The product is used as core material for solid-core flush doors.

Door Cutting – See Door Stock.

Door Frame – The casing into which a door fits when shut.

Door Head – 1. The top rail in a door frame. 2. A horizontal projection or decorative feature over a door.

Door Jamb – The pieces running vertically on either side of a doorway, plus the piece running horizontally at the head, which stop and hold the door shut.

Door Skin – Veneer applied as the surface of a flush door.

Door Stock – Lumber selected for quality and cut to specified sizes for use in doors. Most often obtained from the shop, or cutting, grades of Ponderosa Pine, White Fir, or

Terms Of The Trade

Doric

Douglas Fir.

Doric – Of or pertaining to the first and simplest of five classical architectural orders, or arrangement of columns, developed in Greece and adapted by the Romans.

Dormer – A small projecting structure built out from a sloping roof, and usually bearing a vertical window. Also called a dormer window.

Dosy – Wood that has started to decay.

Dote – An early stage of decay in wood. Usually, the decay can be cut out and the remainder of a piece salvaged.

Double – To use two like framing members, such as studs nailed together, to add strength to a wall or floor.

Double-Arbor Edger – An edger consisting of two circular saws, one working from above and the other from below. Since this reduces the depth of cut for each saw, thinner blades may be used, thereby reducing kerf. The arrangement also increases the rate at which material can be fed through the edger.

Double Bead – A type of moulding consisting of two parallel beads separated by a flat, narrow groove.

Double-Bitted Ax – An ax with two cutting edges.

Double Breasted – A company that runs both union and non-union shops.

Double Canopy – A forest stand having a tall overstory of trees over a second layer of shorter trees.

Double Coursing – The use of two layers of shakes or shingles in covering roofs or sidewalls. The first layer is referred to as undercoursing, for which lower-grade material is often used.

Double-Cut Saw – A saw with teeth on both edges, which cuts regardless of the direction the carriage is moving.

Double Diffusion Treatment – A non-pressure process for treating wood in which green or partially seasoned wood is steeped first in one chemical and then another. The two chemicals diffuse into the wood and then react with each other to form an effective preservative.

Double-End Kiln – A dry kiln with doors at both ends and a track running through it; the charges are loaded through one end and unloaded through the other.

Double-End Trimmed (DET) – Passed through saws to be smoothly trimmed at both ends, commonly in length increments of two feet.

Double-Faced Stock – AA and AB grades of sanded plywood, both interior and exterior, having a good appearance on both sides.

Double-Face Pallet – A pallet having both a top and bottom deck.

Double Floor – A floor in which the common joists are supported by secondary beams, called binders. Also called a framed floor.

Double Grading – See Dual Grading.

Double-Handled Saw – A crosscut saw with a handle on each end, designed to be used by two men.

Double Haul – To handle logs with two machines, such as both a donkey and a yarder.

Double Header – Two joists nailed together to form a beam to serve as a trimmer joist.

Double Hung – A type of window in which there are two moveable sash sections that can be opened vertically, usually counterbalanced by weights built into the adjacent wall.

Double-Inverted Truss – A light-frame truss formed by taking two smaller, equal-size obtuse triangular trusses, inverting them, and joining them at the upward projecting points. This gives a roof a dual slope with equal pitches, while creating a raised-ceiling effect on the inside.

Double-Length Log – A log of 32 feet or more in an area where a 16-foot log is the standard.

Double-Pitch Truss – A light-frame truss having dual slopes, of which a shorter of the two slopes has a steeper pitch.

Double Roof – A roof in which the common rafters are carried on purlins, which in turn rest on a truss or other type of intermediate support.

Downfall

Double Sapwood – A defect in wood in which the sapwood has not been converted to heart wood.

Double Skin Roof – A roof having an upper layer providing the weather protection, and a lower layer forming the ceiling.

Double Step – A W-shaped notch made to reduce the possibility of horizontal shear in a tie-beam supporting a rafter.

Double-Tapered Curved Beam – A laminated beam with the top tapering equally from the middle to either end, and with the bottom of the beam slightly concave.

Double-Tapered Straight Beam – A laminated beam with a top having an equal taper from the middle to both ends, and a flat bottom.

Double Vacuum Process – A method of wood preserving in which wood is immersed in water-repellent preservative for a brief period after first being subjected to a low initial vacuum. After immersion, a high final, or recovery, vacuum is applied to draw off excess preservative. This process is often used to treat millwork.

Double Wall Construction – A light frame wall system consisting of exterior finish siding applied over structural wood sheathing.

Double Wholesaling – Transactions between two or more wholesalers. These usually occur in a rapidly rising market when two or more margins of profit are available, and usually while the stock is in transit. Double wholesaling also occurs when needed stock is not available from a producer and one wholesaler must seek the material from another wholesaler.

Double Wide – As defined by the Commerce Department, a mobile home so designated by a dealer and consisting of more than one section and more than one HUD label number.

Double-Wing Pallet – A type of pallet with top and bottom deckboards that extend beyond the edges of the stringers.

Double Yard – To move logs in two steps, first by yarding them to a yarder tree, then either swinging or roading them to a landing.

Doughnut Hook – A type of hook used in logging; the device has a locking ring that can be turned to keep it closed.

Douglas Fir – Psuedotsuga menziesii. This softwood is found throughout the Western U.S. and Canada, but grows most abundantly on the western slopes of the Cascade Mountains. It is widely used in general construction, as well as in finish applications.

Douglas Fir Bark Beetle – Dendroctonus psuedotsugae. An insect that destroys weakened Douglas Fir trees. Douglas Fir can be weakened by severe climatic conditions such as drought, or by overmaturity, making it susceptible to attack by insects. The adult bark beetle chews into the cambium layer of the tree to lay its eggs. After hatching, the young beetles develop in the cambium layer while feeding off it, often killing the tree. Often the beetles will grow in number in blowdown or firekill and then spread to living trees. Coastal Douglas Fir is more resistant to the activity of bark beetles than Douglas Fir in the Inland regions. However, attacks of short duration can cause significant damage in coastal forests.

Douglas Fir Region – As defined by the Forest Service, the geographical area west of the crest of the Cascade Range in Oregon and Washington.

Douglas Pine – Another name for Douglas Fir.

Douglas Spruce – Douglas Fir.

Dovetail – An interlocking joint used in cabinetry.

Dovetail Moulding – A moulding in which interlocked triangles are used.

Dovetail Saw – A small saw used in carpentry work. Similar to a backsaw, but having smaller teeth and a different handle.

Dowel – A "pin" of wood used to strengthen the joint between two pieces of wood.

Dowel Joint – A joint of two wood members made by using a dowel or dowels to hold them. Commonly used in furniture construction.

Dowel Machine – A machine used to manufacture dowels.

Downfall – The same as Falldown. Pieces that did not meet grade or size requirements in the manufacturing process.

Downgrades

Downgrades – See Degrades.

Down Sizes – In the British timber trade, a term denoting exact sizes off the saw.

Down the Hill! – A logger's warning that a tree is about to fall. The term is more widely used than the traditional cry of "Timber!," since it gives an idea of the tree's direction of fall. Also, Up the Hill!.

Down Timber – Timber on the ground, either due to cutting or to natural causes such as a windstorm.

Dow Saw – An early day gasoline powered saw, used in the pine country of Oregon and California. The saw was mounted on a rubber-tired frame.

Doyle – A widely used log scale, particularly in the South. It tends to give a large overrun on small logs.

Doyle-Baxter Rule – A log rule that combines the Doyle and Baxter log scaling rules. The Doyle Rule underscales small logs, while the Baxter Rule underscales large ones. Combining the two results in a large overrun, no matter what the size of the log. Not widely used.

Doyle-Scribner Rule – Another combination rule that results in a large overrun on all sizes of logs. At one time, the official rule of the National Hardwood Lumber Association. It was then known as the Universal Standard Log Scale.

Doze – Dote, a stage of decay in wood.

Dozer – A bulldozer.

Dozy – A term used to describe wood that shows incipient decay, usually caused by a fungus.

Draft – 1. See Bill of Exchange. 2. The vertical distance, in feet, between the keel of a ship and its waterline.

Draft Chain – A chain used in horse logging to bunch together a turn of small logs for skidding.

Draft Environmental Impact Statement (DEIS) – An environmental impact statement in its preparatory stages. A preliminary assessment of the impact an action, such as building a road, will have on a specific area.

Dragline – A line used in a high-lead log-

ging show to bring the main line back in. Also, a line used to pull logs from a mill pond.

Dragon Beam – A short beam at the corner of a structure, connecting with the angle tie at the inner end, and having a mortise on the outer end where the hip rafter is tied in.

Dragon Tie – A timber or beam angled across the corner of a structure to hold, or tie in, the wall plates. Also called an Angle Tie.

Drag Saw – A power-driven saw that uses a reciprocating motion to saw logs.

Drag Sled – A sled on which one end of a log is placed when being skidded or hauled along the ground in animal logging. Also called a Dray.

Drag Saw

Drainboards – See Counter Stock.

Drammen Standard – An obsolete lumber measure, equal to 120 pieces 1-1/4 inches by 9 inches by 13 feet.

Draw – To control the direction of the fall of a tree away from the direction it is leaning, by using a system of saw cuts and wedges, or jacks.

Drawee – One on whom a check or bill of exchange is issued; usually a bank.

Drawer – One who issues a check or draft.

Draw Knife – A carpentry tool consisting of a cutting blade with handles attached at each end. It is used by drawing it towards the body, with the cutting edge of the knife facing the user. It is used for rounding edges, reducing width or thickness of a board, etc.

Dray – 1. A small sled used in skidding logs. See Drag Sled. 2. A truck or other vehicle used to haul goods.

Drunken Saw

Drayage – 1. The hauling of goods from a cargo or rail dock as part of the overall shipment. 2. The cost of this form of transportation.

Dressed and Matched – Another term for Tongued and Grooved. It refers to boards or planks that have been machined so that each piece has a tongue on one side and a groove on the other.

Dressed Lumber – Lumber that has been processed through a planing machine for the purpose of attaining a smooth surface and uniformity of size on at least one side or edge.

Dressed Size – The actual width and thickness of lumber after planing.

Drew Rule – A type of log rule, once the legal rule in the State of Washington, but now obsolete. It was also called the Puget Sound Rule.

Drip Cap – A type of moulding applied over exterior window and door frames to keep water from seeping under the siding, and to direct it away from window glass. Also called a drip moulding.

Drip Pad – A platform that units of treated lumber are placed upon to capture the drippage of chemicals not absorbed by the wood. The pads are designed to prevent seepage of treatment chemicals into the ground.

Drippage – Excess chemicals that are not absorbed by wood during the treating process and drip off the lumber units.

Drip Torch – An ignition device used to start slash fires or backfires in the forest. It usually contains a jellied fuel that can be ignited and dropped on the object to be burned.

Drive – To float logs down a river. This method of log transport was once widely used, especially in Eastern Canada and the Northeastern U.S. Driving became less common as the distance between the logging areas and a driveable stream increased.

Drive Master – The supervisor of a log drive.

Driver's Delivery Ticket – A receipt kept by the driver of a truck for delivery of the shipment.

Driving Crew – The crew at the head of a log drive whose job entailed keeping logs moving in the main current of the river.

Drop & Pull – A service provided by carriers in which a trailer or other container is placed at a dock for loading or unloading, and then removed when the carrier is notified.

Drop Arch – See Gothic Arch.

Drop Ceiling – See False Ceiling.

Drop Line – A line from a carriage to which chokers are attached.

Drop Moulding – A type of panel moulding lying below the face of the framing.

Dropped Shipment – A trucking term for shipments that are "dropped" enroute to the final destination for further processing. Similar to milling-in-transit privileges in rail shipping.

Drop Shipper – See Office Wholesaler.

Drop Siding – A type of siding used to sheath the exterior of a building.

Drop Sorter – See Bin Sorter.

Drugstore Order – A highly mixed order containing a small quantity of each of a number of lumber and/or plywood items. A little of this and a little of that.

Drum Chipper – A type of chipper used especially to convert lily pads and trim ends to pulp chips.

Drum Debarker – A debarker made from welded steel channels or tubes, open at each end, and inclined toward the discharge end. It is driven by a ring gear or chain and sprocket. Used principally to debark bolts up to eight feet long before they are chipped for pulp.

Drum Log – To yard a short distance, using the drum, or a winch, on a crawler tractor. A temporary set-up, compared to a regular operation using a yarder or donkey.

Drum Sander – A machine consisting of a round drum covered with abrasive material and used to finish lumber or plywood.

Drunken Saw – A type of circular saw designed to operate with a built-in wobble so that the kerf it makes is greater than the thickness of the saw. Used for grooving and

Dry

for other special purposes in carpentry. Also called a Wobble Saw.

Dry – Seasoned, usually to a moisture content of less than 19%.

Dry Belt – A reference to that part of Oregon and Washington east of the Cascades, and to the pine country in general.

Dry Bulb – A sensing device that indicates the temperature of the air, used in kiln drying.

Dry Bulk – Cargo loaded into a vessel unpackaged. Grains and wood chips are examples.

Dry Chain – A moving chain or conveyor, where rough kiln dried lumber was graded before being run through a planer. The process was common in older southern mills. Most dry lumber is now graded after it has been planed.

Dry Clipper – A machine used to clip veneer to desired sizes after the veneer has been dried.

Dry Cooperage – Barrels or casks intended to hold dry goods. Also called Slack Cooperage.

Dryer – An oven-like apparatus used to remove moisture from green veneer by passing the veneer through a heated compartment on a moving belt.

Dry Face – A defect in particleboard in which the outer face fines or flakes readily flake or fall off.

Dry Feet – A name for lumberjacks who never worked on river drives.

Drying Defects – Defects resulting from kiln drying lumber, including casehardening and checking.

Drying Rate – The time it takes to dry lumber to a certain moisture content. The drying rate is affected by kiln conditions and the properties of the wood itself, including its propensity to develop defects from drying.

Drying Shed – A building in which green or treated lumber is placed for air drying.

Dry Kiln

Dunnage

Drying Stresses – Stresses in lumber caused by variations in the shrinkage or expansion of different wood layers, due to differences in moisture content.

Dry Joint – A wood joint that has not been glued.

Dry Kiln – A chamber in which wood products are seasoned by applying heat and withdrawing moist air.

Dry Laminating – The initial assembly or positioning of lam stock before the pieces, which will be made into a beam, pass through the glue application process.

Dry Log Chute – A method of moving logs by gravity alone, without water or external power.

Dry Out – In plywood manufacturing, an unsatisfactory glue bond caused by the glue becoming too dry to adhere properly when pressure is applied in the hot press.

Dry Process Hardboard – Hardboard produced by a process in which the fibers are broken down and dried by direct contact with combustion gases. The fibers are then mixed with resin, formed into a mat, and pressed into a panel.

Dry Rot – A type of decay in seasoned wood, caused by fungi.

Dry Service Condition – A reference to the degree of dryness in wood. Specifically, a service condition in which the average equilibrium moisture content over a year is 15 percent or less and does not exceed 19 percent.

Dry Sheet Stacker – A machine that stacks dry veneer as it moves on a belt from the dryer. Also called a grade bin stacker.

Dry Slide – In early-day logging, a trough made of logs and designed to use gravity to slide logs down a slope.

Dry Top – A tree in which the crown, or top, is dead or dying due to injury or disease.

Dry Wall – 1. A wall constructed without use of plaster. 2 A method of interior wall construction using sheets of sheet rock or similar board nailed to the underlying studs and finished with putty and tape over the joints.

Dual Grading – A method of grading lumber or other wood products to determine grade and volume losses before and after selected manufacturing operations, such as drying. Also called double grading.

Dual Slope Truss – See Double Pitch Truss.

Dubbing Off the End – In particleboard, a narrow tapered condition along the long edge of a sanded panel.

Dublin Standard – A softwood lumber measurement used in Eire, equal to 120 pieces 3 inches by 9 inches by 12 feet. Equal to 270 cubic feet. At one time referred to as the Irish Standard or London Standard.

Duck Board – A board, usually with cleats for footing, designed as a walkway up an incline or over a wet area.

Ductility – A term used to describe the flexibility and elasticity of wood. The ductility of a beam can be measured in the technical study of structural applications of wood.

Due on Sale Clause – A provision in a mortgage that prohibits a loan being assumed by a future buyer. The mortgage must be paid off at the time of sale and the buyer must take out a new one at current interest rates.

Duff – The partially decomposed organic material of the forest floor beneath the litter of freshly fallen twigs, needles, or leaves.

Duke – A tool used to thread a choker under a log.

Duke's Mixture – 1. In the early logging days, a mixture of pipe or roll-your-own cigarette tobacco. 2. A highly mixed order of lumber and/or panel items.

Dummy Tree – A tree rigged on a temporary basis to help raise a spar tree.

Dump – A log dump where log trains or trucks are unloaded.

Dumping – The practice of selling a product in a foreign market at a price less than that charged domestically. The practice is illegal in many countries.

Dunnage – Low-grade lumber or panels used to separate and bind ship cargoes. 2. Stakes, strips, or other pieces used to hold and protect merchandise during railroad or truck shipment. 3. In Southern Yellow Pine,

Dunnage Bags

lumber that is below #2 grade but not lower than #4.

Dunnage Bags – Bags made of rubber, plastic, or a combination of materials which can be inflated to fill spaces between portions of a load, or between the load and the sides of the vehicle carrying it. Some dunnage bags can be returned to the shipper for reuse while others, usually made of plastic-coated paper, are intended for one use only.

Durability – A reference to wood's natural ability to withstand deterioration, defect, or damage from outside forces.

Duramen – The hard inner portion, or heartwood, of a tree.

Duration of Load – The length of time a stress is applied to a structure. The duration of load on a piece of structural lumber will affect that piece's ability to withstand the stress of the load. A structure may withstand the load of snow on its roof for a long period of time, but then reach a point at which it fails, despite the load remaining constant.

Dust Spots – Concentrations of fine material on the surface of a particleboard panel. Generally light in color and characterized by the fineness of the particles.

Dutch Arch – See French Arch.

Dutch Lap – A type of shingle application in which the individual shingles have both a side lap and a head lap.

Dutchman – Any piece of wood used to fill space, level out a load, or remove slack from a binding chain.

Dutch Oven – A chamber in which hogged fuel is dried and volatile components drawn off before the fuel is sent on to the boiler furnace.

Duty – A charge assessed by governments on imports, usually expressed as a percentage of the landed cost. Duties are intended to protect domestic industries, or to meet other national goals, such as conserving foreign exchange.

Dwarf Mistletoe – A parasitic plant that infests conifers, especially Ponderosa Pine. Serious infestation can deform or kill the tree.

Dwarf Wall – Any wall with a height of less than one full story, such as the wall surrounding a crawl space.

Dwelling Unit – Same as Housing Unit.

Dynamic Load – A loading that creates stresses beyond that of its dead weight, such as by movement or vibration.

E

Early Seral Stage Forest – A stage in forest development that includes seedlings, saplings, and pole-sized trees.

Early Wood – See Springwood.

Earned Harvest – A timber management concept once used by the U.S. Forest Service. It allowed the timber manager to "earn" an immediate increase in the allowable cut by applying intensive management techniques that would accelerate future timber growth. For example, the earned harvest concept might allow stepped-up harvests of old-growth stands as a result of more intensive management of younger stands.

Earth First! – A loosely organized, radical environmental group, often associated with "monkey wrenching" practices such as tree spiking and sabotage of logging equipment.

Eased Edge – A part of the planing or surfacing operation in which the edges of dimension and many other products are slightly rounded to reduce splintering. Lumber of 1- and 2-inch nominal thickness may be rounded to a radius of no more than 1/16 and 1/8-inch, respectively.

Eased Joint – A face pattern for decking in which the corners are slightly rounded.

Easement – A right granted by a landowner to another person or agency to use the land for a specific purpose, such as constructing a road or power line across it.

Eastern Cedar – See Eastern Red Cedar.

Eastern Hemlock – Tsuga canadensis. This species, also called Canada Hemlock and, less commonly, Hemlock Spruce, is native to the northeastern U.S. and southeastern Canada. The wood is used for general construction purposes, rail ties, and pulpwood.

Eastern Larch – Larix laricina; Tamarack. A deciduous conifer growing in the Northeastern U.S. and throughout Canada.

Eastern Red Cedar – Juniperus virginiana; a juniper whose natural range covers much of the eastern part of the United States, and as far west as the Great Plains. The wood is used for such items as closet and chest liners, pencils, and various novelty items. Also called Pencil Cedar and Virginia Pencil Cedar.

Eastern S-P-F – Lumber of the Spruce-Pine-Fir group produced in the eastern provinces of Canada, including Saskatchewan and Manitoba. Also used in reference to some lumber produced in the northeastern United

Eastern Spruce

States. See Spruce-Pine-Fir.

Eastern Spruce – Picea rubens; Red Spruce. A native of the northeastern U.S. and Appalachian Mountains.

Easter Spruce Budworm – Choristoneura fumiferana. A predatory forest insect that kills trees by defoliation. Its principal foods are flower buds and needles of Balsam Fir and Spruce.

Eastern White Cedar – See Northern White Cedar.

Eastern White Pine – Pinus strobus. This species, once the principal commercial species in North America, is still an important source of lumber. It is found throughout the northeastern U.S. and Eastern Canada. Its wood is used for a wide variety of products, from construction lumber to matches.

Eastside (SYP) – An unofficial division of the Southern Yellow Pine producing region, consisting of the states of Georgia, Florida, South Carolina, North Carolina, and Virginia. Lumber from this region flows mostly to markets along the eastern seaboard and to Florida.

East Side – The logging country east of the Cascades in Oregon and Washington.

Eastside Measurement Rule – A rule established by scaling bureaus in the Northwest for scaling logs harvested east of the Cascade range. The rule establishes a maximum scaling length of 20 feet, plus trim. Logs longer than 20 feet are scaled as two logs. The rule also requires that diameters are rounded up if the fraction is over one-half, whereas under the westside rule diameters are always rounded down.

Eaves – The portion of a roof that hangs over the sides and ends of a building.

Eaves Course – The first course, or row, of shingles on a roof.

Eaves Plate – A wood beam used to support the feet of rafters when there is no supporting wall for the rafters, only posts or piers.

Ebony – Wood of the genus Diospyros found in the East Indies and Africa. The heartwood, which is black, is prized for its color, durability, and hardness.

Echinus – An ornamental moulding that supports the abacus of a column in Doric architecture.

Ecologist – One who studies ecology, the interrelationships of organisms and their environment. In recent years, the term has come to be used (incorrectly) more or less interchangeably with environmentalist, conservationist, preservationist.

Ecology – The branch of science concerned with the interrelationships of organisms and their environments.

Economy – The lowest recognized grade in lumber. Economy (also #5) permits serious defects in the lumber, including large knots and holes, unsound wood, splits, wane, and others.

Ecosystem – A complex of ecological communities and environments forming a functional whole in nature.

Ecosystem Sustainability – A balance of all the interrelated aspects of an ecosystem that allow the system to maintain and perpetuate itself through time.

Eco-Terrorism – Sabotage practiced by radical environmentalists as a form of retaliation for extracting natural resources. Tree spiking has been a prevalent form of eco-terrorism by those wanting to stop logging on public lands. See Monkey Wrenching.

Edge – 1. The narrow faces of rectangular-shaped lumber. 2. To cut wood products to remove wane and other defects and to produce square edges.

Edge Banding – The process of applying various materials to the edges of panel products for appearance, to provide for the secure attachment of hardware, or to provide an edge suitable for machining. The edge bands can be made of thin, rigid strips of lumber, plastics, metal, or high-pressure laminates.

Edge Banding Machine – A device used to apply edge bands to panels.

Edge Bend – A distortion in wood during the drying process in which a board remains flat, but bends edgeways in its own plane. Also called Cup.

Edge Branding – The process of marking individual pieces of lumber with any of various designs, logos, or other identifying signs. The edge brand is used to give the lumber a sort of "brand identity." It may consist of a

Edge Support

graphic design, the manufacturer's name and/or logo, the "name" of the product, or similar material. Also called Edge Printing, Edge Marking.

Edge Distance – The distance from the edge of a board or member to the point of the nearest fastener.

Edge Effect – The point where a forest and clearing meet, creating an environment suitable for shrub growth. Game and non-game animals favor these edge areas for browsing. Timber cutting can be considered a desirable wildlife management tool because of its "edge effect."

Edge-Glue and Rip (EGAR) – A process that involves gluing together narrow strips of wood and then ripping the glued stock to a desired width. The system enables small log processors to produce wider material than would otherwise be possible.

Edge Glued – Lumber that is glued together edge-to-edge to form a wide piece or panel.

Edge Grain – 1. Vertical grain; wood cut so that the wide surfaces are approximately at right angles to the growth rings. 2 The grain produced on quarter-sawn wood. 3. Veneer cut within 45 degrees of the radius of the log and across the growth rings.

Edge Joint – The joint between the edges of two pieces of lumber or plywood. Edge joints can be butt-jointed, finger-jointed, or scarf-jointed.

Edge Laminated – See Edge Glued.

Edgemark – A trade or grade mark stamped on the edge of a panel, such as high grade plywood with B or better face and back veneers.

Edge Marking – See Edge Branding.

Edge Nailing – Toenailing a piece of lumber on its edge to hide the fastening to another member.

Edge Piling – Stacking wood to be dried on edge, so that the wide face is vertical. Usually done to reduce crook in air drying. In kiln drying, edge piling is done in kilns with vertical air circulation.

Edge Printing – See Edge Branding.

Edger – A piece of sawmill machinery used to saw cants after they come off the head rig, squaring the edges and ripping the cants into lumber.

Edgerman – The sawmill worker who operates an edger.

Edge Roll – A decorative moulding of Greek origin, used in furniture manufacture.

Edger Optimizer – A computerized laser system that shows the optimal cut for edging a cant.

Edgerpicker – A sawmill worker, also known as a "bear rassler," who picks up waste behind the edger and sends it to a chipping machine.

Edge Sealing – The application of a sealant, paint, or other type of coating to the edges of a wood panel, to reduce water absorption by the panel.

Edge Snipe – A narrow, tapered condition along the long edge of a sanded particleboard panel.

Edge Sorter – A device used to sort lumber. The lumber is placed on edge in grooves or slots, and powered rollers move it to the proper sort bin.

Edge Split – A split on the narrow surface of a piece, rather than on the wide, or face, surface.

Edge Stamp – See Edge Branding.

Edge Support – A support, such as panel clips or lumber blocking, installed between framing members at plywood panel edges to transfer loads from one panel to the other across the joint.

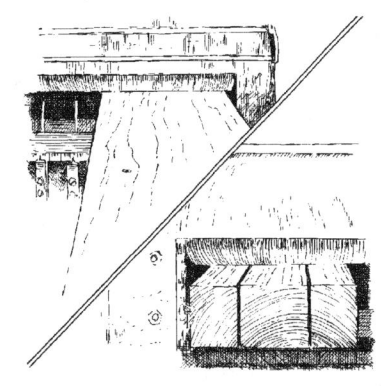

Cant Entering and Coming Out Of Edger

Terms Of The Trade

Edge Tape Ease

Edge Tape Ease – The amount of bevel along the edge of edge-taped shelving.

Edge Taper – Very slight tapering at the edge of sanded panels, caused by the oscillation of the sanding belt.

Edge Treatment – Any of various edge finishing methods used on wood panels, such as banding with wood or plastic, or filling with putty or spackling.

Edge Void – In plywood, a defect in which the edge of an inner ply of the panel has broken away or split during manufacturing, leaving a hole.

Edging – 1. Waste wood produced by an edger when cutting and squaring lumber from a slab or cant. 2. The act of squaring a piece of lumber in the edger.

Edging Strip – The cladding used to cover and secure the edge of a flush door.

Effective Span – The distance between the centers of bearing in a structural member, such as a beam or truss.

Efficiency Apartment – A one-room apartment, or studio, having no room designated specifically for sleeping.

Egg-and-Dart – An ornamental moulding pattern, common in classical architecture, in which shaped etchings are alternated with dart-like vertical anchors.

Eighteen-Patch – An indicator of the maximum number of wood or synthetic patches permitted in certain face-grade plywood sidings. The proprietary name used by the American Plywood Association for this grade is "Sound."

Elastic Constants – A group of three constants, used in testing wood for strength, bending, etc. They include: modulus of elasticity; shear modulus; and bulk modulus.

Elasticity – The property of a material that enables it to change its length, size, volume, or shape in response to force and to recover its original shape after the force is removed. See Modulus of Elasticity.

Elbow Lining – A panel covering a window jamb, from the sill to floor level.

Electron Beam Curing – A method of curing glue bonds by exposing them to an electronic beam.

Electrostatic Particle Alignment – A process used in the manufacture of oriented strand board. Small fiber strands pass through an electrostatic field and are aligned so that their longitudinal axes are roughly parallel.

Electrostatic Precipitator – A pollution control device that uses electrically charged plates to remove particles from air emission sources.

Elephant – The terminal point of a log flume, spread out to facilitate handling and storage of the logs as they arrived.

Elevated Temperature Kiln – A dry kiln operated at a dry bulb temperature above 180 degrees Fahrenheit but below 212 degrees Fahrenheit.

Elm – Any of various trees of the genus Ulmus, native to Europe and North America. The wood is used for such products as furniture, cooperage, flooring, boxes, sporting goods, and in shipbuilding. Most of the commercial sawtimber in the United States is found in the Great Lakes region.

Embossed Hardboard – Hardboard with a decorative pattern pressed into its surface.

Eminent Domain – The power of the government to seize or condemn property for public use upon compensating the owner.

Emperical Design Value – A measurement of a specific lumber item's strength based on trial or experiment.

Empty Cell Process – A process for impregnating wood with preservatives or other chemicals in which air is imprisoned in the wood under the pressure of the entering preservative and then expands to force out part of the injected chemical. See Full Cell Process.

Empty Nesters – A term used by homebuilders and others to describe a married couple whose children have grown up and left home, or "flown the nest." This group represents a potential class of home buyer who is often interested in selling the family home and moving into smaller, more efficient quarters.

Encased Knot – See Knot Quality.

Enclosed Knot – A knot buried in the wood and not visible on the surface. See Knot Quality.

Endangered Species – As defined by the Endangered Species Act, any species "in danger of extinction throughout all or a significant portion of its range."

Endangered Species Act – The Endangered Species Conservation Act of 1969, designed to protect plant and animal species in danger of extinction. Major points of the act include: Determination of species threatened by extinction, acquisition of lands for endangered species, and prohibition against the importation of certain species. The act also provides for international cooperation, organizes a National Wildlife Refuge System, and provides enforcement through penalties for violations.

Endangered Species Committee – A group of federal cabinet officers and appointed others, who may be convened under provisions of the Endangered Species Act. The committee is empowered to override the act under certain provisions. Informally referred to as the God Squad.

End Brand – A mark made on the end of a piece of lumber to indicate the manufacturer or brand name of the lumber.

End Branded and Waxed (EB&W) – Lumber whose ends have been imprinted with the manufacturer's name or logo and sealed with a clear or tinted wax. Waxing seals the ends of the lumber from moisture, and is a cosmetic process that some manufacturers feel aids in the marketing of their production.

End Check – See Check.

End Diffusion Treatment – A type of wood preservation treatment process in which the ends of green or wet poles or piling are steeped in waterborne preservatives that will diffuse out of the water of the treating solution into the water in the wood. This process is not as effective as others using pressure or full-length immersion.

End Distance – The distance between the center of a fastening to the end of a piece of lumber.

Endemic Species – One unique to a specific locality.

End Grain – The end of a piece of wood that is exposed when the wood fibers are cut across the grain.

End Hooks – A type of hook used to lift and load logs, with one jaw of the hook attaching to each end of the log.

End Joints – The joint between the ends of two pieces of lumber or plywood. Ends can be finger-jointed or scarf-jointed in various ways to provide strength to the joint.

Endless Saw – Another name for a band saw.

End Mark – A mark painted or stamped on the end of a log.

End Matched – Lumber that has been matched with a tongue at one end and a groove at the other to provide a tight end-to-end fit between pieces.

Endodermis – Tissue forming the innermost layer of bark.

Endorsement – A signature on a negotiable instrument, transferring it from one party to another. Also, indorsement.

End Piling – A method of storing lumber in which the pieces are placed vertically in bins. This storage method is often seen in retail yards or home centers.

End Sealed – Lumber whose ends have been treated to prevent moisture from entering. This is most often done by coating with wax. See End Branded and Waxed.

End Squeeze Unit – A device used to align the ends of wood products during packaging.

End Stamp – See End Mark.

End Use Mark – A mark or stamp on a panel showing the various end uses, i.e. floor, wall, roof, for which it is suitable.

End User – The ultimate user of a product, such as a builder or remodeler.

End Waxed – Lumber treated by the application of liquid wax, often colored, to retard seasoning checks. See End Sealed.

Engaged Column – A column that helps form a wall.

Engelmann Spruce – Picea engelmanni. This species is found in a wide range, principally along the Rocky Mountains from Northern British Columbia to Arizona. The lumber is light, fine-grained, and strong for its weight; this species is used more often for boards and specialized products than for framing lumber.

Engineered Grades

Engineered Grades – Wood panel grades designed for structural uses such as wall and roof sheathing, subflooring, and other uses where appearance is secondary to strength and structural considerations. As opposed to Appearance Grades.

Engineered Lumber Products – Lumber formed by gluing together veneers, wood wafers, or smaller pieces of solid dimension lumber.

Engineered Panel – A piece of plywood or other panel product designed to meet particular specifications concerning strength, rigidity, etc., and for use in particular applications, especially structural uses.

Engineered Wood Products – Lumber or panels manufactured by using adhesives to hold together oriented veneers, wafers, wood fibers, or dimension lumber.

Engineer's Chain – A survey chain with 100 one-foot links.

English Finish Paper – A smooth-finish paper, widely used in magazines.

English Standard – A measurement of roundwood volume equal to 270 cubic feet.

Entablature – Horizontal members supported by columns in classical construction. A common method of construction in Japan. Also called Trabeation.

Entail – To cut, carve, or etch decorative or ornamental patterns in wood.

Envelope – To enclose a building with sheathing materials.

Environmental Analysis Report (EAR) – An analysis of a proposed action; less stringent than an Environment Impact Report.

Environmental Impact Report – A report required of all agencies of the federal government to accompany proposals for legislation or "other major federal actions significantly affecting the quality of the human environment." The report is an interdisciplinary evaluation of the effects of a plan of action, and alternatives to the proposal. In court tests, the report has been required for a wide variety of proposed actions.

Environmentalist – One who studies or is concerned with the conditions and influences affecting the development of an organism or group of organisms. Now popularly associated with persons or groups seeking to restrict development of resources on public lands such as the national forests.

Environmental Protection Act – A wide-ranging U.S. federal law designed to protect the environment by limiting practices that are harmful to it.

Environmental Protection Agency (EPA) – A U.S. government agency charged with enforcing many of the nation's environmental standards.

Epicormic – Buds or shoots that develop laterally on the trunk of a tree.

Epidermis – Tissue in the bark of trees forming the outer layer of the cortex, just underneath the cuticle.

Epiphytic – Living on the surface of plants.

Epistyle – The architrave, or lowermost member, of a classical entablature.

Epoxy – A type of synthetic resin used in certain paints and adhesives.

Equalizer Beam – A cross beam attached to the underside of a set of stringers (as on a bridge), to distribute the load and equalize vertical and lateral deflection.

Equalizer Saw – A type of saw used in the cutting of shingle bolts to a precise, pre-determined length. The "equalizing" is done at a mill after the bolts have been roughly cut to length in the woods.

Equilateral Arch – An arch having a span equal to its height.

Equilibrium Moisture Content (EMC) – The point at which wood is stable and in equilibrium with the humidity of its surroundings; it is neither taking on nor giving up moisture.

Equipment Register – The "Official Railway Equipment Register," which lists the dimensions of all U.S., Canadian, and Mexican railway equipment.

Equity – The value, less liabilities, of a property. The equity in a house is the market value of the house, less outstanding principal and interest in the mortgage, and taxes. An equity or second mortgage can sometimes be taken out against the net worth of a property.

Even Grain

Eremacausis – The slow oxidation or decay of organic matter, such as wood, due to exposure to the atmosphere.

Erosion Hazard Rating – A measure of a site's susceptibility to erosion, based on soil type and the steepness of the slope.

Errors and Omissions Excepted (E&OE) – A statement by a company issuing an invoice that it reserves the right to correct any errors appearing on the invoice. Most commonly used on invoices originating in England or Canada.

Escrow – Money controlled by a third party until the terms of a sales contract are fulfilled.

Ess-Iron – See Anti-Checking Iron.

Estimated Weight – An estimate of the weight of a thousand board feet of a specific forest products item. Used in estimating the delivered cost of rail shipments.

Estimator – A person who estimates the cost of a building project, based on the type and quantities of materials and the labor required.

Ether Extraction – The removal of substances, not integral parts of the cellular structure, from wood by dissolving them in ether or other solvents that do not react chemically with wood.

Eureka Rate – A reference to a shipping point in Northwest California. Douglas Fir mills in this area have similar freight rates to major market areas, which result in f.o.b. mill prices that usually fall within a narrow range.

Eurocurrency – Currency held by non-residents of a country and deposited in banks outside of the country. For example, German marks owned by a U.S. company on deposit in London.

Eurodollar Deposits – U.S. dollars deposited in banks outside the United States.

Eurodollars – U.S. dollars owned by a non-resident of the United States and deposited in a bank outside the U.S., usually in Western Europe.

European Community – See European Economic Community.

European Economic Area (EEA) – In May 1992 the European Community (EC) and the European Free Trade Association (EFTA) agreed to form a single market allowing for the free movement of goods, services, people, and capital, which would be known as the European Economic Area. The agreement had not been ratified when this book was published.

European Economic Community (EEC) – The formal name for the Common Market, an economic association of Western European countries.

European Free Trade Association (EFTA) – An association formed in 1960 as part of the Treaty of Stockholm. The members agreed to free trade of manufactured goods between member nations, with each country responsible for its own individual trade policy with countries outside the association. Current members are Finland, Sweden, Norway, Austria, Switzerland, and Iceland, though Finland, Sweden, and Norway are applying for entrance into the EC. Denmark, Ireland, and the U.K. belonged to EFTA before joining the EC.

European Larch – Larix decidua. This species, native to Central and Eastern Europe, has been cultivated in North America primarily as a decorative tree. Also called Common Larch.

European Spruce – Picea abies. A species common throughout much of Europe and the former Soviet Union. Also called Whitewood Spruce.

European Terms – An exchange rate expressed as the number of U.S. dollars per foreign currency unit.

Even Aged – A stand of timber that is all of about the same age. This is usually the result of an area of forest being cleared by fire, wind, or harvesting, so that new growth starts more or less simultaneously over the entire area.

Even-Aged Management – The management of a stand of timber so as to keep most trees in the stand at about the same age through cycles of growth and harvest.

Even Flow – A system of forest management designed to keep the rate of timber harvest in a forest constant on a perpetual basis.

Even Grain – Wood fairly uniform throughout the growth ring, showing little or no distinction between springwood and sum-

Evening Up

merwood.

Evening Up – In futures trading, the process of buying or selling to offset an existing position in the market.

Even Texture – Wood in which there is little contrast between springwood and summerwood.

Evergreen – A tree that keeps its leaves the year around; usually a conifer or narrow-leaved tree.

Excelsior – Curled shreds of wood used as a packing material or as raw material for certain board products.

Excelsior Rule – Another name for the Finch and Apgar log measurement rule, which is based on a 5/16-inch saw kerf. This rule gives low values and is considered quite erratic.

Exchange (Futures) – The place at which buyers and sellers meet to trade in commodity futures contracts.

Exchange Bill of Lading – One bill of lading exchanged for another, usually during a stop-off operation.

Exchange Contract – An agreement to exchange one foreign currency for a given amount of another on a specific date.

Exchange Pallet – A pallet circulated among a designated group of shippers and receivers. The ownership of the pallet is transferred along with the ownership of the material shipped on it.

Exchange Rate – The ratio at which the currency of one nation can be exchanged for that of another.

Excurrent Form – The basic form of most softwood species, in which the trees have a dominant main stem with lateral branching off the main stem. By comparison, hardwood species tend to be dendritic, referring to the branching and rebranching.

Exotic – A species of plant that is not native to a particular country; extended to refer to wood paneling or other product made from an imported wood.

Exotic Woods – A designation usually applied to tropical hardwoods which display distinctive grain configurations and which are used for display in paneling, door skins, or furniture.

Expansion Coefficient – An expression of the changes in thickness and width of a wood product as its moisture content increases or decreases. Higher moisture content, until it reaches equilibrium, usually means an increase in dimensions.

Expansion Joint – A small space in the joint between two members to allow for contraction and expansion caused by temperature fluctuations.

Ex Parte – A submission or viewpoint from one side only, as in a controversy. In the interest of one party.

Experiment Station – Any of the nine regional forest and range experiment and research stations operated by the U.S. Forest Service.

Expiration Cycle – In futures trading, the monthly intervals for which contract periods run. For example, lumber futures contracts run in two-month intervals, with expiration dates occurring in January, March, May, July, September, and November.

Ex-Pit – Transactions involving futures contracts that take place off the floor of the exchange.

Export Administration Act of 1969 (PL91-184) – Federal legislation that gives the Secretary of Commerce authority to control exports, including forest products, under certain conditions.

Export Broker – One who arranges the sale or purchase of commodities between two countries.

Export Clear – A high grade of lumber produced for shipment to overseas markets. Most export clears are shipped unsurfaced, unseasoned, and full sawn, and graded according to the R List rules published by the Pacific Coast Lumber Inspection Bureau. Southern Pine clears are an exception. They are shipped kiln dried, mostly in a KD Saps grade peculiar to that species.

Export House – A company that buys domestic goods for further sale to foreign countries.

Export Merchant – See Export House.

Export Trading Company – A company that arranges for buying or selling of commodities between third parties, taking title to the goods on an interim basis.

Exposed Ply – The veneer on the surface of a plywood panel. The ply that is visible or that is directly subjected to its surroundings.

Exposure – The amount of roofing material exposed to the weather. Different sizes of shingles and shakes have different standard exposures.

Exposure Durability Classification – Ratings for APA Performance-Rated Panels designated as Exterior, Exposure 1, or Exposure 2. Exterior panels are designed for continuous exposure to weather or moisture. Exposure 1 panels are intended for protected applications, but where long exposure during construction may be expected. Exposure 2 panels are designed for protected applications with brief or moderate exposure during construction.

Extended Rotation – A rotation plan longer than the time necessary to grow timber to a specific condition of maturity.

Extended Shipment – A sale of goods on which shipment is to take place at a future date that is beyond the seller's normal order file length.

Extender – Organic material added to pure glue in order to increase the volume of the glue, thus reducing its cost. The quality of the glue declines as more extender is added. However, properly controlled, the addition of extenders does not affect the performance of a glue line in practical application.

Exterior – 1. A type of plywood that is produced throughout of veneers that are of C grade or better, and is bonded with a completely waterproof adhesive. Such a panel will retain its glue bond when wet, and is suitable for permanent exposure to the weather. 2. A type of glue-laminated lumber. 3. A type of fire retardant.

Exterior Glue – Glue used in producing plywood intended for exterior applications. Exterior glue lines will resist the elements. See Phenolic Resin Glue.

Exterior Trim – Finish pieces used on the outside of a building, such as eaves, fascia, bargeboards, and mouldings.

Exterior Wall – Any wall enclosing a building that is exposed to outside elements.

Extra – A grade of Northern White Cedar shingles.

Extractives – Substances in wood that are not an integral part of the cellular structure and that can be dissolved out with hot or cold water, ether, benzene, or other relatively inert solvents.

Extraordinary Coverage – An arrangement between a credit insurance company and a policy holder to increase the amount of insurance on certain customers.

Extreme Fiber in Bending – A measurement of the stress applied to the fibers of a piece of lumber by a load or weight. When a load is applied to a piece of lumber it causes the lumber to bend, producing tension in the extreme fibers along the face farthest from the applied load, and compression in the extreme fibers along the face nearest the applied load. This stress is indicated by the symbol "Fb."

Extruded Particleboard – A product produced by forcing machined fiber particles, which have been mixed with resin or other added binder, through a long, heated die. The formation of the panel, the curing, and the pressing take place in one continuous operation. The less common type of particleboard; mat-formed board is more common.

Extrusion Press – A device for manufacturing extruded panels in which the furnish is continuously processed and exits the press in final form.

Exudation – The movement or discharge of resin from softwoods during kiln drying, due to increased fluidity at higher temperatures and because of the pressure exerted by air expansion in the wood.

Eye – A loop in the end of a rope or cable, through which another rope or cable may be threaded.

Eye Dog – A dog with an eye in the head, used by driving it into a log and running a rope or cable through the eye when making up a raft or boom.

Terms Of The Trade

F

Facade – The front, or elevation, of a building, often of decorative architecture. Strictly, the principal front of a building.

Face – The face of a piece of lumber or plywood is that side showing the better quality or appearance.

Face Channel – A rectangular groove cut into the face of a piece of lumber or plywood to provide a decorative, shadow effect.

Face Checking – The partial separation of fibers in the faces of plywood panels.

Face Cord – Sometimes used in measuring firewood, a face cord is four feet high by eight feet long, but only as deep as the length of the pieces. Thus, a face cord may be 4x8 feet, but only 16 inches deep, containing one third of the wood volume of a pulpwood, or standard, cord.

Face Cut – A notch cut into a tree on the side toward which it is to be felled.

Faced Plywood – Plywood that is faced with plastic, metal, or any material other than wood.

Face Edge – The best of the two narrow faces on a rectangular piece of lumber.

Face Grain – The grain on the face of a plywood panel; the face grain should always be placed at right angles to the supports when applying to a roof or subfloor.

Face Mark – A mark made on the face of a piece of lumber, usually in pencil or crayon, and near the edge or end of the piece.

Face Measure – Surface measure; the measurement of the area of a board or panel. Not the same as board measure, except when the piece being measured is one inch thick.

Face Milling – Cutting done on the wide, exposed surface of a piece to produce a design.

Face Nailing – Driving nails through the wide, exposed surface of a board or plank.

Face Oiling – Lightly coating the face of concrete form panels with oil to aid in release after the concrete sets.

Face Side – The better wide side of a rectangular piece of lumber.

Face Stock – See Face Veneer.

Face Veneer – Those veneers of higher grade and quality, used for the faces of plywood panels, especially in the sanded grades.

Terms Of The Trade

Face Width

Face Width — The width of the face of a piece of lumber; in tongued or lapped lumber, it does not include the width of the tongue or lap.

Facing — Thin strips or boards used to cover a rough or inferior surface, to provide a finished and more attractive appearance.

Factor — A financial corporation that buys accounts receivable at a discount, normally assuming the credit risk.

Factoring — A method of financing in which a borrower assigns his customer receivables as collateral.

Factor of Safety — The ratio of the breaking strength of a line or member to the applied load.

Factory Built — A reference to a construction, usually a dwelling, that is built, or at least partially pre-assembled, in a factory rather than "on site." Most factory-built houses are constructed in two or more modules, often complete with plumbing, wiring, etc. The modules are delivered to a building site and assembled there. Finish work is then performed. Factory-built houses are generally less expensive to build because of savings gained through mass production and factory efficiencies, and are quicker to erect.

Factory-Filled Particleboard — Particleboard which has had its edges filled with plastic during manufacture.

Factory Finished — A product that has been coated or stained as part of the manufacturing process.

Factory Lumber — A broad category of lumber that includes stock of various grades and species intended for remanufacturing into items such as furniture, doors, windows, mouldings, boxes, etc.

Factory Primed — A product to which an initial undercoat of paint has been applied.

Factory Select — A grade of shop lumber containing 70% or more of #1 Door Cuttings, but having other defects such as pitch or bark pockets beyond the amounts allowed in the #1 grade.

Faggot — A bundle of sticks or twigs, or a single stick.

Fair Average Quality (FAQ) — A general term applied to ungraded lumber for remanufacture. It implies that all pieces are usable except for minor areas of defect and that they are typical of the average output of the mill.

Fairlead — A system of pulleys or rollers designed to permit the reeling of a line evenly onto a drum from any direction.

Fair Market Value — A price which can be obtained that is fair and reasonable in view of current conditions in the market.

Falldown — 1. Those lumber or plywood items of a lesser grade or quality that are produced as an adjunct to the processing of higher quality stock. 2. A term used in waterborne shipments to indicate that a cargo was not ready for loading when a vessel called for it.

Faller — A person who cuts down trees in a logging operation.

Faller-Buncher — A self-propelled machine used to fell trees by shearing them off near the ground using a hydraulic apparatus. Some models also strip limbs and "bunch" the logs for later pickup. The machines can be used on relatively level ground and are most common in the South.

Faller-Buncher

Faller-Forwarder — A log harvesting machine used to fell trees, which are then stacked in a bin and carried to the landing for loading on a log truck for shipment to a mill.

Faller's Strip — An area of timber designated for one crew of fallers to work in.

Falling Ax — A double-bitted ax used in felling trees before the advent of the power saw.

Falling on the Square – A payment method for loggers, based on the area of a cross-section of the trees felled, rather than on log scale. Also called Big Square, Government Square.

Falling Saw – A long, fairly flexible crosscut saw with a slightly concave back or spine, used to fell timber before chain saws became common. A falling saw was operated by a man at each end alternately pulling the blade through the bole of the tree. The handle of a falling saw was fairly short so that it would not tangle in the operator's clothing. The cutting teeth usually were longer and narrower than those of a bucking saw.

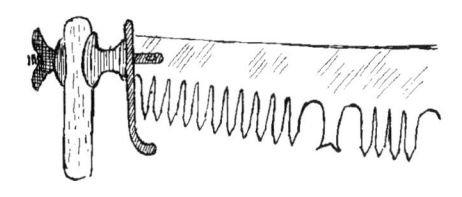

Falling Saw

Falling Wedge – A V-shaped piece of steel, aluminum, or plastic used by driving it into the back cut when felling a tree. Its purpose is to keep the saw from binding, and to help control the direction of the fall.

Fall in Rounds – To fell timber in two or more separate operations in order to minimize breakage.

False Cedar – Wood sharing some characteristics with cedars, including juniper, cypress, and mahogany.

False Ceiling – A ceiling that drops below the floor above to provide space for utility cables, ductwork, etc., or to reduce the area of a room for energy conservation.

False Cypress – Chamaecyparis thyoides, also known as Atlantic White Cedar. This species is native to the Atlantic Seaboard, where it grows along streams and freshwater swamps. Craftsmen favor its light weight and uniform texture.

False Heartwood – Dark innerwood that has been colored by disease or fungi so that it resembles heartwood in color.

False Ring – An extra "annual" ring formed during a year's growth, often due to abnormal weather conditions.

Falsework – A temporary structure erected to aid in the process of construction: Shoring, bracing, concrete forms.

Fancy Butt – A shingle with the butt end machined in some pattern. Fancy butt shingles are usually used on sidewalls to form geometric designs in the shingle pattern.

Fan-Shaped Setting – A logging setting with a set of yarding roads radiating from a common landing.

Fan Tail – A fan-shaped hook or hitch at the rear of a crawler tractor; used when tractor logging without an arch. The fan shape allows the attachment of several chokers simultaneously.

Fan Truss – A basic pitched roof truss with equal slope on either side and the bearing points at the ends.

Farm Logs – Timber obtained from a farmer or small landowner whose principal use of the land is not for growing timber.

FAS – See Free Alongside Ship, Foreign Agricultural Service.

Fascia – A broad, flat horizontal surface, sometimes used to cover a joint, or as the outer edge of a cornice. Also Facia.

Fascia Rafter – A rafter at the end of the rake, or overhanging part of a roof at the gable end.

FAS Price – The price of goods at the loading tackle of a ship, including all costs up to that point. See Free Alongside Ship.

Fastener – Any item, such as a nail, screw, brace, etc., used to join together two construction members.

Fastigium – The apex of a gable or gable-like feature of a building; the ridge of a roof.

Fast Saw – A circular saw whose rim speed is too fast for its size, causing it to wobble as it runs.

Fast Sheet – A window that does not open.

Fast Track – A method used in construction whereby work is started before final plans or specifications are completed.

Fathom – A cubic measurement used in

Fatigue

the British timber trade, equal to 216 cubic feet of stacked wood. Also sometimes used to mean a cube six feet on a side.

Fatigue – The weakening of a material due to overloading by subjecting it to repeated or alternating loads.

Fatigue Strength – The maximum stress that can be sustained for a given number of stress cycles without failure.

Fat Pine – Pitchy wood (of pine or other species) used for starting fires.

Feather – To blend the edge of new material smoothly into an older surface.

Feather Cone Fir – Another name for Noble Fir.

Feather Crotch – See Feather Grain.

Feather Edge – The edge of a tapered board.

Feather Grain – A grain figure produced by cutting in a longitudinal direction through a tree crotch; the resulting pattern resembles a feather. Also called Feather Crotch.

Feather Joint – A joint made by inserting a common tongue into a groove on the squared edge of each of two pieces being joined.

Feather Tip – A shingle or shake with an extra-thin end.

Fed – Short for Federal Reserve Bank.

Federal Funds Rate – The rate at which banks lend reserves to each other. This rate tends to serve as an anchor for other rates, such as the broker loan rate.

Federal Home Loan Mortgage Corporation – A government sponsored organization that provides a secondary market for mortgages. Freddie Mac.

Federal Housing Administration (FHA) – A division of the Department of Housing and Urban Development, FHA works through lending agencies to provide mortgage insurance on private residences that meet the agency's minimum property standards. FHA has also been charged with administering a number of special housing programs.

Federal National Mortgage Association – A corporation that provides a secondary mortgage market for FHA-insured and VA-guaranteed home loans. Fannie Mae.

Federal Reserve – The United States' largest bank, created by Congress in 1913 to provide a stable national financial system. The Fed, as it is often called, is actually 12 banks, with each serving a specific geographic area, but all banks in the U.S. are part of the Federal Reserve system. While accountable to the government, the Fed is owned by the banks. It is run by a seven-member board of governors, who are appointed by the president to serve staggered 14-year terms. The Fed sets the "discount rate," or the interest rate at which smaller banks can borrow money, thus, in effect, regulating the nation's money supply.

Federal Timber Purchasers Committee – A body of the American Forest and Paper Association set up to confront issues and regulations affecting members who purchase U.S. Forest Service and Bureau of Land Management timber.

Feeder – A small spur flume that fed logs to a main flume.

Feed Rate – The rate at which material can be fed to a machine such as an edger or planer without causing a jam.

Feedworks – The collective equipment that feeds work into a machine, such as an edger.

Fee-Owned Timber – Timber that is presently owned free and clear. The term "fee" comes from the legal phrases "fee simple" and "fee simple absolute." A company's fee-owned timber includes timber on land owned by the firm and also may include timber that is owned by the firm but is on land owned by another party.

Fell – To cut down a tree. A faller fells a tree, with a falling saw.

Feller-Buncher – See Faller-Buncher.

Feller-Forwarder – See Faller-Forwarder.

Felling Ax – See Falling Ax.

Felling Break – A break, or fracture, in a log or in a piece of lumber caused by the impact of the tree hitting the ground when it was felled.

Field Man

Felling Cut – The back cut that separates a tree from its stump.

Felling Saw – See Falling Saw.

Felt – In papermaking, a continuous cloth belt that picks up paper from the fourdrinier wire and transports it to the dryer.

Felt Side – That side of the paper that was not against the fourdrinier wire during the papermaking process.

Fence – A straight-edge guide mounted parallel to a saw blade to guide a cant as it is passed through the saw.

Fender Boom – A log boom used to guide other logs in a desired direction.

Fender Log – A log placed so that it acts as a buffer or bumper when hauling a turn of logs around an obstacle or corner.

Fender Skid – A log placed along the lower edge of a slanted skid road, to help hold logs on the road as they are being pulled to a landing.

Ferrule – A metal sleeve or collar attached to the end of a short cable in making a choker. The ferrule fits into the bell of the choker. Also called a Nubbin.

Festmeter – A German term for a cubic meter of solid wood. A cubic meter of stacked wood is called a Raummeter or Ster.

Fiber – A thread-like structure of a plant that contributes to stiffness or strength.

Fiberboard – A general term that refers to any of various panel products such as particleboard, hardboard, chipboard, or other type formed by bonding wood fibers by heat and pressure.

Fiber-Cement Underlayment – A panel made from a fiber-cement mix. Often used in applications where fire resistance is important, such as a substrate for tile around a wood stove.

Fiberglass Reinforced Plastic (FRP) – A coating of glass fibers and resins applied as a protective layer to plywood. The resulting composite is tough and scuff resistant. It is used in construction of containers and truck bodies, and as concrete form.

Fiber Raise – A defect found in hardboard.

Fiber Saturation – The point at which the cell walls of wood are saturated with water but the spaces between the cell walls contain no moisture. This point is usually at about 30% moisture content. Noticeable changes in the dimensions of a piece of wood occur only after water has been evaporated from the cell walls.

Fibril – A fine fiber or filament in a plant.

Fibrillation – The separation of fibrils through vibration or other mechanical action.

Fiddleback Grain – A rippling or undulating grain, common to certain hardwoods such as maple and sycamore. Pieces containing this grain pattern are often used on the backs of violins.

Fid Hook – A small hook used to prevent a larger hook from slipping on a chain.

Field Applied – Material, such as paint, is field applied when it is put on at a job site as opposed to being applied at a factory. Also, the construction or assembly of components in the field.

Field Chipping – The reduction to pulp chips of slash or small trees using a portable chipper in the woods.

Field Cut – A reference to the process of cutting, boring, notching, or trimming lumber panels or other wood products at the jobsite, or "in the field," as required. Specifically, treated lumber that has been field cut needs to have preservative reapplied. See Field Treatment.

Field Gluing – A method of gluing plywood floors in which specially developed glues are applied to the top edges of floor joists; plywood is then laid on the joists and nailed in place. The combination of gluing and nailing results in a stiffer floor construction and tends to minimize squeaks and nail popping.

Field Inspection – The reinspection of lumber or plywood "in the field," usually at the buyer's location. A field inspection is called for by a buyer when he believes the product he receives to be inferior to that specified. See Reinspection.

Field Man – A representative of any of various trade associations. He represents the association "in the field" and is available to answer questions regarding grades, usage, and characteristics of various species and the

Terms Of The Trade

Field Treatment

products produced by his association's members. He also conducts clinics and demonstrations and otherwise promotes his association's products.

Field Treatment — The application of wood preservative "in the field," as opposed to at a treating plant. Such treatment is applied without pressure to cut ends, bored holes, and other newly exposed surfaces of treated wood.

Fifths — The lowest of the common lumber grades normally exported from Scandinavia and Eastern Europe.

Figure — The pattern or design created in wood by abnormal growth. This term is often confused with grain; the two are not synonymous. Types of figure include: faint or conspicuous growth rings, burl, birdseye, curly or wavy ring patterns, streaks, and stripes.

Filer — A saw filer. The person in a sawmill or logging operation who keeps the saws sharp.

Fill — 1. To fulfill a commitment such as by placing an order to cover a sale. To execute a purchase order. 2. Material used to build up an area.

Fill Broker — A broker on the floor of a commodity exchange who, for a fee, executes orders for commission houses. A fill broker does not trade for his own account.

Filled Particleboard — Particleboard to which plastic material has been applied to fill gaps between particles on the edges or faces.

Filler — 1. A small quantity of lumber or plywood purchases to meet a minimum volume or weight requirement for shipment. 2. Material purchased to replace stock sold from inventory. 3. Any material used to fill cracks or voids, especially before the application of paint or other finish. 4. A relatively nonadhesive substance added to an adhesive binder to improve working properties, permanence, strength, or other qualities.

Fillet — A narrow band of wood between two flutes in a wood member; a flat, square moulding separating other mouldings.

Fill-In — A type of buying in which a retailer purchases only those items needed to balance out his inventory and replace items sold out of stock.

Fillister — 1. A groove or rabbet as on a window sash to hold the putty and glass. 2. A plane used for cutting grooves or rabbets.

Film-Faced Plywood — Plywood that has a facing of impregnated vinyl, paper, or similar material. The facing may serve to protect the surface from moisture, or may be decorative, as in printed wood grain patterns.

Film Surfaced Hardboard Siding — Hardboard to which a thin, dry sheet of paper, coated on both sides with a phenol-formaldehyde resin adhesive, has been applied. Such coatings are often printed with grain patterns in imitation of actual veneers, and are used as an inexpensive substitute for the higher-priced all-veneer panels.

Final Environmental Impact Statement (FEIS) — The final version of the environmental effects of an action, required for major federal actions under terms of the National Environmental Policy Act. It is a revision of the Draft Environmental Impact Statement, and includes public and agency responses to the draft.

Final Moisture Content — The average moisture content of lumber at the end of the drying process.

Final Weight — The weight of a kiln sample after drying is complete.

Fin Boom — A type of log boom system in which one end of the boom floats free and can be winched into the current of a river to shunt logs floating down the river into a storage boom.

Finch and Apgar Rule — A log rule based on a 5/16-inch saw kerf. This rule gives low values and is considered quite erratic. Also known as the Finch Rule, Apgar Rule, and Excelsior Rule.

Finch Rule — See Finch and Apgar Rule.

Fines — Fine milled chips used in the production of particleboard. Fines are larger than sander dust or wood flour. The faces of particleboard panels are made of fines, with coarser chips used to make up the inner parts of the particleboard. See Discrete.

Fine Sawn — A term that describes surfaced lumber, or plywood, that has been passed through a saw to gain a textured face. The face of fine sawn lumber is not as rough as unsurfaced lumber, but is more textured that surfaced lumber. Often two boards are placed side by side and passed through a band saw to gain fine sawn faces on one side of each.

Fine Shake – A barely perceptible separation of the wood which occurs between or through the annual growth rings.

Fine Woodwork – Trim, paneling, etc., used for finish and decorative effects.

Fingercone Pine – Another name for Western White Pine, Pinus monticola.

Fingerjoint – A method of joining two pieces of lumber end-to-end by sawing into the end of each piece a set of projecting "fingers" that interlock. When the pieces are pushed together, these form a strong glue joint.

Fingerling – A young fish, especially a young salmon or trout.

Finger Roll – A wavy, ornamental marking or design in wood, with each wave about the width of a finger.

Finial – An ornamental projection, or terminal form at the top a gable, spire, newel, etc.

Finish – 1. A high-quality piece of lumber graded for appearance; often used for interior trim or cabinet work. 2. The surface characteristics of paper.

Finish Carpentry – The work of installing doors, trim, moulding, and the like.

Finished Size – The net dimensions of a piece of lumber after surfacing.

Finish End – The area in a plywood plant where panels are patched and sanded as needed.

Finish Sag – A defect in hardboard.

Finish Skip – A defect in hardboard.

Fink Truss – A type of wooden bridge truss, named after its designer. Also, a type of roof truss.

Finn Hoe – A hoe-like implement with a slightly bowed handle, used for leveling roads or trails.

Finn Saw – A bow saw. A small saw with a bowed handle.

Fir – Although this term is used most often to refer to Douglas Fir (which is a pseudo-fir), it is also a general term for any of a number of species of conifers, including the True Firs. See Abies.

Fir&Larch – A mixture of Douglas Fir and Western Larch, sold together as one species grouping. The two species are intermixed in the inland regions of the Western U.S. and British Columbia. Because they have similar characteristics and are used in similar ways, the two woods are usually mixed together.

Fire – A variation in sheen or luster in wood, due to the reflection of light on non-parallel fibers as in interlocked or curly grain.

Fire Block – See Firestop.

Fire Boss – The person in charge of the fire crews at a forest fire, as opposed to a fire warden, who is more involved in fire prevention.

Fire Compartment – An enclosure, usu-

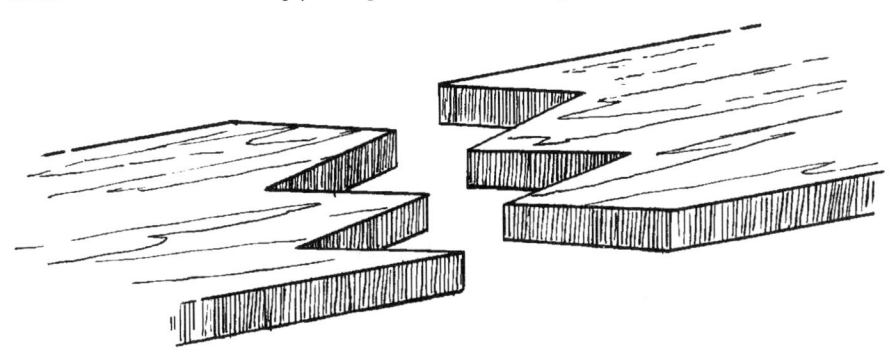

Finger Joint

Fire Danger

ally with a fire-resistance rating, designed to protect contents from fire damage.

Fire Danger — A measure of the likelihood of a forest fire, based on temperature, relative humidity, wind force and direction, and dryness of fuel in the forests.

Fire Door — A metal, or metal-sheathed door, built and installed to resist flames and prevent the spread of fire.

Fire Endurance — The ability of a structural member to maintain its integrity (shape and stiffness) during exposure to a fire. Usually expressed in terms of time: One-hour door.

Fire Finder — A sighting device used in fire lookouts to obtain map coordinates of a fire.

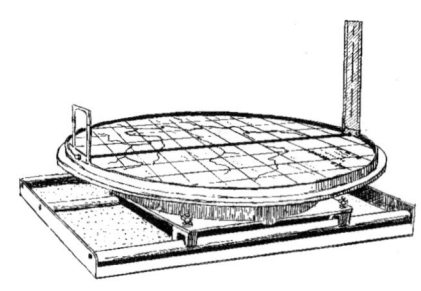

Fire Finder

Fire Management — A forest management technique using small, controlled fires to clear away debris or unwanted brush.

Fireproof Wood — Chemically treated wood that is fire resistive. No wood can be completely fireproof, but wood can be treated so that it is highly resistant to heat and flame and very difficult to ignite under ordinary circumstances.

Fire-Rated System — Wall, floor, or roof constructions of specific materials and designs that have been tested and rated for conformance to fire safety criteria, such as flame spread rate.

Fire-Resistance Rating — A rating system specifying in hours or minutes how long a material or assembly will withstand exposure to flames and heat under test conditions.

Fire-Resistant Door — A door that is designed to confine fire to one part of a structure, keeping it from spreading through the entire building. It may be a solid core wooden door, or one sheathed in metal, depending on its intended location. The doors are rated for the projected time they could be expected to perform their function during a fire. Most building codes require that the door between living quarters and a garage be fire resistant.

Fire Retardant — 1. A chemical applied to lumber or other wood product to slow combustion and flame spread. 2. A chemical, usually phosphate, used to fight forest fires, often by dropping it from an airplane or helicopter.

Fire Road — A road built to provide access to an area in case of fire. Such roads are usually built as part of a fire protection system, rather than at the time a fire is actually burning.

Fire Scar — A burned or charred area on a tree or log, often an entry point for decay-causing organisms.

Fire Season — That period of the year when the fire danger is high due to hot, dry weather.

Fire Separation — A barrier, which may or may not be fire-resistance rated, designed to prevent the spread of fire.

Firestop — A short piece of wood, usually a 2x4 or 2x6, placed horizontally between the studs of a wall. Firestops are equal in width to the studs. They are usually placed halfway up the height of the wall to slow the spread of fire by limiting drafts in the space between the sheathing on the two sides of the wall. Building codes usually do not require fire stops in walls that are less than eight feet high. Also called a Fire Block.

Fire Succession — Fire is one of the disturbances by which existing vegetation is killed, making way for new growth. Some species of trees, such as the closed-cone pines (Lodgepole), are adapted to reproduce after severe burning, and are among the first, after grass and some shrubs, in the line of succession. The cones on these pines open and distribute their seed after being subjected to intense heat.

Fire Tower — A tower built on a vantage point to serve as a post for spotting and reporting forest fires.

Fire Trail — An area that has been cleared to the mineral soil to prevent the spread of fire. May vary in width from a couple of feet to the width of a bulldozer blade.

Fishtail (F/T)

Fire Wall – A fire-resistive wall extending through all levels of a building and designed to arrest the spread of fire.

Fire Warden – A person in charge of enforcing fire regulations such as at a logging site. A fire warden is more involved with fire prevention than with fire fighting.

Fire Watch – A watchman who stays at the logging site after the day's work is completed to watch for fire during the danger season.

Firewood – 1. Wood to be used as fuel. 2. Slang for short pieces used for crating, etc.

Fir Fixed – Rough lumber forming a temporary part of a structure, held in place by nails only.

Firm Destination – A reference to a rail or truck shipment that is routed to a specific delivery point, rather than to some intermediate point for further shipment.

Firm Heart Stain – See Firm Red Heart.

Firm Knot – See Knot Quality.

Firm Order – An order placed at a mill by a wholesaler, after the wholesaler has a buyer for that particular order.

Firm Red Heart – A stage of incipient decay characterized by a reddish color in the heartwood, which does not make the wood unfit for the majority of yard purposes.

Firmwood – The solid wood in a log suitable for manufacture into wood products or chips; soft or rotten wood is excluded.

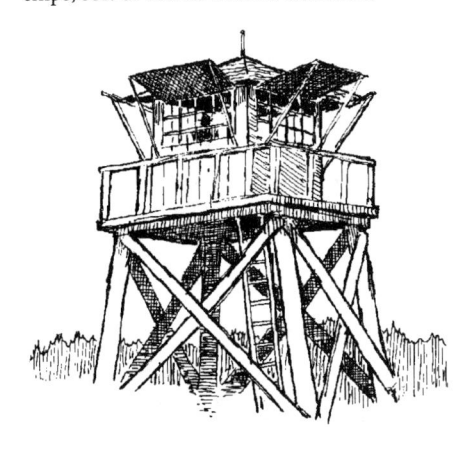

Fire Tower

Fir Region – That part of the western United States and British Columbia in which Douglas Fir is a dominant species. It is generally considered to cover those parts of Oregon and Washington west of the Cascades, Southwestern British Columbia, and Northwestern California.

First Faller – The head man in a falling crew.

First Forest – As defined by the Forest Service, the forest that existed in the South before the first clearing or harvest.

First Growth – Virgin timber; timber that has never been logged.

First In, First Out (FIFO) – A type of accounting for inventory in which items purchased first are assumed to be the first to be sold. An accountant will compute the cost and profit on the oldest or first price in the inventory. Opposite of Last In, First Out (LIFO).

First Loader – The head loader in a logging crew; one in charge of loading logs onto a truck or rail car.

First Notice Day – In futures trading, the first date on which notices of intentions to deliver the actual commodities against futures is authorized.

Firsts and Seconds – Grades of hardwood lumber; the highest standard grades.

Fish & Wildlife Service (FWS) – A U.S. Interior Department agency charged with protecting wildlife and administering the federal Endangered Species Act.

Fisheye – A wood finishing defect.

Fish Joint – A type of joint in which two pieces of lumber are spliced end-to-end using wooden or metal plates that are fastened on either side.

Fish Plate – A wood or metal plate used to join together the ends of two pieces of lumber when making one long piece out of two shorter ones.

Fish Scale – A fancy-butt shingle pattern in which the exposed portion of the shingle is rounded. When grouped with other such shingles the overall effect is that of a pattern of fish scales.

Fishtail (F/T) – A piece of veneer from the

Fissile

outer portion of the block. The first veneer produced from each log rounds the block (block roundup). This veneer has one angled edge, thus the term fishtail. Fishtails are trimmed to gain rectangular pieces and are used most frequently as core material in plywood. Fishtails are of random widths.

Fissile – Capable of being split or cleaved.

Fitter – The person who marked trees for harvest and then marked the felled logs for the bucking crew.

Five-Quarter (5/4) – See Quarter Measure.

FiveX – Shingles 16-inches in length and having a thickness of .40 inches at the butt. Also, 5X.

Fixation – The process by which waterborne preservatives react within the wood to become insoluble or fixed.

Fixed Arbor Gang Rip Saw – A rip saw having the saws set in a fixed position.

Fixed Assets – Assets, such as real property, that are not readily converted to cash.

Fixed Beam – A beam with one or both ends secured in position and direction.

Fixed Costs – Costs that do not change with a change in the volume of output or the rate of operation. An example would be the cost of a mortgage.

Fixed Exchange Rate – An agreement under which a monetary authority of a country keeps the value of its currency within a given percentage of the fixed value of another currency.

Fixed Harvest – See Allowable Cut.

Fixed Knot – See Knot Quality.

Fixed Liabilities – Long term liabilities; debts that have a maturation of more than one year.

Fixed Nosebar – See Nosebar.

Fixed Rate Mortgage – A mortgage on which the interest rate remains the same through the period of the loan, allowing a buyer to make equal monthly payments.

Flagging – Brightly colored plastic ribbon attached to trees or stakes to mark boundaries.

Flag of Convenience – A nation whose registration requirements and/or tax structure makes it an attractive place for foreign ship owners to register their vessels.

Flake – A particle of wood, similar in size to other particles used in the manufacture of panels.

Flake Bin – A receptacle used to store flakes or particles prior to their use in manufacture.

Flakeboard – See Particleboard, Waferboard.

Flake Geometry – The study of the size and shape of flakes, wafers, or strands used to make composite structural panels. It includes the means of their manufacture and their orientation within a panel.

Flaker – A machine that converts round wood and/or mill wastes into flakes for use as the raw material for particleboard or waferboard.

Flake Raise – A defect in particleboard in which face flakes are raised above surrounding flakes, giving a rough appearance.

Flamard – A type of splitting tool similar to an ax.

Flame Grain – A grain figure produced on flat-cut boards or rotary-cut veneer.

Flame-Spread Rating – A measure of the rate of flame spread along the surface of a material. Such ratings are expressed in numbers or letters and are used in describing interior finish requirements in building codes.

Flanker – A log driver who works along the riverbank to keep logs moving in the main channel.

Flash Dam – A dam built on a tributary to provide extra flow to the main river when driving logs. Same as a Flood Dam, or Splash Dam.

Flat Arch – See Jack Arch.

Flatbed – See Flat Car.

Flat Boom – A type of log boom, or raft, in which the logs are arranged parallel to the sides of the boom, rather than helter-skelter as in a bag boom.

Flat Car – A railroad freight car without

Flitched Beam

sides; an open car. Lumber is shipped on flat cars in banded units, which are sometimes wrapped in paper or plastic for protection from dirt and weather. Also, a flatbed.

Flat Car, No Paper (FCNP) – Lumber or plywood loaded on a railroad flat car and not covered by paper.

Flat Car, Paper Under Top Tier (FCPUTT) – Lumber or plywood loaded on a railroad flat car, covered by a strip of weather-resistant paper which is held in place by the addition of a final layer of material.

Flat Car, Paper Wrapped (FCPW) – Lumber or plywood loaded on a railroad flat car after being strapped into bundles and wrapped in a weather-resistant paper.

Flat Cut – To saw wood through its thinnest dimension or thickness.

Flat Goods – Panel products such as plywood, OSB, particleboard, etc.

Flat Grain (FG) – Annual rings (grain) that form an angle of less than 45 degrees with the surface of a piece of lumber.

Flat Moulding – A thin moulding.

Flat Piling – In lumber drying, the placement of the pieces so that the wide faces are horizontal and parallel to the ground.

Flat Raft – See Flat Boom.

Flat Slicing – Slicing veneer parallel to a line through the center of the log. This type of slicing produces a variegated pattern on the veneer.

Flat Stress Skin Panel – A roof or floor deck constructed of plywood sheets glued to framing members to provide greater load carrying capacity than the individual members installed separately.

Flat Truss – A truss constructed with no pitch.

Flat Use Factor – An adjustment factor used to determine the allowable bending design value in lumber used flatwise (when a load is applied to the wide face).

Flecks – Spots or marks on the surface of wood caused by irregularities in the grain or by extraneous matter.

Fleet – Several rafts of logs tied together for transport downriver.

Flight Holes – Worm holes in wood.

Flippers – Arms mounted on a shaft on the saw side of a log carriage and used to turn the log or cant.

Flitch – 1. A log sawn on two or more sides from which veneer is sliced. 2. Thin layers of veneer sliced from a cross-section of a log, as opposed to turning the log on a lathe and peeling from the outer edge in a continuous ribbon. Flitch veneers are often kept in order as they are sliced from a log. This provides a pattern to the veneer after it is laid up in panels. Panels that are laid up with matching flitches are said to have a flitch pattern. 3. A product cut from a log by sawing on two sides and leaving two rounded sides. Usually exported for joinery.

Flitched Beam – A beam built up by two or more pieces bolted together, sometimes

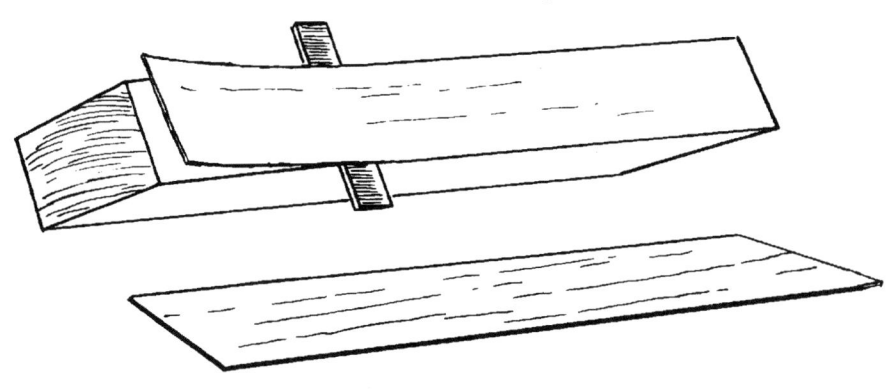

Flat Slicing

Terms Of The Trade

109

Float

with a steel plate in the middle. The pieces, or flitches, are cut from a squared log sawn up the middle. The outer faces of the log are placed together, with their ends reversed to equalize their strength.

Float – 1. The elapsed time between the issuance of a check and the amount being debited against a checking account. 2. In the British timber trade, a measure of wood equivalent to 18 "loads," with a load equal to 50 cubic feet of hewn softwood, or 40 cubic feet of hardwood or unhewn softwood.

Floatage – Logs floating in a pond, river, or lake.

Floated Deal – A reference to wood that has spent time in the water, such as in a log boom; such wood is sometimes discolored.

Floating Blade Gang Ripsaw – A rip saw that allows sizes to be adjusted while running, to vary the width of the pieces being ripped.

Floating Camp – A logging camp with bunks, cookhouse, etc. built on rafts so it could be moved from place to place.

Floating Exchange Rate – A system that allows currency values to fluctuate on foreign exchange markets in response to changes in trade and economic conditions. The present system of floating exchange rates replaced the existing fixed-rate system in March 1973.

Floating Load – A method of loading a flat car in which the load is not anchored to the car. Individual units of lumber or plywood are loaded on the car and groups of the units are banded together. When all units are loaded, they are banded into a single unit. In the winter months, stub stakes are required around the perimeter of the car as a safety precaution.

Flood – To release a head of water stored behind a flash dam to drive logs downstream.

Flood Dam – See Flash Dam.

Floor Arch – See Jack Arch.

Floor Blocking – Bracing placed between the floor joists to stiffen them. See Blocking.

Floor Broker – In futures trading, an exchange member who executes orders for clearing members.

Floor Furring – Furring strips usually applied to a subfloor to provide channels for pipes or electrical conduits under the main floor.

Flooring – A tongued and grooved piece of lumber used in constructing a floor. The basic size of flooring is 1x4 inches, although other sizes are used. Flooring is sold mostly in Superior and Prime grades, and is produced either as vertical grain or flat grain.

Flooring Machine – A machine used to make flooring, in which the lumber is surfaced and tongues and grooves are cut all in one operation.

Floor Joist – A piece of lumber, two to four inches thick and five or more inches wide, used horizontally as a support for a floor. Also, such a support made from aluminum, steel, or other material.

Floor Price – 1. A price set by a manufacturer, below which he refuses to sell. 2. A minimum price guaranteed by a wholesaler for stock released to him on consignment, or for sale without a predetermined price.

Floor Span – 1. The distance, in inches, between the centers of floor joists in a floor system. 2. The span covered by floor joists between supports.

Floor Stock – Products in stock or in inventory at a producer's plant; stock on hand, as opposed to stock scheduled for future production.

Floor Strutting – See Blocking.

Floor Trader – A speculator in futures who owns an exchange membership, enabling him to execute his own trades. Usually trades only for his own account. Also called a Local.

Floor Underlayment – Particleboard, plywood, waferboard, or similar products designed to be used as flooring in a house or other building. The underlayment to which the finished floor surface is applied.

Florida Pine – Another name for Longleaf Pine, Pinus palustris, common to marshy areas of the South. Also known as Georgia Hard Pine, North Carolina Pitch Pine, and Texas Longleaved Pine.

Florida Yew – Taxus floridana. A species of yew tree found in Florida.

Flowback – A reference to the degree a ma-

Foreign Agricultural Service (FAS)

terial will compress before penetration of a cutting tool occurs.

Flower Face – The inside face in tangentially sawn wood.

Flume – A system for transporting logs or rough lumber. It consisted of water flowing down a long wooden trough.

Flume Chaser – A person who patrolled flumes transporting logs or rough lumber. His duties were to break up jams and to spot damage or obstacles in the flume. Also called a flume tender, flume herder, or flume walker. See Chute Tender.

Flunkie – A cook's helper in a logging camp. The flunkie waited on and cleaned tables, washed dishes, and performed other menial chores. Also spelled flunkey, flunky.

Flush Door – A door constructed with a plain, flat surface, covered by a single veneered skin. A common type of door for interior use.

Flush Moulding – A moulding on the same level and/or plane as the wood member or assembly to which it is applied.

Flush Pallet – A pallet having the deck boards or panels flush with the stringers or blocks along its sides.

Flute – A long, rounded groove machined along the grain of a wood member, such as a pilaster.

Fluted Butt – The asymmetrical butt of a tree in which the wood has grown from the ground to the bole to form long furrows or grooves, often enclosing earlier growths of bark. This occurs in most conifers occasionally but is most common in cedar, cypress, and redwood.

Flying Buttress – A type of segmental arch that transfers an outward and downward thrust to a solid, usually masonry, buttress, which in turn transforms the thrust into a vertical one.

Foam Core – The center of a plywood "sandwich" panel, consisting of plastic foam between wood veneers. The foam may be introduced in a liquid form that is forced under pressure into a space between the wood veneer skins, or the skins may be applied to a rigid plastic foam board.

Foils – Cellulose papers used in decorative laminating. Can be impregnated with melamine resins or left untreated.

Folded Plate Roof – A roofing system consisting of sloping "plates" in a repetitive gable arrangement; usually a combination of plywood skins and lumber trusses. A folded plate roof permits a large, clear floor area.

Folding Carton – Packaging material made from non-corrugated boxboard. Cartons are made by passing sheets of boxboard or paperboard through machines which trim, crease, fold, and glue them.

Folding Stair – A hinged set of steps, such as a ladder, which can be raised for storage or lowered for use.

Fool Killer – A pole or limb bent under tension, which can cause injury or death to anyone in its path should the tension be released suddenly.

Footage – A measure of lumber, logs, plywood or other wood product, as in the daily or annual output of a mill, the volume of timber logged, etc.

Football Patch – A type of patch or plug used to repair veneer, tapered on both ends and roughly resembling a football in shape.

Footboard – See Springboard.

Foot, Board Measure – See Board Foot.

Footing Beam – The tie beam in a roof system.

Foot Plate – A board laid across a wall top plate to join the foot of a rafter to an ashlar piece, or short upright.

Force Burn – To burn logging slash in wet conditions when fires must be forced to burn by adding diesel or other fuels to the wet wood. Such burns, while difficult to maintain, are much less likely to get away and start a wildfire.

Foreign Agricultural Service (FAS) – An agency of the U.S. Department of Agriculture which stations attaches overseas to promote consumption of U.S. agricultural products. FAS administers wood products promotional campaigns funded partly by industry organizations and partly by the agency. FAS also administers Commodity Credit Corporation load guarantee programs which guarantee bank loans on sales to developing nations.

Foreign Sales Corporation (FSC)

Foreign Sales Corporation (FSC) – A corporation set up overseas to handle export sales for a U.S. firm. FSCs are normally owned by the U.S. firm involved, but must have nonresidents on the board of directors, and must be actively engaged in international trade. If these conditions are met, part of the FSC's income is exempt from U.S. taxes. FSCs are usually incorporated in nations with little or no income tax. The U.S. government created FSCs in 1985 to replace Domestic International Sales Corporations (DISC), which were shell companies used by U.S. exporters to defer taxes on overseas sales. U.S. trading partners claimed the DISCs were illegal under international trade agreements.

Foreign Testing Organization (FTO) – A certification granted by the Japanese government to wood products organizations in other countries. It authorizes those organizations to grade, test, and oversee application of Japanese Agricultural Standard (JAS) marks on foreign products as required by Japanese building codes.

Foreign Trade Zone (FTZ) – An area located within U.S. boundaries but outside its customs territory. Foreign goods can be imported duty free into a foreign trade zone and then either re-exported without a duty or formally imported into U.S. markets with payment of U.S. duties.

Forepaws – A type of logging dog used to attach logs to each other when yarding to a landing.

Forest – An area, usually fairly large, covered with trees and undergrowth. The "woods."

Forest Biomass – The above-ground portion of woody plants in a forest.

Forest District – An administrative subdivision of a Forest Region in British Columbia. See Forest Region.

Forester – One who practices forestry; a person trained in forest management.

Forest Incentives Program (FIP) – A U.S Department of Agriculture program that offers private landowners financial assistance for timber reforestation practices. The federal government shares up to 65% of the cost of tree planting and timber stand improvement practices. The program was started in 1974.

Forester

Forest Industries – As defined by the U.S. Bureau of the Census, all or part of four industry groups classified under the Standard Industrial Classification System. These include: lumber and wood products; paper and allied products; furniture and fixtures; and gum and wood chemicals.

Forest Industry Lands – Lands owned or leased for one rotation or longer by companies or individuals operating wood-industry plants.

Forest Land – As defined by the U.S. Forest Service, land at least 10% stocked with live trees, or land formerly having such a tree cover and not currently developed for non-forest use. The minimum area of forest land recognized is one acre.

Forest Management – The art of managing forest land for all of its resources.

Forest Management Type – A classification of timberland based on the species and source of trees that make up a plurality of the live trees present.

Forest Mensuration – See Mensuration.

Forest Plan – As defined by the Forest Service, a summary of the analysis of the management situation for each national forest, describing multiple-use goals and objectives and including a description of the desired future condition of the forest.

Forest Region – One of six geographical areas of British Columbia for purposes of forest administration. The regions are Vancouver and Prince Rupert on the coast, and Nelson, Kamloops, Cariboo, and Prince George in the interior.

Forward Buying

Forestry – The science of forest management.

Forest Service – An agency of the U.S. Department of Agriculture, charged with the management and administration of National Forest lands. Among its duties are timber management, recreational development, reforestation, protection of the forest from fire, insects, or disease, and watershed and wildlife management and protection.

Forest Survey – As defined by the U.S. Forest Service, a survey conducted by that organization that provides a continuing inventory of the area, location, and condition of forest lands, amounts and quality of timber volumes available, rates of timber growth, removals and mortality, timber ownership, and trends in timber consumption.

Forked Tenon – A joint formed by a tenon cut into a long rail and inserted into an open mortise.

Forklift – A piece of mechanized equipment used to move units of lumber or plywood. Steel blades, or "forks," slip under the load, which is then lifted hydraulically, moved to the desired location, and lowered into place.

Forklift

Form – See Concrete Form.

Formaldehyde – A water-soluble chemical commonly used as a disinfectant or preservative. Mixed with the resin used in the manufacture of plywood, it creates a chemical reaction that gives a strong adhesive bond between veneers. It is also used in the manufacture of particleboard.

Formaldehyde Scavengers – Chemicals added to particleboard to reduce formaldehyde emissions. The chemicals are added either when the furnish and resin are mixed or after the panel is pressed. The scavengers combine with free formaldehyde to stabilize it and prevent it from leaving the board.

Formation – A characteristic of paper. Formation refers to the distribution of fibers through the paper, as perceived when light passes through the sheet. Good formation refers to a uniform distribution of fibers. Poor formation refers to an uneven distribution, where the fibers appear in clumps.

Formed Plywood – See Moulded Plywood.

Former – A machine used to form particleboard furnish into a mat prior to hot pressing.

Formosa Fir – Cunninghamia konishii. An important plantation species in China and Taiwan. Used in building construction, furniture manufacturing, and finish.

Formula Rule – A type of log rule, used to determine the net yield of a log. Included are any of various formulas based on some ideal geometric solids and adjusted for losses in saw kerf, slab, edging, and other factors.

Formula Tally – The normal assortment of lengths of lumber provided in a load by a certain producer. Such tallies vary from mill to mill, with some mills providing more of certain lengths, such as shorts, than others. The attractiveness of each producer's formula tally is an important factor in determining the price he is able to receive for his stock.

Forst Loader – A gin pole, or gill poke, with a swinging boom, used to unload logs at a log dump.

Fortified Glue – An interior plywood glue consisting of hot-press protein adhesives to which phenolic resin has been added. It contains a mold-resistant agent that counteracts a major cause of delamination in plywood. Not suitable for exposure to severe weather.

Forty – Forty acres, or 1/16th of a square mile; a standard unit of measurement used in surveying and in describing units of forest land.

Forward Buying – Buying for extended shipment in anticipation of future needs.

Terms Of The Trade

Forwarder

Forwarder – See Freight Forwarder.

Forward Exchange Rate – The price of foreign currency to be delivered at a future date, agreed to by the parties involved.

Forward Integration – A term describing manufacturers who operate their own distribution systems.

Forward Market – The future market in foreign exchange.

Forward Premium – In foreign exchange, the amount in excess of the forward rate above the spot rate.

Forward Position – The sum of a trader's purchases or sales transacted for consummation at a future date. May be applied either to futures activities or to trading in the physical commodity.

Foundation Lumber – Lumber used for wood foundations, chosen for its resistance to decay and for its dimensional stability. Specifically, a grade of redwood or cedar lumber. Foundation lumber must be composed totally of heartwood, but be free of heart center.

Four Cutter – A type of milling machine that prepares all four sides of a piece of lumber in one operation.

Fourdrinier – Part of a machine used in papermaking. As part of the papermaking process, pulp is released onto a rapidly moving wire mesh, called the fourdrinier, which carries it to the press and drying sections of the machine. While on the fourdrinier, the pulp fibers lock together to form the paper and some of the water is drained away through the wire mesh.

Four Foot Wood – Fuel wood cut into four-foot lengths to make it easy for measuring volume in cords. Cordwood.

Four L – The Loyal Legion of Loggers and Lumbermen, a "patriotic" organization formed near the end of World War I to counteract the International Workers of the World, or "Wobblies." When the war ended, the Four L was reorganized into an association of employees and management in the Northwest timber industry. Detractors claimed that the Four Ls stood for Lazy Loggers and Loafing Lumbermen.

Four-Quarter (4/4) – See Quarter Measure.

Fourth Forest – As defined by the U.S. Forest Service, the forest that will exist in the decades beyond 2000, after the harvest or clearing of the third forest – the one now existing in the South.

Fourths – A common grade of lumber exported from Scandinavia and Eastern Europe. A better grade than Fifths, but below Unsorted.

Fourths & Better – A grade mix of lumber exported from Scandinavia and Eastern Europe. The mix includes a percentage of fourths, but also contains stock of higher grades.

Four-Way Entry Pallet – One of two basic pallet types, this pallet allows fork-lift blades to be inserted from all sides. The usual design consists of top and bottom deck boards and nine space blocks positioned to allow the entry of fork-lift blades from any side.

Four-Way Matched – End Matched.

Foxiness – Incipient decay in wood, accompanied by a dull red stain. Caused by fungi, and usually attacking trees growing in marshy conditions.

Foxtail Pine – Pinus balfouriana, an alpine tree growing in the western U.S. The name is also applied to Bristlecone Pine.

Fractionals – Industrial cuttings sawn to specific, rather than nominal, measurement.

Frame Construction – A construction system in which the structural parts are wood or dependent on a wood framework for support. The balloon system consists of vertical members running from the foundation to the roof plate, to which floor joists are attached. In platform construction, floor joists of each floor rest on the plates of the floor below, and the bearing walls of each floor rest on the subfloor.

Frame Grade – See Framing.

Frame Saw – A type of powered saw in which a number of blades are secured in a moveable frame, allowing several parallel cuts in a single operation. A gang saw.

Framing – Lumber used for structural members in a house or other building. The skeleton to which roofs, floors, and sides are attached.

Framing Anchor – A prefabricated metal

connector used for joining joists and purlins to supporting wood members in the framing of buildings.

Framing Lumber Composite Price – See Composite Price.

Fraser Fir – Abies fraseri. This species, very similar to Balsam Fir, is found mostly in small areas of Eastern Virginia and Eastern North Carolina.

Frass – The mixture of wood powder, fecal material, soil, etc., left by wood-boring insects in logs and lumber.

f Rating – The measurement of stress (symbolized by the letter "f") in a piece of lumber. Generally, the higher the "f rating," the stronger the piece of lumber. See Design Value.

Freddie – A slang term for a forest ranger, used by some preservationist groups, especially Earth First.

Free Alongside Ship (FAS) – Used in waterborne shipments to denote that the price quoted includes all freight and handling charges from the point of origin to the vessel.

Free Astray – A term applied to freight that has been unloaded at the wrong terminal. It will be forwarded to the correct terminal free of charge.

Free End – The unsupported end of a beam that protrudes horizontally from its attachment to a vertical member.

Free Formaldehyde – Uncombined or unreleased formaldehyde available for release or emission from a particleboard panel.

Free-Growing Forest – A stage in the growth of a new forest in which young trees are healthy and growing without detrimental competition from other trees, shrubs, or plants.

Free In and Out (FIO) – Terms of an agreement under which an exporter is responsible for the costs of loading and unloading the vessel.

Free Logs – Logs without brands or other identifying marks of ownership that have been washed ashore on a river bank or the beach as the result of the breakup of a raft, or due to a storm. Such logs can be claimed by the finder.

Free Moisture – Moisture in cell cavities and intercellular spaces of wood.

Free of Heart Center (FOHC) – Lumber sawn to exclude the pith or heart center of a log.

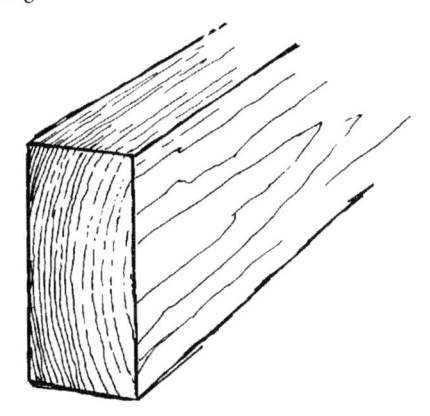

Free of Heart Center (FOHC)

Free on Board (FOB) – A reference to the point to which the seller will deliver goods without charge to the buyer. Additional freight or other charges connected with transporting or handling the product become the responsibility of the buyer.

Free Overside – A term denoting that the buyer is responsible for all costs as soon as the goods leave the ship's side. Also, free overboard.

Free Sheet – Paper manufactured from wood fibers that have been washed free of impurities.

Free Time – Time allowed a shipper to load, or a receiver to unload, before demurrage charges begin.

Free Water – Water that is held in the capillary structure of wood.

Freight Agency – A company that handles demurrage, ordering, and releasing rail cars, and services local rail customers.

Freight Agent – The supervisor of a freight agency.

Freight Auditor – A company which specializes in auditing freight bills for errors.

Freight Bill – A document listing all the freight charges due. The freight bill is presented to the receiver of the shipment upon

Freight Collect

its arrival and is payable before the goods are received.

Freight Collect – Freight charges payable by the consignee or receiver at the shipment's destination, when a freight agent is located there.

Freight Forwarder – One who accepts small lot shipments from shippers and combines them for forwarding in large lots. If international shipments are involved, a forwarder will attend to customs procedures and documents.

Freight Measure – The board measure contents of lumber, when calculated from measurements of actual overall dimensions. It is used only for displacement measurements for freight purposes.

Freight Pattern – The major geographical direction that a commodity moves, i.e. west to east.

Freight Pickup – See Underweights.

Freight Prepaid – Freight payable by the shipper at the point of origin of the shipment or at the head office of the originating railroad.

Freight Rate – The charge assessed by a freight carrier for moving a commodity from one point to another. Rates vary by distance and the type of commodity and the methods of calculating rates differ among rail, truck, and ship carriers. The first two basically calculate rates on units of 100 pounds of weight, while cargo shipments are charged on the cubic volume of the load.

Freight Rebate – A rebate paid by a railroad to a shipper, based on a minimum annual volume of business. Under such agreements, railroads rebate to shippers a dollar amount on a per-car basis. Rebates are usually paid monthly. Contract freight rates between railroads and shippers do not necessarily include rebates.

Freight Ton – See Cargo Ton.

French Cord – A unit of measurement used in Quebec. A French Cord is 8 1/2 feet by 4 feet by 4-1/4 feet.

French Roof – A mansard roof. A roof with two pitches on either side, with the lower slope steeper than the one above it.

French Truss – See Fink Truss.

Fresh Air – Air brought into a kiln dryer to replace vented air.

Fresh Water Immersion – A reference to lumber, timbers, or plywood that have been treated with a waterborne preservative to a retention level of .40 lbs. per cubic foot.

Fresh Wood – Wood that is brittle, with little elasticity, due to poor lateral adhesion between the growth rings.

Fret Saw – A long, narrow, fine-toothed saw used to cut ornamental designs in thin wood.

Frieze – A box cornice wood member, surfaced on four sides and nailed to one wall of a structure where the soffit and building wall meet.

Froe – A tool used in the manufacture of shakes, consisting of a steel blade that is placed against a shake bolt and hit with a mallet to split off the shake from the bolt.

Froe

Frog – The point where two or more log chutes came together.

Frost Cracks – Splits or cracks in the trunk of a tree, caused by extreme cold; such cracks are defects in lumber manufactured from such timber.

Frost Rib – A protrusion or callus caused by repeated opening and closing of a frost crack.

Frost Ring – A brown layer in a growth ring caused by injury to the cambium layer by frost.

Frowy – Soft or brittle wood.

Fuel Ladder – Combustible material that connects burnable ground vegetation and material at the crowns of trees, providing a means for the ground fire to climb into the tree canopy.

Fuel Log – Sawdust or other wood residue compressed into the shape of a small log to be used as fuel.

Fuelwood – Wood salvaged from mill waste, cull logs, branches, etc. and used to fuel fires in a boiler or furnace.

Full – A reference to lumber that is slightly oversize. See Full Sawn.

Full Cell Process – A process for impregnating wood with preservatives or other chemicals in which a vacuum is created to draw air from the wood before admitting the chemical. See Empty Cell Process.

Full Count – The length of a piece of lumber before trimming. For example, studs trimmed to 92-5/8 inches are counted as being a full 8 feet long for purposes of determining board footage.

Full Length Bundling (FLB) – See Old Bundling.

Full Sawn – A grading term used to describe rough lumber that has been cut to full nominal size. Tolerances above the nominal size are allowed in full-sawn lumber, but there is no tolerance for pieces undersize at the time of manufacture.

Full Scale – Gross scale in determining log volume; no deductions are made for defects. Used in determining scale for bushelers who work on a piece rate basis rather than by the hour.

Full Sheet – A whole veneer panel, such as a 4x8 or 4x9 sheet.

Fumigant – Any chemical or chemical compound used to exterminate pests found in lumber or logs.

Functional Discount – A discount from the stated or list price, to provide for the cost of the distribution function.

Fundamental Analysis – An approach to futures market trading that stresses the study of underlying factors of supply and demand in the commodity, in the belief that such an analysis will enable one to profit by being able to anticipate price trends.

Fungicide – A chemical that kills fungi.

Fungistatic – Having the ability to inhibit the growth of fungi.

Fungus Stain – Lumber stain caused by fungus growth in wood. Fungi can be either of the sapwood-staining or decay-producing types.

Furnish – 1. The raw material used to make reconstituted wood-based non-veneer panel products. 2. In papermaking, the mix of fibers, water, dyes, and chemicals poured onto the fourdrineir wire.

Furniture Grade – Lumber of a quality and size suitable for the manufacture of furniture.

Furniture Squares – Standard-sized lengths of wood, usually 2x2 inches, intended for further processing in the manufacture of furniture. Usually hardwood.

Furring – Lumber one inch in nominal thickness and less than four inches in width; frequently the product of resawing a wider piece. Most common sizes are 1x2 and 1x3. Furring is fastened to wall studs to provide a nailing surface. See Strip.

Furtherance – A reference to a rail car shipped without a final destination. Such a car is shipped to a diversion point "for furtherance," with the understanding that the shipper will later give the carrier an ultimate destination.

Fusiform Rust – A type of blister rust disease, caused by the fungus Cronartium fusiform. The disease attacks certain Southern Pine species; similar rusts infect some western pines.

Fust – The shaft of a column.

Future Room – A room in a house roughed in but left unfinished by the builder, with the idea that the homeowner will finish the room at a later time when additional living space is needed.

Futures – Contracts representing a commitment to deliver or receive a specified commodity at a future date.

Fuzzy Grain

Fuzzy Grain – In surfacing lumber, a condition of the board surface in which fibers are not completely severed in the surfacing process and are still partially attached to the surface, giving it a fuzzy appearance.

G

Gable – A side or end of a building enclosed by the end of, or masking the end of, a pitched roof.

Gaff – The hooked point of a pike pole, the tool used to move logs around in a pond or boom.

Gain – 1. A notch in a piece of wood that has been cut out to receive the end of another piece. 2. A bevel in a shoulder at the end of a mortised brace.

Gall – Any of various abnormal growths or excrescence on the surface of a tree, caused by insect damage, fungi, disease, or injury.

Gambrel Truss – A truss designed for a gambrel roof, which has a shallower slope above a steeper one on each side.

Gang Edger – An edger with multiple saws.

Gang Forming – A method of grouping lumber or metal-framed plywood panels to create large formwork sections for concrete.

Gang Mill – A machine having several saws that make parallel cuts.

Gang Rip – To cut a cant into uniform smaller members by passing it lengthwise through a gang saw.

Gang Saw – A machine in which two or more saws are mounted together, either on the same arbor or in the same sash and used to saw logs or cants.

Gap – A defect in plywood in which an edge void occurs on an inner ply.

Gap-Filling Adhesive – An adhesive suit-

Swedish-Type Gang Saw

Gap Stick

able for joining surfaces that may not be in continuous contact with each other.

Gap Stick — A log used to close off a sorting gap in a log boom.

Garden Grades — Various grades of Redwood commons, including Construction Heart, Construction Common, Merchantable Heart, and Merchantable. These are used for fencing, decking, trellises, outdoor furniture, etc.

Garden Tie — A timber, often a used railroad tie, used in landscaping a garden or yard. Also called a Garden Timber, or Landscape Timber.

Garden Timber — See Garden Tie.

Gate Boom — A boom that could be opened or closed to permit or prevent the passage of logs downstream.

Gateway — In transportation, the point at which goods leave one territory for another, or are transferred from one carrier to another for further shipment.

Geared Locomotive — Any of various locomotives in which the power to the drivers was transferred from the cylinders by some type of gear system. Examples include the Shay and the Climax.

Gefle Standard — A measure of roundwood volume equal to 100 cubic feet; used in the export trade.

Gelatinous Fibers — A wood fiber with an inner wall lacking in lignin and having a gelatinous appearance; usually associated with compression wood.

General Agreement on Tariffs and Trade (GATT) — A multilateral organization influential in monitoring trade barriers and in conducting multilateral trade negotiations.

General Line Wholesaler — A firm that deals in a broad variety of products, as opposed to a few specialties.

Genus — A kind or class having common characteristics. In wood or tree identification, a group of species having the broader characteristics in common. For example, all species of fir belong to the genus Abies.

Georgia Hard Pine — Another name for Longleaf Pine, Pinus palustis.

Georgia Pine — Another name for Pitch Pine, Pinus rigida.

Get Away — An escape route used by a tree faller to get out of the way when a tree begins to fall. Often selected and cleared in advance.

Ghosting — See Telegraphing.

Giant Cedar — Another name for Western Red Cedar, Thuja plicata.

Giant Fir — Another name for Grand Fir, Abies grandis.

Gib — 1. A narrow wedge of metal used in a planer as a chip breaker. 2. A heavy metal strap used to fasten two members together.

Gibson Raft — A type of log raft developed by James Gibson of Vancouver, B.C. This ocean-going raft was square shaped and built on a float mat instead of a cradle, like the Benson raft. Most were about 200 feet long and contained about 1 million board feet of logs.

Gigantic Pine — Another name for Sugar Pine, Pinus lambertiana.

Gig Trail — A trail along a river, used to follow a log drive.

Gilchrist — 1. A type of hand-logging jack used to move logs into the water or on and off railcars. 2. A small town in Central Oregon named after a family that established a sawmill there.

Gill Poke — A system employing a swinging boom to push logs off railcars at a log dump.

Gingerbread — Elaborate ornamentation in the trim of a house.

Ginger Pine — An informal name for Port Orford Cedar, Chamaecyparis lawsoniana.

Ginnie Mae — See Government National Mortgage Association (GNMA).

Gin Pole — A rigging system based on a tripod and heavy pullies, used to load logs on open cars.

Girder — A main structural member, placed horizontally to support a vertical load.

Girdle — To cut away the bark in a band around a tree. This will usually result in the

Glue Spreader

tree's death if the bark band is completely removed.

Girt – A horizontal structural member between columns, used to stiffen the frame.

Girth – The circumference of a circular object, such as a log or tree.

Girthing Tape – A specially calibrated measuring tape used to determine the volume of round logs. There are different calibration methods, based on various log rules and systems of timber measurement.

Girt Strip – A board attached to studs to support floor joists.

Glancer – A short log positioned so as to steer logs around a turn or obstacle.

Glass Bead – A type of moulding used to hold glass in place. Also called Glass Stop, Putty Bead, Glazing Bead, or Staff Bead.

Glass Stop – See Glass Bead.

Glassy – See Wetwood.

Glazing Bead – See Glass Bead.

Glens Falls Standard – See Adirondack Standard.

Global Warming – A theory suggesting an increase in the average temperature of the earth's surface due to a trapping of solar energy by atmospheric gasses. See Greenhouse Effect.

Gluability – The ability of wood products to bond together with adhesives.

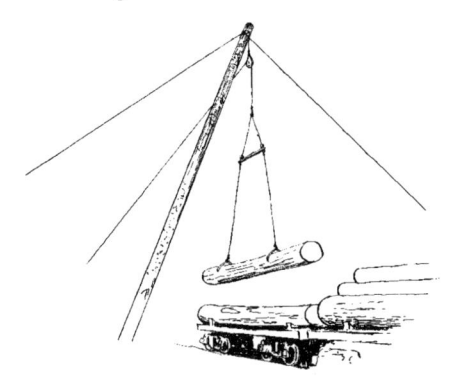

Gin Pole

Glue Bead – A narrow strip of adhesive applied to one of two pieces to be joined. The line of glue applied to the back of a panel that is to be fastened to a wall.

Glue Bleed – A leaking of excess glue from a joint.

Glue Bleedthrough – The seepage of glue through the face of a panel, typically a hardwood with open pores.

Glue Bond – A measure of how well articles are fastened together after being glued.

Glue Bond Test – A test designed to determine the performance of a glue bond. Samples of glued veneers are subjected to various tests, including soaking for interior glues, and boiling or vacuum-press exposures followed by shear testing for exterior glues.

Glued Floor System – A floor construction method in which plywood underlayment or other structural panel is both glued and nailed to the floor joists. The combination of gluing and nailing results in an especially strong floor that is much stiffer and less prone to squeaking and nail-popping than a customary floor that is fastened by nails only.

Glue Jointing – The process of manufacturing wide pieces from a number of narrow ones. The edges of the pieces to be jointed are planed to produce a smooth edge perpendicular to the face. Glue is applied to the edges, which are then pressed together while the glue cures. See Edge Glue & Rip, Veneer Composer.

Glue Laminated (Glulam) – A process in which individual pieces of lumber or veneer are bonded together with an adhesive to make a single piece, with the grain of each piece running parallel to the grain of each of the other pieces.

Glue Line – A layer of glue or adhesive between two pieces of lumber or veneer.

Glue Nailed – A combination of gluing and nailing plywood joints and connections for the stiffest possible construction. See Glued Floor System.

Glue Report – In plywood manufacture, a tabulation of the number of panels and the square footage of plywood that has passed through the gluing process.

Glue Spreader – A machine that spreads glue on veneer pieces prior to layup.

Terms Of The Trade

Glue-Up

Glue-Up – The process of spreading glue on the surfaces of veneers of similar sizes and pressing them together to make a sheet of plywood.

Glulam – A shorthand version of Glue Laminated.

Glulam Appearance Grades – Three grades of glue laminated beams whose appearance has been improved by finish work done after laminating. The grades, in ascending order, are Industrial, Commercial, and Quality.

Glulam Rivet – An oval-shaped fastener used with steel plates to attach glulam members.

Glut – A wooden wedge, made of heavy hardwood, that was used in splitting Redwood, or sometimes used in conjunction with steel wedges to fell a tree.

Glyph – A decorative channel or groove used in construction.

GNMA – See Government National Mortgage Association.

Go-Back Road – A road used by empty trucks returning from the log dump to the woods, so as not to interfere with loaded trucks traveling from the woods, or because the other road is too steep to climb on the return to the landing. Such a road is also called a Come-Back Road, depending on which end you are on.

Go-Devil – A sled or skid-pan designed to keep the leading end of a log off the ground when skidding. Often crudely fashioned out of the fork of a tree. Also called a Travois.

God Squad – Popular name for the Endangered Species Committee, a panel of high-ranking government officials who can override provisions of the Endangered Species Act under certain conditions.

Going – In a stairway, the horizontal distance between two consecutive treads; this is known as the going of the tread. The horizontal distance between the first and last risers on a stairway is known as the going of the flight.

Go Long – To purchase a stock, futures contract, or a commodity, such as forest products, with the expectation of selling at a higher price.

Good Assortment – This term, although vague, is generally understood by traders to mean that a random loading of lumber contains a high percentage of the desired lengths and a small percentage of the "doggy" lengths. Referring to a loading as a "good assortment" implies a selection of lengths that is somewhat more desirable than would ordinarily be produced.

Good One Side (G1S) – A grade of sanded plywood produced in Canada. A plywood panel with a higher grade of veneer on the face than on the back, permitting neat wood patches or inlays; used when the appearance of one exposed surface is important.

Goods and Services Tax (GST) – Canada's version of a value added tax, a system that places a levy on the value added to commodities at each stage of production and distribution.

Good Till Canceled (GTC) – In futures trading, an order to buy or sell at a fixed price. The order is in force until executed or canceled.

Good Two Sides (G2S) – The highest grade of sanded plywood produced in Canada. These panels may have inlays or neat wood patches and are intended for use where the appearance of both sides of the panel is important.

Goose Pen – A large hole burned in the bark of a tree, at the base; this term was most commonly used in the Redwood region.

Goose-Wing Ax – A broad ax with a head resembling a goose wing. Used to hew timbers.

Gopher – 1. A digging tool used to make a hole under a log, through which a choker could be passed. 2. A low-ranking employee who runs errands for a specialist, such as a millwright (GoFor).

Go Short – To sell a stock, futures contract, or commodity before buying it. The expectation is that the purchase price will be lower that the selling price, thus providing some profit margin.

Gothenburg Standard – A unit of measurement, usually used to measure pitwood. It is equal to a pile of roundwood 6x6x5 feet, or 180 cubic feet. At one time, it also meant 120 pieces of sawn wood, with each piece 2x9 inches by 12 feet.

Grade Stamp

Gothic – An early English style of architecture characterized by the use of pointed arches and ribbed vaults.

Gothic Arch – A high, narrow, pointed arch, usually with a joint instead of a keystone at the apex.

Government National Mortgage Association (GNMA) – A federally sponsored private corporation that provides a secondary market for pools of insured mortgages. "Ginnie Mae."

Government Square – See Falling on the Square.

Gowen Cypress – Cupressus goveniana. This species, which often grows as a shrub, is found in the coastal mountains of California. It is not a commercial species.

Grab Hook – A hook with a narrow throat that grabs and holds a link of chain.

Grabinski – A system of cable logging which uses the haulback line to provide extra lift for the logs by running the haulback through a block attached to the butt rigging.

Grab Link – An iron link used to hook something along a chain.

Grabs – Another name for tongs, an implement used to pick up logs.

Grade – A term used in reference to AB veneer. Also used to designate plywood panels by the grade of veneers used as faces.

Graded Rates – Railroad freight rates that are graded upward as the distance from the point of origin increases.

Grademark (GM) – A stamp or symbol indicating the grade, quality and/or intended use of a piece of lumber, plywood, or other wood product. To be recognized as "grade marked," the product must bear an official stamp issued by a grading agency and applied by a qualified grader, or it must be accompanied by a certificate attesting to the grade.

Grade Marked – Lumber or plywood that has been graded for quality and/or specific use and marked with certain symbols attesting to that quality. Such lumber is marked with a grading association or agency stamp.

Grade Mark Reader – See Automatic Grade Mark Reader.

Grader – A worker who examines lumber, plywood, or other wood products and assigns it a grade according to an established set of rules. The grader is usually an employee of the mill, but sometimes is employed by a grading agency which charges the mill for his services. See Approved Grader, Certified Grader.

Grade Recovery – The rate at which various qualities, or grades, are obtained in the sawing of a log.

Grade Sawing – The practice of turning a log on the carriage in order to obtain the highest values or grades.

Grade Stamp – A rubber stamp, issued by a grading agency or association to a client mill and used to indicate the grade of a particular piece of lumber or panel, along with other information. A typical grade stamp

MILL 000 — Mill Identification

CONST — Grade

Species

Grading Agency

S-GRN — Surfaced Green

WESTERN CEDAR

Grade Stamp

Terms Of The Trade

123

Grade Stamped

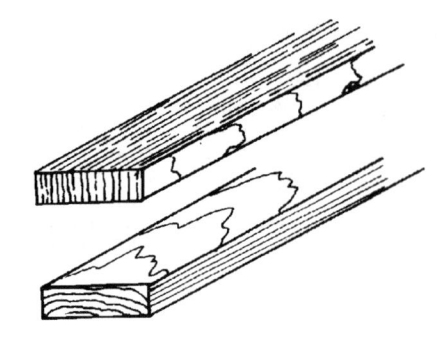

Grain

will include the species, the grade, the producing mill by name and/or agency number, the grading agency, and a designation (for lumber) of whether the stock was dry or green when surfaced.

Grade Stamped – See Grade Marked.

Gradetto – A type of fillet moulding.

Grading Agency – An organization that provides grading rules, gradestamps, and supervisory services to member producers. The agency is financed by assessing users of the service a rate based on their production.

Grading Certificate – In futures trading, a document stating the quality of a commodity, as determined by authorized inspectors or graders.

Grading Rules – A set of criteria by which to judge various pieces of lumber or plywood in terms of strength, appearance, and suitability for various uses. Regional grading agencies draw up rules for grading, based on the voluntary product standards issued by the U.S. Bureau of Standards.

Grading Service – See Grading Agency.

Graduated Payment Mortgage (GPM) – A type of mortgage pay-back schedule that starts payments at a low level during the first few years and gradually increases them by a predetermined amount each year. The idea behind this plan is that it will enable lower-income households to afford a mortgage and that the payments will rise in line with increased income over the years.

Grain – 1. A general term referring to the arrangement, appearance, and direction of wood fibers. Among the many types of grain are fine, coarse, straight, curly, open, flat, vertical, and spiral. 2. In papermaking, the predominate direction in which the fibers are aligned.

Grain Direction – The orientation of the long axis of the dominant fibers in a piece of wood.

Grainer – A shingle machine device used to "lengthen" shingles by overriding the normal ratchet cycle.

Grain Printing – The process of obliterating the original face color and grain pattern by printing a new grain and color over it to represent a more stylish or exotic wood.

Grain Raise – A roughened condition on the surface of dressed lumber in which the hard summerwood is raised above the soft springwood, but not torn loose from it.

Grain Rupture – Breaks in veneer that result from cutting or from irregular grain.

Grain Show Through – A defect in overlaid panels.

Grain Slope – See Slope of Grain.

Grain Sweep – A deviation of grain around a knot, causing cross-grain defect.

Grand Fir – Abies grandis. This species is one of the True Firs, and is classified commercially as part of the White Fir group; it is graded as Hem-Fir.

Grape Stake – A narrow board, sometimes irregular in size, used for fencing.

Grapple – A heavy set of tongs with fine teeth on the inside edge. Developed primarily to eliminate large tong holes in logs. Used with a shovel or crane equipped with a heel-

Grapple

boom, grapples have replaced tongs for loading logs onto trucks.

Grapple Processor – A boom-mounted device to delimb and buck small trees removed in plantation thinning. A Scandinavian development, a grapple processor is an alternative to manual delimbing and bucking.

Grass Line – A light line used in logging; more commonly called a Straw Line or Guinea Line.

Gravity System – A cable logging system in which the mainline is attached to a stump across a canyon and used as a skyline. A heavy carriage holding the chokers rides the mainline by gravity. The haulback line is used to pull or to lower the logs to the landing. Also called a Shotgun System.

Gray Fir – An old, slang term for Western Hemlock.

Gray Pine – Another name for Jackpine, Pinus banksiana.

Grease Dauber – A worker who carried a bucket of grease along a skid road, greasing the skids so that logs could be moved over them more easily. Also called a Grease Monkey.

Grease Monkey – 1. See Grease Dauber. 2. A mechanic who lubricates equipment.

Great Basin Bristlecone Pine – Pinus longaeva. These pines are the oldest living trees, with some known specimens more than 4,000 years old. They are found in a range from Utah to California.

Green – Unseasoned; not dry. Lumber with a moisture content of 19% or more.

Greenchain – A moving chain or belt on which lumber is transported from saws in a mill. The lumber is pulled from the chain by workers and stacked according to size, length, species, and other criteria.

Green End – A manufacturing facility that produces green veneer. "Green end" is used to describe a facility or portion of a facility that barks the logs, cuts them into block lengths, peels and clips the veneer, and sorts the veneer according to grade. A green end usually also separates veneer made from sapwood and veneer from heartwood so that the green veneer can later be properly dried before use in plywood production. In the Douglas Fir plywood producing region, green ends are frequently not adjacent to a plywood layup plant and the green veneer must be transported to another site for layup into plywood.

Greenhouse Effect – The theory that the Earth is gradually warming due to the buildup of certain gases in the atmosphere that trap the sun's heat. Many of these gases are by-products of burning fossil fuels.

Green Logging – The logging of live trees, as opposed to salvage logging.

Green Manure Trees – Trees that add nutrients to the ground as they grow, usually by releasing nitrogen through their roots.

Green Movement – An informal, international collection of political and interest groups whose agendas are centered around protection of the environment.

Green Tree – A live and growing tree.

Green Tree Retention – The practice of leaving live, growing trees on a site during timber harvest as a future source of snags.

Green Weight – The weight of a kiln sample prior to drying. Also called Initial Weight, Original Weight.

Gribble – A marine crustacean that attacks pilings and timbers in piers and bridges. Gribbles bore holes by chewing through the outer layers of wood. Creosote treatment does not prevent gribble damage, but certain chemical fumigants will.

Grillage – A framework of logs or timbers used to provide support in marshy or treacherous soil.

Grip Hook – A type of end hook used in loading logs.

Grips – Another name for tongs used in skidding logs.

Grit Marks – Scratches or similar marks on the surface of a particleboard panel, running in the sander direction.

Grit Sequence – In producing particleboard, the process of sanding the panels with successively finer grit papers to produce uniform smoothness and thickness.

Grit Size – A reference to the coarseness of the abrasive material on a sanding belt. The lower the grit number, the coarser the abra-

Groin Arch

sive material.

Groin Arch – A rib dividing two vaulted surfaces into bays.

Groove – A narrow channel on the face or edge of a piece of lumber or plywood.

Grooved Plywood – A plywood panel with grooves sawn, routed, or embossed along the grain of the face veneer in order to simulate lumber paneling.

Gross Domestic Product (GDP) – The total annual value of the goods and services of a nation's economy, minus exports.

Gross Features – Those characteristics of wood that can be readily distinguished without the use of laboratory tests. Included would be characteristics such as color, weight, grain, and odor.

Gross Measure – The board measure content of a piece of lumber calculated from nominal sizes, as contrasted with a measure taken from actual dimensions.

Gross National Product (GNP) – The total annual value of the goods and services of a nation's economy.

Gross Profit – The revenue from sales, minus the cost of the goods sold.

Gross Register Tonnage (GRT) – The total internal cubic capacity of a ship's cargo space, in terms of units of 100 cubic feet, or equivalent tons.

Gross Sales – The total sales of all merchandise before deducting costs.

Gross Scale – The measurement of the yield of a log, without allowance for loss due to various defects.

Gross Ton – A long ton; 2,240 pounds.

Ground Contact – A level of treatment of wood products intended for use in, or in contact with, the ground, soil, or fresh water. As established by the American Wood Preservers Association, that level is .40 pounds of retained preservative per cubic foot of wood.

Ground Haul – Another name for Ground Lead.

Ground Lead Logging – A logging system in which logs are yarded to the landing by dragging them along the surface of the ground. The system is similar to animal logging, except that a machine, such as a tractor or a high lead, provides the pulling power.

Ground Plate – The lowest horizontal member of a framing system. Also called a Sole Plate.

Groundwood Pulp – Pulping fibers produced by grinding wood against an abrasive wheel.

Group 1, 2, 3, 4, 5 – A classification into five groups of approximately 70 species of timber of varying strength used in the manufacture of plywood. The highest-rated woods are in Group 1.

Grouse Ladder – A logger's term for a mature conifer that has grown in a more or less open area and has retained its limbs along the full length of the tree. Also called a Hooter.

Growing Stock – Live trees of commercial species which meet the minimum merchantability standards for sawtimber, poletimber, or seedling and sapling trees.

Growth Basal Area (GBA) – A measure of the potential of a forest site to grow timber, based on volume growth. GBA uses a basis, such as 15 rings per inch, as a measure of growth. Through a systematic sample, the basal area at which a stand will maintain the basis growth can be determined. Silvicultural treatments can then be prescribed to maintain or create maximum growth through control of basal area.

Growth Layers – Successive layers of growth visible in the cross section of a log corresponding to a tree's seasonal or annual growing periods. Also called Growth Rings.

Growth Ring – The amount of growth in a single year; an annual ring.

Grub Hoe – A thick-handled, heavy tool used in building fire lines and in similar work.

Grub Hole – See Borer Hole.

Guarantor – One who promises to answer for the debt or default of another; a form of collateral security.

Guatambu – A tree species native to Central America that produces hard, strong, moderately heavy lumber of yellowish color. Its veneer is often exported to the United

Gypsum Fiberboard

States, where it is used as faces on western sanded plywood. Also called Lemonwood.

Guessing Stick – Another name for a Cruiser's Stick, a measuring device used by a timber cruiser and consisting of a long stick marked with graduations for measuring tree height, diameter, and estimated volume.

Guillotine – A type of knife fastened in a frame and used to slice and trim veneers using a vertical cutting action.

Guinea Line – A light line or cable used to haul other lines and do a variety of tasks around a logging show. Also called a Straw Line or Grass Line.

Gulf Coast Classification – A grading rule for Southern Yellow Pine export lumber.

Gulf Cypress – Another name for Baldcypress, Taxodium distichum.

Gullet – The space between two teeth in a saw.

Gum – Oleoresin; a compound of resins and natural oils exuded by plants. Gum from certain species is distilled to yield such products as rosin and turpentine.

Gum Ducts – Intercellular canals in woods, especially certain tropical hardwoods.

Gummer – A short-toothed saw once used in felling and bucking.

Gum Pocket – An opening between growth rings which contains or has contained resin or bark, or both.

Gum Seam – Check or shake filled with gum.

Gum Spot – Accumulation of gum-like substance occurring as a small patch. This may occur in conjunction with a bird peck or other injury to the growing wood.

Gum Streak – A well-defined accumulation of gum in a more-or-less regular streak. Classified by size in the same manner as pitch streaks.

Gum Vein – A streak of resin or pitch occurring in some hardwoods.

Gun – To aim a tree in a particular direction while felling it.

Gunning Stick – A device used to deter-

Gusset

mine the direction of the fall of a tree.

Gusset – An insert; especially, a triangular wood or metal brace used to strengthen or reinforce a corner or angle as on a roof truss.

Gut a Show – To skim only the highest grade timber from a stand, leaving the lower-quality timber in the woods. While this was once a common practice, economics and regulations have made such methods a thing of the past.

Gut Chain – A type of binder chain used to draw the outside logs closer together when loading a log truck, in order to make a better bed for the log on top.

Gut Log – The center log in a load.

Gut Robber – A logging camp cook.

Guts and Feathers – Slang terminology for random width and fishtail veneer.

Gutter – A select grade of lumber, usually 4x5 inches, which can be milled to produce a watertight eavestrough. Usually made from Douglas Fir or West Coast Hemlock.

Gymnosperm – The type of trees that bear naked fruit or seeds. Conifers are included in this category. The other major class, Angiosperm, includes most deciduous trees.

Gyppo – An independent logger or small, independent sawmill or other wood-related operation. Also refers to personnel paid on a piecework basis, such as a "gyppo" carloader, or a "gyppo" trucker.

Gypsum – See Sheetrock.

Gypsum Fiberboard – A type of mineral-

Terms Of The Trade

Gypsy Moth

bonded wood composite panel using wood fiber as the furnish and gypsum as the binder.

Gypsy Moth – Porthetria dispar. A moth, native to Europe, that was introduced into North America and is now considered a major danger to deciduous species. The larvae of the gypsy moth feed on the leaves of a tree, defoliating it; several successive attacks are enough to weaken the tree so that it falls victim to drought, disease, or other insects.

Habitat – The native environment of an animal or plant.

Habitat Conservation Area – See Owl Conservation Area.

Habitat Type – All land areas potentially capable of producing similar plant communities, or the same plant association.

Hack – 1. To cut or hit at something carelessly or irregularly; to deal heavy blows. 2. A person lacking, or not applying, knowledge or skill in performing his job. 3. A mark stamped on a log to denote ownership.

Hackberry – Celtis occidentalis. Yellowish grey to light brown wood used in furniture and boxes. Produces an edible, cherry-like fruit.

Hackmatack – Another name for Tamarack, Larix laricina. Of Algonquian origin: Hackmantak.

Haddon Hall – A parquet flooring pattern.

Hairline – A thin, perceptible line showing at the joint between two pieces of wood.

Halfbreed – A type of engine used to power a donkey skidder.

Half-Landing – A flat area between floors of a building joined by stairs.

Half-Principal – A rafter which does not reach the ridge of the roof.

Half Round – 1. A type of moulding whose profile is a half circle. 2. Veneer produced by rotary slicing a flitch, or a log that has been sawn into two equal halves. The flitch is connected to a metal beam and rotated off center to produce a piece of veneer each time the beam revolves past the knife. The veneer produced is similar to flat-sliced veneer.

Half Timbered – A building having the frame and principal supports of timber, with walls filled in with plaster or masonry.

Halve – To form a lap joint by halving the thicknesses of two pieces of wood where they join.

Hammer Beam – A short beam extending inward from the bottoms of the principal rafters in a hammer beam roof truss.

Hammer Mark – A mark on a log or timber that identifies the owner; a brand.

Hammermill – A machine for producing fibers from solid wood pieces by hammering

Terms Of The Trade

Hand Briar

Hand Jack

or flailing them.

Hand Briar – A hand-powered crosscut saw.

Hand Faller – One who fells timber with a cross-cut saw rather than a powered chain saw.

Hand Hook – A special hook used in lifting one end of planks when stacking.

Hand Jack – A small screw jack used to move a log.

Handloading – Loading material onto a freight car or truck a piece at a time, by hand.

Hand Logging – Logging that utilizes man and animal power rather than machine power.

Hand Pike – A pole with a metal point, used to guide or control floating logs.

Hand Ring – A ring attached to a swivel hook that can be grasped to move the rigging used to skid logs.

Hand Saw – Any of numerous types of non-mechanized saws used by hand.

Handsplit and Resawn (HS&RS) – A type of ccdar shake. handsplits are split from cedar bolts using a mallet and froe (a type of steel blade). The pieces are then ripped on a resaw to produce two shakes, each with a rough, split face and a smooth, sawn back.

Hand-to-Mouth – A method of buying in which a retailer purchases only as much stock as meets his immediate needs and avoids building an inventory; a common procedure in a market in which prices are falling.

Hanger – Metal straps from which cross members can be suspended.

Hanging Stile – The vertical part of a door or window to which hinges are attached.

Hanging Wedge – A wide, thin wedge driven into a log at right angles to a crosscut to hold the two cut pieces together until the cut is finished.

Hang-Up – A situation in which a tree, in falling, has become entangled in the crown of another tree.

Hardback – A term used to describe a certain grade of Mldg&Btr lumber. Although often referred to as Hardback alone, the full term is "Hardback D", since it is the D grade to which the term applies. Hardback is D select graded from the good face only. The face must be clear but the back may contain knots if they do not extend through the piece.

Hardboard – A generic term for a panel manufactured primarily from interfelting ligno-cellulosic fibers (usually wood) consolidated under heat and pressure in a hot press to a density of 31 pounds per cubic foot or greater.

Hard Conversion – A conversion from one system of measurement to another in which adoption of the new system is accompanied by a change in the actual sizes of the products involved.

Hard Grained – Wood with dense, close grain.

Hard Hat – A rigid protective helmet, usually of metal or plastic, worn by workers in wood products and other industries.

Hard Maple – Acer saccharum, the Sugar Maple.

Hardness – The property of wood indicated by its resistance to cutting, scratching, denting, pressure, or wear.

Hard Pine – One of the more resinous pines such as Loblolly or Pitch Pine.

Hard Rot – Decay caused by fungi that reduce wood to a brown, crumbly state.

Hard Snag – A recently dead, standing tree

Head Nailing

that typically has an intact top, most of its bark, and most of its limbs.

Hardwood — A general term referring to any of a variety of broad-leaved, deciduous trees, and the wood from those trees. The term has nothing to do with the actual hardness of the wood; some hardwoods are softer than certain softwood (evergreen) species.

Harvest Scheduling — Planning timber sales several rotations into the future to estimate how current sales will affect future harvest levels.

Haulback — A small cable attached to the main line in a high lead logging operation, used to return the main line, along with chokers, from the landing to a cutting area.

Hauling Line — The line used to drag a log to a loading site.

Haul Road — A logging road.

Haunch — 1. That portion of some beams that is deeper where the beam is supported. 2. The part of an arch midway between the base and the highest point.

Hayline — A small cable used to move heavier lines.

Hayrack — A type of log loading boom, rectangular in shape and hung from the spar tree so that the side pieces straddle the tree to hold the boom in place. Two lines and tongs are used with this boom; they are so positioned on the boom that they are in line with the railroad car or logging truck when the boom is swung over it.

Hazel Hoe — A grub hoe used to clear a fire line or trail.

Hazel Pine — Another name for both Sweetgum, Liquidambar styraciflua, and Water Tupelo, Nyssa aquatica. Neither are pines; both are hardwoods.

Head — 1. The top horizontal member of a frame. 2. The highest or foremost part of anything.

Head Block — 1. The main block on a high lead spar tree. 2. A large cross-timber on the front of a donkey sled.

Head Boom — The main boom, consisting of a group of logs chained together, used to contain floating logs in a storage area.

Headbox — In papermaking, the device that feeds pulp slurry onto a continuous, moving band of wire mesh. See Fourdrinier.

Head Dam — A dam used to accumulate water that is later released to float logs downstream.

Head Dog — A large metal stake driven into the front log of a boom.

Header — A beam fitted between trimmers and across the ends of tailpieces in a building frame; a horizontal support at the top of an opening.

Head Haul — The principle movement of a loaded rail car.

Heading — The pieces of lumber from which a keg, or barrel, head is cut. Also, the stock after it has been cut and assembled to form the barrel head.

Headlap — The part of a shingle covered by the shingles in the outer course.

Head Loader — The worker who chooses the logs to be loaded on each truck or railcar.

Head Log — The brow log at a landing.

Head Moulding — A moulding over an opening.

Head Nailing — Nailing shingles near the top instead of at the middle.

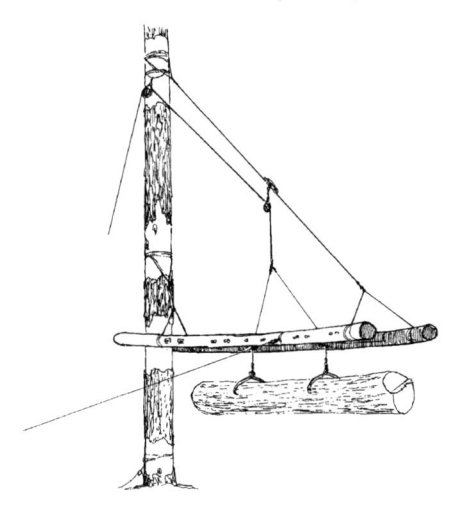

Hayrack

Terms Of The Trade

Head Rig

Band Saw Head Rig

Head Rig – The principal saw in a sawmill, on which logs are first cut into cants before being sent on to other saws for further processing.

Double Circular Head Rig

Head Saw – The principal break-down saw in a sawmill; part of the head rig.

Head Sawyer – One who operates the headrig, or principal saw, in a sawmill.

Head Spar – A tall tree, topped and stripped of branches, to which a cable has been rigged.

Head Tree – 1. The living tree that makes up the head spar. 2. A short horizontal piece of wood placed on top of a post to support a beam.

Headworks – A capstan mounted on a log raft to warp a boom across a lake.

Heart B – A grade of Redwood siding consisting of all heartwood and allowing a limited number of knots and characteristics not permitted in Clear or Clear All Heart. It is graded on one face and one edge.

Heart Boxed – Sawn so that the heart, or pith, is boxed or surrounded.

Heart Center – The pith or center of a log.

Heart Center Decay – A localized type of decay that develops in the pith of some species. It develops in the living tree and does not advance after the tree has been cut.

Heart Check – Seasoning checks in the central core of a timber.

Heart Face – The face side of a piece of lumber that is free of sapwood. See Heart Side.

Heart Off Center – A defect in an otherwise peeler grade log that makes it difficult or impracticable to turn the log on a lathe.

Heart Shake – Shake, or a split, starting in the center of a log or timber.

Heart Side – The side of a piece of lumber which, if it were still part of the log, would be closest to the heart of the log. In flat grain lumber, the side on which the grain is more likely to raise or separate from the piece.

Heart Stain – A marked variation from the normal color of the heart, ranging from pink to brown, and usually in irregular blotches.

Heartwood – That portion of the tree contained within the sapwood; this term is sometimes used to mean the pith. The heartwood is dormant and unnecessary for the tree's continued life; the living part of the tree is contained in its outer parts.

Heat Durability Test – One of various tests used to determine the glue bond quality of plywood. A test specimen is subjected to a flame from a Bunsen-type burner, then examined for delamination.

Heater Boom – A small, round log boom.

Heat Transfer Foil – A type of foil used in the manufacture of decorative laminates. The process involves the transfer of a complete coating system from a carrier film to a substrate using heat and pressure. The foil is printed in reverse sequence on mylar film, with the release coat printed first, followed by a pattern or wood-grain print, the ground coat, and the adhesive.

Hem-Fir (Coast)

Heavies – Shakes produced with a thickness of 3/4 to 5/4 inches at the butt.

Heavy – 1. An ambiguous term indicating that the number of pieces of a certain size or grade is more than the number usually included in a shipment. For example, a load of 2x4, "heavy 16-foot." The opposite of Light. 2. In futures trading, a description of a market in which prices are showing either an inability to rise or a slight tendency to decline. 3. See Heavies.

Heavy Dimension – A term sometimes used to describe squares and timbers four inches in thickness, such as 4x4, 4x6.

Heavy Dressing – See Heavy Shop.

Heavy Peel – Veneer in any thickness greater than 1/10-inch. Most often used to describe veneer greater than 1/8-inch.

Heavy Shop – A thicker-than-standard piece of shop grade lumber. For example, "heavy" 5/4 Ponderosa Pine shop is 1-5/16 inches thick, while standard surfaced 5/4 is 1-5/32.

Heavy Timber – 1. A particular type of construction with good fire resistance. 2. Rough or surfaced pieces having a smallest dimension of at least 5 inches.

Heavy Timber Construction – A type of construction using large pieces of structural lumber to carry the load.

Hectare – A metric measure of land area. A hectare is equal to 10,000 square meters, or 2.47 acres.

Hedge – The establishment of a position in futures opposite to one in cash; designed to transfer risk from the hedger to the speculator.

Heel – 1. The back or bottom part, as opposed to the head. 2. The point on a truss where the top and bottom chords intersect.

Heelboom – A type of log loading boom that uses a single line and grapple. The grapple, or tong, is attached to the log back of the point of balance. When the log is raised, the back end comes up first and "heels" against the boom, forcing the front end of the log to raise. It is then swung over a railroad car or logging truck for loading.

Heel Cut – See Butt Cut.

Heel Tackle – A system of lines and blocks used to tighten a skyline or raise a spar.

Heisler – One of the three most popular geared steam locomotives used in railroad logging. The Heisler was put into service in 1894. See Shay, Climax.

Helicopter Logging – A system of logging in which the logs are removed from the cutting area by helicopter. This method is used in roadless areas or in areas where other logging methods might prove too damaging to the surrounding terrain.

Helm Roof – A steeply pitched roof with four faces resting diagonally and meeting at the top.

Helve – The wooden handle of a tool, such as an ax.

Hem-Bal – A combination of Western Hemlock and Balsam Fir produced in British Columbia for overseas markets.

Hem-Fir – A species combination used by grading agencies to designate any of various species having common characteristics. Included in the Hem-Fir group are California Red Fir, Grand Fir, Noble Fir, Pacific Silver Fir, Shasta Fir, White Fir, and Western Hemlock. Of these the last two are the most important in terms of volume. These species were given a common designation for identification and standardization of recommended design values and because some species cannot be visually separated in lumber form.

Hem-Fir (Coast) – An unofficial designation developed to differentiate between Western Hemlock and the True Firs in the Hem-Fir group, because of shipping weights and

Heelboom

Hem-Fir (Inland)

individual characteristics. Hem-Fir (Coast) refers to stock produced in Western Oregon, Western Washington and British Columbia and is generally understood to be primarily Western Hemlock.

Hem-Fir (Inland) – An unofficial designation developed to differentiate between Western Hemlock and the True Firs in the Hem-Fir group. Hem-Fir (Inland) refers to stock produced in Northern California and the Inland West, and is generally understood to be White Fir or a directly related species.

Hemicellulose – A gummy wood substance, intermediate in complexity between sugar and cellulose.

Hemlock – Tsuga heterophylla. This species, also called Western Hemlock, West Coast Hemlock, and, less commonly, Pacific Hemlock, is an important commercial species. It is found in a wide range in Washington, Oregon, California, Northern Idaho, and British Columbia. It is used in general construction and is also used heavily in the manufacture of pulp. Under grading rules adopted in 1970, this species is grouped under the designation "Hem-Fir." It is sometimes referred to as "Coast Hem-Fir" to distinguish it from White Fir and other species in the Hem-Fir group.

Hemlock Show – 1. A logging site composed predominantly of Hemlock. 2. An archaic term for any logging site that contained poor-quality timber.

Hemlock Spruce – Tsuga canadensis, Eastern Spruce.

Hem-Tam – A combination of Eastern Hemlock and Tamarack produced in the Northeastern United States and Eastern Canada.

Herbicide – A chemical substance that kills plants.

Herringbone Felling – To fell timber in a herringbone pattern toward the center of a skyline road.

Herringbone Figure – 1. A method of laying up face veneers where alternate joints show a V effect, while inverted V effects appear in intervening joints. 2. A parquet flooring pattern.

Hewing Dog – A metal bar used to hold a log steady while hewing.

Hewn Timber – A timber that has been squared with an ax or adz.

Hickey – A tool carried by a brakeman on logging trains. The brake hickey is designed to use with a brake wheel. It is thrust between the spokes of the brake wheel and hooked over the shaft to provide added leverage when applying brakes.

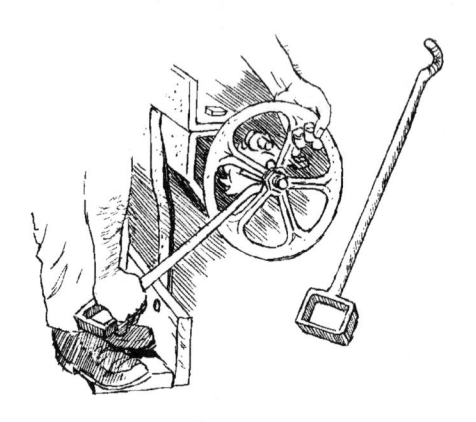

Hickey

Hickory – North American trees of the genus Carya: pecan, shagbark, shellbark, mockernut, and pignut.

Hickory Shirt – A heavy-duty cotton work shirt, often worn by woods workers. Characterized by narrow, light blue vertical stripes.

Hidden Defect – A defect in a log that is not apparent to the eye.

Hiding Cover – Vegetation used by wildlife for security.

Highball – To work at a high rate of speed, usually smoothly and efficiently. A fast, skilled logging operation is often said to be a "highball show."

Highclimber – A logger who climbs tall trees to top and limb them so they may serve as spar trees.

High Cube Car – A rail car with larger dimensions than a regular box car.

High Density Overlay – The surfacing of one or both faces of a plywood panel with a cellulose-fiber sheet or sheets containing not less that 45% resin solids, to provide a finished product that is hard and smooth so that further finishing is not necessary.

Himalayan Spruce

High Frequency Gluing – A gluing process often used in constructing laminated beams, but also used in other wood gluing applications. High frequency electronic waves are passed through the wood and glue to create a bond. An extremely rapid gluing process.

High Frequency Press – The press used in high frequency gluing.

High Grading – In logging, going through an area and taking out only the best quality logs. Also applicable to any process in which only the "cream" is taken.

High Humidity Treatment – Temporarily raising the humidity of the air circulating in a dry kiln to provide special treatment.

High Lead – A method of logging in which the logs are yarded from the cutting area to a landing using a cable system that holds the logs partially or totally off the ground to avoid obstructions. The cable system runs from a spar tree or pole to an anchor stump, with one end of the line rigged high on the spar tree to provide ground clearance.

High Line – A term indicating that a particular piece or shipment of lumber or other product is near the top end of the grade in which it falls. A high line piece of lumber nearly qualifies for the grade next above the one with which it is stamped. A high line shipment contains a large proportion of such pieces.

High Moisture Gluing – The layup of veneer using a resin that will bond with veneers having a higher moisture content, usually up to 12%, than the maximum under traditional gluing, which is about 5-7%.

High Pressure Laminate – A sheet of material formed from multiple layers of kraft paper saturated with phenolic resin, a decorative layer of paper saturated with melamine resin, and a thin top sheet of paper saturated with melamine resin. The layers are pressed together under high heat and pressure to form a stiff plastic sheet.

High Rigger – A specialist who rigs, or attaches cables to, a spar tree to yard logs to a landing.

High Site – As defined by the U.S. Forest Service, land that is capable of growing 85 cubic feet or more of wood per acre per year in fully stocked natural stands.

High Spar – A steel spar skidder.

High-Strain Bandsaw – A thin-kerf bandsaw operated at high tension to saw accurately with little waste.

High Temperature Drying – A method of drying lumber using a dry-bulb temperature in excess of 212 degrees Fahrenheit.

High Temperature Kiln – A dry kiln operated at a dry-bulb temperature above 212 degrees Fahrenheit.

Highway Logs – Logs purchased from a logger or trucker who brings a load to a manufacturing center for sale to the highest bidder. Also called Road Logs.

Highway Truck – A truck equipped for use on public, rather than private, roads. See Off-Highway Truck.

High Wheels – See Big Wheels.

Himalayan Spruce – A softwood species native to India that produces lumber used in

Highclimber

Hip

packing cases and other inexpensive applications.

Hip – The angle at the intersection of two inclined roof surfaces.

Hip and Ridge – Shingles manufactured for use on the portions of roofs referred to as hips and ridges, the creases in roofs formed by the planes of roof sections intersecting.

Hipped Roof – A roof with inclined ends instead of gables.

Hip Truss – A type of roof truss sloping upward from both ends to a flat center section.

Historical Exchange Rate – The rate applying at the date that an asset or liability was acquired, or at the date of subsequent change in the accounting valuation of the asset or liability.

Hit and Miss – A series of surfaced areas with skips not over 1/16-inch scant between them.

Hitchhiker – A log caught or entangled with other logs being drawn to a landing.

Hit or Miss – To skip-surface a piece of lumber for part or the whole of its length, provided that it is nowhere more than 1/16-inch scant.

Hoardings – In the European timber trade, small pieces of lumber used to construct a fence or barricade.

Hoedag – A tool shaped somewhat like a grubbing hoe and used for hand planting conifer seedlings. Also, hoedad.

Hog – A machine used to grind wood into chips for use as fuel or for other purposes; the wood used is usually waste wood unfit for lumber or other uses.

Hogged Fuel – Fuel made by grinding waste wood in a hog. Used to fire boilers or furnaces, often at the mill or plant at which the fuel was processed.

Hogshead – A barrel with a capacity of 48 to 54 gallons.

Hoist – A tripod used for loading logs.

Hokkaido Spruce – Picea glehnii. This conifer, native to the Far East, has properties similar to Yezo Spruce, one of the most important plantation trees in Japan.

Holdback – Another name for a haulback line.

Holddown – 1. A limit on the amount by which rail freight rates could be increased on a given commodity. Usually applied by carriers to preserve their competitive position on a specific item. Until the deregulation of transportation in the early 1980s, holddowns often were applied to increases in freight rates on lumber originating in the West to maintain a competitive relationship with southern lumber in Midwest markets. 2. See Veneer Holddown.

Holding Boom – A series of floating logs chained together end-to-end to hold logs in storage.

Holding Dam – An earthen dam used to store water for log drives.

Holding Ground – An area of water in which stored logs were held by floating booms for later release.

Holding Wedge – See Hanging Wedge.

Holding Wood – The part of a tree left uncut until the last, to aid in guiding the direction of the fall.

Hold Point – See Diversion Point.

Hold Track – See Diversion Point.

Hole Saw – A thin, narrow-bladed saw, or a barrel or ring saw, used to cut holes in panels or other surfaces.

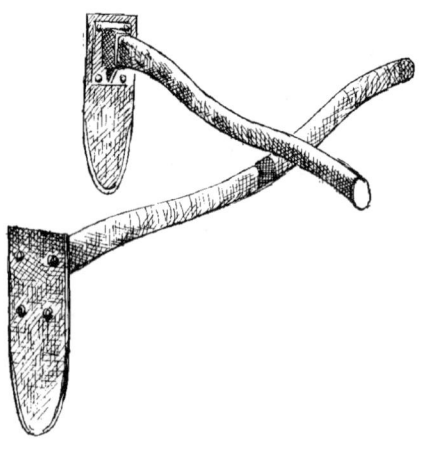

Hoedags

Hooktender

Holistic Forestry – A type of forestry that treats the ecosystem as a self-equilibrating mechanism and that espouses only minimal, site-specific interference with natural processes.

Hollow Backed – Boards or mouldings that have shallow grooves in the back to improve seating on uneven surfaces, or to reduce shipping weight.

Hollow Butt – A log with the center hollowed out by rot.

Hollow Core – Doors constructed with stiles and rails around the perimeter that are covered by a flat, veneered skin. Such doors usually have cross-bracing at one or two points but are otherwise hollow. See Flush Doors, Solid Core.

Home Center – A building supply store that carries a broad line of furnishings and appliances, window and floor coverings, etc., in addition to construction materials.

Home Loan Bank Board (HLBB) – The supervisory agency of the federally chartered savings and loan industry. HLBB establishes regulations on reserves and administers the depositor insurance program.

Home Owners Warranty Corporation (HOW) – A program under the National Association of Home Builders, through which builders warrant the structural qualities of new houses.

Home Tree – The spar tree at a landing.

Homogeneous Board – Particleboard manufactured with the same kind, size, and quality of furnish throughout its thickness.

Honduras Cedar – Another name for Spanish Cedar.

Honeycomb – A type of decay indicated by large pits in the wood.

Honeycomb Core – A sandwich core material for hardwood plywood that is constructed of thin sheet materials or ribbons formed to honeycomb-like configurations. Also used as a lightweight core in flush doors.

Hoofler – One who attaches the hook to logs to be loaded.

Hook Angle – The angle on a cutting tool affecting the ease in which the tooth penetrates the material being machined.

Hookaroon – See Pickaroon.

Hooker – The hooktender or foreman of a yarding crew.

Hook Hole – A perforation or puncture resulting from the use of hooks or tongs in moving a log or cant.

Hooks – See Climbing Irons.

Hooktender – The foreman of a high lead

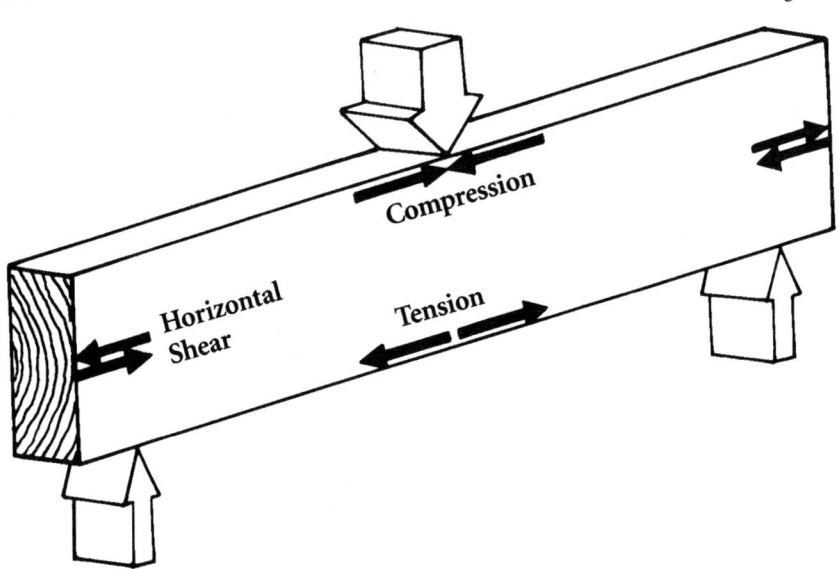

Horizonal Shear and Fiber Stresses

Terms Of The Trade

137

Hoop Pine

logging crew, who supervises all phases of yarding and loading logs.

Hoop Pine – Araucaria cunninghamii. This conifer, native to Australia, was once heavily logged and is now making a comeback in plantations in that country.

Hooter – A logger's term for a mature conifer that has grown in a more-or-less open area and has retained its limbs along the full length of the tree. Also called a Grouse Ladder.

Hootnanny – A device used to hold a crosscut saw while sawing a log from underneath.

Hoot Owl – A method of logging in which operations are carried out in the cool, early morning hours before heat and low humidity force the closure of the woods due to fire danger.

Hoppus Foot – A unit of measurement used primarily in the United Kingdom, India, Australia, and New Zealand. Hoppus measurement is used to measure the cubic volume of logs; one hoppus foot is roughly equivalent to 10 board feet.

Horizontal Resaw – A single or multiple bandsaw, mounted horizontally and used to break down slabs or cants from a headrig.

Horizontal Shear – A measurement of the resistance to shearing along the longitudinal axis of a piece of lumber. When a load is applied to a piece of lumber supported at each end, there is a stress over each support that tends to slide the fibers over each other horizontally. The internal force that resists this action is the horizontal shear value of the wood. The shearing action is maximum at the center of the depth of the piece. This stress rating is indicated by the symbol "Fv."

Horizontal Siding – Any exterior wall covering installed parallel to the ground.

Horn – 1. The extension of a stile, jamb, or sill. 2. The stub of a broken branch left on a log.

Horse – A piece of lumber that supports the treads and risers of a staircase.

Horse Dam – A temporary dam in a stream.

Horsefeathers – Beveled strips applied to

Steamed Logs in Hot Pond

Humboldt Undercut

wood shingle roofs when reroofing with asphalt shingles. Usually low-grade spruce, 3/8x4".

Horse Logging – A logging method in which horses are used to drag the logs to the landing for loading. Although not widely used today, this method is still employed by small operators, or in areas that cannot be logged using tractors because of potential damage to soils, etc.

Host Country – In international trade, the country in which a foreign subsidiary is located.

Hot and Cold Bath – Another name for thermal treatment. See Thermal Process.

Hot Deck – The supply of logs currently being used in a sawmill or veneer plant. Opposite of Cold Deck.

Hot Logging – To log and ship directly to a mill without intermediate storage.

Hot Melt Adhesive – An adhesive applied at an elevated temperature that becomes solid at room temperature.

Hot Pond – A vat of heated water used to condition logs before peeling into veneer, or flaking to produce furnish for waferboard or oriented strand board.

Hot Press – The method of producing plywood whereby adhesion of layers in the panel is accomplished by using a heat process, under pressure, to cure the gluelines.

Hot Water Extraction – The removal of a soluble substance by leaching with hot water.

24-Opening Hot Press

Hourly Rating – A measure of the ability of a type of construction to withstand fire. A one-hour rating means that the assembly will not collapse or transmit flame or high temperature for one hour after a fire starts.

Housed Mortise and Tenon Joint – A way of gaining extra support in a mortise and tenon joint by grooving the face of the mortised piece to accept the tenoned member.

Housewrap – A sheet of material placed between the wall sheathing and siding of a house to prevent air infiltration.

Housing Permit – See Building Permit.

Housing Start – The beginning of the construction of a new housing unit. A start is defined as having occurred when excavation for the foundation of the building begins. Monthly housing start figures are a closely watched measure of the health of the building industry and allied industries, such as forest products.

Housing Unit – As defined by the Commerce Department, a single room or group of rooms intended as separate living quarters for a family, a person living alone, or a group of unrelated persons living together.

Howe Truss – A wood roof truss design for large spans.

Hub Tree – See Head Tree, Head Spar.

Huckle – Green spruce dimension lumber of standard thickness and 1/4-inch scant of nominal size in width. It was used mainly in Eastern Canadian markets until about 1970, but is no longer produced in quantity.

Hudson Bay Pine – Another name for Jackpine, Pinus banksiana.

Hudson's Bay Ax – A single-bitted light ax, modeled after one provided by the Hudson's Bay Co., and often used to mark or "blaze" trees.

Humboldt Face – See Humboldt Undercut.

Humboldt Scale – A log measurement used in the Redwood country.

Humboldt Undercut – An undercut chunk taken out of the stump side in power saw felling to provide a log with an end cut straight across.

Terms Of The Trade

Hummer Head

Hummer Head – A cutterhead on a debarker. Also called a rosser head.

Humpback – A log truck returning to the woods with its trailer on its back.

Humpback Tip – A defect in Red Cedar shakes in which the tip of the shake is of an excess thickness.

Humped Shipment – A rail shipment that has been damaged when another car has slammed into it, jarring the contents. Humping is a method of making up freight trains by allowing individual cars to roll down a slight incline until they hook up with the cars that preceded them. It was a common cause of damaged shipments, but the term is used more broadly to describe shipments damaged by any sudden impact to the rail car. Actual humping damage is less common today due to the use of more sophisticated equipment in rail yards.

Humping – The use of sloped tracks in a rail yard to assemble trains. Spurs in the yard may be sloped for long distances in order that cars can roll along them without a locomotive. Cars are directed to a spur where a train is being made up by signals from the yard tower.

Humus – Organic material in soil, formed by the decomposition of leaves, etc.

Hundred – See Standard.

Hung Tree – A tree that hangs up in another tree when felled.

Hunting License Sale – A slang reference to the area salvage sales conducted by the U.S. Forest Service. See Area Salvage.

Huon Pine – A softwood tree native to Tasmania.

Husk – On a circular saw headrig, that part of the system including the arbor, saw, saw guide, and splitter.

Hydrapulper – An open-topped tank in which baled pulp is mixed with water to create a pulp slurry which can then be fed onto a moving wire mesh to make paper.

Hydraulic Barking – A method of removing bark from logs using water jets.

Hydraulic Cutting – The use of a water jet in paper making to trim the edges of a wet web of paper.

Hydrometer – An instrument used to measure the specific gravity of a liquid.

Hygrometer – An instrument used in measuring the moisture content of circulating air.

Hygroscopicity – The ability of a material, such as wood, to absorb moisture readily.

Hygroscopic Water – Water contained within the cell walls of unseasoned wood. Also called "bound" water.

Hypothecate – To pledge, without delivery of title or possession, as in assigning invoices for collateral.

Hypsometer – A device for determining the height or elevation of an object.

Hysteresis – The tendency of dried wood exposed to any specified temperature and relative humidity conditions to reach equilibrium at a lower moisture content from a drier condition than when losing moisture from a wetter condition.

Humboldt Undercut

I Beam – A beam whose cross section resembles the letter "I"; one in which the top and bottom chords (such as 2x4s) are connected by thinner material (such as plywood).

Ice Allowance – An allowance for the weight of ice or snow on a rail car load so that it is not included when figuring freight charges.

Idaho Cedar – Another name for Western Red Cedar.

Idaho Pine – Another name for Western White Pine.

Idaho White Pine – Another name for Western White Pine.

Identification Index – An index to the relative stiffness of plywood panels. No longer in use. See Span Rating.

Idler Car – A flat car used in the movement of bulky items that extend beyond the length of the car carrying them. The shipment does not rest on the idler car, but overhangs it.

Imbricated – The pattern formed by overlapping tiles or shingles on a roof.

Immature – A reference to trees that have grown past the regeneration stage, but are not yet mature.

Immersion Tank – A tank containing wood preservative in which lumber is treated by absorbing the chemicals.

Impact Insulation Class – An evaluation system that rates the capacity of floor assemblies to control impact noise such as footfalls.

Impact Resistance – The ability of an object to withstand forceful blows or violent contact without losing its integrity.

Imperfect Manufacture – Damage, such as torn grain or machine burn, done to a product during manufacture.

Impingement Drying – See Jet Drying.

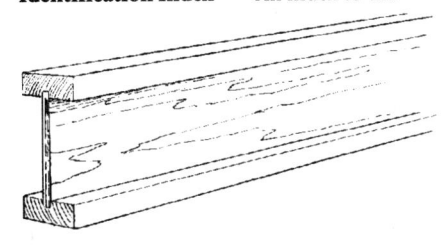

I Beam

Terms Of The Trade

Importance Factor

Importance Factor – A factor used in building design to measure the consequence of collapse relating to the use and occupancy of the structure.

Impost – The cap, or top, of a support for an arch.

Impreg – Veneer infused with resin, which is then dried, stacked, and cured under low pressure.

Impregnation – Preservation of a product by penetrating it in a vacuum with an oil, mineral, or chemical solution.

Improved Wood – Wood treated to reduce absorption of moisture, usually through impregnation with a synthetic resin under pressure.

Inbark – Bark enclosed in the wood of a tree by growth and subsequently exposed by manufacture.

Incense Cedar – Libocedrus decurrens. This species ranges from Northern Oregon to Southern California. Its wood is aromatic and is extremely durable when seasoned. It is used in pencil manufacture, and for many of the same uses as Western Red Cedar.

Incentive Per Diem – A rental charge applied to off-line rail cars to encourage their quick return.

Incentive Rate – A reduced freight rate provided for rail shipments that meet a specified minimum weight. Used to encourage fuller utilization of rail equipment, and to recapture traffic lost to other forms of transportation.

Incidental Take – As used in the language of the Endangered Species Act, to "take" an individual member of a protected species while conducting lawful activities such as forestry or land development. See Take.

Incipient Decay – The early stage of decay in which the disintegration has not proceeded far enough to soften or otherwise perceptibly change the quality of the wood.

Incising – Cutting slits into the surfaces of a piece of wood prior to preservative treatment to improve absorption.

Incline – A system that permitted logs to be lowered down a steep slope on railroad cars. On some inclines, logs were lowered by cable from a stationary engine. Others used a power plant that traveled up and down the incline.

Incline Roller – A roll or spool used to guide yarding lines.

Included Sapwood – Irregular areas of light-colored wood included in the darker heart wood.

Inconvertible Currency – A currency that cannot be converted to another, usually because of exchange control regulations.

Incoterms – International Chamber of Commerce rules for the interpretation of trade terms.

Increased Coverage – See Extraordinary Coverage.

Increment Borer – An auger-like instrument with a hollow bit, commonly used to extract cores from trees for growth and density determinations. Also called an Increment Corer.

Increment Corer – See Increment Borer.

Indentation – A depression on the surface of a particleboard panel, caused by caul defects or by foreign material stuck to the caul or press platen.

Indented Rings – The growth rings of a piece of wood that, when seen in cross section, contain small, recurring indentations.

Indian Pine – Another name for Loblolly Pine.

Indicator Species – A plant or animal species that signifies certain environmental conditions.

Indigenous – In wood technology, a species of wood native to a particular area or region; one that has not been introduced.

Indirect Quotation – An exchange rate quoted as certain number of units of home currency per one unit of foreign currency.

Industrial – 1. A grade of Idaho White Pine, equivalent to #4 common in other species of boards. 2. Industrial corestock particleboard, used in the manufacture of furniture, doors, etc. 3. A general term for lumber destined for remanufacture or further seasoning.

Industrial Account – A customer who is

primarily a manufacturer of products such as window sash, boats, or truck bodies. Usually a direct buyer of specific items from a manufacturer or wholesaler.

Industrial Grade – The lowest of three appearance grades of glue laminated beams. Intended for use where appearance is secondary, as in industrial buildings.

Industrial Paper – Heavy duty paper used in packaging, etc.

Industrial Roundwood – All commercial roundwood products except firewood.

Infill Framing – Smaller members interspersed between the load-bearing columns in post-and-beam construction, to which panels enclosing the structure can be attached.

Infiltration – The process through which organic matter has been encompassed during a tree's growth, but is not a part of the wood.

Infrastructure – The network of transportation, communications, and other facilities that support the economic and social activities of a nation.

In-Grade Testing – Testing of the design values of lumber within a particular grade. An in-grade testing program was undertaken in the late 1970s by U.S. grading agencies and the U.S. Forest Products Laboratory to develop data to more accurately define design values of various species, sizes, and grades of lumber.

In-Haul Line – The main line of a high lead logging system.

Inholding – Land belonging to one landowner that is located in, and surrounded by, land owned by another.

Initial Absorption – The absorption of preservative before pressure is applied.

Initial Moisture Content – The moisture content of wood at the start of the drying process.

Initial Weight – See Green Weight.

Inland Hem-Fir – See Hem-Fir (Inland).

Inland Red Cedar – Western Red Cedar growing in the Inland West region of the U.S.

Inland Region – This region is generally considered to include those parts of Oregon and Washington east of the Cascades, along with Idaho and Montana. Also sometimes referred to as the "Inland Empire."

In-Line Joint – A butt joint made by placing two pieces end-to-end and fastening them together with a splicing piece nailed on each side of the joint.

Inner Bead – A small moulding attached to the inside of a window frame, against which the sash containing the glass slides.

Inner Plies – Those layers of veneer used between the face and back of a piece of plywood.

Inquiry – A solicitation by a potential

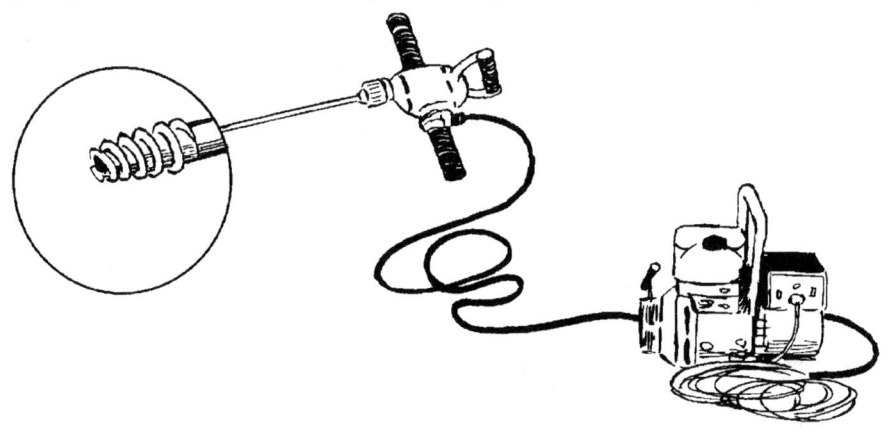

Increment Borer

Insert

buyer to a seller concerning a particular item or items sought by the buyer. The inquirer seeks to ascertain if the seller has the item available and its cost; an inquiry is not considered an offer to buy.

Insert – A patch, plug, or shim used to replace a defect in a plywood veneer.

Inserted Tooth Saw – A saw to which specially hardened teeth have been attached.

Inside Sales – Selling done from an office or other central location, as opposed to selling conducted "on the road."

Insignis Pine – Another name for Radiata Pine, Pinus radiata.

Inspection Certificate – See Certificate of Inspection.

Instant – A credit term meaning "this month."

Insulation Board – A board made from ligno-cellulosic fibers, usually wood or cane, which are interfelted to create the principal source of bond. Asphalt or other materials may be added in manufacture, but insulation board is not consolidated under heat and pressure in a separate manufacturing step, as are particleboard and hardboard.

Insulation Value – The ability of a material to resist heat flow. Stated as "R," or thermal resistance value.

Integrated – 1. A production operation containing more than one processing plant at a single location, such as a complex including both a sawmill and a pulp mill. 2. A company that controls production and distribution steps from the raw material to the location of a finished product in a marketplace. See Vertical Integration.

Intense Fire – One that burns hot enough to consume much of the forest floor along with most of the vegetation and surface fuels in a stand.

Intensive Management – Management practices intended to increase the fiber production of a forest. Techniques include site preparation, genetic selection, planting, weed and pest control, fertilization, thinning, and harvesting.

Intercoastal – Between sea coasts; shipments of forest products by waterborne carrier from the western U.S. to the eastern seaboard. Shipments from British Columbia are broadly classed as Intercoastal, although technically they are exports from Canada.

Intergrown Knot – See Knot Quality.

Interior Bulkhead Door – A moveable wall inside a rail boxcar, used to help secure a load.

Interior Glue Line – A type of bonding used in the production of plywood. "Interior" refers to the fact that plywood constructed with this type of glue is suitable for interior, or protected, applications. The glue is not suitable for outdoor use, since repeated exposure to moisture may cause delamination.

Interior Region – In British Columbia, that region east of the Cascades, on a line projected from Hope to Terrace.

Interior Underlayment – A type of particleboard used as subflooring.

Interlaced – 1. Strips of wood that have been interwoven, as in a fence. 2. Wood grain in which the fibers are interwoven.

Interlaced Arches – Arches that pass over two openings so that they intersect.

Interlocked Grain – A condition in lumber or other wood products in which fibers are inclined in one direction in a number of annual rings, then gradually reverse and are inclined in an opposite direction in succeeding growth rings.

Interlock Yarder – A yarder in which the main and haulback drums can be coupled to re-use the power provided.

Intermediate Crown Class – Trees that are under the general forest canopy layer and receive little light from above and no light from the sides. They have much competition for space from neighboring trees.

Intermediate Glue Line – A type of glue used in the manufacture of plywood. Its adhesive qualities are higher than those required for interior panels, but do not meet the accepted standards for exterior panels.

Intermediate Moisture Content – The moisture content of wood during the drying process. Measured after the initial moisture content but before the final moisture content.

Intermediate Trees – See Intermediate

Crown Class.

Intermodal Transportation – A shipment carried by a combination of types of transport, such as truck-rail-truck.

Internal Bond – The particle-to-particle bond in reconstituted panel products, measured in pounds per square inch. Internal bond is tested by gluing metal blocks to the face of a panel and measuring the force needed to separate the particles.

Internal Bond Strength – A measure of a particleboard panel's integrity, tested by applying tension perpendicular to the panel surface. Measured in pounds per square inch.

International 1/8-Inch Scale – This log scale, a forerunner of the International 1/4-inch Scale, was developed about 1900. Like its successor, it was one of the few rules to incorporate a basis for dealing with taper in a log. Also known as Clark's International Rule, for its developer, Judson Clark.

International 1/4-Inch Scale – This log scale, a modification of an earlier rule using a 1/8-inch kerf, is based on an analysis of the loss of wood fiber incurred in the conversion of sawlogs to lumber. It is one of the few rules incorporating a basis for dealing with log taper. One of several widely used log scales.

Internode – The length of a stem between branches or leaf attachments.

Interrupted Arch – An arch-shape pediment from which the center has been cut away.

Interstate Commerce Commission (ICC) – The federal agency regulating railroads and trucking lines.

Intertie – A horizontal member just above the doorway in an interior wall.

In the Round – Felled trees or logs before manufacture. Round logs.

In the White – Natural, untreated, or unpainted wood.

Intolerant – Plant species that cannot survive under adverse conditions, such as dense shade.

In-Transit Privileges – These permit changes in the degree of manufacture or treatment during shipment while retaining the original freight rate.

Intraplant Switch – The respotting, by a railroad, of rail cars on a customer's property.

Intumescence – The swelling that occurs in a fire-retardant coating when it is heated.

In-Use Moisture Content – The moisture content that wood attains in the environmental conditions of usage.

Inventory – As defined by the U.S. Forest Service, the net volume, in cubic feet, of growing stock trees.

Inverted Arch – An upside-down arch placed between piers to distribute pressure.

Inverted Market – In futures trading, a market in which the nearer months are selling at premiums to the more distant months; characteristically, a market in which supplies are tight.

Invisible Supply – In futures trading, a reference to uncounted stocks of a commodity in the hands of wholesalers and producers, which cannot be identified accurately but are theoretically available to the market.

Invoice – An itemized list of goods shipped, and their prices; a bill.

Ionic – One of the five classical orders of Greek architecture.

Iowa Commons – A term used to describe construction lumber specified by the Iowa State Highway Commission. The specifications of the commission are very similar to the #1 and Construction grades described in the grading rules of the WCLIB and WWPA.

Irish Standard – See Dublin Standard.

Iron Stain – A blue-black stain on oak and other woods containing tannin; caused by contact with iron under damp conditions.

Ironwood – A hard, heavy wood such as Hornbeam (Carpinus caroliniana) in North America.

Item – A quantity of lumber or other product of a given size, grade, length, etc.

J

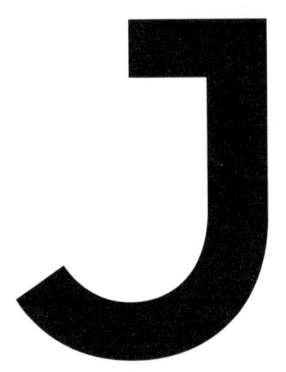

Jack – 1. A tool used in felling trees. Using a jack, a faller can overcome a tree's natural lean and fall the tree in a particular, desired direction. 2. A tool used to stack lumber; it acts as a fulcrum on which pieces of lumber can be levered from one pile to another. 3. Short for lumberjack.

Jack Arch – An arch with horizontal or nearly horizontal upper and lower surfaces; a straight or flat arch.

Jack Beam – A beam that supports another beam, eliminating the need for a column.

Jack Chain – A chain used to convey logs from the pond into the sawmill.

Jacket Board – A board produced incidentally when cutting a log into lumber. The jacket board is usually developed from the first slab cut by the head rig.

Jack Ladder – A type of conveyer used to bring logs up into a manufacturing plant. Same as a Jack Chain.

Jack Pine – Pinus banksiana. This species is found in East Central Canada and the Great Lakes states. It is generally small in size, and is used primarily for studs and pulpwood.

Jack Rafters – Short rafters that support the roof in a hip, or between a valley and ridge.

Jack Saw – A hand-operated drag saw that can be folded.

Jackscrew – See Screw Jack.

Jackstraw – 1. A log deck in which logs have been piled without order. 2. A pile of anything in which individual items are left as they fell.

Jack Works – A loading dock parallel to railroad tracks, from which logs are transferred to rail cars.

Jacob's Staff – A bar suspended from the axle of "big wheels" log transporters and used to raise logs. Also called a Johnson Board.

Jagger – A broken strand projecting from a worn cable.

Jags – Odds and ends left in an inventory; quantities too small to make up a unit.

Jail Hook – A large, partially closed hook designed to prevent a chain or cable from slipping out when the line goes slack.

Jalousie

Jalousie – A window blind or shutter made with horizontal slats mounted at an angle to give protection from the elements.

Jam – A pile of logs caught on an obstruction in running water.

Jamb – Either of the sides of an opening; the vertical pieces at the sides of a doorway.

Jambliner – A casing for an interior door.

Jamb Stock – Material from which jambs are manufactured, for use at the sides of a doorway or window.

Jammer – A type of block and tackle used on an A-Frame to lift logs for loading.

Jam Pike – A type of heavy pike pole used by river men in log drives. See Pike Pole.

Japanese Agricultural Standard (JAS) – Japanese grading rules for lumber used in platform construction in Japan. Also known as the 1974 Standard for Platform Frame Construction.

Japanese Fir – Abies sachalinensis. A coniferous tree growing in the Far East, yielding light, pale-colored wood. Also called Todomatsu.

Japanese Redwood – Cryptomeria japonica. Another name for Sugi, a straight-grained, deciduous tree native to Asia and commonly used for plywood.

Jap Square – An obsolete term for roughly squared logs, usually 12x12 or larger, shipped to Japan in the 1930s for further processing.

J-Bar – A hanger, or jack, used to support a logging cable.

Jeffrey Pine – Pinus jeffreyi. This pine is found in Southern Oregon and Northern California. It resembles Ponderosa Pine and its wood is marketed as Ponderosa.

Jelecote Pine – Pinus patula. This species, a native of Mexico, is sometimes referred to as the "most feminine" of all the Pines, due to its delicate, drooping needles. Also called Spreading-leaf Pine.

Jemmy John – See Pede.

Jerkinhead – A gable roof with a secondary slope that forms a hip.

Jerrybuilt – Poorly constructed, flimsy.

Jersey Pine – Another name for Virginia Pine.

Jesting Beam – A beam with no structural purpose, used to adorn a building.

Jet Drying – A process of applying heated air at high velocity from small nozzles perpendicular to a drying surface. Also called Impingement Drying.

Jew Plank – An obsolete term for scant-sawn plank shipped to Atlantic Seaboard markets.

J-Grade – Stock that has been segregated from regular production to meet the specifications of the Japanese market for 2-inch dimension.

Jib Crane – A crane which has a derrick from which the load is suspended.

Jigsaw – A narrow saw mounted vertically in a frame for sawing curves.

Jim Crow Load – A load consisting of a single large log.

Jinnie – One of several names for a drag used to haul logs from the woods to the skidway.

Jitney – A small passenger vehicle following a prescribed route.

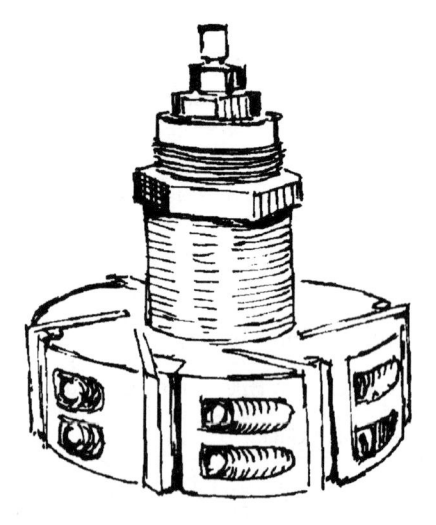

Jointer Head

Juniper

Jobber – A wholesaler; one who buys goods in quantity from a manufacturer and resells them to retail stores.

Jobsite – A construction site, where building is taking place.

Johnson Board – See Jacob's Staff.

Joinery – A term used in Europe to denote the higher grades of lumber suitable for such uses as cabinetry, millwork, or interior trim.

Joint – The place where two or more pieces of material meet.

Jointed Core – Core veneer that has had its edges machine-squared to permit the tightest possible layup.

Jointed Lumber – Lumber that has had its edges machined square to provide the tightest possible fit between pieces.

Jointer – The machine used to square edges of lumber or panels, especially to prepare them for edge gluing.

Joint Line – Two or more railroads sharing the same line.

Joint Move – Rail car movement involving two or more railroads.

Joint Rate – A rate that two or more transportation units have agreed will be charged to move goods from a point located on one transportation system to a point on another system.

Joint Through Rate – A freight rate established to cover interline movement. It is different from a joint rate in that it may be composed of a combination of joint or local rates. Generally, the only legal rate between points where it has been established.

Joint Treatment – The method of sealing the space between panels that is left to provide for expansion. Sealing may be provided by caulking, Z flashing, shiplapped joints, etc.

Joist – A piece of lumber two to four inches thick and six or more inches wide, used horizontally as a support for a ceiling or floor. Also, such a support made from steel, aluminum, or other material.

Joist Hanger – A pre-formed metal device used to hold joists at right angles to another structural member. They act somewhat like a stirrup to provide secure support for the

Joist Hanger

ends of joists, eliminating toe-nailing.

Joist Spacing – The distance between joists, usually measured from the center of one joist to the center of the next.

Jones Act – A law, in effect since 1920, that requires shippers to use American-flag vessels when shipping goods between U.S. ports. As a consequence of the law, it is less expensive to ship wood products from Alaska to Japan than from Alaska to other U.S. points.

Jumbo Block – A very heavy block used in cable logging.

Jumbo Shake – A shake that is split and or sawn to a thickness of 1-inch or more at the butt.

Jump – 1. To move a spar tree by alternately loosening and tightening guy lines as another line pulls the butt forward. 2. To move a log caught on an obstruction by rigging the choker to make it "jump" over the obstruction.

Jumper – A small wooden sled used to haul pulpwood.

Jump Saw – A circular cross-cut saw that can be raised and lowered.

Junction Point – The connecting point where two or more rail lines meet.

Juniper – Any of 50 to 70 species of trees and shrubs. Juniperus virginiana is Eastern Red Cedar, widely distributed in the Eastern U.S. and Ontario. There are 10 western junipers, of which Juniperus communis is most widespread.

Terms Of The Trade

Junkbutt

Junkbutt – The badly splintered end of a felled tree that has been cut back to sound wood.

Just-In-Time Buying – The practice of waiting as long as possible to buy, and then taking only enough stock to meet immediate needs. A common practice in a weak or shaky market.

Juvenile Wood – The initial wood formed adjacent to the pith, often characterized by lower specific gravity, lower strength, higher longitudinal shrinkage, and different microstructure than mature wood. Also called core wood, pith wood, crown-formed wood.

K

Kahikatea – Podocarpus dacryaioides. This species, indigenous to New Zealand, yields fine-grained pale yellow to yellow-brown wood used for general construction purposes. Also called New Zealand White Pine.

Katydid – Another name for the Big Wheels used to move logs in the western pine region.

Kauri Pine – Agathis australis. A softwood tree indigenous to Malaysia, Australia, New Guinea, New Zealand, and Fiji. It produces lumber suitable for a variety of uses, from joinery and pattern-making to general construction and crates. Not a true pine.

KD Furniture – Furniture that has been "knocked down," or disassembled, for shipment, usually to a consumer.

KD Saps – A Southern Yellow Pine export clear grade. It requires that 80% of the pieces be free from knots on both sides.

Keel Arch – An inverted arch with the keystone at the lowest point.

Keel Moulding – A moulding that, in section, resembles a ship's keel.

Kerf – The width of a saw cut. This portion of a log is lost as waste when it is sawn for lumber, although the residue can be used as fuel or for other purposes. The size of a kerf is dependent on saw thickness, saw type, sharpness, and other factors.

Kerf Chip – The piece cut out of material by a saw; sawdust.

Kerfing – In millworking, longitudinal saw cuts or machined grooves of varying depths made on the unexposed faces of mill-

Kerf

Kerosene Bottle

work members to relieve stress and prevent warping.

Kerosene Bottle – A bottle carried by fallers in the cross-cut saw days. The kerosene was used to prevent the saw from binding on resin or gum.

Key – A wedge of wood or metal inserted in a joint to limit movement.

Keyhole Saw – See Hole Saw.

Key Length – Lumber of specific lengths favored for a particular use or application. Each width of dimension lumber has certain key lengths, e.g 14- foot in 2x10 and 16-foot in 2x12. In the past, 2x4-16s were key lengths because two eight-foot studs could be cut from them on the jobsite.

Key Log – The primary log in a jam. Once the key log was freed, the jam would break up.

Khasya Pine – Pinus khaya. Native to India, Burma, Thailand, Indochina, and the Philippines. A light-colored wood used in home building and mining. Also called Benguet Pine.

Kick – The throwing back of wood from machinery due to defect or careless handling.

Kick Back – 1. The reaction of a tree which, when felled, kicks back toward the faller. 2. A cant or board ejected from a circular saw when the saw teeth bind and the cant is not held firmly enough. 3. The excess preservative released from the wood when the pressure in a treating cylinder is released.

Kick Board – A board, usually 1x12, used as part of a fence. The kick board is attached horizontally to the bottom of a fence at ground level.

Kickout – The failure of a temporary support or brace.

Kilderkin – A barrel with an 18-gallon capacity.

Killig Pole – In the early logging days, a pole used to push against a tree being felled to guide its direction of fall.

Kiln – See Dry Kiln.

Kiln Burn – A darkening or scorching on the surface of lumber that sometimes occurs when the lumber is dried in a kiln.

Kiln Charge – One full load for a kiln; the amount of lumber processed in a kiln at any one time.

Kiln Checks – Small seasoning checks that occur during the drying process.

Kiln Dried – Lumber that has been seasoned in a kiln to a predetermined moisture content.

Kiln Dried After Treatment (KDAT) – Treated lumber that has been seasoned in a kiln to a predetermined moisture content following the treating process.

Kiln Dried Saps – See KD Saps.

Kiln Sample – A piece cut from a board and placed in the kiln charge, so that it may be removed for examination, weighing, or testing.

Kiln Schedule – A sequence of temperatures used to kiln-dry lumber with a minimum of defects.

Kiln Seasoned – See Kiln Dried.

Kiln Stick – A 1x2 or 2x4 piece used between layers of wood to improve air circulation within the pile.

Kiln Truck – A wheeled framework designed to hold a load of lumber for drying in a kiln. Used in kilns with tracks.

Kiln Wet – Lumber that has been removed from the kiln before it has dried to the required moisture content.

King Log – The key log in a log jam.

King Post – The vertical piece in the center of a roof truss.

Kingpost Truss – A type of pitched roof truss containing a single vertical web at the center.

King William Pine – Athrotaxis selaginoides. A workable, straight-grained wood used in cabinets, pattern work, and general carpentry. Also called King Billy Pine, Tasmanian Pine.

Kinks – A form of warp in which there are sharp deviations from flatness or straightness due to exceptionally abrupt grain distortions, such as around knots, or due to the piece being sharply bent by misplaced stickers in stacking for drying.

Knot Quality

Kip – A unit of weight or force equal to 1,000 pounds.

Kiwi Pine – Another name for Radiata Pine, Pinus radiata.

Knee Bolter – A type of saw and carriage used in preparing shingle bolts.

Knee Brace – An angle brace between horizontal and upright members, used to make a structure more stable.

Knee Wall – A short wall between roof rafters and ceiling joints.

Knife Check – Checks occurring on the face of lumber or plywood due to dull knives or lathe blades.

Knifegrinder – See Set-Up Man.

Knife Marks – Imprints or markings of machine knives on the surface of dressed lumber or on veneer, usually due to dull or chipped knives.

Knobcone Pine – Pinus attenuata. A three-needle pine found on dry slopes of Southwestern Oregon, California, and Nevada.

Knocked Down – Taken apart for easy shipment; an unassembled box.

Knot – A branch or limb embedded in a tree and cut through in the process of manufacturing. Knots are classified according to size, quality and occurrence. In lumber, the size classifications are: Pin knot, one not over 1/2-inch in diameter; Small, a knot larger than 1/2-inch but not over 3/4-inch; Medium, larger than 3/4-inch but not over 1-1/2-inches; Large, over 1-1/2-inches in diameter.

Knot Bumper – A logger who works in a landing area, cutting limbs and knots off of logs. Also, a brand name for a type of ax.

Knot Cluster – See Knot Occurrence.

Knot Hole – The hole that occurs in a piece of wood when a knot, or embedded branch, falls out.

Knot Occurrence – Knots are classified by the way they occur in a piece of lumber. Types of occurrences include: 1. Branch knots, two or more divergent knots sawed lengthwise and tapering toward the pith at a common point. 2. Corner knot, one located at the intersection of adjacent faces. 3. Cluster, two or more knots grouped together, the fibers of the wood being deflected around the entire unit. 4. Single knot, one occurring by itself, the fibers of the wood being deflected around it. 5. Spike, a knot sawed in a lengthwise direction.

Knot Quality – In addition to size, knots are classified according to quality. Classifications include: 1. Unsound, a knot that contains any degree of decay. 2. Encased, a knot whose rings of annual growth are not intergrown with those of the surrounding wood. 3. Intergrown, a knot partially or completely intergrown on one or two faces with the growth rings of the surrounding wood. 4. Loose, a knot not held tightly in place by growth or position, one that cannot be relied on to remain in place. 5. Fixed, a knot that will hold its place in a dry piece under ordinary conditions; one that can be moved under pressure but not easily pushed out of the surrounding wood. 6. Pith, a sound knot containing a pith hole not over 1/4-inch in diameter. 7. Sound, a knot that is solid across the face, as hard as the surrounding wood, and shows no indications of decay. 8. Star-checked, a knot having radial checks. 9. Tight, a knot fixed by growth or position so as to retain its place. 10. Firm, a knot that is solid across its face but contains incipient decay. 11. Watertight, a knot whose annual rings of growth are completely intergrown

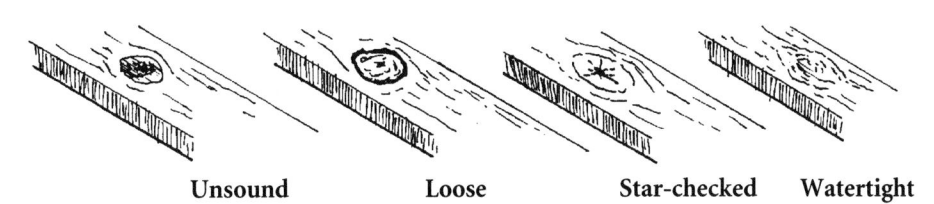

Unsound   Loose   Star-checked   Watertight

Knot Quality

Terms Of The Trade

Knot Saw

with those of the surrounding wood on one surface of the piece, and which is sound on the surface.

Knot Saw – A small circular saw used to cut defects from shingles.

Knotting Ax – A light, short-handled, double-bitted ax used to clear roads.

Knotty Paneling – Paneling, often of pine, sawn to expose firm knots as an appearance feature.

Knotty Pine – See Knotty Paneling.

Knuckleboom Loader – A jointed loading boom whose action imitates the human arm.

Knucklejoint – The curb joint in a mansard roof.

Koku – A Japanese unit of measurement, equivalent to 110 board feet, or 0.255 of a cubic meter.

Korean Pine – Pinus koraiensis. A plantation conifer commonly grown in Korea and China. It has a wide variety of uses ranging from home construction to boat building.

Kraft – A heavy paper or paperboard made from wood pulp using a method of boiling wood chips in a sodium sulfate solution. Kraft paper is typically used for packaging materials such as corrugated paper or grocery bags.

Kyan's Process – A way of preserving wood by infusing it with bichloride of mercury.

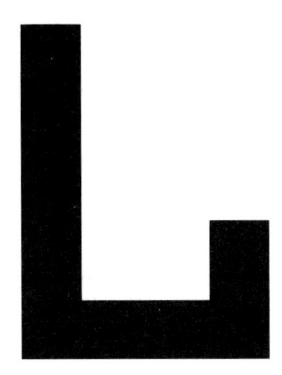

Label – A moulding that extends across the top of a door or window and downward for a distance on the sides.

Lac – A resinous substance deposited on trees in southern Asia by the female lac insect. It is collected and used in the manufacture of shellac and other varnishes.

Laced Column – A support used in temporary buildings. It consists of four timbers held together by diagonal braces on the sides.

Laced Corner – A method of laying shingles on sidewalls. The corner shingles of each course are laid alternately on the faces of the two walls.

Ladder Rails – The two long side pieces of a ladder to which the rungs are attached. Ladder rails are a special grade of kiln dried lumber, usually Douglas Fir, Western Hemlock, or Sitka Spruce. See Ladder Stock.

Ladder Rounds – The rungs of a ladder, on which one stands.

Ladder Stock – A high grade of lumber, usually entirely without knots or defect, restricted to pieces showing a growth rate of no less than six annual rings per inch and meeting strict slope of grain requirements. Ladder rails and ladder rail stock are seasoned and surfaced to meet additional requirements to provide serviceability and safety.

Lagging – Lumber used with mining timbers to shore up a mine or pit. It usually consists of low grade planking, which is used on the outside and above the supporting set of timbers.

Lamb's Tongue – A type of moulding used to form the sash bars that divide, into smaller squares, the glass in a window frame.

Laminate – To bond together two or more pieces of wood to make a single piece, using adhesive and pressure. Also, the product of such a procedure.

Laminated Root Rot – A fungal disease caused by Phellinus weirii. It attacks most conifer species in the western United States and Canada. The infection spreads from tree to tree via root contact. Infection in a young stand of trees can occur when roots of the young trees contact residual infested stumps and roots from preceding stands. The fungus is slow-acting, and symptoms may not be visible for 5 to 15 years after the initial infection. The disease takes its common name from the appearance of wood affected by the later stages of decay; the wood tends to sepa-

Laminated Veneer Lumber (LVL)

rate in layers along annual rings, giving the appearance of being laminated.

Laminated Veneer Lumber (LVL) – Structural wood members constructed of veneers laminated to make a "flitch" from which pieces of specific sizes can be trimmed.

Laminated Veneer Products – See Laminated Veneer Lumber.

Laminboard – A compound board consisting of a core of small strips of wood glued together and covered by veneer faces. See Blockboard.

Laminwood – See Laminboard.

Lam Stock – Special grades of wood used in constructing laminated beams.

Lancet Arch – A Gothic arch with a radius of curvature greater than the span.

Land Bridge – Part of a shipping system in which freight is shipped by water, unloaded at a port, shipped by rail or truck across a body of land, then reloaded on a ship to complete shipment to another country. For example, the continental U.S. may serve as a land bridge for a shipment originating in Europe and destined for Japan.

Landed Costs – The total cost, including freight, insurance, fees, etc., required to place an inventory in a consuming area. Usually used in reference to waterborne shipments.

Landing – 1. A collecting point for logs; the place to which logs are yarded for loading and transportation from the woods. 2. A floor or platform between flights of stairs.

Landing Cant Hook – A short-handled version of the cant hook, a peavey-like pole used to handle logs on land.

Landing Charges – Fees levied by a port on imports passing through the port.

Landing Hooker – The loading foreman at a landing.

Landing Tree – A tree or spar at a loading point, or landing.

Land Sales Contract – A contract in which the seller retains title to property until the buyer has paid the full purchase price.

Landscape – 1. A portion of land that can be seen from one viewpoint. 2. To improve the appearance of an area by planting or changing the ground contours.

Lap – 1. A situation in which one piece of material lies over an adjacent piece. 2. Debris (slash) remaining after logging.

Lap Joint – The joint formed when one piece of material is placed partly over another and bonded by nails or adhesive.

Lap Siding – See Bevel Siding.

Larch – Larix occidentalis. This softwood species, officially Western Larch but also called Mountain Larch and Western Tamarack, is native to Eastern Oregon and Washington, Idaho, Montana, and the southern interior of British Columbia. It is used for construction lumber and plywood, and is often intermixed with Douglas Fir since the two have very similar structural qualities. It is one of two conifers that sheds their needles in winter.

Large Chamber Test – A controlled environmental chamber test designed to measure formaldehyde emissions of panels bonded with urea formaldehyde.

Larrigans – See Shoepack.

Laser Line – A line of light projected on a cant, used as a cutting guide at the edger.

Lash Pole – A cross piece used to hold floating logs together in a log raft.

Last In, First Out (LIFO) – A method of accounting for inventory in which it is assumed that goods bought last are sold first. This allows automatic updating of inventory values.

Last Trading Day – The day on which trading ceases for the maturing (or current) delivery month in the futures markets.

Lateral Brace – A temporary purlin attached to the top chords of roof trusses to support them during construction.

Lateral Yarding – The movement of logs toward a landing.

Lateral Yarding Distance – The maximum distance from the landing within which logs can be yarded.

Late-Successional Forest – A forest seral stage that includes mature and old-growth age classes.

Late Wood – See Summerwood.

Latewood Percentage – The amount of summerwood in the growth rings of a wood product. An important factor in determining density and other characteristics.

Lath – A thin, narrow wooden strip, used as a backing for wall plaster or other materials, or as a fencing material.

Lath Bolt – A piece from which lath is sawed.

Lathe – A machine upon which logs are peeled to yield veneer for plywood.

Lathe Charger – The device that positions a log, or block, on a lathe for peeling.

Lathe Check – A characteristic of peeled veneer resulting from the peeling process in which the veneer is bent as it is separated from the block. The depth of a lathe check is influenced by the pressure of the nose, or roller, bar.

Lathe Chuck – See Chucks.

Lattice – A small, plain, S4S moulding originally used in trellis work.

Lauan – A term used to describe various species of Asian timber, particularly those originating in Southeast Asia.

Lawson Cypress – Another name for Port Orford Cedar, now rarely used.

Lay – 1. The position of a felled tree. 2. The directions in which strands of rope or cable are wound.

Lay Bead – A horizontal bead moulding.

Lay Days – A specified period of time allowed for loading and unloading a vessel. All time over the agreed lay day period is paid as demurrage by the charterer to the ship's owner.

Lay Off – To mark a felled tree for sawing into standard lengths.

Lay Time – Time allowed to a charterer, under terms of a contract, for loading and unloading a vessel.

Lay Up – The process of manufacturing plywood. The term is used to describe the assembly of veneers into panels after glue has been applied in preparation for pressing. Lay up also is often used to describe all the phases of plywood production from veneer to plywood, including pressing.

Lay Up Plant – A plywood manufacturing facility. The term can be used to refer specifically to the portion of a facility that assembles veneer in preparation for pressing. However, the term is often used to describe an entire plywood manufacturing plant. A lay up plant does not necessarily produce its own veneer; many include only a glue spreader, an assembly line, and presses.

Leach – 1. To cause water or other liquid to penetrate through something. 2. To remove soluble materials from a substance by leaching.

Leader – 1. The growing tip of a conifer. 2. A foreman or sub-foreman who directs a group of workers.

Leads – Thin strips of wood, often used in picture framing.

Leaf – An individual unit in the foliage of a plant.

Leaf Grain – Another term for flat grain lumber.

Leakage – The loss of heat from a dry kiln, usually through and around doors or through cracks in the walls or ceiling.

Leased Car – A rail car leased by a shipper (normally a manufacturer) to help ensure a regular supply of cars, especially in periods of shortages. The lessee pays a monthly rental to the lessor and the railroads participating in the round trip of the car pay a mileage allowance to the lessor, who may in turn apply this allowance to the rental fee.

Leave Strip – A strip of uncut timber left as a buffer adjacent to a stream or highway, or between cutting units.

Leave Tree – A tree left standing in a cutting unit as a future source of seed, or as wildlife habitat. In a shelterwood project, they are left as shade to protect young seedlings.

Lebanon Cedar – Cedrus libanotica. A light, brown, brittle cedar of Asia Minor.

Ledger – 1. A horizontal member used in concrete forming to support the joists. 2. A horizontal member extending between the posts in a scaffold.

Ledger Board

Ledger Board – 1. A horizontal board attached to studs to support floor joists.

Leg – 1. A prop used to support something. 2. One of the sides of a triangle or forked object.

Length – 1. A specific length of lumber, such as 16-foot. 2. The overall measurement of the bottom chord of a truss.

Leningrad Standard – See Petrograd Standard.

Lenticel – A lens-shaped pore on a tree trunk or branch.

Lesser Known Species – A collection of tropical hardwoods that are identified by local, rather than botanical, names.

Less Than Carload (LCL) – This term, or the notation "less than truckload (LTL)," indicates that the volume of a particular lumber or plywood purchase is less than the volume shipped in a full rail car (or truck). These quantities are usually purchased at warehouses or distribution centers for local delivery, rather than direct from a mill. They usually bring a higher price than a full carload of the same commodity.

Less Than Containerload (LCL) – See Less Than Carload.

Less Than Truckload (LTL) – See Less Than Carload.

Less 5% – An indication that the price shown includes a 5% discount to the wholesaler or distributor from the manufacturer. Thus, a wholesaler purchasing stock at $100, less 5%, would actually pay $95 to the mill. This method of pricing, once common in commodity sales, is now rarely used. Most mills now sell on a "net" basis, subject only to a 2% discount for payment within a specified period.

Less 5% & 3% – This phrase indicates that the price shown will be discounted first by 5%, and then by 3%, to arrive at a net figure. Thus, a price of $100, "less 5% and 3%," would be equivalent to a net price of $92.15. This discount was common for sanded plywood sales but is no longer used for plywood.

Less 2% – An indication that the price shown will be discounted 2%, usually for payment within a specified period. Thus, a price of $100, "less 2%," is equivalent to a net price of $98.

Let-In – To admit or to incorporate something in a structure.

Let-In Bracing – A board notched into studs diagonally to provide lateral rigidity.

Letter of Credit – A letter issued by a bank on behalf of a buyer of merchandise that entitles the seller to draw funds from the bank up to a stipulated amount. Sometimes requested by export shippers of forest products as a form of financial protection.

Level Return – Horizontal pieces of lumber forming a soffit under a roof overhang.

Liberian Pine – Tetraberlinia tubmaniana. A large, very straight tree growing in the coastal region of Liberia. Used domestically for general construction and furniture, it is also exported and sliced for veneer for use in Scandinavian furniture.

Lidgerwood Skidder – Apparently the first mechanical skidder or yarder, built in Michigan about 1882.

Lien – A legal claim on property as security for a debt.

Lift – 1. A mechanical appliance used to raise items. 2. A step or bench in multiple-layer excavations. 3. The British term for elevator.

Lift Capacity – The amount of weight, or volume, that a lift can handle.

Lift On, Lift Off – A method of loading lumber or other cargo on a ship, using cranes and cargo slings. The opposite of Roll On, Roll Off.

Lift Truck – A vehicle equipped with two sturdy arms which can be slipped under a load to support it while it is being lifted. A forklift.

Light – An ambiguous term indicating that the number of pieces of a certain size or grade is less than the number usually included in a shipment. Opposite of Heavy.

Lighter – A barge used to transport goods over short distances or to deliver to or unload from a larger vessel.

Light-Frame Construction – A building method that uses relatively small framing members to form a skeleton.

Light Framing – Lumber that is two to

Lineal Moulding

four inches thick, two to four inches wide, and graded Construction, Standard, or Utility. Most often a 2x4. Used in a wide variety of general construction applications. The corresponding joist and plank grades are #1, #2, and #3.

Light Regime – The amount of sunlight reaching various levels of the forest canopy.

Lights – Shakes produced with a thickness of 1/2 to 3/4 inch. Also referred to as Mediums.

Light Shake – A type of defect not over 1/32" wide.

Light Side – The side of a log that floats upward in a pond.

Lightwood – Wood containing an unusually high amount of resin or pitch; usually from a coniferous species.

Lignin – A substance related to cellulose that combines with cellulose to form the woody cell walls of plants, and the cementing material between them. Lignin is extracted during pulping and is used in other processes such as leather tanning and rubber formation, and as a source of organic chemicals.

Lignocellulosic – A term describing woody tissue. It is derived from the two basic substances found in wood, lignin and cellulose.

Lily Pad – A round piece cut from the end of a log. Sometimes converted to chips for pulping, and sometimes sold for use as stepping stones in a landscape arrangement, or sold as fuel. See Pond Lily.

Limb – 1. To cut branches off a tree or log. 2. A branch growing on a tree.

Limber Pine – Pinus flexilus. A medium-sized pine growing at high altitudes in the Rocky Mountains.

Limbwood – Firewood cut from branches.

Limit Move – The maximum price movement allowed in a futures contract during one day's trading.

Limit Order – In futures trading, an order in which the customer sets a limit on either the price or the time of execution, or both. Opposite of Market Order.

Limit State – The point at which a structure ceases to fulfill the function for which it was designed.

Limit States Design (LSD) – The fundamental method of wood design used in Canada. A system used to determine the standard allowable stresses for lumber and panels.

Limnoria Tripunctata – A marine organism that attacks wood pilings.

Line – 1. A rope or cable. 2. A boundary. 3. To place objects in a line.

Lineal Moulding – Mouldings sold on a random-length basis, as distinguished from

Lily Pads

Terms Of The Trade

Linear Expansion

cut-to-length mouldings, which are trimmed to specific lengths.

Linear Expansion – A measurement of the growth along the length and width of a particleboard panel when it is exposed to various humidity levels.

Linear Foot – A measurement of length, equal to the actual length of a piece of lumber. Thus, a piece of lumber 12 feet long contains 12 linear feet. The width and thickness of the piece are not considered in this type of measurement.

Linebar – A fixed, or moveable, metal plate or fence at the edge of a roll case, against which a piece of lumber rides as it goes through a resaw or edger.

Linebar Resaw – A resaw with a stationary bandsaw and a moveable linebar which is set to determine the width or thickness of the piece of lumber being resawn.

Line of Credit – The maximum amount of credit that a bank will allow a borrower over a stated period. Also, the maximum credit that a seller will allow a buyer.

Linerboard – Paperboard made for use as a facing material in corrugated or solid fiber boxes.

Liner Service – A shipping company carrying break-bulk cargo over fixed routes on a regular schedule.

Line Yard – An establishment for retail sales of building materials; one of a chain utilizing a common purchasing office and administrative facilities.

Link Saw – An early-day chain saw.

Lintel – A horizontal beam supporting the weight above an opening.

Linville Truss – A girder containing a lattice of vertical and diagonal members forming a series of N-shaped bays.

Lipping – The process of facing an exposed edge, such as particleboard, with a veneer or strip of solid wood.

Liquid Assets – Things of value that can be exchanged or sold quickly, such as stocks and bonds.

Liquidation – The act of closing out a futures position; usually applied to long positions. Liquidating a short position is usually referred to as "short covering."

Liquid Market – In futures trading, a reference to a market where selling and buying can be accomplished with ease, due to the presence of a large number of interested buyers and sellers willing and able to trade substantial quantities at small price differences.

List – A sheet provided by manufacturers or wholesalers to their customers containing asking or "list" prices of stock offered for sale.

List Code – A word, phrase, number, or symbol used to distinguish a particular mill or wholesale offering list. The list is referred to by the code so that there is no confusion between it and previously published lists.

Listel – A square fillet in a moulding.

List Price – See Asking Price.

Little Sugar Pine – Idaho White Pine, Western White Pine.

Live Knot – A sound, firm knot.

Live Load – The weight borne by a structure resulting from the presence of mobile objects such as people; a design factor in calculating the requirements for construction of a load-bearing surface such as a floor or roof.

Live Log Deck – A deck from which logs are being taken to a mill. See Cold Deck, Hot Deck.

Live Rolls – Powered rollers used to move lumber or cants in a sawmill.

Liverpool String Measure – A formula used to measure the cubic volume of logs or poles.

Live Sawing – A method by which a log or bolt is sawn directly into boards or dimension lumber without the log being turned, or cut into cants.

Live Skyline – A skyline that can be raised or lowered to facilitate yarding.

Load – The external forces acting on a structure. See Live Load, Dead Load.

Load Binder – A cable, chain, or belt used to secure a load of logs or finished products to a flatbed truck.

Load Combination Factor – A factor used

in building design to measure the reduced probability of a number of loads from different sources acting on the structure simultaneously.

Load Duration Factor – A mathematical value that can be applied to lumber design values to adjust for the length of time a structure must support a given load.

Loaded Full Visible Capacity (LFVC) – A box car loaded flush, or essentially so, with the top of the access door. When a car is loaded to its full visible capacity it qualifies for freight rate reductions based on minimum weights even though, because of small car size or light-weight wood, the actual weight is less than the minimum required.

Loaded Miles – A reference to the actual number of miles a product will be hauled by a truck; used in calculating freight rates. Does not include the distance an empty truck must travel to the mill in order to pick up the product.

Loader – The machine used to load logs onto a truck or rail car. Also, the operator of such a machine.

Load Factor – A building design factor that takes into account the variability of loads and load patterns.

Loading Bitch – A log loader.

Loading Boom – The arm used to swing logs from a landing to a rail car or truck.

Loading Diagram – The cross-sectional plan of the various parts of a rail car, showing the location of the various lengths and/or sizes loaded in a car. Often supplied automatically by flat car shippers and by box car shippers of mixed cars.

Loading Machine – A steam-powered log loader mounted on a railroad car.

Loading Tongs – Very large tongs used to pick up logs.

Loading Tree – A small spar tree used for loading only.

Loading Tripod – A device for loading logs. It consists of three long timbers joined at the top, from which a pulley block is suspended.

Load Path – The arc followed by a turn of logs being carried along a skyline. Used in planning to determine ground clearance.

Loan-to-Value Ratio – In real estate, the ratio of the dollar amount of the mortgage loan on a piece of property to the total value of the property.

Loblolly Pine – Pinus taeda. One of the Southern Yellow Pines, this species takes its name from the fact that it often grows in moist depressions called loblollies. It is the fastest growing and most plentiful of the southern pines. The species is found in a range from Texas to Delaware.

Local – A speculator in futures who owns an exchange membership, enabling him to execute his own trades. He usually trades only for his own account, and is also referred to as a floor trader.

Local Management Area – As defined by the U.S. Forest Service, a management planning area generally not exceeding 20,000 acres in a single national forest watershed. As defined by the Bureau of Land Management, a tree seed zone established by the Western Forest Seed Tree Council.

Local Market – An area in the general proximity of a producer, or distributor.

Local Point of Delivery – The first location, such as a concentration yard or a rail siding, to which roundwood timber or other timber products are transported after harvest.

Loading Tongs

Locie

Locie – One of the early-day small logging locomotives. Pronounced "Lokee."

Lock Corner – The corner of a box or drawer in which two sides are cut to interlock, as in a dove tail.

Lock Down – A strip of wood laid across a raft of logs, through which pins were driven into the outside logs to hold the raft together.

Lockie – See Locie.

Lock Rail – The door rail that carries the lock.

Locomotive Cord – Wood cut in two-foot lengths and piled 2x4x8 feet as fuel for the old wood-burning engines.

Lodge – A tree that hangs up in another tree when it is felled.

Lodgepole Pine – Pinus contorta. This species, a principal raw material for studs, is found in a wide range in the Northwestern U.S. and Canada. The primary pine in Spruce-Pine-Fir (S-P-F) and Engelmann Spruce, Lodgepole (ES-LP) mixtures of studs and dimension. The Lodgepole Pine takes its name from the use various Indian tribes made of it: using the tall, straight trees as frames for their lodges.

Loft Ladder – A folding ladder attached at the top to a hinged trap door that opens downward to allow access to a loft or attic space.

Log – The stem of a tree after it has been felled. The raw material from which lumber, plywood, and other wood products are processed.

Log Body – A truck trailer built to transport logs or other material that may be chained in place.

Log Boom – See Boom.

Log Brand – A mark placed on the end of a log to designate ownership of it, similar to a brand that designates cattle ownership. Log brands are placed on the log with a small sledge that can be used with one hand. The impression made by a log brand can be read even after the end of the log has been trimmed, since the impression, applied with force, compresses the grain of the wood a distance into the log. Like cattle brands, log brands are registered.

Log Cabin – A type of siding, rounded on one side to resemble a log. See Cabin Log.

Log Chute – A trough made of lumber through which logs were floated. Also called a log flume.

Log Cleaner – Any of various machines used to "clean" logs of their bark by using knives, water pressure, or other methods. A debarker.

Log Conditioning – A process in which logs are steam-bathed to improve the quality and recovery in the milling process.

Log Deck – A pile of logs; a deck in use is called a hot deck, while one where logs are stored for later use is called a cold deck.

Log Dog – 1. A projection, or stop, on an endless chain used to draw logs into a sawmill. 2. Jaws or other devices used to secure a log to a saw carriage.

Log Drive – The movement of loose logs down a river to a point where they are fashioned into a raft or boom. Seldom used now.

Log Dump – The place where logs are unloaded from trucks or trains. Sometimes the logs are dumped directly into a mill pond, while at other times they are unloaded and stacked in a mill yard.

Log Gang – A type of initial log breakdown in which the entire log is passed through a set of reciprocating saws.

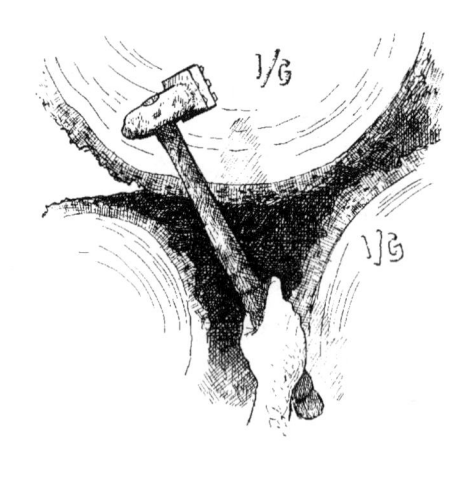

Log Brand

Log Truck

Logger – One who works in the woods performing any of a variety of jobs related to the harvesting of timber.

Logger's Can Opener – An ax.

Logger's Smallpox – Scars inflicted during a fight by the spikes in a logger's calk shoes.

Logging Camp – A temporary "town" for loggers built in the woods and generally abandoned when the nearby timber was cut. It consisted of a bunkhouse, cook house, and attendant buildings.

Logging Chance – See Chance.

Logging Show – See Show.

Logging Sleigh – A sled built to haul small logs (usually pulpwood) to a central point.

Logging Wheels – See Big Wheels.

Log Haul – The conveyor, or endless chain, on which logs are hauled into a mill.

Log Haul-Up – See Log Haul.

Log Jack – See Log Haul.

Log Jam – In river-driving days, the pile up of logs on a rock or gravel bar. Log jams still occur occasionally as a result of flooding.

Log Lift – The giant mechanical jaws used to transfer logs from a vehicle, or from the water, to a deck.

Log Maker – See Bucker.

Log Mark – A symbol showing the ownership of a log, usually stamped in the end of a log with a branding hammer or chopped into the side with an ax.

Log Patrol – One or more persons who recover stray logs lost while being floated to a mill or other destination. The patrol may capture such logs and return them to the boom company or the log owner, collecting a fee for its services.

Log Pile – See Log Yard.

Log Pond – A small body of water, usually man-made, used for the temporary storage of logs, usually at a mill.

Log Reducer – A type of slabbing chipper used in a small-log sawmill.

Log Rule – Any one of various methods of determining the net yield of a log, usually expressed in terms of board feet of finished lumber (or in terms of cubic volume). Among the commonly used log rules are Scribner, Brereton, and the International 1/4-inch Rule. In British Columbia, the British Columbia Firmwood Cubic Scale is the official rule.

Log Run – The full yield of a log. This term is sometimes used when purchasing the full cut of a sawmill. See Mill Run.

Log Saw – The initial breakdown saw in a mill.

Log Scale – A measure of the volume of wood in a log.

Log Scaling Procedure – The methods used by log scalers in measuring log volumes.

Log Scanner – A device that automatically measures a log on a carriage, and indicates the best opening cuts.

Log Stacker – A vehicle equipped with movable jaws of any of a variety of designs, used to unload logs from logging trucks and transport them around a storage yard. Many log stackers are capable of lifting the entire load of a logging truck in a single bite.

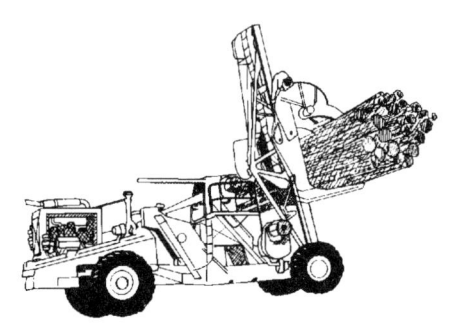

Log Stacker

Log Stud – A stud that has been cut from a log, in contrast to one that has been cut from a peeler core.

Log Truck – A vehicle used to transport logs. Log trucks consist of a cab for the engine and driver, and a trailer on which logs are placed. The trailer usually has an adjustable carriage, or reach, in order to accommodate loads of various lengths. The trailer can usually be carried over the cab when not in

Log Turner

Log Truck

use. Log trucks gained wide use during the 1930s, replacing rail lines as the principal means of log transport from the logging site.

Log Turner – An articulated arm used in turning logs on a carriage. The arm can be extended to roll a log from the carriage, with the log then being repositioned by hydraulic bumpers.

Log Washer – A high-pressure water system used to clean logs of dirt, gravel, and other debris before the logs reach the headrig. When logs are debarked, this step can be eliminated.

Log Way – A ramp on which logs are moved up from a pond or waterway into a sawmill. Also slip, gangway, Log Jack, Jack Ladder.

Log Wrench – A peavey.

Log Yard – The southern equivalent of a log deck.

London Guarantee – A credit insurance company that regularly provides credit insurance to forest products traders.

London Standard – See Dublin Standard.

Long – 1. One who buys a commodity for delivery at a future date. Also, one who has purchased a futures contract. 2. An adjective describing the state of being long: "He took a long position." 3. A long length of lumber.

Long-Bodied – A tree with a long stem that is free of branches.

Long Butt – A chunk cut off the bottom log of a tree because of defect.

Long Car – A skeleton flat car used to transport long logs.

Long Corner – The corner of a cutting unit that is uneconomic to log; often left to provide a seed source.

Long Hedge – The purchases of a futures contract to offset the forward sale of an equivalent quantity of a commodity not yet owned.

Longhorn Beetle – Any of various insects of the family Cerambycidae that infest dead or dying resinous conifers, particularly after fires. They do not reinfest seasoned lumber.

Longleaf Pine – Pinus palustris. This species is native to the Southeast and Gulf Coast. Commercially, it is grouped with other species as "Southern Yellow Pine." It is an important commercial species for lumber and plywood, as well as for naval stores (turpentine, resins, etc.). It closely resembles Slash Pine.

Long Lengths – A loose term generally referring to boards or dimension lumber longer than the lengths that are common for the species or region. In the Inland West, long lengths are widely understood to be pieces 18 feet or longer. In other regions, the phrase usually refers to dimension 22 feet or longer.

Long Log – 1. A log in the Douglas Fir region, as contrasted with the 16- to 20-foot logs of other areas; 40 feet is a common length for logs in the Douglas Fir area. 2. A tree-length log.

Long-Log Country – The Douglas Fir region.

Long Logger – A logger on the West Coast, where logs are bucked as long as 40 feet.

Long-Log Measurement – The scaling of logs using the Westside Measurement Rule, which sets at 40 feet the maximum length for scaling a log. Logs longer than 40 feet are scaled as two logs.

Long-Log Scaling – The scaling of logs more than 20 feet long.

Long Price – The cost of goods after duties are paid.

Longs – 1. Long lengths. 2. Those who have taken long positions in cash or futures markets.

Longshoreman – A worker who loads and

Low-Stump Falling

unloads ships. A dockworker.

Long Span – 1. The distance between supports in a structure, usually spanned by a truss or heavy timber. 2. A logging operation where logs are yarded over a long distance.

Long-Term Sustained Yield (LTSY) – The maximum amount of timber that can be harvested annually.

Long the Basis – A trading technique in which a trader purchases a cash commodity and sells a futures contract against unsold inventory. This is done to provide protection against an increase in the cash price. Also called a Short Hedge.

Long Ton – 2,240 pounds. See Short Ton, Metric Ton.

Looper – A measuring worm whose larvae are a serious threat to West Coast timber.

Loose Knot – See Knot Quality.

Loose-Loaded Box (LLB) – A railroad box car into which lumber has been loaded by the piece rather than in strapped units.

Loose Logs – Logs that, in the days of the river drives, had escaped being rafted. Also called Scrabble, or Prize Logs.

Loose Moulding – Beading used in glazing, or mounting glass in a frame.

Loosened Grain – A condition in which a small portion of the surface wood on a piece of lumber is loosened but not displaced.

Loose Side – The bottom side of peeled veneer as it comes off the lathe. This is the side that comes from the inner or heart side of the log and had contact with the knife, whether the veneer is peeled or sliced. The loose side contains checks or linear fractures because of the bending of the wood at the knife edge and is usually the side facing the glueline when the veneer is used as a face or back ply.

Lop – To cut branches from a tree or log.

Lot Loaded – A railcar in which the load is arranged so that specific portions of it can be unloaded separately at two or more destinations.

Lots – Pieces of land of various sizes and shapes.

Louvered Door – A door constructed with a series of horizontal slats, or louvers, arranged to allow ventilation while limiting light and vision.

Lovely Fir – A slang term for Pacific Silver Fir, Abies amabilis.

Low Basis Weight Paper – A paper ranging in weight from 23 to 30 grams per square meter, used in production of decorative laminates. Sometimes called micro-paper or rice paper, and sometimes impregnated with resin.

Low-Density Fiberboard – A manufactured board in which the fibers have been subjected to only enough pressure to bind them; insulation board.

Low-Density Wood – Wood in which the harder summerwood growth is in small proportion to soft springwood, resulting in reduced stiffness.

Low Grade – A general term describing framing lumber graded as Utility and #3 or lower.

Lowland Fir – Another name for Grand Fir, Abies grandis.

Low Lead – A ground lead or cable in a yarding operation.

Low Pressure Laminate (LPL) – A decorative paper, either pre-printed or of a solid color, that has been saturated with resin. It is bonded to a board surface under heat and pressure, without the need for additional adhesive.

Lowry Process – One of the "empty cell" processes for treating wood with preservative. The Lowry Process begins with preservative being pumped into the treating cylinder without either an initial air pressure or vacuum being applied. When the cylinder is full of preservative, pressure is applied until the wood can absorb no more preservative; the cylinder is then drained and surplus preservative is removed from the wood by a final vacuum.

Low Site – As defined by the U.S. Forest Service, land capable of growing 20 to 49 cubic feet of wood per acre per year in fully stocked natural stands.

Low-Stump Falling – The modern practice of cutting timber as close as possible to the ground. The opposite of cutting from

Low-Temperature Drying

springboards above the swell of the butt.

Low-Temperature Drying – A process of drying by dehumidification by condensing the moisture removed from the lumber and recirculating the heated air.

LP-2 – A reference to a treatment level for pressure-treated lumber. This level requires .25 lbs. of preservative for each cubic foot of lumber.

LP-22 – A reference to a treatment level for pressure-treated lumber. This level requires .40 lbs. of preservative for each cubic foot of lumber.

Lumber – 1. A wood product manufactured from logs by sawing, resawing and, usually, planing, with all four sides sawn. ("Timber" is used in place of "lumber" in many countries.) 2. To log, or to manufacture lumber. 3. Miscellaneous discarded articles such as furniture.

Lumber Body – A truck body equipped with rollers so that a lumber or plywood package can be rolled off at the delivery point.

Lumber Committee – A committee of the Chicago Mercantile Exchange responsible for keeping the CME's lumber futures contract in workable order. The committee is made up of exchange members active in the lumber contract. The lumber committee is advised by a lumber advisory committee, which consists of representatives of the cash trade producers, wholesalers, retailers, and association executives.

Lumber Contract – A futures contract traded on the Chicago Mercantile Exchange. The contract unit consists of 160,000 board feet of kiln dried Std&Btr random length 2x4 of Spruce-Pine-Fir produced in Western Canada, or of Hem-Fir, Engelmann Spruce, Lodgepole Pine, or Alpine Fir produced in the Western U.S.

Lumber Core – Strips of lumber used as the core of a panel.

Lumber Core Panel – A panel constructed of a lumber core and veneer face and back.

Lumber Drummer – A wood products salesman who covered an established route of customers, before inexpensive telephone access.

Lumberer – A regional term for one who works in the lumber industry; a logger or millworker.

Lumber Hooker – A Great Lakes sailing vessel used to haul lumber to market before steamships or railroads were available.

Lumbering – One term that describes the process of cutting timber and converting it into wood products.

Lumberjack – One who works at any of a variety of jobs related to the harvesting of timber. The word properly is applied to workers in the northeastern United States and Eastern Canada. In all other areas, logger is more common.

Lumberman – A generic term describing any person involved in the manufacturing or marketing of lumber, plywood, or other wood products.

Lumber Pit – The arena in a futures exchange where a lumber futures contract is traded.

Lumber Raft – A collection of lumber fastened together so that it could be floated to another location.

Lumber Recovery Factor (LRF) – The volume of lumber recovered (in board feet) per cubic foot of log processed.

Lumber Roller – A metal framework containing a series of cylindrical rollers over which lumber was rolled into a boxcar.

Lumber Stretcher – A mythical tool that rookie sawmill employees are sent in search of.

Lumber Tally – A measure of sawn lumber, expressed in board feet.

Lumber Transfer Yard – See Border Point.

Lumber Yard – 1. A retail outlet selling lumber and, usually, other building materials. 2. A storage area at a sawmill.

Lumen – A cavity enclosed by cell walls or the canal of a tubular organ.

Lump-Sum Sale – A method of selling timber in which payment is based on the estimated volume included in the timber sale. This method contrasts with "scale" sales, where payment is based on the volume measured after harvest.

M

M1 – A measure of money supply that includes all money in immediately spendable forms, i.e. currency and money deposited in checking accounts.

M2 – Another measure of money supply that includes M1 and adds money in savings accounts and time deposits.

M3 – The broadest measure of money supply. Includes M1 and M2 plus the financial instruments of large institutions.

Macaroni – Sawdust in long shreds.

Machine Bite – A depressed cut in the end of a piece of lumber, made by machine knives during surfacing.

Machine Burn – Darkening or charring on a piece of lumber caused by overheating of machine knives during surfacing or moulding.

Machine Direction – In particleboard production, the panel orientation that corresponds to the direction the product moved through the machine that manufactured or machined it. Also called parallel direction.

Machine Evaluated Lumber (MEL) – Lumber evaluated by calibrated mechanical grading equipment which measures certain properties and sorts the lumber into various strength classifications. MEL must also meet certain visual requirements.

Machine Gouge – An unwanted groove in a piece of lumber, caused by a machine knife cutting below the desired depth.

Machine Grading – A mechanical method of measuring stiffness and assigning a stress grade on a production-line basis. See Machine Stress-Rated Lumber, Continuous Lumber Tester, Stress-O-Matic.

Machine Run – The product after the graded rough stock has been surfaced and not separated by grade following surfacing.

Machine Shake – A shake given a "split face" appearance by running a shingle through a machine that grooves one side. Often made from rebutted and rejointed shingles and used in sidewall applications.

Machine Stress-Rated Lumber – Lumber that has been evaluated by mechanical stress-rating equipment. The force required to deflect a piece by a specified amount is measured to determine the modulus of elasticity. The lumber must also meet certain visual grading requirements.

Mackinaw – A short wool plaid coat, the

Terms Of The Trade 167

Main Alley

standard overcoat for a lumberjack in the early days in the eastern woods.

Main Alley — In air drying, the roads in a yard used for the transport of lumber and other wood products.

Main Couple — The principal truss in a timber roof.

Mainline — A heavy cable used to yard logs to a landing.

Main Rafter — A roof member extending at right angles from the plate to the ridge.

Managed Fire — A fire that is allowed to burn under nominal control to achieve a specific purpose, such as eliminating small fuel or brush in a forest, or to increase forage by eliminating some of the competition for water and space.

Managed Forest — Forested lands managed for several purposes, frequently with maximum timber production the main objective. Forest management includes the harvesting and restocking of timber, protection of watershed and wildlife values, and fire and disease control.

Management Area — One or more areas having a common management direction. May or may not be contiguous.

Mansard — A roof with a nearly flat top and steep slopes on all sides. The steep portions are often covered by decorative plywood or wood shakes.

Mantel Tree — A beam across the opening of a fireplace.

Manual Release — The hand-clearing of brush, without the use of herbicides, to lessen competition around desired trees.

Manufactured Housing — Housing units partially or completely built in a factory.

Manufacturer — See Producer.

Manufacturer's Representative — A person who acts as a sales agent for a producer. May be a wholesaler, and may represent more than one manufacturer. Usually paid a set fee or percentage for his services.

Margin — 1. A stipulated amount of money that traders in futures must deposit with a broker each time a position is established. The margin deposit serves as a performance guarantee. Adverse price movements may result in a demand for additional cash deposits; these are termed margin calls. 2. The amount added to the cost of goods by a distributor as profit or a markup. 3. A narrow strip or border around an object.

Marginal Cropland and Pasture — A U.S. Forest Service term denoting cropland or pasture that would yield higher rates of return to the owner if planted to trees.

Marginal Producer — One who is just meeting production costs at current sales levels; the one who will be the first to shut down in a poor market.

Margin Call — A demand for additional money to maintain a leveraged position in futures trading. A margin call occurs when the market goes against a trader's position. See Margin.

Marine Borers — Mollusks and crustaceans that destroy wood piling used in supporting wharves, piers, and other structures that are more or less in constant contact with saltwater. Mollusks bore into the wood for food and shelter, while the action of crustaceans is usually on or near the surface of the wood. Creosote treatment, or a covering over the wood, are the usual means of combating marine borers.

Marine Exterior Plywood — Plywood adaptable to boat hull construction. Must be exterior type of grades AA, AB, BB, with high density overlay or medium density overlay, using only Douglas Fir or Western Larch. In marine plywood there are restrictions on core gaps, splits, and edge-grain joints on the inner plies.

Marine Framing — Pressure-treated dimension lumber intended for use in applications where the material will be in contact with salt water. Such lumber may be of any grade, but must be treated to a preservative level of 2.5 lbs. per cubic foot.

Marine Insurance — Insurance against loss or damage that may occur while forest products are stowed in an ocean-going vessel.

Maritime Pine — Pinus pinaster. A pine of Southern Europe, used mainly for mine timbers.

Maritimes — The Canadian provinces of New Brunswick, Nova Scotia, and Prince Edward Island.

Mark – A symbol stamped on the end or side of a log to indicate ownership.

Market – 1. A place, either physical or abstract, where goods are bought and sold. 2. The current price or value of an object. 3. To sell an object by marketing it.

Market If Touched (MIT) – In futures trading, a price order that automatically becomes a buy or sell order if the price is reached.

Market Letter – A periodical that follows lumber and panel markets, reporting prices, market conditions and trends, industry news, and other information. Usually sold by subscription.

Market Logs – Privately held timber, usually from non-industry or woodlot ownerships, sold on an open market.

Market Order – In futures trading, an order to buy or sell futures contracts that is to be filled at the best possible price and as soon as possible. The opposite of limit order, which may specify requirements as to price or time of execution. See Limit Order.

Market Penetration – An individual manufacturer's share of the total demand for specific goods.

Market Pulp – Wood pulp produced for sale rather than for internal use in manufacturing paper products. It is usually bleached kraft pulp, used in fine papers and tissues.

Market Value – The price of a property or goods under existing market conditions.

Marking Ax – See Brand, Branding Ax.

Marking Gun – A spray can of paint used to mark standing timber for cutting.

Marking Hammer – A swamping hammer used to mark logs for identification.

Marks – 1. Imperfections such as tool marks on finished goods. 2. Symbols stamped on goods to indicate qualities or ownership.

Marquetry – A mosaic of varicolored woods.

Massed Pitch – An excessive concentration of pitch.

Mastic – An aromatic resin used in making varnish. A tough, chewy substance.

Mat – Logs or timbers laid down to provide a solid base or foundation for machinery.

Matched – 1. Veneers cut from adjoining sections of a log and matched to provide continuity of pattern. 2. See Matched Lumber.

Matched Lumber – Lumber that has been worked with a tongue on one edge and/or end and a groove at the opposite edge and/or end, to provide a tight joint when two pieces are fitted together.

Matcher – A person or machine that matches veneers or boards. See Jointer, Veneer Composer.

Match Splints – The thin pieces from which wooden matches are made. Also match blocks.

Matchwood – 1. Billets of wood suitable to cut into match splints. 2. Wood splinters.

Mat-Formed Particleboard – The most common type of particleboard, in which coated particles are formed into a mat (having substantially the same width and length as the finished board) before being flat pressed. The particles may be in the form of granules, chips, flakes, slivers, strands, shavings, or wafers. The coating consists of a binder and wax, with the binder being either liquid or powder resin.

Mat Fracture – An irregular opening or an extreme low-density area in the surface of a particleboard panel, caused by the mat being pulled apart before pressing.

Mat-Layered Particleboard – A type of mat-formed particleboard or other reconstituted panel having distinct layers of material, with particles at the core different in size and/or shape than those on or near the surface. For example, such a panel might have large particles at the core and fine material on the surface to increase smoothness.

Matte Finish – A flat or non-glossy finish on coated paper.

Mattock – A heavy digging tool with a hoe blade on one side of the head and a pick or ax on the other.

Mattress Stock – 1. Dry lumber, usually whitewoods and chiefly 1x2, 1x3, or 1x4, precision trimmed to length and used to build

Mature Tree

Mattock

the frame base of a box spring mattress. Also known as bed-frame stock. The term is also used to describe 2x3 and 2x4 intended for re-sawing to the required sizes and lengths. 2. 1x4s used to make mats to be sunk into a stream to reduce flow and erosion.

Mature Tree – A tree that is capable of producing seed or pollen; one that is sexually mature.

Mature Wood – See outer wood.

Maturity – 1. In futures trading, that period within which a futures contract can be settled by delivery of the actual commodity; the period between the first notice day and the last trading day of a commodity futures contract. 2. The point at which a tree has reached its full growth, after which new growth will be offset by deterioration.

Maul – A heavy hammer used for driving stakes or wedges.

Maximum Price Fluctuation – In futures trading, the maximum amount a contract price can change in either direction during one trading session.

MBF – The standard abbreviation for 1,000 board feet of standing timber, logs, or lumber.

McCloud – A type of grubbing hoe used to dig a fire trail or break. One side has a wide, heavy blade for cutting roots or scraping dirt; the other side is a coarse rake for moving debris. See Hazel Hoe.

McNab Cypress – Cupressus macnabiana. This non-commercial species is found in the inner portion of the northern coastal mountains of California.

Meadow Pine – Another name for Slash Pine, Pinus elliotii.

Mean Annual Increment (MAI) – The average annual increase in timber volume of a stand of trees. Typically, a stand increases in timber volume until the age of culmination, which may be from 40 to 250 years depending on the species and site conditions. After culmination, MAI slows but does not stop.

Measurement Ton – See Cargo Ton.

Mechanical Discharge – The unloading of lumber or plywood from a rail car or truck by use of a forklift or other machine, instead of by hand; the latter method is sometimes used when lumber is loaded loose, or not in banded units.

Mechanically Graded Lumber – See Machine Evaluated Lumber.

Mechanically Stress Rated – See Machine Stress Rated.

Mechanical Properties – The strength and stiffness characteristics of wood.

Mechanical Pulping – A pulp-making process in which the raw material is broken down mechanically, usually by tearing or grinding pulpwood into fibers. In mechanical pulping, the lignin in the wood is not removed. This causes the pulp to turn yellow with time. Mechanically processed pulp is used for inexpensive paper such as newsprint. See Chemical Pulping.

Median Home Price – For a given number of home sales, the median is the price in the middle (an equal number of sales occur above and below the median).

Medium-Density Fiberboard – A dry-formed panel product manufactured from wood fibers combined with a synthetic resin or other suitable binder and compressed in a hot press to a density of from 31 to 50 pounds per cubic foot.

Medium-Density Overlay – The surfacing process is the same as in High-Density Overlay, except that the percentage of resin solids required is 17% and the finished product provides a smooth, uniform surface intended for high quality paint finishes.

Medium Grain – Lumber that exhibits an average of approximately four or more annual growth rings per inch on one end of the piece. The ring count is a measure of the

Mexican Drooping Juniper

strength of the piece as related to the rate of growth of the tree from which it was manufactured. A piece that averages one-third or more summerwood may also qualify as medium grain.

Mediums – See Lights.

Medium Shake – 1. A type of defect not over 1/8" wide. 2. A wood roofing product, usually cedar, manufactured in a 1/2"x24" size.

Medium Site – 1. As defined by the U.S. Forest Service, land capable of growing 50 to 85 cubic feet of wood per acre per year in fully stocked natural stands.

Medullary Rays – Ribbons of tissue formed across the growth rings of trees. They allow the radial transfer of sap, and in many woods produce decorative figures. See Rays.

Meeting Rail – A strip of wood or metal forming the horizontal bar separating the upper and lower sash of a window.

Melamine Glue – A thermosetting resin formed by the chemical interaction of melamine and formaldehyde. It is used as an adhesive, and as a coating for various materials.

Memel Fir – Another name for Pinus sylvestris, or Baltic Redwood. Also called red and yellow deal, Scots or Baltic Fir or Pine. There are 17 trade names for this species commonly used in the U.K.

Mensuration – In forestry, the measurement of timber, both standing and harvested.

Menzies Spruce – Sitka Spruce, Picea sitchensis.

Meranti – A pinkish-to-red tropical wood used in veneers and cabinet work, often as a substitute for mahogany.

Mercer Tables – These tables, used in India and Pakistan, show the contents, in cubic feet, of logs and sawn timbers of given dimensions, along with timber price calculations in rupees.

Merchandiser – A mechanical log-handling system that sorts full-length logs and dispatches them to a sawmill, chipper, or plywood plant, as appropriate.

Merchantable – 1. An export grade that describes a piece of lumber suited for general construction use; this grade is described in the R List grading and dressing rules. 2. The lowest of three Redwood garden grades.

Meristem – A tissue capable of active cell division, thereby adding new cells to the plant body.

Merkus Pine – Pinus merkusii. A pale beige wood found in Burma, Thailand, Java, Sumatra, and the Philippines. It contains much transparent resin, is prone to blue staining, and is relatively nondurable. Uses are interior trim and fittings, and general construction. Also known as Indochina Pine, Sumatra Pine, and Mindoro Pine.

Mesic Area – One that has a balanced supply of water and is neither wet nor dry.

Messenger Cable – A haulback line in a log yarding operation.

Metal Detector – A device used in many mills to detect old metal, such as spikes driven into trees and subsequently overgrown, ahead of the saws.

Metal Overlaid – Plywood that has a metal face permanently bonded to it.

Metrication – The act of converting an existing system of measurement to the metric system.

Metric Foot – A compromise measurement in the European timber trade, slightly longer than 13 inches, or one-third of a meter.

Metric Ton – A unit of weight equal to 1,000 kilograms, or approximately 2,205 pounds.

Metropolitan Statistical Area (MSA) – A geographic area consisting of a large population nucleus together with adjacent communities having a high degree of economic and social integration with that nucleus. It generally includes a city of at least 50,000 population, or an urbanized land area of at least 50,000 population with a total metropolitan population of at least 100,000 (75,000 in New England).

Mexican Cedar – Cedrela mexicana. Not a true cedar, this species is actually a hardwood. It takes its common name from its fragrance, which is similar to a true cedar's.

Mexican Drooping Juniper – Juniperus flaccida. This species is found in Mexico and

Terms Of The Trade

Mexican Pinyon Pine

southwest Texas in the form of large bushes or small trees. It can be distinguished from other junipers by its distinctive pendant branchlets.

Mexican Pinyon Pine – Pinus cembroides. This species is found mainly in Mexico. Its seeds are harvested, but its wood is of little commercial value except as posts and fence posts.

Michigan Ax – A popular double-bitted ax that originated in Michigan during the early logging days.

Microclimate – The climate in the immediate vicinity of an organism or of a local habitat.

Microwave Drying – The re-drying of partially dry veneer in a microwave system, which redistributes moisture evenly throughout the sheets, making them suitable for layup.

Middle Cut – A log cut from the middle portion of a tree stem, above the butt cut.

Middlings – A term used for the middle grades in several European gradings.

Midstory – That portion of vegetation that forms the intermediate vertical structural position, below the overstory.

Mildewcide – A chemical that kills mildew.

Mill – A manufacturing plant in which logs are converted into products such as lumber or plywood.

Mill Bright – Lumber that is fresh from the mill and that has not begun to stain or weather.

Mill-Brite Treating – A process of treating lumber with a proprietary product to protect its appearance and to prevent staining or discoloration.

Mill Certified – See Mill Grade.

Mill Deck – A log deck near the manufacturing equipment.

Milled Wood – Wood that has been finished by passing through a machine such as a planer or moulding head.

Mill Grade – Plywood that conforms generally to size, thickness, and glue line requirements, but does not have all the quality characteristics necessary for grading agency approval.

Milling – The act of planing or shaping a surface.

Milling in Transit – A privilege extended to rail shippers by carriers that allows shipments of lumber moving from sawmills to be diverted to a moulding or millwork plant for remanufacture before moving on to a final destination. Freight rate tariffs usually provide for the delay of a shipment for milling in transit without penalty or loss of through-rate privileges. However, such shipments are usually subject to milling-in-transit charges and weight losses due to remanufacture. Since deregulation, many railroads have eliminated milling-in-transit rates.

Mill Log Deck

Mill List – A listing of items for sale by a producer. The list, which is mailed or faxed to potential customers, contains such information as type of product, species, price, lengths and widths, shipping information, and volumes available.

Mill Number – A number assigned to a mill by a grading agency and used to identify the mill on the grade stamp.

Mill Oiled – Concrete form panels that have been treated with oil at the place of manufacture. The oil helps the form release after the concrete has cured.

Mill Pond – A pond constructed at a mill site to hold logs before drawing them to the saw or lathe.

Mill Race – In the early days of sawmilling, a watercourse directed to move the water wheel that furnished power to the mill.

Mill Realization – The net proceeds to the manufacturer from the sale of products.

Mill Run – The normal output of a sawmill. When stock is offered for sale as "mill run," it is understood to be the typical grade mix and tally of the mill, with neither more nor less of the desired lengths, widths, etc., contained in the load.

Mill Scale Rule – See Mill Tally Rule.

Mill Specifications – A method of selling (usually plywood) in which mills designate minimum and/or maximum amounts of grades and thicknesses they will supply in a given shipment.

Mill Tally Rule – A type of log scale rule based on the board footage of lumber recovered from the log. In constructing a mill scale rule, a sample of logs is first measured in the round. Then, as each log is sawed, the lumber is measured to determine the board foot yield of the log. By measuring a large number of logs, an average yield can be determined. This method of log volume measurement is not widely used today. Also called Mill Scale Rule.

Millwork – Lumber that has been remanufactured into door and window parts or decorative trim. Generally made from the shop grades of Ponderosa Pine, Sugar Pine, White Fir, Douglas Fir, or Western Hemlock.

Millwright – The person in a sawmill or plywood plant who maintains and repairs machinery and other equipment.

Mine Prop – See Pit Prop.

Mineral-Bonded Wood Composite – Molded panels or boards which contain about 10-70 wt% of wood particles or fibers and about 30-90 wt% of mineral binder. The properties of the composites are influenced by the matrix and also by the amount and nature of the woody material and the density of the composites. Composites are classified according to their density and binder.

Mineral Streak – A discoloration in wood that does not affect performance.

Mine Timbers – Timbers used to line a mine tunnel to prevent collapse.

Minimum Bid Price – The lowest price acceptable to the agency selling timber; equal to the appraised price.

Minimum Price Fluctuation – In futures trading, the smallest increment of price movement possible for a given commodity. In lumber futures, the minimum is 10 cents.

Miscut – A mismanufactured piece of wood.

Misery Harp – See Misery Whip.

Misery Whip – A hand-powered crosscut saw used to fell and buck trees in the days before power saws.

Mismanufacture – A general term that includes all blemishes or defects that may occur in manufacturing a wood product, such as torn grain, skip surfacing, chipped grain, and others.

Mismatched Lumber – Worked lumber that does not fit tightly at all points of contact between adjoining pieces, or in which the surfaces of the adjoining areas are not in the same plane. There are five degrees of mismatch: 1. Slight mismatch, barely evident; 2. Very light mismatch, not over 1/64-inch; 3. Light mismatch, not over 1/32-inch; 4. Medium mismatch, not over 1/16-inch; 5. Heavy mismatch, not over 1/8-inch.

Mismatching – A process in veneer lay-up in which distinctly different individual pieces are laid up side by side to give a random plank effect to a decorative panel.

Mississippi Raft – A type of lumber raft used on the Mississippi River.

Missouri Selects

Missouri Selects – A tongue-in-cheek reference to Utility and #3 grade dimension lumber.

Mistrim – A piece inaccurately trimmed to length.

Mitered Corner – A corner in which two pieces intersect and are trimmed so that the miter bisects the angle.

Miter Joint – See Mitered Corner.

Mix – See Regular 30% Mix.

Mixed Car – A carload of forest products consisting of a variety of items, sizes, species, etc. Mixed-car quantities generally command a higher price than full carloads of the same items.

Mixed Grain – Any combination of edge grain and flat grain.

Mixed Stand – A tract of timber consisting of trees of two or more species.

MMBF – One million board feet.

MMSF – One million square feet.

Mobile Home – As defined by the Commerce Department, a movable dwelling, eight feet or more in width and 40 feet or more in length, designed to be towed on its own chassis. The transportation gear is integral to the dwelling when it leaves the factory. The unit is built so there is no need for a permanent foundation, although units are often put on such foundations and are not moved after their initial placement.

Mobile Home Component – See Mobile Home Stock.

Mobile Home Decking – A type of particleboard used primarily for subfloors in mobile homes; it is usually manufactured in 12- or 14-foot lengths to fit the most common sizes of mobile homes.

Mobile Home Stock – Any of various lumber items intended for use in the construction of mobile homes. Such stock is usually cut to certain preferred lengths and/or widths that fit well with standard mobile home sizes.

Mobile Slasher – A portable machine used to buck long pulpwood logs into shorter lengths in the woods.

Mobile Spar – See Spar Pole.

Mobile Stacker – A self-propelled machine that stacks logs in a deck.

Model Building Code – See Model Code.

Model Code – A building code developed by a regional affiliation of building officials and periodically reviewed or revised. Model codes are adopted, usually with variations, by building code jurisdictions to govern construction practices.

Modified Wood – Wood that has been processed by chemicals, compression, heat, or other means to impart properties lacking in the original wood. Included are resin-treated wood (Impreg), and resin-treated compressed wood (Compreg).

Modoc Cypress – Cupressus bakerii. A rare species found in the Siskiyou Mountains of Southern Oregon and Northern California. Of no commercial value.

Modular Housing – A type of housing in which major components are assembled in a factory and then shipped to the building site to be joined with other components to form the finished structure. The components are usually of uniform incremental sizes, permitting some flexibility of design while maintaining the structure of individual elements. Sometimes called "prefabricated" or "prefab" housing by laymen; these terms are avoided by the industry because of negative connotations.

Module – 1. A component of construction fabricated off-site. 2. A unit of measurement in classic architecture.

Modulus of Elasticity (MOE) – A measurement of stiffness in a wood product, found by determining the relationship between the amount a piece deflects and the load causing the deflection. Factors affecting the MOE include size, span, load, and the

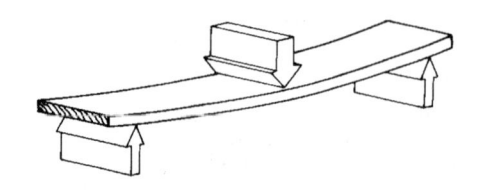

Modulus of Elasticity (MOE)

Mortgage Insurance

species being tested.

Modulus of Rigidity – A measure of the constant stiffness of a piece of lumber or plywood; the degree to which the distance between any pair of points remains fixed under all loads.

Modulus of Rupture (MOR) – A measurement of the load required to break a wood product.

Moisture Barrier – A membrane of treated paper or plastic designed to halt the migration of vapor through a wall or floor.

Moisture Content – The weight of the water in wood, expressed as the percentage of the weight of the oven-dry wood.

Moisture Detector – A device used to measure moisture content.

Moisture Gauge – See Moisture Detector.

Moisture Gradient – A condition of moisture difference within the wood.

Molding – A variant spelling of Moulding.

Mold Resistance – A requirement that certain types of plywood be made with an adhesive possessing a mold resistance equivalent to that created by adding, to plain protein glue, five pounds of pentachlorophenol or its sodium salt per 100 pounds of dry glue base.

Molly Hogan – A rough splice used to temporarily link pieces of cable in a logging operation.

Monkey Block – A small utility block that slides on one line to support another line.

Monkey Wrenching – A term applied to the practice of vandalizing heavy equipment on logging or construction sites. Often associated with radical environmental groups bent on stopping those operations.

Monoculture – The use of land for growing only one type of crop. In forestry, emphasis on only one species of tree.

Monoecious – Plants with both male and female parts in different structures but on the same individual.

Mono Truss – A pitched, light-framed truss with three webs.

Montane Forests – Forests characterized by variation in treelines, depending on the annual rainfall, temperature, shelter, and soil conditions. Montane forests occur in Mexico, Peru, Chile, East Africa, China, Tibet, and Western Australia.

Monterey Cypress – Cupressus macrocarpa. This species is found primarily along a small portion of the Central California coast. It is not a commercial species, but is used as an ornamental.

Monterey Pine – Pinus radiata. Of little commercial significance in the United States, where it is indigenous to the coastal areas of Central California, Monterey Pine has been widely planted in Australia, New Zealand, South Africa, Spain, and Chile. In these areas, plantations produce sawtimber in relatively short times, with 30-year-old trees reaching 100 feet in height and 30-inch diameters.

Montezuma Bald Cypress – Taxodium mucronatum. This close relative of the Baldcypress is found in southernmost Texas and in Mexico.

Monticello – A pattern for Canadian hardwood parquet flooring. The flooring is made of small slats of hardwood assembled into a patterned sheet and glued to a backing sheet.

Mooley – A cant hook, sometimes spelled muley. A tool similar to a peavey, but having a toe ring and lip instead of a pike to handle logs on land.

Moose Cat – 1. A log that goes onto the deck or landing in the proper manner. 2. Anything unusually large, or an unusually good logger.

Mormon Pine – Another name for Cottonwood.

Morse Amendment – A limitation on the export of federal timber attached to the Foreign Assistance Act of 1968 by Sen. Wayne Morse (D-Ore). It restricted exports of federal timber cut west of the 100th meridian to 350 million board feet per year.

Mortgage – An agreement between a borrower and a financial institution to finance part of the cost of purchasing a home. In exchange for the money, the borrower pledges his interest in the property to the lender as security.

Mortgage Insurance – A policy that insures repayment of a mortgage in event of a

Mortise

default. This insurance allows lenders to offer mortgages for lower down payments and at lower interest rates. Insured mortgages can be sold readily in secondary markets.

Mortise – A series of slots in the end of a piece of lumber into which a series of projections, called tenons, on another piece of lumber can be fitted to form a corner joint. Also, the act of forming a joint using a mortise and tenon arrangement.

Mortise Ax – A poll ax that has one cutting edge, with the other edge a narrow, chisel-like cutter used for cutting holes through poles and posts.

Mother Tree – See Seed Tree.

Mottle – Figures in wood that give the impression of texture although the surface is smooth.

Mottling Effect – An irregular appearance in an area or an entire surface of a finished particleboard or hardboard panel due to heavy application of finishing material, poor drying, or incompatible solvents.

Moulded Plywood – A panel product made from veneer and shaped in a mold under pressure to any of various shapes.

Moulder – A moulding machine.

Moulding – A shaped strip of wood, plastic, or other material, used as a decorative trim in residences and other structures. Usually, this trim is used to hide joints.

Moulding&Better (Mldg&Btr) – A grade combination purchased by moulding producers. It consists of the grades Moulding Stock, D Select, and C&Btr Select in combination. The percentages of each grade included vary from mill to mill. Mldg&Btr is produced primarily from Ponderosa Pine, Sugar Pine, Douglas Fir, and White Fir and is usually shipped in the rough.

Moulding Rip – A strip of wood, suitable for remanufacture into a moulding, that is sawn from a piece of moulding stock.

Mountain Beaver – See Boomer.

Mountain Cedar – Another name for Alligator Juniper, Juniperus deppeana.

Mountain Fir – See Alpine Fir.

Mountain Hemlock – Tsuga mertensiana. This species usually is found at higher elevations than the more abundant Western Hemlock. Its lumber is grouped for grading purposes under the Hem-Fir designation.

Mountain-Pacific Group – A freight rate territory including most Rocky Mountain states.

Mountain Pine – Idaho White Pine, Western White Pine.

Mountain Pine Beetle – Dendroctonus ponderosae. An insect that attacks several species of pine in the western U.S. It kills trees in groups or stands. No specific control method has been found, though regular stand thinnings help.

Mountain Spruce – Engelmann Spruce.

Movement – Occurs when moisture content goes below 30%. Water leaves the cell walls, causing them to shrink and come closer together. Timber movement can be measured across the grain, but is negligible along it because the cells do not become significantly shorter in length.

MRO Items – Supplies for an industrial firm categorized as Maintenance items, Repair items, or Operating supplies.

MSF – The standard abbreviation for 1,000 square feet, surface measure, of plywood or other panel products.

Mudsill – A plank or timber resting directly on the ground to support construction.

Mulay Saw – A stiff, upright saw once used in waterpowered sawmills.

Mule-Ear Knot – A spike knot; see knot occurrence.

Mullen Test – A measure of bursting strength in paper.

Mulligan – 1. A thick soup or stew. 2. A truck or bus used to haul a logging crew; a crummy.

Mullion – A vertical member dividing panes in a multiple-opening window or panels in a door.

Multi-Layered Particleboard – A type of mat-formed particleboard having distinct layers of material, with the material at the core different in size and/or shape from the material on and near the surface of the panel. For

Mycorrhizae

example, such board may have large flakes at the core and fine particles at the surface.

Multilevel Canopy – A forest stand in which several levels of shrubs and tree branches are present.

Multi-Opening Press – A hydraulic press which makes many sheets of a panel product simultaneously. The press is moved vertically so that each opening can accept raw materials from the conveyor on which they are formed.

Multiple Bandsaw – A headrig or resaw consisting of two or more bandsaws that cut simultaneously on the same log or cant.

Multiple-Family Structure – A housing structure containing separate living units for different households. It may be an apartment building, condominium, duplex, etc.

Multiple Ring – A growth ring containing several false rings.

Multiple Use – A system of forest management in which forested lands are used for a variety of purposes, including timber harvesting, recreation, wildlife management, and others.

Multispan Skyline – A skyline having one or more intermediate supports.

Muntin – A short vertical or horizontal bar used to separate panes of glass in a window or panels in a door. The muntin extends from a stile, rail, or bar to another bar.

Murray Pine – Another name for Cypress Pine, Callitris glauca. This species, native to Australia, is neither a true pine nor cypress.

Muzzle Loader – 1. In the early logging days, a bunk into which the logger crawled from the foot of the bed. Also called a Shotgun Bunk.

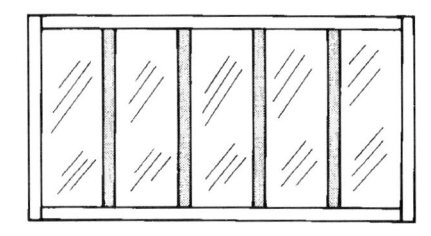

Mycorrhizae – Fungi that grow among the outer cells of plant rootlets and form a symbiotic relationship with their host. They help the roots absorb nutrients and water from the soil and often protect against disease.

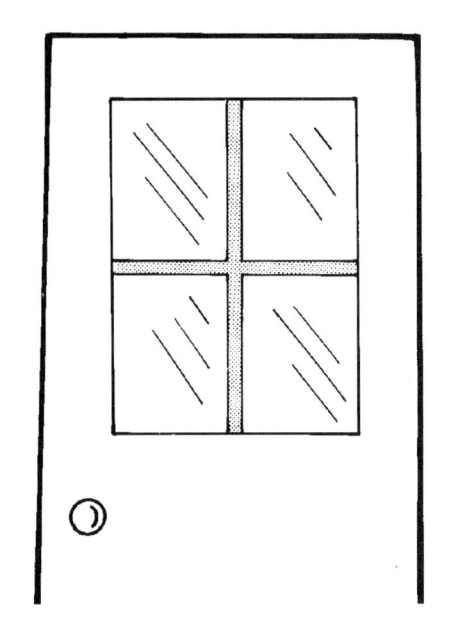

Muntin

Mullions

N

Nailability – A measure of whether a product has good nail holding properties.

Nailed Laminated Beam – A beam constructed of two or more members that are nailed together to form a stronger and stiffer member than would be possible with a single piece.

Nail Glued – A construction technique in which panels are attached to studs or joists using both glue and nails to achieve maximum rigidity. See Glue Nailed.

Nailing Edge – The edge of a joist or stud to which covering material is nailed; wane reduces the usable nailing edge.

Nailing Strip – A board, usually two to four inches wide, attached to concrete or metal structural members to accept nails.

Nail Pop – A flaw in wall construction, where the nail has moved outward relative to a wall panel; usually due to lumber shrinkage after installation, or to improper wallboard application. Also called Backout.

Nail Pull – A tool for extracting nails.

Nail Schedules – The size and spacing of nails used with various materials.

Narrow Gauge – A type of railroad used in the early logging days. The tracks were no wider than four feet, eight and one-half inches, and often narrower; three feet was a common width.

Narrow Grain – Slowly grown (fine grain) wood having narrow, usually inconspicuous growth rings in contrast to coarse or open grain.

Narrow Ringed – Fine grained; closely spaced growth rings.

Narrows – The narrow widths of dimension or boards, usually 2x4, 2x6, and sometimes 2x8.

National Environmental Policy Act (NEPA) – In effect since January 1, 1970, this act sets as policy for the federal government the use of all practicable means "...to create and maintain conditions under which man and nature can exist in productive harmony..." The act establishes the Council on Environmental Quality and requires the preparation of environmental impact statements for major actions affecting the environment.

National Forest – Federal lands set aside by the government to be administered for a variety of purposes, including timber harvest-

National Grading Rule (NGR)

ing, wildlife management, recreation, and others. National Forests are administered by the U.S. Forest Service, an agency of the U.S. Department of Agriculture.

National Grading Rule (NGR) – The general rule covering grade strength ratios, nomenclature, and descriptions of grades for softwood dimension lumber conforming to the American Softwood Lumber Standard. Regional rules prepared by rules-writing agencies must conform to the National Grading Rule for dimension lumber to be certified as meeting the American Lumber Standards.

National Grading Rule Committee (NGRC) – A committee of the American Softwood Lumber Standards Committee which established and maintains the National Grading Rule for dimension lumber under the provisions of Product Standard 20-70. The committee is composed of representatives of regional rules-writing agencies, organizations of building officials, homebuilders, architects, and consumers plus representatives of the Federal Housing Administration, Defense Supply Agency, Forest Products Laboratory, and National Bureau of Standards.

National Lumber Grades Authority (NLGA) – The organization responsible for writing and maintaining Canadian lumber grading rules.

National Park – An area set aside by the federal government for the use and enjoyment of the citizens of the country. The area usually has some particular scenic attraction, or group of attractions. As a rule, timber harvesting is not allowed in national parks, although certain salvage operations may sometimes be authorized.

Natural Circulation Kiln – A dry kiln that depends on temperature differences to induce air circulation through the stickered loads.

Natural Decay Resistance – The ability of various types of wood to resist decay; some woods have high resistance, but most are relatively low.

Natural Finish – A finish on wood that allows the grain to show; a clear finish.

Natural Finish Veneer – High quality veneer with few or no repairs, that is suitable for a natural finish.

Natural Pine – A type of forest in which 50 percent or more of the naturally established stand is Southern Pine.

Natural Seasoning – Air drying.

Nature Conservancy – A national conservation group whose aim is to preserve areas of environmental significance. The Conservancy is unique in that it purchases the areas it wishes to set aside.

Naval Stores – A general term for the chemicals that can be extracted from wood, derived from the days when wooden vessels were caulked with pine tar and pitch. Turpentine is distilled from gum resin extracted from Southern Yellow Pine, and other chemicals are used in the production of adhesives, carbon paper, gasoline additives, lubricants, inks, and detergents.

Naval Stores

Nearbys – The closer-in months in which futures trading is being conducted.

Near-Rift – Lumber that meets all the requirements for edge-grain stock except the required number of annual rings per inch. Also may be lumber that has an average of at least six annual rings per inch across the face at each point in length and has only one edge of grain on the face, but forms an angle of less than 45 degrees with the face side.

Necking – 1. The connecting moulding be-

Newel

tween the parts of a shaft in a column. 2. Small mouldings around table legs, etc., in cabinet work.

Necktie – A choker.

Needle – The small leaf of a conifer.

Needle Fire – A light burn, affecting only the needles of trees.

Needle Point Grain – Same as rift grain. The surface or figure produced by a longitudinal plane of cut which is at approximately 45 degrees to both rays and growth rings. The term is used especially for White Oak.

Negative Amortization – A situation in an adjustable rate mortgage in which rising interest rates result in interest charges that exceed the monthly payment. Unpaid charges may be added to the term of the mortgage, lengthening it, and reducing the buyer's equity.

Negotiable – An instrument, such as a check, that can be transferred with the rights originally created by it.

Negotiable Warehouse Receipt – A legal document, issued by a warehouse, describing and guaranteeing the existence of a specific quantity of a commodity in the warehouse.

Nematode – See Pinewood Nematode.

Nested Bundling – See New Bundling.

Net – What remains after all deductions. A net price is one from which commissions, or other expenses, have been deducted.

Net Annual Growth – The measure of the growth of a tree, or stand of timber, after deductions for decay, wind breakage, etc.

Net f.o.b. Mill – The net mill price to the buyer. Does not include discounts, freight charges, or other fees.

Net Measure – The content of lumber, in board feet, when calculated from measurements of actual dimensions, including tongue or lap.

Net, Net – The price basis upon which futures and export trading in forest products is conducted. Obtained by deducting all trade discounts from cash quotations.

Net Register Tonnage – A method of measuring the size of ships. In determining the net figure, deductions from the Gross Register Tonnage are made; these deductions include machinery, crew quarters, water ballast, etc.

Net Scale – The measurement of a yield of a log after deduction for defects.

Net Surfaced – The actual size of a piece of lumber after being surfaced or planed.

Net Ton – Same as a short ton; 2,000 pounds.

Net Ton Mile – The movement of a ton of freight for one mile.

Net Tonnage – The total cubic space of a vessel available for cargo, calculated as one gross ton for each 100 cubic feet of capacity.

Neutral Axis – An imaginary line through the center of gravity of a structural member.

Neutral Section – The longitudinal section of a structural member where the stresses from tension and compression are offset.

New Brunswick Rule – This log scale rule, one of the oldest board foot rules on record, was made the statutory rule for the province of New Brunswick in 1845.

New Brunswick Spruce – Picea mariana, Black Spruce.

New Bundling – A method of packaging random lengths of siding or other select grades by which pieces of varying lengths are nested to form a package of a single, standard length.

Newel – An upright post about which the steps of a circular staircase wind; also, the post at the foot or on the landing of a straight stairway.

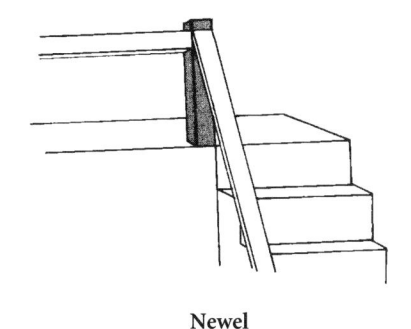

Newel

Terms Of The Trade

New England Hemlock

New England Hemlock – Tsuga canadensis, Eastern Hemlock.

New England Pine – Pinus strobus, Eastern White Pine.

New Forestry – Sometimes used synonymously with Ecosystem Management, this concept for forest management has not been clearly defined by public agencies in the U.S. In general, however, this strategy de-emphasizes commodity production, such as timber harvesting. Instead, timber is balanced against all other non-commodity values over the forest landscape. Where harvesting does take place, clearcut harvest units are generally smaller than traditional units, if employed at all. Selective or shelterwood cuttings figure prominently in harvesting because they retain more of the forest's structure.

Newsboard – Cheap paper board made from waste newsprint.

Newsprint – A low-grade paper used chiefly for printing newspapers. See Mechanical Pulping.

New Zealand Red Pine – Dacrydium cupressinum. This species, indigenous to New Zealand, is also known as Rimu. It is used chiefly for flooring, furniture, paneling, and interior trim.

New Zealand White Pine – Podocarpus dacryaioides. Also known as Kahikatea, the wood of this species is pale yellow to yellow-brown. The grain is straight with fine texture and the growth rings are indistinct.

N-Grade – 1. In moulding, stock intended for natural or clear finishes. The exposed face must be of one single piece. 2. In plywood, cabinet quality panels for natural finishes.

Nicaraguan Cedar – Another name for Mexican Cedar, Cedrela mexicana.

Niche Market – A special market in which a company has the best potential to succeed; usually a narrow market segment.

Niche Product – A product that is manufactured and marketed for specialized uses. Niche products are readily differentiated from other products.

Nick – Another name for a notch or undercut on a tree.

Nigger – A device on a log carriage that turns smaller logs.

Nineteen-Inch Standard – See Adirondack Standard.

Nitrogen Fixation – The process by which atmospheric nitrogen is transformed into nitrogen compounds that can be used by growing plants.

N List – A set of export clear grading rules published by the Pacific Lumber Inspection Bureau. The N List is more restrictive than the R List, principally because no sapwood is allowed. Japan is the main consuming area for N List clears.

Noble Fir – Abies procera. This species is found at relatively high altitudes and is of minor commercial importance in the manufacture of wood products. However, it produces good quality material and is highly regarded in the log export market. The species also is cultivated as a Christmas tree because of its symmetrical shape and upstanding, bluish needles.

Node – 1. The place on a plant stem which bears the leaf or leaves. 2. The point on a truss when two or more members meet.

Nog – 1. A small block of wood. 2. A projecting block built in a wall to hold a shelf. 3. A projection on a log left from a sawn-off branch.

Nominal Measure – The nominal or common-named sizes of lumber, usually expressed in terms of the nearest inch regardless of actual surface, or net, sizes.

Nominal Price – In commodity trading, the declared price for a futures month sometimes used in place of a closing price when no recent trading has taken place in that particular delivery month. Usually an average of the bid and asked prices.

Nominal Size – The size designation for most lumber, plywood, and other panel products, used for convenience. In lumber, the nominal size usually is greater than the actual dimension; thus, a kiln dried 2x4 ordinarily is surfaced to 1-1/2 x 3-1/2 inches. In panel products, the size is generally stated in square feet for the surface dimension and in increments of an eighth of an inch for thickness.

Non-Bearing Wall – A partition which does not support the weight of a higher floor, or the roof.

Non-Certified – Plywood which does not meet prescribed quality standards and has not been certified as to grade by a grading agency. See Mill Grade.

Noncombustible Construction – That type of construction in which a degree of fire safety is attained by the use of noncombustible materials for structural members and other building assemblies.

Non-Commercial Forestlands – Land incapable of yielding crops of industrial wood, or potentially productive land set aside for non-timber use.

Non-Contiguous Trade – Trade between ports of the same nationality located on different land masses.

Non-Declining Yield – A method of forest management in which timberlands are harvested in such a manner as to ensure that the volume of timber cut will not decline in future years, so that the land may be harvested in perpetuity without depleting the timber base.

Non-Dense – A reference to the specific gravity of wood. Lumber classified as "Non-Dense" has five or fewer annual rings per inch, and/or less than one-third summerwood, measured at either end.

Non-Forest Land – As defined by the U.S. Forest Service, non-forest land has never supported forests, or is land that was formerly forested but is currently developed for non-forest uses.

Non-Industrial Private Forest – Forest land owned by farmers, other individuals, and corporations that do not also operate wood-processing plants.

Non-Point Pollution – Pollution from a general source or area, that cannot be identified as having a specific origin.

Non-Pressure Process – Treating wood by allowing it to soak in a preservative to absorb it naturally.

Non-Reversible Pallet – A pallet having a top deck configuration different from the bottom deck.

Non-Sale Area – An area in a national forest or district where no timber sales are scheduled over the next five years.

Non-Stocked Areas – Timberland that is less than 10 percent stocked with growing-stock trees.

Non-Structural Panel – Any of various panels such as particleboard, insulating board, hardboard, medium-density fiberboard, and others, which building codes preclude from use in structural applications.

Non-Tariff Trade Barrier – An action taken to exclude unwanted imports without actually levying a tariff against the item in question. For example, rigid specifications that can be met by domestic producers but that are incompatible with foreign manufacturers' standards may be established to effectively bar an import.

Nootka Cypress – Chamaecyparis nootkatensis, Alaska Yellow Cedar. Also called Nootka False Cypress.

Nootka Pine – Psuedotsuga taxifolia, Douglas Fir; also Nootka Fir.

No Prior Selection – A notation on an offering of lumber that indicates that, if the loading is marked with a grade such as "Standard & Better," the higher grades have not been pulled out and that some higher grades can be expected. However, "No Prior Selection" is a term that is neither defined nor enforced by existing grading rules.

Norfolk Island Pine – A species closely related to Hoop Pine.

North Bend System – A method of yarding logs in which the carriage travels on a line anchored at both ends.

Northern Carolina Pitch Pine – Another name for Longleaf Pine, Pinus palustris.

Northern Pine – A general term refering to both White Pine and Red Pine.

Northern Spotted Owl – Strix occiden-

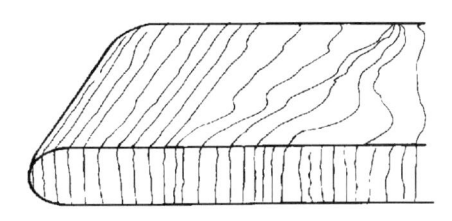

Nosed Board

Terms Of The Trade

Northern White Cedar

talis caurina. This secretive, docile owl is found in forests west of the Cascade Range from southern British Columbia to Northern California. Its controversial listing as a threatened species in the United States in 1990 caused millions of acres of productive forest land to be set aside for its protection.

Northern White Cedar – Thuja occidentalis. This species, also known as Eastern White Cedar and Eastern Arborvitae, is normally found in Southeastern Canada, the Great Lakes states, and New England. Like western cedars, it is resistant to decay and is used for such purposes as shingles, fence posts, and tank stock.

Northern White Pine – Another name for Eastern White Pine, Pinus strobus.

Norway Pine – Pinus resinosa, Red Pine.

Norway Spruce – Picea abies, European Spruce.

Nose – To round off the edge of a board. Also, to round off the end of a log so that it will drag or pull more easily; this is also known as Sniping.

Nose Auger – A tool used to bore large holes in a tree or timber.

Nosebar – A solid bar mounted across the head of a veneer lathe parallel to the axis of the peeler block to control compression of the veneer against the knife during peeling. See Roller Bar.

Nosed – Having a rounded edge. See Bullnosed.

Notch – 1. An angular cut or groove made in an object to receive a crosspiece. 2. An old term for an undercut in felling a tree.

Notch Effect – The locally increased stress at a point in a member which changes in section at a sharp angle. Close to a right angle notch, the stress can be three times as high as the average across the reduced section.

Notcher – A worker who cut a notch in a tree to make it fall in a certain direction.

Notice Day – In futures trading, the day on which delivery notices may be issued.

Notice of Intention to Deliver – See Delivery Notice.

Notice of Shipment – A notice sent to a consignee by a shipper, stating that the consignee's order has been shipped. It usually includes such information as the car number, route, and date of shipment.

Novelty Ripping – A method of ripping that produces a very smooth edge by moving lumber at a relatively slow speed through thin saws.

Novelty Siding – Siding with a lower edge intended to be decorative.

Nubbin – 1. A knob or protuberance. 2. An undeveloped fruit.

Nub Cut – A vertical cut made on the outside edge of the bottom chord of a truss, to ensure uniform spans and tight joints. Also called a Butt Cut.

Number 2 and Better (#2&Btr) – A mixture of joist and plank lumber grades, with the lowest being #2. The "&Btr" signifies that some percentage of the mixture is of a higher grade than #2 (but not necessarily of the highest grade). In light framing, the corresponding term is Standard and Better.

Number 3 and Better (#3&Btr) – Similar to the above except that #3 is the lowest grade included in the mix. In light framing, the corresponding term is Utility and Better.

Nursery – A plantation where trees are grown from seed for future transplanting on cutover forest lands.

Nut Pine – See Pinyon Pine.

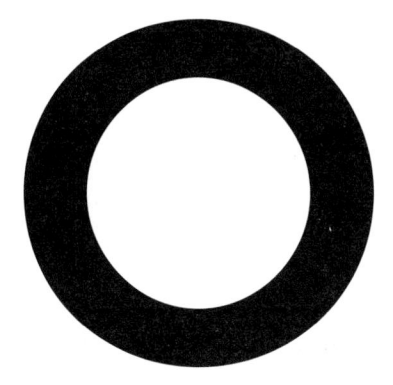

Oak-Barked Cedar – Another name for Alligator Juniper, Juniperus deppeana.

Oblique Arch – A skew arch.

Oblique Butt Joint – A butt joint at an angle other than 90 degrees to the length of the piece.

Oblique Grain – Spiral grain relative to the axis of a tree.

Occasional Pieces – A term generally understood to mean not more than 10% of the total pieces in a quantity of wood products.

Ocean-Going Raft – A log raft constructed so that it can be towed on the open sea. See Benson Raft.

Ocote Pine – Pinus oocarpa. This species grows in the higher elevations of Mexico and Central America. Its properties are similar to those of the Southern Pine group.

Odd Lengths – Odd lengths of lumber not trimmed to standard measure; usually shorts or trim ends.

Odds and Sods – A term used to describe accumulations of the less-desired lumber items; used mainly by Canadian traders.

Offal – The by-products of lumber production: trim ends, short pieces, narrow edgings, etc. that have value for other purposes. For example, trim ends are sometimes sorted by size and sold to toy manufacturers.

Off Bearer – A worker in a sawmill or veneer plant who handles the material as it comes from the headrig or lathe and directs it to the next step of processing.

Off Bearer

Terms Of The Trade

185

Offer

Offer — In futures trading, the indication of a willingness to sell a futures contract at a given price.

Offering List — A list of items for sale, published by a mill or wholesaler and distributed to potential customers. The list usually includes a description of the item, shipping information, price, and terms of sale.

Off Grade — A wood product that fails to meet the requirements of a particular grade.

Off-Highway Truck — A truck intended for use on private logging roads, carrying loads that exceed the size and weight restrictions that apply to public highways.

Office Wholesaler — A wholesaler who trades lumber or plywood without actually taking physical possession of the commodity; one who does not maintain a distribution yard.

Offset — 1. The liquidation of a purchase of futures through the sale of an equal number of contracts of the same delivery month, or the covering of a short sale of futures contracts through the purchase of an equal number of contracts of the same delivery month. Either action transfers the obligation to make or take delivery of the actual commodity to another principal. 2. A type of paper.

Offset Peel — Veneer peeled from a log that was placed on the chucks of the lathe off center.

Offshore — Destinations or markets that are across an ocean and can only be reached by waterborne shipment.

Off the Air — See Off the Market.

Off the Market — A position taken by a lumber or plywood producer when, for a variety of reasons, he does not wish to offer stock for sale. This posture might be taken because of an extended order file, a lack of stock, or as a tactic designed to ensure a higher price in a rising market.

Ogee — A moulding contour much like the letter "S"; the union of concave and convex lines.

Ogee Arch — In masonry, an arch in which the keystone is located at the lowest point of the arch. Used to distribute weight over a foundation.

Oilborne Preservative — One of the two general classifications of wood preservatives (the other being waterborne salts). Examples of oilborne preservatives include creosote and various chlorinated phenols, such as pentachlorophenol.

Oil Bottle — Commonly an old whiskey bottle filled with kerosene. Used in the early logging days to clean a saw gummed with pitch.

Oiled and Edge Sealed — A process used to resist moisture and preserve plywood concrete form panels; oiling and sealing in-

Oil Bottle

creases the number of times a panel can be used, and makes the panel easier to release from the concrete.

Oil Soak Treatment – A method of treating wood with preservative by placing it in a solution of pentachlorophenol or similar oil for several hours or days, without subjecting the wood to vacuum or pressure. This method of treatment works best with the pines.

Oil Spot – A dark-colored spot on the surface of a particleboard panel, caused by oil dripping on the mat or panel from machinery.

Old Bundling – A method of packaging siding in which each piece is of equal length. Also called full-length bundling. Most shippers use "new bundling," in which pieces of various lengths are nested.

Old Growth – Biologically, a stand of timber which is near its climax; such trees may be 200 years old or more. In timber management planning, old growth also refers to timber that is older than the rotation age planned for future forests; this definition may include trees that are 100 years of age, or less.

Old Growth Deficit Forest – A forest which cannot provide the volume per acre which could be supplied by a younger, faster-growing forest.

Old Growth Surplus Forest – A forest containing a greater volume of timber than could be expected from managed second growth through one rotation.

Oleoresin – A natural combination of resinous substances and essential oils occurring in or exuding from plants. See Gum.

On Center – A measurement of the distance between the centers of two repeating members in a structure; e.g. 16 inches on center, or 16" o.c.

One-Hour Rating – A measure of fire resistance, indicating that an object can be exposed to flame for an hour without losing structural integrity or transmitting excessive heat.

One-Off Visit – In international trade, a nonscheduled call at a port.

On Grade – A wood product that meets the requirements of a particular grade.

On Hand – In stock or inventory; available for immediate shipment.

Ontario Rule – The official log rule of the province of Ontario, this rule was adopted in 1952. It applies to logs 4 to 40 inches in top diameter, and 8 to 18 feet long. The Doyle rule, which was the official rule of the province for a number of years, is still sometimes called the Ontario Rule.

On the Floor – A reference to plywood that has accumulated in the producing mill's warehouse; often it is offered for sale at a reduced price.

On the Ground – Lumber that has accumulated in a producing mill's inventory; often it is offered for sale at a reduced price.

On the Market – A situation in which a supplier is offering stock for sale at the prevailing market price.

On the Stump – Timber that has not yet been felled.

On Track – In futures trading, a type of deferred delivery in which the price is set f.o.b. the seller's location and the buyer agrees to pay freight costs to his destination.

Open Assembly Time – In plywood manufacture, the amount of time that elapses between the application of a glue and the making up of an assembly prior to the application of heat and pressure.

Open Cell Process – A process for fixing preservative in wood under pressure. The chemical is retained in the cell walls only, with the cells left empty.

Open Contract – In futures trading, a contract that has been bought or sold without the transaction having been completed by subsequent sale or repurchase, by actual delivery of the physical commodity, or the receipt of the commodity.

Open Defect – Splits, checks, holes, cracks, open joints, or other similar defects that interrupt the smooth continuity of a panel product.

Open-End Rate – A rail freight rate that allows shippers a lower rate if the load reaches a specified minimum weight, and to receive an even lower rate on weights exceeding the minimum.

Open Face – The surface of veneer against

Open Flat

the knife during peeling or slicing; may contain knife checks.

Open Flat – A method of shipping lumber or plywood in which the product being shipped is loaded on a railroad flat car without the benefit of paper wrapping or other protective covering. Used mainly with unseasoned lumber or veneer.

Open Forest – A term used in international forestry to describe savannahs where trees and shrubs are the dominate vegetation.

Open Grain – 1. Lumber which is not restricted as to the number of rings per inch or the rate of growth. 2. Hardwood with coarse, open pores.

Opening Price – In futures trading, the price recorded during the period designated by the exchange as the official opening.

Open Interest – The number of unliquidated futures contracts in a specific month. Open interest is equal to either the number of long positions or the number of short positions, since each contract is made up of one long and one short.

Open Joint – A joint in which two pieces of material that are joined together are not entirely flush. A joint that is not tight.

Open Market Price – 1. The price that is prevalent in the current market for a specific product. 2. Selling levels for shop lumber that are established on a day-to-day basis. These prices are distinguished from contract business, for which prices are usually established at one-month intervals.

Open Order – An order to a futures broker that is good until executed or canceled.

Open Outcry – In commodity futures trading, virtually every offer to buy or sell must be called out publicly, and may be accompanied by hand signals. Those who scream the loudest often make the most deals.

Open Pitch Pocket – An accumulation of resin in wood that has been exposed by manufacture.

Open Position – The difference between the long and short positions in a given currency.

Open Side – See open face.

Open Side Block – 1. A block with a hinged side plate permitting a line to be placed in the sheave without threading. 2. A knockdown block.

Open Soffit – The undersurface of a subordinate part of a building that has not been closed off by boards or panels.

Open Storage – Storage in open-air lots, either paved or unpaved.

Open Tank – A tank for treating wood with preservative at atmospheric pressure.

Operating Differential Subsidy (ODS) – A subsidy paid by the federal government to certain operators of U.S.-flag vessels. The subsidy equals the difference between the cost of operating a vessel under the U.S. flag and the cost of operating it under foreign flags on a particular trade route.

Operator – 1. The owner or contractor of a logging operation. 2. The actual operator of a piece of equipment.

Optimizer – Any of various pieces of sawmill equipment designed to maximize the yield from a log or cant by using scanners, linear positioning, and computers to determine the best way to saw, edge, or trim the wood. Among the types are small-log, edger, rip saw, trimmer, and headrig carriage optimizers.

Option – In futures trading, the month in which a specific contract will expire: the January option. See Nearbys, Deferreds.

Oral Auction – A method of selling timber, usually from a national forest or other public land, in which potential buyers vie with each other by bidding orally on each separate "sale" or tract. The highest bidder is awarded the right to purchase the timber at his last bid price. Bidding always starts at a minimum price set by the seller.

Orangeburg – A standard paneling pattern used in decorative plywood. Orangeburg panels have random-width grooving, with the width between each groove following a pattern of 4-8-4-7-9-6-4-6 inches.

Orange Peel – A defect in hardboard that produces a moderately roughened surface.

Order – 1. A type of column and its entablature. There are five orders in classic architecture: Doric, Ionic, Corinthian, Tuscan, and Composite. 2. One market transaction.

Outdoor Wood

Order Bill of Lading – A special type of rail bill of lading, the original of which must be surrendered to obtain delivery of the car. The waybill specifies this requirement to avoid automatic delivery at destination.

Orderchaser – A person, such as an assistant shipping clerk or checker, who keeps track of shipments leaving a mill.

Order File – A measure of the sales made by a producer, usually expressed in terms of the time it will take him to produce and ship an order, such as in a "two-week order file."

Oregon and California Lands (O&C) – Approximately two million acres of public domain lands in Western Oregon that were granted to the Oregon & California Railroad and the Coos Bay Wagon Road Co. late in the 19th century to finance improved transportation facilities. Failure to meet the terms of the grant resulted in the lands being taken back by the U.S. government. They are presently administered by the Department of Interior, Bureau of Land Management, and are a major source of public timber in Oregon. Because the lands were removed from local property tax rolls by the revestment, the counties in which they are located receive 75% of timber sales revenue, with the U.S. Treasury receiving the balance. Of the counties' share, one-third is used to finance management and improvements on the lands.

Oregon Cedar – Another name for Port Orford Cedar.

Oregon Larch – Pacific Silver Fir and Noble Fir. Lumber from these two species shared the Oregon Larch designation for many years in sales to the Orient.

Oregon Maple – Acer macrophyllum. Big Leaf Maple used in furniture, especially the burls, and as core veneer in some plywood.

Oregon Pine – Another name for Douglas Fir in some overseas markets.

Oregon Spruce – Another name for Sitka Spruce.

Oregon White Cedar – Another name for Port Orford Cedar.

Oregon White Fir – Another name for Grand Fir.

Oregon White Pine – Another name for Ponderosa Pine.

Oriel – A projecting window with its walls supported by brackets.

Oriented Core – A type of oriented strand board having aligned fibers in its core layers. Some OSB panels have random cores.

Oriented Strand Board (OSB) – Panels made of narrow strands of fiber oriented lengthwise and crosswise in layers, with a resin binder. Depending on the resin used, OSB can be suitable for interior or exterior applications.

Origin – The point where rail car shipment begins.

Original Weight – See Green Weight.

...Or Longer – A designation, usually abbreviated "OrLgr," that indicates that lengths longer than those specified may be supplied; usually understood not to exceed 24-foot pieces.

Orthotropic – A mode of growth that is more or less vertical.

...Or Wider – A designation, usually abbreviated "OrWdr," that indicates pieces wider than those specified may be supplied.

OS&D Report – A report on a shipment that indicates whether it was over or short of the required number of pieces, and whether any were damaged.

Osborne Fire Finder – A round, flat plate representing the compass, with a sighting device, used to determine the map coordinates of a forest fire. It was developed by Bush Osborne of the U.S. Forest Service.

Oscillating Saw – A power saw utilizing a straight blade that oscillates in short strokes.

Osmosis – The tendency of dissimilar liquids and gases to diffuse through a membrane or porous structure.

Other Removals – As defined by the U.S. Forest Service, the net volume of growing-stock trees removed from the inventory by cultural operations such as timber-stand improvement, land clearing, and changes in land use such as a shift to wilderness.

Ottawa Red Pine – Another name for Norway Pine, Pinus resinosa.

Outdoor Wood – A merchandising name for wood treated for use in contact with the

Outer Ply

ground, or in decks or benches. A trademark of Koppers Company, Inc.

Outer Ply – The outermost veneer of a plywood panel.

Outer Wood – Wood produced after cambial cells have attained maximum dimensions; mature wood.

Out-of-Round – 1. A form of warp. The elliptical shape assumed by turned circular green wood items upon drying, due to the difference in tangential and radial shrinkage. 2. A circular saw with its periphery not a true circle.

Out-of-Square – Not square; having edges that are not exactly parallel.

Outrigger – A piece of dimension lumber that extends beyond the rake of the roof to support a fascia rafter.

Outs – See Shop Outs.

Outsider – A bidder on a public timber sale who does not have production facilities in the general vicinity of the sale. One who enters the bidding against local buyers and takes the timber to another area for manufacture or export.

Outside Salesman – One who travels to the customer, calling on him in the field.

Out Trade – Futures market transactions in which buy and sell orders do not match up at the end of the day due to errors by brokers, who have the financial responsibility to correct them.

Ovendry – Containing no water, or a moisture content of 0%.

Ovendry Ton – A quantity of wood pulp, sawdust, or other wood residue that weighs 2,000 lbs. at zero percent moisture content. Also called a bone-dry ton.

Ovendry Unit – A quantity of wood pulp, sawdust, or other wood residue weighing 2,400 lbs. at zero percent moisture content. Also called a bone-dry unit.

Overall Dimensions – The measurements of a piece of lumber that are used to compute the space occupied. For example, the overall width of a piece of tongue and groove lumber is the width of the face plus the tongue.

Overall Rise – The vertical distance from the bottom edge of the bottom chord of a truss to the uppermost point of the truss.

Over Arbor – An edging machine in which circular saws are mounted on a shaft (the arbor) so that the saws cut the material from above. The main advantage of this system is that there is less sawdust buildup on the saws, arbor, and guides. Also called an Overhead Arbor.

Over Bark – A method of measuring timber volume that includes the tree's bark. See Under Bark.

Overbid – The difference between the appraised price (minimum bid price) of a timber sale and the actual selling price.

Overbought – In futures trading, a term describing a market that has sharply advanced.

Overcut – 1. A trim allowance of several inches left on the end of a log. 2. In timber harvesting, to cut more than allowed.

Overhang – The extension of the top

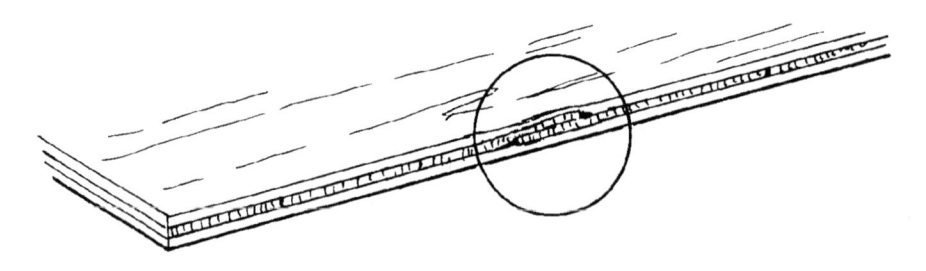

Overlap

Overtopped Trees

chord of a truss beyond the heel, measured horizontally.

Overlaid Panels – Plywood with a surfacing material added to one or both sides. The material usually provides a protective or decorative characteristic to the side, or a base for finishing. Materials used for overlays include resin-treated fiber, resin film, impregnated paper, plastics, and metal.

Overlap – In plywood manufacture, a defect in panel construction caused by one of two adjacent veneers overriding the other.

Overlay – The surfacing of a plywood face with a solid material other than wood. See Overlaid Plywood.

Overlength – See Overcut.

Overload – A load on a log truck that is in excess of the maximum weights allowed on public roads.

Overmaturity – The point at which timber has begun to decline in commercial value because of size, age, decay, and other factors. Many of the trees in an old-growth forest are overmature and are, in fact, dying of old age.

Overripe – See Overmaturity.

Overrun – The volume of lumber actually obtained from a log in excess of the estimated volume of the log, based on log scale.

Overs – In particleboard and fiberboard production, particles that are too large for the particular production process. They are culled out from the classifier and rerouted to be reduced to usable size.

Overscale – The difference between a log scale taken in the woods, and the same logs measured in water, where the former scale is greater.

Overshot Wheel – A water wheel used to power a sawmill. The wheel is turned by water flowing over it. See Undershot Wheel.

Overside Delivery – Unloading a ship to a smaller vessel or lighter.

Oversold – A condition occurring when a seller of forest products finds himself with a longer order file than he wants and/or can handle in a timely manner. When this occurs, the seller usually goes off the market by refusing to take additional orders until his order file is reduced.

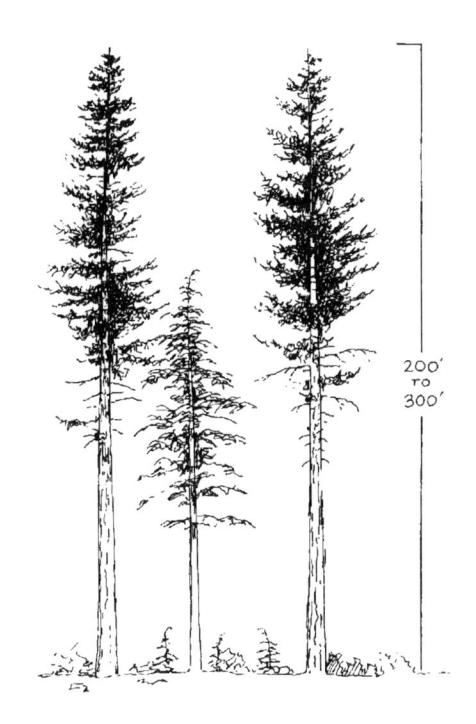

Overstory

Overstory – The older and taller trees in a forest of mixed species or age groups. The overstory forms a canopy that reduces the light available to the smaller trees, resulting in slow growth. One of the objectives of selective logging is to release the smaller trees by removing the overstory of mature trees.

Overstory Removal – A logging technique in which the tallest trees in a stand are harvested without purposely removing the smaller trees.

Over-the-Counter – Small quantity sales at a retail lumber yard. See Over-the-Shoulder.

Over-the-Shoulder – A reference to small-volume retail customers such as a home remodeler or do-it-yourselfer, who might carry his purchases of building materials home over his shoulder.

Overtopped Crown Class – This class includes trees that make up the underlayer of a forest canopy and receive very little light. Unless released, such trees usually do not survive to maturity. See Overstory.

Overtopped Trees – See Suppressed Trees,

Terms Of The Trade

Overweights

Overtopped Crown Class.

Overweights – The underpayment of rail freight charges that results when the actual weight of a forest products shipment exceeds the estimated weight. The additional charge is traditionally paid by the shipper.

Over Without Bill – Freight without a bill of lading or freight bill.

Ovolo Sticking – A specific shape of moulding, worked onto the wood itself instead of being added as a separate piece.

Owl Conservation Area – An area formally designated by the Forest Service or Bureau of Land Management for protection of the northern spotted owl.

Owner-Built House – A house built for owner occupancy, on the owner's land, under the supervision of the owner acting as his own general contractor. In most cases, a house built partly by the owner and partly with paid help.

Oxen – The primary method by which logs were moved to landings in the early pine days. Many camps used horses for hauling and oxen for skidding.

Oxidation Stain – A stain that occurs when a mineral in the wood combines with oxygen.

P

Pacific Coast Cypress – Another name for Alaska Yellow Cedar.

Pacific Coast Spruce – Another name for Sitka Spruce.

Pacific Coast Yellow Cedar – Another name for Alaska Yellow Cedar.

Pacific Dampwood Termite – Zootermopsis angusticollis. These destructive insects, found in coastal areas from British Columbia to Baja California, require wood with a high moisture content. They are often found in the bark of fallen conifers, or in forest cabins or beach houses where soils are moist and humidity is high.

Pacific Hemlock – Another name for Western Hemlock.

Pacific Red Cedar – Another name for Western Red Cedar.

Pacific Silver Fir – Abies amabilis. This species is found in British Columbia, Washington, and Oregon. The name comes from the silvery appearance of the undersides of the tree's needles. Its wood is classed in the Hem-Fir group.

Pacific Yew – Taxus brevifolia. This species, generally small in size, was not a commercially important tree until scientists discovered that its bark contained taxol, a promising drug for the treatment of ovarian cancer. Its wood is heavy and strong and has long been used for such purposes as archery bows. Yews are usually found growing in the shade of larger trees.

Pack – The bundling in which shakes and shingles are shipped. In shakes, the most prevalent pack is a 9/9. This describes a bundle packed on an 18-inch wide frame with nine courses, or layers, at each end. The most common pack for shingles is 20/20. Because of their smoother edges, shingles can be packed tighter than shakes; a bundle of shakes usually contains a net of about 16 inches of wood across the 18-inch width of the frame.

Packaged Lumber – Lumber strapped in standard units, usually pulled to length and wrapped in paper or plastic.

Package-Loaded Kiln – A trackless compartment kiln used to dry packages of lumber. It usually has large doors so that it may be loaded using a forklift.

Pad Saw – A keyhole saw.

Pad Stain – In wood finishing, a stain applied to blend in off-color regions of wood.

Terms Of The Trade

Paintability

Paintability – A measure of whether a product may be finished with any good quality paint system. For best results with wood, the surface must be primed or sealed prior to painting.

Paint Grade – A description of a wood product that is more suitable for painting than for a clear finish.

Paint Marking – A method of identifying the ownership of logs in the days of river drives by marking them with various paint colors. This method was later replaced by log branding.

Pairing Veneers – Matching full sheets of veneers (faces and backs) together to reduce handling when laying up panels at the glue spreader.

Pairs – Two side members of door jambs, frames, or casing trim.

Pale – One of the stakes in a palisade; a picket in a fence.

Paling – A short board or piece of wood.

Pallet – A portable platform used as a base for storing, stacking, and transporting goods in a unit.

Palletized – A term used frequently in the shingle and shake industry. Both items are often shipped on pallets from the mill for ease in handling while in transit. These shipments are referred to as palletized loadings.

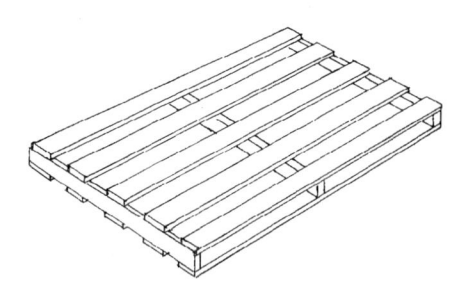

Pallet

Pallet Stock – Lumber used to make materials-handling pallets. In softwoods, usually a #4 grade of dimension.

Pan – A large flat metal plate curved up in front upon which the front end of logs were placed to make skidding easier and to prevent the ends from digging up the trail.

Panel – 1. A sheet of plywood, particleboard, or other similar product, usually of a standard size, such as 4x8 feet. 2. A chord segment of a truss, between two panel points.

Panel Clip – A specially shaped metal device used in joining panels in roof construction. The clip substitutes for lumber blocking, and helps spread the load from one panel to the next.

Panel Door – A door constructed with panels, usually shaped to a pattern and installed between the stiles and rails which form the outside frame of the door.

Panel Grade – The appearance or structural grade of a plywood panel, determined by the veneer grades used in the construction of the panel.

Paneling – The material used to cover an interior wall. Paneling may be made from a 4/4 select milled to a pattern; either hardwood or softwood plywood, often prefinished or overlaid with a decorative finish; or hardboard, also usually prefinished.

Panelized Housing – A building method in which entire wall sections of a house are assembled in a factory and connected at the building site. See Factory Built.

Panel Length – The distance between the points on a truss chord where the webs are attached by connector plates.

Panel Mould – A decorative moulding, originally used to trim raised panel wall construction.

Panel Patch – See Patch.

Panel Point – The point on a truss where a web or webs intersect a chord.

Panel Product – Any of a variety of wood products such as plywood, particleboard, hardboard, oriented strand board, or waferboard, sold in sheets or panels. Although sizes vary, a standard size for most panel products is 4x8 feet.

Panel Saw – A power saw held in a framework and used in cutting panels to size.

PANLIBHON – An acronym for the principal flags of convenience used by U.S. shipowners: PANama, LIBeria, and HONduras.

Parquet Flooring

Pan Skidding – Skidding with the use of a large, steel skidding pan pulled by a caterpillar tractor.

Paper – A substance made from fibrous material, usually in thin sheets.

Paper Birch – Betula papyrifera, a North American birch with a tough bark.

Paperboard – A stiff cardboard composed of layers of paper, or paper pulp, compressed into a sheet.

Paper Cap – A method of wrapping lumber for rail or truck shipment, in which each unit is covered with a cap made of paper or plastic that covers the top and four sides of the unit.

Paper Overlay – Paper prepared for application to the face of a panel after first being printed in four colors with the grain and color of a more valuable wood, or in a decorative design.

Paper Plan – A timber harvest plan using available maps and inventory data as the basis for field work to establish the final logging plan for an area.

Paper Rate – A published freight rate under which no traffic actually moves.

Paper Wood – Pulpwood logs.

Paper Wrap – A method of packaging wood products for shipment on a truck or railroad flat car, with the paper designed to protect the product from dirt and the elements.

Papreg – A paper product produced by impregnating sheets of high-strength paper with synthetic resin and then laminating the sheets to form a dense, moisture-resistant product.

Par – In futures trading, a reference to the standard delivery point, or to quality specifications of a commodity represented in the contract.

Paraform – Paraformaldehyde, an additive used with wood flour as a hardener in adhesives. See Resorcinal Resin Adhesive.

Paragraph 99 Wood – A grade of Ponderosa Pine commons selected to provide shop-type cuttings suitable for fingerjointing by moulding and millwork plants. The name is derived from paragraph 99 of the factory lumber section of the Western Wood Products Association grading rule book, where this grade is described.

Parallam – A proprietary name for a type of parallel strand lumber.

Parallel Chord Truss – A type of truss in which the top and bottom chords are parallel. Also called a Flat Truss.

Parallel-Laminated Veneer – A product in which the veneers have been laminated with their grains parallel to one another. A technique used in furniture and cabinetry to provide flexibility over curved surfaces, and in the production of laminated-veneer structural products.

Parallel Siding – Siding that is not beveled; siding whose edges are of the same thickness. Also called Square-Edged Siding.

Parallel Strand Lumber – A structural wood product made by gluing together long strands of wood which have been cut from softwood veneer.

Parana Pine – Araucaria angustifolia. This softwood, found in Paraguay, Argentina, and parts of Brazil, is not a true pine. Principal uses include framing lumber, interior trim, sash and door stock, furniture, and veneer.

Parapet – In architecture, a protective railing or low wall along the edge of a balcony, roof, or terrace.

Parbuckle – A bight of line placed around a log, causing it to roll when the line is pulled.

Parcel – A loosely used term in the export trade denoting a small quantity of wood.

Parenchyma – Soft wood tissue involved in the distribution and storage of carbohydrates. It is composed of thin-walled, brick-shaped cells with pits that may be axial or radial.

Par Grade – In futures trading, the grade of a commodity used as the standard of the contract. In lumber futures, Std&Btr is the par grade. Also called Basis Grade.

Parity – A reference to the official exchange rate between two countries.

Parquet Flooring – A floor covering composed of small pieces of wood, usually forming a geometric design.

Terms Of The Trade

Parry Pinyon Pine

Parry Pinyon Pine – Pinus quadrifolia. A rare species found in Southern California and northern Baja California.

Partial-Cut Sale Unit – An area within a timber sale that has a silvicultural prescription to cut only part of a stand. Examples include thinning and salvage operations.

Partially Air Dried (PAD) – Seasoned to some extent by exposure to the atmosphere, without artificial heat, but still considered green or unseasoned.

Participating Carrier – Each transportation line involved in a tariff is a participating carrier.

Particleboard – A generic term used to describe panel products made from discrete particles of wood or other ligno-cellulosic material rather than from fibers. The wood particles are mixed with resins and formed into a solid board under heat and pressure.

Parting Bead – A vertical guide strip on a double-hung window frame separating the sashes.

Parting Slip – A long, narrow, vertical strip of wood that hangs from the pulley level to the bottom of the cased frame of a sash window and prevents the sash weights from colliding when the window is being opened or closed.

Parting Stop – A small wood piece used in the side and head jambs of double-hung windows to separate the upper and lower sashes.

Part-Time Drying – A method of kiln drying involving discontinuous operation of the kiln. Usually necessitated by the interrupted supplies of fuel, steam, or power. Also called Day-Time Drying.

Party Car – A railroad car shared by two or more shippers, each of whom loads a less-than-carload quantity for shipment to a shared destination.

Party Wall – A common wall between two living units.

Pass Line – A light cable used to haul gear up a spar tree.

Pasteurized Wood – Lumber that has been heat-treated to remove insect pests; required for exports of some North American species to the European Community.

Patch – A piece of wood or synthetic material used to fill defects in the plies of plywood. Also, Plug.

Patch Cutting – An arrangement of logging units in which small areas are clear cut as single settings separated by standing forest.

Patching Machine – A machine that cuts out the defect in a piece of veneer and replaces the defect with a solid piece of veneer used as a patch. Often referred to by the brand name of the machine, such as Raimann or Skoog.

Patio Decking – A grade designation for western decking, which can be of any species. Patio decking has radius edges, a nominal thickness of 1-1/4", and a nominal width of 5-1/2". There are two grades, Patio 1 and Patio 2.

Patina – A sheen, or glow, on an object as a result of oxidation or use.

Patten – The base of a column.

Pattern – Any of a number of standard shapes, moulds or configurations to which lumber is machined.

Paul Bunyan – A mythical logger of the Great Lakes region who, with his blue ox, Babe, performed mighty feats of logging. Paul moved to the Northwest when the Great Lakes timber had been cut.

Paving Blocks – Wood blocks, generally soaked in creosote, used for surfacing city streets.

Payne's Process – A method of fireproofing wood by first treating it with an injection of sulphate of iron, then infusing the wood with a solution of sulphate of lime or soda.

Peacock's Eye – A circular marking in wood, such as bird's eye in maple.

Peaked Roof – A roof rising either to a point or a ridge.

Peaker – The top log on a truckload of logs.

Peak Joint – The joint at the apex of a roof truss.

Peavey – A tool used in turning logs; it consists of a lever and a moveable, curved hook.

Pendulum Saw

Pecan – Carya illinoensis. One of the largest native hickories, its wood is used in furniture and flooring, while it is grown commercially for its nuts in Texas and the Mississippi River valley.

Peck – Channeled or pitted areas or pockets sometimes found in cedar or cypress.

Peckerwood – Small logs, usually second-growth or understory, suitable for dimension production.

Peckerwood Mill – A small sawmill, usually one that cuts small logs, or "Peckerwood."

Pecky – Characterized by peck, channeled or pitted areas or pockets found in cedar and cypress.

Pede – 1. In the early logging days, a handcar used on a railway. Also called a Jemmy John.

Pedicel – The stalk of a flower or fruit.

Pediment – A low, triangular, ornamented crowning in front of a building or over doors and windows.

Peel – 1. To produce veneer by revolving a peeler block against a knife. 2. The veneer itself, especially its surface quality. See Peel Quality.

Peeler – A log from which veneer is peeled on a lathe, for the production of plywood. A peeler-grade log most frequently is from an old-growth tree, with a high proportion of clear wood.

Peeler Core – That portion of a peeler block that remains after the veneer has been taken. Peeler cores are often used as raw material for the production of studs or landscape timbers.

Peeler Log – See Peeler.

Peeling Bar – A tool used to remove bark from a log; a spud.

Peeling Chisel – 1. A chisel used to remove bark. 2. A spud, barking spud, or barking iron.

Peel Quality – A reference to the smoothness, tightness, and thickness uniformity of veneer.

Peewee – Another name for a peavey.

Peewee Log – A small, but merchantable, log.

Peggies – British term for small random shingles usually sold by weight.

Pencil Cedar – Eastern Red Cedar.

Pencil End Trimmed – Lumber that is not double end trimmed or precision end trimmed to length, but rather has been marked by a pencil or crayon to the desired length and tallied accordingly. Usually shop lumber.

Pencil Ripped – Lumber that has been pencil-marked to show where it might be ripped or edged. See Pencil End Trimmed.

Pencil Rot – A type of decay found in cedar.

Pencil Slat – A thin slice of wood from which pencil parts are cut.

Pencil Square – The bolt from which pencil slats are cut.

Pencil Stock – Pieces of Eastern Red Cedar or Incense Cedar from which pencils are manufactured. Pencil stock consists of squares eight inches in length, or in multiples of eight inches, and equal to the thickness of the piece in width.

Pendentive – An arch that cuts off the corners of a square building internally, so that the superstructure may become an octagon or dome.

Pendulum Saw – A swinging circular saw suspended as a pendulum, and usually used to cut logs to length as they enter the manu-

Peavey

Penetration

facturing plant.

Penetration – A term referring to the relative resistance of woods to impregnation by preservatives. According to the structure of the wood, some are easily injected, while others are very resistant. Douglas Fir and some species of spruce are difficult to treat, while long-leaf pines are readily injected.

Penny – This term originally described the price, per hundred, of nails. Now it is used as a measure of nail length and is abbreviated by the letter d. In general, the larger the number, the larger the nail.

Penta – Short for pentachlorophenol, a wood preservative.

Pentachlorophenol – A chemical used in wood preserving; it is usually applied under pressure so that it will penetrate the wood.

Pent Roof – A roof with a slope on one side only.

Per Acre Material (PAM) – Dead timber and logging residue sometimes sold by the Forest Service or other land manager for its salvage value. Since values are usually too low to justify close measurement of the volume and type of material, it is priced "per acre" based on sampling a small plot.

Per Car Charge – See Per Car Rate.

Per Car Rate – A type of rail freight rate calculated on carload quantity rather than weight. It encourages the maximum utilization of rail cars, up to their weight limits, because the more goods loaded into a car, the lower the per unit freight cost.

Per Diem Charge – The amount paid by one carrier to another for each day the payee's equipment is on the payor's line.

Perforator Test – A formaldehyde test designed as a plant quality control test. It extracts free formaldehyde from particleboard, using toluene.

Perfections – Shingles with 18-inch edges and a thickness of .45 inches at the butt.

Performance Bond – A guarantee that a contractor will perform a job according to the terms of the contract, or the bond will be forfeited.

Performance Standard – A standard for products designed to meet specific end-use applications. A performance standard emphasizes end-use criteria rather than materials and methods used in manufacture. See APA Performance-Rated Panels.

Periderm – The cork-producing tissue of a tree.

Perimeter Insulated Raised Floor (PIRF) – An engineered foundation floor system for crawl space construction. Insulation is applied only to the inside of the perimeter foundation wall, eliminating the need for underfloor insulation.

Permanent Wood Foundation (PWF) – A foundation system in which treated wood products are used in place of concrete. PWF improves heating and cooling capabilities and can be installed in weather conditions that would prevent pouring of a concrete foundation. Originally called the All-Weather Wood Foundation, the PWF name was adopted in 1984.

Permeability – The ease by which a fluid such as a preservative flows through a porous material such as wood in response to pressure.

Permit – A certificate that authorizes a specific action; a permit to build a structure or to gather firewood. A Building Permit.

Perpendicular Felling – A system in which timber is felled at right angles to ground contours.

Personal Property – The property of an individual or firm which is movable, such as office furniture or tools.

Per Thousand – Short for per thousand board feet or per thousand square feet; a unit of measure of timber or finished products.

Peruvian Cedar – See Spanish Cedar.

Petersburg Standard – See Petrograd Standard.

Petiole – A leaf stalk.

Petrified Wood – Wood that has been converted into a stone substance by the action of mineral-laden water.

Petrograd Standard – A unit of measure of softwoods used in the European timber trade. It is equal to 165 cubic feet, or 1,980 board feet.

Piedmont

P-Grade – In moulding, stock intended for opaque paint finishes or overlays. Can be fingerjointed and/or edge glued.

Phantom Freight – A method of determining delivered prices by including freight costs from the farthest point to destination, regardless of origin. The amount included in the delivered price that is in excess of actual freight costs is the phantom freight cost. See West Coast Freight (2).

Phase I, II, III – The various stages of the government's wage and price control program of 1971-1973. Each of the various phases included rules and regulations affecting lumber and plywood prices and marketing.

Phellem – Cork, an outer tissue of bark.

Phelloderm – Inner tissue of a tree, formed from phellogen and containing chlorophyll.

Phellogen – A layer of tissue in a tree giving rise to cork tissue on the outside and phelloderm on the inside.

Phenol – A product of the petroleum industry used in the production of phenolic resin, exterior plywood glue. Phenol is made from benzine. It exists naturally in coal tar and wood tar; however, the phenol from these sources is rarely used in the production of plywood glue.

Phenolic Resin Glue – An adhesive used for bonding exterior plywood. Phenolic resin is produced in a reaction between phenol and formaldehyde. An extender is usually added to the phenolic resin prior to use in the plywood manufacturing process.

Phenoxy Herbicides – Chemical compounds that can kill or damage many species of broadleafed plants by promoting uncontrolled division and expansion of the plants' cells.

Phloem – A bundle of vascular tubes and fibers that transports food from the leaves to other parts of a plant.

Pholad – Also known as a stoneborer, this marine organism pierces wood, etc., by rasping with its shell.

Phosphate – The most commonly used chemical in forest fire suppression. Aircraft are used to "bomb" fires with a solution containing the chemical. After suffocating the fire, the phosphate remains in the soil and benefits the growth of new vegetation.

Photosynthesis – The complex chemical process that takes place in a tree's leaves by which the tree produces the materials necessary for its growth.

Piano Trimmer – The worker who operates the trim saw when boards come from the head saw.

Picea – The general botanical classification of the spruces.

Pickaroon – A short, sharp tool used to move logs or timbers.

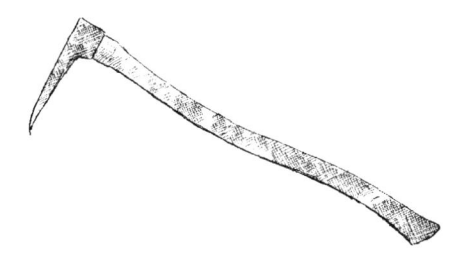

Pickaroon

Pick Ax – A tool with an ax blade on one side and a hoe blade on the other. Also called a Mattock.

Picket – A sharpened or pointed stake, post, or pale, usually used as fencing.

Pickling – Slang for the preservative treatment of wood.

Picture Mould – A type of moulding used to support hooks for picture hanging. It is applied around a room's circumference near the ceiling line.

Piece Stuff – Lumber cut to specific lengths, often by special order.

Piece Tally – A description of a parcel of wood products that lists contents by widths and lengths.

Piece Work – Cutting logs or pulpwood by the piece, rather than by the hour. Also called Busheling.

Piedmont – The geographic area between the Coastal Plain and the Appalachian Mountains in Alabama, Georgia, the Carolinas, and Virginia. It is characterized by gentle slopes

Pier

and an elevation range of from 100 to 600 feet.

Pier – 1. A support of brick or concrete. 2. A landing place projecting into a body of water.

Pier Caps – Metal or wooden covers protecting the tops of pilings used to support a pier.

Pig – A short, hollowed log that was used to transport tools from the landing to the woods. Also, a truck trailer, either a van or flatbed.

Piggyback – A shipment that is loaded in one conveyance, but carried part of its route on another vehicle. Forest products, especially pre-cut pieces or partly assembled components, often are loaded into highway trailers which are then carried on rail cars to a destination city. There, the trailers are off-loaded and the shipment is driven over streets to a jobsite.

Pig Iron – Hardwood logs, so called because they were heavier than pine, spruce, or hemlock.

Pigment Figure – Distinctive patterns formed by uneven extractive deposits within the heartwood. Examples are Rosewood and Zebrawood. The layering effect of pigmentation may be independent of the growth-ring layering.

Pig's Foot – A claw-like hook on a heavy rope, used to steady or guide a log during loading.

Pig Tail – An open loop of metal driven into a tree trunk to guide a light line.

Pike Pole

Pike Pole – A long pole with a spear-type point and a hook on one end. It is used to move logs around in a mill pond.

Pike Staff – A tool similar to a pike pole, but lighter.

Pilaster – A rectangular, circular, or semi-circular member used as a simulated column in entrances and other door openings and in fireplace mantels.

Piling – Round timbers or poles that are driven into the ground to support a load, as a foundation for a structure, or as part of a dock or moorage.

Piling Unmerchantable Material (PUM) – A provision of some timber sales contracts requiring that logging debris be piled in the logged area (rather than being left where it fell) for later disposal, usually by burning. See Yarding Unmerchantable Material.

Pillow – A wood block used as a support.

Pinch Bar – 1. An iron bar used to pinch logs tightly together. 2. A bar used to move logging railroad cars short distances.

Pin Dote – Small, rotten spots on the ends of logs.

Pine – Any of various softwoods of the genus Pinus.

Pine Beetles – Insects that bore into the bark of pine trees to lay eggs. The larvae of the pine beetle feeds off the cambium layer of the tree, eventually killing it. Trees killed by the beetles can be spotted easily in the forest as their needles turn reddish brown. The wood is salvageable, but the beetles often carry the spores of blue stain fungus.

Pine Country – Used on the West Coast to refer to the area east of the Cascade Mountains in Oregon and Washington.

Pine Engraver – Ips Pini. This insect is found in boreal forests of North America south to Tennessee. It lays eggs in tunnels burrowed below the bark of a dead or dying tree, giving the tree the appearance of having had a design "engraved" on it when the bark falls off. Large outbreaks can attack healthy stands of several species of spruce and all pines.

Pine Hog – An early-day term for a timber baron.

Pitch Seam

Pine Oil – A strong solvent used in paints. Made from the oleo-resin of pine trees, or synthetically.

Pinery – Pine country.

Pine Tar – A blackish-brown liquid distilled from pine wood; used as an antiseptic externally and an expectorant internally. Pine tar is also used to make the grips of tools sticky.

Pine Tongs – Extra large skidding tongs that open up to accommodate a pine log five feet in diameter.

Pinewood Nematode – A roundworm parasite carried from tree to tree by a beetle native to North America. To keep the nematode from infesting European forests, the European Community banned imports of green lumber beginning June 1, 1993.

Pin Hole – A small, round hole made by a pin-hole borer.

Pinhooker – An unlicensed dealer in timber or timberland, particularly in the southern U.S. Operates by securing options and selling during the option period. Usually a derogatory reference.

Pin Knot – A knot with a diameter no larger than 1/2-inch.

Pink Pine – New Zealand Silver Pine.

Pinus – The general botanical classification for the pines.

Pinyon Pine – Pinus monophylla, P. cembroides, P. quadrifolia, P. edulis. A group of small pines, 20 to 40 feet in height, occurring in scattered groves in the semi-arid areas of the West. They produce an edible seed, mostly used as topping for a salad. Trees exposed to constant winds take on a sprawling form. Also called Nut Pine; also spelled Pinon Pine.

Pioneer Species – A plant species that is among the first to establish itself in an open area following a fire or other process that clears the area.

Pipeline – The distribution chain for forest products, from producer to retailer. When the pipeline is "empty," there is little product in the hands of wholesalers and retailers; the reverse is true when the pipeline is "full."

Pipe Stave Stock – Lumber used in the manufacture of pipe staves. The edges must be suitable for constructing watertight joints. Pipe stave stock is of high quality, with only minor defects allowed.

Piss Fir – A slang term for green White Fir, derived from its characteristic odor.

Piss Fir Willie – Slang for a forest ranger in Northern California.

Pistol Grip – Describes the shape of a tree with a sharp bend near the butt, often caused by the weight of snow.

Pit – 1. The location in a commodity exchange where trading in a specific product takes place; i.e., the lumber pit. 2. A hollow or cavity in the ground where one sawyer would stand when using a pit saw. 3. A thin part of the cell wall of wood tissue. 4. A void on the surface of a piece of particleboard.

Pitch – 1. An accumulation of resin in the wood cells in a more-or-less irregular patch. Classified for grading purposes as light, medium, heavy, or massed. 2. The angle or inclination of a roof, which varies according to climate and roofing materials used. 3. The set, or projection, of teeth on alternate sides of a saw to provide clearance for its body.

Pitch Blister – An open pitch pocket on the finished surface of wood.

Pitch Butt – A pitch-soaked bottom log of a tree.

Pitched Roof – The most common type of roof, usually with two slopes of more than 20 degrees to the horizontal, meeting at a central ridge.

Pitch Exudation – See Exudation.

Pitch Pine – Pinus rigida. This pine is found in a wide area, from Maine to Northern Georgia. Lumber from it is graded under rules established by the Northeastern Lumber Manufacturers Association.

Pitch Pocket – An opening between growth rings which usually contains or has contained resin, or bark, or both. Classified for grading purposes as very small, small, medium, large, closed, open, or through.

Pitch Ring – Pitch accumulated around the annual growth ring of a tree.

Pitch Seam – Shake or check filled with

Terms Of The Trade

Pitch Select

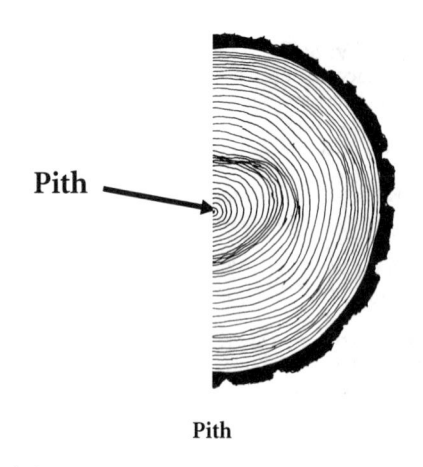

Pith

pitch.

Pitch Select — D Select or better, except that the grade admits any amount of medium to heavy pitch. Massed pitch is admissible, but limited to half the area of an otherwise high line piece. Dimensions are 4 inches and wider, 6 feet and longer in multiples of one foot.

Pitch Streak — A well-defined accumulation of pitch in a more or less regular streak. Classified for grading purposes as small, medium, or large.

Pith — The small, soft core in the structural center of a log.

Pith Fleck — A narrow streak resembling pith on the surface of a piece of lumber, usually brownish and up to several inches in length, resulting from the burrowing of larvae in the growing tissue of the tree.

Pith Knot — See Knot Quality.

Pith Ray — The medullary rays which bind wood across the grain or growth ring.

Pith Shake — See Heart Shake.

Pith Wood — 1. Wood formed near the pith of the tree, often characterized by wide growth rings of lower density and abnormal properties. 2. See Juvenile Wood.

Pit Kiln — A dry kiln with a fan system located in a pit below the tracks carrying the kiln charge.

Pit Prop — A timber used as a support in an excavation or mine.

Pit Sawing — See Whipsawing.

Pitted Sap Rot — A decay caused by fungus in the sapwood of felled conifers.

Pit Wood — See Pit Prop.

Plagiotrophic — The growth of branches, stems, and/or roots in a horizontal direction.

Plainsawn — Lumber sawn so that the annual rings form angles of 0 to 45 degrees with the surface of the piece.

Plain Slicing — See Flat Slicing.

Plane — 1. A flat surface. 2. A tool used to smooth or shape wood. 3. To run sawn wood through a planer to smooth its surface.

Planed All Round — A piece that has been surfaced on all four sides.

Plane of Weakness — The plane along which a body under stress will tend to fracture. This may exist by design, by accident, or because of the nature of the structure and its loading.

Planer — A machine used to surface rough lumber.

Planer Chain — The moving conveyor belt upon which lumber is moved from the planer to various stacks, according to length, grade, etc.

Planer Ends — See Planer Trim.

Planer Heads — Sets of cutting knives mounted on cylindrical heads which revolve at high speed to dress lumber fed through them. Top and bottom heads surface or pattern the two faces, while side heads dress or pattern the two edges or sides.

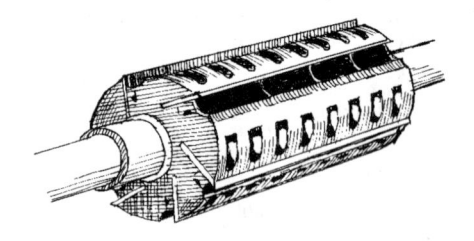

Planer Head

Planer Knife — One of the sharp blades used in a planer head.

Planerman — See Set-Up Man.

Planer Split – 1. A split or check in a board, caused by the flattening of a cupped board by the feed rolls of a planer. 2. A reference to lumber divided longitudinally into two or more pieces as it passes through the planer. See Splitterhead Rip.

Planer Trim – Short pieces trimmed off the ends of planed lumber to attain specific lengths; also called Planer Ends.

Planing Allowance – The allowance required in setting saw sizes to allow a planer to smooth the lumber; the amount removed by a planer.

Planing Mill – An installation where lumber is surfaced. Also refers to mills where lumber is remanufactured to a customer's specifications.

Plank – A piece of lumber two or more inches thick and six or more inches wide, designed to be laid flat as part of a load-bearing surface, such as a bridge deck.

Plank Decking – Heavy decking intended as a load-bearing surface.

Planking – Material used for flooring, decking, or scaffolding.

Plank Road – A logging or mill town road built of planks laid directly on the ground. Used extensively in the early logging days. On very steep grades narrow wooden cleats were nailed to the planks to provide better traction. Also called a Tram Road.

Plank Truss – Any truss work constructed of heavy timber such as planking in a roof truss or in a bridge truss.

Plantation – Woodlands in which at least 50 percent of the trees have been established by planting or direct seeding.

Plasterboard – A composition sheet in any of various thicknesses, used as a base for a thin finish coat of plaster.

Plastic Glue – Resin bonding materials used in joining wood pieces. They include: 1. Thermosetting resins such as phenol-formaldehyde, urea-formaldehyde, and melamine resin. 2. Thermoplastics such as acryl-polymers and vinyl-polymers. 3. Casein plastics. 4. Natural resin glues.

Plasticity – The capability of being molded, or being made to assume a desired form; a property of wood that allows it to retain its form when bent.

Plastic Wood – A paste for filling holes and open joints in wood.

Plate – A horizontal structural member that forms the top or bottom of a stud wall; the member that directly supports the rafters.

Platen – A flat plate in a hot press, usually one of many in a multi-opening press used in the manufacture of panel products.

Platenboard – See Mat-Formed Particleboard.

Plate Shear – Failure parallel to the grain or plies of a member under load.

Plate Stock – Plates are pieces of lumber used in construction to which the studs are fastened at top and bottom to form a wall. The term Plate Stock usually refers to a general class of commodity-type 2x4 lumber used as plates.

Platform – An area raised above the level of the surrounding floor, used as a work station.

Platform Framing – A framing system in which the vertical members are only a single story high, with each finished floor acting as a platform upon which the succeeding floor is constructed. The common method of house construction in North America.

Pleasing Match – A type of veneer matching in which the veneer pieces are matched by color similarity and not necessarily grain characteristics.

Plenum – 1. A chamber under a structure that is closed, at a higher pressure than the surrounding atmosphere, and used in heating and cooling systems in place of extensive duct work.

Plen-Wood System – A system for distributing air for heating and cooling using the entire under-floor area of a building as a plenum chamber; the system eliminates the need for duct work in some structures. Proponents of the system cite savings in both construction costs and in the costs of heating and cooling.

Plies – 1. A reference to the number of identical trusses joined together to form a girder. 2. The individual layers of veneer that make up a sheet of plywood.

Plinth Block

Plinth Block – A block at the base of a pilaster. A block of wood placed at the bottom of a side door casing to terminate the casing as well as the base.

Plot Cruise – To project timber volume in an area by estimating the log yield in standing trees at intervals on either side of a compass course.

Plow – In moulding, a rectangular slot of three surfaces cut with the grain of the wood.

Plug – See Patch.

Plug and Touch Sand (P&TS) – Plywood sheathing and underlayment grades that have had holes and other surface defects in the C-grade face veneer patched with wood plugs or a plastic filler. The patch is then touch sanded to remove any high spots.

Plug Boom – A boom of logs connected by ropes passed through holes bored in the ends of the logs. Wooden plugs driven into the holes wedged the ropes that pulled small groups of logs to the main boom.

Plugged Crossply – See Plugged Inner Ply.

Plugged Inner Ply – An inner ply of C-plugged grade veneer where a defect has been filled to provide a solid core.

Plugged Lumber – Lumber in which a defect has been filled by plastic material to provide a smooth paint surface.

Plugger – See Patcher.

Plugs and Fillers – Wooden pieces inserted into pieces of lumber to improve their appearance and usefulness. The quality of the inserts and workmanship must be in keeping with the quality of the grade. In dimension and other lumber graded for strength, inserts are limited to the same size and location as knots.

Plug Tenon – A short tenon projecting from the head or foot of a post to stabilize it.

Plumb Cut – The vertical cut at the foot of a rafter where it fits over the wall plate; also, the vertical cut at the top ridge.

Plum Figure – Irregular patches on the face of wood where new growth has followed the contour of an indent or bending of the tree.

Plumule – The rudimentary stem in an embryo plant.

Plus Tree – A tree considered to possess superior genetic qualities.

Ply – A single layer or sheet of veneer. One complete layer of veneer in a sheet of plywood.

Plyform – The trademark owned by the American Plywood Association for concrete form panels produced by its members.

Plymetal – Plywood faced on one or both sides with sheets of galvanized steel, aluminum, or other metals.

Plyron – A trademark of the American Plywood Association applying to panels with hardboard faces on both sides. Plyron is used in the manufacture of countertops, shelving, cabinet doors, etc.

Plywood – A flat panel made up of a number of thin sheets, or veneers, of wood in which the grain direction of each ply, or layer, is at right angles to the one adjacent to it. The veneer sheets are united, under pressure, by a bonding agent.

Plywood Contract – A futures contract for plywood traded at the Chicago Board of Trade for many years but abandoned in 1984. As this book was being published, the Board was proposing a new contract in plywood/OSB, to begin in January 1994.

Plywood Layup – The point in the production of plywood where glued veneers are assembled into panels and inserted into a curing press.

Plywood List – See Sanded List.

Plywood Pit – The arena of a commodity exchange where the plywood futures contract was traded.

Plywood Research Foundation (PRF) – A subsidiary of the American Plywood Association, made up of APA members and associate members engaged in plywood-related activities, such as manufacturers of adhesives, chemicals, equipment, etc.

Pocket – A log pen at a sorting works.

Pocket Rot – A type of decay found in cedar.

Pocket Sorter – See Bin Sorter.

Pond Pine

Pocosin Pine – Another name for Pond Pine, Pinus serotina.

Point – A tooth for an inserted-tooth saw.

Pointed Arch – A Gothic or Tudor arch.

Points – A reference to changes in prices: The stock market went up two points ($2); or interest rates increased a point from 11% to 12%. A basis point is 1/100 of a point.

Poisson's Ratio – The ratio between lateral and longitudinal strain resulting from uniform stress below the proportional limit of a structural member.

Pole – A long, usually round piece of wood, often a small diameter log with the bark removed, used to carry utility wires or for other purposes; often treated with preservative.

Pole Ax – To strike down, as with a pole ax, a medieval weapon. See Poll Ax.

Pole-Frame Construction – A construction system using vertical poles or timbers to which modular units of a house are attached.

Pole Pine – Another name for Ponderosa Pine, Pinus ponderosa.

Pole Plate – A horizontal beam, heavier than a wall plate, that carries the feet of rafters.

Pole Road – 1. A road like a railroad track, generally built over swamps, made of 10-inch or larger logs that were doweled together at the ends. The top was roughly dressed to fit iron wheels on which logs were carried to the river or the landing on railroad-type cars. 2. A Tram Road.

Poletimber – Growing trees 5.0 to 10.9 inches in diameter at breast height, with a cubic foot volume of wood at least 50% free from defect. They are free of any disease, defect, or deformity that would likely prevent them from becoming sawtimber.

Pole Trailer – A specially constructed log trailer designed to carry extremely long poles, usually employing a disconnected rear section with independent steering, much like a long-ladder firetruck.

Pollarding – The continuous lopping of the top, or poll, of the tree to encourage fresh growth.

Poll Ax – A single-bitted ax with a flat poll or head. See Pole Ax.

Polymerization – The curing that occurs when wood is impregnated with chemicals that are then transformed into plastic. The curing, or polymerization, links together monomers into multiple molecules (polymers) in which form the plastic is hard and stable. A composite structure of wood and plastic is thereby formed.

Poly (Paper) Under Top Tier (PUTT) – A method of loading open cars in which a sheet of polyethylene film or treated paper is spread over the load for protection from the weather. This covering then is held in place by placing a final layer or tier of lumber over it. See Flat Car Loadings.

Poly Wrap – A system of protecting lumber in transit and storage, similar to paper wrap, but using plastic instead.

Pond – A body of water at a mill in which logs are stored. The water facilitates easy handling of the logs, which can be moved and sorted by a single pond man, or "Pond Monkey."

Pond Boss – The man in charge of work in a log pond.

Pond Dry – A reference to green or unseasoned lumber; as "dry" as when the log was pulled from the pond.

Ponderosa Pine – Pinus ponderosa. Also known as Western Yellow Pine, this species is found in a wide range that reaches from British Columbia to Mexico, and from the Pacific Coast to the Dakotas. The wood is widely used in general construction, most often as boards, but is more valued for its uses in millwork and in cuttings for remanufacture.

Pond Lily – The trim end of a log that floats flat in the pond and gives the appearance of an oversized lily pad.

Pond Man – One who handles and sorts logs in a mill pond.

Pond Monkey – See Pond Man.

Pondosa Pine – A common name which has been used for both Western White and Western Yellow Pine.

Pond Pine – Pinus serotina. This pine, a minor species of the Southern Yellow Pine

Terms Of The Trade

Pond Saw

Pony Band Saw

group, is found along the Atlantic Coast from Southeast Virginia to the Florida panhandle. Lumber from this species carries a "Mixed Pine Species" stamp.

Pond Saw – A saw mounted at the edge of a pond to trim logs before they are moved into the mill; the trim may be either for proper length or to remove splintered or broken ends.

Pontoon – A small raft carrying a windlass and grapple, used to recover sunken logs. Also called a Sinker Boat.

Pony Rig – A smaller version of a piece of manufacturing equipment. A sawmill may utilize a headrig for large logs and a smaller pony rig for small logs. A pony resaw may be operated in conjunction with a main resaw to handle smaller cants.

Pool Car – A shipment by rail in which several less-than-carload lots ordered by different companies are brought together in a single car to obtain the lower carload shipping rate.

Pool Drive – A river drive in which logs of various ownerships were consolidated.

Poor Adhesion – A condition that develops when a finish or laminate is applied over a filler and proper bonding does not occur.

Poor Pine – Another name for Spruce Pine.

Pop – 1. A delaminated area in a plywood panel; the same as a blow or blister. 2. See Nail Pop.

Poplar – A member of the willow family. In North America: Populus tremula, Aspen; P. balsamifera, Cottonwood; P. tacamahaca, Balsam Poplar. Its wood is used in furniture core stock, excelsior, etc.

Popple – Another name for Aspen.

Pore – The cross section of a vessel, a conductive tube in hardwoods formed by the end-to-end arrangement of cells whose end walls are open.

Pore Bleed – The migration of pigments or solvents from wood pores after stain or filler has been applied.

Porosity – The density of wood is a measure of its gross porosity. Its porosity exists either in the form of cell cavities, the interconnecting pit system, resin ducts and intercellular spaces, or as voids within cell walls. Porosity has such an important influence on mechanical and other physical properties of wood that it is the most useful index of the suitability of wood for many end-product uses.

Porous Wood – Wood, usually a hardwood, containing pores or vessels that will absorb finishing material unless they are filled.

Portable Hog – A movable machine used to produce ground fuel from wood or bark that is otherwise unusable.

Portable Sawmill – A small mill that can be moved readily by trailer or its own wheels. Used to cut rough lumber in the woods.

Portable Spar – See Spar Pole.

Portal Crane – A gantry crane situated on an elevated open structure (portal), and which is moved on rails.

Port Charges – The charges that cover pilot, towing, and wharf services.

Porter – An early steam locomotive used in logging.

Portland Rate – A reference to a shipping point in Oregon. Producers in this area have similar freight rates to major markets, which result in f.o.b. mill prices that usually fall within a narrow range.

Port of Entry (POE) – A port that provides custom house services to collect duties on imports.

Port Orford Cedar – Chamaecyparis lawsoniana. A cedar common to the coastal belt of Western Oregon and extreme Northern California. It has limited markets in the U.S., mostly for items such as bleacher seats, but its light-colored wood is greatly desired in Japan for exposed use in houses.

Position – 1. A trader's open contracts in the futures market. 2. A reference to a wholesaler's buying or selling strategy at a given moment. A wholesaler who has sold a product before buying it is said to hold a short position, or more simply, is "short." A wholesaler who has purchased stock that he has not yet sold is said to hold a long position, or is "long." 3. A reference to a shipping period, as in "Feb/March position."

Position Trading – An approach to futures trading in which the trader either buys or sells contracts and holds them for an extended period, as distinguished from a day trader, who will normally initiate and offset his position in a single trading day.

Post – A piece of lumber used in a vertical position to support a beam or other structural member in a building, or as part of a fence. Although 4x4s are often referred to as posts, most grading rules define a post as having dimensions of five inches by five or more inches in width, with the width not more than two inches greater than the thickness.

Postage Stamp Rate – A freight rate that is uniform throughout a large territory.

Post and Beam Construction – Traditional open-structure method for constructing single-family wooden houses in Japan. Constructed with a series of 4x4 posts and 4-1/8-inch beams made from clear lumber, with a minimum of nails and solid walls. Most walls are sliding and therefore removable.

Post and Girt – Wood-framed buildings consisting of load-bearing wood posts, widely spaced and connected with horizontal members called girts.

Post and Lintel – A description of trabeated construction; that is, upright supports bearing horizontal beams or lintels.

Post-consumer Wastepaper – Material that has lived out its usefulness as a consumer item. Examples include newspapers, discarded office paper, etc.

Post-impregnated Paper – Paper that is treated with resin after manufacture, for use in the production of decorative laminates.

Post Pallet – See Block Pallet.

Post Pointer – A fencing machine used to produce a slanted, usually pyramid-shaped, top on a post to encourage drainage.

Potentiometer – A instrument used to measure the temperature in a dry kiln.

Pot Life – The length of time that an adhesive remains usable after it has been mixed.

Powder Monkey – A person who uses dynamite or other explosives in road construction, etc.

Powder Post Beetles – The larvae of lyctus beetles that bore through wood for food, leaving undigested powdery remnants in their burrows. Also called deathwatch beetles.

Power Cutting – See Climb Cutting.

Powered Backup Roller – The backup roller helps hold a peeler block against the knife of a veneer lathe. A powered roller also helps turn the block, allowing the core to be peeled to a smaller (3-1/2 inch) diameter. Without the powered roller, attempts to peel this small often result in "spin out" as the chucks that turn the block on the lathe tear out.

Powersaw – See Chainsaw.

Pratt Truss – A type of flat truss, having parallel top and bottom chords and alternating perpendicular and angled webs.

Prebunching – The act of gathering individual logs at an intermediate point for later handling or loading; smaller logs can then be handled in batches.

Precision End Trimmed – Lumber trimmed square and smooth on both ends to a uniform length, with a manufacturing tolerance of 1/16-inch over or under length in a maximum of 20% of the pieces.

Precommercial Thinning – The removal of selected trees in a young stand so that the remaining trees will have more room to grow to marketable size.

Precompression – The process of passing

Preconsumer Wastepaper

lumber through a series of pressure rollers prior to drying it.

Preconsumer Wastepaper – Trimmings and wastepaper generated in the manufacturing and printing processes.

Precuring – The premature curing of an adhesive due to press temperatures being too high, a too-rapid resin-curing speed, or a malfunctioning press. Precuring can result in plywood delamination or a poor quality surface in particleboard.

Precut – A lumber item, usually a stud, that is cut to a precise length at the time of manufacture, so that it may be used in construction without further trimming at the jobsite.

Predrilled – Lumber, such as roof decking, that has been drilled at the mill to accommodate bolts or other hardware.

Predrying – A drying process used to accelerate the evaporation of free water. Stickered loads of lumber are placed in a building and heated air is circulated over the wood. The process is similar to regular kiln drying, except that much lower temperatures are used.

Prefilled – A panel of reconstituted wood whose surface has been made smooth by the application of a solvent-based filler before being shipped. Such panels have decorative overlays or laminates applied to them.

Prefinished – Lumber, plywood, moulding, or other wood product with a finish coating of paint, stain, vinyl, or other material applied before it is taken to the jobsite.

Preframed – A construction term for wall, floor, or roof components assembled at a factory.

Prefreezing – A method of improving the reaction of lumber to the drying process by freezing stock at temperatures from –5 to –100 degrees Fahrenheit prior to drying.

Prehauler – A machine used to carry logs from the cutting area to the landing. Also called a Forwarder.

Preheater – In a continuous laminating process, a device that heats the veneer or lumber prior to the application of adhesive.

Preimpregnated Paper – Paper treated with resin during the paper-making process for use in the production of decorative laminates.

Preload – 1. To load logs onto a carrier for subsequent transport. 2. To prepare several logs for loading as a unit on a truck or rail car by fastening them into a bundle with binders.

Prelog – The removal of understory trees as poles or pilings to avoid breakage during the main logging.

Premium – 1. In commodity futures trading, a sum above the value of the item in the cash market. 2. Of better quality than another product. 3. A grade of radius edge decking. 4. A grade of hardwood plywood. 5. A proprietary name for six-patch plywood siding, used by the American Plywood Association.

Premium Grade – A general term describing the quality of one item as superior to another.

Premium Warehouse – The highest of three grades of pallets recognized by the National Wooden Pallet and Container Association.

Prepay – The payment of a freight bill before the product is shipped. Prepayment is based on an estimate of these charges, with actual charges being determined when the shipment is completed. Carriers sometimes give incentives, such as discounts or favorable currency exchange rates, to encourage prepayment of freight bills. The recipient of these benefits is often subject to negotiation between mills and wholesalers.

Prepress – A machine used to apply, without heat, pressure to a load of plywood, prior to the load being inserted into the hot press.

Prescribed Burning – See Controlled Burning.

Preservationist – A term applied to one who objects to the use of natural resources because of a belief that such use will destroy basic values of the resource. Often used to refer to a member of various groups opposed to the expansion of industrial/commercial uses of public lands.

Preservative – Any substance applied to wood that helps it resist decay, rotting, or harmful insects.

Preserved Wood Foundation (PWF) –

Primary Wood Products

See Permanent Wood Foundation.

Press – See Hot Press.

Press Cycle – The time required in a press to complete an entire operation.

Press Load – The number of sheets of plywood that can be cured at one time in a press.

Pressmen – Workers who load glued veneer assemblies from the spreaders into the hot press or into an automatic loader which then feeds the assemblies into the hot press.

Press Roll – A roller that pressures a cant against a feed (or live) roll, directing the cant into a machine for further processing.

Pressure Guide – A movable fence or bar that applies pressure to hold a cant or peeler in place while it is being sawn or peeled. See Roller Bar, Line Bar, Powered Backup Roller.

Pressure Preserved – Wood that has been treated with preservative in a closed container, under pressure.

Pressure Process – The process of treating wood under pressure in a closed container. Pressure is usually preceded or followed by a vacuum. See Full Cell, Empty Cell Processes.

Pressure-Refined Fiber – A type of furnish for particleboard or fiberboard, produced by pressurized attrition mills.

Pressure Treating – A process of impregnating lumber or other wood products with various chemicals, such as preservatives and fire retardants, by forcing the chemicals into the structure of the wood using high pressure.

Presteaming – The process of subjecting wood to be dried to saturated steam prior to drying.

Presto Log – A brand name for a fuel log made of sawdust. The sawdust is compressed in special machines with the resulting heat causing the natural resins in the wood to bind the sawdust into a "log" about 15 inches long. The Presto Log process was one of the earliest commercial uses for residues developed by western sawmills.

Prestressed Beam – A beam in which internal stresses have been introduced to increase its strength. Usually, this is accomplished by constructing a beam so that it is deflected slightly upward to offset the downward deflection that will result from a load being applied.

Price – The amount that can be obtained for a good or service.

Price at Time of Shipment (PTS/PATS) – A method of pricing in which a buyer and a seller agree that the price of a particular item will be that price prevailing when the item is actually shipped. The price listed by a market reporter or other third party is often used as the prevailing price.

Priced Out of the Market – A situation that exists when the price asked for a product is higher than potential buyers will pay. A tactic sometimes used by sellers to stop the inflow of orders. See Defensive Pricing.

Price Limits – In futures trading, the maximum price advance or decline from the previous day's settlement price permitted for a contract in one trading session. The price limits are set by the rules of an exchange for each commodity.

Price List – A listing of products for sale, and the prices asked for each item, published by a producer or wholesaler and circulated to potential buyers.

Price Reporter – A publication that reports wood products prices. See Market Letter.

Prickly Pine – Another name for Ponderosa Pine, Pinus ponderosa.

Primary Cut – The initial cut by a faller into a tree.

Primary Marks – A defect in particleboard in which occasional deep scratches or marks occur on finished sanded board. Caused by the primary course grit sanding heads and not entirely removed by finish sanding heads.

Primary Members – The main load carrying member of a structural system, including the columns, end wall posts, rafters, or other main support members.

Primary Producer – A manufacturer who produces commodity lumber and panel products from raw materials such as logs, veneer, furnish, etc.

Primary Wood Products – Logs, cants, and commodity grades of lumber. Also, commodity grades of plywood, waferboard, oriented strand board, and similar panels.

Prime

Prime – A grade of finish lumber, ranking below Superior, the highest grade, and above E, the lowest grade of finish. Finish graded Prime must present a fine appearance and is designed for application where finishing requirements are less exacting.

Prime Rate – The index interest rate charged by commercial banks on loans to businesses. Depending on a variety of factors, the actual rate charged on a given loan may be above or below the prime.

Primitive Area – An area having the characteristics of a wilderness but not officially designated as such. Certain areas were designated primitive areas while their suitability to be classified by Congress as a wilderness area was determined. Other areas, not classified as primitive but without roads, also have been under study in recent years.

Prince Albert Fir – Another name for West Coast Hemlock.

Princess Pine – Another name for Jackpine, Pinus banksiana.

Princess Post – Any subsidiary vertical timber between the queen posts and the wall used to stiffen a queen-post truss.

Principal Post – A door post in a framed partition.

Principal Rafters – The main rafters in the roof truss that carry the purlins and on which the common rafters are laid.

Print – 1. A process of opaquing over the neutral grain of a panel or moulding piece and overprinting a different grain or color to simulate a more-desired wood. 2. The price or prices shown by a market report. Transactions are sometimes based "on print," or "print plus" or "print minus" a specific figure.

Private Car – A rail car owned or leased by a party for its exclusive use and not under the control of a railroad.

Private Carrier – In international trade, a vessel that transports only the goods of a person or company that owns the vessel. Private carriers operating U.S. built, owned, and registered ships are not subject to provisions of the Jones Act.

Private Track – Railroad track outside the jurisdiction of a railroad, usually a spur or siding that has been assigned to the exclusive use of a party through a lease or written agreement.

Prize Log – An unbranded log floating free of any boom, subject to claim by whomever captures it.

Producer – A primary manufacturer of wood products; a mill or number of mills under one corporate head.

Producing Region – An area in which certain species are harvested and processed; e.g., British Columbia is the principal producing region for Western Spruce-Pine-Fir, the southern U.S. is the producing region for Southern Yellow Pine.

Product Developing – The full range of grades that develop in the manufacture of a particular item. A buyer who purchases 2x6 #3, resawn to 1x6 boards, "product developing," is agreeing to take all of the grades that develop in the remanufacturing process.

Productivity Class – See Site Index.

Product Shipped – See Product Developing.

Product Standard – A published standard that establishes: (1) dimensional requirements for standard sizes and types of various products; (2) technical requirements for the product; and (3) methods of testing, grading, and marking the product. The objective of product standards is to define requirements for specific products in accordance with the principal demands of the trade. Product standards are published by the National Bureau of Standards of the U.S. Department of Commerce, as well as by private organizations of manufacturers, distributors, and users.

Product Standard 1-83 – A product standard for plywood developed cooperatively by the U.S. Department of Commerce and the construction and industrial plywood industry. P.S. 1-83 established requirements for the production, marketing, and specifying of construction and industrial plywood. The standard covers virtually all softwood plywood grades. See Performance Standards.

Profile – To cut or saw to a particular pattern.

Profile Density – Variation in density in particleboard from face to core.

Profiler – A machine used to cut or saw

Pulaski

lumber to a particular pattern.

Profile Ripped – See Novelty Ripped.

Pro Forma Invoice – An invoice sent before the order has been shipped in order to obtain payment before shipment.

Program Trading – Computerized buying or selling programs. Some of these programs are triggered automatically when prices reach a certain level. Computer-based activity can often accentuate sudden swings in the price of a commodity or stock, or cause dramatic shifts in the entire market.

Progressive Kiln – A dry kiln in which the total charge of lumber is not dried as a single unit but as several units, such as kiln truckloads, that move progressively through the dryer. The kiln is designed so that the temperature is lower and the relative humidity higher at the entering end than at the discharge end.

Prompt Shipment – An inexact term generally understood to mean that the shipment will take place immediately or in the very near future, usually within a few days of when the order is placed.

Proof Loading – 1. A method of testing the mechanical properties of a structural member by subjecting it to weight or pressure. 2. The point at which the links of a chain begin yielding under load.

Proof of Delivery – A freight bill receipt signed by the consignee acknowledging delivery.

Proof Testing – One phase of manufacture of glu-lam beams, in which end joints are tested for strength.

Propeller Twist – Twisted grain in a Red Cedar shake that prevents it from lying flat and causes it to take the shape roughly resembling an airplane propeller.

Proportional Rate – A rate used to equalize freight costs through one gateway with the rate through another.

Proposed Species – One under consideration for listing as an endangered or threatened species.

Prosenchyma – Non-living wood cells that function in conduction and support. Includes tracheids, vessels, and fibers, and accounts for most of the volume of wood structure.

Protective Association – An organization of land owners designed to pool their fire fighting or patrol efforts.

Proximo, Prox – A credit term meaning next month.

PS20-70 – The code designation for National Bureau of Standards Voluntary Product Standard 20-70, covering softwood lumber.

Psychrometer – An instrument for measuring water vapor in the atmosphere, utilizing both wet- and dry-bulb thermometers. A wet-bulb thermometer is kept moistened and is cooled by evaporation, giving a slightly lower reading than the dry-bulb thermometer. Because evaporation is greater in dry air, the difference between the two thermometer readings is greater in a dry atmosphere.

Public Delivery Track – Railroad track open to use by the general public in loading or unloading rail cars.

Public Reload Center – A point from which materials may be sold and reloaded for delivery to a customer. See Border Point.

Public Sustained Yield Unit (PSYU) – A geographically defined area in Canada over which the government retains management control.

Published Rate – A rail rate officially filed with the Interstate Commerce Commission and available to the public.

Puget Sound Pine – An archaic term for Douglas Fir.

Puget Sound Rule – See Drew Rule.

Pulaski – A tool used in fighting forest fires, consisting of a single-bitted ax and a

Pulaski

Terms Of The Trade

Pullboat Logging

hoe-like trenching blade, attached to a wooden handle. It was developed by Edward C. Pulaski, a ranger in the U.S. Forest Service, in 1910.

Pullboat Logging – A method of logging cypress in the swamplands of the southern U.S. The system employed a scow-mounted skidder to pull logs to a central location. There they were made up into rafts and floated to a sawmill. The system was first developed in the late 19th Century, and was still in use as late as the early 1960s.

Pulled to Length (PTL) – A designation that denotes lumber in a load has been separated by length and packaged in units containing single lengths.

Puller – 1. A worker on a sorting chain who pulls lumber from the chain and stacks it according to width, length, and grade, or some combination of these factors. An off-bearer; also called a chainman or chain hand. 2. A device used in extracting resin to be made into turpentine.

Puller

Pulling Station – A spot on a sorting chain, where a puller or chain hand is positioned to sort the various pieces of lumber that move along the chain. Each chain normally has several such stations, with each puller responsible for pulling certain grades, lengths, etc.

Pull-Out – Any one of several select or high grades removed, or pulled out, from a quantity of lumber before that lumber is marketed as common grades.

Pull Saw – A circle saw, mounted on a movable frame, which could be maneuvered by hand as a trimming saw.

Pull Up – A place on the bank of a river where logs that had been pulled out and floated down from the woods were pulled out of the water.

Pulp – A soft, moist mass of wood fiber used in the manufacture of paper. Pulp is made by reducing wood chips to fibers, either by grinding them up, or by chemical means, and then turning the fibers into a slurry. See Pulping Liquor.

Pulpboard – A crude form of paperboard composed of ground wood pulp strengthened by the addition of sulphite or sulphate pulp.

Pulp Chip – The wood chip from which pulp is made, usually made from mill edgings and small timber.

Pulp Hook – A metal hook that provides a hand grip for moving four-foot pulpwood logs.

Pulping Liquor – In pulpmaking, an acid (sulphite) or alkaline (sulphate) liquor used in a cooking process to break down wood lignin to free the fibers.

Pulp Rule – A scale stick used in determining a volume of pulp wood.

Pulp Sticks – Individual pieces of pulpwood.

Pulp Stone – The stone, or grinding wheel, used to reduce wood to fibers in the groundwood pulping process.

Pulpwood – Wood used to produce pulp used in the manufacture of paper products; pulpwood is usually wood that is too small, of inferior quality, or the wrong species to be used in the manufacture of lumber or plywood.

Pulpwood Slasher – A machine used to cut pulpwood logs to designated lengths.

Pump Jack – A hydraulic jack used to roll logs or tip over a tree. See Jack.

Pumpkin Pine – 1. A White Pine tree yielding a superior grade of lumber. 2. Cork Pine.

Puncheon – 1. Roughly dressed, heavy timber used as flooring, or as a footing for a foundation. 2. Short timbers supporting

Pyramiding

horizontal members in a coffer dam.

Puncher – One who operates heavy machinery such as a bulldozer or yarder.

Punk – 1. The person who passes signals in the woods, as between choker setters and the yarder operator (See Whistle Punk). 2. One new to working in the woods. 3. Rotten wood.

Punky – Rotten or inferior wood.

Pup Hook – A small hook at the end of a loading line or chain.

Puppy – A type of choker pin, or iron plug, used in yarding trees in pullboat logging of cypress. Choker chains were attached to the pins, with the system replacing the traditional tongs, which tended to slip off the cypress logs.

Purchase Order – A document sent to a seller by the buyer, listing details of the order such as stock descriptions, price, shipping instructions, etc.

Pure Stand – A tract of timber consisting of trees of a single species.

Purlin – A timber laid horizontally to support the rafters or trusses of a roof.

Push – A foreman.

Push Block – A shaped block to protect the hand when using a circular saw or spindle moulder.

Push-Out Test – A test of adhesive strength. Two or more surfaces are affixed to one another, and a hole is then drilled through all but the one surface to be tested. Pressure is then applied through the hole until the bond is broken.

Puttied Split – A split in a wood product such as a panel surface that has been filled with putty, usually an epoxy, then sanded.

Put to Bed – To complete a sale.

Putty Bead – See Glass Bead.

Pyramiding – In futures trading, the tactic of using the profits on a previously established position as margin for adding to that position.

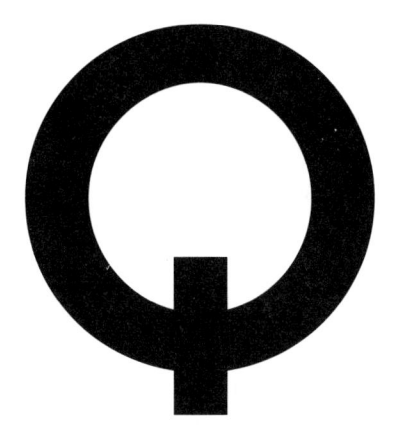

Quaggy – Timber riddled with shake in the center.

Quality – A grade of Idaho White Pine, equivalent to D Select in other species.

Quality Cruise – A timber cruise that tallies the grades of logs as well as the volume.

Quality Grade – One of three grade designations for glue-laminated beams. Quality beams are intended for use where appearance is a primary concern. Also a grade designation for Idaho White Pine boards.

Quality Mark – The mark of an agency accredited by the American Lumber Standards Committee Board of Review indicating conformance to treatment processing and treated products rules. The mark, when affixed to wood products treated with preservatives, certifies that all of the actions and quality certification requirements under the agency's quality control and inspection procedures have been met by both the treater and the quality control agency which licenses the use of the mark by treating plants.

Quartered Lumber – Lumber that has been quarter-sawn approximately radially from the log.

Quartered Veneer – Veneer that has been sliced in a radial direction; that is, at right angles to the growth rings. The term quartered comes from the use of blocks that have been cut into quarters before slicing. Quarter slicing brings out the presence of medullary rays; quarter-sliced veneer appears striped.

Quarter-Girth Measurement – A formula for finding the approximate cubic volume of a round log. A quarter of the girth is assumed to be the equivalent square. The area of the square, multiplied by the length of the log, equals the approximate cubic volume.

Quarter Measure – A reference to the thickness of lumber, especially select, industrial, and board material, which utilizes a nominal one-quarter-inch scale. Thus, 4/4 is a nominal 1-inch, 5/4 is 1-1/4 inches, 6/4 is 1-1/2 inches, etc.

Quarter Point – The point on a Fink or Howe truss where the webs connect with the top chord.

Quarter Round – A type of moulding used as a base shoe, an inside corner moulding, or to cover any 90-degree recessed junctures.

Quartersawn – Lumber sawn so that the annual rings form angles of 45 to 90 degrees with the surface of the piece.

Terms Of The Trade

Quarter Section

Quarter Section – One-fourth of a one-square-mile land section, or 160 acres.

Quarter Sliced – See Quartered Veneer.

Quay – A wharf where ships are loaded or unloaded.

Quay Charges – A fee charged to a vessel for the use of a quay.

Quebec Board – A piece of lumber 2-1/2 inches by 11 inches by 12 feet. Also called the Quebec Deal or English Deal. One hundred pieces of this size are called a Quebec Standard.

Quebec Choker – A peavey, used for moving logs.

Quebec Deal – See Quebec Board.

Quebec Pine – Pinus resinosa, also known as Quebec Red Pine, Canadian Red Pine, or Norway Pine.

Quebec Spruce – Picea alba, P. glauca, White Spruce.

Quebec Standard – A unit of lumber measurement consisting of 100 Quebec Boards. Also, a log rule.

Queen Post – The two principal vertical members in a roof truss.

Queensland Pine – A common name for Hoop, Bunya, and Kauri Pines.

Queen Truss – A truss having two vertical tie posts, or queen posts.

Quick Turner – A proprietary device used to turn logs at the head rig.

Quilted Figure – A distinctive profile sometimes found in the wood of Bigleaf Maple, characterized by crowded bulges in the grain direction.

Quirk – A narrow, flat groove forming part of a moulding.

Quoin – An exterior corner of a structure.

Quotation – An offer to sell at a specific price in response to an inquiry. A prospective buyer will often get a quotation, or "quote," from several sources on a specific item.

R

Rabbet – A rectangular cut in which two surfaces are cut on the edge of a member, parallel with the grain. Also, a Rebate.

Rack Car – A rail car equipped with stakes.

Racking Strength – A measure of the ability of a structure, such as a wall, to withstand horizontal pressure or wrenching transmitted from side to side.

Rack Saw – A log saw, or one having wide teeth.

Radial – Coincident with a radius, from the axis of the tree or log to the circumference. A radial section is a lengthwise section in a plane that extends through the center line of the log.

Radial Layup – 1. The production of plywood with the direction of the grains of adjacent pieces of veneer being parallel. Radial layup plywood is used primarily in making furniture, since it is usually flexible and can be curved. 2. Parallel-laminated veneer or laminated veneer lumber (LVL) which is used for various structural purposes. See Laminated Veneer Lumber.

Radial Sawn – See Quarter Sawn.

Radial Section – The section of lumber cut along a plane containing the pith.

Radial Shake – Shake starting at the circumference of a log and crossing the growth rings. The opposite of ring or cup shake, which occurs between adjacent growth rings.

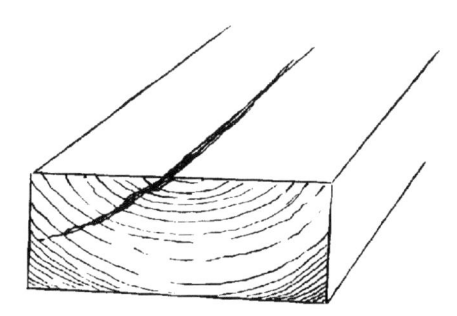

Radial Shake

Radial Stress in Tension – A measure of stress in a curved wood beam subjected to bending. The designation "in tension" indicates that the bending moment increases the radius (makes the member straighter).

Radiata Pine – Pinus radiata. This species is widely planted in New Zealand and Australia, and is also exported from Chile. In the

Terms Of The Trade

Radicle

U.S., it is commonly called Monterey Pine. Also called Kiwi Pine, Insignis Pine.

Radicle – The first root to emerge from a seed.

Radio-Controlled Carriage – A carriage in a yarding operation, operated under remote control through radio signals.

Radio-Frequency Edge Gluing – A method of curing glue quickly by subjecting the bond to radio waves.

Radio-Frequency Electronic Press – A press that uses radio waves to cure glue.

Radius Edge Decking (RED) – A board of nominal 5/4 thickness with rounded edges the length of one surface. Most frequently manufactured from Southern Pine or cedar, it is used primarily for construction of exterior decks on residential homes.

Raft – A floating assembly of logs bound together for transport.

Rafter – 1. A piece of lumber that extends from the ridge of a roof to the eaves and serves to support the roof covering. 2. A person who tends lumber in a river rather than logs; also known as a "River Pig." 3. A boat used to tow logs or lumber.

Rafting Dog – See Dog.

Rafting Ground – An area of a river where log rafts were put together.

Rafting Works – An area near the mouth of a river where logs were sorted or held until needed.

Raft Stick – A long, slender pole to be used as a boomstick.

Rag Paper – Paper made wholly or in part from cotton fibers.

Rafting Ground

Ramin

Rail Head — A loading point, or the nearest point of access to a railroad.

Railing — 1. A solid wood band around one or more edges of a plywood panel. 2. A balustrade.

Rail Market — The abstract arena in which wood products are traded for rail shipment, as opposed to truck or cargo shipments.

Rail Rate — A price charged by rail carriers for transporting goods.

Rail Reform Act of 1980 — The basic legislation that led to deregulation of the railroads, allowing them to make rate or route decisions with little or no oversight by the Interstate Commerce Commission. The Staggers Act, after its key sponsor.

Railroad-Controlled Car — A freight car owned or leased by a railroad for its use in serving any of its customers.

Railroad Tie — A piece of industrial lumber used to support rails on a roadbed. In Britain and other countries, a "Sleeper."

Rails — 1. The horizontal members that form the outside frame of a door, including pieces used as cross-bracing between the top and bottom rails. 2. The horizontal members of a fence, between posts. 3. The side pieces of a ladder to which rungs or steps are attached.

Rail Shipment — A method of shipping wood products by railroad as opposed to truck or cargo shipment.

Rail Spur — A short rail line attached to a main line at one end.

Raimann — A machine that cuts a football-shaped patch and inserts it into a defect in veneer. See Raimann Patch, Patching Machine.

Raimann Patch — A patch, elliptical in shape, used to fill voids caused by defects in the veneers of plywood panels. Sometimes called a "football patch" and one of the two patch designs allowed in A-grade faces.

Rain Day — A day on which producers of air dried Southern Pine could not load because of weather, and were not charged demurrage on a rail car held at their siding. Now obsolete.

Raindrop — A figure in wood grain.

Rain Forest — Any forest in temperate or tropical climates where significant annual rainfall is the dominant factor in the growth of vegetation.

Rain Pants — Lightweight, water-resistant outer pants worn by modern loggers. See Tin Pants.

Rainwet — Lumber that has excess moisture content because of exposure to rain after it was dried. Also, surfaced lumber that has been stained or weathered by exposure to rain.

Raised Grain — A roughened condition on the surface of dressed lumber in which the hard summerwood is raised above the softer springwood, but not torn loose from it.

Raised Moulding — A moulding not on the same level or plane as the wood member or assembly to which it is applied.

Raising Plate — A horizontal timber carrying the feet of other structural members.

Rake — 1. The overhanging part of a roof at a gable end. 2. See Raker.

Rake Angle — Same as cutting angle.

Raker — A sort of tooth in a saw, designed to clear chips from the kerf behind the cutting teeth.

Raker Gauge — A tool used with a saw file to ensure that the raker teeth on a crosscut saw are correctly sized to work with the cutting teeth.

Rally — A revival of action or vigor in wood products trading.

Ramin — Gonystylus bancanus. This hardwood is native to Southeast Asia. Plywood made from this species is often exported to

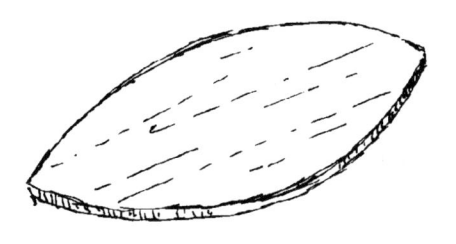

Raimann Patch

Terms Of The Trade

Rampart Arch

the U.S., mainly for interior doors and other decorative uses.

Rampart Arch – An arch with one end higher than the other.

Ram Pike – A snag, or a standing tree from which the top and limbs have been broken off.

Ramrod – The foreman or "push" on a specific job.

Ram's Horn – A figure in wood grain.

Random Core – An oriented strand board panel in which the inner layers of strands or wafers are not aligned in a particular direction.

Random Grain – A combination of vertical and flat grain.

Random Lengths (RL) – 1. Lumber of various lengths, usually in even two-foot increments. Lumber offered as random-length will contain a variety of lengths which can vary greatly between manufacturers and species. A random-length loading is presumed to contain a fair representation of the lengths being produced by a specific manufacturer. 2. A service that regularly publishes information about wood products markets.

Random Matched – Pieces of unequal size combined in one panel.

Random Paneling – Board paneling of varying widths of the same grade and pattern. Plywood paneling grooved to represent random width paneling.

Random Sheet – A sheet of veneer of virtually any width. Random sheets are used as inner plies in layup of plywood, or joined edge to edge to make full-sheet faces.

Random Waferboard – A mat-formed panel product in which all of the wood strands or wafers are randomly distributed.

Random Width (RW) – 1. Wood products of various widths. 2. Veneer clipped in various nonstandard widths, usually less than two feet wide. 3. Shingles or shakes that are manufactured and sold in various widths within a certain length, thickness, and grade. 4. Lumber, usually for factory or industrial uses, that is sold in random widths.

Random Width, Random Length (RWRL) – A designation that indicates that lumber so labeled contains an assortment of widths and lengths. Although all types of lumber may be packaged and sold in this manner, it is more common in the marketing of boards than in dimension or other lumber items. It is particularly common in the marketing of Idaho White Pine, and shop of various species.

Raspberry Jam – This Australian hardwood, Acacia acuminata, is named for its distinctive odor. It is not an important commercial species.

Rate – The price charged by a railroad or truckline to move a product.

Rate Bureau – A group of railroads that establish joint rates.

Rated Sheathing – Panels that have been tested to meet specific load and deflection conditions from impact, point loads, and uniform loads when the panels span two or more supports.

Rate Manual – A compilation of freight rates for one mode of transportation.

Rate Matrix – A transportation rate tariff, usually containing mileage or other scales.

Rate of Growth – The rate at which a tree lays on wood, measured in the number of annual growth rings per inch.

Rate of Growth

Rate Territory – A geographic division that establishes the jurisdiction for rate-making purposes.

Rattlings – Debris from a sawmill.

Raummeter – A German term for one cubic meter of stacked wood. Also called a stere.

Raw Board – A term used for particleboard panels as they come off the sander and before laminates are added.

Raw Material – Primarily logs from which wood products are manufactured. Also used to refer to veneer, sawdust, shavings, or chips used in making products.

Ray Fleck – A speck of medullary ray.

Raymond Jammer – A steam-powered log loader working from a railroad track.

Rays – Cells in wood fiber which store food and are arranged in horizontal bands across the grain in a radial pattern. In some species, such as oak and beech, rays can be seen easily in finished wood. Rays exist in both softwoods and hardwoods. Scientific name: parenchyma.

Raze Knife – A tool used in the British timber trade to inscribe the cubical content of a log on the log itself.

Reach – A beam used on log trucks to connect the trailer to the tractor. The adjustable trailer carriage can be moved forward or backward on the reach to accommodate different log lengths. See Stinger.

Reaction – In futures trading, a decline in prices following an advance.

Reaction Wood – Wood with a special structure or chemical composition developed to help the tree overcome stress from leaning or crooked growth. It is typically difficult to work and unpredictable due to the release of stress.

Real Property – Property that cannot be easily moved: land, mineral rights, a factory.

Rearing Crew – Men who followed behind a log drive on a river, clearing the banks of beached or snagged logs.

Rebate – See Rabbett.

Reburn – A forest fire burning over an area previously burned.

Rebutt – See Rebutted and Rejointed.

Rebuttable Presumption Against Registration (RPAR) – A step in the process of determining whether certain chemicals, generally herbicides and pesticides, are safe for use. The Environmental Protection Agency issues its "presumption" that the chemicals are not suitable for registration, and invites interested companies, agencies, or individuals to support or rebut that position.

Rebutted and Rejointed (R&R) – Shingles whose edges have been machine-trimmed to be exactly parallel and whose butts have been retrimmed at precisely right angles. Used primarily in sidewall applications.

Receiver – A person appointed by a court to hold and protect a property until the legal rights of parties have been established. One who receives the property of a bankrupt and administers the payment of debts.

Receiving Boom – A boom used to corral floating logs in a river until they are used.

Recessed Arch – An arch within and behind another arch.

Reciprocal Switching Agreement – An agreement between rail carriers that they will absorb each other's switching costs when serving the same point.

Reciprocating Saw – A saw operated in a back-and-forth, or up-and-down, motion extending from an engine or other power source.

Reconditioning – A method of diminishing collapse in lumber by applying a high-temperature saturated steam treatment.

Reconstituted Wood – Wood products constructed from fibers or particles.

Recovery Boiler – A furnace used to burn recovered cooking liquor, a by-product of papermaking, to produce steam and reprocess cooking chemicals.

Recovery Plan – A plan for the conservation, surviva, and re covery of threatened or endangered species.

Recycled Paper – Paper made from at least 50% recycled fibers.

Red Alder – See Alder, Alnus rubra.

Redbook – The Lumbermens Redbook, a listing of lumber companies and credit ratings, published periodically by the Lumbermens Credit Association, Inc.

Red Cedar – See Western Red Cedar, In-

Red Cockaded Woodpecker

cense Cedar, Eastern Red Cedar.

Red Cockaded Woodpecker – A bird species native to parts of the South from Texas to Virginia. Listed by the U.S. Fish and Wildlife Service as "endangered."

Red Cypress – Taxodium distichum, also known as Baldcypress.

Redding Rate – A reference to a shipping point in Northern California. Producers in this area have similar freight rates to major markets, which result in f.o.b. mill prices that usually fall within a narrow range.

Red Fir – 1. See California Red Fir. 2. An archaic description of Douglas Fir lumber made from smaller, younger timber principally from the Coast Range and Southern Oregon.

Red Gum – Liquidambar styraciflua. American Red Gum or Sweet Gum. These species are often used in furniture making.

Red Heart – An incipient stage of decay.

Red Knot – A slang term for a knot caused by cutting through a live pine branch.

Red Label – A grade of shingle between Blue Label (#1) and Black Label (#3), graded by the Cedar Shake and Shingle Bureau.

Red Meranti – Shorea species. Any of a number of tropical hardwoods, mainly used as veneers. Lauan.

Red Oak – Quercus rubra and others; Southern Red Oak.

Red Pine – Pinus resinosa. This species, commonly called Norway Pine, is found in the Great Lakes states, the northeastern U.S., and Eastern Canada. The wood is used for general construction and for remanufacturing into such items as sash, moulding, flooring, and crating.

Redress – Financial compensation for a loss caused by the actions of another.

Red Rot – An incipient stage of decay.

Redry – To return material to a dry kiln or veneer dryer for additional drying when the material is found to have a higher moisture content than desired.

Red Silver Fir – Abies amabilis, Pacific Silver Fir.

Red Spruce – Picea rubens. This species, also called Eastern Spruce, is found in Southeastern Canada, the New England states, and along the Appalachian Mountains as far south as North Carolina. In addition to general construction applications, the wood is often used for such products as ladder rails, and is also a source of pulpwood.

Red Stripe – Fungi that have entered cracks in wood and caused decay.

Red Tag – The stoppage of construction at a jobsite by a building inspector because a material or procedure fails to meet building code standards or regulations.

Red Top – The dying crown of a tree that is diseased or under insect attack.

Redwood – Sequoia sempervirens. This species is found only in limited areas of Northern California and Southern Oregon. It is resistant to decay and is used for many of the same purposes as cedar, especially siding and paneling. Another species of Redwood, Sequoia gigantea, grows in the Sierra Mountains of Central California. It is protected from harvest.

Redwood Region – The region of Northern California west of the Coast Range where Redwood trees grow.

Redwood Special – A type of chain saw used to cut large logs, especially Redwood. It has extra space between the teeth to expedite the removal of chips from the kerf.

Reeding – A moulding pattern, or a surface made up of closely spaced, parallel, half-round profiles.

Reel – A roll of paper wound directly from the papermaking machine. The master roll from which smaller rolls are cut.

Refractory Wood – 1. Material that is hard to work. 2. Material that retains its shape and characteristics when subjected to high temperatures.

Refiner Mechanical Pulp – A type of woodpulp used in papermaking, obtained by processing wood chips in a disc refiner, which grinds the chips to fibers and fiber fragments.

Reforestation – The process of rebuilding a forest after it has been logged, or after a fire or other natural processes such as disease kill the timber. Reforestation is accomplished

Reload Pond

Reforestation: Planting a Seedling

through a variety of methods, including the planting of seedlings, the sowing of seed, or natural regeneration from "seed trees." Before replanting, the ground usually is cleared of most of the debris, and efforts are made to limit the growth of brush and grasses that would compete with the seedlings for water and light.

Regeneration – The regrowth of plants and trees in an area that has been logged or burned.

Region – A Forest Service administrative unit. Region 6, for example, includes the national forests of Oregon and Washington.

Regional Forester – A Forest Service official responsible for administering a single region.

Regional Wholesaler – A wholesaler located in a consuming area. One who covers a certain region or territory.

Reglet – A small rectangular moulding.

Regrade – To check the quality of a load of wood products a second time, changing grade designations as necessary. See Reinspection.

Regular 30% Mix – CD 8-foot veneer loaded in specified proportions of the four widths. The 30% mix usually contains 35% 54-inch widths, 35% of 27s, 20% random width, and 10% fishtails. The portions of the 54s and 27s may vary from 30% to 40%, but the combined amount of random width and fishtails is constant at 30%. The 30% mix formula has fallen into disuse except as a general market indicator. The improvement in manufacturing techniques, and the gradual shift to second-growth logs, has allowed veneer mills to recover greater volumes of 54s, and proportionately less of the other widths.

Regulated Forest – A managed forest with equal acreage in all age classes from planting to the year of harvest.

Reinspection – A process in which a wood product received by a buyer and thought by him to be of a lesser grade than that specified is re-examined by a grading agency authorized to make reinspections. Generally, the re-inspected material is considered to be of the proper grade if 95% of it meets the requirements of the stated grade.

Reject – A piece of lumber or a panel that fails to meet a certain grade requirement.

Relaskop – A patented instrument used by foresters to measure tree heights and/or slope gradients by trigonometric means.

Relative Humidity – The amount of water vapor in the air as a percentage of the maximum amount the air could hold at a given temperature. See Absolute Humidity, Dew Point.

Release – To free trees from competition by eliminating brush or other growth that is crowding them.

Released Slash – Residue in a logging area that has been sufficiently burned or has decomposed enough to permit the logger to be released from responsibility should a fire occur.

Relief-Grain Surface – A surface to which a grain pattern has been applied, by printing or embossing, to simulate the texture of real wood grain.

Reload – 1. A warehouse or distribution facility located relatively near producing regions. A reload operation purchases inventory in quantity, blends various items to customers' specifications, and reships them as mixed cars. 2. See Border Point. 3. A location where truckloads of logs are assembled from off-highway vehicles and reloaded on highway trucks or rail cars.

Reloader – One who uses a reload. Can be a producer, wholesaler, or a retail organization such as a chain or co-op.

Reload Pond – A pond where logs are stored for sorting and reshipping.

Terms Of The Trade

Relog

Relog – To go back to a logging operation to retrieve smaller or lower-quality trees after an initial logging.

Reman – An abbreviation for remanufacture or remanufacturing. A process of converting a common product to a more specialized or higher grade product by further manufacturing.

Renewable Resource – A natural resource, such as timber, that renews itself over time by regrowth.

Repair – A patch applied, usually to plywood, to fill or replace a defect.

Repeat – The distance between identical design elements in panels. The most widely used is an 18-inch repeat, although they can range from 3 to 54 inches.

Repetitive Member – One of a series of framing or supporting members such as joists, studs, planks, or decking that are continuous, or spaced not more than 24 inches apart, and are joined by floor, roof, or other load-distributing elements. In repetitive-member framing, each member is connected to, and receives some shared support from, the others.

Repetitive Member Design Value – See Repetitive Stress Rating.

Repetitive Stress Rating – The strength rating of lumber (fiber stress in bending) applicable when three or more pieces, spaced no more than 24 inches apart and joined by flooring or sheathing, support loads on the flooring or sheathing. Repetitive stresses are applied on joists and rafters. The repetitive stress rating for a particular species, size, and grade of lumber is always higher than the single stress rating for that lumber.

Replevin – An action to have goods, which were unlawfully removed, returned to the original possessor.

Reprod – Reproduction. Young growth in an area previously cleared by logging or fire.

Reproduction Area – An area of forest land on which young trees have started to grow after logging or a fire. The trees may have been started by broadcast seeding, hand planting of seedlings, or from natural seed sources.

Resaw – 1. To saw a piece of lumber along its horizontal axis. 2. A bandsaw that performs such an operation.

Resawn Board – A piece of lumber, most commonly 11/16-inch thick, obtained by re-sawing a piece of 6/4 common. Used mostly for sheathing and industrial applications. Produced most often from Ponderosa Pine and White Fir.

Resawn Lumber – Lumber that has been sawn on a horizontal axis to produce two thinner pieces. See Resawn Board.

Residual Biomass – The organic material left on the ground after an event such as logging, or a fire. Slash.

Residual Green Tree Reserve – Green trees left standing on a logging site to provide a local seed source or animal habitat, or for other purposes.

Resilience – The property of a wood member that allows it to recover from strain.

Resilient Floor Coverings – Vinyl- or asphalt-based floor coverings manufactured with enough "give" to resist permanent deformation or denting due to dropped objects, shoe heels, etc.

Resin – A natural vegetable substance occurring in various plants and trees, especially the coniferous species. Used in varnishes, inks, medicines, and plastic products. Also, any of a variety of synthetic products having many of the properties of natural resin and used in the production of plastics or other products.

Resin Canal – See Resin Ducts.

Resin Ducts – The canals between wood cells of the tree in which resins are found. Resin ducts are often clearly visible in cross sections of wood.

Resin Fortified Glue – A protein-based glue to which a resin, such as phenolic resin, has been added to improve resistance to mold and bacteria. At higher levels of resin fortification some improvement in bonding may result if longer press times are used.

Resin Spots – Hard pieces of dark foreign material in the face layer of a particleboard panel. Composed of glue and wood dust.

Resorcinol Resin Adhesive – A synthetic resin adhesive made with resorcinol-formaldehyde resin using a hardener, usually composed of wood flour and paraform. The ad-

Ribbon Joist

hesive provides an exterior quality glueline and will cure at room temperature. It is used in the manufacture of laminated beams or scarf joints.

Resource Allocation Model (RAM) – A timber management planning model that was widely used by the U.S. Forest Service. The model served to predict future standing timber inventories.

Resource Management Plan – A land-use plan developed by the Bureau of Land Management under current regulations and in compliance with the Federal Land Policy and Management Act.

Resources Planning Act (RPA) – The Forest and Rangeland Renewable Resources Planning Act of 1974. The act directs the Secretary of Agriculture to make assessments, every 10 years, of the U.S. range and forest lands, and of all renewable resources within them.

Respond – A pilaster forming a pair, or matching another pilaster or column.

Retail Chain – Two or more retail yards operated by the same company, usually under one name.

Retailer – One who sells directly to the ultimate user of a product, such as a building contractor, remodeler, etc. The last link in the distribution chain.

Retail Terms – A credit term used in defining the terms of payment of invoices. Commonly, these call for payment within a set period after delivery of the goods.

Retention by Assay – A method of determining preservative retention in treated wood by extraction and analysis of specified samples.

Reticulate Veins – Veins that resemble the threads of a net; the smaller veins in broadleafed trees.

Retort – A vessel used to treat wood by applying various chemicals under pressure.

Return – The continuation, in a different direction, of a moulding or projection, usually at right angles.

Returnable Pallet – A pallet designed to be used for more than one trip.

Reusable Pallet – See Returnable Pallet.

Reveal – The side of an opening in a wall to accommodate a door or window.

Reverse Board & Batten – A siding pattern in which the wider boards are nailed over the battens, producing a narrow inset.

Reversible Siding – Resawn board siding that may be installed with either the surfaced or sawn side exposed.

R-Factor – A measurement of a property's resistance to the passage of heat, or thermal conductivity. The higher the R-Factor, the greater the resistance.

Rhombs – A hexagonal pattern for parquet flooring.

Rib – 1. One of a series of parallel structural members backing sheathing. 2. A curved rafter.

Ribbing – A more-or-less regular corrugation of the surface of wood, caused by differential shrinkage of springwood and summerwood. Also called crimping or washboarding.

Ribbon Board – A horizontal brace used in balloon framing where the board is applied to notches in the studs; a let-in brace.

Ribbon Coursing – A sidewall pattern for shakes and shingles.

Ribbon Face – See Ribbon Stripe.

Ribbon Grain – See Ribbon Stripe.

Ribbon Joist – See Band Joist.

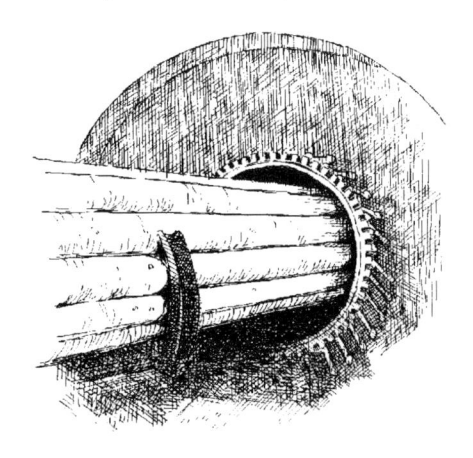

Pressure Retort

Terms Of The Trade

Ribbon Stripe

Ribbon Stripe — A pattern on quartered veneer that has the appearance of a ribbon.

Rick — A pile of any kind of loose material, such as firewood, contained in a framework.

Ride — The side of a log facing the ground while it is being dragged.

Ridge Beam — A horizontal timber to which the tops of rafters are fastened.

Ridge Board — See Ridge Beam.

Ridge Cap — A layer of wood or metal topping the ridge of a roof.

Ridge Cut — The cut at the top of a hip rafter.

Ridge Pole — The highest horizontal beam of a roof supported by rafters.

Rift Crack — A radial crack in a log.

Rift Cutting — The production of veneer by slicing or sawing a log at right angles to the radius of the log. A parallel grain pattern results. The process is similar to the production of half-round veneer, but a quartered log is used.

Rift-Cut Veneer — Veneer that has been sliced or sawn at an angle of 45 degrees to the annual rings.

Rift Grain — A grain pattern resulting from rift cutting, or slicing/sawing a log at right angles to the radius of the log. See Rift Cutting.

Riga Last — A timber measuring up to 65 cubic feet in the round, or 80 cubic feet of squared timber.

Rigger — The logger in charge of installing the rigging used to draw logs to a landing.

Rigging — The cables, blocks, lines, hooks, etc., used in the yarding of logs.

Rigging Crew — The loggers who handle the rigging at a logging operation.

Rigging Slinger — A member of a logging crew who supervises chokersetters, selects logs to be yarded, handles tangles in rigging, and signals when to start and stop lines.

Rigid Frame — A structural component in

Rigger

River Boss

which the studs and rafters are joined with plywood gussets, creating a rigid frame that acts like an arch. Rigid frame construction reduces the need for interior supports.

Rim Joist – A joist applied to both ends of the floor joists to provide stability and lateral support while preventing rotation.

Rim Speed – The rate at which the teeth of a circular saw revolve.

Rind Gall – Surface wounds in a tree that are later covered by new growth.

Ring – 1. A growth ring. 2. An area on the floor of a futures exchange in which commodities are traded. Rings are usually reserved for commodities with lighter trading; commodities with heavier volumes are traded in the floor's pits.

Ring Boom – A small boom used to gather logs that escaped from the main boom.

Ring-Cut Flaker – A machine used to produce flakes for furnish in the production of waferboard, OSB, and similar products.

Ring Debarker – A machine consisting of a stationery outer ring and a revolving inner ring which holds curved cutting tools to remove bark from logs.

Ring Dog – A dog with a large ring through its head for carrying cable.

Ring Failure – See Shake.

Ring Porous – A condition in which a growth ring contains a wide variation in the size and number of pores.

Ring Rot – Decay following the direction of the annual rings.

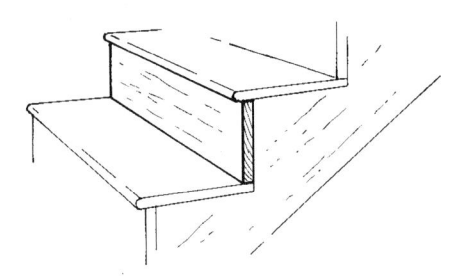

Riser

Ring Shake – Cup shake between adjacent growth rings.

Rip – To saw a piece of lumber along its longitudinal axis.

Riparian – Areas associated with or influenced by streams, ponds, or lakes.

Riparian Ecosystem – A functioning plant and animal community centered around a riparian area.

Riparian Rights – Rights of a landowner to water on or abutting his property.

Ripped & Bundled – A service provided at an extra cost by some producers in which a specified number of pieces of lumber, obtained by ripping, are tied together in a package at the buyer's request.

Ripped Lumber – Lumber that has been sawn and resawn lengthwise to reduce its width, or to make two or more narrow pieces from a single wide piece.

Ripper – A ripsaw.

Rippled Dressing – Uneven dressing or surfacing usually caused by misaligned, unbalanced, or blunt planer knives.

Ripple Marks – 1. See Rippled Dressing. 2. A figure caused by buckling fibers due to compression in a growing tree.

Rip Saw – A saw used to cut lumber lengthwise.

Rip Saw Optimizer – See Optimizer.

Rise – 1. The difference in diameter between two points on a log due to taper. 2. The increase in height of a set of steps or a roof; pitch.

Rise and Run – A carpentry term used to denote the angle of an incline, as on a roof.

Riser – A vertical member between two stair treads.

Rive – To split shingles from a bolt, using a froe.

Rived Bolt – A piece or chunk of wood, usually cedar, split from a log, using wedges.

River Boss – The man who was in charge of river drives in the Northeast.

River Drive

River Drive – A method of transporting logs to a mill via a river.

River Hog – A logger who also worked on river drives. Also called a River Pig, River Rat, or River Jack.

River Jack – See River Hog.

River Mills – A group of millwork manufacturers, located in the Upper Midwest on the Ohio, Mississippi, and other rivers. Originally, they used the rivers to power some of their equipment as well as for transportation.

River Pig – See River Hog.

River Pirate – A person who stole logs from their rightful owners on a river drive.

River Rat – See River Hog.

River Scale – Water scale; logs measured while in the water.

R List – A set of grading rules published by the Pacific Lumber Inspection Bureau that describes the export grades of Douglas Fir, Western Hemlock, Sitka Spruce, and Western Red Cedar lumber.

Road Ban – A restriction placed on road usage during periods of thaw (breakup) in the spring. The thawing of a frozen road takes place at the surface and, with the base still frozen, water does not drain off. Until the base thaws, or the surface dries, a road is vulnerable to severe damage from vehicular traffic.

Road Credit – A credit earned by a purchaser of national forest timber for building roads to gain access to the timber. The cost of building the road is deducted from the amount owed for the timber.

Road Gang – Logging crew members responsible for road construction and maintenance.

Roadless Area – A forest area essentially undisturbed by man; specifically, those areas of a national forest that have not been opened up for timber harvest.

Roadless Area Review and Evaluation (RARE) – A program conducted by the U.S. Forest Service to inventory roadless lands in the national forests and to evaluate them for future use designations, principally to determine which areas had potential as wilderness areas; those areas not so designated were to be opened to timber management. RARE I was conducted in 1973 and involved studies of about 56 million acres. Complaints from conservationists that the agency's evaluation was inadequate led to RARE II, beginning in 1977; this involved a study of about 67 million acres. Some decisions reached as a result of RARE II were overturned in federal court. Others, however, have been the basis of agreements establishing wilderness and multiple-use areas.

Roadless Islands – Roadless areas that are surrounded by permanent waters, or are markedly distinguished from surrounding lands by topographical or ecological features, such as precipices, canyons, thickets, or swamps.

Road Logs – See Highway Logs.

Roadrailer – A piggyback trailer having wheels for both highway and track usage; does not require a separate rail car.

Robertson Raft – The raft design that was first successful for towing large quantities of logs. Designed by Hugh Robertson of New Brunswick.

Rock Elm – Ulmus racemosa. A lighter colored and finer textured wood than common elm. Used primarily for veneer.

Rocking Chair Money – Unemployment compensation.

Rock Saw – A saw used to detect rocks or metal in a log that might damage the headsaw.

Rocky Mountain Bristlecone Pine – Pinus aristata. Pines of this species, a close relative to the Great Basin Bristlecone Pine, P. longaeva, are among the oldest living trees known. They are found mostly in Colorado and New Mexico.

Rocky Mountain Douglas Fir – Pseudotsuga menziesii var. glauca.

Rocky Mountain Juniper – Juniperus scopulorum. This species is found in a broad range, from British Columbia to New Mexico. Its wood is used primarily for posts and fuel.

Rocky Mountain Ponderosa Pine – Pinus ponderosa var. scopulorum.

Rod Engine – A type of logging locomotive in which the pistons were connected directly to the drive wheels.

Rod Mill – A machine that manufactures cylindrical objects, such as broom handles.

Roe Figure – The appearance of a radial surface when stripes less than one foot long are formed by irregular interlocked grain.

Roll – A technique for freeing a log hung up on a stump by first circling the center of the log with a cable, then rolling it sideways by tightening the line. See Parbuckle.

Roll Case – A series of rollers across which stacks of lumber or plywood can be moved to another location.

Roll Coater – A machine used to apply finish material to the face of a plywood panel.

Roller – See Transit.

Roller Bar – A round metal bar set in a channel across the head of a veneer lathe, parallel to the axis of the block, and driven so the surface speed of the bar is the same as that of the block. It applies pressure at the knife gap, compressing the wood fiber without creating the friction that is encountered with a solid nosebar. See Nosebar.

Roller Check – Cracks in wood caused by a piece of cupped lumber being flattened between machine rollers.

Roller Nosebar – See Roller Bar.

Roller Split – Same as Roller Check.

Rolling Shear – A stress generated in plywood. Each ply of a piece of plywood is subject to horizontal shear when a load is placed on the piece. Since a ply is fixed in relation to the ply or plies glued to it, the fibers in the wood tend to roll over each other.

Rolling Stock – Railroad cars.

Roll On, Roll Off (Ro-Ro) – A method of loading bulk carrier ships in which wheeled vehicles are used to drive aboard the ship and set the lumber in place in the hold. Opposite of Lift On, Lift Off.

Rollway – A landing or dump where logs are stored while awaiting transportation.

Roman Arch – A round arch.

Romanian Pine – Another name for European Spruce, Picea abies.

Rood – A unit of land measurement equal to 40 square rods, or 1/4 acre.

Roof – In air drying, a cover on top of the stacked wood to protect the upper layers from exposure to the weather.

Rolling a Log with Peaveys

Roof Boards

Roof Boards – Boards used as sheathing, attached to rafters as a base for other roofing materials.

Roof Decking – See Decking.

Roofers – Lumber, usually 1x4s, used as backing for shingles or shakes on a roof.

Roofing Felt – Waterproof sheets of fiber usually laid under other roofing materials.

Roof Sheathing – Boards or panels nailed to roof rafters on which the shingles or other roof covering is laid.

Roof Square – The four bundles of shingles that are required to cover 100 square feet of roof, when properly applied.

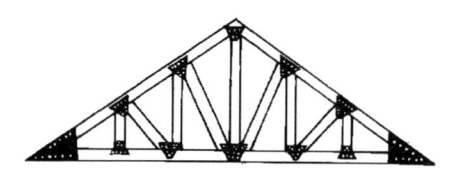

Roof Truss

Roof Truss – An engineered building component supporting the roof in place of rafters. Roof trusses are usually constructed in a triangular shape with a number of interconnected pieces that spread a load evenly across the truss.

Room Temperature Setting Adhesive – A glue, based on a phenolic formula, that cures at room temperature and below, and at a faster rate than other adhesives.

Rooter – A log that has dug into the ground while being yarded.

Root Rot – Decay in a tree's root system caused by a fungus, of which the most common is Fomes annosus. Generally, the fungus enters through a wound and grows through the heartwood into the root system.

Rope-Fed Carriage – A system used in early sawmills that used ropes to bring logs into contact with the headsaw.

Rope Moulding – A moulding pattern simulating the twisted strands of a piece of rope.

Ropy Finish – An uneven surface defect in hardboard.

Ro-Ro – See Roll On, Roll Off.

Rosin – See Resin.

Ross – To remove the bark of a log.

Rosser – A person who barked logs manually, using a rossing tool.

Rosser Head Debarker – A type of mechanical debarker which utilizes a cutting tool on a pivoting arm to remove bark from a log being rotated.

Rossing Tool – A tool used to remove bark from a tree; a spud.

Rosy – Irregular, overlapping wood grain.

Rotary Clipper – A knife that rotates with the flow of veneer and clips the pieces to size, as opposed to the traditional guillotine-style clipper.

Rotary-Cut Veneer – Veneer peeled from a round log by turning the log against a knife to produce a continuous sheet of wood of a uniform thickness. The common method of making softwood veneers.

Rotary Drum Blender – A rotating cylindrical machine used in the manufacture of oriented strand board or waferboard. It combines wafers with resin before the panels are formed into mats.

Rotary Figure – Wood grain in veneer that has been peeled on a lathe.

Rotary Saw – Same as a circular saw or circle saw.

Rotation Age – The period of time required to establish and grow a timber crop to a specified size. Rotation ages vary according to species, soil conditions, and climate.

Rotten Knot – A knot in a more advanced state of decay than the surrounding wood.

Rotten Tree – A tree of a commercial species that does not contain a sawlog, usually because of rot. A tree in which rot accounts for more than 50 percent of the total cull volume.

Rough – Not dressed or surfaced. The surface texture is the same as when the piece was first sawn or peeled.

Routing

Rough-Backed Board (RBB) – A board that has been resawn from thicker material, with the sawn side left rough. Rough-backed boards are often used as siding or paneling to give a rustic affect.

Rough-Barked Fir – Grand Fir, Abies grandis.

Rough Cut – Uneven areas of rough grain surrounded by smooth grain on the face of veneer. Also called Rough Peel.

Rough Dry – Lumber that has been seasoned but not dressed.

Rougher Headed – Lumber that has been run through a planer with notched knives. The lumber has a rough-sawn texture, but is accurately sized.

Rough Floor – Unfinished floor material over which the finished floor surface is laid.

Rough Full Sawn – Unsurfaced lumber sawn to full specified size.

Roughing In – Installation of all concealed electrical lines or plumbing, before finishing or installation of fixtures.

Rough Lumber – Lumber which has not been dressed or surfaced but has been sawn, edged, and trimmed.

Rough Peel – See Rough Cut.

Rough Sand – In particleboard manufacture, an area of a sanded panel that was not sanded with the finish sanding heads. The surface feels and appears rough.

Rough Sawn – 1. Lumber that has not been planed or sanded. 2. A type of plywood siding in which the face has not been dressed, to give a rustic effect.

Rough Tree – 1. A tree of a commercial species that does not contain a sawlog, usually because of roughness, poor form, splits, cracks, etc., and has less than one-third of its gross volume in sound wood. 2. Any live tree of a noncommercial species.

Round – 1. A moulding which may be semicircular to full round, as in a closet rod. 2. A turn of wire rope around a drum.

Round Arch – An arch of semicircular shape; a Roman arch.

Round-Edge Lumber – Lumber with bark on both edges.

Round Hook – A half-round hook through which a chain will slide, like a slip noose in a rope.

Round Knot – See Knot Occurrence/Quality.

Round Saw – See circle saw.

Round Stuff – Logs.

Round Ties – Round railroad ties, used on spur railroad lines in the woods.

Round Turn – The situation in which the long or short position of a futures trader is offset by making an opposite transaction, or by accepting or making actual delivery.

Roundup – See Block Roundup.

Roundwood – The cubic volume of logs, bolts, and other round sections as they are cut from the tree.

Roundwood Equivalent – The volume of logs required to produce a given quantity of lumber, panels, pulp, paper, or other wood products.

Route – A legal description of how a rail car will move between two points.

Router Patch

Router Patch – A wood patch in plywood with straight sides and rounded ends, similar to a tongue depressor, used to fill voids caused by defects. One of two patch designs allowable in A grade faces. Also known as a Davis Patch.

Routing – 1. The process of determining how a shipment will move from origin to des-

Terms Of The Trade

Royals

tination. 2. The method of removing a defect when a router patch or Davis patch is to be inserted in a piece of plywood.

Royals – Shingles of 24-inch lengths and a thickness of 1/2-inch at the butt.

Roy Rule – This rule, the official log rule of the province of Quebec, is applied to logs 3 to 44 inches in small-end diameter, and 4 to 20 feet in length. Logs over 20 feet are measured by the Quebec Cubic Foot Scale.

Rubber Man – Any of several reciprocating devices used to pull a hand-powered saw opposite a logger working alone. Tire inner tubes were sometimes used.

Rub Tree – A tree used as a pivot point when hauling logs to a landing; the rub tree protects the remaining trees.

Rueping – An empty-cell method of wood preservative treatment. See Empty Cell Process.

Ruff Sawn – A designation for plywood paneling or siding that has been saw-textured to provide a decorative, rough sawn appearance.

Rule – 1. A regulation issued by organizations governing the grading or measurement of wood products. 2. A flat strip of wood used for measuring.

Run – The drying of a single charge of lumber in a kiln.

Runner – An employment agent in the days of logging camps.

Running Days – Days of operation. On a railroad, running days include Saturdays, Sundays, and holidays.

Running Foot – A linear foot; a measurement of the actual length of a piece of lumber, without regard to the thickness or width of the piece.

Running Inch – A linear inch; a measurement of the actual length of a piece of lumber. See Running Foot.

Running Skyline – A logging system employing two or more suspended moving cables, usually called the main and haulback lines, that provide lift and travel to a load carrier.

Run Off Sander Belt – A condition that occurs when a corner or edge of a panel does not get sanded. The area is thicker than the rest of the panel.

Run to Pattern – Lumber that has been machined to a particular configuration, such as shiplap, centermatched, etc.

Ruptured Grain – Breaks in veneer resulting from cutting or irregular grain.

Russel Car – A short car once used on logging railroads in the western pine country.

Russian Coupling – A bucked log that was not cut cleanly through.

Russian Fathom – Seven feet cubed, or 343 cubic feet.

Rust Infection – A plant disease caused by fungi. Rust diseases among gymnosperms affect needles, cones, and stems. Stem rust diseases cause malformations in the host tree.

Rutger's Process – A process of pressure preservation consisting of a solution of oil and salt.

R Value – The resistance to heat flow of a material. The higher the R Value, the more effective the insulation.

S

S1S1E – Surfaced one side and one edge.

S1S2E – Surfaced one side and two edges.

S2E – Surfaced two edges.

S2S – Surfaced two sides.

S2S1E – Surfaced two sides and one edge.

S4S – Surfaced four sides.

Safety Swede

Sack – 1. To draw boomsticks into a circle to close up a bag boom (log raft) for towing. 2. A log boom.

Sacker – The tail-end man on a river drive crew.

Sack Raft – A log boom.

Sacome – The profile of a moulding.

Saddle Joint – A notch cut in a horizontal timber to provide a good footing for a vertical member. The notch is cut in an inverted V shape to fit an opposite cut on the end of the joining member.

Saddle Roof – A gabled, pitched roof.

Safe Load – The proportion of the ultimate breaking strength of a member to which it is safe to load it.

Safe Side – In unloading logs from trucks or rail cars, the side away from the dump.

Safety Swede – A lever used to tighten binders on loaded trucks.

Sag – 1. The amount of deflection of a member between supports. 2. A slump in a finish coat, such as paint that was not properly cured.

Sailer

Sailer – A limb or other chunk of wood broken loose by a falling tree.

Sale – 1. A unit of timber offered for sale as a separate entity, usually designated by a particular name, such as "Cougar Ridge Sale," or "Salt Creek Salvage Sale," etc. 2. A transaction between a buyer and seller.

Sales Agent – A broker or wholesaler who sells the production of a mill without actually taking title to that production and who collects a fee or commission for his services.

Salt Treatment – One method of preserving wood, using any of various waterborne salts to impregnate the wood. Among the more widely used systems are Wolman Salts and Osmose Salts.

Salt Water Immersion – A level of treatment of wood products intended for use in, or in contact with, salt water. As established by the American Wood Preservers Association, that level is 2.50 pounds of retained preservative per cubic foot of wood.

Salt Water Pine – Another name for Slash Pine, Pinus elliottii.

Salvage Logging – Logging that involves harvesting only dead or dying timber.

Salvage Sale – A sale involving a timber stand that has been ravaged by some disaster, such as a fire, disease, insect kill, or windstorm. Such a sale often involves salvaging dead or dying timber before it is destroyed by decay or insects.

Sample Board – In wood drying, a board from which samples are cut and tested to determine moisture content.

Sample Tally – See Formula Tally.

Sampson – One of several devices used to lift or move a log.

Sandability – In wood finishing, the ease by which a coating can be sanded without dragging or gumming the sanding medium.

Sanded – Panel products that have been processed through a machine sander to provide a smooth surface on one or both sides. In sanded plywood, A or B grade veneers are used for one side of the panel.

Sanded-Face Shingle – A shingle with re-trimmed edges and butt that has been sanded to remove saw marks, etc. It is usually applied to a wall as part of a decorative effect.

Sanded List – A list of prices for sanded plywood by which all standard grades and thicknesses were related to the stated price of 1/4-inch AD Interior. The sanded list is no longer used, although prices are still sometimes related through various thicknesses and grades.

Sander – A machine designed to smooth wood, and to remove saw or lathe marks and other imperfections. Sanders range in size from hand-held to large drums or belts capable of surfacing a full-size panel.

Sander Dust – The residue from a sanding operation, usually drawn off by vacuum to a bag house for storage. Sander dust is extremely fine and can be volatile.

Sander Hesitation – A defect in a panel that results when it stops under a sander head.

Sander Skip – An area of a sanded panel that was not sanded when the surrounding area was, because the panel was thinner than the setting on the sander heads.

Sander Stop – A low spot on the surface of a particleboard panel, perpendicular to the sander direction, that occurs when the panel stops in the sander with the belts still running.

Sand Hill – A steep section of a logging road spread with sand to slow heavily loaded sleighs; used in the early logging days in Eastern Canada.

Sanding Loss – The decrease in size of a wood product due to surfacing with a sander. This loss is less than if surfacing were done with blades.

Sand Pine – Pinus clausa. This pine is found almost exclusively in North-Central Florida, where it grows in very sandy soil. The wood is used mostly for pulp.

Sand Through – A particleboard defect in which the face layer has been sanded off, exposing the core.

Sandwich Beam – See Flitched Beam.

Sandwich Film – A type of vinyl overlay consisting of an opaque base that is usually top-printed, with a clear layer laminated on top.

Saturation Point

Sandwich Panel – A panel formed by bonding two thin facings to a thick, and usually lightweight, core. Typical facing materials include plywood, single veneers, hardboard, plastics, laminates, and various metals such as aluminum or stainless steel. Typical core materials include plastic foam sheets, rubber, and formed honeycombs of paper, metal, or cloth.

Santa Lucia Fir – Abies bracteata. This rare species is found only in California's Santa Lucia mountains. It is not a commercial species.

Sap – The circulating fluid in a tree. On exposure to air it turns gummy. In the days of hand-powered saws, a bottle of turpentine or other solvent was a part of the tool kit to provide lubrication. See Saw Oil.

Sap Fir – A colloquialism for sap-heavy timber such as White Fir.

Sap Grade – A grade of Southern Yellow Pine export lumber. Also KD Saps.

Sap Is Down – See Sap Is Stopped.

Sap Is Running – A reference to a period in springtime when a tree puts on most of its new growth. Also, Sap Is Up.

Sap Is Stopped – A reference to a tree in dormancy. Also, Sap Is Down.

Sap Is Up – See Sap Is Running.

Sapling – A young, growing tree, too small to be merchantable.

Sapper – See Knee Bolter.

Sappie – A slang term, used mostly in Canada, to designate an inferior tree – one that has heavy pitch, for instance.

Saps – Pieces of lumber that are chiefly sapwood. See KD Saps.

Sap Stain – A discoloration of the sapwood.

Sapwood – The outer layers of growth between the bark and the heartwood that contain the sap.

Sapwood Tree – A tree with light-colored heartwood, showing little difference from the sapwood.

Sash – The portion of a window that holds the glass.

Sash Bar – A strip separating panes of glass in a window. A Muntin.

Sash Door – A door having its upper portion glazed.

Sash Gang – A multiple, or "gang" saw in which a series of blades is fixed vertically between two horizontal members. The entire assembly is then moved up and down to rip cants that are moved through the saw on rollers. Also, Swedish Gang Saw.

Sash Saw – A ribbon of toothed steel, having a handle that extends from one end of the blade to the other in an extended U shape.

Satisfaction – A payment or performance that satisfies the terms of an agreement.

Saturation Point – The stage at which the cell walls are saturated with water, but the cell cavities are free of water. This occurs at about a 30% moisture content, based on the ovendry weight. Also, Fiber Saturation Point.

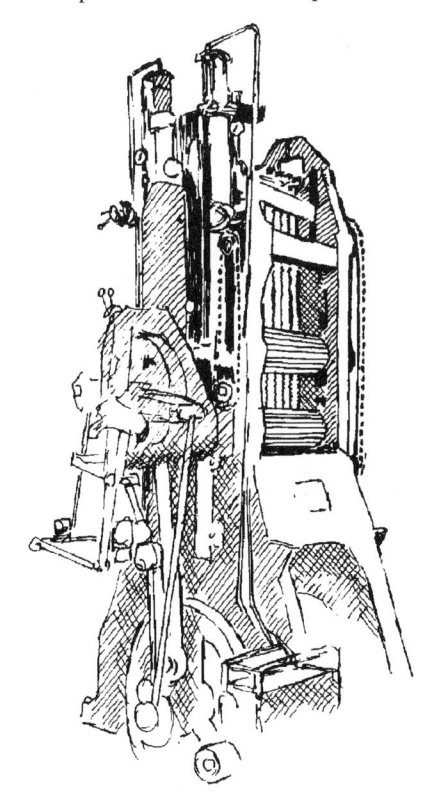

Sash Gang

Savannah

Savannah – A grassy, mostly treeless plain, usually in the tropics or subtropics.

Saw – 1. A slang reference to a timber faller in the pine country. 2. See Saws.

Saw Alive – See Cut Alive.

Sawara White Cedar – Chamaecyparis pisifera. This species, native to Japan, is widely used in the U.S. as an ornamental.

Saw Arbor – The shaft and bearings that hold a power-driven saw.

Saw Bar – The steel frame around which the chain runs on a chain saw.

Saw Boss – The person in charge of a cutting crew in the woods.

Sawbuck – A device used to hold fuel logs when sawing firewood. A saw horse having legs in a "X" configuration on each end. This is the origin for the slang term for a $10 bill, from the "X" of the legs of a sawbuck and the Roman numeral X.

Saw Butted – Trimmed by a saw on both ends.

Saw Collar – A device fastened to the outside of a saw blade to hold it on the arbor.

Saw Crew – A Cutting Crew.

Saw Dentist – A saw filer. So called because he works to sharpen the saw's teeth.

Saw Doctor – The mechanic who keeps the saws in condition; a saw filer.

Sawdust – Small particles of wood removed by the saw in cutting.

Sawdust Concrete – A type of concrete in which the aggregate consists mainly of wood sawdust.

Sawdust Eater – A sawmill worker.

Sawdust Hook – A short-handled, toothed tool used to clear sawdust away from sawmill machinery.

Sawdust Savage – A worker in a sawmill, although sometimes applied to a logger.

Sawfalling – A general term for the developing (lower) grades of Scandinavian export lumber.

Saw Filer – See Filer.

Saw Fitter – Same as Saw Filer.

Saw Guide – That part of a bandsaw that keeps the saw cutting in a straight line.

Sawhand – A worker in a sawmill.

Sawhorse – A portable frame or trestle used to hold wood while sawing.

Sawing Around – Turning the log on a saw carriage between passes through the saw, to obtain the highest grade or greatest volume.

Sawing Fat – Sawing lumber at a thickness greater than necessary. A wasteful practice.

Sawing Stool – A British term for sawhorse.

Sawing Through and Through – A method of sawing in which a log is sawn in one direction only. This method produces a combination of flat-grain and edge-grain boards. Other methods of sawing include "sawing around" a log, which produces flat-grain boards only, and quartersawing, which produces mostly edge-grain boards.

Sawing Variation – The variation in thickness of a piece of wood due to lateral movement of a saw.

Sawmill – A manufacturing plant in which logs are converted to lumber by running them through a series of saws.

Sawn – Cut with a saw or saws.

Sawn Lath – An unsurfaced strip of wood, usually 3/8-inch thick, 1-1/2-inches wide, and 32 or 48 inches long. Used as a foundation for plaster on interior walls, and as inserts in chain link fencing.

Sawn Oversize – See Cut-Full Lumber.

Sawn Through and Through – See Cut Alive.

Sawn Veneer – Veneer that has been cut from a block with a saw rather than peeled on a lathe, or sliced off by a blade. Sawn veneer is sometimes said to be more solid than sliced or peeled veneer. Because of saw-kerf waste, it is more costly to produce.

Saw Oil – A lubricant and solvent, such as kerosene or turpentine, used on a saw when felling or bucking trees. The saw oil dissolves sap, which turns sticky when exposed to air. See Bottle Hook.

Saw Pit – 1. The space under a machine saw that allows the saw to complete its motion, and that receives the sawdust. 2. See Whipsawing.

Saws – Toothed steel devices used to cut wood. The principal saws used in wood-products production include: 1. Band: An endless ribbon toothed on one or both edges, held in tension on two pulley wheels and powered by one or both of them. 2. Chain: Usually portable, a gas-powered saw utilizing an articulated chain with cutting teeth running around a bar of flat steel; used in felling trees and bucking logs. 3. Circular: A circular steel blade fitted with cutting teeth and mounted on an arbor. 4. Drag: A powered reciprocating saw used to buck logs. 5. Gang: A number of toothed steel ribbons, fitted in a sash or frame, operating together. 6. Rock: A circular saw that removes a wide kerf on the upper surface of a log; used to remove stones or debris before a log enters the headrig. 7. Sash: A saw fitted in a frame which moves vertically. 8. Slashers: A set of circular saws operated in combination for quick cross cutting of lengths of wood before chipping or grinding into pulp fibers, or as fuel. 9. Swing: A circular saw suspended on a pendulum; used in cross cutting. 10. Twin: Two circular saws mounted one above the other to cut in the same plane; double arbor saws.

Saw Set – A tool used to bend the teeth of a crosscut saw slightly so that the sawblade has clearance to cut.

Saw-Sized Lumber – Lumber uniformly sawn to the net size for surfaced lumber, and not planed on the faces, although the corners may be eased, or rounded slightly. A variation in sawing of not more than 1/32-inch under and 1/8-inch over is permitted in 20% of the pieces.

Sawsmith – A mechanic who keeps saws in good working order.

Saw Tex – See Saw Textured.

Saw Textured – A texture put on a piece of siding or paneling by a saw or knurled drum to give it a textured, rough, and/or resawn appearance.

Sawtimber – Logs of sufficient size and quality as to be suitable for conversion to lumber or other products.

Saw Vise – A vise used to hold a saw firmly in place while its teeth are sharpened.

Sawyer – 1. A worker in a sawmill who operates the head rig, or main saw, making the initial cuts on a log. 2. In the early logging days, one who felled trees and sawed them into logs; these workers are now called fallers and buckers, respectively.

Sawyer Beetle – This destructive insect attacks logs cut from most coniferous trees, and will also infest dead standing timber. The larvae of the beetle bore holes in the wood. The holes facilitate the entrance of stain and decay-causing fungi. Monochamus species.

Saxony – A pattern of parquet flooring.

Scab – 1. The initial growth over an injury to a tree that seals and protects it. 2. A worker who takes a striker's place on the job. Offensive.

Scaffold Plank – A piece of lumber at least 1-1/4 inches thick and at least eight inches in width, that is graded under a special set of criteria that includes a high stress rating. As implied, such lumber is often used as planking for scaffolds.

Scald – An injury to the cambium layer of a tree due to direct exposure to sunlight.

Scale – 1. A measure of the volume of wood in a log or logs, usually expressed in board feet and based on any of various log scaling rules. See Log Scale. 2. To measure a log to determine its volume. 3. The place where logs are measured to determine their volume. See Scaling Station.

Scale Bill – A document containing the volume, or board footage, of a load. Also, Scale Ticket.

Scale Off – That portion of a board or other product not charged for because of excessive defects.

Scaler – One who determines the net yield of logs by measuring them and applying one of a variety of formulas, or log rules. Scaling may take place at the site of the logging, at the mill, or at a scaling station located between the two points.

Scaler's Stick – The measuring device used by a log scaler to help estimate the board-foot volume of a log.

Scale Shack

Scale Shack – See Scaling Station.

Scale Ticket – A tag attached to the end of a log after it has been scaled. Information obtained from scaling the log is written on the ticket.

Scale Wood – Logs sold by board foot volume, rather than weight. Opposite of Weight Wood.

Scaling Bureau – An agency or company that provides log scaling services. The scaler works for the scaling bureau rather than for either the buyer or seller of the logs, with the bureau assessing a fee for its services.

Scaling Station

Scaling Station – A place where logs are scaled. A typical scaling station has a long ramp on which the scaler walks while measuring the logs on the truck, and a scale "shack" where the scaler does his paperwork.

Scalping – 1. In reforestation, the scraping away of vegetation to bare mineral soil around a newly planted seedling to reduce competition for water and nutrients. 2. In futures trading, the practice of trading for small gains by establishing and liquidating a position quickly, usually within the same day.

Scanner – A device used to determine the dimensional aspects of logs, lumber, or veneer prior to any one of the steps in the manufacturing process. Scanners feed information to computers, which determine how best to use the material in the next step of production. In sawmills, scanners can determine the size of logs so that the computer can tell the sawyer the number of passes and thicknesses of cuts to make in the log. In veneer plants, scanners detect defects in the veneer so it can be clipped properly and accurately. Scanners usually use photoelectric beams or laser beams.

Scant – Less than standard or required size.

Scant Face – A piece of lumber whose broad side, or face, is less than the required width.

Scantling – 1. A piece of lumber of small size; ordinarily yard lumber two inches thick and less than eight inches wide. 2. Framing lumber in the United Kingdom and Australia.

Scarf Joint – A joint made by chamfering, or beveling, the ends of two pieces of lumber or plywood to be joined. The angled cut on each piece is made to correspond to the other so that the two pieces being joined are flush.

Scarification – The process of breaking up the soil surface of a logged site in preparation for planting. A heavy disk or toothed tool is dragged over the site, usually by a crawler tractor, to break up the ground and any slash left from the logging operation. Scarification is sometimes used in lieu of slash burning.

Scheme Arch – Another name for a Segmental Arch.

Schoolmarm – A conifer whose natural leader was damaged, with two of the uppermost limbs bending upward to lead the tree's growth, producing two separate trunks part way up the tree.

Schnitzelbank – A bench used when hand-shaping shingles or shakes. A common device in the early logging days.

Scissor Lift – A lifting platform, with the lifting accomplished by pairs of legs that rise in a scissor motion.

Scissors Truss – A roof truss with tension members extending from the foot of each principal rafter to the upper half of its opposite member.

Scoot – 1. A slang term for hardwood lumber of inferior quality. 2. Another name for a Go-Devil.

Score – Waste from veneer production resulting from the trimming of the veneer at the peeling lathe. Peeler blocks are usually slightly longer than the length of the veneer that is to be produced from them. Spur-type

Screw Jack

knives at each end of the lathe cut into the block as it turns. This scoring will yield veneer of the desired length with straight edges and parallel sides. Also called spur trim.

Score Knives – Knives on a veneer lathe that cut into the block as it is turned, assuring the veneer will have straight edges and be exactly the desired length.

Scorer – In hand-squaring timbers, the man who notched out the rough dimensions on a log so that a hewer could square it.

Scoring Ax – The ax used to score timbers before hewing them square with a broadax.

Scotch Pine – Pinus sylvestris. An imported European conifer widely used in reforestation.

Scotia – A deep, concave moulding more than 1/4 round in sections.

Scots Fir – Another name for Scotch Pine.

Scots Pine – Another name for Scotch Pine.

Schoolmarm

Four-Saw Scragg Mill

Scow – A small boat used in forming log booms.

Scrabble Log – See Prize Log.

Scragg Mill – An arrangement of four fixed saws used to break down logs or peeler cores of fairly uniform sizes. The Scragg produces two slabs, two 2-inch cants, and a 4-inch cant in a single operation. These can then be reduced to 2x4s and 4x4s in a resaw.

Scratcher Teeth – One type of teeth in a crosscut saw. They are designed to sever fibers at each edge of the kerf, before the raker teeth pull the chips from the cut.

Scratch Sanding – Sanding a panel using a coarse-grit medium to create very shallow striations on the surface.

Scratch Stick – A tool consisting of a wooden handle and a metal point, used to mark logs when scaling them.

Screen Mould – A moulding originally used in the construction of screens and now used extensively in cabinet work and finished carpentry where a clear strip is required, as on the edge of a shelf made of plywood or particleboard.

Screw Holding – A measure of the force required to withdraw a screw directly from the face or edge of a board. Measured in pounds.

Screw Jack – A type of jack used to move logs in the early days of logging. Also called a Jackscrew.

Terms Of The Trade 239

Screw Roller

Screw Roller – Live rollers with coarse threads that change the direction of material moving over a conveyor.

Scribner – A widely used log scale rule, originally developed in 1846. It is designed to measure the actual net yield of a log, in board feet, and is one of a number of "diagram" rules.

Scribner-Doyle Rule – This is a combination log rule that uses Scribner values for small logs, and Doyle values for large logs. It is the statutory rule of Louisiana.

Scroll Knob – The butt end of an ax handle.

Scrub – Small, unmerchantable timber and brush, usually growing where soils are poor or conditions are extreme.

Scrub Pine – A common name for a number of pines, including Jackpine, Lodgepole Pine, and Pinyon Pine.

Scuffled – A rough-sawn surface that has been lightly planed or sanded to retain, but subdue, saw marks.

S-Dry – A description of lumber seasoned to a moisture content of 19% or less prior to surfacing.

Sealed Bidding – A method of selling timber, usually from federal lands, in which potential buyers submit a sealed bid that is equal to, or higher than, the minimum acceptable bid set by the seller. The highest bidder is awarded the right to harvest the timber at his bid price.

Sealer – A coating applied to a wood surface as a base for varnish or other finish coating.

Seal Number – An identifying number on a device used to secure a door on a rail car or motor vehicle. The seal number is recorded when the seal is applied; if the number on the seal differs when delivery is made, it is an indication that the seal was replaced and that the contents of the car may have been tampered with.

Sea Shed – A cargo module used on a container ship to convert it into a break-bulk carrier.

Seasonally Adjusted Annual Rate (SAAR) – A calculation of economic activity in which the actual activity in a month is adjusted to remove seasonal influences. Seasonal adjustment attempts to account for month-to-month variations resulting from normal changes in weather conditions, and differences in the number of working days. A seasonally adjusted annual rate of housing starts developed for any given month can be used in comparisons of trends with the SAARs of previous periods. However, a seasonal adjustment is not a forecast for future months.

Seasoned – Not green; having a moisture content of 19% or less.

Seasoning – The process of evaporation and extraction of moisture from green or partially dried wood.

Seasoning Checks – Small splits, or checks, that occur in wood grain if moisture is withdrawn too rapidly.

Seawall – A wall or embankment designed to prevent encroachment from the sea. Can be made of wood, masonry, earth, or a combination of materials.

Secondary – A wholesaler; one who buys and resells goods.

Secondary Beam – A beam supported by other beams instead of columns or walls.

Secondary Wood Products – Primary wood products that have been physically altered by changing their dimension, shape, chemical composition, appearance, or other properties. Remanufactured products.

Second Clear – A grade of Eastern White Pine shingles. Usually shown as "2nd clear."

Second Faller – The assistant, or second man, in a falling crew.

Second Forest – The forest that became established in the South after the harvest of the region's original "old-growth" forest. The second forest was the source of the bulk of the timber harvested in the South from the 1930s through the 1960s.

Second Growth – Timber that has regrown after a virgin stand was logged or burned.

Second Loader – The worker in a logging operation who assists in the loading of logs on a truck by standing on the cab of the truck and directing both the truck driver and loading engineer in placing the logs on the truck.

Semi-Rigid Clear Film

Seconds – A grade of lumber used in the hardwood industry and sometimes in the overseas trade; as in Firsts & Seconds.

Second Seasoning – The further seasoning of wood to allow it to reach equilibrium with its surroundings.

Secret Fixing – A carpentry method in which pieces are joined in such a way that the fasteners cannot be seen on the surface.

Section – 1. A topographical measure of land area, equal to one mile square, or 640 acres. One of the 36 divisions in a township. 2. Veneer clipped to standard widths of 54 and 27 inches. The actual width may vary from 48-54 inches, or 24-27 inches. The most desired pieces of veneer because of the ease of using them in assembling a panel. 3. A part of a flat log raft.

Section Corner – The point where the boundary lines of sections of land intersect.

Section 37 – A mythical area in the woods; there are only 36 sections in a township.

Sectorwood – A method of wood processing, patented by Weyerhaeuser Company, in which round logs are first quartered and then cut into pie-shaped pieces called sectors. These pieces are then glued together to form wood two inches thick and up to three or four feet in width. This wood can then be ripped to the desired widths. The process is designed to greatly increase the yield from small logs.

Seed Tree – A tree left standing in a logging operation to provide seed for natural regeneration of the logged-over area.

Segmental Arch – Another name for a Gothic arch.

Segment Ground – A saw that has been ground so that the back is thinner than the toothed edge. Hollow ground.

Segment Saw – A round saw made up of pie-shaped sections.

Seismic Design – Construction designed to withstand earthquake force.

Select – 1. A high quality piece of lumber graded for appearance. Select lumber is used in interior and exterior trim, and cabinetry. It is most often sold S4S in a 4/4 thickness, but may also be produced S2S in a variety of thicknesses, usually for remanufacturing. 2. A grade of Canadian exterior plywood.

Selected – Pieces that have been selected for particular features, such as tight knots.

Selection Thinning – Thinning an area of forest by selecting and removing trees to reduce competition.

Selective Cutting – A method of timber harvesting in which only selected trees in a stand are cut at any one time. The remaining trees are allowed to continue to mature and produce seed.

Select Merchantable – 1. A grade of boards intended for use where knotty type lumber of fine appearance is required. 2. An export grade of sound wood with tight knots and close grain, suitable for high quality construction and remanufacture.

Select Structural – The highest grade of Structural Joists and Planks. This grade is applied to lumber of high quality in terms of appearance, strength, and stiffness.

Select Tight Face (SEL TF) – A grade of Canadian exterior plywood, having a B-grade face, C-grade inner plies, and a C-grade back.

Select Tight Knot (STK) – A grading term frequently used for cedar lumber. Lumber designated STK is selected from mill run for the tight knots in each piece, as differentiated from lumber that may contain loose knots or knotholes.

Self-Acting Saw – A saw which has a mechanical feed as an integral part.

Self-Loader – A type of log truck equipped with machinery that enables the driver to load the logs on the truck without the aid of a separate loading device. Usually used by small, "gyppo" operations, often consisting of only one person.

Seller's Market – A condition in which demand for goods is greater than supply, giving sellers the upper hand in negotiations.

Semi-Chemical Woodpulp – Woodpulp that has been processed by chemical treatment to partially delignify the wood before further processing in a refiner.

Semi-Detached Housing – Dwellings that share a common wall but are otherwise separate from each other.

Semi-Rigid Clear Film – A type of vinyl

Semi-Specified Loading

Self Loader

overlay, printed on the reverse side to protect the print.

Semi-Specified Loading – A loading in which the customer stipulates a maximum or minimum number of pieces of a certain size that would be acceptable. For example, a carload of random-length 2x4s to contain a minimum of 2,000 pieces of 16-foot.

Semi-Split – A trade name used by the Cedar Shake and Shingle Bureau for a product with a partially sawn and split face.

Sender – A member of a loading crew who guided logs up a skidway.

Sensitive Species – As defined by the U.S. Forest Service, those plant and animal species for which population viability is a concern, as evidenced by a significant current or predicted downward trend in population or density, or by a significant current or predicted downward trend in habitat capability that would reduce a species' existing distribution.

Sequoia – Another name for Giant Sequoia, Sequoia gigantea.

Sequoia Silver Spruce – Another name for Sitka Spruce, Picea sitchensis.

Seral Species – A species associated with an early stage in the development of a biotic community.

Serbian Spruce – Picea omorika. A species of spruce found in Europe, particularly in Yugoslavia.

Service Condition – A reference to the degree of dryness in wood. A dry service condition is one in which the average equilibrium moisture content over a year is 15 percent or less and does not exceed 19 percent. A wet service condition refers to all conditions other than dry.

Serviceability Limit States – Conditions limiting the intended use and occupancy of a structure. These include deflection, joint slip, vibration, and permanent deformation.

Servo-Mechanism – A control system utilizing a mechanism that is actuated and controlled by low-energy signals.

Set – 1. The location from which a pullboat operated in the logging of cypress. Similar to the landing in conventional logging. 2. A semipermanent deformation in lumber caused by tensile and compressive stresses in drying. See Compression Set, Tension Set. 3. The degree to which a saw's teeth are bent so that the cutting edge makes a wider cut than the back of the saw, to prevent binding. 4. A two-man cutting team. 5. See Saw Set.

Set Aside – 1. A timber sale reserved for auction to small businesses (defined as having less than 500 employees) so that they do not have to compete in auctions against larger firms. This is intended to protect them against any size advantage the larger firms might have. 2. Forest land removed from the timber base.

Sett – The use of more than one truck or wagon to transport a long log.

Setter – The worker who adjusted the saw on a headrig, at the direction of the head sawyer.

Setting – The area of a logging operation from which logs are yarded to a single landing.

Settlement Price – In futures trading, the price established by a clearinghouse at the close of the daily trading session. The settlement price is used as the official price for establishing gains and losses, margin requirements, and the next trading day's price limits. While the term "settlement price" is sometimes used interchangeably with "closing price," such usage is inexact, since there can be a range of closing prices at the end of a trading session. The settlement price is usually established at or near the midpoint of a closing range, when such a range exists. If there is only one closing price, it becomes the settlement price.

Settling Pond – A pond in which incom-

Sheathing

ing water is held while sediment carried by it sinks to the bottom.

Set-Up Man – One who sets knives and machines for surfacing lumber. Also called a Planerman, or Knifegrinder.

Setworks – The portion of the headrig carriage that precisely positions the log or cant to be sawn.

Seventeen-Inch Rule – A cubic foot log rule. Because a square inscribed inside a circle 17 inches in diameter would have 12 inches on a side, a log 17 inches in diameter and one foot long would yield one cubic foot of square timber.

Seventy-Five, Twenty-Five (75/25) – A mixture of lumber grades indicating that 25% of the load is of one grade (usually the lowest acceptable) and the remainder consists of pieces of higher grades.

Severance Tax – A tax assessed by a state, county or other unit of government on timber when it is harvested.

Sewer Plank – Timbers, mostly in the sizes of 3x8 and 3x10, 18- and 20-foot lengths, which are used to repair or construct drainageways, especially in older cities.

S-Green – A description of lumber surfaced while at a moisture content of more than 19%.

Shade Pine – Another name for Sugar Pine.

Shade Tolerant – A tree species that is able to germinate and grow in the shade of other trees; one that does not require full sunlight in its early stages of growth. Usually the species that becomes dominant as older trees die.

Shadow Guide – A sawing guide created by projecting the shadow of a cord on a cant to help in aligning it with a saw.

Shake – 1. A lengthwise grain separation between growth rings, or a break through the rings (radial shake), usually the result of high winds. Among the recognized types and degrees of shake are: fine, slight, medium, open, cup, round, ring, shell, through, and pith. 2. Roofing material produced from wood (most often a cedar). Shakes have at least one surface with a natural grain-textured split surface.

Shake Bolt – See Bolt.

Shaku – A Japanese unit of measurement, equal to 30.303 centimeters, or about one foot.

Shales – An obsolete term for shingles.

Shank – 1. The part of a tool connecting the handle to the working part. 2. A device for locking teeth into an inserted-tooth saw.

Shanty – A small wooden building, usually temporary and usually haphazardly constructed.

Shanty Boat – See Wanigan.

Shantymen – Lumberjacks who lived in shanties in the eastern woods.

Shasta Red Fir – See California Red Fir.

Shaving – A very thin slice of wood, used in some types of panels.

Shaving Machine – A machine that makes shavings for use in construction of some types of panels.

Shay – A popular type of steam locomotive, used in early-day logging operations. It was first built by Ephraim Shay, Haring, Michigan, in 1877 and was driven by a geared mechanism attached directly to each axle. It was the first geared locomotive and was powerful but slower than conventional siderod engines.

Shear – The tendency of wood fibers, under stress, to slide longitudinally.

Shear Parallel to Grain – A strength property of wood determined by applying a load to a piece of wood notched on the end. The load is applied in line with the grain so that the step formed by the notch is sheared from the rest of the piece. Any piece of wood subjected to a transverse load will experience shear parallel to the grain. The shear strength of wood across the grain is much stronger than the shear strength parallel to the grain, and this property is rarely considered in structural applications of wood.

Shear Wall – A diaphragm wall designed to withstand wind or earthquake loads on a structure.

Sheathing – Plywood, waferboard, oriented strand board, or lumber used to close up side walls, floors, or roofs preparatory to the installation of finish materials on the surface. The sheathing grades are also com-

Sheathing Layup Plant

monly used for pallets, crates, and certain industrial products.

Sheathing Layup Plant – The factory in which veneers are combined to make sheathing plywood.

Sheave – The wheel of a pulley, or block.

She Balsam – Another name for Fraser Fir, Abies fraseri.

Shed Stock – See Uppers.

Shed Upper – See Uppers.

Sheer Boom – A log boom placed diagonally across a river to guide logs into a sorting works or holding boom.

Sheer Log – A log used as a bumper or guide to cause other logs to sheer away from an obstacle while they are being yarded.

Sheet – The same as a panel; "a sheet of particleboard."

Sheeting – Planks used to line the sides of an excavation. Also, sheathing.

Sheeting Lumber – A low grade of lumber.

Sheet Plant – A manufacturing plant that makes corrugated-board boxes, after purchasing the board from converting plants. See Converting Plant.

Sheet Rock – A construction panel used for interior wall finish. Usually constructed of reconstituted gypsum bound in heavy paper.

Sheet Slinger – See Sheet Turners.

Sheet Turners – Workers in a plywood layup plant who place faces, backs, and intermediate sheets in the manufacture of the panel.

Sheffield Test – In papermaking, a test for smoothness.

Shelf Cleat – A moulding commonly used in closets to support a shelf; also called a shelf strip.

Shellac – A type of varnish manufactured by dissolving lac, a resinous substance produced by the lac insect, in alcohol or other solvents. See Lac.

Shell Shake – Cup or ring shake.

Shelterwood Logging – A method of harvesting timber in two or more successive cuttings in such a manner that the residual trees provide protection from sun and wind during the period in which a new crop of trees is being established.

She Pine – Another name for Australian Brown Pine, Podocarpus elatus.

She Pitch Pine – Another name for Slash Pine, Pinus elliottii.

Shide – A shingle (chiefly British).

Shim – 1. A long, narrow repair of wood or suitable synthetic not more than 3/16-inch wide, used in replacing defects in plywood. 2. A piece of shingle or other small piece used as a wedge in construction.

Shim Hoe – An adze.

Shingle – Roofing material made from wood or other material. Wooden shingles are usually made from Western Red Cedar, but other species are also used. Shingles come in various sizes and grades; all have sawn faces and backs. Shingles are tapered, with a standard thickness at the butt.

Shingle Bench – A device used when shaping shingles or shakes by hand. Also called a Schnitzelbank.

Shingle Bolt – The bolt or block of wood from which shingles are sawn.

Shingle Crib – A raft constructed of booms, in the center of which shingle bolts are loaded for towing over water.

Shingle Machine – The saws and carriage used in the manufacture of shingles.

Shingle Press – A machine used in bundling shingles.

Shingle Sawyer – See Shingle Weaver.

Shingle Thief – A tool used by roofers to remove damaged shingles without harming undamaged ones.

Shingle Tow – String-like shavings that are a by-product of Western Red Cedar shingle production. Shingle tow is often used as packing around seedling roots during shipment from nurseries, to keep the roots moist.

Shingle Weaver – A person who makes shingles with a shingle machine; a shingle

Shook

Shingle Weaver

sawyer. A member of the Shingle Weavers Union (LPIW), including sawyers and packers.

Shinglewood – Another name for Western Red Cedar.

Ship Decking – Full-sawn vertical grain pieces, knot-free on the faces, used in the construction of ship decks.

Ship Knee – A brace obtained from the point where a tree trunk turns into a large flat root.

Shiplap – 1. Lumber that has been worked to make a lapped, or rabbetted, joint on each edge so that pieces may be fitted together snugly for increased strength and stability. 2. A similar pattern cut into plywood or other wood panels used as siding, to assure a tight joint.

Shipper – One who dispatches goods by ship, rail, truck, or other conveyance.

Shipper's Agent – A transportation broker who arranges for equipment and performs other services for the actual shipper of freight.

Shipper's Certificate – A form filled out by a shipper and presented to an outbound carrier at a transit point, requesting reshipping privileges on material previously brought into the point for further manufacture or sorting. The certificate includes shipping instructions and the inbound carrier's freight bill.

Shipper's Load & Count (SL&C) – A notation made on bills of lading for the purpose of relieving the carrier of any claim for shortages discovered by the consignee.

Shipper's Pool – A system designed to return the same empty rail cars to a shipper for storage and then loading.

Shipping – The lowest of three pallet grades recognized by the National Wooden Pallet and Container Association.

Shipping Charges – See Landing Charges.

Shipping Cull – Wood that has been damaged in shipment.

Shipping Days – The number of days agreed to for the loading of a vessel.

Shipping Dry – A reference to wood that has been sufficiently seasoned to prevent fungi attack or deterioration on board ship.

Shipping Marks – The trade/grade marks of exporters, denoting the quality and source of wood shipments.

Shipping Pallet – A pallet designed to be used for a single trip from shipper to receiver, then disposed of.

Shipping Position – A seller's estimate of the time required after an order is placed until it can be shipped.

Shipping Ton – A volume of wood taking up 42 cubic feet of space.

Ship Plank – Various kinds of framing, planking, and decking used in the construction or maintenance of a ship or barge. Of a lower quality than ship decking.

Ship Worm – A marine insect (teredo) that attacks wood in water.

Shipwright Ax – A heavy ax used to shape ship timbers.

Shive – 1. A piece of wood from which a bung is made for a cask or barrel. 2. A particle of wood appearing as an impurity in a paper product.

Shoe Moulding – Base shoe used at the bottom of a baseboard to cover the space between the finished flooring and the baseboard.

Shoepack – Leather boots with moccasin soles, worn by early-day lumberjacks. Also called Larrigans.

Shook – Sawn or split pieces of wood used in construction of boxes or barrels.

Terms Of The Trade

Shop

Shop – Lumber that is graded for the number and sizes of cuttings that can be taken from it. Used in the manufacture of other products such as door and window parts.

Shop&Btr – A grouping of board grades that includes shop, moulding, and selects. An informal trading term used to describe the high-grade portion of a mill's production; not an official grade description.

Shop Cutting Panel – A plywood panel that has been rejected as not conforming to the requirements of standard grades, but that can be sold for remanufacturing or recutting into applications other than those specified in grading rules, or a product standard.

Shop Outs – Shop-type lumber that falls below the official shop grades, but will yield some cuttings.

Shore Pine – Another name for Lodgepole Pine, Pinus contorta. In particular, this name refers to pines found along the coast, where they are often contorted or twisted by persistent winds.

Short – 1. A trader who sells a commodity he does not yet own with the expectation that the item will be available at a lower price later. Also, an adjective describing the state of being short; "he took a short position." 2. A short piece of lumber. See Shorts.

Shortage Claim – A claim filed against a supplier because of a deficiency in the quantity of material received.

Short Cord – See Face Cord.

Short Covering – A purchase to offset a previous transaction in which an item was sold prior to having been bought. Used in reference to both futures and cash market trading. See Cover.

Short Face – A sales term used when describing tongue-and-groove siding that includes the tongue within the stated width. Also called narrow face.

Short Grain – Wood in which part of the grain runs diagonally to the length of the piece; subject to failure under load.

Short Ground – A hump or break in the ground's surface. A tree could be broken if felled across it.

Short Hedge – In futures trading, the sale of contracts to eliminate or lessen the possible decline in value of ownership of the physical commodity.

Shorthorn – A common slang reference to the pine bark beetle. From its Latin name: Dendroctonus brevicomis, or tree-killing shorthorn.

Short in the Grain – A wood defect characterized by brittle fractures.

Shortleaf Pine – Pinus echinata. This species, one of the Southern Yellow Pine group, is found in a broad range from Texas to as far north as Pennsylvania and New Jersey.

Short-Log Country – The Inland West, where logs are commonly trimmed to 16 or 20-foot lengths, or their multiples.

Short Logger – A log truck with no trailer.

Short Logs – Logs that are no more than 16 to 20 feet long; common lengths in pine logging.

Short Rate – A generalized description of the distance relationship between a supplying point and consuming area expressed in reference to freight rates; relatively nearby market areas as contrasted to a more distant consuming area on a long rate.

Short Rotation Forest Crop – Trees that grow to merchantable size in relatively few years, such as 30. They can be harvested and a new crop started quickly.

Shorts – Short pieces of lumber. The lengths described as shorts vary widely by species, products, and regions. Generally, dimension of 12 feet or less is described as short, while boards of 6 feet or less are also shorts.

Short Sale – A transaction in which an item is sold below the current market price prior to having been bought. The expectation in a short sale is that the item can be purchased later at a price that is even lower than that at which it was sold.

Short Squeeze – A situation in which traders are unable to profitably purchase items that they have sold short.

Short Stuff – Short pieces of pulpwood, logs, shinglebolts, etc.

Short the Basis – In futures trading, the forward sale of a cash commodity hedged by the purchase of a future against the cash posi-

Siding

tion.

Short Ton – The standard 2,000 pound ton used in the United States. The long ton equals 2,240 pounds, and the metric ton 2,240.6; these are widely used in the export trade.

Shortwood – Pulpwood logs less than 10 feet in length.

Shotgun Bunk – In the early-day logging camp, a bunk that was "loaded" by crawling in from the foot. Also called a Muzzle Loader.

Shotgun System – See Gravity System.

Shoulder Trade – Buyers of building materials who usually pay cash and transport their purchases themselves. See Over-the-Shoulder.

Shovel Loader – A power shovel used as a portable loader after the digging apparatus is removed.

Show – A logging operation.

Shrinkage – 1. The amount of dimensional loss of a piece of wood when it has been seasoned in some manner. 2. Log loss during a river drive.

Shrink Wrap – A system of protective wrapping using plastic that is applied and then shrunk by heat. Used primarily to wrap shingles and shakes, and pre-finished paneling.

Shut Out – A term used in waterborne shipments to indicate cargo not loaded due to deficiency in a vessel's space.

Shuttle Logging – The process of yarding logs to one location, where they are stored temporarily before being moved to a landing for loading.

Siamese Cat – Two tractors linked by cable which is dragged through the woods to tear down brush and small trees. The practice, called "chaining," is intended to improve forage and tree growth by reducing competition for space and water.

Siberian Spruce – Picea obovata. A species native to the Far East.

Side – A logging operation; the men and equipment involved in cutting and moving logs to one landing.

Sidecasting – During the construction of a logging road, the blading of waste soil and debris over the downhill side.

Side Cut – 1. A piece of lumber, usually a board, produced incidentally as a by-product of cutting for other products such as dimension. 2. To saw a tree in increments around its circumference when the saw is not long enough to pass all the way through.

Side Grain – Any grain on a longitudinal surface, as opposed to end grain.

Side Hill Gouger – An imaginary woods creature, having two long legs on the downhill side and two short legs on the uphill side. It can travel around hills in only one direction; if it turned around it would tip over.

Side Hill Load – An uneven load of logs, with the bigger ones all at one side.

Sidelap – In roofing, a pattern of laying the second and succeeding courses of shingles so that the joints between them are staggered relative to those of the lower courses. The side lap should be at least 1-1/2 inches.

Side Mark – A type of log brand made on the side of a log rather than the end. Used mainly in the days of river logging, since it was easier to see when the log was in the water.

Sidenotching – Cutting a notch in the side of a tree (other than the undercut notch) to prevent splitting, or when a saw is too short.

Side Push – Same as a Side Rod (def. 1).

Side Rod – 1. The foreman at a logging "side." 2. The device on a railroad locomotive that transmits power from the mainrod to the wheels.

Side Spooler – A type of steam donkey having a single engine and a single spool.

Side Sticks – Boom sticks at the side of a log raft.

Sideswiper – A limb that lashes out sideways when broken during yarding.

Sidewall – The exterior wall of a building.

Sidewinder – See Sideswiper.

Siding – 1. Lumber or panel products intended for use as the exterior wall covering on a house or other building. 2. A railroad

Sierra Club

track that allows one train to pull off the main line so that another may pass.

Sierra Club – A major U.S. environmental group that traces its roots back to early environmentalist John Muir. Fund-raising and lobbying efforts are geared toward protection of the world's wild lands and natural resources.

Sierra Club Legal Defense Fund – A law firm, not part of the Sierra Club, representing a number of clients in environmental litigation.

Sierra Juniper – Another name for Western Juniper, Juniperus occidentalis.

Sierra Lodgepole Pine – Pinus contorta var. murrayana. A variation of Lodgepole found in the Sierra Nevada Mountains.

Sight Draft – An instrument of payment negotiated through banks. Negotiable documents are attached, such as an order bill of lading, thus ensuring payment by the consignee to the negotiating bank in exchange for the documents and prior to the delivery of the goods.

Sight Gun – A device to aid in determining where a tree will fall; a triangle sawn out of a board or made with light sticks. The base is set into the undercut and the top of the triangle shows the line of fall.

Signal Man – A Whistlepunk.

Silica – A mineral secretion in some trees that makes the wood resistant to insect attack.

Sill – The horizontal member forming the bottom of a window or exterior door frame. As applied to general construction, the lowest member of the frame of the structure, resting on the foundation and supporting the frame.

Silver Fir – See Pacific Silver Fir.

Silver Grain – The figure produced in quarter-sawn wood by medullary rays.

Silver Spruce – Another name for Sitka Spruce.

Silver Tip – 1. A young Shasta Red Fir. 2. A gray-haired man.

Silvex – A phenoxy herbicide, 2,4,5-TP.

Silvics – The study of general characteristics of forest trees, with particular reference to locality.

Silviculture – The theory and practice of controlling the establishment, composition, care, and development of stands of trees to achieve the objectives of management.

Simple Span – A method of installing plank decking in which all pieces are the same length and rest on two supports.

Simple Straight Beam – A glulam beam having the same thickness throughout its length.

Simplicity – A parquet flooring pattern.

Single Arbor – An edger or trimsaw with one shaft containing multiple saws.

Single Bit – An ax with one cutting edge.

Single Course – One layer applied to a structure, as in one course of shingles.

Single-End Kiln – A kiln with a door at one end only; the charges enter and exit through the same door.

Single-Face Pallet – A pallet having only a top deck.

Single-Family Structure – A detached housing unit built for occupancy by members of one family, or group.

Single Floor – A wood floor in which the joists reach from wall to wall.

Single Jack – A logger who works alone as a faller.

Single Knot – See Knot Occurrence.

Single-Leaf Pinyon Pine – Pinus monophylla. A type of Pinyon Pine found in the Southwest, having single needles.

Single Line – The movement or rate on one railroad.

Single Member – A joist or rafter bearing a load without assistance from other members.

Single-Member Design Value – See Single Stress Rating.

Single Opening Press – A panel production process used to make thin panels, particularly of particleboard.

Sized Green

Single-Pitch Roof – One that slopes in a single direction; a lean-to roof.

Single Roof – A roof that is supported by common rafters instead of trusses, purlins, or principals.

Single Span – A structural member that spans an opening without intermediate support.

Single Stress Rating – The strength rating of lumber (fiber stress in bending) used when the individual piece is responsible for carrying an entire, specific load. Single stresses are applied on structural lumber in beam, girder, post, and truss chord uses. The single stress rating for a particular species, size, and grade of lumber is always less than the repetitive stress rating (where the load is shared by a number of members) for the same lumber.

Single-Tapered Straight Beam – A type of glulam beam having a flat bottom and a top that tapers in one direction, from the wide end to the narrow end.

Single-Use Pallet – See Shipping Pallet.

Single Wide – As defined by the Commerce Department, any mobile home unit so designated by a dealer. There is only one section and only one HUD label number.

Single-Wing Pallet – A pallet with the top deck extending beyond the edge of the stringers. If a bottom deck is present, it is flush with the stringers.

Sinkage – The loss by sinking of logs stored or being transported on water.

Sinker – A log whose specific gravity is so high that it sinks when put into water.

Sinker Boat – A small boat used in the recovery of sunken logs.

Sinker Stock – Lumber or other wood product produced from sinker logs. The green moisture content is very high and the rate of drying can be slow.

S-Iron – See Anti-Checking Iron.

Site Built – The construction of a structure at the site where it is to remain.

Site Class – See Site Index.

Site Index (SI) – A measure of the potential of a forest site to grow timber, based on height growth. The SI for a single tree equals the height of the tree in feet, divided by the age of the tree, multiplied by 100. The SI for an area is the average of several single tree SIs.

Site-Potential Tree – A tree that has attained the maximum height possible, given site conditions where it occurs.

Site Preparation – The process of preparing an area for planting, often through the use of controlled burns, herbicides, and mechanical devices.

Site Productivity – The measure of inherent capability of land to grow timber, based on fully stocked natural stands.

Sitka Spruce – Picea sitchensis. Light in weight, but particularly strong, this species is still used in aircraft construction and for other special uses. The range of Sitka Spruce is a narrow belt extending along the Pacific Coast from Alaska to Northern California.

Six-Patch – A grade of plywood siding. The term refers to the maximum number of patches allowed in each panel. The proprietary name used by the American Plywood Association is "Premium."

Six-Quarter (6/4) – See Quarter Measure.

Sixths – The lowest Scandinavian lumber export grade.

Sixty, Twenty-Five, Fifteen (60/25/15) – A mixture of lumber grades, sometimes used in marketing Western Red Cedar lumber. The numbers designate 60% of a load as Construction, 25% as Standard, and 15% as Utility.

Sixty, Twenty, Twenty (60/20/20) – A mixture of lumber grades sometimes used in marketing unseasoned Hem-Fir, and some minor species. The numbers designate that 60% of a load is Construction, 20% Standard, and 20% Utility.

Size – An additive introduced to particleboard furnish prior to forming, to improve water resistance.

Sized Dry – Surfaced or sawn to a specific size after being dried.

Sized Green – Surfaced or sawn to a specific size while still green, and subject to further shrinkage. The National Grading Rule for dimension lumber sets slightly larger sizes

Terms Of The Trade

Sized Lumber

for green lumber than for dry to reflect shrinkage.

Sized Lumber – Lumber uniformly manufactured to net surfaced sizes. Sized lumber may be rough, surfaced, or partly surfaced on one or more faces. See Saw Sized Lumber.

Size Effect – In lumber, the phenomenon that the bending strength (Fb rating) of a piece of lumber decreases as the size of the piece increases. For example, when comparing a 2x4 and 2x8 of similar qualities and characteristics, the bending strength of the 2x8 will be less than that of the 2x4.

Size Factor – One of various adjustment factors affecting allowable design values in wood.

Sizer Sander – A machine that surfaces lumber or panel products to a specific size by abrasion.

Sizing – The application of diluted glue or adhesive to hardwood veneer, to prepare the wood for application of the standard concentration of glue. Sizing reduces the amount of standard glue that will be absorbed. Sizing is often used when woods of different densities are glued together.

Sizing Saw – A saw that trims large timbers to the desired dimensions.

Skeleton Car – A log-hauling railroad car, having its trucks connected by a center beam, but having no floor, sides, or ends.

Skeleton Construction – A building method in which all loads and stresses are transmitted through a rigid framework of metal or concrete to the structure's foundation.

Skewback Saw – A type of handsaw having a curved back to lessen weight while maintaining stiffness.

Skid – A pallet having no bottom deck.

Skid Camp – A logging camp where buildings were mounted on skids for ease of changing locations.

Skidder – A mechanized piece of logging equipment used to drag, or skid, logs from the cutting area to the landing. Skidders usually have wheels and rubber tires, rather than endless tracks such as those found on crawler tractors.

Skidding Chain – A chain used to pull a turn of logs. A Bunching Chain.

Skidding Pan – A metal sheet placed under the front end of logs to reduce friction when ground skidding.

Skid Greaser – A worker who applied any of various lubricants to the wooden cross members in a skid road. The lubricant facilitated the movement of logs across the skids as they were pulled by teams of oxen or horses. Also called a Swabber.

Skid Road – A road or path upon which logs are dragged from the cutting area to the landing. In animal logging days, a skid road was often constructed by placing short logs

Skidder

Slash Burning

or poles at right angles to the direction of the movement of logs. Towns built up around the skid roads leading to Puget Sound in Washington State, and the vicinity of the roads was where loggers gathered for amusement; these sections became known as a "Skid Road," which was later corrupted to "Skid Row."

Skid System – Pre-planned routes for skidding tractors on harvest units designed to minimize soil disturbance and protect younger, unharvested trees.

Skid Trail – A path through the woods created when logs are skidded.

Skidway – 1. A Skid Road. 2. A loading dock built of logs.

Skimming Off the Cream – See High Grading.

Skinner Saw – A saw that trims and sizes the eight-foot side of a plywood panel as it leaves the press. The four-foot side is trimmed by a cut-off saw.

Skin Panel – See Door Skin.

Skin Wood – Pitchy wood, helpful in starting fires. Also called skin timber.

Skip – An area on a piece of lumber that a planer fails to surface, classified for grading purposes as slight, shallow or small, and deep or heavy.

Skip Dressing – Lumber surfaced so lightly that planer heads skipped portions. There are various degrees of skip; the most common allow skips up to 1/16-inch deep.

Skirtboard – A baseboard.

Skoog – A brand of veneer-patching machine.

Skookum – A Northwest Indian word meaning strong or powerful evil spirits. The word was used by early-day loggers to describe anything that was strong, big, or powerful.

Skulch – Wastewood, usually logs, of little commercial value; culls.

Skunk Spruce – Another name for White Spruce, Picea glauca.

Skybound – A tree that is difficult to fell.

Sky Hook – A mythical hook, one end of which fastens to the sky. Loggers will wish for one to get them out of various jams and hang-ups.

Skyline – A large cable (up to 2 inches in diameter) used to partially or totally suspend logs over long spans. See Skyline System.

Skyline System – Any of several cable logging systems used to suspend logs for protection of the soil, for crossing streams without damage, or to yard logs for distances of up to a mile where road access would create too great an environmental impact or is not economical. Skyline systems may use intermediate supports to reduce the sag in long cables.

Slab – The exterior portion of a log removed by the saw, having one flat and one curved surface.

Slabbed – 1. Describes a log that has been roughly sawn on one or more sides. 2. Describes a log which has had a part broken off in skidding or loading.

Slab Chipper – A machine that cuts pulp chips from the slabs first sawn from a log.

Slab-on-Grade Construction – A type of construction in which the floor is a concrete slab poured after plumbing and other equipment is installed.

Slab Saw – A resaw.

Slab Wood – Edgings or other waste wood in a sawmill.

Slack Cooperage – Cooperage intended to hold dry items.

Slacker – Another name for a skyline cable.

Slack Line – A standing skyline that can be raised or lowered during yarding.

Slash – Debris, such as limbs, bark, broken pieces of logs, etc., left over after a logging operation.

Slash Burning – The process of disposal of logging debris by controlled burning. The practice has drawn objections in recent years because of pollution problems associated with the burning. Land management agencies generally favor burning as a means of preparing the ground for reproduction because it reduces future fire hazard.

Terms Of The Trade

Slasher Deck

Slasher Deck – Part of a oriented strand board plant in which logs are sawn to uniform lengths before entering the waferizer.

Slashers – Circular saws mounted at fixed distances on one or more arbors. Slashers are used to reduce long logs to set lengths, or to reduce pulpwood to short lengths for grinding.

Slash Figure Check – The separation of fibers along the growth rings of a flat-sawn surface.

Slash Grain – See Flat Grain.

Slash Knot – A spike knot.

Slash Pine – Pinus elliottii. One of several pine species grouped under the designation of Southern Yellow Pine. Slash Pine is native to the southeastern and Gulf Coast states. It is fast-growing and matures early. Its wood closely resembles that of the Longleaf Pine, another of the SYP group.

Slash Saw – A type of reciprocating saw used in the early sawmilling days.

Slat – A thin, narrow strip of wood used in the manufacture of crates; lath.

Slat Deck – Narrow boards, with spaces between equal to the width of the boards, used to provide nailing strips in applying wood shingles.

Slating – A term used in the British timber trade to denote square-sawn softwood 1/2- to 1-inch thick and 1- to 3-inches wide.

Sled – A horse-drawn sled used to haul logs across snow or ice. Also called a Sleigh or Sledge.

Sled Patch – A rectangular patch with right angle corners. Used in voids caused by defects in the veneers of plywood panels.

Sledge – See Sled.

Sleeper – 1. A fire that was apparently out, but returned to life. 2. A British term for a railroad tie. 3. See Idler Car.

Sleeper Floor – A type of subfloor built on the ground or on a concrete slab to support the finished floor.

Sleeve – A hollow tube with threads on the inside, used to adjust the tension of metal rods.

Sleigh – See Sled.

Sliced Veneer – Veneer that is cut from a block using a knife, with the resulting slices coming off as individual pieces rather than the one long, continuous sheet that results from peeling on a lathe.

Slicer – A machine that slices veneer from a log. The log is not turned as it is sliced for veneer, but held stationary on a carriage and moved across the knife. Various methods of slicing result in different grain patterns on the veneer. Slicers are most often used in the manufacture of hardwood veneer.

Slicewood – Knife-cut sheets of wood with a thickness greater than one-fourth inch.

Slick – See Spud.

Sliding Hook – A hook, to which chokers are attached, that can be moved along a skidding line.

Slim Bin – See Big Bin.

Slime – A term used in the early logging days to describe Hemlock sap.

Slip Matched – One method of matching sliced veneer in which each sheet is joined side-by-side, without turning the figure.

Slip Sheet – Protective paper placed over the faces of pre-finished plywood paneling to protect them during transport.

Sliver – A narrow, thin piece of wood cut or broken from a larger piece, usually along the grain.

Slope – The ratio of vertical rise to horizontal run, as in a roof. See Pitch.

Slope of Grain – The deviation of the line of fibers from a straight line parallel to the sides of a piece.

Slotted Saw – A circular saw with cutouts in the blade to reduce friction and heat.

Slough Knot – A knot or knothole on the corner of a piece of lumber.

Slough Pig – A man sent to work logs out of sloughs and bays during the days of river drives; usually a less-experienced or less-skillful river man.

Slow-Release Pressure Treating – A variation of pressure treating of wood in which the pressure is released slowly with the expectation that more treating solution will remain in the wood.

Sluice – 1. An artificial channel carrying water; a flume. 2. A gate controlling water flow in a sluice. 3. The act of opening the sluice gate to let water flow through a sluice.

Slumgullion – A sort of stew, with a consistency between that of hash and soup.

Slurry – A mixture of water and wood fiber, from which paper is made.

Smalian's Formula – One of a number of formulas used to calculate the cubic volume of a log. Because it tends to overestimate or underestimate the correct volume, depending on the log's shape, the formula is seldom used. Also called Smalian's Rule.

Small Clear Specimen – A piece of wood, approximately 2x2 inches in size, that is free of defects. It is used to test the properties of the species from which it came.

Small Log Mill – A sawmill designed specifically for the processing of small-diameter logs. Rapid handling of logs throughout the mill is usually a characteristic of a small log mill. Logs from 5 to 14 inches in diameter are generally used, but some mills can process smaller logs. The mills are also usually designed to generate a high percentage of chips as by-products rather than sawdust, by the use of chipping devices in place of, or in combination with, saws.

Small Square – A small timber, usually a 4x4. See Baby Square.

Smoke Dried – Seasoned by exposure to the heat and smoke of fire maintained beneath or within the stack of lumber.

Smoke Eater – One who fights forest fires.

Smokejumper – A forest fire fighter, trained to parachute to fires in remote locations.

Smooth Face Sawing – The production of saw-sized dimension lumber that does not require surfacing on the wide faces.

Snag – A standing dead tree, or portion of a tree, from which most of the foliage, limbs, etc., have fallen.

Snake – A wavy saw cut due to improper tension or fitting.

Snatch Block – A logging pulley with a side release.

Sneezewood – This tropical hardwood, Ptaeroxylon obliquum, gets its name from the irritant properties of its sawdust, which often causes sneezing.

Snipe – 1. To round off the end of a log to make it pull or skid more easily. 2. A bevel on the edge or end of a particleboard panel that exceeds sanded specifications.

Sniped Log

Sniped Dressing – The loss of wood on the face of the last few inches of a piece of lumber, usually caused by a fault in the in-feed or out-feed rollers of a planer.

Snoose – Snuff or chewing tobacco.

Snow Break – Branches and tops broken out of trees by heavy snow.

Snow Interception – The tendency for overstory trees and mid-level vegetation to catch and hold some falling snow, reducing snow depth on the forest floor. This helps wildlife to move and feed.

Snubber – Any of various devices designed to slow the movement of something down a hill. In the early logging days, sleighs were sometimes snubbed by wrapping a rope around a stump and letting the sleighs down slowly. Drum and cable systems were also used.

Soaking Pond – A pond where peeler blocks were conditioned (softened) for peeling by soaking in water, usually heated. Now largely superseded by vats constructed especially for the purpose of conditioning blocks. See Vats.

Soak Test – A test of glue bond. Pieces with an interior glue line are soaked in cool water; exterior glue bonds are tested in boiling water.

Soda Pulp

Soda Pulp – Pulp produced mainly from hardwoods and containing short fibers; often used in printing papers.

Soffit – The underside of an eave or other part of a building.

Soft – A reference to a market condition when supply slightly exceeds demand and sellers are sometimes vulnerable to counter-offers.

Soft Conversion – A conversion from one system of measurement to another in which measurements are expressed in the new system while actual sizes remain the same.

Soft Elm – Ulmus americana. Another name for White Elm, used for veneers, furniture, and cooperage.

Soft Fir – Fine-grained, old growth Douglas Fir.

Soft Maple – Acer rubrum, A. saccharinum. Red Maple and River Maple, softer than Rock or Sugar Maple.

Softness – The property of wood that is indicated by a relative lack of resistance to cutting, denting, scratching, pressure, or wear.

Soft Pine – Any of various pines, including Weymouth Pine, Northern White Pine, and Eastern White Pine.

Soft Rot – Decay in wood, where the residue is chiefly cellulose.

Soft Textured – A term used by some pine and fir producers, primarily in Oregon and California, to describe their sawn products. Wood from these areas is often finer in grain and softer in texture than wood from areas farther north.

Softwood – A general term referring to any of a variety of trees having narrow, needle-like or scale-like leaves, generally coniferous. The wood from such trees. The term has nothing to do with the actual softness of the wood; some "softwoods" are harder than certain of the "hardwood" species.

Solar Dryer – A wood dryer that raises the dry-bulb temperature of the air being circulated through the wood by using solar energy.

Sole Plate – See Ground Plate.

Solid Color Film – A type of vinyl overlay used in the production of decorative panels. Can be left plain, printed with a pattern, or embossed.

Solid Core – 1. The inner layers of a plywood panel which contain no open irregularities such as gaps or open knotholes, and whose grain runs perpendicular to the outer plies. Primarily used as underlayment for resilient floor covering. 2. A flush door containing particleboard or wood blocks to completely fill the area between the door skins; used in entries and as fire-resistant doors.

Solid Cross (X) Band – A cross band in plywood consisting of plugged veneer allowing limited open defects or splits. The term is no longer used by softwood plywood manufacturers, who have substituted plugged inner plies or plugged crossbands as a more accurate description. See Plugged Inner Ply.

Solid-Deck Pallet – A pallet having no spaces between the deckboards.

Solid Jam – A log jam that stretches from bank to bank on a river.

Solid Moulding – A moulding produced from a single piece of wood, as distinguished from finger-jointed mouldings which are produced from more than one piece of wood joined together end to end.

Solid Pile – A stack of plywood that has just left the press and has been placed on a flat surface and weighted down while it cools.

Solids Concentration – The percentage (based on weight) of resin solids present in an adhesive. Also called Solids Content.

Solids Content – See Solids Concentration.

Solid-Tooth Saw – A saw whose teeth are an integral part of the saw itself, rather than removable pieces. See Inserted-Tooth Saw.

Solid Wood – Wood having the same structure it had in the living tree. Wood that has not been pulped, waferized, defibrated, etc.

Solid Wood Content – The actual volume of solid wood, exclusive of air space, bark, or other matter, in a given measure of wood.

Solid Wood Equivalent – The amount of wood fiber, in any form, that is equivalent to that found in a given volume of solid, green wood of the same species.

Solvent-Borne Adhesive – A type of glue containing polymeric material dissolved in a volatile organic solvent. Characteristics of such adhesives include good coatability, high heat resistance, and high bond strength.

Solvent Drying – A method of drying lumber by using a volatile liquid to draw off the moisture. The solvent is recaptured when the moisture is condensed and drained off.

Solvent Extraction – See Solvent Drying.

Soon As Possible (SAP) – An inexact shipping term indicating that a shipment will be made as soon as possible. Also, ASAP, "as soon as possible." Such indefinite shipping terms allow the shipment of an order to be delayed as long as 30 days unless a specific, earlier time limit is established.

Sorption – The binding of one substance to another by adsorption, absorption, or persorption.

Sorrel – A recently dead tree.

Sort – A concentration of logs by the specifications desired by individual buyers, i.e. a China Sort (C Sort), a Korea Sort (K Sort), etc.

Sorter – 1. A mechanical device that sorts lumber for thickness, width, or length by dropping or ejecting pieces into separate compartments. Types include drop sorters, edge sorters, and tray sorters.

Sorting Grounds – See Booming Grounds.

Sorting-in-Transit – A privilege extended to rail shippers by some carriers that allows cars to be stopped at an intermediate point for the purpose of mixing and reloading items to meet specific customer requirements. A sorting-in-transit charge is assessed, but the car retains the through freight rate from the initial point of origin to the ultimate destination.

Sorting Table – A table or platform in a sawmill or plywood plant on which products are carried past graders to pullers who put the various sizes and grades in appropriate piles.

Sorting Works – See Boom Works.

Sort Line – A conveyor from which wood products are sorted for grade and size.

Sort Yard – An area where logs are sorted according to species, size, or quality.

Sound – 1. Free of decay. 2. A grade of hardwood plywood. 3. A proprietary name for eighteen-patch plywood siding, used by the American Plywood Association.

Sound Cull – A tree with excessive defect caused by its form, roughness, etc.

Sound Knot – See Knot Quality.

Sound Tight Knot – See Select Tight Knot.

Sound Transmission Class (STC) – A method of rating airborne sounds to determine the comfort level of a particular living space. The higher the STC rating, the better the airborne noise control performance of a structure.

Sound Wormy – Wood that is basically sound, but that contains small wormholes or pinholes.

South American Cedar – See Spanish Cedar.

Southern Balsam Fir – See Balsam Fir.

Southern Cypress – Another name for Baldcypress, Taxodium distichum.

Southern Pine – See Southern Yellow Pine.

Southern Red Cedar – Juniperus silicicola. This species is very similar to Eastern Red Cedar. It is found in wet lowlands and swampy areas along the Southern Atlantic and Gulf Coasts.

Southern White Cedar – Another name for Atlantic White Cedar, Chamaecyparis thyoides.

Southern Yellow Pine – A species group, composed primarily of Loblolly, Longleaf, Shortleaf, and Slash Pines. Various subspecies also are included in the group. The Southern Yellow Pine region refers to the southeastern United States, from Texas to Virginia.

South Florida Slash Pine – A variation of Slash Pine, Pinus elliottii.

Southwestern White Pine – Pinus strobiformis. This species is found in the southwestern U.S and northern Mexico. It is of little commercial value.

Spacer Blocks – Short pieces of wood that

Spalt

are placed between joists to keep them vertical.

Spalt – See Spaults.

Spalted Wood – Partially decayed wood characterized by discolorations on the surface.

Span – The measure of distance between two supporting members.

Spandrel Panel – The panel that lies between columns in a building, and between the top of a window and the sill of another just above.

Span Index – No longer in use. See Span Rating.

Spanish Cedar – Cedrela mexicana. Native to Central and South America, this species is not a true cedar, but rather a hardwood. It is used in the manufacture of pencils, furniture, cigar boxes, and boats. Also called Brazilian Cedar, Cedro, Honduras Cedar, Mexican Cedar, Nicaraguan Cedar, Peruvian Cedar, South American Cedar, Tabasco Cedar.

Span Mark – See Span Rating.

Span Rating – The recommended center-to-center spacing of supports for structural panels. The rating is carried as part of the grademark and indicates the spacing in inches for various types of applications. For example, 32/16 on a sheathing panel shows 32 inches as the maximum spacing of supports when that panel is to be used as roof sheathing, and 16 inches when it is used as subflooring.

Span Roof – A common roof, with an equal single pitch on each side.

Spark Arrester – A baffle over a smokestack or chimney to prevent sparks from escaping. Originally, spark arresters were intended for wood-fueled steam engines, but they are also required on gasoline engines used in the woods.

Spark Catcher – Same as Spark Arrester.

Spar Pole – A man-made tower, usually of metal, designed to take the place of a spar tree in a logging operation. The spar pole has the advantage of portability and eliminates the need for topping and rigging a spar tree.

Spar Timber – Large, straight timber used for ship masts.

Spar Tree – A tree that has been stripped of limbs and top, and rigged with cables in a high-lead logging show. The spar tree supports the rigging used to yard logs from the cutting area to the landing.

Spaulding Rule – At one time, the legal log measurement rule in California. It was worked out in 1868 by N.W. Spaulding.

Spaults – Waste ends from shingle blocks.

Spec – See Specification, Speculation.

Special – See Special Offering.

Special Drawing Rights (SDR) – A type of international currency created by the International Monetary Fund to facilitate trading between countries.

Specialized Wholesaler – A wholesaler whose business is concentrated on special, often proprietary, products rather than on commodities such as dimension.

Special Offering – An offer made by a producer or distributor to sell a particular lumber, plywood, or other forest product item, usually at a discount from the list price for that item. Offerings are usually made on items that are in surplus, or that are particularly slow movers.

Special Overlay – A surfacing material used to coat wood panels and which has char-

Spar Pole

Spent Liquors

acteristics that do not fit the specific descriptions of high density or medium density overlays.

Special Pattern – A reworking of a piece of lumber to prepare it for a specific application, such as siding. Special patterns are variations of the standard patterns designated by grading agencies.

Special Service Charges – Additional charges levied by manufacturers for extra work on a product. In plywood, this would include cutting tongue and groove patterns, oiling, etc. In lumber, charges are levied for running boards to a pattern.

Specialties – A general term referring to products with special uses and not falling into other lumber categories such as dimension or boards, or into panel categories such as sheathing.

Specialty Grade – Hardwood plywood made to order to meet specific requirements of a customer. Usually entails special matching of face veneers.

Species – A category of biological classification; a class of individuals having common attributes and designated by a common name. "Species" is always properly used with the "s" when referring to trees or other biological classifications; specie refers only to money in coin.

Species Group – A group of generally related tree species, such as the True Firs (Abies) or Southern Pines (Pinus), to which common grading and design values have been designated.

Specifications – A detailed description or listing of requirements, in the case of a buyer (customer specifications), or mill-tailored offering, in the case of a seller (mill specifications).

Specific Gravity – The ratio of the density of one substance to another when used as the standard. Water is the standard for determining specific gravity of solids and liquids; hydrogen is used for gases.

Specific Heat – The ratio of the heat required to raise the temperature of a given weight of material one degree Fahrenheit, compared to the heat required to raise the same weight of water from 62 to 63 degrees, Fahrenheit.

Specified – Lumber that is sold on the basis of length, rather than as a random-length loading. A specified length would be a 2x4-16 foot, for example. Specified lengths are generally priced according to the popularity of the various lengths, with the so-called key, or popular, lengths priced higher than the less-desired lengths.

Specifier – A person who prepares written instructions to builders, listing information about materials, style, and workmanship for the job.

Speck – See White Speck.

Speculation – The purchase (or sale) of stock with the expectation of being able to sell (or buy) it later at a profit. In the futures market, trading with the expectation of profiting from the trade alone, as opposed to hedging.

Speculator – A person involved in speculation. In the futures market, one who takes a position for any purpose other than hedging. See Hedge.

Speeder – A small rail car, with its own power, or one that is powered by the passengers. Used to transport work crews and supplies to sites along the railroad.

Speed Sander – A high-speed surfacing machine for either lumber or panel products that is equipped with abrasive-coated sanding heads or belts. The heads are positioned to sand the top and bottom surfaces (and edges, if desired) simultaneously.

Speed Sander

Spent Liquors – A by-product of the paper making process containing carbohydrate and lignate decomposition products, which can be fermented into ethyl alcohol or used

Terms Of The Trade

Sphaeroma Terebrans

in other processes to make animal feed and vanillin flavoring. Spent liquors can also be used as fuel or in the production of a solvent, dimethyl sulfoxide (DMSO).

Sphaeroma Terebrans – A marine organism that damages untreated wood.

Spider Shake – A lengthwise separation of wood between or through annual growth rings and set in a radial pattern.

Spike Knot – See Knot Occurrence.

Spike Top – A tree with a dead top, often one that has lost branches, leaving only the central bole as a spike.

Spile – 1. A peg or plug of wood. 2. A spout for directing the flow of sap from Sugar Maples. 3. A heavy wooden stake. 4. A small log used in the construction of a splash dam.

Spindle – 1. A shaft used as the axis of rotation; an arbor or mandrel. 2. A narrow, turned piece of wood.

Spin Out – A peeler core that breaks loose from the lathe chucks holding it at each end before the peeling of veneer is completed.

Spiral Grain – Fibers that extend spirally around, instead of vertically along, the bole of a tree.

Splashboard – Wood or other material placed against a wall to help keep it clean and dry.

Splash Dam – A temporary dam constructed across a slow-moving or shallow stream to build up a head of water that is strong enough, when released, to wash logs downstream.

Splay – 1. To form with an oblique angle; bevel. 2. To spread out or extend.

Splayed Edge – A bevel across the full thickness of a piece.

Splayed Joint – A spliced joint, one in which the two pieces being joined are beveled and overlap without increasing the cross-sectional area.

Splay Knot – A spike knot.

Splice – The point on a truss at which two chord members are joined together to form a single member.

Splice Plate – A plate laid over a joint and fastened to the pieces being joined to provide stiffness.

Splice Point – The point where two chords of a truss are connected.

Splicer – A machine used to join pieces of veneer to make larger sheets by jointing and edge-gluing two pieces at a time. See Veneer Jointer.

Spline – A piece of metal or wood used to join two pieces of wood, such as decking, together.

Splinter – A small, thin sharp piece of wood broken from a larger piece. 2. To split or break something into splinters.

Splash Dam

Spread Trading

Splinter Draw

Splinter Draw – Pieces that pull out of a tree butt as it is felled, leaving them on the stump.

Splinter Pull – See Splinter Draw.

Splints – Waste edgings developed in trimming shingles and shakes.

Split – A lengthwise separation of a piece of lumber extending from one surface through the piece to the opposite surface or to an adjoining surface. Classified for grading purposes as short, medium, or long split. In plywood, a separation of wood fiber completely through a veneer.

Split Level – A structure having floors on more than one level when the difference in some floor levels is less than one story.

Split Pattern – A divided mould used in casting metal.

Split Products – The posts, rails, stakes, or bolts split from Redwood or cedar logs.

Splitter – A device mounted behind a saw to prevent cants from falling onto the saw, or to prevent the saw from binding.

Splitterhead Rip – One of several processes by which a piece of lumber is divided longitudinally into two or more pieces. In splitterhead ripping, a piece of lumber, usually dimension, is split in two along its length by a series of knives as it passes through the planer.

Splitting Gun – A pipe driven into a log too large to handle. Filled with explosives, it will split the log when detonated.

Splitting Saw – A saw used to split shingle bolts into quarters, before they are cut into shingles.

Splitting Wedge – A heavy metal wedge used to split rails or firewood.

Spoke Bolt – A small log from which wheel spokes were split.

Spoolwood – Small blocks of hardwoods, intended for the manufacture of spools or bobbins.

Spot – To place a rail car in a particular location for loading or unloading.

Spot Exchange Rate – In international trade, the price paid to exchange currencies for immediate delivery.

Spot Fire – A small fire started by sparks blowing out from the main blaze.

Spot Lumber – See Spot Price.

Spot Market – See Spot Price.

Spot Month – The most current month in which futures trading is being conducted.

Spot Price – A term used by futures traders to describe the price at which the physical commodity is currently selling, as opposed to the price in the futures market. The Cash Price.

Spotter – 1. An individual who was responsible for centering a veneer block on the lathe properly. This job has been eliminated by the use of mechanical lathe chargers. 2. The person who directs the yarder operator on a logging show.

Spread – 1. A futures transaction in which the purchase of one commodity is offset by the sale of the same, or a different, commodity because of an advantageous price relationship between the two positions in different contract months. Also called a straddle. Sometimes, the term arbitrage is used to describe this type of transaction. 2. To apply glue to veneer prior to layup. Also used as a quantitative measure of the pounds of adhesive applied per thousand square feet of glue line. See Veneer Gluing. 3. In international exchange, the difference between the buying and selling rates for a currency.

Spreader – A machine that spreads glue on veneer prior to layup.

Spreading-Leaf Pine – Another name for Jelecote Pine.

Spread Trading – A strategy in futures

Terms Of The Trade

Springback

trading in which a trader buys one contract and simultaneously sells another, related contract. This tactic reduces the trader's risk.

Springback – The tendency of a pressed particleboard panel to return to its original uncompressed state.

Springboard – A board on which a faller stands while felling a tree, used primarily in the days of hand-sawing and rarely seen today. The board was inserted into a notch cut in the tree, usually at a considerable height. Placing the springboards high enable fallers to avoid the resin and the saw binding usually encountered when sawing nearer the ground, especially where the butt of the tree had cross-grain swell or was flared. Trees are felled today by cutting as close as possible to the ground, to maximize the volume of usable wood.

Spring Breakup – See Breakup.

Spring Pole – A pole used to guide a whistle punk's signal wire before the use of portable radio. Also used in one-man handsawing to guide the unmanned end of the saw.

Spring Set – The cutting teeth of a saw, set alternately to each side so that the kerf is slightly larger than the thickness of the blade.

Springwood – More or less open and porous tissue marking the inner part of each annual ring of a tree, formed early in the period of growth.

Sprout – A young tree growing from a stump or root.

Spruce – Picea species. Yellow to reddish-white wood, usually straight grained, light, and soft. See White Spruce, Red Spruce, etc.

Spruce Budworm – An insect that damages spruce trees. Eggs of the spruce budworm are laid on the tree branches by the adult moth. Young budworms feed on the new growth of the tree branch primarily, but also eat the older needles. Defoliation results, killing the tree.

Spruce Fir – See Red Spruce.

Spruce Gum – Sap extruded by spruce trees. Sometimes used by early-day loggers as a substitute for chewing tobacco.

Spruce Pine – Pinus glabra. A minor species found in the South, this pine bears a close resemblance to spruce. The wood is considerably weaker than the major Southern Yellow Pine species. Lumber from this species must be stamped "Spruce Pine."

Spruce-Pine-Fir – Canadian woods of similar characteristics that have been grouped for production and marketing. The S-P-F species have moderate strength, are worked easily, take paint readily, and hold nails well. They are white to pale yellow in color. The largest volume comes from Western Canada (British Columbia and Alberta) where the principal species in the group are: White Spruce, Engelmann Spruce, Lodgepole

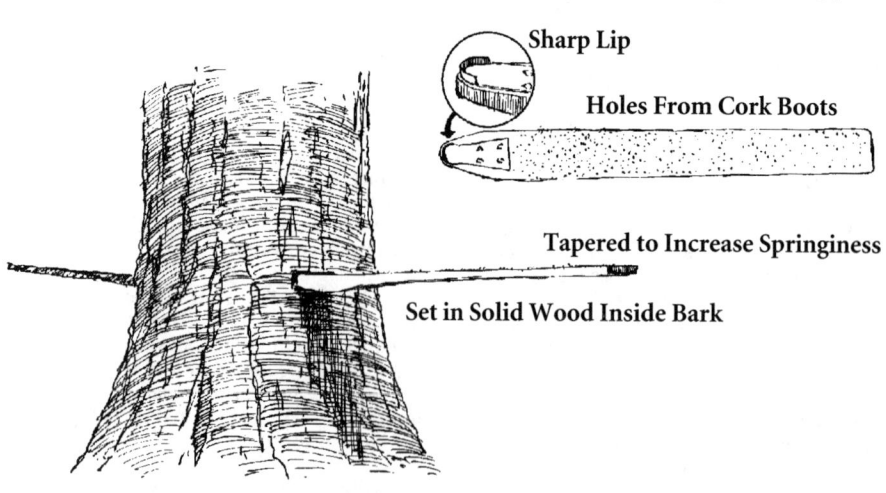

Sharp Lip

Holes From Cork Boots

Tapered to Increase Springiness

Set in Solid Wood Inside Bark

Springboard

Pine, and Alpine Fir. The principal species in the group originating in Eastern Canada are: Red Spruce, Black Spruce, Jack Pine, and Balsam Fir. Some lumber production in the New England states also is marketed as Spruce-Pine-Fir and includes those species.

Spruce-Pine-Fir (South) – A species grouping developed in 1991 by the Western Wood Products Association as a result of the In-Grade Testing Program. The grouping, available as a stamp to western U.S. lumber producers, includes Engelmann Spruce, Lodgepole Pine, and Sitka Spruce, singularly or in any combination.

Sprung Moulding – A moulding that has its interior corner beveled off to better fit a right angle joint.

Spud – A hand tool used to strip bark from logs. Also called a Rossing Tool or a Slick.

Spunk – Punky, partly decayed wood.

Spur – See Rail Spur.

Spur Beams – Short timbers used in domes, turrets, etc. to carry the feet of ribs or rafters.

Spurs – See Climbing Irons.

Spur Trim – See Score.

Square – A quantity of shingles or shakes sufficient to cover 100 square feet of area when applied in a standard manner; the basic sales units of shingles and shakes.

Square Cut – A cut at the end of a top chord of a truss, perpendicular to the slope.

Spuds

Squared Log – A timber hewn or sawed to a square, usually intended for remanufacture.

Squared Stuff – Hewn timbers.

Square Edge and Sound – A specification for Southern Yellow Pine timbers.

Square-Edge Siding – See Parallel Siding.

Square Foot – A unit of area measurement equal to a square 12 inches on each side. The standard unit of measurement for panel products. The measurement is usually qualified by inclusion of a "basis" of measurement, such as 4,000 square feet, 3/8-inch basis (thickness). Thicker panels would account for greater footage on a 3/8 basis, while thinner panels would account for less.

Square Pitch – A roof having rafters that rise 45 degrees from the plates and meet at a right angle at the ridge.

Square Roof – See Square Pitch.

Squaw Hitch – A bight of line put around the end of a log that is partly buried to aid in extricating it.

Squaw Link – A link used to connect two broken pieces of chain as a temporary repair.

Squaw Log – A log that is rotten on the butt end.

Squaw Wood – Small pieces of wood, preferably pitchy, that aid in starting a fire. Also, Skin Wood.

Squirrel – A counterweight, often a chunk of wood, that rides up and down a spar tree to pull a loading boom into position.

Squirrel Block – See Squirrel, Monkey Block.

Squirrel Tree – One with a great many branches, mainly useful as a perch for squirrels. See Grouse Ladder.

Stack – Lumber or panel products piled in an orderly manner.

Stacker – A machine, usually equipped with forks or clamps, that arranges lumber or logs in piles. See Forklift.

Stack Train – A train made up of shipping containers stacked two deep on flat cars. The concept was developed by steamship lines to facilitate the movement of waterborne freight

Stadium Plank

beyond the docks.

Stadium Plank – Lumber that is 1-1/4 to 3 inches in thickness and at least 4 inches in width, is well manufactured and free of heart center. As implied, such lumber is often used for outdoor seating and walkway boards for bleachers and stadiums.

Staff Bead – See Glass Bead.

Stage Cut – To cut timber in successive stages to reduce breakage and protect understory reproduction.

Stage of Construction – The Department of Commerce lists two stages of construction, Start and Completion. A start occurs at the time of excavation for the footings or foundation. A completion occurs when all finished flooring or carpeting has been installed.

Stagged – Cut off. Loggers often stag their pants so that the bottom of each pant leg ends near the top of their boots. Stagging helps loggers avoid catching their pants on brush or equipment. Shirts are also sometimes stagged at the tail or arms for the same reason.

Staggered Coursing – A method of applying shakes or shingles to sidewalls of a building. The shakes are placed so as to give an uneven, random appearance to the finished sidewall. Opposite of Ribbon Coursing.

Staggered Setting – An approach to timber harvesting in which harvest units, separated by uncut units of at least the same size, are scattered across the landscape.

Staggers Rail Act of 1980 – The basic legislation that led to the deregulation of the railroads. Under it, the railroads were allowed to decide many tariff and routing questions that previously had been under the direct jurisdiction of the Interstate Commerce Commission.

Staghead – See Spike Top.

Staging – A platform constructed to give workers access to the job. In timber felling by hand, boards were laid across springboards to provide a platform around a tree.

Stag Tree – A tree whose top has been broken off.

Stain – 1. Discoloration on or in lumber, or other wood product, other than its natural color. Stain may be caused by fungal growth, weathering, or the oxidation of metallic substances in a log. It is classified for grading purposes as light, medium, or heavy. 2. A pigment applied to a wood surface to accent the grain pattern.

Stair Tread Grade – A grade of particleboard. The product is designed to be used for interior treads that are subsequently covered with carpeting or resilient flooring.

Stakes – Poles or posts used on flat cars to help hold the load in place while in transit.

Stamp – See Grade Stamp.

Stamp Ax – An ax or hammer with a design on its striking surface to brand the ends of logs for identification.

Stamping Hammer – See Stamp Ax.

Stamping Iron – See Stamp Ax.

Stand – An identifiable group of trees or section of timber occurring in a particular area.

Standard – 1. A grade of lumber suitable for general construction and characterized by generally good strength and serviceability. In light framing rules, the Standard grade applies to lumber that is two to four inches thick and two to four inches wide. It falls between the Construction and Utility grades. 2. A grade of Idaho White Pine boards equivalent to #3 Common in other species. 3. A grade of radius edge decking. 4. In the British timber trade, a quantity of lumber that equals 1,980 board feet.

Standard and Better (Std&Btr) – A mix of lumber grades suitable for general construction. The "and Better" signifies that a portion of the lumber is actually of a higher grade than Standard (but not necessarily of the highest grade). The proportion of higher grades included is a factor in determining market value.

Standard Bundling – Packaged paneling and siding. Stock 1/2-inch thick is bundled 8 feet and longer, 10 layers deep; bundles 10 feet and longer may include three layers of 3- to 7 foot lengths. Stock 3/4-inch thick is bundled 8 feet and longer, six layers deep. Bundles 10 feet and longer may include two layers of 3- to 7-foot lengths.

Standard Cubic Load – A unit of measure used in the export trade, equivalent to 50 cubic feet, or 600 board feet.

State Trees

The official trees of each of the 50 states are:

Alabama: *Southern Pine*

Alaska: *Sitka Spruce*

Arizona: *Paloverde*

Arkansas: *Shortleaf Pine*

California: *Redwood*

Colorado: *Blue Spruce*

Connecticut: *White Oak*

Delaware: *American Holly*

District of Columbia: *Scarlet Oak*

Florida: *Sabal Palmetto Palm*

Georgia: *Live Oak*

Hawaii: *Candlenut*

Idaho: *Western White Pine*

Illinois: *White Oak*

Indiana: *Tuliptree*

Iowa: *Oak*

Kansas: *Cottonwood*

Kentucky: *Coffeetree*

Louisiana: *Baldcypress*

Maine: *Eastern White Pine*

Maryland: *White Oak*

Massachusetts: *American Elm*

Michigan: *Eastern White Pine*

Minnesota: *Red Pine*

Mississippi: *Magnolia*

Missouri: *Flowering Dogwood*

Montana: *Ponderosa Pine*

Nebraska: *Cottonwood*

Nevada: *Singleleaf Pinyon Pine*

New Hampshire: *White Birch*

New Jersey: *Red Oak*

New Mexico: *Pinyon Pine*

New York: *Sugar Maple*

North Carolina: *Shortleaf Pine*

North Dakota: *American Elm*

Ohio: *Ohio Buckeye*

Oklahoma: *Redbud*

Oregon: *Douglas Fir*

Pennsylvania: *Eastern Hemlock*

Rhode Island: *Red Maple*

South Carolina: *Palmetto Tree*

South Dakota: *Black Hills Spruce*

Tennessee: *Tuliptree*

Texas: *Pecan*

Utah: *Blue Spruce*

Vermont: *Sugar Maple*

Virginia: *Flowering Dogwood*

Washington: *Western Hemlock*

West Virginia: *Sugar Maple*

Wisconsin: *Sugar Maple*

Wyoming: *Cottonwood*

Standard Dozen

Standard Dozen – A British term denoting 12 pieces of 2x12 12-foot.

Standard Gauge – A railroad track system in which the rails are four feet, eight and one-half inches apart.

Standard Industrial Classification (SIC) – A system used by the U.S. government to collect and disseminate information about various industries.

Standard Matched – A type of tongue and groove lumber in which the tongue and groove are offset, rather than centered as in center matched.

Standard Sawn – A term used to describe rough lumber that has been cut to sizes and specifications described in grading rules of rules-writing agencies. For example, under WCLIB rules, a rough timber with a nominal thickness of 8 inches has a standard-sawn thickness of 7-3/4 inches. Variations of 1/2-inch over and 1/8-inch under this standard-sawn size are allowed.

Standard Shop – Shop lumber surfaced to a standard thickness. Standard surfacing for 5/4-inch Ponderosa Pine shop is 1-5/32-inch, for example; 5/4 shop surfaced to a thicker dimension is described as having "heavy" surfacing.

Standard Surfacing – The surfaced size of a piece of lumber established in grading rules. This phrase is usually used in reference to shop lumber, which can be surfaced to a variety of thicknesses to meet specific customer needs or production requirements. See Standard Shop.

Standard Transportation Commodity Code Tariff (STCC) – A system of classifying all commodities shipped by railroads; each commodity is assigned a seven-digit code number.

Standard Unit – A stack of lumber, plywood, or other wood product securely fastened together in a unit containing a specified number of pieces and/or of a particular length, width, or height. In lumber, a standard unit is generally considered to be: 2x4 208 pieces (13 wide and 16 high), 45-1/2 inches wide and 25 inches high; 2x6 128 pieces (8 wide and 16 high), 44 inches wide and 25 inches high; 2x8 96 pieces (6 wide and 16 high), 43-1/2 inches wide and 25 inches high; 2x10 80 pieces (5 wide and 16 high), 46-1/4 inches wide and 25 inches high; 2x12 64 pieces (4 wide and 16 high), 45 inches wide and 25 inches high. In panel products, most units are either 30 or 33 inches high. The most common unit of 1/2-inch particleboard contains 60 sheets, while the common unit of 1/2-inch plywood sheathing contains 66 sheets. However, some units of panel products are 36 inches high, or 72 sheets of 1/2-inch material.

Standard Warehouse – One of three pallet grades recognized by the National Wooden Pallet and Container Association.

Stand Density – A measure of tree stocking volume on a specific site, usually expressed in terms of the number of trees, basal area, or volume.

Standing Timber – Trees that have not been cut, but are of merchantable size.

Standing Tree – A live tree used as a spar tree.

Stand Size Class – A classification of forest land based on the predominant size of timber present.

Star-Checked Knot – See Knot Quality.

Start – See Housing Start.

Starter Board – A 6- or 8-inch board used at the eave of a roof to provide a solid nailing surface for the first course of shingles or shakes. Also used in reroofing to replace the old shingles at the eaves.

Starter/Finish Course – A course of shakes used at the eave (starter) and ridge line (finish) of a roof, utilizing 15-inch, rather than 24-inch, shakes.

Starting Bar – In the early logging days in the Lake States, a metal bar used to break loose log sleighs that had frozen to the ice or snow.

Starved Joint – A glued joint that did not receive an adequate amount of adhesive and is faulty.

Statement – The summary of a financial account, showing the balance due or credits accrued.

State Trees – See previous page.

Static Bending – The application of loads across a piece of wood to determine strength properties, such as modulus of elasticity and modulus of rupture.

Stick Scaling

Station Line – A phone line that is usually answered only by the person to whom it is assigned. By calling a station line, the caller can be assured of reaching the person to whom he desires to speak without the expense or trouble of calling person-to-person.

Statute of Limitations – A law that establishes the period of time in which a debt may be collected.

Stave – A narrow strip of wood used in the construction of barrels or buckets.

Stave Bolt – The bolt from which wooden staves are cut.

St. Croix Scale – An early-day method of measuring lumber volumes.

Steam Bending – A method of manipulating wood using steam and pressure. Some woods can be rendered supple and pliable by steaming them, and can then be bent to a desired shape, such as for furniture. When cooled and dried, the wood retains the form to which it has been shaped, without damage to the fiber.

Steam Chest – A container in which wood is steamed for bending or forming.

Steam Dago – A drag saw that was driven by compressed air.

Steamed Wood – Wood that has been softened in preparation for bending or for producing veneer.

Steam Hauler – A steam-powered tractor, used to haul sleighs of logs over icy roads in the early logging days in the Lake States.

Steaming – A process in which logs are heated with steam or hot water in special vats prior to peeling them into veneer. Steaming results in smoother veneer and improved recovery from the log. A similar process is used to prepare wood for bending or shaping.

Steam Jammer – A steam-powered log loader.

Steam Vat – A container used in steaming to soften logs or flitches before peeling or slicing veneers; sometimes referred to as a steam chest.

Steep Grain – Severe cross grain.

Stem – The trunk of a tree.

Stem-Formed Wood – See Adult Wood.

Stemwinder – A geared locomotive.

Step – The difference in height between panels when butted together, due to thickness variations.

Step Joint – A notched joint used in construction.

Stepping – Lumber designed to be used for stair treads. Stepping is vertical-grained and is customarily shipped kiln-dried, surfaced three sides and bull-nosed on one edge. Besides the C&Btr and D grades of solid wood, stepping is also made from particleboard for use where it will be covered.

Step Sawing – See Stage Cut.

Stere – One cubic meter, or 1.31 cubic yards. A common unit of measure for logs and lumber in Europe.

Sterilization – The process of treating wood with chemicals or by steaming to kill fungi or insects.

Sterling – A grade of Idaho White Pine boards, equivalent to #2 Common in other species.

Stettin Fir – Redwood.

Stevedore Pallet – A heavy-duty pallet designed to be used at seaports.

Stick Built – A term describing frame houses assembled piece by piece from lumber delivered to the site with little or no previous assembly into components. The more typical type of residential construction.

Sticker – A narrow strip of wood placed at right angles between layers of lumber to facilitate air circulation in drying the lumber, either in a kiln or by air seasoning.

Sticker Stain – A stain on dry lumber resulting from the use of a sticker with a mineral or fungal content.

Sticks – 1. Extra-long logs, poles, or piling. 2. The boomsticks of a raft. 3. 100-inch pulpwood logs.

Stick Scaling – A method of determining the volume of a log by using a scaling stick to measure the small-end diameter, inside the bark.

Stiffener

Stiffener – See Lumber Stiffener.

Stile – The upright or vertical members forming the outside pieces of the frame of a door.

Stinger – The reach pole of a logging truck, especially when the trailer is mounted on the tractor, and the reach projects upward and forward somewhat like a scorpion's tail.

Stinking Cedar – Another name for Western Red Cedar, Thuja plicata.

Stirrup Logs – Smaller logs serving as bunkers, or "Cheese Blocks," to prevent a large log from rolling while being transported by truck or flat car.

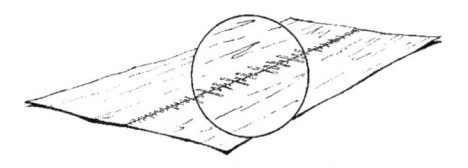

Stitched Veneer

Stitched Veneer – Veneer sheets composed of random width pieces of veneer sewn together with heavy thread. Several stitch lines run across the width of each piece of stitched veneer. In veneer production, the random width pieces are run through a large sewing machine and reclipped in desired (usually standard 48-54-inch) sizes. Stitched veneer usually is used in the core plies of plywood.

Stitcher – A machine that joins veneers by stitching them together edge to edge. Unlike glue jointing, stitching may be used on either green or dry veneer. See Veneer Composer, Glue Jointing.

St. John's Spruce – Canadian Spruce.

Stock – 1. Material carried in inventory for resale. 2. To purchase material for inventory; to stock up. 3. The main stem of a tree.

Stock Gang – A gang saw that cuts similar sections from a log or cant.

Stockholm Tar – A wood preservative obtained by the distillation of resin from pine or fir.

Stocking – The quantity of trees in a specified area. Expressed in terms of a percentage of maximum capacity.

Stocking Wholesaler – A wholesaler who buys goods in quantity from manufacturers and stores them for resale to retail dealers or industrial customers.

Stock Panel – A standard-sized panel kept in inventory for resale.

Stock Rustler – The person who buys veneer for a plywood layup plant.

Stock Sizes – Common sizes of lumber or panels that are kept in inventory.

Stock Woodwork – Mouldings that are stocked in inventory.

Stomata – Pores on leaves or stems.

Stone-Ground Wood – Wood fibers obtained for pulp production by grinding pieces of wood against an abrasive wheel.

Stone Pine – Cembran or Swiss Pine.

Stool – A moulded interior trim member serving as a sash or window frame sill cap.

Stooling – The growth of shoots from a tree stump to produce a second growth from the original roots. Some trees, such as Redwood, regenerate in this fashion.

Stop – A type of moulding nailed to the face of a door frame to prevent the door from swinging through. Also used to hold the bottom sash of a double-hung window in place.

Stop Loss Order (Stop) – A buy or sell order in futures to be executed when prices reach a specified level; generally used to limit losses in case of an adverse price movement.

Stopover – A provision in rail freight tariffs allowing a car to stop between its origin and final destination to complete loading or to partially unload without losing through-rate privileges. It is useful when a customer requires a mixture of items, not all of which are available from a single source, and when two or more customers "pool" a car so that none has to buy a full-car quantity.

Stopover Car – See Stopover.

Storage Boom – A boom used to hold logs at a sawmill.

String Measurement

Straddlebuggy

Storied Rays – Wood rays that, when viewed on a tangential section, are in horizontal rows.

Story – That portion of a building between the floor and the ceiling or roof, or the next floor above in the case of a multi-story house. A basement is not counted as a story, even if finished.

Stove – A dry kiln.

St. Petersburg Standard – See Petrograd Standard.

Straddle – See Spread.

Straddlebuggy – A lumber carrier with an extremely high center that enables it to straddle a unit of lumber and move it by lifting it on arms that extend from either side.

Straddle Truck – See Straddlebuggy.

Straight Beam – See Simple Straight Beam.

Straight Car – A loading of forest products consisting entirely of one type of item and usually limited to one species, grade, and width. There may be a variation in length, such as in a random-length loading of dimension.

Straight Grain – A piece of wood in which the principal cells run parallel to its length.

Straight Joint – A butt joint.

Straight Length – A single length of lumber, such as 16-foot, or a unit or load of such a length.

Strapping – 1. Flexible metal bands used to bind lumber or plywood into units for ease of handling and storage. 2. Another name for furring.

Strawline – A small light cable, usually pulled by hand and used in logging to move larger lines or tackle blocks.

Straw Medium – A corrugating medium having as its raw material straw from wheat, oats, or other grain. Widely used in Europe.

Stray – An unbranded log floating loose, or at the side of a road.

Streak – Localized incipient decay.

Streaks – A defect in particleboard which results in narrow, slightly raised streaks along the length of a panel. Caused by metal in a previous board which strips grit from the sanding belt.

Stressed Skin Panel – A panelized roof, floor, or wall component constructed of plywood glued to one or both edges of framing members to provide greater load carrying capacity than the individual framing members acting individually.

Stress Grades – Lumber grades having assigned working stress and modulus of elasticity values in accordance with accepted basic principles of strength grading and meeting the provisions of the American Softwood Lumber Standard.

Stress-O-Matic – A brand of machine that tests lumber to determine modulus of elasticity. See Machine Stress Rated.

Stretch Wrap – A method of applying plastic wrap under tension; used primarily to wrap shingles and shakes.

Striated Face – The face of a plywood panel that has been given closely spaced, shallow grooves to provide a vertical pattern.

Stringer – A horizontal timber used to support floor joists or other cross members.

Stringing – A process for joining veneers to be used as core stock. As veneer edges are brought together by a crowder, nylon strings, coated with hot-melt adhesive, are applied to the veneer surface and set by cold wheels. From four to six strings may be applied to an 8-foot sheet, depending on thickness.

String Measurement – A method of log measurement in which string or tape is used

String Tied

to determine the girth of the log, which is then multiplied by the length, according to any of various formulas.

String Tied – A bundle of small pieces such as lath, mouldings, etc., tied by twine. Also, String Tied & Bundled (ST&B).

Strip – 1. Board lumber one inch in nominal thickness and less than four inches in width; frequently the product of ripping a wider piece of lumber. The most common sizes are 1x2 and 1x3. See Furring. 2. Developing items in veneer production. See Sections (2).

Strip Adjustment – An arrangement giving timber fallers an adjustment in pay due to rough ground or scattered timber.

Strip Burning – Burning slash in strips across a logged area instead of burning the entire area.

Strip Cruise – An old method of cruising timber, by following a compass course through the stand, counting trees on a strip on either side of the line.

Stripe Figure – Ribbon grain in quarter-sawn wood.

Strip Thinning – The removal of selected trees from an immature stand on a relatively narrow straight course.

Strobili – Cones from conifers.

Stroke Sander – A machine with a sanding face that oscillates or has a reciprocal motion, as opposed to one that employs an endless belt of abrasive.

Structural Joists and Planks (SJ&P) – Lumber two, three, or four inches thick and six inches or wider, graded for its strength properties. Used primarily for joists in residential construction and graded (in descending order) Select Structural, #1, #2, and #3. The #1 and #2 grades are usually marketed in combination as #2&Btr.

Structural Light Framing (SLF) – A category of dimension lumber up to four inches in width which provides higher bending strength ratios for use in engineered applications such as roof trusses. It is often referred to by its fiber strength class, such as 1750f for #1&Btr Douglas Fir, or as stress-rated stock.

Structural Panel – Any of various panels, including plywood and OSB, designed to be used in applications where strength and stiffness are required. Such uses include roof, wall, and floor sheathing, structural diaphragms, etc.

Structural Panel Composite Price – See Composite Price.

Structural Sandwich Panel – Any of a variety of panels constructed by combining wood and plastic foam. One type uses plywood or OSB/waferboard as the face and back, foam as the core, and framing lumber on the edges as reinforcement. Another type consists of a series of wood I-joists or pieces of framing lumber interspersed with foam. The panels are used for such applications as bearing walls, foundations, floors, and roofs.

Structural Veneer – Veneers used in the construction of structural plywood panels, as opposed to decorative veneers.

Strutting – See Blocking.

Stub – 1. A timber used on a flat car to keep the load in place. 2. The broken off stump of a tree.

Stubbies – Fifteen-inch shakes used for starter and finish courses on roofs. Stubbies are manufactured by trimming back blowouts, or falldown, in the production of 24-inch shakes. See Starter/Finish Course.

Stub Stake – A timber or stake used on a flatcar to keep a load in place, required on floating loads during the winter and spring due to icy conditions.

Stud – A framing member, usually cut to a precise length at the mill and designed to be used in framing building walls with little or no trimming before it is set in place. Studs are most often 2x4s, but 2x3s, 2x6s, and other sizes are also included in the stud category; studs may be of wood, steel, or composite material.

Stud Bolt – A bolt firmly anchored in, and projecting from, a structure such as a concrete pad, and used to fasten dissimilar materials together.

Stud Finder – A tool used to locate studs in a wall, usually by employing a magnet that reacts to the nails fastening the wall sheathing to the studs.

Stud Grade – A grade of framing lumber under the National Grading Rule established by the American Lumber Standards Committee. Lumber of this grade has strength and stiffness values that make it suitable for use as a vertical member of a wall, including use in load-bearing walls.

Stulls – Mine timbers.

Stump – 1. The end of a tree remaining in the ground after the tree was felled. 2. To break a tree by felling it across a stump.

Stumpage – 1. Standing timber; trees on the stump before they are felled. 2. The monetary value of standing timber calculated before the tree is cut. This originated from the early practice of charging a set price per tree cut, determining the total charge by counting stumps.

Stumpage Charge – In Canada, the fee paid by a company or individual for the right to harvest timber on Crown lands.

Stumpage Rate – The rate per unit of measurement that a faller is paid for his work.

Stump Deduct – A penalty that was assessed against fallers for leaving too high a stump in hand-logging days.

Stump Figure – Decorative grain obtained from the base and roots of a tree. See Stump Veneer.

Stump Jumper – Slang for a choker setter.

Stump Loading – A method of harvesting pulpwood in which trees are felled and bucked into bolts and a truck is driven from stump to stump while the bolts are loaded, either manually or with the use of a hoist. This method is most often used in flat, dry areas of the South.

Stump Scale – An approximate estimate of the volume of timber removed from an area, made by counting and measuring the stumps.

Stump Shot – The removal of stumps by use of an explosive to clear a right of way or a landing.

Stump Veneer – Veneer that has been produced from the roots of a tree. Used in hardwood plywood manufacturing because of its grain configurations. See Stump Figure.

Stumpwood – See Stump Figure, Stump Veneer.

Sturd-I-Floor – A trade name registered by the American Plywood Association for a panel designed specifically for use as combined subfloor/underlayment in residential floor applications. It is available in several thicknesses, each keyed to a recommended spacing of floor joists from 16 to 48 inches.

Sturd-I-Wall – APA 303 siding panels intended to be attached directly to studs, as combined sheathing/siding, or over non-structural wall sheathing. A registered grade-trademark of the American Plywood Association.

Sub – See subcontractor.

Subalpine Fir – Abies lasiocarpa. One of the true firs, this species is grouped for commercial purposes under the Hem-Fir designation.

Subalpine Larch – Larix lyallii. Found on slopes of the Northern Rocky Mountains, this species is of no commercial value.

Subcontractor – A secondary contractor who performs a specific job, such as framing, plumbing, etc.

Subdominant Species – One growing below the tallest layer of vegetation in a forest.

Subject to Prior Sale – A notation seen on offering lists, indicating that any of the items offered therein may be sold prior to the list being received by other potential buyers, and thus may not be available.

Sub Prior – See Subject to Prior Sale.

Subrogate – To substitute a claim against one person for a claim against another. The act of one person who substitutes for another as a creditor.

Subsidiary – A separate corporation controlled by another corporation and standing on its own for credit purposes.

Substitution of Logs – A procedure in which a company exports logs obtained from private or state sources and then substitutes logs from federal forests to meet the raw material supply needs for its domestic operations. Such substitution is specifically banned by federal regulation.

Substrate – A layer of material that supports something applied to its face.

Subterranean Termite – See Western Subterranean Termite.

Succession

Succession – The process by which the composition of a forest is changed as trees of a dominant species die out, or are cut, and are replaced by other species.

Successional Species – The species that succeeds a previously dominant species; in timber, usually highly shade tolerant.

Sucker – A sprout growing from the roots at the base of a tree or from a branch, not a main limb or trunk.

Suckerdown Block – In balloon logging, a block that can be lowered to make chokers accessible on the ground.

Sudd – A floating barrier of logs.

Sugar Maple – Acer saccharum. A maple with sweet sap that is drawn off as the source of maple syrup. The tree also provides a hard wood which is used in the manufacture of furniture.

Sugar Pine – Pinus lambertiana. This species, found in Northern California and Southern Oregon, is light, smooth, and easily worked. It is widely used in millwork, pattern work, and various interior applications. The Sugar Pine takes its name from the sugary, sweet-tasting deposits of resin which are exuded from its bark after injury to the tree.

Sugi – Cryptomeria japonica. Commonly called Japanese Redwood or Japanese Cedar, this conifer is a major plantation tree in Japan and Taiwan. The wood is used in general construction as well as in paneling and furniture.

Sugler – A man who wet the ground under Redwood logs to make it easier for oxen to skid them.

Sulky – An arch mounted on wheels.

Sulphate Pulp – Pulp produced by cooking wood fibers in an alkaline solution to remove lignin and other impurities. This is known as the kraft process. The pulp is used in the production of wrapping papers, and in duplicating and typing paper due to its strength.

Sulphite Pulp – Pulp produced by cooking wood fibers in an acid solution to remove lignin and other impurities. It is used in the manufacture of tissues and lightweight papers.

Summer Beam – A beam serving as a lintel over an opening.

Summerwood – The dense fibrous outer portion of each annual ring of a tree, formed late in the growing period, although not necessarily in the summer. The opposite of Springwood.

Sun – A tenth part of a Shaku, a Japanese unit of measurement for logs. A sun equals 1.19 inches.

Sun Checking – Checking in a log caused by drying and exposure to the sun. Logs stored in a pond are less likely to sun check than are those stored on land. Log decks are often sprayed with water to resist checking.

Sunken Joint – A small, narrow depression on the face of a piece of plywood. Sunken joints occur over joint gaps in the core plies of plywood.

Sun Scald – Damage to a tree caused by excessive exposure to the sun.

Sun Shield – A plywood panel, board, or other shield placed to protect the ends of lumber piles from the direct sun while air drying. The shields help minimize checking and splitting.

Supercalender – In papermaking, a series of smooth metal rollers over which pulp is passed to produce a smooth surface.

Superficial Foot – A square foot, one inch thick. A board foot. Also called a super foot.

Superior – The highest grade of finish lumber under WWPA rules. This grade is recommended and used where finest appearance is important. Some pieces are absolutely clear. Superior is equal to C&Btr under SPIB and WCLIB rules.

Super Trees – Genetically superior seedlings that grow much faster than their ordinary counterparts, developed from superior seed and usually nurtured under controlled climatic conditions in greenhouses.

Supply – The amount of goods currently available to satisfy demand.

Supply and Demand – The relationship between the availability of goods and the demand for them. The "Law of Supply and Demand" holds that the price of a product will move in the same direction as demand and opposite to the direction of supply.

Support Tree – A tree into which another has been felled, preventing it from falling to the ground.

Suppressed Pine – Small Ponderosa Pine that has grown under adverse conditions. It usually has dark bark as opposed to the reddish bark found on most mature Ponderosa Pine. Also called Blackjack Pine or Bull Pine.

Suppressed Trees – Trees whose crowns are below the general canopy, and who receive no direct light.

Supreme – A grade of Idaho White Pine equivalent to B&Btr-1&2 Clear; the highest grade of select lumber.

Surbase – Mouldings immediately above the base of a pedestal.

Surcharge – An additional cost added to the basic price of a commodity or service.

Surety – A pledge by one party to perform a given act if another fails to do so in accordance with an agreement.

Surface Check – See Check.

Surfaced – Refers to lumber that has been dressed by a planing machine for the purpose of attaining smoothness of surface and uniformity of size. Surfacing may be done on one side or edge, or all sides.

Surface Inactivation – See Veneer Drying.

Surface Measure – A method of measuring an area or materials that gives a measurement of area only and does not take thickness into account. For example, a 2x6 eight feet long would measure four square feet on a surface measure basis, but eight board feet on a board foot basis.

Surface Pull – Defects in the surface of a particleboard panel, caused by particles being pulled from the panel during sanding.

Surface Shake – A type of shake (defect) occurring on only one side of a piece.

Surge Deck – An area near the mill where logs are stored temporarily, providing a continuous supply in the event delivery from the log yard is interrupted.

Surplus – Any excess of a product, size, grade, length, etc., so designated by a seller. Producers often publish special sales notices on which surplus items are offered to potential buyers, sometime at prices well below "list" price levels.

Surround – A decoration around something, such as a floor or window.

Survey Stakes – Small pieces of wood, usually 1x2 or 2x2, which have been cut and pointed for driving into the ground to mark a survey line or some boundary of construction.

Suspended Ceiling – A finished ceiling suspended from a framework that drops down from the actual room height.

Sustainable Development – The development of forests to meet current needs without prejudice to their future productivity, ecological diversity, or capacity for regeneration.

Sustained Yield – The yield of timber that a given forest area can sustain indefinitely at a given intensity of management.

Swabber – See Skid Greaser.

Swage Saw – A stiff circular saw whose thickness has been reduced by grinding below the teeth. Hollow ground.

Swallow Tail Stump – See Barber Chair.

Swamp – To clear brush and other obstructions from a landing or in construction of a road; to clean out.

Swamp Cedar – Another name for Atlantic White Cedar, Chamaecyparis thyoides.

Swamp Cypress – Another name of Baldcypress, Taxodium distichum.

Swamper – A cleanup man around a mill or logging operation. Also, an extra man who works with a forklift, setting spacers or blocks between units when yarding or loading trucks or flat cars.

Swamping Ax – A wide, sturdy, double-bitted ax used in rough work.

Swamp Pine – A common name for both Slash Pine, Pinus elliottii, and Loblolly Pine, Pinus taeda.

Swamp Sauger – A mythical animal of great strength who was said to live in swamps.

Swamp Spruce – Canadian Black Spruce.

Sway Bar

Sway Bar — A bar used to connect two log cars.

Swede — A modifier for a large number of tools and other items in the hand-logging days.

Swede Saw — A short saw, usually used to cut pulpwood.

Swedish Fiddle — See Misery Whip.

Swedish Steam — Loggers' slang for hand power.

Sweep — The curvature or bend in a log, pole, or piling, classified as a defect.

Sweeper — A sapling that has been bent over in yarding and is swept back and forth by succeeding turns.

Sweetening — Improving the grades or lengths in a load as an enticement to buy.

Swell — 1. The flare at the butt end of a log. 2. A defect in particleboard consisting of a thickness increase caused by excessive moisture pickup or wetting.

Swell Butted — A log that has a swelled or flared butt.

Swelling — An increase in the size of wood due to an increase in moisture content.

Swifter — 1. A device consisting of a chain that was put around two objects and then twisted, bringing the objects together. 2. A cable, rope, or cross timber used to join boomsticks on either side of a raft.

Swing Boom — A boom across a river that could be opened and closed.

Swing Chain — The short chain that attached logs to an arch, or big wheels.

Swing Chaser — The man who uncouples chokers from logs at the landing and also fastens the chokers for their return to the logged area.

Swing Dog — Another name for a Cant Hook.

Swing Donkey — A skyline donkey in a yarding operation, used to swing logs from the yarding engine to another spot.

Swing Jammer — Same as Swing Yarder.

Swing Saw — A saw mounted on an arm and pendulum for crosscutting material.

Swing Yarder — A yarder capable of positioning logs on either side of itself.

Swirl — Irregular grain usually caused by a knot or other defect in the wood.

Swirl Crotch — Figured veneer obtained from the crotch of a tree where its grain fades into the grain from the normal stem.

Switch — The movement of rail cars from one location to another within the switching limits.

Switch Hog — A switch engine.

Switching — In futures trading, the tactic of liquidating an existing position and simultaneously reinstating that position in another future of the same commodity.

Switching Charge — A surcharge levied by a railroad for moving a car to, or from, a siding. A charge is made when a car, delivered to a destination by one carrier, must be switched to a siding on a line owned by another carrier. In some instances, railroads make reciprocal arrangements and most have free switching areas within which they will move a car once without charge.

Switch Tie — An extra-long railroad tie, used to span the area beneath a rail switch.

Sycamore — Platanus occidentalis. The American Sycamore, Buttonwood, or Planetree, a large hardwood native to the eastern United States.

Symbiosis — The living together of two dissimilar organisms, especially when the relationship is beneficial to both. Also called mutualism.

Symmetrical Construction — A plywood panel in which the plies on one side of the center ply are balanced in thickness with those on the other side. Balanced construction.

Symmetrical Truss — A truss with the same configuration of members and design loading occurring on each side of the truss centerline.

Synthetic Resin Patch (Plug) — A patch composed of a synthetic substance, such as epoxy, used to fill voids caused by defects in the veneers of a plywood panel.

T

T1-11 – See Texture 1-11.

Tabasco Cedar – See Spanish Cedar.

Table Joint – Any of various joints in which the fitted surfaces are parallel to the edges of the pieces being joined, with a vertical break in the middle; this break is termed the table. Such joints are used in lengthening structural members.

Table-Mountain Pine – Pinus pungens. This pine is found primarily in the Appalachian states. It is not a commercial species.

Tabulated Design Value – Design values

Tailhold and Tail Block

Tag

based on normal loading conditions, before being modified by various adjustment factors such as temperature, load duration, stability, etc.

Tag – A grade of strong, dense paper.

Tagline – A short piece of cable that connects a choker to the main part of the yarding system.

Taiga – Subarctic coniferous forests of North America and Eurasia; small trees.

Tail – The bottom part of a shingle.

Tail Block – A pulley that is attached to an anchor stump, through which a cable is passed and used to return the mainline and chokers to the cutting area from the landing.

Tailhold – An anchor stump to which a tailblock is attached.

Tailhook – Tongs used to skid logs.

Tailored Specs – A detailed description or listing of requirements in a load of lumber or plywood, assembled by either a customer (customer specifications) or seller (mill specifications). Such loadings are tailored to have a high percentage of preferred items, if customer specified, or a high percentage of accumulated items, if mill specified.

Tailpiece – 1. A short beam or rafter placed in a wall and supported by a header. 2. A handle on the bar end of a two-man power saw.

Tailrace – Water diverted from a river or other flowing body to power a sawmill.

Tailsawyer – See Off Bearer.

Tailspar – A spar pole or tree at the far end of a skyline logging system, which elevates and supports one end of the skyline. Also called a back spar.

Tailtree – A tree used as a tailspar.

Taiwan Fir – Abies kawakamii. A commercial species native to the Far East.

Taiwan Spruce – Picea morrisonicola. A

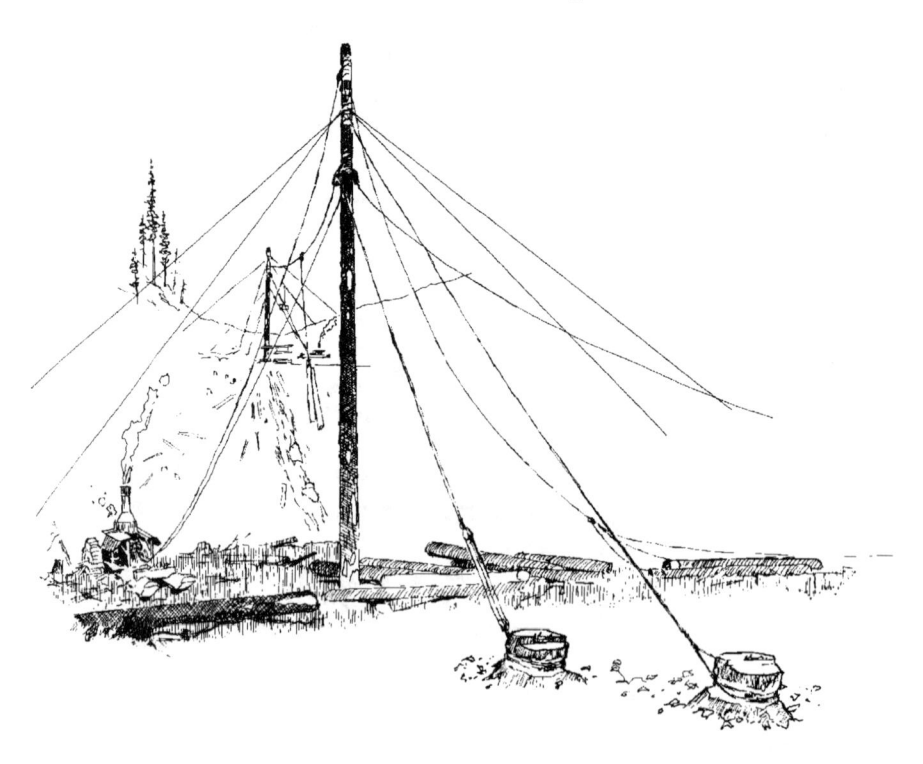

Tailtree

commercial species native to the Far East.

Take – As used in the language of the Endangered Species Act, "to harass, harm, pursue, hunt, shoot, wound, kill, trap, capture or collect" any protected species.

Takeoff – The preparation of a list of materials, taken from the plans and specifications of a building project. Included are the kinds of material, and the number, size, weight, volumes, etc.

Tall Oil – A byproduct of the paper-making process that is used in the production of naval stores. By distilling tall oil, rosin and fatty acids are produced. These chemicals are used in many products including adhesives, carbon paper, inks, lubricants, and gasoline additives.

Tally – A numerical breakdown of the various lengths and/or widths in a load of lumber. The price of a random-length load is generally dependent on the tally, with those loads having a high proportion of the desired lengths bringing the higher price.

Tally Board – A board on which a tallyman records information such as the number of pieces, sizes, etc.

Tallyman – A worker in a sawmill who tallies, or calculates, the volume of lumber produced and ready for shipment by counting the units or pieces and recording them by lengths and widths.

Tally Stick – A device used to tally shop lumber. It consists of a wooden stick with marks showing widths multiplied by lengths.

Tamarack – Larix laricina. This species, also called Eastern Tamarack, is common in the northeastern states; its range extends as far as Southern Alaska, however. As a member of the larch family, it is one of the few conifers that sheds its needles in the fall.

Tamarack Pine – Another name for Lodgepole Pine, Pinus contorta.

Tambours – Narrow strips of wood, mounted on canvas or other flexible material to form a flexible shutter to close up cabinets, roll-top desks, and the like.

Tanbark – Bark from various species of trees, used to tan hides. Also, the shredded bark used to cover the floor of an arena, as for a circus.

Tallyman

Tangent End – The bent end of a laminated beam. The beam is bent at an angle, rather than simply curved.

Tangential Section – A longitudinal section through a tree perpendicular to a radius. Tangential sawing is used to produce flat-grained lumber.

Tank Stock – Lumber suitable for use in the production of water tanks, tubs, and containers for certain chemicals that would damage metal tanks. It is usually two or more inches in thickness, eight or more inches in width, and of redwood, cedar, or other species resistant to decay.

Tannin – Any of various chemical compounds derived from wood, especially oak, and used in the curing of leather. Also called tannic acid.

Tape – 1. Paper or cloth with adhesive on one side that is used to join veneers prior to gluing. It is also placed on veneer pieces to facilitate handling. 2. An adhesive-backed strip used to cover the unfinished edge of a plywood or reconstituted wood panel.

Tapeless Splicer – A machine that joins pieces of veneer together, edge to edge, with glue and without tape.

Taper – 1. A gradual diminution of thickness, diameter or width in a log or piece of lumber. 2. A bevel on the edge of a particleboard panel that exceeds sanding specifications.

Taper Sawing – A method of sawing logs in which the cuts are made parallel to the bark rather than to the longitudinal axis of the log; this results in a greater percentage of straight-grained lumber.

Tapersawn – A trade name used by the Cedar Shake and Shingle Bureau for shakes fully sawn on both faces.

Tapersplit – Shakes produced by using a

Tap Hole

mallet and froe (a sharp steel blade) to obtain split faces on both sides. The taper of the shake is a result of reversing the block and splitting the shake from a different end after each split.

Tap Hole — An incision made in the bark of a tree to draw off its sap, as in the gathering of turpentine or maple syrup.

Taping Machine — A machine used to join pieces of veneer together, using tape made of paper or cloth with adhesive on one side; now largely outmoded by stitchers and veneer jointers.

Tapline — A short, or feeder, line railroad, usually owned or controlled by the customers using it.

Taproot — The main root of a tree. The taproot usually descends more or less vertically while sending out smaller roots laterally.

Tar — A dark, viscous product obtained by the destructive distillation of various organic substances such as coal or wood. Often used as a protective or waterproof coating.

Tare — The weight of a rail car, truck, or other conveyance when empty. The tare is deducted from the gross weight of the vehicle and its contents to determine the weight of the freight in figuring freight charges.

Tariff — A schedule of charges, such as those published by rail carriers listing current freight rates.

Tasmanian Pine — See King William Pine.

Taxation Tree Farm (TTF) — In Canada, an arrangement under which a company agrees to manage freehold land on a sustained yield basis in return for tax concessions.

Tax In — A notation that the tax has been included in the price shown. A designation commonly used in quoted prices on certain Canadian lumber items delivered to Canadian destinations to show that the federal sales tax has been figured into the price.

Taxol — A chemical derived from yew trees and used to treat certain kinds of cancer.

Taxonomist — One who identifies, names, and classifies organisms.

Tax Out — A notation that the Canadian federal sales tax is not included in the price.

See Tax In.

T-Beam — A beam whose cross section resembles a T.

Team Track — A rail siding accessible to the public. A siding where cars may be unloaded at destination by firms having no rail facilities at their locations.

Tear Strength — A measurement of resistance to tearing.

Teazel — An angle post used in the construction of a timber-frame building.

Tecate Cypress — Cupressus guadalupensis. This non-commercial species is found in Southern California, Baja California, and on Guadalupe Island.

Technical Analysis — A method of analyzing futures markets and trends using technical factors of market activity such as price change patterns, rates of change, and fluctuations in volume and open interest, in an effort to predict future price movement.

Technical Trader — A futures trader who bases his buying and selling decisions primarily on conditions that develop within the futures market rather than on developments in the market for the physical commodity. See Chart Trader.

Technical Type — Hardwood plywood manufactured with a completely waterproof glue bond and with veneer meeting special criteria with respect to thickness and quality. Intended for applications such as marine and aircraft, where strength and maximum moisture resistance are required.

Telegraphing — Show-through on a smooth overlaid plywood panel surface, due to defects in the material beneath the surface. Also called Ghosting.

Telex — A teletypewriter exchange service. A Telex machine is equipped with a device for translating a message onto perforated paper tape, which can then be run though a reader to be transmitted. The tape permits corrections to be made before the machine is connected to the exchange. Because of this and the tape's constant speed of transmission, charges for use of the exchange normally are less than if the message were sent directly by an operator.

Temperature Factor — An adjustment factor modifying the tabulated design value of

Termites

wood.

Tempered Hardboard – High-density hardboard that has been impregnated by resin and heat-cured. The resulting product is water resistant and has increased strength and hardness.

Tender – 1. An offer showing a willingness to buy or sell at a specific price and conditions. 2. In futures, the act on the part of a seller of a contract of giving notice to the clearinghouse that he intends to deliver the physical commodity in satisfaction of a futures contract. 3. A hooktender. 4. A railcar attached to a steam locomotive for carrying fuel and water; also, a ship providing similar services in a fleet.

Tennessee Red Cedar – Juniperus virginiana. A pioneer species found in most of the eastern U.S. It is more commonly known as Eastern Red Cedar.

Tenon – A projecting, tongue-like part of a wood member designed to be inserted into a slot (mortise) of another member to form a mortise and tenon joint.

Tenoner – A machine used to form tenons.

Tenon Saw – A small backsaw used for cutting tenons; also called a miter saw.

Tensile Modulus – A measure of tensile loading in pounds per square inch at the point of failure of a wood member or joint.

Tensile Strength – The greatest longitudinal stress a material can resist without tearing apart. Measured in pounds per square inch.

Tension Failure – The pulling apart or rupturing of wood fibers as a result of tensile stresses.

Tension Parallel to Grain – A measurement of the strength of wood when tension is applied in the same direction as that of the grain; tension is the pulling apart of the fibers. Modulus of rupture is more commonly used in practical applications as a conservative, substitute measurement.

Tension Perpendicular to Grain – A measurement of the strength of wood when tension is applied across the direction of the grain; tension is a force that pulls apart the fibers.

Tension Wood – Abnormal growth on the top or uphill side of a leaning tree.

Tenth Prox (Proximo) – The tenth day of the month following the present. A term of sale that sets the tenth of next month for payment for all purchases made this month.

Tepee Burner – See Wigwam Burner.

Teredo – A marine borer that damages untreated wood by boring holes in it.

Terminal – A finial. The terminal end, usually ornamental in nature, of a spire, newel post, pinnacle, etc.

Terminal Bud

Terminal Bud – A characteristic of conifers in which all upward growth takes place as an extension of the trunk through a leader and terminal bud.

Terminal Parenchyma – Parenchyma cells at the edge of a growth ring of a tree.

Termination Day – The final day in which trading may take place in a futures contract. Contracts outstanding at termination of trading in that delivery month must be settled by delivery of the commodity or by agreement for monetary settlement.

Termites – Insects that destroy wood by eating the wood fiber. Termites are social insects that exist in most parts of the U.S. They are most destructive in the coastal states and the Southwest. Termites can enter wood through the ground or above the ground, although the subterranean type is most com-

Territorial Wholesaler

mon in the U.S. They eat the softer springwood first, and prefer sapwood over heartwood.

Territorial Wholesaler – A term used to describe a wholesaler who operates in a specific region, as contrasted with national wholesalers.

Texture – The relative size and arrangement of wood cells.

Texture 1-11 (T1-11) – A registered trade name of the American Plywood Association for siding panels with special surface treatment (such as saw textured), and having grooves spaced regularly across the face.

Thawpond – A mill pond in which frozen logs are thawed in heated water, prior to processing.

Thermal Process – A type of wood preservation treatment in which the wood is heated in the preservative for several hours and is then submerged in cold preservative for several more hours. Creosote or penta are the preservatives most commonly used with this treatment method, which is also called the hot and cold bath treatment.

Thermomechanical Pulping (TMP) – A process in which wood chips are heated and softened by steam before being ground into fibers.

Thermoplastic – A material that is capable of being repeatedly softened by heat, and hardened by cooling. Some glues and resins used in the wood industry are thermoplastic, although most are thermosetting.

Thermosetting – A material, such as an adhesive, that sets when heat is applied; a thermosetting glue does not soften when later subjected to heat.

Thick and Thin – A thickness variation within a panel or between two panels.

Thick Panels – Plywood panels 5/8-inch and thicker.

Thick Veneer – See Heavy Peel.

Thief Stick – See Scaler's Stick, Cheat Stick.

Thin Butt – A defect in Western Red Cedar shakes in which the butt end of the shake fails to meet minimum thickness requirements.

Thin Edge – A defect in shakes in which the thickness of 24-inch shakes, within 10 inches of the butt, is less than half the minimum specified thickness.

Thinning Sale – A timber sale in which only selected trees are harvested, thinning the timber stand and providing room for more rapid growth of the remaining trees.

Thin Veneer Plywood – A panel made from thin veneers, none of which is more than 1/10-inch in thickness.

Third Clear – The highest grade of shop lumber. Officially called Factory Select or #3 Clear, this grade will yield a high percentage of cuttings, but represents a small portion of a mill's total shop production.

Third-Flag Fleet – Ships that carry goods between countries other than the one whose flag they fly.

Third Forest – The forest established in the southern U.S. in the period from the 1930s to the 1960s. This forest is and/or will be the source of much of the timber used by the industry through the year 2000.

Third Point – The point on a Fink truss where the web connects with the bottom chord.

30% Mix – See Regular 30% Mix.

Thoroughly Air Dried (TAD) – Lumber that is air dried sufficiently to meet the grading rule requirements for dry lumber.

Thrall Car – An all-door boxcar manufactured by the Thrall Co.; often used as a generic term for all-door cars, regardless of the manufacturer.

Threatened Species – As defined by the Endangered Species Act, any species "likely to become an endangered species within the foreseeable future." See Endangered Species.

Three-Eighths Basis (3/8" Basis) – A measurement of production used in the structural panel industry. Most often, it is used in describing capacity and production figures. The 3/8-inch basis describes a volume of panels as if all had been made 3/8-inch thick regardless of the actual thickness of the panels being described. This provides a common denominator when comparing capacities, volumes, and output figures. Thus, a plywood plant that produces mainly 1/2-inch sheathing will still give capacity and pro-

Tight Side

duction figures on a 3/8 basis. This plant may produce one million square feet of 1/2-inch plywood over a specific period; however, the output would be reported as 1.333 million square feet on the 3/8-inch basis.

Three Grade – A term describing 6x12&wdr #1, 25% #2 (Select Merchantable developing). The term refers to the three grades included in the mix, which is shipped primarily to the Australian market.

Three-Hinged Arch – A glued-laminated wood arch designed in two parts which are pin connected, or hinged, to each other and to their supports. Such arches are designed for convenience of transportation and erection.

Three-Layer Board – Most often, a particleboard with finer materials on the faces than in the core, as opposed to homogeneous, or single-layer board. Layered board is pressed in a single mat, with the fine materials laid on the caul first, followed by the coarser core material, then another layer of fines. Nearly all non-structural particleboard in North America is made in this manner.

Three-Minute Dip – A method of wood preservation in which the wood receives a superficial treatment by dipping it briefly into the preservative. The three-minute dip is a common method of treating window sash, frames, and other millwork with a water-repellent preservative.

Three-O-Three Siding – See APA 303 Siding.

Threshold – The entrance to something, as the sill of a doorway, or "he was on the threshold of his career."

Thrift Institutions – Repositories for personal savings, principally savings and loan associations and mutual savings banks.

Through and Through – Parallel saw cuts made the full depth of a piece; gang saw ripping. See Cut Alive.

Through Bill – A bill of lading that covers the shipment of goods from origin to destination, involving connecting carriers.

Through Check – See Check.

Through Rate – A freight rate charged on a shipment through connecting carriers. A through rate requires a route designated as a through route, a through bill of lading, uninterrupted movement, continuous possession by a carrier, and no reduction in bulk.

Through Shake – A defect extending from one surface of a piece to the opposite or adjoining surface.

Throw – To fell a tree in a particular direction.

Throwing – A British term for felling trees.

Thrust – The horizontal pressure of an arch at the crown and abutments.

Thumb Moulding – A small moulding used on the edge of a table top or other board. The profile resembles the shape of a thumb.

Thwart Marks – Indentations left by stickers on lumber that has been piled.

Tick – In futures, the minimum amount that a price can change, either up (an uptick) or down (a downtick). In lumber futures, a tick is 10 cents.

Tideland Spruce – Another name for Sitka Spruce.

Tidewater Red Cypress – Another name for Baldcypress.

Tie – See Cross Tie.

Tie Hack – A worker who hewed ties by hand.

Tie Piler – A tool used for lifting ties.

Tier – A line of pieces across the courses of a stacked load of lumber.

Tiger Grain – See Curly Grain.

Tight-Bark Pole – A pole cut during the winter when the cambium dried and shrank slowly so that the bark remained in place.

Tight Cooperage – See Cooperage.

Tight Knot – See Knot Quality.

Tightlining – 1. A method of lifting logs or rigging over obstructions in high-lead logging by tightening the haulback line. 2. Moving rigging from one point to another by tightening the main line.

Tight Side – 1. The upper side of peeled veneer as it comes off the lathe. This side of the

Terms Of The Trade

Tileboard

veneer was closest to the bark. When veneer is sliced, it is the side that is away from the knife. The tight side is usually the exposed side of a face or back ply. 2. In lumber, the side of a sawn piece that was closest to the bark, and the side on which grain rise is less likely to occur. See Bark Side.

Tileboard – A hardboard panel that has been embossed with a pattern and then coated with epoxy. The resulting product is designed to look like ceramic tile, for use in kitchens, bathrooms, etc.

Tillamook Burn – A series of forest fires in Western Oregon in 1933, 1935, and 1945, covering a total of more than 350,000 acres. The burned area was replanted by the State of Oregon, with the new trees reaching small-log sawtimber sizes in the 1980s.

Tiller End – The end of a pitsaw held by the top sawyer.

Timber – 1. Standing trees, stumpage. 2. A size classification of lumber that includes pieces that are at least five inches in their smallest dimension; also classified as beams, stringers, girders, etc. 3. In the British and Australian trades, this term is used to describe all sizes of lumber.

Timber Beast – A logger.

Timber Bind – This term describes problems that can occur when compression wood exists in a block being peeled into veneer. The lathe knife can bind in the compression wood, making it difficult or impossible to peel the block.

Timber Carnival – A competition in which persons vie in a series of events based on tasks performed by loggers in the woods. Included are such events as log birling, high climbing, ax throwing, log bucking, and chopping.

Timber Cruiser – See Cruiser.

Timber Deed – See Cutting Rights.

Timber Exchange – In the British timber trade, a place where lumber is bought and sold.

Timber Growth – A measure of timber output representing the amount of timber produced in the forest and still on the stump for present and future consumption.

Timber Harvest Plan (THP) – A document describing how a timber harvest will be executed. Required by law in some states.

Timbering – Sawn wood of various sizes, used to support the sides of excavations.

Timberland – Forest land that is producing or is capable of producing in excess of 20 cubic feet per acre per year of industrial wood in natural stands. Such lands have not been withdrawn from timber utilization by statue or administrative regulation. However, areas currently inaccessible and inoperable are included.

Timber License – A license to cut and remove Crown timber in British Columbia.

Timber Mark – A brand stamped into the end of a log.

Timber Mortality – The volume of trees that die annually from natural causes such as insects, disease, fire, windthrow, and other factors.

Timber Removals – The net volume of growing stock trees removed from the inventory by harvesting, cultural operations such as timber stand improvement, land clearing, or changes in land use.

Timber Sale Unit – An area within a timber sale which has a silvicultural prescription for a clearcut, shelterwood, or seed tree harvest method. Also, an area to be cleared for road or building construction.

Timber Shaver – 1. A spud, or tool, used to remove bark. 2. A person who barks logs or poles by hand.

Timber Stand Improvement – The process of pruning, thinning, and controlling weed/brush growth in a stand of timber, in order to increase the growth rate and value of the trees.

Timber Supply – As defined by the Forest Service, the volume of roundwood harvested or available for harvest in the future.

Timber Sword – An instrument with a slot at the point to hold the end of a tape measure. Used to pass the rule under a log when measuring its circumference.

Timberyard – A log storage area.

Time Charter – A ship hired for a definite period of time. See Voyage Charter.

Tool Marks

Time Draft – A document similar to a sight draft, except that a time draft stipulates that payment be made within a certain period after date of acceptance by the buyer.

Time Spread – A technique in futures trading that involves buying and selling contracts of the same commodity, with different delivery months.

Tin Hat – A safety hat worn by woodworkers, especially loggers. Although originally made of metal, the "hard hat" now is often made of plastic.

Tin Pants – Heavy, water-repellent pants, made of canvas of other heavy material and worn by loggers when working in wet conditions.

Tip – The thin end of a shingle.

Tipple – A short conveyor, one end of which can be raised or lowered, that directs sheets of veneer into various trays as they come from the lathe. Also, the outfeed belt system as it comes from a dryer.

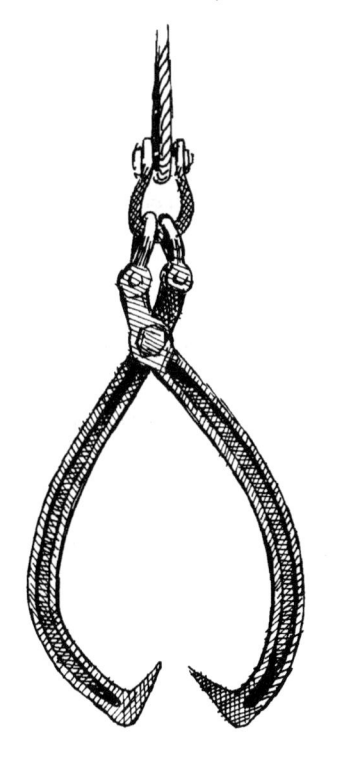

Tongs

Tit – In the early logging days, the hand throttle on a donkey or locomotive.

Toe Nail – To connect two pieces of wood by nailing obliquely through one into the other.

Toe Ring – The movable iron hook on a cant hook.

Tolerance – The amount of variance above or below a given size, width, thickness, or length allowed under the terms of various product standards or grading rules.

Tolerance in Sawing – The accuracy of a saw cut, which depends on type of saw (band or circular), sharpness, tension, speed, and other factors.

Toluene Extraction – A method of extracting substances from wood by removing them in a solvent solution.

Tombstone – See Barber Chair.

Ton – 1. A unit of weight equal to 2,240 pounds (long ton) or 2,000 pounds (short ton). 2. A measurement equal to 50 cubic feet of sawn or hewn wood, used in India and England; formerly "tun."

Tonawanda Pine – Pinus strobus. Eastern White Pine.

Tongs – An implement used to pick up logs. Tongs usually have spiked points for biting into logs to establish a sure grip.

Tongue – One edge of a piece of lumber that has been rabbetted from opposite faces, leaving a projection intended to fit into a groove cut into another board.

Tongue and Groove – Lumber machined to have a groove on one side and a protruding tongue on the other, so that pieces will fit snugly together, with the tongue of one fitting into the groove of the other.

Tonnage Wood – See Weight Wood.

Tonne – A metric ton, consisting of 1,000 kilograms, or approximately 2,200 lbs.

Ton Timber – In the early logging days, a timber that was 12 inches square and 40 feet long.

Tool Marks – Marks left on a finished wood product due to an imperfection in a sawing or surfacing tool.

Terms Of The Trade

Tooth

Tooth – 1. A reference to the rough finish on certain types of papers. 2. A sawtooth.

Top Barker – One who removed bark from the exposed top side of logs before they were yarded by oxen or horses. See Under Barker.

Top Chord – The inclined or horizontal member that establishes the upper edge of a truss. In conventional framing, a rafter.

Top-Hung Window – A casement window hinged at the top.

Top Load – Logs piled two or more tiers high on a truck or rail car. One tier of logs is known as a bunk load.

Top Loader – The head loader; the person in charge of loading operations at the landing.

Top Log – A log cut from the uppermost section of a tree.

Top Plate – A member on top of a stud wall on which joists rest to support an additional floor or form a ceiling.

Top Rail – The top horizontal member of a door.

Top Sawyer – In whipsawing, or pit sawing, the sawyer in the uppermost position.

Top Skin – Part of a stressed-skin panel, used in roof, floor, and wall construction. The top skin should be no less than 3/8" for roof applications and no less than 1/2" for floor applications.

Topwood – Fuelwood cut from the unmerchantable tops of trees.

Torn Grain – Part of the wood torn out in surfacing. Classified for grading purposes as slight, medium, heavy, or deep.

Torrey Pine – Pinus torreyana. This rare species is found in a small area of Southern California. Not a commercial species.

Torus – A large bead; a rope-like moulding.

Total Rise of a Roof – The vertical distance between the plate level and the ridge of a roof.

Total Run – The horizontal distance spanned by a rafter.

Total Tree Chipping – See Whole Tree Chipping.

Touch Sanding – A light surface sanding.

Touchwood – Decayed wood used as tinder in starting a fire.

Tough Ash – Fraxinus excelsior. European White Ash, widely used in bent-wood products.

Toughness – A reference to the ability of wood to absorb a relatively large amount of energy, to withstand repeated shocks, and to undergo considerable deformation before failing.

Tow – 1. The fibers from cedar and redwood bark. 2. A log boom made up to be handled by one tug.

Tower – See Spar Pole.

Tower Skidder – A skidder with an attached steel tower.

Township – In surveying, 36 square miles, or sections.

Toy Stock – Lumber selected and cut to specified sizes for use in the manufacture of toys.

Trabeation – A type of construction utilizing horizontal members supported by columns; a common method of construction in Japan. Also called Entablature.

Tracer – A document seeking information regarding the location of a shipment, sent by a local freight agent at the request of the consignee to various other agents along the route of the shipment.

Tracheid – The elongated xylem cells in wood, adapted for support or for the conduction of resin.

Tractor – 1. A self-propelled vehicle used in skidding logs to a landing. 2. In early logging days, a steam-powered (later gasoline-powered) vehicle with three or four wheels, used to pull sleighs or log carts.

Tractor Wheels – A set of big wheels pulled by a tractor; a forerunner of the arch.

Trade – 1. A futures transaction, as in "200 trades took place." 2. A collective reference to those involved in buying and selling lumber, the trade.

Travois

Trader

Trade Association – An organization of businesses in the same line of work, formed to promote their common interests.

Trade Discount – A deduction from the list price allowed a retail dealer by the manufacturer or wholesaler, or by one firm in selling to another in the same line of business.

Trader – One who buys or sells forest products, usually at the mill or wholesale level. Often used loosely to refer to anyone involved in buying or selling, at any level of the distribution system.

Trade Route Concept – A requirement that directly-subsidized ship operators serve specific ports on a regular basis.

Trading Company – A company engaged primarily in foreign trade.

Trading Floor – 1. The floor of an exchange where trading takes place. 2. The area in a sales office where wood products are traded, usually by phone.

Trailer on Flat Car (TOFC) – A truck trailer carried on a flat car; piggyback.

Trainmaster – The person responsible for train movements.

Tramp – A nonscheduled vessel. Also called a tramper.

Tramp Metal – Bits of metal, such as spikes driven into a tree and overgrown, that can damage saws.

Tram Road – See Plank Road.

Transaction Date – In international trade, the date on which a foreign exchange rate contract is agreed upon.

Transfer Price – The price at which intracompany trades are consummated; for example, from a firm's sawmill to a company-owned wholesale warehouse.

Transit – A loading of forest products, usually a rail car, that is shipped unsold and is then offered for sale while enroute and before reaching a point where it must be diverted to a final destination.

Transiter – Anyone who buys wood products without having sold them first and ships them, usually by rail, toward the marketplace without a specific buyer or destination.

Transit Time – The train operating time between cities.

Transit Trade – A countertrade arranged by a broker in a third country. See Countertrade.

Transload – The transfer of goods from one type of hauling equipment to another.

Transmission Crossarm – See Crossarm.

Transmission Timber – A pole used to carry electrical or telephone lines; a utility pole.

Transom – An opening above a door, usually containing a hinged sash.

Transom Stock – 1. An intermediate horizontal member used to strengthen a door or window opening. 2. Horizontal members of the stern of a boat.

Transpiration – The process by which plants release water into the atmosphere.

Transverse Section – A cross-section from a piece of wood, at right angles to the pith.

Trap Tree – A tree deliberately girdled or felled to attract bark beetles. Also called a Bait Log.

Traumatic Canal – Resin canals parallel to growth rings, caused by injury to the tree.

Traveling Block – A moveable pulley that travels along a cable while supporting a load.

Travois – See Go-Devil.

Terms Of The Trade

Tray

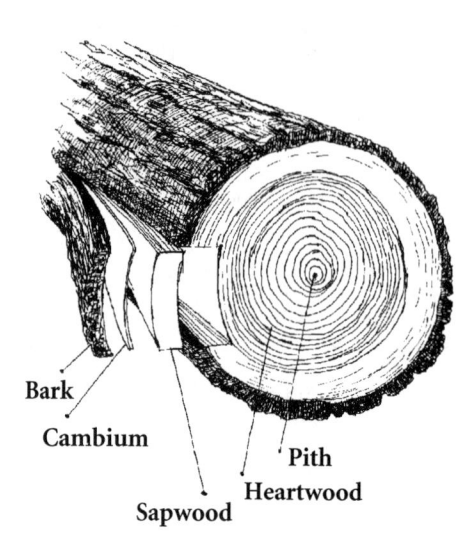

Bark
Cambium
Pith
Heartwood
Sapwood

Tree Cross Section

Tray – A conveyance used in transferring veneer from the lathe to the clipper. Trays are rubber belt conveyors that serve as temporary storage areas for veneers coming from high-speed lathes. Trays are loaded by a short conveyor, called a tipple, that can be raised or lowered at one end.

Tread – The horizontal part of a stair. Historically, treads have been made from 5/4x12" vertical grain lumber called stepping. In recent years, however, most stepping has been made from particleboard that is given a bullnosed edge.

Treated – Wood products infused or coated with any of a variety of stains or chemicals designed to retard fire, decay, insect damage, or deterioration due to weather.

Treating-in-Transit – A privilege extended by some rail carriers that allows wood products to be diverted into a plant to receive treatment before being moved on to a destination. Carriers allow such shipments to take the through rate, which is lower than the local rates from the sawmill to the treating plant, and from the treating plant to the customer.

Treating Plant – An operation where wood products are treated with preservative or fire retardant.

Treating Service Only (TSO) – A company that treats wood products for others for a fee.

Treating Vat – A tank used for non-pressure preservative treatments, such as cold soaking, dipping, or steeping.

Treble Damages – A punitive award that may be made in the case of trespass from one forest ownership to another, or in the case of theft committed while trespassing. Between private parties, timber trespass may result in a civil suit to establish trespass and the volume and value of timber taken; the plaintiff may seek an award equal to three times the value of the timber. In trespass involving public lands, criminal charges may also be filed.

Tree – 1. A perennial plant with supporting stem and branches, usually growing to considerable height. 2. A wooden member on a machine or structure.

Tree Class – A group of trees, classified by size, age, etc.

Tree Farm – A parcel of land on which trees are planted, cultured, managed and harvested as a crop. Some tree farms grow Christmas trees; others grow trees to be harvested for various wood products. A Certified Tree Farm is one operated under guidelines established by the American Forest Institute.

Tree Farm License (TFL) – In British Columbia, a license issued by the provincial government granting a company the right to harvest a certain annual volume of timber from a certain area of government land.

Tree Iron – A metal plate attached to a spar tree to support blocks or straps.

Treejacking – A method of controlling the direction of fall of a tree, using hydraulic jacks. The jacks are placed in a notch cut in the tree, then expanded to tip the tree in the desired direction. Using a jack, a faller can overcome a tree's natural lean and place it in a particular direction to avoid damage to the tree or to facilitate bucking and yarding. With the use of jacks, it has become common to fell trees uphill to minimize breakage.

Tree-Length Logging – Logging in which the logs are not cut to specific lengths before being transported.

Tree Measurement Sale – A timber sale in which volume is cruised and sold in cubic feet, in effect accounting for the volume

True Firs

within the entire tree. Federal agencies are slowly implementing this method to replace sales sold on a board foot basis, which does not account for volume within the taper of the tree.

Tree Plate – A metal plate fastened to a spar tree to protect it from damage caused by cables.

Tree Seed Zone – In Bureau of Land Management lands, an area delineated by the Western Forest Tree Seed Council. Such areas contain similar climatic and geographical conditions.

Tree Spiking – A tactic sometimes used by extremist environmentalist groups in an attempt to block logging. Spikes are driven into the tree in such as manner that they are not visible. Hitting the spike while sawing in the woods or at a sawmill can damage the saw and harm the saw operator. Metal detectors are sometimes used in sawmills to locate the spikes, and ceramic spikes have been used to thwart this detection.

Tree Squeak – A mythical bird, said to be the source of the noise made by trees rubbing together in the wind.

Trespass – An unlawful intrusion on another's property. See Treble Damages.

Tri-Bearing Truss – A multi-panel truss with three bearing points, one on each end and one in the middle.

Trim – 1. Millwork, primarily mouldings and/or trim to finish off (trim around) window and door openings, etc. 2. See Trimback Allowance.

Trimback Allowance – The extra length allowed when bucking logs to permit squaring during the manufacturing process. Also called Trim.

Trimbacks – Odd lengths developed in the manufacture of cut-to-length fingerjointed mouldings.

Trim Ends – Short lengths of lumber trimmed off in the manufacturing process. Trims are made to achieve uniform lengths or to remove defects. Also, planer ends.

Trimmer – A beam that receives the end of a header in floor framing. 2. A logger who lopped limbs from felled trees. 3. The operator of a trim saw.

Trimmer Optimizer – See Optimizer.

Trimmings – 1. Sawmill debris such as edgings. 2. Slash.

Trims – Moulding, and other finish materials.

Trim Saw – A set of saws, usually circular, used to cut lumber to various lengths by lowering individual blades to make contact with the lumber as it passes beneath the saws on a moving chain.

Trip – To use a jack or wedges to cause a tree to fall in a specific direction.

Trip Hook – A quick-release hook used with a chain to move logs.

Trituration Wood – Wood ground into fine particles or fibers, as furnish for particleboard, fiberboard, etc.

Trolley – The carriage that travels on a skyline.

Truck Market – The arena in which lumber and panels are traded for truck shipment, as opposed to rail shipment. The truck market is particularly suited to relatively short hauls and smaller volumes.

Truck Shipment – The shipment of goods by truck.

True Cedar – Cedrus libanotica, Lebanon Cedar.

True Firs – A collective term for a group of firs of the species Abies, including White

Treejacking

Terms Of The Trade

True Wood

Fir, Grand Fir, etc.

True Wood – Heartwood.

Truss – An assembly of members that forms a rigid framework to support the roof or other part of a building.

Trussed Floor – A floor resting on trusses.

Truss Plate Institute – An organization providing technical assistance, design and construction standards, and research to truss manufacturers and users.

Tube Rot – A type of decay in cedar, similar to pencil rot.

Tult – In the British timber trade, a measurement of timber consisting of 12 logs, each 18 feet in length.

Tun – See Ton (2).

Tupelo – Nyssa aquatica, Water Tupelo; N. sylvatica, Black Tupelo. A light, tough hardwood of the southern and eastern United States, used for paneling and turnings.

Turn – One or more logs yarded at one time to the landing.

Turnaround – 1. The roundtrip time of a ship, including loading and unloading. 2. An wide area at the end of a logging road in which a log truck can turn around.

Turner – See Log Turner.

Turning – 1. A product turned on a lathe. 2. The act of producing an object on a lathe.

Turning Plant – A remanufacturing plant that makes various products such as newel posts, balusters, etc.

Turning Square – A bolt of wood intended for shaping on a lathe.

Turnover Notice – A document presented to a freight agent that indicates the original consignee of a shipment is turning the shipment over to another consignee, with the second one responsible for freight charges on the shipment.

Turnover Proceeding – An action under bankruptcy law that transfers the property of a bankrupt to a receiver for administration.

Trim Saw

Type II Glue Bond

Turpentine – An oleoresin derived from conifers, especially Longleaf Pine.

Turpentine Pine – Another name for Longleaf Pine, Pinus palustris.

Turtle Club – An organization for persons who, because they were wearing a protective "hard hat," escaped serious injury or death when struck on the head by a falling limb or other dangerous object.

Tussock Moth – A moth of the family Lymantriidae, whose larvae feed on certain species of conifers. Tussock moth infestations seem to occur on a cyclical basis and, when widespread, cause a high percentage of tree mortality in an infested area.

Twenty-Foot Equivalent Unit (TEU) – A measurement unit used in calculating the volume of ship containers of various dimensions. A TEU is 20'x 8' x 8'. Thus, a 40-foot container would equal two TEUs.

Twig Burr – Decorative wood grain that grows around or over twigs that have been broken or cut off.

Twist – A distortion in wood caused by the turning or winding of the edges of a board so that the four corners of any face are no longer in the same plane.

Twister – A device used to move heavy objects such as logs by twisting a chain or rope with a lever stuck through it. A turnbuckle.

Two-Four-One (2-4-1) – Structural wood panels, at least 1-1/8" thick, designed for single-floor applications over joists spaced 48 inches apart; used also as roof sheathing in heavy timber construction. A registered trade name of the American Plywood Association.

Two-Span Continuous – A method of installing plank decking in which pieces rest on three supports and are of the same length.

Two-Tiered Market – A phrase describing a market situation in which there are substantial differences between mill-to-wholesaler and wholesaler-to-retailer trading. This usually involves an exceptionally wide price difference but also can describe a variation in the sales pace, as when wholesalers move to increase their transit offerings before there has been a corresponding acceleration in sales to retailers.

Two-Way Entry – A basic pallet design that permits the insertion of forklift blades from opposite sides, but not from all sides. Usually consists of top and bottom deck boards and three evenly spaced stringers.

Two-Wheeler – A set of big wheels.

TWX (Twix) – A teletypewriter operating at different speeds and requiring different switching devices than do Telex machines.

Tyee – 1. Northwest Indian word for chief. 2. A trade name for a kind of logging equipment.

Tyloses – A bubble-like ingrowth that forms in some trees when changing sapwood to heartwood; the extension of a ray into adjacent inactive matter.

Type I Glue Bond – Hardwood plywood manufactured with a glue bond having maximum moisture resistance as required in exterior applications.

Type II Glue Bond – Hardwood plywood manufactured with a moisture-resistant glue bond and intended for interior use.

U

Ukay – A marketing term in the British timber trade signifying a product is, or is equal to, a grade used in the United Kingdom: Ukay No. 1 Merchantable. Also, the United Kingdom itself.

Ultimate Load – The load at which a component or structure will fail.

Ultimate Strength – The maximum resistance to load of a member before it breaks or ruptures.

Ultimo – A credit term meaning last month. See Proximo.

Ultrasonics – The technology of using high frequency sound to locate defects in timber or lumber for use in digital form in decision-making computers.

Ultraviolet Radiation Curing – The curing of glue by subjecting it to ultraviolet rays.

Umbrella – A fully rigged spar tree with all the lines attached.

Umbrella Rate – A freight rate that is intentionally held high to protect a high-cost carrier. Also, charges for goods or services set high to protect inefficient members of a cartelized industry.

Unallocated Forest – A forest has not yet been allocated for timber management and does not have road access.

Unbalanced Construction – A condition that occurs when individual components or layers of a laminate do not respond equally to changes in moisture, thus causing warp.

Unbalanced Panel – A plywood panel in which the face and back veneers are of substantially different thicknesses.

Unbleached Kraft – Kraft pulp in its natural brown stage before being subjected to chlorine and other chemicals to bleach out the lignin.

Uncalendered Paper – Paper not smoothed by calendering.

Under Bark – A method of measuring timber volume that excludes the tree's bark.

Under Barker – In animal logging days in the Northwest, logs were barked in the woods to reduce weight, making them easier to yard. Using a spud, the top barker removed all the bark he could reach. The log was then rolled, and the bark that had been on the under side of the log was removed by the under barker.

Undercourse

Undercourse – Low grade (usually #3) shingles used as the initial layer of material on a double-coursed sidewall of a building.

Undercut – The cut or notch made in a tree to govern the direction in which it will fall.

Undercutter – A log bucker's tool which was used to support his crosscut saw upside down as he cut the underside of a log.

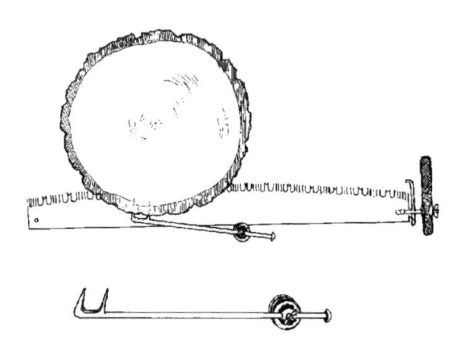

Undercutter

Undergrowth – The smaller trees and brush growing under the larger trees that make up the forest canopy.

Underlayment – Structural wood panels designed to be used under the finished flooring in a structure.

Under-Run – A loss in inventory volume, so that the amount manufactured or sold was less than was indicated by the volume of raw material.

Undershot Wheel – The power source to a water sawmill, generated by a wheel turned by water flowing under it. See Overshot Wheel.

Underside – The back, the opposite of the face.

Understory Trees – Trees whose tops do not penetrate the canopy formed above them by taller trees.

Underweight – A situation in which the actual weight of a wood products shipment is less than estimated at the time of sale. Historically, wood products prices were quoted f.o.b mill, plus rail freight charges to the destination, resulting in a delivered cost to the buyer. In calculating the freight charges, the approximate weight of the shipment was estimated. The actual charges, however, were based on the exact weight of the shipment and if this was less than estimated a refund would be due; this traditionally went to the shipper. In recent years, there has been a trend toward the use of actual weights or delivered prices.

Undressed – Lumber products that have not been surfaced.

Unedged – Lumber whose edges have not been squared; waney.

Uneven-Aged Management – A timber management program in which only the mature trees are removed, leaving younger or small stock for further growth.

Uneven Grain – A grain pattern produced from trees exhibiting distinct differences between earlywood and latewood.

Uneven Texture – Wood in which there is sharp contrast between springwood and summerwood.

Unhook Man – A chaser; the worker in a logging operation who unhooks the choker from the log at the landing.

Unidirectional Layup – See Radial Layup.

Unidirectional Plywood – Plywood in which the adjacent pieces of veneer are parallel.

Uniform Commercial Code (UCC) – A set of regulations governing business transactions, designed to unify methods of conducting business between the various states. Most states have adopted the code.

Uniform Freight Classification (UFC) – A list of regulations governing the movement of freight on railroads.

Uniform Load – An evenly distributed load along a beam or truss.

Unimpregnated Paper – Untreated paper used in the production of decorative laminates. See Preimpregnated, Postimpregnated.

Union Drive – In the days of river drives, a cooperative effort between several log owners, who shared expenses.

Uniseriate – A ray in wood consisting of only one row of cells.

Utility

Unit – A stack of lumber or panels, usually of a standard size. See Standard Unit.

Unitized – A wood product securely gathered into a standard unit, usually fastened with steel straps and often covered by tough paper or plastic.

Unitized Cargo – Any type of cargo packed in containers or on pallets for easy loading and handling on a ship.

Unitized Double Door Box (UDDB) – A description of forest products packaged in standard units and loaded in a railroad box car containing double doors (an opening eight feet or wider).

Unit Tally – See Block Tally.

Unit Train – A train made up of 50 or more carloads of one commodity.

Universal Standard Log Scale – Another name for the Doyle-Scribner log rule, at one time the official rule of the National Hardwood Lumber Association. A combination rule, this scale produces a large over-run on all sizes of logs.

Unmerchantable – Logs or products that are faulty and not salable.

Unsanded – Plywood whose faces have not been smoothed.

Unscrambler – A piece of sawmill equipment that straightens out jumbled accumulations of lumber that collect on a transfer chain before the lumber is further processed. The lumber pieces are separated and delivered, one layer deep, to the machine in an orderly manner.

Unseasoned – Lumber that has not been dried to a specified moisture content before surfacing. The American Softwood Lumber Standard defines unseasoned lumber as that having a moisture content above 19%.

Unsorted – A description used in Scandinavia and Russia for lumber shipped from a mill unsorted as to grade.

Unsound – Containing decay.

Unstable – Describes wood species that change greatly in shape or volume while seasoning; subject to cup, bow, or twist.

Up and Down Saw – A vertical saw used in the days of water-powered sawmills.

Upcharge – An additional charge for performing some extra service or providing special processing.

Upgrading – Making more valuable products by remanufacturing low-grade material.

Upper – A high quality piece of lumber graded for appearance; a select piece.

Upright Machine – A machine used in sawing shingles that allows an operator to also joint or edge as a single process. The shingle block is mounted on a carriage and passed by a thin-gauge saw. On alternate strokes, the block is automatically tilted to produce shingles with the butts either up or down.

Upset Price – The lowest price that a seller will accept. See Appraised Price.

Up to Grade – Products that meet or exceed the requirements of a specific grade.

Urea Resin Glue – Urea-formaldehyde resin, an adhesive used in the manufacture of hardwood plywood and interior particleboard panel products. Urea is a soluble, crystalline material found in the urine of mammals. It is also produced synthetically for the manufacture of plastics and adhesives.

Usury Laws – Laws that limit the amount of interest that can be charged on a loan. These limits vary from state to state; in some states, the limits are applied only to certain types of loans, and there are some states that have no usury laws.

Utah Juniper – Juniperus osteosperma. This species, native to the Great Basin states, is used locally for fuel, posts, and, occasionally, interior trim.

Utility – 1. A grade of softwood lumber

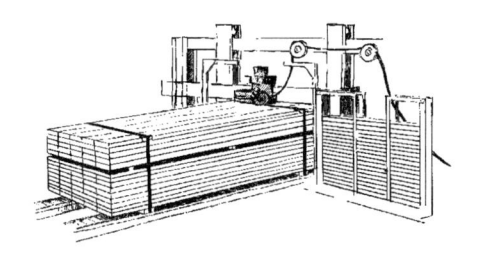

Packaging Units

Terms Of The Trade

Utility and Better (Util&Btr)

used when a combination of strength and economy is desired. It is suitable for many uses in construction, but lacks the strength of Standard, the next highest grade in light framing, and is not allowed in some applications. 2. A grade of Idaho White Pine boards, equivalent to #4 common in other species. 3. A grade of fir veneer that allows white speck and more defects than are allowed in D grade.

Utility and Better (Util&Btr) – A mixture of light framing lumber grades with the lowest being Utility. The "and Better" signifies that some percentage of the mixture is of a higher grade than Utility (but not necessarily of the highest grade). In joist and plank grades, the corresponding term is #3&Btr.

Utility Log – A log that does not meet the grade requirements of a sawlog or peeler, but which will yield at least 50 percent of its gross volume in wood chips.

Utskott – A term used in Scandinavia to describe low grade lumber (fourths or fifths). The word literally means "throw outs."

U-Value – A measure of thermal transmittance. Specifically, a measure of how many BTUs of heat per hour will pass through one square foot of a wall or floor when the air temperature on one side is one degree Fahrenheit higher than the air temperature on the other side.

V

V – Any of several longitudinal cuts made on the face of pieces of lumber or panels. The face veneer of plywood paneling is V-grooved to relieve the flat appearance of the surface; the grooving usually creates a pattern resembling random-width boards placed side by side. Usually, V grooves in paneling are stained darker than the surface. In lumber, edges are sometimes chamfered to create a V where pieces are placed edge to edge. A V may also be machined the length of the piece to provide decoration. A V pattern also may be used to form tongue and groove connections on either lumber or

Veneer Lathe

Vacuum Chamber

panels.

Vacuum Chamber – A device used to test the performance of panels under uniform loads.

Vacuum Drying – A method of drying wood by subjecting it to alternating periods of heated atmosphere, or to fluid and pressures below the normal atmospheric level.

Vacuum Kiln – See Vacuum Drying.

Vacuum Lifter – A suction attachment mounted on a crane that takes the place of a hook or sling.

Vacuum Pressure Test – A glue-bond test applied to exterior type plywood, and interior panels with exterior glue (Exposure 1).

Vacuum Soak Test – A glue-bond test applied to interior type plywood with intermediate glue.

Vagility – The capacity of any organism to become widely dispersed.

Valley – The place where two planes of a roof meet at a downward, or V, angle.

Value-Added Product – A product whose value has been changed by further processing, such as remanufacturing, or by marketing, such as the wholesale function.

Value-Added Tax (VAT) – A sales tax based on the addition to the value of consumer goods or services at each stage of production or distribution.

Valuer – Another name for a timber cruiser.

Van – An enclosed motor vehicle used to carry freight. Also, an enclosed trailer.

Vapor Barrier – 1. Material placed on the warm side of a wall to prevent the movement of vapor through the wall. A plastic or paper sheet, or paint. 2. In kiln drying, a material having a high resistance to vapor movement that is applied to the kiln surfaces to prevent moisture migration.

Vapor Drying – A method of drying wood by subjecting it to the hot vapors produced by boiling any of various organic chemicals, such as xylene.

Vapor Transmission – The migration of water vapor through the walls or ceiling of a closed structure. In a house without vapor barriers, the vapor tends to condense within

Veneer Composer — Veneers Edge Glued into a continuous strip, then clipped to 54-inch widths

Veneer Clipper

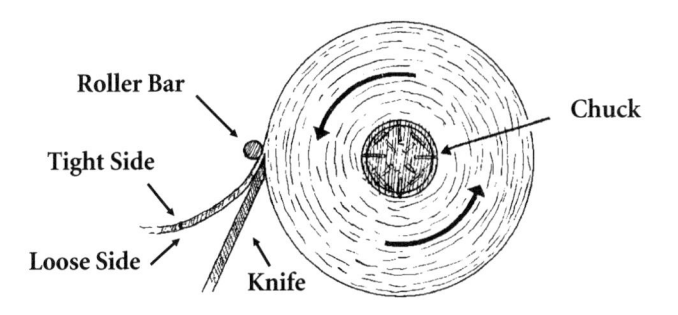

Veneer Peeling (diagram labels: Roller Bar, Tight Side, Loose Side, Knife, Chuck)

a wall after it has moved from the warmer inner wall surface to a cooler outer surface.

Variable Rate Mortgage (VRM) – See Adjustable Rate Mortgage.

Variation in Sawing – A deviation from the line of cut.

Varigated Grain – An uneven, non-uniform grain pattern in veneer.

Vascular Tissue – The living plant tissue that conducts water and nutrients through the tree while also providing physical support.

Vats – Large containers used for steaming logs or submerging them in hot water prior to peeling or slicing them into veneer, or cutting them into wafers. The steaming or heating of logs makes them easier to process and can increase recovery. Vats were first widely used in hardwood veneer manufacturing but are also frequently used in the manufacture of softwood plywood panels, waferboard, and oriented strand board.

Vault – An arched roof.

Vegetative Reproduction – Asexual formation of offspring by sprouting, layering, etc. The offspring of such reproduction are genetically identical to the parent.

Vein of Pine – A term used in the Lake States to describe a clump of pine trees growing within a deciduous forest.

Veneer – Wood peeled, sawn, or sliced into sheets of a given constant thickness and combined with glue to produce plywood. Veneers laid up with the grain direction of adjoining sheets at right angles produce plywood of great stiffness and strength, while those laid up with grains running parallel produced flexible plywood most often used in furniture and cabinetry. See Laminated Veneer Lumber.

Veneer Adhesives – Several basic substances are used in the gluing of veneers to produce plywood. These include blood, soybean, and phenolic resins. Other adhesives made from urea, resorcinol, polyvinyl, and melamine are sometimes used in edge gluing, patching, and scarfing. Among the principal adhesives are: 1. Soybean glue, a protein-type adhesive made from soybean meal and usually blended with blood and used in certain panels for interior use. 2. Blood glue, made from animal glue from slaughterhouses, dried and supplied in powder form; it also is intended for interior uses. 3. Phenolic resin, produced from synthetic phenol and formaldehyde. It cures only under heat and undergoes chemical changes which makes it impervious to attack by micro-organisms. It is used in undiluted form for the production of exterior plywood; however, it may be extended by the addition of other substances in the production of interior plywood.

Veneer Book – See Book.

Veneer Chucks – Steel prongs, or fingers, used in the geometric center of veneer blocks to hold them while they are turned against a knife. Many present-day chucks consist of a ring of outer prongs and a set of smaller inner prongs. Both may be engaged during the early stage of peeling but, as the diameter of the block is reduced, the outer ring of chucks is retracted while the smaller inner chuck completes the operation.

Veneer Clipper – A long knife, or guillotine, attached to air cylinders which produce a rapid down and return movement. The clipper cuts veneer to standard widths, or cuts out defects. Fully automatic clippers utilize an electronic device and computer to produce optimum widths while limiting the defects. Open defects exceeding the predeter-

Veneer Composer

mined sizes are detected as the veneer passes over a sensing plate where light, passing through the defect, triggers the clipper to remove it. Scanners also are available that can detect defects by color variations. Green veneer is clipped oversize to allow for shrinkage during drying and to permit a final trim to size.

Veneer Composer – A machine that takes random-width veneer and manufactures each piece into a specified-width sheet by stitching, stringing, or edge gluing.

Veneer Core – The round wood remaining after the block is peeled to its smallest possible diameter. Historically, veneer cores have been sawn into studs, or chipped to provide raw material for paper making. However, recent techniques involving "powered backup rollers" and "centerless lathes" allow blocks to be peeled to 2-inch diameters; these are sent to the chipper. A powered backup roller continues the rotation of the block against the knife after the chucks have been completely withdrawn. The centerless lathe, a newer development, does not use chucks. Instead, one stationary and two powered steel rolls center a block and rotate it against the knife. The centerless lathe was designed to accommodate small-diameter logs, with the first models limited to blocks up to eight inches in diameter.

Veneer Dryer – See Dryer.

Veneer Drying – Before drying, sheets of veneer must be segregated between heartwood and sapwood, since the latter contains more moisture and takes longer to dry. A series of rolls carry the veneer through the dryer, which is an enclosed shell containing fans, ducts, and baffles for circulating and directing heat to the various lines, or levels, of veneer being dried. Heat is provided by steam produced by the combustion of natural gas, propane, or mill residues. As water is released by the heated veneer, it is converted to steam which, mixed with the hot air, keeps the wood pores open to assure even drying. When sufficient moisture is not present, a condition similar to "casehardening" in kiln dried lumber occurs. This presents problems in the gluing operation and is known as surface inactivation.

Veneered Edge Gluer – A machine in which random width veneer sheets are glued edge to edge to form full sheets.

Veneered Particleboard – A panel with a particleboard core and a veneer face and/or

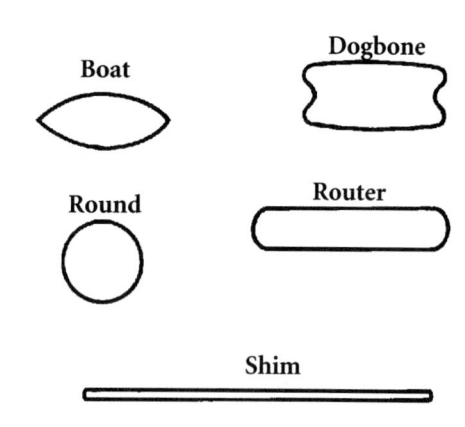

Veneer Repair

back. The veneer is usually decorative and the panel is used in the construction of furniture. However, structural members, known as composite panels, are also made in this fashion.

Veneer Gluing – Wood veneers are not normally produced in quantity in the 48x96-inch dimension of most panels; narrower pieces have to be joined to achieve this size. Many techniques have been developed to accomplish this; veneers are stitched together, connected by "strings" or tape, or, most often, jointed and edge glued. In jointing and edge gluing, a stack of veneer several inches thick is clamped together and passed by cutters until the edge of the mass has the appearance of solid wood. Behind the cutter heads is a glue applicator which coats the freshly cut edges. The stack of veneer is then reversed and the process is repeated on the opposite edge. The pieces are then fed individually into a machine which utilizes a series of crowders to crowd the edges together to complete the bond. The result is a long, continuous sheet which can then be clipped to the width required.

Veneer Hammer – A device used in fine veneering, such as in making furniture, which can be worked across the face of a piece to squeeze out excess glue.

Veneer Hog – A machine used to grind unusable sheets of veneer into chips for use as fuel or for other purposes.

Veneer Holddown – The part of a veneer clipper that holds down the veneer to assure proper alignment with the clipper blade.

Vertical Grain (VG)

Veneer Knife – A large, sharp, steel blade used to shear veneers from wood blocks, much like a carpenter's plane removes a shaving. The veneers that are produced are used in furniture, cabinetry, and paneling. See Veneer Saw.

Veneer Leaves – Pieces of sliced veneer used in various matching techniques.

Veneer Log – A log used in the manufacture of veneer. A "peeler."

Veneer Matching – Laying up face veneers to achieve a particular pattern.

Veneer Plant – A place where veneer is manufactured. In the softwood industry, this is usually accomplished by peeling the veneer from a wood block on a lathe; the product usually is used structurally. In the hardwood industry, veneers are most often sliced or sawn from a block to obtain grain patterns that are distinctly different from rotary peeled veneer.

Veneer Recovery Factor (VRF) – The volume of veneer recovered, in square feet per cubic foot of log processed.

Veneer Repair – The grade of veneer may be improved by patching to eliminate defects such as knotholes, pitch pockets, and voids. Patching machines cut out the defect in specific configurations, while also cutting a like-shaped patch from another piece of veneer and automatically gluing these into the void. Later, defects in the finished panel that were not noticed in the veneer stage may be patched with a synthetic material or a piece of sound wood.

Veneer Saw – A special type of circular saw used to produce high-quality veneers; used primarily on burls, crotches, and very hard woods that do not lend themselves to slicing. See Veneer Knife.

Veneer Splicing – The edge-joining of sliced veneer in hardwood veneer operations.

Veneer Stitching – See Stitched Veneer.

Veneer Stringing – A process just short of stitching in which inner plies are held in position by strings during manufacture. This minimizes core gap and overlap.

Veneer Table – A grading station on a green or dry veneer chain.

Veneer Tape – Tape used to connect pieces of random width veneer to form a specified width. The use of tape has declined with the introduction of the veneer composer, which stitches or glues veneer pieces together.

Veneer Tray System – A transfer system in which veneer is carried in trays from the lathe to the clipper.

Veneer Welder – See Composer.

Vertical Edger – An edging machine consisting of band, rather than circular, saws; used to edge large cants.

Vertical Grain (VG) – Lumber that is sawn at approximately right angles to the an-

Veneer Table

Vertical Integration

nual growth rings so that the rings form an angle of 45 degrees or more with the surface of the piece.

Vertical Integration – 1. The structuring of a company so that the production and distribution of its products is controlled by company branches. 2. The expansion of a company by acquisition of other firms along the line of distribution, such as the purchase by a manufacturer of warehousing and retailing companies.

Vertical Resaw – A band resaw mounted vertically to break down cants from the headrig.

Vessel Revenue – The portion of total ship revenue attributed to the ship and the services it provides. It is derived by subtracting port charges from total revenue.

Vessels – A type of wood cell, found only in hardwoods, through which water travels through the tree. Also called Pores.

Vessel Ton – Cargo capacity equaling 100 cubic feet of space.

Veteran – In the British timber trade, a tree more than two feet in diameter at breast height.

V-Groove – A pattern in which a V-shaped groove is machined along the edge of a piece of lumber or panel to receive a corresponding V-shaped tongue on another piece, so that the two pieces fit snugly together. See V.

Vibratory Conveyor – A device that moves material, such as particleboard furnish, while at the same time separating the pieces by size.

Vine Props – Timbers used in vineyards to support the vines.

Vinyl Overlay – An overlay applied to panel products, mouldings, etc. Usually printed with a color and grain, and needing no further finishing.

Virgin Forest – A forest essentially undisturbed by man, from which timber has never been harvested.

Virginian Pencil Cedar – Another name for Eastern Red Cedar, Juniperus virginiana. Not a true cedar, but rather a juniper.

Virginia Pine – Pinus virginiana. This is another minor member of the Southern Yellow Pine group. It is grouped for grading purposes with Pond Pine, under the stamp "Mixed Pine Species."

Visual Grading – The grading of lumber, plywood, veneer, or other products by a person who follows specific rules. Appearance, the presence of knots, wane, splits, and all other characteristics are taken into consideration by a grader when visually inspecting a wood product.

Visually Stress-Rated Lumber – Lumber that has been graded for strength based on its appearance, rather than by mechanical means.

Visual Override – The act of giving machine stress-rated lumber a lower grade than that indicated by the machine test because the piece has visible defect not apparent to the machine.

Vivo – The shaft of a column.

V-Joint – A type of tongue-and-groove joint in which the receiving piece has a v-shaped groove and the other has a corresponding projection.

V-Joint

Void – A hole in one or more of the plies of a plywood panel that occurs when the veneers are not butted firmly together, or due to a knothole or split.

Voluntary Coordinating Agreement (VCA) – A freight rate and switching agreement between two or more railroads to allow the movement of traffic through a common marketing corridor. Often designed to attract business from truck carriers competing in the same corridor.

Voyage Charter – A ship hired for a particular voyage or series of voyages. See Time Charter.

W

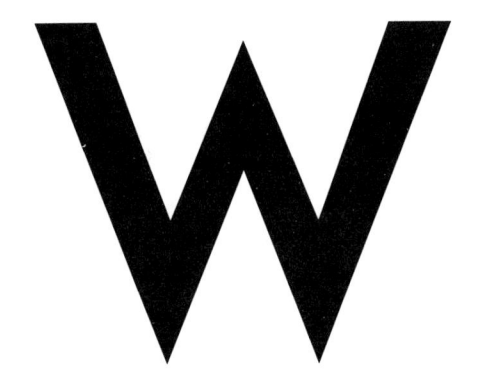

Wade Saw – A type of drag saw, used in the early logging days.

Wafer – A relatively large, flat flake cut from wood in the manufacture of waferboard or oriented strand board.

Waferboard – A panel product made of discrete wafers of wood bound together by resin, heat, and pressure. Waferboard can be made of timber species, such as Aspen, that are not suitable for lumber or plywood manufacture.

Waferizer – A machine that converts wood bolts to wafers for use in waferboard or oriented strand board.

Wagon Vault – Another name for a barrel vault.

Wainscot – A lower interior wall surface (usually extending three to four feet up from the floor) that contrasts with the wall surface above it; an interior wall composed of two different interior wall surfaces, one above the other.

Wainscoting Cap – A moulding designed to finish the top of a wainscot.

Waiver – An action by which a legal right is surrendered.

Wale – 1. Planking placed horizontally across a structure to strengthen it. 2. Horizontal bracing used to stiffen concrete form construction. 3. The planks on the side of a wooden ship.

Walking Boss – A logging superintendent in charge of several operations. Originally, one who visited several camps under his supervision, usually by traveling on foot.

Wanigan

Wallboard

Wallboard – A manufactured sheet material used to cover large areas. Wallboards are made from many items, including wood fibers, asbestos, and gypsum. In North America, the most common is "sheet rock," a gypsum-based panel bound by sheets of heavy paper. It is used to seal interior walls and ceilings in place of wet plaster.

Wall Plate – The top plate in construction, placed on top of studs and bearing the joists of the next floor above.

Walnut – Juglans regia, English Walnut; J. nigra, Black Walnut; J. cinerea, Butternut. The last two, native to North America, are used for veneer and furniture stock, in addition to their edible nuts.

Walter Pine – Spruce Pine.

Wampus Cat – A mythical woods beast.

Wandering Heart – Lumber in which sections of pith appear on the surface after sawing because the log was crooked.

Wane – Bark, or the lack of wood from any cause, on the edge or corner of a piece of lumber. In plywood, thin-to-open areas in veneer sheets that result from outer log surface irregularities.

Waney Cant – A slab cut from a log, having a sawn face and back, and rounded edges.

Wanigan – A floating cookhouse in the days of river drives. Of Algonquin origin, a "Wangan" was a container of odds and ends.

Warehouse Pallet – A double-face pallet intended for general warehouse use.

Warehouse Receipt – A receipt given for goods placed in storage, usually negotiable.

Warp – Any variation from a true or plane surface, including bow, crook, cup, or any combination of these.

Warp Restraint – The process of applying external loads to a pile, package, or load of wood products to prevent or reduce warp while drying.

Warranty – An expressed or implied guarantee that a product will perform as represented.

Warren Truss – A truss consisting of horizontal top and bottom chords, separated by sloping members, and without vertical pieces.

Washboarding – See Ribbing.

Washed Stock – Recycled paper after ink and other contaminants have been removed by a series of washings and bleachings.

Washington Fir – Another name for Douglas Fir.

Waste Hog – A machine that reduces mill residues to hogged fuel.

Wastewood – The edgings and scraps left after processing a log, to be converted into pulp chips.

Water Bar – Dirt placed on a logging road to divert water away from the roadbed, to prevent erosion.

Waterborne Preservative – Preservative salts in a water solution that are transferred to the wood during the treating process.

Waterborne Shipment – Any shipment of forest products that is moved on water by a ship or barge.

Water Core – See Wetwood.

Watermark – 1. In papermaking, a design or logo impressed into the paper. 2. A brand or symbol stamped into logs on a river drive, to identify the owner.

Waterproof Adhesive – An adhesive which, when properly cured, is not affected by water.

Water Repellent Anti-Travel Stain Treated (WRATS) – A treatment applied to the surface of lumber to protect its appearance during shipment.

Water Repellent Lumber – Lumber that has been treated with a water-repellant additive, either topically or under pressure, to reduce checking, splitting, and weathering.

Water Scale – The measurement of logs while they are still in the water.

Watershed – The area of land that drains naturally into a stream or complex of streams. The management of watersheds in the national forests is a principal function of the Forest Service. Some watersheds have been set aside specifically to assure a supply of pure water to a city, e.g., the Bull Run watershed which supplies Portland, Oregon.

Waterslide – A flume.

Water Soak – See Wetwood.

Water Spots – Visual defects in hardboard.

Watertight Knot – See Knot Quality.

Waviness – A defect in hardboard.

Wavy Dressing – A manufacturing defect involving an unevenness greater than that found through knife marks. Characterized as: Very Light, not over 1/64" deep; Light, not over 1/32" deep; Medium, not over 1/16" deep; Heavy, not over 1/8" deep; and Very Heavy, over 1/8" deep.

Wavy Grain – A grain pattern in wood in which the fibers collectively take the form of waves or undulations.

Waybill – A document prepared by the carrier of a shipment of goods, identifying the car and its contents, along with its route and other details of shipment.

Weather Boarding – Siding applied to the exterior of a building.

Weather Checking – Small splits in a wood product due to alternate shrinking and swelling of the surface fibers due to variations in moisture content.

Weather Exposure – See Exposure.

Weathering – The mechanical or chemical disintegration and discoloration of the surface of wood, caused by exposure to light, the action of dust and sand carried by the wind, and the alternate shrinking and swelling of the surface fibers caused by continual variation in moisture content brought on by changes in the weather.

Weatherlife – The length of time a roofing material will protect the interior of a building from the elements.

Weather Stain – Discoloration in lumber caused by exposure to the weather.

Weatherstripping – Any of various materials such as wood, felt, metal, plastic, etc, used to cover joints between doors and their jambs, windows and their sills, and similar applications, to keep out rain, air, etc.

Web – A supporting member in a truss; one that joins the chords, or top and bottom members, together.

Wedge – A triangular-shaped piece of steel

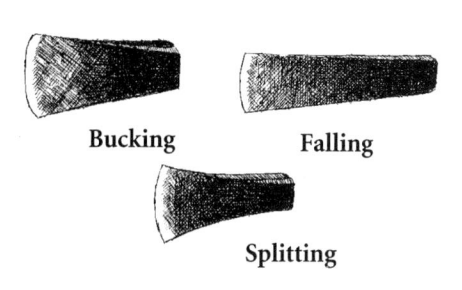

Bucking   Falling

Splitting

Wedges

or plastic, used when felling and bucking trees to keep saws from binding. Also used to split wood by pounding the wedge into the wood with a maul.

Weed Trees – Any vegetation of little or no marketable value to the harvesters of a forest. With improved technology and new products, many species once considered weed trees have become valuable raw material. An example is Aspen, now widely used in waferboard/OSB; until the 1940s, Western Hemlock was seldom used in construction and was considered a weed tree by many manufacturers well into the 1950s.

Weeping Pine – Pinus excelsa. Another name for Himalayan Pine. So called because of its long, drooping needles.

Weeping Spruce – Another name for Brewer Spruce.

Weight – The amount a shipment weighs, qualified as gross, the weight of the goods and container; net, the weight of the goods alone; tare, the weight of the container alone.

Weight Agreement – An agreement between shippers and carriers to use estimated weights on goods not specifically included in classifications and tariffs.

Weighting – The placement of weights on lumber being dried to minimize warping.

Weight Wood – Logs sold by weight rather than by board foot volume. Also called Tonnage Wood. Opposite of Scale Wood.

Well Assorted – An imprecise phrase implying that the pieces in a lot are of lengths or widths that are somewhat more desirable than those normally obtained in manufacture.

West Coast Freight – 1. The freight rates

West Coast Hemlock

applicable to shipments from mills located west of the Cascades Mountains in Washington and Oregon, and on the Northern California coast, into generally eastern consuming regions. 2. A practice of deducting from the delivered cost of southern plywood an amount representing freight charges as if the shipment had originated on the West Coast. See Coast Index.

West Coast Hemlock – See Hemlock.

West Coast Index – See Coast Index.

West Coast Spruce – Another name for Sitka Spruce, Picea sitchensis.

Western Balsam – See Grand Fir.

Western Drywood Termite – Incisitermes minor. These destructive insects are native to the southwestern U.S. They establish colonies in very dry wood, and can attack any part of a structure.

Western Hemlock – See Hemlock.

Western Jackpine – See Lodgepole Pine.

Western Juniper – Juniperus occidentalis. This species, found in Oregon and Washington to elevations of 10,000 feet, is also called Sierra Juniper.

Western Larch – See Larch.

Western Pine – Any of several pines growing in the Western United States or Canada, including, Ponderosa, Sugar, and Western (Idaho) White Pine.

Western Red Cedar – Thuja plicata. This species in found principally along the western edges of British Columbia, Washington and Oregon. The wood is soft, straight-grained, and extremely resistant to decay and insect damage. It is used extensively in roof coverings, exterior sidings, fences, decks, and other outdoor applications.

Western Silver Fir – Abies amabilis. A minor species included in the Hem-Fir grouping.

Western S-P-F – Lumber of the Spruce-Pine-Fir group produced in British Columbia or Alberta. See Spruce-Pine-Fir.

Western Spruce – 1. Another name for Sitka Spruce. 2. A casual reference to Western S-P-F.

Western Subterranean Termite – A destructive insect found in western North America, from British Columbia to Mexico. The lower structural members of wooden structures are especially vulnerable to this insect.

Western Tamarack – Another name for Larch.

Western White Pine – Pinus monticola. Commonly called Idaho White Pine, this species is found in a wide range throughout the western U.S. and British Columbia. It is easily worked and is favored for shelving, cabinets, and a variety of specialized uses.

Western Woods – A species designation that, under current grading rules, may include any combination of western softwood species, converted to lumber.

Western Yellow Pine – Ponderosa Pine. Rarely used.

Westside (SYP) – 1. An unofficial division of the Southern Yellow Pine producing region, consisting of Texas, Arkansas, Oklahoma, and Louisiana west of the Mississippi. Products from this region are most often marketed in the central southern states, the Midwest, and the West.

West Side – The area west of the Cascades Mountains in Oregon and Washington; contrasted with east side, the pine country.

Westside Measurement Rule – A rule established by scaling bureaus in the Northwest that sets at 40 feet the maximum length for scaling a log harvested on forests west of the Cascades (also called long log measurement). Logs longer than 40 feet are scaled as two logs. The rule also states that log diameters be rounded down to the nearest inch; they are never rounded up.

West Virginia Spruce – See Red Spruce.

Wet Bulb – A thermometer that utilizes evaporation of moisture from a water-saturated cloth on its bulb to measure temperature.

Wet Cemented – Plywood in which the veneers have been glued up before being dried.

Wet Cooperage – Barrels or casks built to hold liquids.

Wet Core – A zone of exceptionally high moisture content in the interior of a piece of

White Cedar

lumber.

Wet Finishing – The process of applying any of various types of paint, lacquer, or other finishes to particleboard for such applications as shelving, furniture, store fixtures, and cabinetry.

Wetlands – Low-lying areas of land such as marshes that are saturated with water for extended periods. They are considered beneficial for wildlife, plant diversity, flood control, and pollution filtration. They are often protected by various regulations that govern use, building, etc.

Wet Pockets – See Wet Core.

Wet Process Hardboard – Hardboard manufactured by a process in which a wood slurry is combined with a resin binder and is then dried, first on a screen and later under pressure. The pressure imparts high density to the board and also sets the binder.

Wet Rot – Fungal decay of wood exposed to alternate wet and dry conditions.

Wets – See Kiln Wet.

Wet Service Factor – One of various adjustment factors modifying tabulated design values for lumber. Applied when moisture content will exceed 19% for an extended time period.

Wet Sheet Stacker – A machine that stacks green veneer as it moves along the belt from the lathe.

Wet Wall – A plaster or stucco wall that sets up as the material dries.

Wet Weight – The weight of wood or paper solids before drying.

Wetwood – Wood of high water content having a water-soaked appearance; a condition sometimes found in living trees. The condition is also called Glassy, Water Core, Water Soak.

Weymouth Pine – Yellow Pine, Northern White Pine.

Wharf – A structure built along or at an angle from the shore of navigable waters, so that ships may lie along side to receive or discharge cargo or passengers.

Wharfage – A charge for use of the port surface over which cargo moves.

Wheels – See Big Wheels.

Whiffletree – In animal logging, the bar or singletree to which the harness is attached. Also called a singletree.

Whippy – A small log that is springy or flexible.

Whipsawing – A primitive method of sawing logs into lumber in which a handsaw is worked vertically through a log that has been suspended in a frame or over a pit. One man works from the top of the log, with another positioned under it. Also called Pitsawing.

Whiskers – Jaggers in a wire cable.

Whistle Boy – See Whistle Punk.

Whistle Punk – A signalman who, with a radio, horn or other device, transmits signals between the various parts of a logging operation. One of his most common duties is to signal the landing that a turn of logs is ready for yarding.

White – Untreated. See In the White, White Wood.

White Balsam – White Fir.

Whitebark Pine – Pinus albicaulis. A tree that grows at isolated high elevations in the West.

White Cedar – 1. Atlantic White Cedar. 2. Another name for Port Orford Cedar. 3. Another name for California Juniper.

Whipsawing

White Cooperage

White Cooperage – Smaller containers such as churns, tubs, etc.; often made from Sycamore or Poplar.

White Cypress – Another name for Baldcypress, Taxodium distichum.

White Cypress Pine – Callitris columellaris. A conifer native to Australia, this species is neither a true pine nor cypress. It is used extensively for framing, posts, and poles in that country.

White Deal – European Spruce.

White Finger – An ailment involving the nerves and blood vessels in the hands of loggers and some construction workers. It is apparently caused by the effect of grasping certain power tools, such as chainsaws, for long periods of time.

White Fir – Abies concolor. The most important of the true firs, this species is found in a wide range in the western U.S. Northern California accounts for the majority of White Fir (or Inland Hem-Fir) lumber produced in the U.S. The wood is straight-grained, fine-textured, and relatively light. It is used in general construction and for such specialized uses as mouldings and doors.

White Hemlock – Eastern Hemlock.

White Lumber – Lumber not yet treated with preservative.

White Oak – Any of several species of American oaks whose wood is more white than red, principally Quercus alba.

White Pine – Pinus strobus, Northern White Pine; P. monticola, Idaho White Pine; P. lambertiana, Sugar Pine.

White Pocket – See White Speck.

White Rot – Fungal decay that removes lignin, leaving a white substance, chiefly cellulose.

White Silver Pine – Another name for New Zealand Silver Pine.

White Speck – A fungus, Fomes pini, that develops in a living tree. It does not develop after the tree has been cut, but causes clusters of small white areas in the wood. The term "white speck" or "speck" is frequently used in the veneer and plywood industries to describe Utility grade veneer, which is produced from wood containing white speck.

Also known as White Pocket.

White Spruce – Picea glauca. This species is found predominately in British Columbia and Alberta. It is marketed as part of the Spruce-Pine-Fir group and is an important source of general construction lumber; it is also used extensively in pulp production.

White Water Man – A person who directed logs through river rapids in the days of log drives.

White Wood – 1. Wood products intended for treating, but not yet treated. 2. A designation applied to a number of species, such as White Fir.

Whole Log Mill – A mill equipped with Scragg or chipper-saw equipment to reduce a log to cants in one pass.

Wigwam Burner

Wholesale Distributor – A stocking wholesaler. Also sometimes called a stocking distributor.

Wholesaler – One who purchases material from a producer for the purpose of resale to retailers, remanufacturers, or industrial users.

Wholesale Terms – A discount allowed from the invoice price if payment is made within a specific period. See After Date of Invoice.

Whole Timber – Unsawn timbers used as balks in construction.

Whole Tree Chipping – A system of con-

Wire Brushing

verting trees into chips in which the chipper is operated in the woods at or near the cutting area. The entire tree, including small branches, is fed into a chipper and the chips are blown into a truck for transportation to a mill for further processing.

Wicking – The action of a material that draws a liquid substance from one point to another. Some products will draw moisture from the exterior of a wall to its interior. See Vapor Transmission.

Wide Area Telephone Service (WATS) – A WATS line enables a caller to phone anywhere in a designated area for a monthly charge based on the total amount of time used, rather than for the individual calls.

Wide Ringed – Coarse-grained wood.

Wides – The wider widths of dimension or board lumber, usually 10- and 12-inch widths.

Widia Saw – A circular saw with hardened inserted teeth, used on very hard hardwoods.

Widowmaker – A limb that poses danger to a logger through the possibility of it falling from a tree and hitting him.

Wigwam – Two or more trees that lodged together at their tops when felled.

Wigwam Burner – A metal structure, shaped roughly like an Indian wigwam or teepee, in which mill wastes are burned. Now rarely seen, partly because mill wastes are being utilized to a much greater degree, and partly because the burners can be a major source of air pollution.

Wilderness – A wild, undeveloped area essentially unaffected by man. An area designated by law to be left in a natural state.

Wilderness Society – A major U.S. environmental group, founded in 1935, that focuses lobbying and fund-raising efforts toward preservation of wilderness, as well as protection of wildlife, forests, parks, and other lands.

Wildlife Tree – A tree, often hollow or with a large hole, designated to provide wildlife habitat; a "coon tree." A tree left standing for wildlife use while those around it were felled.

Wild Pine – Scotch Pine. So called because of the tendency in some plantings to-

Witness Tree

ward an extreme crookedness of the young boles.

Willawa-Willie – See Piss Fir Willie.

Willow – Any of various species of the genus Salix. Salix nigra, Black Willow, is the largest of as many as 100 species of willow found in North America.

Windbarrier – See Windbreak.

Windbreak – A row or group of trees planted to give protection from the wind, especially on farmland.

Windfall – A tree that has been blown down by the wind. Also called Windthrow.

Windfirm – Trees able to withstand strong winds.

Windlean – Standing timber leaning in one direction due to strong, prevailing winds.

Windshake – Ring shake caused by wind damage.

Wind Slash – See Windfall.

Windthrow – See Windfall.

Wing Log – The outer log of a load or raft.

Winter Cut – Poles cut during the winter, believed less subject to checking than those cut in the spring.

Winter Show – A logging area used in the winter. Winter shows are usually at low elevations and have graveled roads so logging can continue in inclement weather.

Wire Brushing – Abrading the surface of plywood or board paneling to give it an aged

Terms Of The Trade

Wire Rope

or weathered effect.

Wire Rope – A flexible steel rope made of many strands twisted around a core; used in logging.

Witch – A chain-and-lever system used to bind lumber together in a raft.

With the Grain – See Along the Grain.

Witness Tree – A tree used by surveyors to mark the location of a survey corner; the tree is located near the corner and is inscribed with survey data.

Wobble Saw – See Drunken Saw.

Wobblies – International Workers of the World, an early labor union of loggers and miners in the Pacific Northwest. Attempts at organization and bargaining from World War I through the Great Depression of the 1930s led to pitched battles between workers and company supporters, including the police. At least one Wobblie was lynched in Western Washington.

Wold – A small forest. British.

Wolf Link Saw – An early chain saw.

Wolf Tree – One that has grown faster than its neighbors. Usually of little value for lumber.

Wolman Salts – Aqueous wood preservatives applied by vacuum and pressure impregnation, immersion, or spraying. Wood treated with Wolman Salts is odorless and may be painted. A trademark of Koppers Company, Inc.

Wood – The part of a tree within the cambium, used in the production of a wide variety of items due to its lightness and strength.

Wood-Based Panel – Any of various panels formed from wood veneers, flakes, particles, etc. Examples include plywood, oriented strand board, particleboard, hardboard, and fiberboard.

Woodbuck – See Woodsplitter.

Wood Butcher – A do-it-yourself carpenter.

Wood Cement Particleboard (WCP) – A high density board manufactured in Europe for use on exteriors, or where fire resistance is needed. Wood particles are combined with Portland cement, or other minerals, as a binder.

Wood Chemicals – Any of various extractives from wood, including lignins, tannins, terpenes, resin acids, phenols, and others.

Wood Cutter – One who cuts wood for fuel. Also, a regional term for a timber faller.

Woodcutter's Eczema – A skin irritation affecting loggers. Caused by contact with various lichens or liverworts found on treebark. Also called Wood Poisoning.

Wooden Railroad – In the early logging days, a temporary rail line using wooden rails.

Wood Everlasting – An informal name for old-growth cypress.

Wood Failure – A measure of glue bond quality between two plies in a plywood panel or lumber laminate in a laminated beam. Wood failure is usually estimated by submitting a sample to a shear test, and is a measure of the percentage of wood remaining on the glueline. If 90% of the wood fails in this test, the bond is said to have 90% wood failure and is considered a strong bond. In this example, only 10% of the glue bond between the panels failed to hold.

Wood Fiber Content – The actual solid wood structure, not including decay, moisture, voids, etc., contained in a volume of wood.

Wood Flour – Wood particles that have been processed to the consistency of flour. Wood flour has a variety of uses in composition products, plastics, and as a filler or extender.

Wood Head – Slang for a logger.

Wood Hick – Slang for a logger (used chiefly in the Lake States).

Woodlands – A term commonly used in the South for forested areas, especially those with mixed hardwood and softwood species.

Wood Log – A log grade ranking above cull but below #3. A wood log must have a solid wood content of #3 common or better lumber of at least one third of the gross scale amount.

Woodlot – A small timbered area, usually part of a farm, from which trees may be harvested.

Working Edge

Wood Maul – A heavy hammer with a block of hardwood as its head.

Wood Meal – See Wood Flour.

Wood Oil – Tung oil used in the manufacture of varnish, putty, etc.

Wood Pickling – Slang for wood preservation through the use of any of various chemicals.

Wood-Plastic Composite (WPC) – Wood impregnated with chemicals, which are then cured to make a rigid plastic. The resulting product is harder, tougher, and less susceptible to abrasion. It is used primarily to make novelty items such as jewelry, chess pieces, and the like.

Wood Poisoning – See Woodcutter's Eczema.

Wood Pulp – Wood reduced to pulp, a slurry of wood fibers, by mechanical or chemical means.

Wood Rack – An open container or U-shaped support in which fuel wood is stacked. Also, a wood rick.

Wood Ray – See Rays.

Wood Reduction – The process of reducing wood in the form of logs to lumber, chips, wood flour, or other products.

Wood Room – The location in a pulp plant where wood is chipped. Also, the point in some plants where the decision is made on whether a log is to be chipped or directed to processing into lumber or other products.

Woods – The forest where logging operations occur. Loggers or lumberjacks work in "the woods" or "the bush," rarely in the forest. See Bush.

Woods Boss – See Bull of the Woods.

Woodsplitter – A workman who split rounds into firewood for use in a steam donkey boiler in the woods. Also called a Woodbuck.

Woods Push – See Bull of the Woods.

Woods Run – Unsorted logs, the entire output of a logging show. See Camp Run.

Wood Tar – A substance distilled from wood.

Wood Wool – Another name for excelsior.

Woodworker – 1. A person who performs a variety of tasks having to do with the processing of timber into lumber, plywood, or other products. Although the term can be applied to loggers, it most often is used to describe workers in a factory. 2. One who makes cabinets, furniture, etc.

Woodworker's Asthma – A hypersensitive reaction to wood dust, characterized by breathing difficulties.

Wood Yard – A place where fuel wood is stored and cut to size.

Woolly Grain – See Fuzzy Grain.

Workability – A reference to the degree of ease with which a species of wood may be cut, shaped, smoothed, or otherwise processed.

Worked Lumber – Dressed lumber that has also been matched, shiplapped, or patterned.

Working Capital – The excess of current assets over current liabilities.

Working Charge – A charge added to the basic price of a lumber or panel product to cover the cost of extra processing or special services. These charges may include running to pattern, cutting tongues and grooves, etc. Also, a Special Service Charge.

Working Circle – A general area of forest land tributary to a specific processing location.

Working Edge – The face edge of a piece of lumber.

Woodsplitter

Terms Of The Trade

Working Face

Working Face – The face of a piece of lumber.

Working Life – The time period after mixing in which an adhesive remains usable. Also called Pot Life.

Working Qualities – See Workability.

Working Stress – See Allowable Stress.

Worm Hole – See Borer Hole.

Worm Holes No Defect (WHND) – A statement that worm holes existing in a shipment of lumber cannot be considered a defect; used in reference to hardwood and some cedar lumber.

Wormy – A term used to describe wood that has been attacked by any of a variety of borers.

Wound – An injury to a tree that penetrates the bark to, or through, the cambium layer.

Woven Corner – See Laced Corner.

Wow – A warp or bend in lumber.

WP Pattern – Any of various standard millwork patterns, originally described by the Western Pine Association (now the Western Wood Products Association).

Wrack – A low (sixth) grade of wood from the Baltic region.

Wrap-Around Mortgage – A financing package in which an existing mortgage is kept in place at its original interest rate, and a new mortgage is issued at a current interest rate to cover the balance due on the sale of a property.

Wrapper – See Binder.

Wrapping – A method of applying narrow strips of veneer around a curved surface, such as a piece of furniture.

Wrought Timber – Lumber planed on one or more surfaces.

XYZ

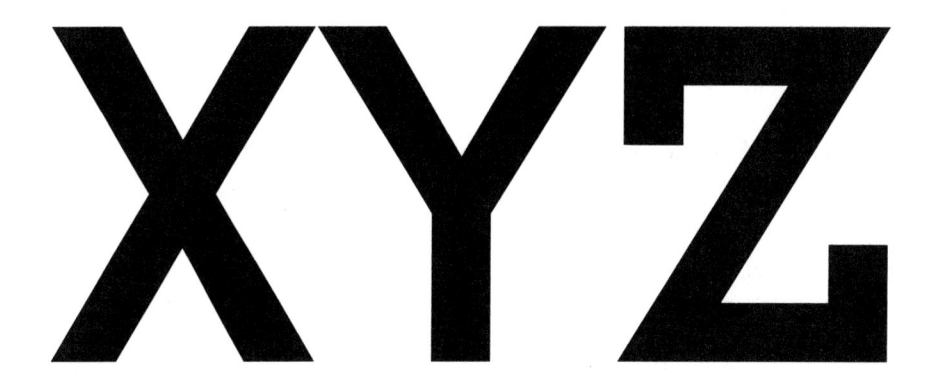

X-Band – See Crossband.

Xeno Currency – Another name for Eurocurrency.

Xenograft – A tissue graft involving two different species.

X-Tree – A tree marked to be used as a spar tree.

Xylem – See Sapwood.

Yakima Pine – Another name for Ponderosa Pine.

Yard – A place where wood products are stored or made available for sale. There are mill yards, distribution (wholesale) yards, and retail yards.

Yarder – A machine used to haul logs from the cutting area to the landing.

Yarding – The process of hauling logs from the cutting area to the landing.

Yarding Unmerchantable Material (YUM) – A feature of some U.S. Forest Service timber sale contracts that requires the purchaser to yard logging residue to a landing or other specified location.

Yard Keeper – In the British timber trade, an importer who stores timber.

Yard Lumber – Lumber of those grades, sizes, and patterns which is generally intended for ordinary construction and general building purposes.

Yard Man – An employee who works in the yard of a retail store.

Yardmaster – The person who controls all switching movements in a railyard.

Yarder

Terms Of The Trade

Yard Stain

Yard Stain – Stain that develops in air drying.

Yellow Cedar – Another name for Alaska Yellow Cedar.

Yellow Cypress – Another name for Alaska Yellow Cedar.

Yellow Fir – The heartwood of old-growth Douglas Fir, which has a yellow cast when sawn.

Yellow Pine – 1. Northern White Pine. 2. A casual reference to Southern Yellow Pine.

Yellow Spruce – Sitka Spruce.

Yew – A fine-grained, elastic coniferous tree of the genus Taxus. Varieties grow in many parts of the world. English Yew was the basis of the long bow. The bark contains taxol, a substance that appears to combat some types of cancer.

Yezo Spruce – Picea jezoensis. This species, native to northeast Asia, is an important plantation tree in Japan.

Yield – The amount of product recovered from a given quantity of raw material.

Yield Table – A table designed to predict how much timber of a given species could grow in a perfectly stocked stand with a specified site index.

Young Growth – Reproduction of trees in a logged area.

Young Stand – As defined by the Forest Service, an immature forest stand, typically 20-40 years old.

Zebrawood – Connarus guianensis. A tropical hardwood with strikingly marked grain, used for decorative purposes in cabinetry, paneling, etc.

Zero Discharge – The concept of no discharge of contaminated or processed water from a manufacturing facility. Although zero discharge is a goal of some anti-pollution regulations, it is common for regulatory bodies to issue permits for the discharge of wastes that have been subject to the "best practicable treatment."

Zero Lot Line – A system of locating a dwelling on the extreme edge of a lot when building, in order to maximize the use of the available land, especially in areas of high-density housing.

Z Flashing – Z-shaped metal flashing applied between panels of plywood siding to shed water.

Zig-Zag Moulding – See Chevron.

Zone of Rate Freedom (ZORF) – A territory in which a carrier may lower or raise rates without being subject to legal protest from shippers or other carriers.

Section II

ABBREVIATIONS

A

A – A high grade of softwood veneer, suitable for a natural finish and exposed use.

AA – 1. After arrival of freight. 2. A grade veneer on the face and back of high grade sanded plywood. 3. Always afloat.

AAC – 1. After arrival of car. 2. Annual allowable cut.

AAR – 1. Association of American Railroads. 2. Against all risks.

AB – 1. A combination of veneer grades on the face (A) and back (B) of sanded plywood. 2. Alberta (postal code).

ABS – American Bureau of Shipping.

AC – Veneer grades on the face (A) and back (C) of sanded plywood.

ACE – Allowable cut effect.

ACI – American Credit Indemnity Co.

AD – 1. Veneer grades on the face (A) and back (D) of sanded plywood. 2. Air dried.

ADA – Americans with Disabilities Act.

ADAT – Air dried after treating.

ADF – After deducting freight.

ADF&D – After deducting freight and duty.

ADFD&E – After deducting freight, duty, and entry fees.

ADI – After date of invoice.

ADT – Air dried ton.

AFA – American Forestry Association.

AFB – Allowance for bark.

AFI – American Forestry Institute.

AFL – American Federation of Labor

AFPA – 1. American Forest and Paper Association. 2. Alberta Forest Products Association.

AFRA – American Forest Resource Alliance.

AITC – American Institute of Timber Construction.

AK – Alaska (postal code).

AL – 1. All lengths. 2. Alabama (postal code).

ALA – Alaska Loggers Association.

ALS – American Lumber Standard.

ALSC – American Lumber Standards Committee.

ALY – Allegheny Railroad.

A&MR – Arcata & Mad River Railroad.

AM – Amplitude Modulation.

AMEX – American Stock Exchange.

ANSI – American National Standards Institute.

APA – 1. American Plywood Association; 2. American Pulpwood Association.

APHIS – Animal and Plant Health Inspection Service.

API – American Paper Institute.

AR – Arkansas (postal code).

ARF – American Railroad Foundation.

ARM – Adjustable rate mortgage.

AS – 1. Along side. 2. American Samoa (postal code).

ASAP – As soon as possible.

ASCE – American Society of Civil Engineers.

ASD – Allowable stress design.

ASQ – Allowable sale quantity.

ASQC – American Society for Quality Control.

Assn, Assoc – Association.

Asst – 1. Assorted or assortment. 2. Assistant.

AST – At ship's tackle.

ASTM – American Society for Testing and Materials.

ATA – American Trucking Association.

AT&SF – Atchison, Topeka & Santa Fe Railroad.

ATSDR – Agency for Toxic Substances and Disease Registry.

Av, Ave, Avg – Average.

AW – All widths.

AWC – American Wood Council.

AW&L – All widths and lengths.

AWMAC – Architectural Woodwork Manufacturers Association of Canada.

AWPA – American Wood Preservers Association.

AWPB – American Wood Preservers Bureau.

AWPI – American Wood Preservers Institute.

AWPPW – Association of Western Pulp & Paper Workers.

AWS – American Wood Systems.

AWWF – See PWF.

AZ – Arizona (postal code).

B

BACT – Best available control technology.

Bal – Balance.

BAT – Best available technology.

B&B, B&Btr – B grade and better.

BB – A plywood panel with B-grade veneer on both the face and back.

BBC – Basic building code.

BC – 1. A plywood panel with a B face and a C back. 2. British Columbia (postal code).

BCOL – British Columbia Railway.

BCT – Best conventional technology.

BD – A plywood panel with a B face and a D back.

Bd – Board.

Bd Ft, BF – Board feet, or foot.

Bdl – Bundle.

BDT – Bone dry ton.

BDU – Bone dry unit.

B/E – Bill of entry.

BEPS – Building Energy Performance Standards.

Bev – Beveled.

Bev Sdg – Beveled siding.

BH – 1. Boxed heart. 2. Breast height.

BHND – Boxed heart no defect.

BI – Burning index.

BIA – Bureau of Indian Affairs.

B/L – Bill of lading.

BLM – Bureau of Land Management, Interior Department.

BLS – Bureau of Labor Statistics, Labor Department.

BM – Board measure.

BMP – Best management practice.

BN – 1. Burlington Northern Railroad. 2. Bull nosed.

BN1E – Bull nosed one edge.

Terms Of The Trade

B&O

B&O – Baltimore & Ohio Railroad.

BOCA – Building Officials and Code Administrators, International.

BOD – Biological oxygen demand.

BOF – Best opening face.

BS – 1. Both sides. 2. Breaking strength.

B&S – Beams and stringers.

B/S – Bill of sale.

BSI – British Standards Institute.

BSND – Bright sapwood no defect.

BSS – British Standards Specification.

BT – Berth terms.

Btr – Better.

BTU – British thermal unit.

C

C – 1. Allowable stress in compression in pounds per square inch. 2. Celsius.

CA – California (postal code).

CABO – Council of American Building Officials.

Carno – Car number.

CB – Center beaded.

CB1S – Center bead one side.

CB2S – Center bead two sides.

CBOT, CBT – Chicago Board of Trade.

CC – 1. Cubic centimeter. 2. Cubic content. 3. Country cut.

CCA – Chromated copper arsenate.

CCB – Chromated copper boron.

CCC – Commodity Credit Corporation.

CCF – 100 cubic feet or Cunit.

CCMC – Canadian Construction Materials Center.

CCW – Counter clockwise.

CD – 1. A combination of veneer grades on the face (C) and back (D) of a sheet of plywood. 2. Cash discount.

Cdr – Cedar.

CDX – CD plywood with exterior (X) glue line.

CEA – Commodity Exchange Authority.

CEC – Commodity Exchange Commission.

Ceil – Ceiling.

CEO – Chief executive officer.

CETA – Comprehensive Employment and Training Act.

C&F – Cost and freight.

CF – Cubic foot or feet.

CFA – Canadian Forestry Association.

CFM – 1. Customs fund measure. 2. Cubic feet per minute.

CFPA – Central Forest Products Association.

CFS – 1. Container freight station. 2. Cubic feet per second.

Cft – Cubic foot or feet.

CFTC – Commodity Futures Trading Commission.

CG – 1. Center groove. 2. Center of gravity.

CG2E – Center groove two edges.

CH – Standard (British).

CHBA – Canadian Home Builders Association.

CHPA – Canadian Hardwood Plywood Association.

CHU – Critical habitat unit.

CIF – Cost, insurance, freight.

CIF&C – Cost, insurance, freight & commission.

CIF&E – Cost, insurance, freight & exchange.

CIO – Congress of Industrial Organizations.

CITW – Canadian Institute of Treated Wood.

CL, C/L – Carload.

CLA – Canadian Lumbermen's Association.

CLF – Hundred lineal feet.

Clg – Ceiling.

CLIS – California Lumber Inspection Service and Testing Agency.

CLMA – Cariboo Lumber Manufacturers Association.

Clr – Clear.

Clr&Btr – Clear and better.

CLS – Canadian Lumber Standard.

CLSAB – Canadian Lumber Standards Accreditation Board.

CLSC – Canadian Lumber Standards Committee.

CLT – Continuous lumber tester.

CM – Center matched.

CME – Chicago Mercantile Exchange.

CN – Canadian National Railroad.

CNW – Chicago & Northwestern Railroad.

C&O – Chesapeake & Ohio Railway.

CO – Colorado (postal code).

COFC – Container on flatcar.

COFI – Council of Forest Industries (B.C.).

Com, Cmn – Common.

Comrl – Commercial decking.

Con, Const, Contr – Construction.

CONASA – Council of North Atlantic Shipping Associations.

COO – Chief operations officer.

COS – Cash on shipment.

CP – Candlepower.

CPA – Canadian Particleboard Association.

CPD – Charterers paying dues.

CPR – Canadian Pacific Railroad.

CPSC – Consumer Product Safety Commission.

CPU – Canadian Paperworkers Union.

CR – Consolidated Rail Corporation (Conrail).

CRA – California Redwood Association.

CRT – Columbia Research & Testing Corporation.

CS – Caulking seam.

C&S – Commons & selects.

CSA – Canadian Standards Association.

CSG – Consign, consignment.

Csg – Casing.

CSP – Canadian softwood plywood.

Cst – 1. Cost. 2. Coast.

CT – Connecticut (postal code).

Ctr – Center.

CTS – Cut to size.

Cu, Cub – Cubic.

CuFt – Cubic foot or feet.

CuM – Cubic meter.

CV – Center V.

CV1S – Center V 1 side.

Terms Of The Trade 315

CV2S

CV2S – Center V 2 sides.

CVTS – Cubic volume total stem.

CW – Clockwise.

CWC – Canadian Wood Council.

CWD – Coarse, woody debris.

CWO – Cash with order.

CWPB – Canadian Wood Preservers Bureau.

CWT – Hundredweight.

CX-Band – C grade cross band inner ply in plywood underlayment.

Cyp – Cypress.

CZ – Canal Zone (postal code).

D

d – Penny (as in 16d nail).

D2S – Dressed two sides.

D4S – Dressed four sides.

D&B – Dun & Bradstreet.

DBA – Doing business as.

DBB – Deals, battens, boards.

DB Clg – Double-beaded ceiling.

DBH – Diameter at breast height.

Dbl T&G – Double tongue and groove.

DB Part – Double-beaded partition.

D&CM – Dressed and center matched.

DC – 1. Direct current. 2. District of Columbia (postal code).

DCA – Designated conservation area.

DD – Double door.

DDB – Double door boxcar.

DE – Delaware (postal code).

DEIS – Draft Environmental Impact Statement.

DET – Double end trimmed.

Dex – Decking.

DF – Douglas Fir.

DF&L – Douglas Fir & Larch.

DFP – Douglas Fir plywood (chiefly Canadian).

DFPA – Douglas Fir Plywood Association (now APA).

DH – Double hung.

D&H – Dressed and headed.

Dia – Diameter.

DIB – Diameter inside bark.

Dim – Dimension.

DISC – Domestic International Sales Corporation. See FSC, Foreign sales corporation.

DIY – Do it yourself.

Dkg – Decking.

DL – Dead load.

DM – Double moulded.

D&M – Dressed and matched.

DMSO – Dimethyl sulfoxide.

Dn – Dense.

DNR – Department of Natural Resources (Washington State).

DOB – Diameter outside bark.

DOC – Department of Commerce.

DOE – Department of Energy.

DOT – Department of Transportation.

D&RGW – Denver & Rio Grande Western Railroad.

DVJM – Double V-jointed matching.

D/S – Drop siding.

D S/L – Double shiplap.

DTA – Differential thermal analysis.

DWAT – Dead weight all told.

DWCC – Dead weight cargo capacity.

DWT – Dead weight ton.

E

E – 1. Edge. 2. Modulus of elasticity.

EA – Environmental assessment.

EAR – Environmental analysis report.

EB1S – Edge bead one side.

EB2S – Edge bead two sides.

E&CB2S – Edge and center bead two sides.

E&CV2S – Edge and center vee two sides.

EC – European Community.

Econ – Economy.

ED – Equivalent defect.

EDF – Environmental Defense Fund.

EDI – Electronic data interchange.

EE – 1. Eased edges. 2. Errors excepted.

EEA – European Economic Area.

EEC – European Economic Community.

EEOC – Equal Employment Opportunity Commission.

EER – Energy efficiency ratio.

EFTA – European Free Trade Association.

EG – 1. Edge grain. 2. Edge glued.

EGAR – Edge-Glue and Rip.

EHF – Extremely high frequency.

EIS – Environmental impact statement.

EL – Edge laminated.

ELP – Engineered lumber product.

EM – End matched.

EMC – Equilibrium moisture content.

Eng. Sp., ES – Engelmann Spruce.

E&OE – Errors and omissions excepted.

EPA – Environmental Protection Agency.

ESA – Endangered Species Act.

ESM – End standard matched.

E-SPF – Eastern Spruce-Pine-Fir.

EV – Edge vee.

EWP – Engineered wood products.

Ext – Exterior.

F

F – 1. Face. 2. Fahrenheit.

f – Extreme fiber stress in bending.

FA – Facial area.

FAA – Free all average.

Fac – Factory.

FAO – Food and Agricultural Organization (United Nations).

FAQ – Fair average quality. (Used in international trade.)

FarmHA – Farmers Home Administration.

FAS – 1. Free alongside ship. 2. Firsts and seconds. 3. Foreign Agricultural Service.

FB

FB – Extreme fiber stress in bending. Or, fb.

FBM – Board foot measure.

FBT – Full berth terms.

FC – Flat car.

Fc – Compression parallel to grain.

FCC – 1. Forest Conservation Council. 2. Federal Communications Commission.

Fc⊥ – Compression perpendicular to grain.

FCL – Full container load.

FCNP – Flat car, no paper.

FCPUTT – Flat car, paper under top tier.

FCPW – Flat car, paper (or poly) wrapped.

Fdn – Foundation.

FE – Feathered edge.

FEA – Federal Energy Administration.

FEIS – Final environmental impact statement.

FEMA – Federal Emergency Management Agency.

FET – Federal excise tax (U.S.).

FFA – Full freight allowance.

FG – Flat grain.

F&G – Feathered and grooved.

FGL – Fortified glue line.

FHA – Federal Housing Administration.

FHLMC – Federal Home Loan Mortgage Corporation; Freddie Mac.

FHVA – Fine Hardwood Veneers Association.

FIB – Free into barge.

FIC – Forest Industries Council.

FIFRA – Federal Insecticide, Fungicide, and Rodenticide Act.

FIFO – First in, first out.

Fin – Finish.

FIO – Free in and out.

FIOS – Free in and out, stowed.

FIOT – Free in and out, trimmed.

FIP – Forestry Incentives Program.

FIR – Forest Industrial Relations.

F&L – Fir & Larch.

FL – Florida (postal code).

Flg – Flooring.

FM – 1. Flush moulded. 2. Festmeter. 3. Frequency modulation.

Fm – Fathom.

FMC – Federal Maritime Commission.

FmHA – Farmers Home Administration.

FMV – Fair market value.

FNMA – Federal National Mortgage Association; Fannie Mae.

FOB – Free on board.

FOHC – Free of heart center.

FOK – Free of knots.

FOQ – Free on quay.

FOR – Free on rail.

FOT – Free on truck.

FOW – First open water.

FP – Flat, paper.

FPM – Feet per minute.

FPRS – Forest Products Research Society.

FPS – Feet per second.

FRA – Federal Railroad Administration.

FRDA – Farm and Rural Development Administration.

Freddie Mac – See FHLMC, Federal Home Loan Mortgage Corporation.

FRP – Fiberglass reinforced plastic.

FRR – Fire resistance rating.

FRT – Fire retardant treated.

Frt – Freight.

FRTW – Fire retardant treated wood.

FS – Forest Service.

FSC – Foreign sales corporation.

FSP – Fiber saturation point.

FST – Federal sales tax (Canada).

FT – Full Terms.

Ft – 1. Tension parallel to grain. 2. Foot, feet.

F/T – Fishtail.

Ft BM – Feet, board measure.

FTO – Foreign testing organization.

FTPA – Federal Timber Purchasers Association.

Ft SM – Feet, surface (square) measure.

FTZ – Foreign trade zone.

Fv – Horizontal shear.

FWS – Fish and Wildlife Service.

G

G – Girth.

GA – Georgia (postal code).

GAAP – Generally accepted accounting principles.

GAO – General Accounting Office.

GATT – General Agreement on Tariffs and Trade.

GBA – Growth basal area.

GBL – Government bill of lading.

GM – Grade marked.

GMV – Gram-molecular volume.

GNMA – Government National Mortgage Association; Ginnie Mae.

GPM – Graduated payment mortgage.

Gr, Grn – Green.

G/R, G/Rfg – Grooved roofing.

GRT – Gross register tonnage.

Gr Wt – Gross weight.

GS, G/S – Grade stamped.

GSM – Good, sound merchantable.

GST – Goods and services tax.

GT – Gross ton.

GTC – Good till canceled.

GU – Guam (postal code).

H

Ha – Hectare.

HB – Hollow back.

HDO – High density overlay.

Hdwd – Hardwood.

Hem – Hemlock.

Hem-Bal – Hemlock-Balsam Fir.

Hem-Fir – Hemlock-White Fir (Abies).

Hem-Tam – Hemlock-Tamarack.

HF – 1. Hem-Fir. 2. High frequency.

HF-C – Hem-Fir (Coast).

Terms Of The Trade

HF-I

HF-I – Hem-Fir (Inland).

HG – Home grown (British).

HI – Hawaii (postal code).

HLBB – Home Loan Bank Board.

H&M – Hit and miss.

HorM – Hit or miss.

HOW – Home Owners Warranty Corporation.

HPL – High pressure laminate.

HPMA – Hardwood Plywood Manufacturers Association (now HPVA).

HPVA – Hardwood Plywood & Veneer Association (formerly HPMA).

Hrt – Heart.

Hrt CC – Heart cubical content.

Hrt FA – Heart facial area.

Hrt G – Heart girth.

HS – Hand split.

HS&RS – Hand split and resawn.

HUD – Department of Housing and Urban Development.

HV – High voltage.

Hvy – Heavy.

I

IA – Iowa (postal code).

IAPR – International Association of Pallet Recyclers.

IC – 1. Incense Cedar. 2. Illinois Central Railroad.

ICBO – International Conference of Building Officials.

ICC – Interstate Commerce Commission.

ID – Idaho (postal code).

IFA – Industrial Forestry Association.

IIC – Impact insulation class.

IL – Illinois (postal code).

ILA – International Longshore Association.

ILMA – Interior Lumber Manufacturers Association.

ILWU – International Longshore Workers Union.

IMG – Intermediate glue line.

IN – Indiana (postal code).

In – Inch, inches.

Incl – Including.

Ind – Industrial.

INR – Impact noise rating.

Int – Interior.

IPD – Incentive per diem.

ISO – 1. Insurance Services Office. 2. International Standards Organization.

ITA – International Trade Administration.

ITC – International Trade Commission.

IWA – International Woodworkers of America.

IWP – Idaho White Pine.

IWW – International Workers of the World (Wobblies).

J

JAS – Japanese Agricultural Standard.

JIT – Just-in-time.

J&P – Joists and planks.

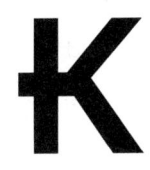

Jtd – Jointed.

K

K – Thermal conductivity.

KD – 1. Kiln dried. 2. Knocked down.

KDAT – Kiln dried after treating.

Kg – Kilogram.

Km – Kilometer.

KS – Kansas (postal code).

Kw – Kilowatt.

KY – Kentucky (postal code).

L

L – Linear, length.

LA – Louisiana (postal code).

Lam – Laminate, laminated.

Lbr – Lumber.

LC – Letter of credit.

LCA – Lumbermens Credit Association (Redbook).

LCL – 1. Less than carload. 2. Less than containerload.

Ld – Load.

L&D – Loss and damage.

Ldg – Loading.

LF – 1. Light framing. 2. Low frequency.

LFR – Lumber recovery factor.

LFt – Linear foot, feet.

LFVC – Loaded to full visible capacity.

Lgr – Longer.

Lgth – Length.

LIFO – Last in, first out.

Lin – Lineal, linear.

LKS – Lesser known species.

LL – 1. Loose loaded. 2. Live load.

LLB – Loose loaded box.

LLP – Longleaf Pine.

Lng – Lining.

Lngr – Longer.

LP, LPP – Lodgepole Pine.

LPIW – Lumber, Production, and Industrial Workers.

LPL – Low pressure laminate.

LR – Log run.

LRF – Lumber recovery factor.

LRFD – Load and Resistance Factor and Design.

LSD – Limit states design.

LSL – Laminated strand lumber.

LSM – 1. Lumber sales manager. 2. Local sales manager.

LT – Long ton.

LTIC – Laminated Timber Institute of Canada.

LTL – Less than truckload.

LTSY – Long-term sustained yield.

LTY – Lumber transit yard.

LUA – Lumbermen's Underwriting Alliance.

LVL

LVL – Laminated veneer lumber.

M

M – 1. Thousand. 2. Meter.

M1S – Moulded one side.

M³ – Cubic meter.

MA – Massachusetts (postal code).

MAI – Mean annual increment.

Max – Maximum.

MB – Manitoba (postal code).

MBA – Mortgage Bankers Association.

MBF – Thousand board feet.

MBFM – Million board feet measure (as sometimes used in Canada).

MBM – Thousand feet board measure.

MC – 1. Moisture content. 2. Mixed car.

MD – Maryland (postal code).

MDF – Medium-density fiberboard.

MDO – Medium-density overlay.

ME – Maine (postal code).

MEL – Machine-evaluated lumber.

Merch – Merchantable.

MF – Melamine formaldehyde.

Mfg – Manufacturing.

Mfr – Manufacturer.

MG – 1. Medium grain. 2. Mixed grain.

MHC – Mobile home components.

MHD – Mobile home decking.

MHI – Manufactured Housing Institute.

MHMA – Mobile Home Manufacturers Association.

MI – Michigan (postal code).

Mismfr – Mismanufacture.

MIT – Market if touched (futures term).

M-I-T – Milling-in-transit.

ML – Mixed load.

MLB – Maritime Lumber Bureau.

Mldg – Moulding.

Mldg&Btr – Moulding and better.

MLIB – Maritime Lumber Inspection Bureau.

MMBF – Million board feet.

MMC – Money market certificate.

MMSF – Million square feet.

MN – Minnesota (postal code).

MO – Missouri (postal code).

MOE – Modulus of elasticity.

MOR – Modulus of rupture.

MOS – Moulded on solid.

MP – Missouri Pacific Railroad.

MR – Mill run.

MRVD – Thousand recreation visitor days.

MS – 1. Mixed species. 2. Mississippi (postal code).

MSA – Metropolitan statistical area.

MSF – Thousand square feet.

MSR – Machine stress-rated.

MT – 1. Metric ton. 2. Montana (postal code).

MUF – Melamine urea formaldehyde.

Mult – Multiple(s).

MW – 1. Mixed width. 2. Milwaukee Railroad. 3. Midwest.

N

N – 1. Special grade of veneer selected for appearance. 2. Nosed.

N1E – Nosed one edge.

N2E – Nosed two edges.

NA – 1. Not available/applicable. 2. Neutral axis.

NAFTA – North American Free Trade Agreement.

NAHB – National Association of Home Builders.

NAIL – National Association of Independent Lumbermen.

NAWLA – North American Wholesale Lumber Association.

NB – 1. Nested bundling. 2. New Brunswick (postal code).

NBC – National Building Code.

NBCC – National Building Code of Canada.

NBM – Net board measure.

NBMDA – National Building Material Distributors Association.

NB/NGH – No bark/no grub holes.

Nbr – Number.

NBS – National Bureau of Standards.

NC – 1. North Central. 2. North Carolina (postal code).

ND – North Dakota (postal code).

NDS – National Design Specifications.

NDT – Nondestructive testing.

NE – 1. Northeast. 2. Nebraska (postal code).

NELMA – Northeastern Lumber Manufacturers Association.

NEPA – National Enviromental Policy Act.

NES – 1. National Evaulation Service. 2. Not elsewhere specified.

NEWLA – New England Wholesale Lumber Association.

NF – National forest.

NFA – National Futures Association.

NFDRS – National Fire Danger Rating System.

NFPA – National Forest Products Association. (Now AFPA).

NGM – No grade mark.

NGRC – National Grading Rule Committee.

NH – New Hampshire (postal code).

NHLA – National Hardwood Lumber Association.

NHPMA – National Hardwood and Pine Manufacturers Association.

NIE – Not indicated elsewhere.

NIPF – Nonindustrial private forest.

NIST – National Institute of Standards and Technology.

NJ – New Jersey (postal code).

NLBMDA – National Lumber and Building Material Dealers Association.

NLEA – National Lumber Exporters Association.

NLGA – 1. National Lumber Grades Authority. 2. National Lumber Grading Association.

NLMA – 1. Northeastern Lumber Manufacturers Association. 2. National Lumber Manufacturers Association.

NLPA – Newfoundland Lumber Producers Association.

Terms Of The Trade 323

NM

NM – New Mexico (postal code).

No – Number.

NOE – Not elsewhere enumerated.

No GS – No grade stamp.

NOI – 1. Notice of intent. 2. Not otherwise indicated.

NOM – Norwegian official measure.

Nom – Nominal.

NOS – Not otherwise specified.

NPA – National Particleboard Association.

NPDES – National Pollution Discharge Elimination System.

NPS – No prior selection.

NRCC – National Research Council of Canada.

NRDC – Natural Resources Defense Council.

NRLDA – National Retail Lumber Dealers Association (now NLBMDA).

NRME – Notched, returned, and mitered ends.

NRT – Net register tonnage.

NS – 1. Nova Scotia (postal code). 2. Norfolk Southern Railway.

NTPC – National Timber Piling Council.

NW – 1. Northwest. 2. Norfolk and Western Railway.

NWFA – National Wood Flooring Association.

NWPCA – National Wooden Pallet and Container Association.

NWMA – National Woodwork Manufacturers Association.

NWP – Northwestern Pacific Railroad.

NWT – Northwest Territories.

NWTA – North West Timber Association.

NWWDA – National Wood Window and Door Association.

NY – New York (postal code).

NYME – New York Mercantile Exchange.

NYSE – New York Stock Exchange.

O

OB – Over bark.

OC – 1. On center. 2. Open charter.

O/C – Overcharge.

O&C – Oregon & California lands.

OD – Oven dry.

ODS – Operating differential subsidy.

ODT – Oven dry ton.

O&E – Odd and even.

OECO – Organization for Economic Cooperation and Development.

O&ES – Oiled and edge sealed.

OG – 1. Old growth. 2. Open grain.

Og – Ogee.

OH – Ohio (postal code).

OI – Open interest.

OK – Oklahoma (postal code).

OLMA – Ontario Lumber Manufacturers Association.

OMB – Federal Office of Management and Budget.

ON – Ontario (postal code).

OR – 1. Owner's risk. 2. Oregon (postal code).

O&R – Ocean and rail.

324   Random Lengths

Ord – Order.

OS – 1. One side. 2. Overside delivery.

OSB – Oriented strand board.

OS&D – Over, short, and damaged.

OSHA – Occupational Safety and Health Administration.

OVE – Optimum value engineering.

OW – Overweight.

P

P – Planed.

P1E – Planed one edge.

P2E – Planed two edges.

P1S – Planed one side.

P2S – Planed two sides.

P1S1E – Planed one side, one edge.

P2S1E – Planed two sides, one edge.

P1S2E – Planed one side, two edges.

P4S – Planed four sides.

PA – Pennsylvania (postal code).

PAD – Partly air dried.

PAH – Polycyclic aromatic hydrocarbon.

Pal – Palletized.

PAM – Per acre material.

PAR – Planed all 'round.

Par, Para – Paragraph.

Part – Partition.

Pat – Pattern.

PATS, PTS – Price at time of shipment.

PB – Particleboard.

PBI – Industrial grade particleboard.

PBU – Particleboard underlayment.

Pc – Piece.

PCEC – Pacific Coast European Conference.

PCF – 1. Per cubic foot. 2. Pounds per cubic foot.

PCFB – Pacific Coast Freight Bureau.

PCP – Polychlorophenol

PCUF – Plugged crossband under face.

PE – 1. Plain end/edge. 2. Prince Edward Island (postal code).

PEG – Polyethylene glycol.

PEL – Permissible exposure limits.

PET – Precision end trimmed.

PF – Phenol formaldehyde.

PFC – Platform frame construction.

PFF – Public Forestry Foundation.

PFS – Plywood Fabricator Service.

PGE – Pacific Great Eastern Railroad (now BCOL).

PHND – Pinholes no defect.

PIRF – Perimeter insulated raised floor.

Pkg – Package or packaging.

Pky – Pecky.

PLF – Pounds per lineal foot.

PLIB – Pacific Lumber Inspection Bureau.

Pln – Plain.

PLV – Parallel laminated veneer.

PMA – Pacific Maritime Association.

PO – Purchase order.

POC – Port Orford Cedar.

Terms Of The Trade

POD

POD – Pay on delivery.

POS – Point of sale.

PNW – Pacific Northwest.

PP – Ponderosa Pine.

PPA – Plywood Pioneers Association.

PPE – Planed plain edge.

PPI – Producer Price Index.

PPWC – Pulp, Paper, and Woodworkers of Canada.

PQ – Quebec (postal code).

PR – Puerto Rico (postal code).

PRA – Prinicipal residence account.

PRP – Performance-rated panel.

PRF – Plywood Research Foundation.

PS – 1. Product standard. 2. Petrograd Standard.

PSE – Planed square edge.

PSF – Pounds per square foot.

PSI – Pounds per square inch.

PSJ – Planed and square jointed.

PSL – Parallel strand lumber.

PSYU – Public Sustained Yield Unit.

P&T – 1. Plug and touch. 2. Posts and timbers.

PTG – Planed, tongued and grooved.

PTL – 1. Pulled to length. 2. Pittsburgh Testing Laboratory.

P&TS – Plugged and touch sanded.

PUM – Piling unmerchantable material.

PUTT – Paper (or poly) under top tier.

PW – Paper wrapped.

PWF – Preserved wood foundation; Permanent wood foundation.

Q

QG – Quarter girth.

QLMA – Quebec Lumber Manufacturers Association.

QMS – Quality management system.

QSD – Quality services division.

Qtd – Quartered.

R

R – Moment of resistance.

RAM – 1. Resource allocation model. 2. Reverse annuity mortgage.

RARE – Roadless Area Review and Evaluation.

RB&B – Reverse board and batten.

RBB – Rough-back board.

R&B – Rabbet and bead.

RC – 1. Red Cedar. 2. Rotary cut.

RCRA – Resource Conservation and Recovery Act.

RCRI – Rail Cost Recovery Index.

RCS&HSB – Red Cedar Shingle & Handsplit Shake Bureau (now Cedar Shake and Shingle Bureau).

R&D – Research and development.

Rdm – Random.

RED – Radius edge decking.

SG

Reg – Regular.

REL – Random even lengths.

Reman – Remanufacture.

RF – Radio frequency.

Rgh – Rough.

RI – Rhode Island (postal code).

RIS – Redwood Inspection Service.

RL – Random length.

Rnd – Round, rounded.

R&O – Rail and ocean.

ROEL – Random odd and even lengths.

RoGrn – Rough green.

ROI – Return on investment.

Ro-Ro – Roll on, roll off.

R&R – 1. Rebutted and rejointed. 2. Repair and remodeling.

RS, R/S, Rsn – Resawn.

RTA – Ready to assemble.

R&T – Rail and truck.

RW – 1. Random width. 2. Redwood.

R&W – Rail and water.

RW&L – Random width and length.

RWRL – Random width, random length.

S – Surface, side, square, shear.

S1E – Surfaced one edge.

S2E – Surfaced two edges.

S1S – Surfaced one side.

S2S – Surfaced two sides.

S1S1E – Surfaced one side, one edge.

S1S2E – Surfaced one side, two edges.

S2S&CM – Surfaced two sides and center matched.

S4S – Surfaced four sides.

SA – Sales agent.

SAAR – Seasonally adjusted annual rate.

SAF – Society of American Foresters.

SAP – Soon as possible.

SBA – 1. Small Business Administration. 2. Structural Board Association.

SBC – Standard Building Code.

SBCC – Southern Building Code Congress.

SBCCI – Southern Building Code Council International.

SC – South Carolina (postal code).

SCC – Standards Council of Canada.

SCL – 1. Seaboard Coast Line Railroad. 2. Structural composite lumber.

SD – South Dakota (postal code).

Sdg – Siding.

SDR – 1. Saw, dry, and rip. 2. Special drawing rights.

S-Dry – Surfaced dry.

SE – Southeast.

SEC – Securities and Exchange Commission.

Sel – Select.

SE&S – Square edged and sound.

SE Sdg – Square edged siding.

Sel TF – Select tight face.

SFPA – Southern Forest Products Association.

SG – 1. Slash grain. 2. Specific gravity.

Terms Of The Trade 327

S-Grn

S-Grn – Surfaced green.

SGSSND – Sapwood, gum spots and streaks no defect.

SHD – Shipped dry.

SHEX – Sundays and holidays excluded.

SHINC – Sundays and holidays included.

SIC – Standard industrial classification.

SIT – 1. Stopping in transit. 2. Storing in transit.

SJ&P – Structural joists and planks.

SK – Saskatchewan (postal code).

SKU – Stock keeping unit.

SL – Snow load.

S/L – Shiplap.

S&L – Savings and loan institution.

SL&C – Shipper's load and count.

SL&T – Shipper's load and tally.

SLF – Structural light framing.

SLMA – Southeastern Lumber Manufacturers Association.

SM – 1. Sales manager. 2. Surface measure. 3. Standard matched. 4. Single moulded.

S&M – Sunk and moulded.

SN – Shipping note.

Snr – Sooner.

SOHA – Spotted owl habitat area.

SOO – Soo Line Railroad.

SP – 1. Sugar Pine. 2. Southern Pine. 3. Southern Pacific Railroad.

SPA – Southern Pine Association (now SFPA).

SPD – Shipowner pays dues.

Spec – 1. Specification. 2. Speculation.

S-P-F – Spruce-Pine-Fir.

SPIB – Southern Pine Inspection Bureau.

SPMC – Southern Pine Marketing Council.

Sq, Sqr – Square.

SR – 1. Strength ratio. 2. Southern Railway. 3. Stress rated.

SRB – Stress-rated board.

SSND – Sap stain no defect.

ST – Short ton.

Sta – Station.

ST&B – String tied and bundled.

STC – Sound transmission class.

STCC – Standard transportation commodity code.

Std – Standard.

Std&Btr – Standard & better.

Std Lgths – Standard lengths.

Ster – Sterling.

STK – Sound/Select tight knot.

Stk – Stock.

Stpg – Stepping.

Struc – Structural.

Sup Ft – Superficial foot.

Surf – Surfaced.

SW – 1. Sound, wormy. 2. Southwest.

SWE – Solid wood equivalent.

SWG – Standard wire gauge.

SWST – Society of Wood Science and Technology.

SYP – Southern Yellow Pine.

T

T – Tangential.
TAD – Thoroughly air dried.
Tbr – Timber.
TCF – Totally chlorine free.
TCFB – Transcontinental Freight Bureau.
TDW – Tons dead weight.
TECO – Timber Engineering Company.
TEU – Twenty-foot equivalent unit.
TFL – Tree farm license.
T&G – Tongue and groove.
TG&B – Tongued, grooved, and beaded.
TG&V – Tongued, grooved, and V-jointed.
Thkr – Thicker.
THP – Timber harvest plan.
TIT – Treating in transit.
TL, T/L – Truckload.
TLO – Total loss only.
TMP – Thermomechanical pulping.
TN – Tennessee (postal code).
TOB – Tape over bark.
TOC – Timber Operators Council.
TOFC – Trailer on flat car.
TPI – 1. Truss Plate Institute. 2. Timber Products Inspection and Testing Service.
TPIC – Truss Plate Institute of Canada.
TPM – Timber Products Manufacturers Association.
T&R – Truck and rail.
Trk – Truck.
TRS – Total reduced sulphur.
TR&W – Truck, rail, and water.
TSA – Timber supply area.
TSCA – Toxic Substance Control Act.
TSO – Treating service only.
TSP – Total suspended particulate.
T&T, Trk&Trlr – Truck and trailer.
TT – Trust Territories (postal code).
TTF – Taxation tree farm.
TX – Texas (postal code).

U

UB – Under bark.
UBC – Uniform Building Code.
UCC – 1. Uniform Commercial Code. 2. Uniform Code Council.
UDD – Unitized double door.
UDDB – Unitized double door box car.
UE – Unedged.
UF – Urea formaldehyde.
UFC – Uniform Freight Classification.
UHF – Ultra-high frequency.
UL – 1. Underwriters' Laboratories. 2. Underlayment (also U/L).
ULC – Underwriters' Laboratories of Canada.
ULSC – Underlayment, solid center/core.
UP – Union Pacific Railroad.

UPC

UPC – Universal product code.

UPI – United Paperworkers International.

US – 1. Unsorted. 2. United States.

USA – United States of America.

USDA – United States Department of Agriculture.

USDI – United Stated Department of the Interior.

USFS – United States Forest Service.

UT – Utah (postal code).

Util – Utility.

Util&Btr, Ut&Btr – Utility & Better.

UV – Ultraviolet.

UW – Underweights.

V

VA – Virginia (postal code).

VAT – Value added tax.

VCA – Voluntary coordinating agreement.

VG – Vertical grain.

VHF – Very high frequency.

VI – Virgin Islands (postal code).

VJM – V-joint matching.

VOC – Volatile organic compounds.

Vol – Volume.

VPS – Voluntary Product Standard.

VRF – Veneer recovery factor.

VRM – Variable rate mortgage.

VT – Vermont (postal code).

W

WA – Washington (postal code).

WATS – Wide Area Telephone Service.

W/B – Waybill.

WBMA – Western Building Materials Association.

WCH – West Coast Hemlock.

WCLA – West Coast Lumbermens Association (now WWPA).

WCLIB – West Coast Lumber Inspection Bureau.

Wdr – Wider.

WE – Waney edged.

WF – White Fir.

WFIA – Western Forest Industries Association.

WHND – Worm holes no defect.

WI – Wisconsin (postal code).

Wk – Week.

WL – Wind load.

WLMA – Western Lumber Marketing Association.

WO – 1. Week of. 2. Wait order.

WPA – Western Pine Association (now WWPA).

WPMA – Western Plywood Manufacturers Association (Canada).

WPPC – Wood Products Promotion Council.

W&R – Water and rail.

WRATS – Water repellent anti-travel stain

(treated).

WRC – Western Red Cedar.

WS – 1. White Spruce. 2. White speck.

W-SPF – Western Spruce-Pine-Fir.

WSSA – Wood Shake and Shingle Association.

Wt – Weight.

WTA – Western Timber Association.

Wth – Width.

WTCA – Wood Truss Council of America.

WV – West Virginia (postal code).

WW – White woods.

WWD – Weather working days.

WWMMP – Western Wood Moulding and Millwork Producers.

WWP – Western White Pine.

WWPA – Western Wood Products Association.

WWTA – Western Wood Truss Association.

WY – Wyoming (postal code).

X

X – Exterior glue line.

X-Band – Cross band.

Y

YP – Yellow Pine.

YT – Yukon Territory (postal code).

YUM – Yarding unmerchantable material.

Z

Z – Modulus of section.

ZORF – Zone of rate freedom.

Terms Of The Trade

Section III

USEFUL INFORMATION

Patterns and Sizes • Metric Conversions
Characteristics of Some Common Softwood Species
Common Knot Types and Other Lumber Characteristics
Common Wood Joints

Paneling and Siding

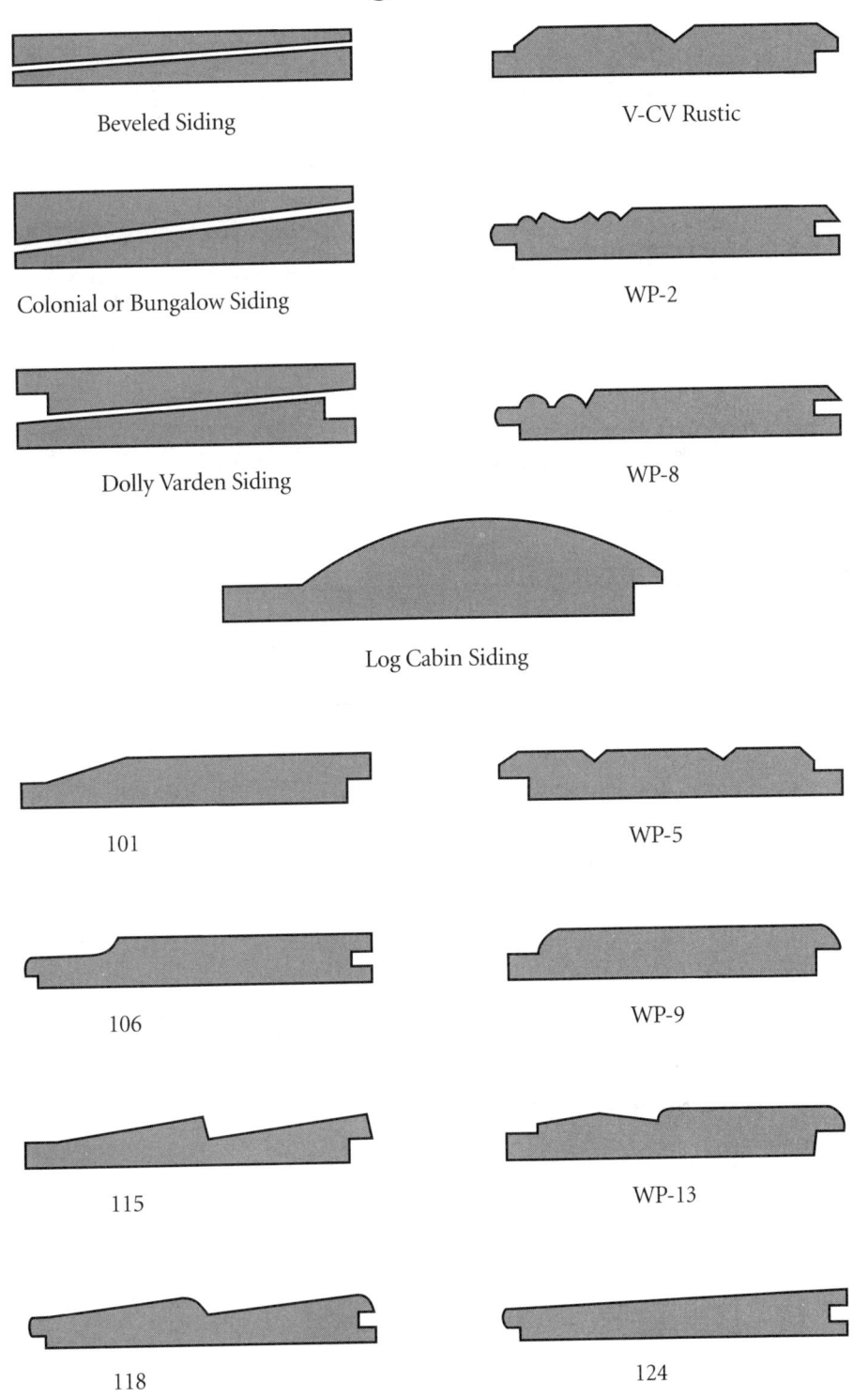

Beveled Siding

V-CV Rustic

Colonial or Bungalow Siding

WP-2

Dolly Varden Siding

WP-8

Log Cabin Siding

101

WP-5

106

WP-9

115

WP-13

118

124

Terms of the Trade

334

Decking and Flooring

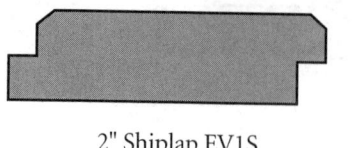

2" Shiplap EV1S

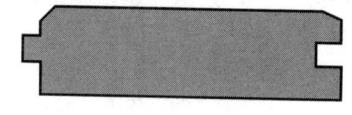

2" S2S CM EV1S Decking

Shiplap

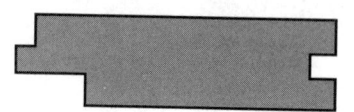

2" Channel Decking

S2S & CM T&G

1-1/4" Flooring D&M

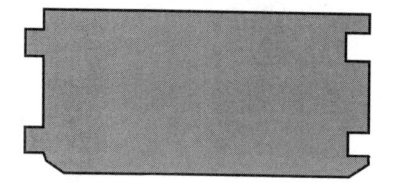

3x6" WP-305a

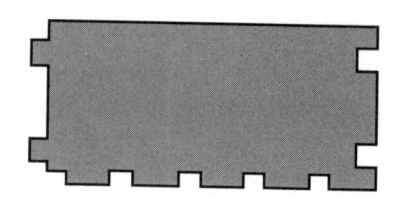

3x6" WP-305b

Ceiling and Partition

1x6" EV Ceiling
(S2S & CM EV1S)

1x6" E&CV Partition
(S2S & CM E&CV2S)

S2S & CM E&CB2S

1x4" Beaded Partition

1x4" Boston Pattern

Random Lengths

Miscellaneous Patterns

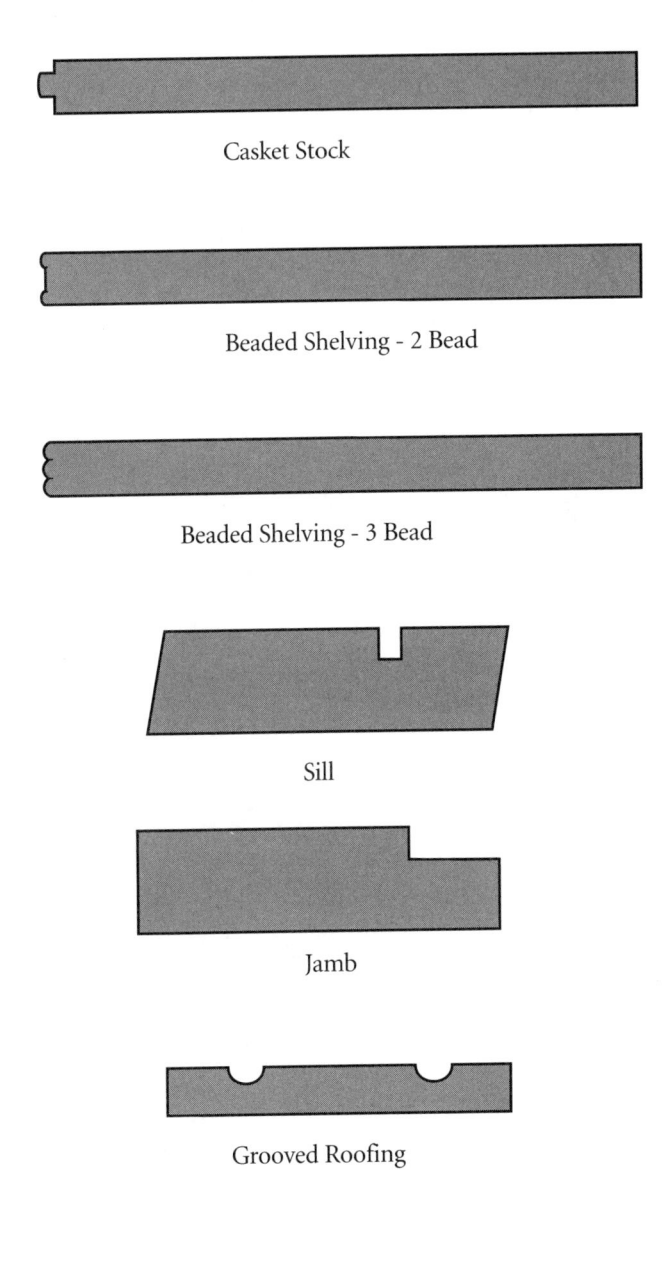

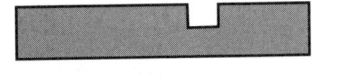

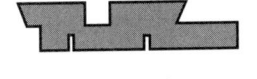

Casket Stock

Beaded Shelving - 2 Bead

Beaded Shelving - 3 Bead

Sill

Jamb

Grooved Roofing

Pulley Stile

Patent Lath

Moulding and Millwork

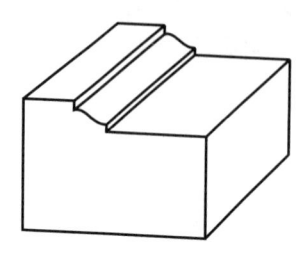

Brick Moulding	Back Band	Flat Astragal
Casing	Stop	Half Round
Panel Mould	Screen Mould	Quarter Round
Stool	Drip Cap	Glass Bead

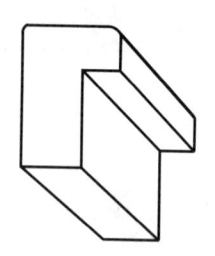

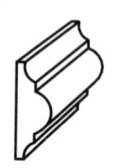

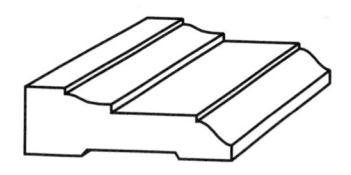

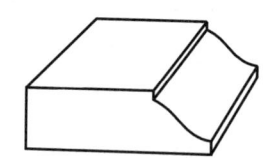

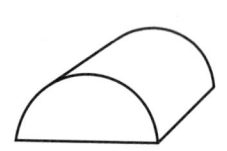

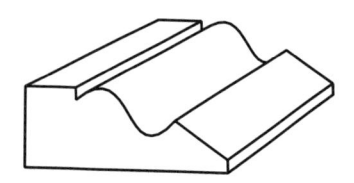

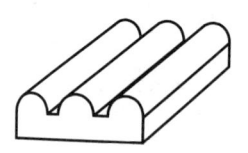

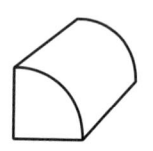

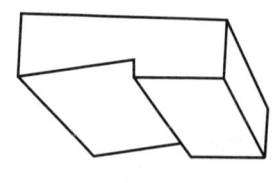

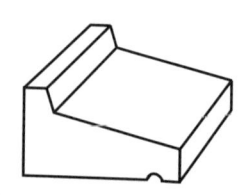

Moulding and Millwork

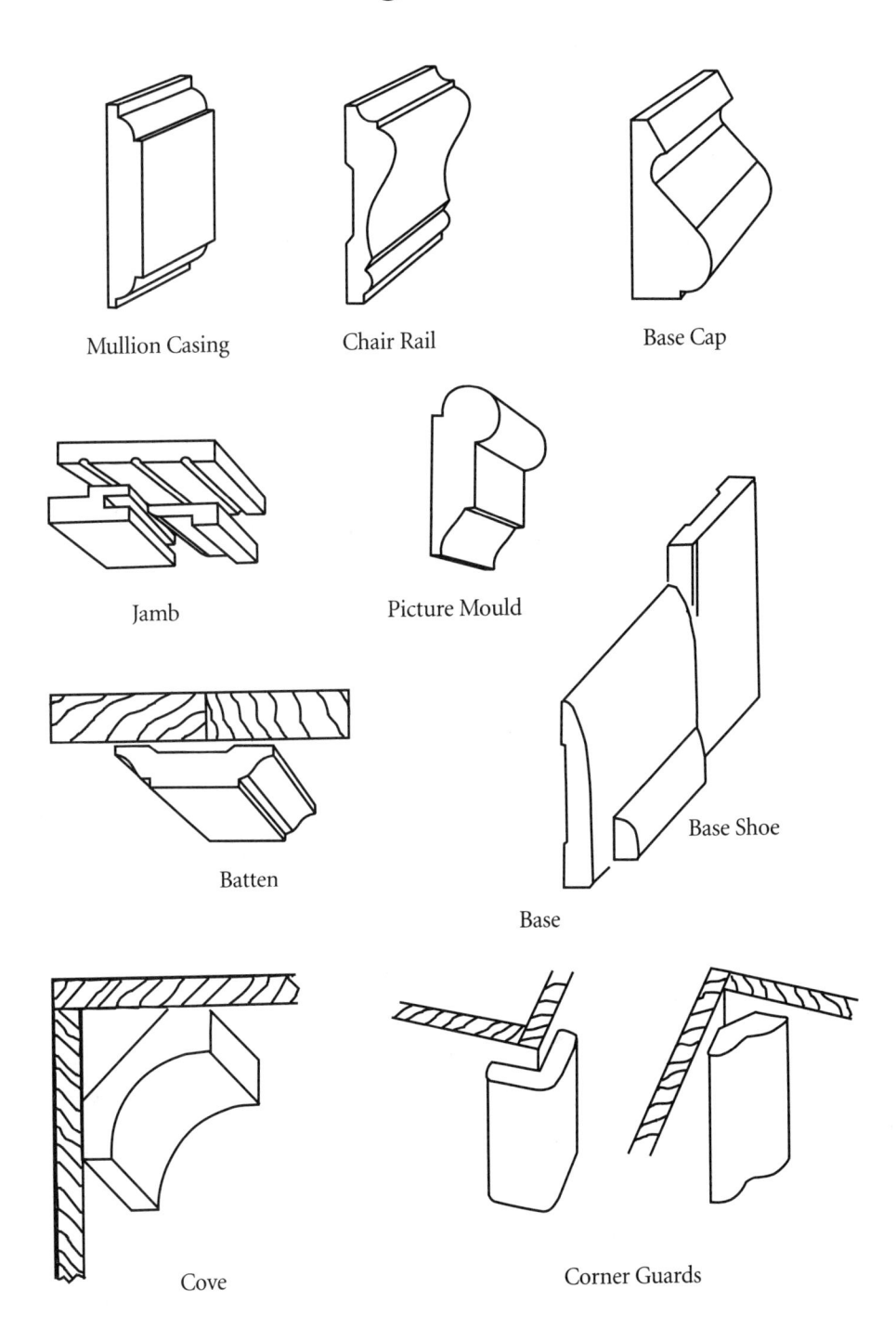

Mullion Casing

Chair Rail

Base Cap

Jamb

Picture Mould

Batten

Base

Base Shoe

Cove

Corner Guards

Terms of the Trade

Characteristics of Some

A. Douglas Fir – Needles: 1" long, grow from all sides of the stem in a spiral. Height: 150′ - 200′. Diameter: 2′ to 6′.

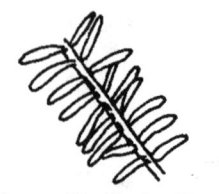

C. Western Hemlock – Needles: ¼" to ¾", rounded tips, grow from the sides of stems in pairs. Height: 130′ to 150′. Diameter 2′ to 4′.

D. Noble Fir – Needles: Curve up in thick, even growth, blue-green. Height: 120′ to 150′. Diameter: 2′ to 3′.

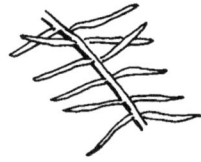

B. White Fir – Needles: 1½" to 2½", grow oppositely in paris from the sides of stems. Height: 120′ to 200′. Diameter: 1½′ to 4′.

E. Ponderosa Pine – Needles: 6", grow 3 to a cluster; patchy yellow-orange bark at maturity. Height: 125′ to 200′. Diameter: 2′ - 5′.

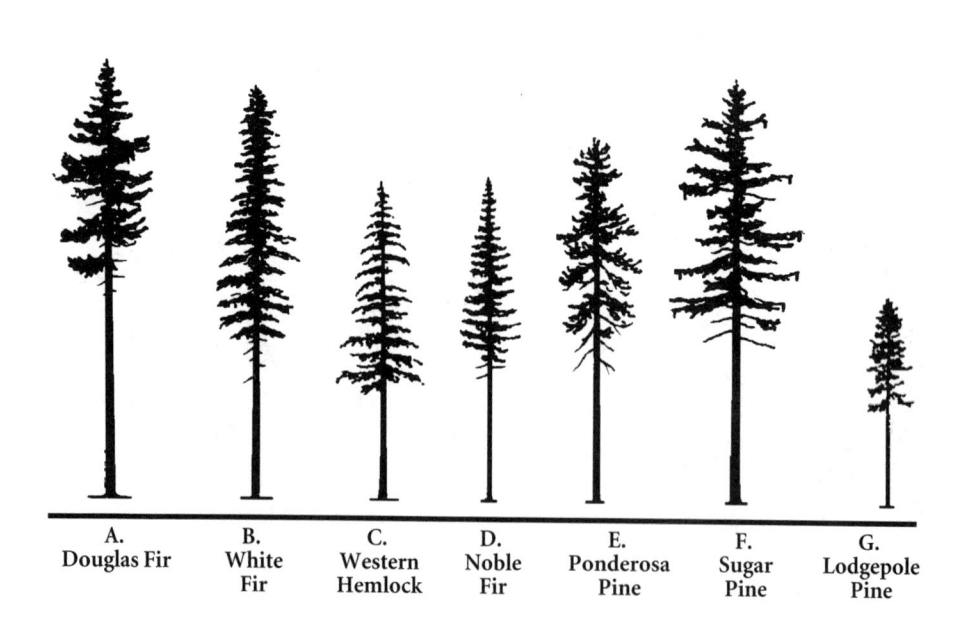

| A. Douglas Fir | B. White Fir | C. Western Hemlock | D. Noble Fir | E. Ponderosa Pine | F. Sugar Pine | G. Lodgepole Pine |

Common Softwood Species

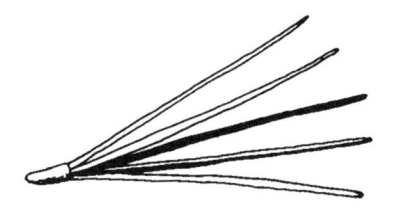

F. Sugar Pine – Needles: 3", 5 to a cluster, blue-green, red-dish bark, very large cones. Height: 160' to 200'. Diameter: 2' to 7'.

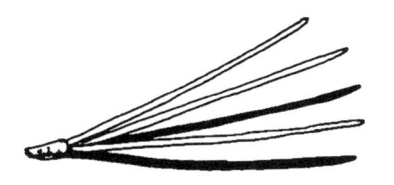

H. Western White (Idaho) Pine – Needles: 3", 5 to a cluster, blue-green; gray bark. Height: 150' to 175'. Diameter: 2' to 4'.

I. Loblololly Pine – Needles: 6" to 9", 3 to a cluster, pale green. Height: 90' to 100'. Diameter: 2' to 3'.

G. Lodgepole Pine – Needles: 2" to 3", 2 to a cluster, yellow-green. Height: 70' to 100'. Diameter: 1' to 2'.

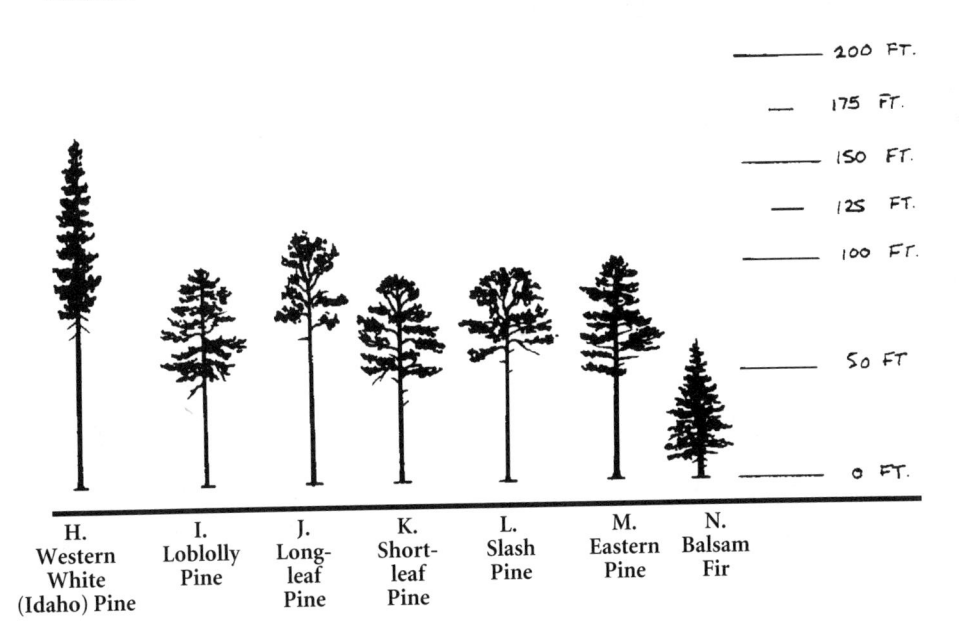

- 200 FT.
- 175 FT.
- 150 FT.
- 125 FT.
- 100 FT.
- 50 FT.
- 0 FT.

H. Western White (Idaho) Pine | I. Loblolly Pine | J. Longleaf Pine | K. Shortleaf Pine | L. Slash Pine | M. Eastern Pine | N. Balsam Fir

Terms of the Trade

Characteristics of Some Common Softwood Species, continued

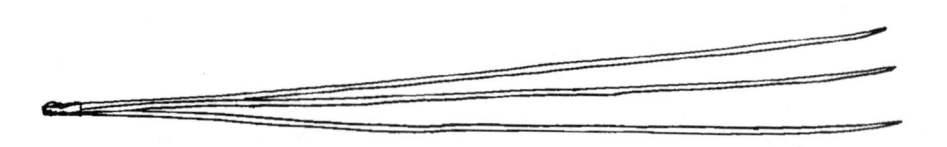

J. Longleaf Pine – Needles: 8" to 18", 3 to a cluster, dark green. Height: 100′ to 200′. Diameter: 2′ to 3′.

K. Shortleaf Pine – Needles: 3" to 5", 2 or 3 to a cluster, dark bluish green. Height: 80′ to 100′. Diameter: 2′ to 3′.

L. Slash Pine – Needles: 8" to 12", 2 or 3 to a cluster, dark green. Height: 100′. Diameter: 2′ to 3′.

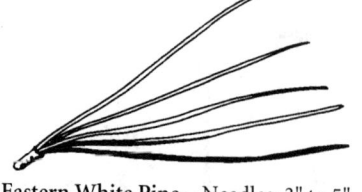

M. Eastern White Pine – Needles: 3" to 5", 5 to a cluster, blue green; dark brown bark. Height: 100′. Diameter: 1′ to 2′.

N. Balsam Fir – Needles: ½" to 1", dark green, grow from the sides of the stem in pairs. Height: 60′. Di-

Common Wood Joints

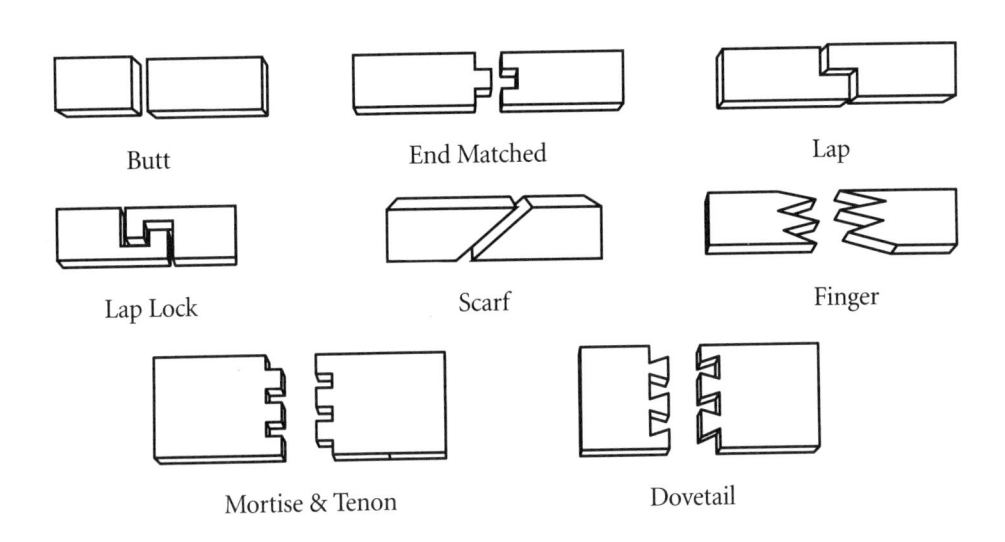

Butt

End Matched

Lap

Lap Lock

Scarf

Finger

Mortise & Tenon

Dovetail

Metric Conversions

If You Know	And Want To Find	Multiply By:
inches	millimeters	25.4
inches	centimeters	2.54
millimeters	inches	.03937
centimeters	inches	.3937
feet	meters	.3048
meters	feet	3.280
MBF, full sawn*	cubic meters	2.36
cubic meters	MBF, full sawn*	.424
MSF, ⅜″ basis	cubic meters	.885
cubic meters	MSF, ⅜″ basis	1.13
MBF, Scribner log scale	cubic meters	4.52
cubic meters	MBF, Scribner log scale	.221
acres	hectares	.4047
hectares	acres	2.4711

*Nominal sawn lumber is usually converted to cubic measure by the same factors. Actually, there are approximately 638 board feet of nomical sized lumber in a cubic meter, making the mathematically correct conversion factors 1.57 and .638

Terms of the Trade

Common

Knots are the most frequently found characteristics in lumber. A knot occurs when a branch or a limb embedded in the tree is cut through in the manufacturing process. Knots are classified according to size, type, and location.

Sound, encased, fixed, round knot through two wide faces.

Sound, watertight, tight, intergrown knot with radial checks.

Round knot hole through two wide faces, resulting from a loose knot.

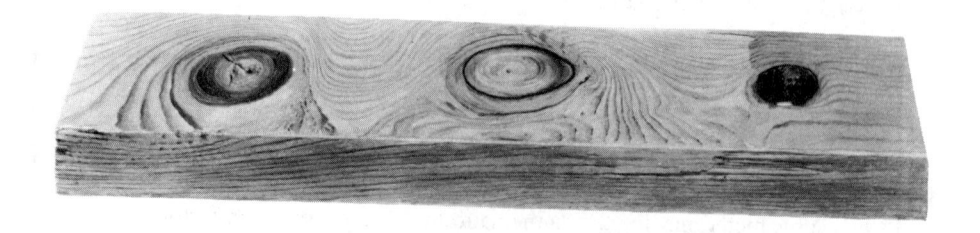

Artwork Courtesy of Western Wood Products Association

Knot Types

While knots are generally classified as defects, some, because of size or quality, do not affect the grade or usability of the piece. Some of the more common knot types are shown below, as they appear on the lumber face, and in the cross section.

Intergrown round knot through all four faces.

Sound, tight, intergrown, watertight spike knot through three faces.

Sound, tight, round pith knot through two narrow faces.

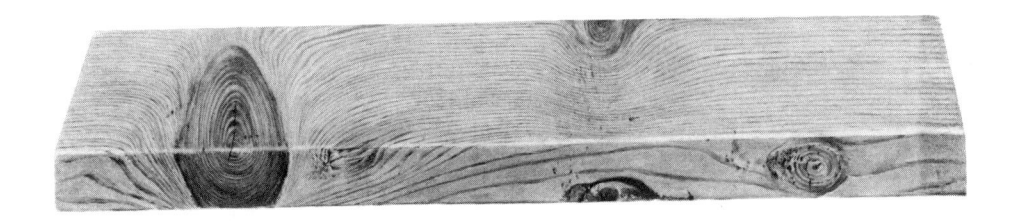

Terms of the Trade

Other Lumber

In addition to knots, there are numerous other characteristics of lumber that have an effect on its appearance, strength, stiffness, and usability. Some of the more common characteristics are shown below.

Wane – The presence of bark or the lack of wood from any cause on the edge or corner of a piece of wood.

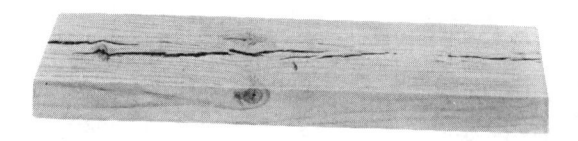

Shake – A lengthwise separation of the wood between or through the growth rings.

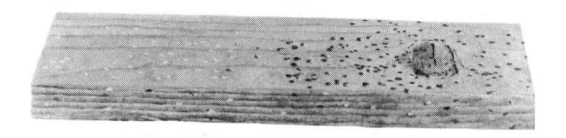

White Speck and Honeycomb – Conditions casued by a fungus in the living tree. White speck is characterized by small white pits or spots. Honeycomb is an advanced stage of white speck; the pits are deeper or larger. Neither condition is subject to further decay unless the lumber is used under wet conditions.

Artwork Courtesy of Western Wood Products Association

Characteristics

Split – The lengthwise separation of a piece of lumber extending from one surface or to an adjoining surface.

Decay – This is the disintegration of the wood due to the action of wood-destroying fungi.

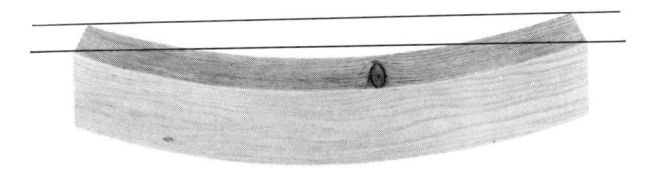

Crook – A deviation from a flat plane of the narrow face of a piece of lumber, from end to end.

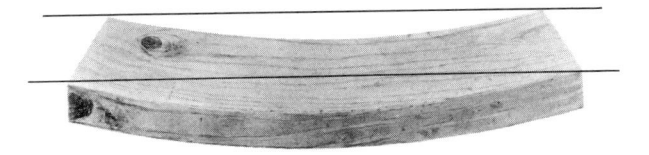

Bow – A deviation from a flat plane of the wide face of a piece of lumber, from end to end.

Twist – A deviation from the flat planes of all four faces of a piece of lumber by a spiraling or

Minimum Dressed Sizes Lumber

Dimension

Nominal Size	Actual Size		Metric Equivalent (to nearest whole mm)	
	Dry	Green	Dry	Green
2x2	1½x1½	1⁹⁄₁₆x1⁹⁄₁₆	38x38	40x40
2x3	1½x2½	1⁹⁄₁₆x2⁹⁄₁₆	38x64	40x65
2x4	1½x3½	1⁹⁄₁₆x3⁹⁄₁₆	38x89	40x90
2x5	1½x4½	1⁹⁄₁₆x4⅝	38x114	40x117
2x6	1½x5½	1⁹⁄₁₆x5⅝	38x140	40x143
2x8	1½x7¼	1⁹⁄₁₆x7½	38x184	40x191
2x10	1½x9¼	1⁹⁄₁₆x9½	38x235	40x241
2x12	1½x11¼	1⁹⁄₁₆x11½	38x286	40x292
3x4 etc.*	2½x3½	2⁹⁄₁₆x3⁹⁄₁₆	64x89	65x90
4x4 etc.*	3½x3½	3⁹⁄₁₆x3⁹⁄₁₆	89x89	90x90

Boards & Finish

Nominal Size	Actual Size		Metric Equivalent (to nearest whole mm)	
	Dry	Green	Dry	Green
1x2	¾x1½	²⁵⁄₃₂x1⁹⁄₁₆	19x38	20x40
1x3	¾x2½	²⁵⁄₃₂x2⁹⁄₁₆	19x64	20x65
1x4	¾x3½	²⁵⁄₃₂x3⁹⁄₁₆	19x89	20x90
1x5	¾x4½	²⁵⁄₃₂x4⅝	19x114	20x117
1x6	¾x5½	²⁵⁄₃₂x5⅝	19x140	20x143
1x8	¾x7¼	²⁵⁄₃₂x7½	19x184	20x191
1x10	¾x9¼	²⁵⁄₃₂x9½	19x235	20x241
1x12	¾x11¼	²⁵⁄₃₂x11½	19x286	20x292
⁵⁄₄x2 etc.*	1x1½	1¹⁄₃₂x1⁹⁄₁₆	25x38	26x40
⁶⁄₄x2 etc.*	1¼x1½	1⁹⁄₃₂x1⁹⁄₁₆	32x38	33x40

* Other widths, same as above.

Note: Metric sizes show are merely equivalents, rounded to the nearest whole millimeter.

Board Footage

	6'	8'	10'	12'	14'	16'	18'	20'	22'	24'	26'
2x2	2	2⅔	3⅓	4	4⅔	5⅓	6	6⅔	7⅓	8	8⅔
2x3	3	4	5	6	7	8	9	10	11	12	13
2x4	4	5⅓	6⅔	8	9⅓	10⅔	12	13⅓	14⅔	16	17⅓
2x5	5	6⅔	8⅓	10	11⅔	13⅓	15	16⅔	18⅓	20	21⅔
2x6	6	8	10	12	14	16	18	20	22	24	26
2x8	8	10⅔	13⅓	16	18⅔	21⅓	24	26⅔	29⅓	32	34⅔
2x10	10	13⅓	16⅔	20	23⅓	26⅔	30	33⅓	36⅔	40	43⅓
2x12	12	16	20	24	28	32	36	40	44	48	52
1x2	1	1⅓	1⅔	2	2⅓	2⅔	3	3⅓	3⅔	4	4⅓
1x3	1½	2	2½	3	3½	4	4½	5	5½	6	6½
1x4	2	2⅔	3⅓	4	4⅔	5⅓	6	6⅔	7⅓	8	8⅔
1x5	2½	3⅓	4⅙	5	5⅝	6⅔	7½	8⅓	9⅙	10	10⅚
1x6	3	4	5	6	7	8	9	10	11	12	13
1x8	4	5⅓	6⅔	8	9⅓	10⅔	12	13⅓	14⅔	16	17⅓
1x10	5	6⅔	8⅓	10	11⅔	13⅓	15	16⅔	18⅓	20	21⅔
1x12	6	8	10	12	14	16	18	20	22	24	26

Lumber

Feet	Meters
6'	1.83m
8'	2.44m
10'	3.05m
12'	3.66m
14'	4.27m
16'	4.88m
18'	5.49m
20'	6.10m
22'	6.71m
24'	7.32m

Panels

Thickness	Metric
¼"	6.36mm
5/16"	7.94mm
⅜"	9.53mm
15/32"	11.91 mm
½"	12.70mm
19/32"	15.09 mm
⅝"	15.88mm
23/32"	18.26 mm
¾"	19.05mm

4 x 8' = 48 x 96" = 1,200 x 2,440mm*
4 x 10' = 48 x 120" = 1,220 x 3,048mm*

* Metric sizes shown are merely equivalents, rounded to the nearest whole number.

Terms of the Trade

Board Footage in Standard Units of Lumber

Pieces per Unit	8'	10'	12'	Length 14'	16'	18'	20'
2x4							
(192)[1]	1,024	1,280	1,536	1,792	2,048	2,304	2,560
(208)[2]	1,109	1,387	1,664	1,941	2,219	2,496	2,773
(294)[3]	1,558	1,970	2,352	2,734	3,146	3,528	3,910
2x6							
(128)[1,2]	1,024	1,280	1,536	1,792	2,048	2,304	2,560
(189)[3]	1,512	1,890	2,268	2,646	3,024	3,402	3,780
2x8							
(96)[1,2]	1,024	1,280	1,536	1,792	2,048	2,304	2,560
(147)[3]	1,568	1,960	2,352	2,744	3,136	3,528	3,920
2x10							
(80)[1,2]	1,067	1,333	1,600	1,867	2,133	2,400	2,667
(105)[3]	1,400	1,750	2,100	2,450	2,800	3,150	3,450
2x12							
(64)[1,2]	1,024	1,280	1,536	1,792	2,048	2,304	2,560
(84)[3]	1,344	1,680	2,016	2,352	2,688	3,024	3,360

1 – Common in the South, and from some western mills.

2 – Common in the West

3 – Common in British Columbia Interior

Plywood Square Footage (3/8" basis)

Panel Width	60"	72"	84"	96"	108"	120"	132"	144"
5/16" Thickness								
36"	12.5	15.0	17.5	20.0	22.5	25.0	27.5	30.0
48"	16.7	20.0	23.3	26.7	30.0	33.3	36.7	40.0
60"	20.8	25.0	29.2	33.3	37.5	41.7	45.8	50.0
3/8" Thickness								
36"	15.0	18.0	21.0	24.0	27.0	30.0	33.0	36.0
48"	20.0	24.0	28.0	32.0	36.0	40.0	44.0	48.0
60"	25.0	30.0	35.0	40.0	45.0	50.0	55.0	60.0
1/2" Thickness								
36"	20.0	24.0	28.0	32.0	36.0	40.0	44.0	48.0
48"	26.7	32.0	37.3	42.7	48.0	53.3	58.7	64.0
60"	33.3	40.0	46.7	53.3	60.0	66.7	73.7	80.0
5/8" Thickness								
36"	25.0	30.0	35.0	40.0	45.0	50.0	55.0	60.0
48"	33.3	40.0	46.7	53.3	60.0	66.7	73.3	80.0
60"	41.7	50.0	58.3	66.7	75.0	83.3	91.7	100.0
3/4" Thickness								
36"	30.0	36.0	42.0	48.0	54.0	60.0	66.0	72.0
48"	40.0	48.0	56.0	64.0	72.0	80.0	88.0	96.0
60"	50.0	60.0	70.0	80.0	90.0	100.0	110.0	120.0

Panel Length

Particleboard Square Footage (3/4" basis)

Panel Width	Panel Length							
	60"	72"	84"	96"	108"	120"	132"	144"
3/8" Thickness								
36"	7.5	9.0	10.5	12.0	13.5	15.0	16.5	18.0
48"	10.0	12.0	14.0	16.0	18.0	20.0	22.0	24.0
60"	12.5	15.0	17.5	20.0	22.5	25.0	27.5	30.0
1/2" Thickness								
36"	10.0	12.0	14.0	16.0	18.0	20.0	22.0	24.0
48"	13.0	16.0	19.0	21.0	24.0	27.0	29.0	32.0
60"	17.0	20.0	23.0	27.0	30.0	33.0	37.0	40.0
5/8" Thickness								
36"	12.5	15.0	117.5	20.0	22.5	25.0	27.5	30.0
48"	16.7	20.0	23.3	26.7	30.0	33.3	36.7	40.0
60"	20.8	25.0	29.2	33.3	37.5	41.7	45.8	50.0
3/4" Thickness								
36"	15.0	18.0	21.0	24.0	27.0	30.0	33.0	36.0
48"	20.0	24.0	28.0	32.0	36.0	40.0	44.0	48.0
60"	25.0	30.0	35.0	40.0	45.0	50.0	55.0	60.0